1484

WITH SHIELD AND SWORD

BOOKS BY WARREN W. HASSLER, JR.

General George B. McClellan: Shield of Union

Commander of the Army of the Potomac

Coauthor, *Civil War Books: A Critical Bibliography,* 2 volumes

Crisis at the Crossroads: The First Day at Gettysburg

The President as Commander in Chief

With Shield and Sword: American Military Affairs,
Colonial Times to the Present

With Shield and Sword

AMERICAN MILITARY AFFAIRS, COLONIAL TIMES TO THE PRESENT

Warren W. Hassler, Jr.

IOWA STATE UNIVERSITY PRESS • AMES

1 9 8 2

ACKNOWLEDGMENTS

Figures 2.1, 2.2, 2.3, 9.1, and 10.2. Reprinted by permission of G. P. Putnam's Sons from *The United States in War and Peace* by Oliver Lyman Spaulding. Copyright ©1937 by Alice Chandler Spaulding.

Figures 4.1, 6.1, and 15.1. From *Military Heritage of America* by R. Ernest Dupuy and Trevor N. Dupuy. Copyright ©1956. Used with permission of the publisher, The Bobbs-Merrill Company, Inc.

Figure 6.2. From *The Story of the Mexican War.* Copyright ©1950 by Robert Selph Henry. Used with permission of the publisher, The Bobbs-Merrill Company, Inc.

Figures 7.1, 7.2, 7.3, and 8.1. From *Abraham Lincoln* by Benjamin Thomas. Copyright ©1952 by Benjamin Thomas. Reprinted by permission of Alfred A. Knopf, Inc.

Figure 10.1. From *The United States and World Sea Power* by E. B. Potter. Copyright ©1955. Used with permission of Prentice-Hall, Inc.

Figures 12.1 and 12.2. From *War through the Ages,* New and Enlarged Edition by Lynn Montross. Copyright 1944, 1946, ©1960 by Harper & Row, Publishers, Inc. Reprinted by permission of the publisher.

Figures 14.1 and 14.3. From *Strategy* by Basil H. Liddell Hart. Copyright ©1954. Courtesy of Frederick A. Praeger.

Figure 14.2. From *Crusade in Europe* by Dwight D. Eisenhower. Copyright ©1948 by Doubleday & Company, Inc. Reprinted by permission of Doubleday & Company, Inc.

Figure 14.4. From *A Guide to Naval Strategy* by Bernard Brodie, Revised Edition. Copyright ©1958 by Princeton University Press. Reprinted by permission of Princeton University Press.

Figure 14.5. From *A Military History of the Western World,* Volume 3, by Major General J. F. C. Fuller. (Funk & Wagnalls). Copyright ©1956 by J. F. C. Fuller. Reprinted by permission of Harper & Row, Publishers, Inc.

Figure 15.2. From *Freedom and Crisis: An American History,* Third Edition, by Allen Weinstein and Frank Otto Gatell. Copyright ©1981 by Random House, Inc. Reprinted by permission of Random House, Inc.

©1982 The Iowa State University Press. All rights reserved. Composed and printed by The Iowa State University Press, Ames, Iowa 50010

First edition, 1982

Library of Congress Cataloging in Publication Data

Hassler, Warren W.
  With shield and sword.

  Bibliography: p.
  Includes index.
  1. United States—History, Military.   I. Title.
E181.H36   973   82-15379
ISBN 0-8138-1627-0   AACR2

HENRY A. VAUGHN
AND THE
MEMORY OF LORETTE H. VAUGHN

CONTENTS

PREFACE

*[There has been] a generally dawning realization
that war, war preparations, military tactics and
strategy, military manpower questions, [and]
military economics, are not problems arising only
suddenly and sporadically in moments of international "emergency"; they are continuous factors
within the fabric of our society. Military institutions and their consequences are as essential
elements of our social and political history as are
religious, economic, legal or partisan political institutions.*

WALTER MILLIS

WRITING of the American Civil War, Walt Whitman prophesied:
"A great literature will yet arise out of the era of those four years,
those scenes—era compressing centuries of native passion, first-
class pictures, tempests of life and death—an inexhaustible mine for the
histories, drama, romance, and even philosophy, of peoples to come—indeed
the verteber of poetry and art (of personal character too) for all future
America—far more grand, in my opinion, to the hands capable of it, than
Homer's siege of Troy, or the French wars to Shakspere." He might well have
been speaking of the entire military history of the United States from the
earliest colonial settlements to the Persian Gulf crises of the 1980s.

Studies abound in various aspects of American military affairs. Ever since
the first encounters with the Indians in the forested North American
wilderness, Americans have wavered between abhorrence of things military
and fascination with the art of arms.

But with comparatively few exceptions, American military historians have
tended to chronicle either certain wars of the United States or have employed a
specialized topical approach to some phases of the nation's martial institutions. There is a dearth of recent comprehensive studies that incorporate and
integrate military operations and policy with the personalities and characters
of leading civilian and uniformed figures who have been the protagonists in
American armed endeavors. It is hoped that the present study will provide an
up-to-date and integrated survey of American military activities across the
span of some three centuries.

Although now outdated, there have been several milestone studies of considerable scope dealing with America's military history. One of the most important of these early efforts was the pioneer work by Emory Upton, *The
Military Policy of the United States* (1904), which examined the evolution of
the way we went to war and survived militarily between the conflicts from the
colonial wars to the second year of the Civil War. In 1955 C. Joseph Bernardo
and Eugene H. Bacon in *American Military Policy* covered the period from
1775 through the Korean War; like Upton's, this book largely ignores military
operations and the role of the principal individuals involved in the development of national military policy.

i x

In 1924 William A. Ganoe wrote an institutional account of America's ground forces, *The History of the United States Army* (revised in 1942). Oliver L. Spaulding in 1937 produced a documented operational history of *The United States Army in War and Peace* that ends with the First World War. This topic was continued through the Korean War by R. Ernest and Trevor N. Dupuy in their *Military Heritage of America* (1956) and was broadened in scope and brought up to the mid-1960s by Russell F. Weigley in *History of the United States Army* (1967).

Harold and Margaret Sprout in 1939 in *The Rise of American Naval Power* (revised in 1942) covered naval policy from the Revolution through the First World War in the same manner that Upton, and Bernardo and Bacon had for the land forces. Recent works that deal with both naval operations and policy are those by Kenneth J. Hagan, editor, *In Peace and War: Interpretations of American Naval History, 1775–1978* (1978) and Paolo E. Coletta, *The American Naval Heritage in Brief* (1980), which trace the evolution of the navy from the earliest days of sea power to the 1980s. Operational histories of the service afloat by such writers as E. B. Potter, Chester W. Nimitz, and Dudley W. Knox are numerous. And there are a number of books dealing with the Marine Corps and the United States Air Force.

But there is a paucity of integrated, comprehensive studies of the land, sea, and air forces of the United States in their operational and policy areas, during and between wars, and analyses of the characters of their leaders. A survey, first published in 1956, *Men in Arms* (revised in 1978), by Richard A. Preston, Sydney F. Wise, and Herman O. Werner, attempts a broader approach, as does the important though episodic and now outdated work by Walter Millis, *Arms and Men* (1956). More modern, though highly selective in what it ably covers, is Russell F. Weigley, *The American Way of War* (1973). And there are brief though brilliant and perceptive sketches in Theodore Ropp's *War in the Modern World* (1959) that need to be brought up to date.

The time is overdue for a documented study that discusses the participation of significant individuals interacting with American military operations on land, sea, and in the air and their search throughout history for a viable military policy in times of peace and war. A study of the shortcomings and achievements in the military annals of the United States invites an understanding of the epic of the American people in arms.

The author would like to thank and to acknowledge the assistance of a host of friends and colleagues, chief among whom is George T. Ness, Jr., in the research and writing of this book. I appreciate also the financial assistance provided by the Institute for the Arts and Humanistic Studies and its director, Professor Stanley Weintraub, of the Pennsylvania State University.

Warren W. Hassler, Jr.

Pennsylvania State University
University Park, Pa.
1981

WITH SHIELD AND SWORD

CHAPTER ONE

Indians and Frenchmen

On the obscure strife where men died by tens or by scores, hung questions of as deep import for posterity as on those mighty contests of national adolescence when carnage is reckoned by thousands.

FRANCIS PARKMAN, 1 8 6 5

 WHEN THE DRUMS echoed restlessly in the North American wilderness, they signaled not only four colonial wars between the French and Indians on the one hand, and the British and their American colonists on the other, but they heralded a later brutal war between England and her erstwhile colonies that would leave a legacy of new problems—civil and military—for the infant republic.

Unlike wars fought on the more open, cultivated European countryside, the four major colonial wars waged in America between 1689 and 1763 were fought on heavily forested terrain. Logistic support for the contending hosts was a nightmare; little artillery or cavalry could be used, and primitive Indians made independent raids or acted as auxiliaries. Because large professional forces in North America were rare, the customary rules of European warfare were often ignored. Thus the Americans were slow to develop a real military tradition. Howard H. Peckham, historian of these wars, concludes:

> The challenge of developing a continent made army life, in fact, an unattractive career. Advancement in military science as an end in itself carried no appeal to Americans, although they retained an amateur's receptivity to new tactics and organization and weapons, untempered by the heat of tradition.[1]

This, of course, could prove a mixed blessing. Just as the American colonists brought English political institutions with them across the Atlantic, so too did they bring some British military practices.

In addition to the regular army, England had a militia system. Whereas in the British Isles the militia was homogeneous under one command, in North America each colony had its own tiny militia, independent of the others, and lacking in any unified command. In America the militia was preferred over the standing army, and it was effective against localized and isolated Indian raids.

3

But the militia was far from successful against the French and their semiorganized Indian allies in the four colonial wars that erupted as an aftermath of the Glorious Revolution and the ascendancy of William and Mary to the English throne.[2]

The fighting that was to be done on the wild shores of the New World was performed with a variety of weapons. The standard army shoulder piece was the single-shot, muzzle-loading flintlock musket, having a ¾-inch bore, running some 4 feet in length, weighing up to 15 pounds, and sometimes equipped with a cumbersome bayonet. A good marksman might hit an opponent at 50 yards. In addition, the Americans possessed a bayonetless Pennsylvania (or Kentucky) rifle, a long, light, unique piece that employed a ½-inch bullet. It was customarily used as a hunting weapon on the frontier, and the rifle became invaluable for the crack-shot Americans. In the artillery, 4-, 8- and 12-pounder muzzle-loading cannon were employed, firing a solid iron ball, or grape and canister. A range of knives, swords, pistols, and tomahawks were used. The French as well as the English colonists in North America adapted readily to the Indian style of individual fighting, but the red-coated British regulars adhered stiffly to rigid linear formations and similarly unrealistic tactics. Only slowly and painfully did light infantry and ranger-type forces emerge.[3]

WITH THE OUTBREAK of the War of the Grand Alliance (known also as the War of the League of Augsburg and in North America as King William's War [1689–1697]) events moved swiftly. A heavy raid by pro-English Iroquois Indians against Montreal led French King Louis XIV to appoint, albeit reluctantly, the seventy-year-old Count Frontenac as Governor of Canada. A brigadier general at the age of twenty-six, ruthless and self-assured, Frontenac had previously served a ten-year term as governor. In this post he had shown strong energy and determined purpose marred only by self-approbation and a domineering, quarrelsome ill temper.

Before the new determination of England and her colonists to employ joint operations was tried in earnest, laurels were won by a Massachusetts expedition launched against Port Royal, Acadia. A colorful personality was chosen to lead this 1690 venture—Sir William Phips, a thirty-nine-year-old native of Pemaquid (Bristol, Maine), who as a younger man had worked as a ships carpenter and contractor. In 1687 Phips learned of a sunken Spanish treasure galleon off Hispaniola, organized a salvaging operation that located the vessel, and became a rich man. In England Phips was knighted by James II. He returned to Boston, joined the North Church, and achieved not only wealth but unimpeachable respectability.

The expedition, made up of 736 raw Massachusetts militiamen and fourteen ships, sailed on 9 May 1690. Phips had little trouble in seizing his objective, and the French commander of Port Royal surrendered the pitiful fort and his 72-man garrison in hopes of saving the town. Phips not only destroyed the fort, but, thinking some of the citizenry guilty of a breach of the capitulation terms, permitted his men to loot the town. The resourceful commander and his expedition returned in triumph to Boston on 30 May. To the resentment of the people of Massachusetts, Port Royal was handed back to France at the end of the war.[4]

Stop   The popular Phips was given command of a Massachusetts force of 2,200 soldiers; with thirty-four ships, he pushed off on 21 August 1690 against Quebec. Eight lengthy weeks were needed before that mighty bastion was sighted on 17 October, the delay caused in part by the search for a pilot who knew the treacherous St. Lawrence River. The weather had by then turned cold. Frontenac, with 2,000 regulars and militia, rejected Phip's demand to capitulate. The latter disembarked over 1,200 men east of Quebec at the mouth of the St. Charles River, but these were checked by 600 French soldiers. Nor were the Americans assisted by the sinking of their six cannon in the muddy tributary.

Skirmishing ensued. Without coordinating with the troops, the warships bombarded the city, but they suffered more damage than they inflicted. With limited food supplies and ammunition about exhausted, the men were recalled to the ships, which dropped down the river for repairs (Phips himself did some actual work on several vessels). Thirty Americans were killed and 60 wounded; 30 French were slain and 17 captured. When smallpox struck, Phips ordered the expedition home, not knowing that in another week Quebec might have yielded because of its own food shortage. Three ships were lost, and through accidents on these craft and disease, some 200 more men perished. Phips arrived back in Boston in later November, followed haphazardly by limping ships. Although not censured by the people for his evinced incapacity, Phips nonetheless sailed for England. The ill-fated expedition had cost Massachusetts £50,000. Although fruitless, the effort did preempt any further French invasions during the winter of 1690–1691.[5]

In early 1691 Lt. Gov. Jacob Leisler, a bungling usurper, was executed in New York by Royal Gov. Henry Sloughter. To appease their eager Iroquois allies, Sloughter agreed to a joint raid against the St. Lawrence River line to be led by Maj. Peter Schuyler, an Albany merchant and Indian affairs commissioner, with 120 New York volunteers and 150 Iroquois braves. Schuyler's expedition up Lake Champlain began on 22 June 1691. On the night of 1 August he surprised the larger French and Indian garrison of over 400 and attacked without success the fortified La Prairie. During their withdrawal to canoes at Fort Chambly, the Americans blundered into an ambush; after their initial repulse, they smashed the enemy and successfully regained their starting point. Further New York efforts were halted by the sudden death of Governor Sloughter on 23 July, although their Iroquois allies continued their raids in the spring of 1692.[6]

Again lacking cooperation between the colonies, Massachusetts nevertheless began an offensive in Maine. The 300 troops were commanded by Maj. Benjamin Church, an active, adroit, but blustering soldier who fifteen years before had crushed King Philip's rebellion. In early September 1691 the expedition sailed up Casco Bay and captured an enemy fort at what is now Brunswick and another at what was to be Lewiston. Scoring several other minor successes, and always inflicting heavier losses than he suffered, Church returned to Boston only to find the Massachusetts populace dissatisfied that more decisive results had not been achieved.[7]

The action fronts were comparatively quiet until the summer of 1696. Then Pierre Le Moyne Iberville attacked Fort William Henry at Pemaquid, but its faint-hearted commander, Capt. Pascoe Chubb, with adequate troops and cannon, surrendered after only a few shots were fired. The French then leveled the fort. Major Church retaliated by raiding Penobscot Bay as far up the coast as the Bay of Fundy. But the pendulum swung back again in the French favor when Iberville boldly struck the east coast of Newfoundland and damaged British warships at Fort Nelson in Hudson's Bay. That same summer the seventy-six-year-old Frontenac, carried in a chair by Indians, invaded New York colony with 2,000 regulars, militia, and Indians and defeated the Onondagas and Oneidas. Although the French soon withdrew and Benjamin Fletcher sent food to the Indians, the Iroquois were convinced that New York would not defend them. These were the last consequential military operations of the war, although the Indians in Maine conducted some raids in 1697.[8]

The Iroquois agreed to make peace with the French, but they would not do so with Frontenac's Indian allies. The count would not consent to a settlement on these terms, although King Louis XIV favored it. But the great powers in Europe made peace on 30 September 1697. By the treaty of Ryswick, all conquests in North America, including Port Royal, were restored. The French casualties in the war amounted to perhaps 300 killed as compared to the possible deaths of 650 English and Americans. The Indian associates of France lost perhaps over 100, while the pro-British Iroquois may have suffered more than 650 slain.[9]

THE SECOND COLONIAL WAR (1702–1714) began in Europe with a quarrel over the Spanish throne. It was known as the War of the Spanish Succession and as Queen Anne's War in North America. The struggle was limited in the Western Hemisphere to the West Indies, Florida, the Carolinas, and New England. Iroquois neutrality for once freed New York from raids and invasions, and New Yorkers saw clearly that the only way to defeat the French and Canadians was to dispatch a strong, joint, army-navy expedition from England to strike Quebec.

In the South in October 1702 Gov. James Moore of Carolina, an adventurer and planter, led 500 militiamen and 300 Indians in an assault on St. Augustine in Spanish Florida. They seized a few outposts, sacked the town, and were turned back after a seven-week siege at Fort San Marcos. Upon their return to Port Royal, South Carolina, they found that not only had the expedition cost Carolina £8,500, but Moore had lost the governorship. Moore, an intrepid individual, reacted to this setback positively; he led a successful independent attack in 1703 with 50 militia and approximately 1,000 Indians. After winning the battle, Moore's force ransacked thirteen Spanish-dominated Indian missions between St. Augustine and Tallahassee; that was the limit of his accomplishments.[10]

In the North some 500 Abenakis, who had made pledges to the English to maintain peace in the summer of 1703, were enticed by Philippe de Rigaud de Vaudreuil, the able new French governor of Canada, to launch scattered raids from Wells to Casco Bay and York. In February 1704 the infamous sack of Deerfield on the Connecticut River in Massachusetts took place, with 158 inhabitants and soldiers killed or captured. In retaliation, a Massachusetts expedition of 550 troops under the capable Col. Benjamin Church sailed from Boston on 21 May 1704 and raided Abenaki villages from Penobscot Bay to Port Royal, Nova Scotia. However, the stronghold was too powerfully held, and on 14 July they began the voyage back to Boston, having lost but 6 men while capturing 100. The action prompted peace negotiations to begin between Massachusetts and the French in 1705, but these talks failed.[11]

One man who perceived that the French in Canada could be defeated only with English leadership and military assistance was Samuel Vetch, a thirty-eight-year-old Scot. Vetch, who had been charged with trading with the enemy, was a commercial man who had recently arrived in New England and had married the daughter of Robert Livingston. Vetch journeyed to England and used his persuasive powers to convince the British officials of the need for a massive effort against Canada; his efforts bore fruit two years later, in February 1709. He was appointed a colonel and was promised the governorship of Canada when that French possession was captured. Vetch sailed for Boston in the company of the former governor of Virginia, Col. Francis Nicholson, a stalwart who favored unified colonial action.[12]

The British-American plan called for 1,500 troops from Connecticut, Pennsylvania, New Jersey, and New York, under Nicholson's command, to assemble in May 1709 at Albany and then to move upon Montreal. It was hoped that the Iroquois would rally to the British side and assist in the operation. In addition, 1,000 New England militiamen were to join English forces for a water attack on Port Royal and Quebec. The American colonies prepared in earnest for the mission only to learn in October, through the discouraged Vetch, that the campaign had been cavalierly postponed. The colonists sent Nicholson to Queen Anne to seek revival of the operation.[13]

Victory finally crowned the allies' efforts. London approved Nicholson's plan to head a force of 500 British marines and colonials in an assault, not on Quebec but on Port Royal, and the colonists were to provide ships and supplies. It was agreed that Vetch was to be administrative head of the area conquered. Reaching Boston in July 1710 Nicholson prepared for the operation, which got under way in September. Port Royal, on level terrain with only a tiny garrison of less than 300 troops, had no other recourse than to surrender on 20 October to the overwhelming force of 3,500 New England militiamen and the regiment of British marines. The stronghold was renamed Annapolis Royal by Nicholson, and Vetch became governor of Nova Scotia.[14]

Earlier in the war on the continent, the Duke of Marlborough's brilliant victories at Blenheim and Ramillies had enhanced Whig prestige. But with the Tories recently back in control of the government, the triumphant Nicholson's renewed appeal for the conquest of Quebec was endorsed in London, and the British agreed to send English regiments to America and to pay for them. The strategic plan involved one army under Vetch to join the redcoats in the expedition against Quebec while the other army under Nicholson was to move against Montreal. The expedition arrived on time in Boston near the end of June 1711; there were 5,000 British soldiers and nearly seventy ships. But there were problems: the local citizens were not happy at the presence of this massive English force; the British general had never commanded troops before; and the British admiral was pessimistic about success.[15]

The huge expedition of 6,000 British and 1,500 American soldiers sailed on 30 July 1711, but they encountered contrary winds, squalls, and fog at the mouth of the St. Lawrence. Hampered by an incompetent pilot, eight of the tacking ships were wrecked on the rocks with the loss of 150 sailors and 740 British soldiers. At a council of war, all army officers wished to press on, but the admiral and ship captains of the Royal Navy declined, citing the difficulties of pushing upriver with inept pilots. The expedition was terminated and sailed directly back to England except for the colonial troops and ships that were returned to Boston. So angry was Nicholson, stranded at Lake Champlain, at this sad turn of events that he hurled his wig on the floor and stamped on it. The British admiral was cashiered upon his arrival in England, but it was too late to redeem the situation. Too exhausted for a third offensive against Canada, the English and Americans braced for an anticipated French counterinvasion. Fortunately, it did not materialize.[16]

The Tories, now in power, removed Marlborough from supreme command in December 1711 and concluded the Treaty of Utrecht with France in April 1713. By this peace settlement France gave Newfoundland and Acadia to England, recognized Britain's claim to Hudson's Bay, and ceded to England the islands of Nevis and St. Kitts in the Caribbean. The treaty also saw Spain yield the strategic areas of Gibraltar and Minorca to Britain, who had captured them earlier. France recognized the Iroquois as British subjects, although the Iroquois did not! But France still retained Cape Breton Island, commanding the best entrance into the Gulf of St. Lawrence, and began constructing powerful fortifications at Louisbourg.

The casualties in Queen Anne's War, besides the 900 British lost in the ill-fated St. Lawrence sortie, involved hundreds who perished at Guadeloupe. Perhaps only 50 or 60 Canadians and Spaniards lost their lives in battle. Possibly 150 American colonists were killed in the Carolinas and approximately 200 New Englanders paid the supreme sacrifice.[17]

AMERICANS swiftly became participants in a third colonial war. A mammoth English force of 9,000 troops (3,500 were Americans in a regiment enrolled on the British establishment) was taken by Admiral Edward Vernon, who had previously captured Porto Bello, Panama, to assail Colombia's seaport, Cartagena. The soldiers were at the mercy and command of incompetent Brig. Gen. Thomas Wentworth, who had advanced at a glacierlike pace. The force landed outside of Cartagena on 3 March 1741, but it took three weeks before Wentworth could arrange to have his troops open fire. Although the Americans did fairly well, the ill-advised attacks by Wentworth were hurled back. Then the rains descended and yellow fever struck. Vernon reembarked the soldiers on 17 April. An effort to recoup lost prestige by moving against Cuba only wasted more time. The expedition ended with only 600 Americans alive of the 3,500 who had started.[18]

King George's War (1740–1748), as it was known in North America, erupted unofficially in October 1740 after the death of Emperor Charles VI and the resulting embroglio over the succession to the Austrian throne. In 1742 Robert Walpole resigned and the new prowar ministry sent money to Maria Theresa, subsidized Hessian and Hanoverian soldiers, and threw a British army into Holland.

In North America, Spain seized the initiative in May 1742 by mounting an invasion of Georgia and the Carolinas by 3,000 men from Cuba via St. Augustine. But Gen. James Oglethorpe, who had been refused troops by South Carolina, nonetheless beat off an attack on Fort William at Cumberland Island in June. A week later he repelled another assault by 3,000 Spanish soldiers against Fort Fredericka on St. Simon's Island. However, Oglethorpe's countermove against St. Augustine in 1743 failed to capture that stronghold, although much damage was inflicted in the surrounding area. In that same year the British army in Holland, led in person by King George II (the last time an English monarch would be at the head of an army), repulsed a French attack at the Battle of Dettingen, and war was formally declared by the two countries in March 1744.[19]

In the early summer of 1744, French Capt. Francois Duvivier sailed from Louisbourg at the head of an expedition against Annapolis Royal, defended by some 100 troops under the command of Maj. Paul Mascarene. The British fortifications were not in good condition, but the firm defenders succeeded in beating off the feeble French attacks. Duvivier gave up the enterprise too easily and returned to Louisbourg, where he released some previously captured English prisoners. The latter, who had had time to study the defenses and battery positions while incarcerated within Louisbourg's walls, reported this intelligence to Gov. William Shirley of Massachusetts, with the suggestion that Cape Breton Island be seized.

Plans of the master fort builder, Vauban, had been used to construct the powerful fortifications at Louisbourg on Cape Breton Island between the years 1720 and 1740. Some 250 cannon were to be on the ramparts atop thirty-foot stone walls. Actually, as Lt. John Bradstreet pointed out, there were fewer than 100 guns in position, the garrison contained only 600 discontented French regulars, and the fortified town was dominated to the west by higher ground.[20]

In early January 1745 the fifty-year-old Gov. William Shirley, with pressure from Boston merchants, finally won approval from the Massachusetts Court for an expedition from that colony against Louisbourg. It was to be buttressed by naval aid from England's Commodore Peter Warren. Command of the big operation was entrusted to the prosperous and distinguished merchant from Kittery, Maine, the forty-eight-year-old William Pepperrell, who was a militia colonel and president of the Massachusetts Council. With the citizens' great enthusiasm for the venture, Pepperrell's personal popularity was a key asset. In addition, despite his lack of military experience and other limitations, he was a determined, enterprising, and intelligent individual who possessed sound common sense.[21]

The large expedition, embracing 34 cannon, 3,950 New England militiamen, 115 ships, and 4 British warships, sailed on 29 April 1745. The landings outside of Louisbourg on the following two days were scarcely opposed by the French. Errors and lack of expertise on the American side were more than counterbalanced by good luck and enemy blunders. Warren cooperated effectively with Pepperrell and captured several valuable French supply ships. Progress among the allies in the seven-week siege was delayed by the ill-disciplined and occasionally drunken state of the Yankee fishermen, farmers, and mechanics making up the soldiery. But the steady pounding of the fortress by Pepperrell's artillery was a contributing factor toward success; over 9,600 projectiles were hurled into the stronghold, and only one structure was unhit. With food provisions running low, the French commander surrendered his 600 regulars and 1,300 Frenchmen, their wives, and children on 17 June.[22]

The treaty of Aix-la-Chapelle was signed on 18 October 1748. By its terms, much to the anger and smoldering resentment of New England, Louisbourg and Cape Breton Island were given back to France, while Madras was returned to England. Much blood and treasure had been spent in North America. Probably 500 Americans had been killed and over 1,100 had died of disease (not including the losses of the Cartagena expedition); possibly only 350 French had been killed, although the debacle of the naval expeditions had yielded another 2,500 deaths by disease.[23] Yet all the sacrifices seemed futile to the American colonists if strongholds and territory gained from the enemy were returned to the French, leaving their expansion unchecked.

THE BASIC ISSUE that fomented trouble again in North America and helped lead to the fourth colonial war was the interest of Virginia speculators in the Ohio Valley at the same time the French advanced in earnest into that region to set up missions and forts. Not only did the French begin building forts rapidly after 1748, but they also bent every effort to entice the Indians away from the British side.

Events moved inexorably toward hostilities, encouraged by the aggressive policy of Marquis de Duquesne, an obstinate and arrogant man who became governor of New France in 1752. He was a member of the family of the prominent French naval leader of that name, and he inspired respect by his lofty bearing and air of command. Not satisfied with merely extending French commerce into the Ohio Valley, Duquesne was determined to expand French rule there as well. A strong fort was to be built by Capt. Francois Le Mercier at the forks of the Ohio where the Allegheny and Monongahela Rivers joined to form the Ohio River. In the spring and summer of 1753 three forts were built in Pennsylvania along the route: at Presque Ile (Erie); Fort Le Boeuf (Waterford); and at Venango (Franklin), at the mouth of French Creek where it empties into the Allegheny.[24]

Strong reaction to the French threat came from an obese, sixty-year-old Scot, the ambitious Lt. Gov. Robert Dinwiddie of Virginia. Although he was irascible in temperament, Dinwiddie had gained much administrative experience from long years in the colonial service. In October 1753 he received permission from London to construct forts in the West, but the British government insisted that Virginia must first try to remove the French menace by negotiation. So Dinwiddie immediately sent George Washington, a twenty-one-year-old major and "person of distinction," and six others to warn the French away. The contingent traveled by way of Cumberland, Maryland, the Monongahela (Braddock, Pennsylvania), and the forks of the Ohio (which Washington saw as an excellent site for a fort), then down the Ohio to Logstown. The force pushed on to Venango by 4 December 1753 and were cordially greeted by the French. Washington pressed forward to Fort Le Boeuf by 11 December, but the French there politely refused to leave. So he started back on 23 December and reached Williamsburg on 16 January 1754. He delivered an observant, superior report of French intrigue that he rightly perceived as hostile and directed against the English colonies.[25]

The patriotic young Virginian was already motivated by a high sense of public duty. Historian Francis Parkman characterized Washington at the formative period of his career thusly:

> He was respected and generally beloved, but he did not kindle enthusiasm. His were the qualities of an unflagging courage, an all-enduring fortitude, and a deep trust. He showed an astonishing maturity of character, and the kind of mastery over others which begins with mastery over self. At twenty-four he was the foremost man, and acknowledged as such, along the whole long line of western border.[26]

The French promptly leveled a fort begun by some Virginians at the forks of the Ohio and commenced building a much larger one, Fort Duquesne. Meanwhile, Washington with 120 troops marched to the Monongahela at Redstone Creek (two miles north of present-day Brownsville) and there awaited reinforcements. Moving by way of present U.S. Highway 40, Washington reached Great Meadows (between Chestnut Ridge and Laurel Hill) on 24 May, and his force of 40 men clashed with a French force five miles east of modern Uniontown. In this engagement French Ens. Joseph Coulon de Jumonville and 9 other enemy troops were killed and many captured. The French response was to mass an overwhelming force to counterattack Washington's small command.[27]

At Great Meadow, Washington built a crude, circular stockade, 7½ feet high and 53 feet in diameter, called Fort Necessity (ten miles southeast of present-day Uniontown). He had nearly 450 soldiers but lacked flour and horses. Then his Indian allies deserted. The French force appeared on 3 July and skirmishing commenced. It was a hopeless situation for the Americans. With 13 killed, 54 wounded, nearly 100 ill, complicated by wet powder, no transportation, and but three days' food, Washington yielded and gained the honors of war—meaning that he could march his men back to Virginia.[28]

A major effort was now under way to capture Fort Duquesne, while provisions were being gathered in early 1755 at Fort Cumberland. Maj. Gen. Edward Braddock, chosen by the Duke of Cumberland, arrived in Williamsburg in late February to assume command of the predominantly British army. The sixty-year-old Braddock had had over forty years of army experience: much of it had been in the Low Countries, though more in garrison than on the battlefield. He had been a popular governor of Gibralter and was a member of the famous Coldstream Guards. Braddock was plain speaking, brave, and an officer of honor and fidelity. But he could also be dogmatic, imperious, impatient, and overly self-confident, with an uncritically high opinion of regulars and too low a view of Americans. The young George Washington served as a volunteer aide-de-camp on Braddock's staff.

The British plan of grand strategy was threefold: Braddock was to capture Fort Duquesne and drive the French away from its vicinity; he was then to assist Gov. William Shirley in seizing Fort Niagara; and New York Indian Agent William Johnson and the northern militia were to attack Fort St. Frederic at Crown Point. But there were many snarls in the plan. Even though Braddock and two part-strength Irish regiments were at Fort Cumberland by 10 May 1755, local American civilians undermined preparations for the Fort Duquesne expedition by their laziness, indifference, and greed. In addition, many of the British officers were inefficient, dense, and unresourceful.[29]

After herculean efforts, Braddock's column was at last organized and supplied. His force of 2,500 was composed of three independent companies of regulars and two Irish regiments, several companies of Virginians, small numbers of militia from North Carolina and Maryland, some backwoodsmen, a few friendly Indians, and some wagoners. The column left Fort Cumberland on 7 June 1755, but it averaged only a poor two miles per day. Asked by Braddock how to expedite the march, Washington recommended pressing on with some artillery and a detachment, allowing the wagons to struggle on in the rear with the rest of the force. The result was that 1,450 soldiers moved forward a little faster. Most of the officers expected the French and Indians to attack as Braddock's army crossed to the left bank of the Monongahela River in order to advance two miles before they recrossed some eight miles from Fort Duquesne.[30]

As Braddock's van reached this latter point on 9 July, with adequate close-in flankers and skirmishers but inadequate long-range reconnaissance, it was attacked by Capt. Claude P. P. Contrecoeur's force of approximately 108 French regulars, 146 Canadian militia, and about 650 Indians. Surprised by the enveloping enemy, the redcoats made easy targets and were in such a tight formation that they could not reply effectively. The battle was brief and vicious. Braddock was mortally wounded; that half of the force was finally extricated from the death trap should be credited to Washington's fine composure and dexterity in fighting on that terrain. As against enemy losses of but 23 killed and 16 wounded, British casualities reached the staggering total of 63 officers and 914 enlisted men killed alone. It was an appalling disaster and one of the greatest victories for the French and Indians.[31]

Governor Shirley became the commander in chief after Braddock's death, and although he was a civilian and impatient with military administrative details, he had courage and zeal. His dynamic and offense-minded outlook intimidated some of the fainthearted colonial governors, and his military sense

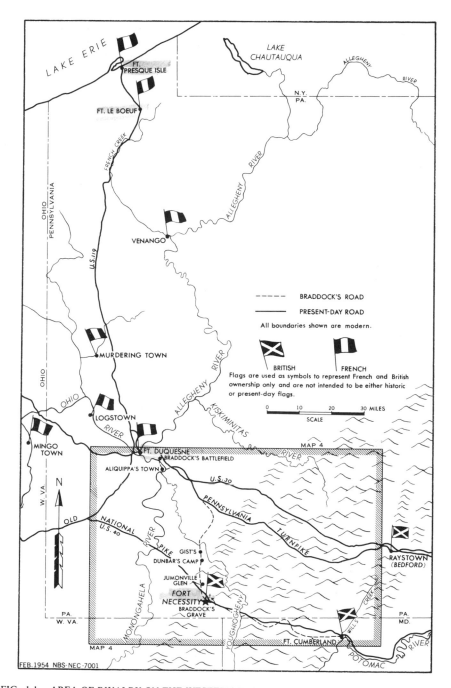

FIG. 1.1. AREA OF RIVALRY ON THE WESTERN FRONTIER, 1753 (*Courtesy National Park Service*).

was in some ways superior to that of Britain's first three professional commanders in chief. Benjamin Franklin declared that Shirley "was sensible and sagacious in himself, and attentive to good advice from others, capable of forming judicious plans, quick and active in carrying them into execution." One of Shirley's wisest decisions and most innovative tactical accomplishments was his formation of the famous light infantry force known as Capt. Robert Rogers's Rangers, a group chosen from New Hampshire woodsmen.[32]

Rogers was a singular figure. His boyhood had been spent in the rough surroundings of a village on the frontier. He was not uneducated, but he had resorted to the smuggling trade with Canada before the war. When hostilities developed, he first raised a company composed largely of New Hampshiremen and then a battalion of rangers. Historian Francis Parkman commented that Rogers had "a strong, well-knit figure, in dress and appearance more woodsman than soldier, with a clear, bold eye, and features that would have been good but for the ungainly proportions of the nose." Violent and ambitious, Rogers could be unscrupulous and was at one time charged with complicity in forgery. But he was skilled in woodcraft, and was energetic, resourceful, and resolute.[33] In March of 1756 the Earl of Loudoun (John Campbell) succeeded Shirley as British commander in chief.

On the French side, the incompetent governor of Canada, the Marquis de Vaudreuil-Cavagnal, provided a stark contrast in leadership qualities to the able forty-four-year-old Marquis de Montcalm. Vaudreuil disliked Montcalm and other regular French officers and troops. This jealous man was a double-dealer and lacked force of character. Montcalm, on the other hand, showed strong traits and high attainments. He had fought with distinction at Philipsbourg in Bohemia from 1741 to 1744, and in Italy. He had been wounded several times in 1745 at Piacenza, and again the following year he had been creased. Montcalm was animated and a lover of good books. He could be emotional and imprudent, as well as vain and ambitious, and his conduct was marred by occasional vehement utterances. Yet he was a dashing figure with a fertile imagination, and a man of honor and character; he was, withal, a commander of ability.[34]

Montcalm's talents were quickly displayed. Proceeding from Fort Frontenac (Kingston, Ontario), he handily captured Fort Oswego on 13 August 1756, the English suffering eighty-one killed. Unfortunately Montcalm could not control his Indian allies. Lord Loudoun's reaction was to call upon the American colonies for militia and supplies; when these were not forthcoming he became convinced that the British army would have to operate on its own noncolonial resources. Such colonies as Pennsylvania and Virginia (the latter under the leadership of Col. George Washington) strengthened their western frontiers against the pro-French Indians, and Virginia constructed Fort Loudoun at Winchester. New York and New England were to be defended by militia, but only New York provided its full quota. Nonetheless the commander in chief had achieved for the first time a degree of military union with the colonies, and he had been able to deploy colonial forces where he saw fit.[35]

In December 1756 William Pitt (the elder), later Lord Chatham, came to power in England. Though he was poor, he came from a rich and influential family. Pitt was a magnificent war leader—dynamic, talented, and patriotic. Although conceited and theatrical, he was nonetheless a courageous and lofty-principled soul who loved both liberty and the people. This incorruptible leader had unwavering faith in England's cause, possessed superior intellectual powers, and was a fine grand strategist and judge of military commanders.[36]

According to historian Douglas Leach, the French leader Montcalm "showed little sign of real distinction," but he acknowledged that the French general was

> Appalled and disgusted by the rampant graft he saw in the civil administration of Canada, [and] he was handicapped by his military subordination to Governor Vaudreuil. Montcalm was not given a free hand in planning overall strategy or even particular operations, but had to accept the tasks given him by the governor. In executing his assignments he did well, producing notable victories at Oswego and Lake George and thus sparing Canada the serious danger of British attack from Lake Ontario and Lake Champlain. Certainly the French victories of 1756 and 1757 were in part the result of steady, methodical leadership on the part of the French general, who assessed every circumstance carefully and deployed his available forces to the best advantage.[37]

Pitt was not able as yet to mobilize in concert the superior resources of the English colonies—a problem that had thwarted Braddock and frustrated Loudoun.

In August 1757 Montcalm and 6,000 soldiers and 2,000 Indians advanced from Fort Ticonderoga against Fort William Henry at the head of Lake George. The defenders numbered 1,300 at this fort and 3,400 at Fort Edward to the southeast on the Hudson River. But British General Webb procrastinated over calling in reinforcements. The skirmishing was followed by a siege that led to the surrender of Fort William Henry on 9 August. The French Indians cold-bloodedly butchered 87 sick and wounded prisoners before Montcalm's desperate personal efforts finally ended the massacre. Nor was equipment available for Loudoun's contemplated move against Fort Ticonderoga. To add to Pitt's gloom at this time, word was received of the defeat and resignation in Germany of the Duke of Cumberland.[38]

In an attempt to redeem the situation, the incompetent new commander in chief, James Abercromby, moved upon Fort Ticonderoga on 5 July with a force of 16,000. Delays in food deliveries had scarcely allowed Montcalm time to hurry his troops down to Fort Ticonderoga, where he found himself outnumbered five to one. But Abercromby blundered by not taking time to place his superior artillery atop nearby and dominant Mount Defiance and by attacking too hastily and rashly on 8 July. The six waves of gallant British regulars who assaulted the French fort were repulsed by abatis and deadly French fire. In this debacle the British lost 464 killed, 1,117 wounded, and 29 missing—a total of approximately 10 percent of their force. French casualties of all kinds were some 400. Abercromby felt impelled to retreat.[39]

But Pitt had ordered a concomitant blow against Louisbourg that summer, to be commanded by the steady, reliable, forty-one-year-old Maj. Gen. Jeffery Amherst. His second in command was the sickly, emaciated Brig. Gen. James Wolfe, whose father, a major general, was an officer of distinction. By the age of sixteen James was a regimental adjutant in Flanders, showing "a precocious faculty for commanding men." He had fought well at Dettingen, Culloden, and Rochefort. The bold and decisive Wolfe, whose piercing eyes commanded attention, was not a storybook soldier in appearance. Besides a receding chin and forehead, he had an irresolute mouth, narrow shoulders, and a slender, delicate body. This redheaded young general had read Zenophon's *Anabasis* on mountain warfare, and many other military classics, had studied Latin and mathematics in his spare time, and was well versed in dancing, fencing, and horsemanship. As an officer, Wolfe made and held friends readily, and though he was diligent, he was often impatient and needlessly stern. In short, he was a thorough professional and a soldier of integrity.[40]

The expedition against Louisbourg, supported by a naval force under Adms. Edward Boscawen and Sir Charles Hardy, left Halifax for Cape Breton Island on 28 May 1758 with 9,000 British regulars and 500 American provincial soldiers. Initial landings near Louisbourg took place on 8 June. The French garrison of perhaps 6,000 was composed of regulars, militia, and Indians. The siege was pushed for over six weeks, with parallels advanced and large numbers of bombs, shells, and hot shot hurled into the stronghold. On 9 July the French tried a desperate but futile sortie. Damage to French ships, buildings, and defenses mushroomed. With only four rampart cannon able to fire, the tenacious Governor de Drucour was finally compelled to surrender on 26 July. This not only gave the British Cape Breton Island and Ile St. Jean (Prince Edward Island), but the Gulf of St. Lawrence was now cleared. Later, in 1760, the English blew up the remaining fortifications at Louisbourg.[41]

The British administered yet another blow to the enemy, this time in Pennsylvania. The commander of their forces, the ailing, fifty-one-year old Brig. Gen. John Forbes, was persuaded in early May 1758 to hack a road through the wilderness westward with 5,000 colonial militiamen and 1,700 regulars, from Carlisle via Fort Bedford, in order to capture Fort Duquesne. Colonel George Washington accompanied the expedition and played an important role in the operations. With Forbes's illness becoming serious, a key part in the day-to-day activities devolved upon a skilled Swiss-born professional, Lt. Col. Henry Bouquet. As Forbes's road was pushed westward, the 3,000 French troops inside Fort Duquesne were deserted by most of their Indian allies and their low food stocks remained unrelieved.

The British colonial effort continued. Colonel James Burd began constructing Fort Ligonier at Loyalhanna Creek on 3 September. However, Maj. Gen. James Grant lost 215 of his 840 troops in a loudly heralded attack near Fort Duquesne. But the French and Indians, in their turn, were repelled in their 12 October attempts to seize Fort Ligonier; so were their efforts to capture horses at this fort one month later—Forbes had stationed some 5,000 soldiers there. The crucial decision of this vast campaign was made by the dying Forbes—"Iron Head" to his soldiers—when he overruled his officers who wanted to winter at Ligonier and ordered his army to press on. The French, with severely reduced supplies because of their loss of Fort Frontenac, decided to blow up and burn Fort Duquesne. This was done on 24 November and the French fell back to Fort Venango. Lieutenant Colonel Hugh Mercer was directed by Forbes to rebuild on a more massive scale the captured bastion at the forks of the Ohio. When this was accomplished, the new stronghold was renamed Fort Pitt. General Forbes was carried back to Philadelphia, where he died on 11 March 1759. He has been remembered ever afterward as the able, dedicated hero of one of the pivotal operations of the fourth colonial war.[42]

In England Pitt's increasing power was matched by his enhanced popularity with the people. He acted decisively, replacing Abercromby with Amherst, who assumed command at Lake George in September 1758. While the British Navy was cutting the Canadian lifeline to France, Pitt's forces were capturing trading posts in Africa and India. Amherst was to move by way of Crown Point and seize Montreal; then Fort Niagara was to be taken. Pitt directed Wolfe at the same time to exercise independent command of 12,000 soldiers and to move via Louisbourg and the St. Lawrence upon Quebec, the most formidable citadel in North America. Amherst executed his part of the plan effectively, capturing Fort Ticonderoga on 26 July 1759 and Fort St. Frederic at Crown Point on 31 July. But obstacles slowed the rebuilding of these two forts and Amherst's invasion of Canada was delayed.[43]

The stage was set for the epic climax of the entire four colonial conflicts: the crucial contest between Montcalm and Wolfe for Quebec. Wolfe's impressive force of 8,500 troops (all seasoned regulars including Col. William Howe's battalion of light infantry, but with the exception of a battalion of colonial rangers) and a massive squadron of 49 warships and 119 transports under the command of Vice Adm. Charles Saunders sailed from Louisbourg. They arrived on 27 June at the island of Orleans and then moved to Point Levis, opposite Quebec. The location of Quebec atop Cape Diamond on the north bank of the St. Lawrence permitted French surveillance of the British camps several hundred feet below. Montcalm had some 16,000 troops, but only five battalions were French regulars. Wolfe's early feints upstream were abortive, and his attack against Montcalm's left flank near the Montmorenci Falls on 31 July was repulsed with the loss of 440 men as against only 60 French casualties. The summer weeks fled by, and Admiral Saunders kept reminding Wolfe that he should either triumph or retire, because the English ships would be in danger of being iced in by October.

Frustrated, discouraged, and in poor health, Wolfe finally and rather desperately accepted a plan that he had requested from his brigadiers, despite their strained relations. They proposed to land upstream from the citadel, following a steep goat trail up from the Anse au Foulon (known since as Wolfe's Cove) to the flat, grassy Plains of Abraham. French carelessness and Montcalm's conviction that the enemy would attack only to the east of Quebec contributed to their success. British audacity enabled Howe's 200 light infantrymen, accompanied by Wolfe, to surprise the 100-man guard at the path on the night of 12 September—the French assuming the British were attached to the French supply boats expected from upriver.

By daylight Wolfe had perhaps 4,500 of his soldiers drawn up in defensive line of battle on the plains. It was a brilliant feat. Montcalm had done well thus far in the campaign, but he was handicapped by a lack of artillery, which was under the control of his enemy, Vaudreuil. Montcalm hurriedly gathered an equal force of 4,500, half of them regulars, and gallantly yet too hastily charged the English lines in a typical European-style battle. Holding their fire until the enemy was within sixty yards, the redcoats with one crashing volley blasted the attackers off their feet and forced them to retreat. This critical action decided the control and destiny of North America. Both Montcalm and Wolfe were mortally wounded. Casualties amounted to 658 British and possibly 1,000 French. The city surrendered on 18 September. Its loss sealed the doom of New France.[44]

In the meantime the cautious Amherst, behind schedule in his movement against Montreal, dispatched Maj. Robert Rogers and 200 of his rangers to take St. Francis. This point, some fifty miles below Montreal, was the site from which Christian Indians had made a number of raids into New York and New England, and had pillaged and massacred indiscriminately. Rogers scored well. In a surprise attack on the town on 6 October his rangers killed 200 Indians while losing only 1 man. However, 49 of Rogers's troops were lost during their swift withdrawal southward under Indian pressure.[45]

In 1760, to the southwest, Amherst advanced decisively upon Montreal. He directed troops from Louisbourg to join James Murray at Quebec to permit Murray's move up the St. Lawrence. Some 3,400 soldiers were to advance on 10 August from Lake Champlain northward upon Montreal, while Amherst and Brig. Gen. Thomas Gage's troops led the main body from Fort Oswego down the St. Lawrence to Montreal. Amherst's circumspect but coordinated timing was flawless, with the three British columns reaching the island of Montreal by the end of the first week of September. The Canadians deserted Levis, leaving only French regulars, and again the incompetent Governor Vaudreuil meddled ineptly in strategy and tactics. Vaudreuil finally realized that capitulation was his only alternative and yielded Montreal on 8 September 1760, giving England all of Canada. The capable operations of Amherst and Wolfe had won for Britain a vast empire twelve times the area of England.[46]

The final operation of significance in the French and Indian War occurred when the Swiss-born Col. Henry Bouquet, who had been prominent in the Forbes expedition, led a relief excursion to Fort Pitt from Carlisle via Bedford. A bloody engagement was fought on 5–6 August 1763 at Bushy Run; after an initial setback, Bouquet deftly turned the tables on the Shawnees and Delawares and roundly defeated them. Douglas Leach declares that the victory at Bushy Run was "a clear vindication of British military discipline and valor when properly sustained in the wilderness by modified tactics based on experience." Although he lost some fifty men killed, sixty wounded, and five missing, Bouquet saved Fort Pitt and helped clinch the peace negotiations then being negotiated abroad.[47]

THE FOUR COLONIAL WARS, though of considerable importance, seem relatively insignificant because the numbers and casualties were comparatively low. In the first war, no more than 2,000 troops were in action at any time or place; in the second conflict, the number increased to 5,000 soldiers operating in 1712 in England's futile Quebec expedition; the third war was a smaller affair; and only in the fourth contest were 25,000 troops raised by Pitt for service in North America. Battle casualties were quite light most of the time, usually under 10 percent, except in Wentworth's debacle at Cartagena, where losses ran 55 percent, and in Braddock's defeat, where casualties amounted to 67 percent. However, fearful field and camp diseases took a high toll at such places as Louisbourg in 1746 and at Oswego in 1756.

The contributions of American provincial forces were not inconsequential. In King William's War, Phips's Massachusetts militiamen captured Port Royal, Acadia. In Queen Anne's War, 1,500 Americans under Francis Nicholson and Samuel Vetch again took Port Royal. In King George's War, 4,000 New England soldiers under Pepperrell captured Louisbourg. Only in the fourth French and Indian War was American participation less noteworthy. Even then some colonial troops were with Forbes in his capture of Fort Duquesne, with Braddock in his ill-fated venture, and in the Lake Champlain-Lake George area, not to mention the exploits of George Washington, Robert Rogers, Henry Bouquet, and other able soldiers.

There were some lessons, however, that were not well learned. "The experience of four colonial wars," Howard Peckham concludes, "did not disabuse the Anglo-Americans of the adequacy of militia, nor did it render a professional standing army more palatable. The latter was a specific complaint in the Declaration of Independence." Nor did the British ever comprehend colonial hatred of military service in the regular forces; the provincials preferred the militia, when they chose to serve at all. Where there were powerful motivations, skilled leadership, and short-range objectives, American militia could on occasion perform well, as they had at Port Royal in 1710, at Louisbourg in 1745, and at Fort Frontenac in 1758. Otherwise, the superiority of regular forces was amply demonstrated. Weapons changed little, although the former supremacy of fortified strongholds against artillery could now be questioned. And the obvious value of closely coordinated amphibious operations would quickly be forgotten in ensuing conflicts.[48]

Unfortunately for future harmonious relations between the Americans and their mother country, mutual distrust had grown and been nourished during the four wars against the French and Indians. Suspicion and resentment smoldered for some dozen years until it burst out in a great conflagration that rocked the civilized world, so momentous were the pervasive issues involved.[49]

Washington at the Helm

If Historiographers should be hardy enough to fill the page of History with the advantages that have been gained with unequal numbers (on the part of America) in the course of this contest, and attempt to relate the distressing circumstances under which they have been obtained, it is more than probable that posterity will bestow on their labors the epithet and marks of fiction; for it will not be believed that such a force as Great Britain has employed for eight years in this Country could be baffled in their plan of Subjugating it by numbers infinitely less, composed of Men sometimes half starved; always in Rags, without pay, and experiencing, at times, every species of distress which human nature is capable of undergoing.

GEORGE WASHINGTON, 1 7 8 3

BEFORE THE TIMES that tried men's souls evoked hostile military action, relations between Great Britain and her thirteen American colonies after the end of the French and Indian War had been deteriorating. The announcement by the English government of a proclamation line along the crest of the Appalachians in 1763 beyond which the provincials were not to pass caused resentment, as did the Sugar Act of 1764 and the Stamp Act of 1775. By the terms of the Quartering Act of 1775, citizens, without consultation, were ordered to house many of Britain's 8,500 redcoats stationed in North America. Americans, who considered themselves improperly represented in Parliament, were also angered by the Townshend Acts that levied duties upon such imports as tea, paper, lead, paint, and glass. The so-called Boston Massacre on 5 March 1770, in which several colonists were slain on the Common in that troubled port, led the British prime minister, Lord North, to rescind all taxes except that on tea. The famous Boston Tea Party of 1773 was followed by the punitive Intolerable Acts of 1774; the port of Boston was closed and the provincial assembly was dissolved. With the convening of the First Continental Congress that year, the drift toward war was inexorable.[1].

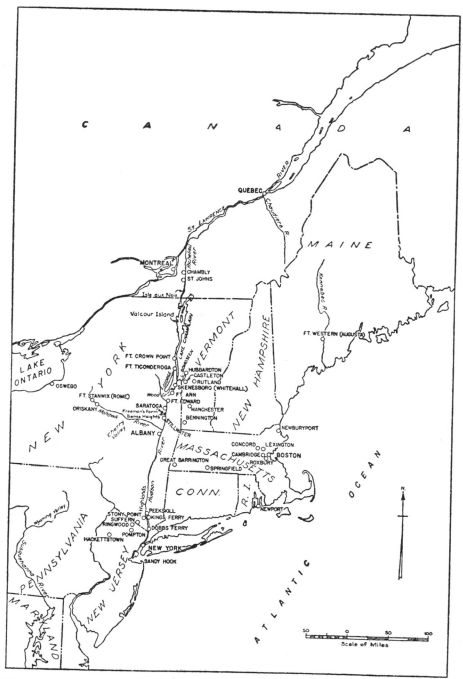

FIG. 2.1. NORTHERN COLONIES

Both sides faced formidable obstacles, not the least of which was the opposition each suffered at home. Two and one-half million colonists were pitted against the nine million people of Great Britain. Nor was the wild terrain in North America conducive to regular land operations by artillery, cavalry, or infantry. Gen. Thomas Gage, the fifty-six-year-old British commander in chief in North America, needed all his best qualities to cope with the provincial hostility around his headquarters city of Boston. His views of the Americans were generally sound, though not appreciated in London. Gage warned that the provincials would fight if provoked and that they could be defeated only by heavy British reinforcements sent 3,000 miles across the seas. He bent over backward to avoid hostilities but was ordered to use military force to prevent armed gatherings and to seize munitions that Americans were collecting in Massachusetts. Gage, a good soldier, reluctantly complied, though his heart was not in it.[2]

Boston, with a population of sixteen thousand, was alive with rumors of patriots collecting arms and ammunition to the west around Concord. When Gage learned of this he dispatched a force under the overall command of the slow-witted and corpulent Lt. Col. Francis Smith to seize these caches on 18 April 1775. The seven hundred British regulars were under the immediate command of Maj. John Pitcairn; he liked the provincials personally but regarded them as inept fighters. Paul Revere and Will Dawes warned that the British were coming and local citizens of Middlesex County began to bestir themselves in the cool hours before daylight. Shortly after dawn on 19 April Pitcairn confronted some seventy of these minutemen drawn up in two ragged lines of battle on the green at Lexington, led by forty-five-year-old Capt. John Parker, a veteran of Rogers's Rangers. Pitcairn rode boldly among the locals, demanding that they lay down their arms, but to no avail. A shot was fired, by whom no one knows, and musketry crashes were exchanged for a few moments; the minutemen reluctantly withdrew, leaving eight of their own dead and ten wounded on the dewy grass. One Britisher was wounded.[3]

Pressing on to Concord, the British succeeded in capturing only small quantities of munitions and weapons; most of the stores had already been dispersed by the alerted colonials. "By the rude bridge that arched the flood" of the river—the north span—the "embattled farmers" shocked the British with "the shot heard 'round the world," and repulsed them. Having accomplished as much of their mission as they could, the King's men started back toward Boston, but they were persistently peppered along the route by shots from the aroused colonists who fired from behind walls, barns, trees, and rocks. At Lexington the hard-pressed enemy was reinforced by over 900 troops rushed from Boston by Gage. But the harried British could only limp back into the city with losses totaling 274; Lieutenant Colonel Smith was seriously though not fatally wounded. Of the perhaps 3,500 Americans who sniped Indian style at the enemy column, some 93 were casualties. Gage might well have said to his superiors in England, "I told you so!" Nothing succeeds like success, and word of this provincial accomplishment spread so rapidly that almost simultaneously thousands of armed locals moved to encircle the royal troops in Boston.[4]

But aid from England was at hand for the uncomfortable Gage and his garrison. On 26 May 1775 His Majesty's 36-gun frigate *Cerberus* sailed into Boston harbor and dropped a precious cargo. This was the "triumvirate of reputation"—Major Generals William Howe, Henry Clinton, and John Burgoyne; two would become British commanders in chief in North America, and all would play pivotal roles in the war of American independence. It should be noted that none of these experienced officers had ever commanded truly large numbers of soldiers in the field, nor had any of them seen combat for over a dozen years.[5]

True to Gage's prediction, the fighting at Lexington and Concord had stimulated, not lessened, colonial opposition. The provincial assembly of Massachusetts authorized raising 13,600 troops; New Hampshire approved 2,000; Rhode Island, 1,500; and Connecticut, 6,000 soldiers. A rabble army of New Englanders, bickering and miserably organized, began erecting siege works around Boston.[6] But it was on another front—northwestward from Boston, at Fort Ticonderoga and Crown Point and at Lakes Champlain and George—that fighting next erupted, again with success for the patriots.

The American officers who would win laurels with their capture of these two famous British strongholds were Ethan Allen of Vermont and Benedict Arnold of Connecticut. The thirty-seven-year-old Allen was a tall, thin, broad-shouldered backwoodsman of great strength and trumpetlike voice, leader of a colorful group known as the Green Mountain Boys. He had served briefly in the French and Indian War with boldness, bluntness, and fearlessness. Though he had little formal schooling, he was an avid reader with a ready wit and a remarkable vocabulary of swearwords. This proud patriot was tough and audacious with boundless self-confidence and native cunning. In short, he was what the times required of a rebel leader.[7]

Benedict Arnold was thirty-four years old when he entered the war as a captain in the Connecticut militia. At the age of seventeen he fought in the last colonial war and then became a prosperous New Haven pharmacist, bookseller, and merchant who dispatched his own ships to the Caribbean. This handsome man had a commanding appearance—well built and muscular though of medium height, he was clear eyed, black haired, and dark skinned. Arnold was athletic, graceful, and swift in his body movements, as well as a brave fighting man who personally led his troops. His was a quick and original mind, and he demonstrated outstanding military merit. Unfortunately for the American cause, Arnold was imperious, arrogant, restive under orders, hypersensitive to supposed slights, and easily influenced by flattery. These character flaws would fatally counterbalance his many undeniable talents and lead ultimately to outrageous and treasonable conduct.[8]

And action was at hand for these two officers. Ticonderoga, on Lake Champlain, was a strategic, fortified position that controlled, along with Crown Point to the north, the classic invasion route of the Hudson, southward to New York and northward to Montreal. It was toward this rather dilapidated fortress that Ethan Allen and a force of some 350, including his Green Mountain Boys, moved in May 1775. On the night of 9 May, assisted by Arnold, Allen and about 83 of his men approached the fort by a cart path, surprised the sentry, and forced the sleepy and astonished commander—with Allen's sword over his head—to surrender the fort and its garrison of 45 tired old soldiers to "the great Jehovah and the Continental Congress." The following winter, in a remarkable feat, young Henry Knox would drag the sixty captured cannon by ox-drawn sleds across the snow and ice to aid George Washington in the capture of Boston. Two days after Allen's victory at Ticonderoga, the British hastily demolished and evacuated Crown Point, and provincials under the command of Seth Warner promptly seized it. Only after these twin set-backs did Gage on 12 June issue a tougher proclamation (written by General Burgoyne) calling upon the rebels to yield. But he acted in vain.[9]

The Americans encircling Boston in June tightened their semisiege by moving on to the Charlestown peninsula and rapidly throwing up slight fieldworks and a redoubt on Breed's Hill and flimsy works to the rear on Bunker Hill. The chief patriot commander on Breed's Hill, where the main engagement would be fought, was the tough-minded, bald-headed farmer, Col. William Prescott, a veteran of the French and Indian War. Over six feet tall, Prescott was muscular, broad shouldered, and clean-cut, with strong features. His manners were simple but courteous; although his formal educa-tion was limited, he was well read, cool, steady, and possessed a commanding presence. His orders were obeyed instantly by the troops, who respected this amateur commander who was so professional in his training methods and thinking. Assisting Prescott at the lesser rallying point on Bunker Hill to the rear was Israel Putnam. In the lines on Breed's Hill Dr. Joseph Warren, though a mere volunteer, brought up supplies, organized regiments around Boston, served as chairman of the Committee of Safety, and presided over the provincial congress. The thirty-four-year-old physician, courteous and modest in manner, was an ardent patriot—dynamic, impulsive, and intemperate in his demands for independence.[10]

On the bright sunny day of 17 June General Gage determined to give the Americans a demonstration of British might and prowess. He ordered Howe to launch a frontal assault by 2,500 of his redcoats on the 1,600 rebels at Breed's Hill. Gage could easily have cut off the locals at the narrow Charlestown neck of the peninsula to the north-northwest, but this he shunned. Citizens in large numbers crowded the Boston rooftops to witness this full-blown European type of open attack—a martial spectacle. And they were not disappointed. Reserving their fire until they could allegedly see the whites of the eyes of the gallant British coming forward in beautifully dressed lines, Prescott's locals twice hurled back the head-on charges with frightful losses to the enemy. Although Howe, Clinton, and Prescott led charmed lives in the raging combat, Dr. Warren, shot through the head, and Maj. Pitcairn, of Lexington fame, were slain.

Howe's third attack, to the flanks as well as to the front, finally forced the retreat of the minutemen from Breed's Hill when their ammunition was ex-pended. After a brief stand on Bunker Hill, the patriots were obliged to flee to safety across the narrow Charlestown neck. But they had gained a splendid moral victory, inflicting upon the British casualties of 228 killed and 826 wounded—a loss of 42 percent—as against provincial losses of 140 killed, 271 wounded, and 30 prisoners. While the colonists could and did make excellent propaganda of the so-called Battle of Bunker Hill, this engagement deluded them into believing that their untrained and undisciplined minutemen could stand up every time in line of battle to the enemy regulars. This misapprehension would be slowly unlearned at great cost in men and money.[11]

MEANWHILE the Continental Congress, with John Adams taking the lead, named George Washington, forty-three, their commander in chief. He assumed command of the Continental army under the Cambridge elm on 2 July 1775: a finer choice could not have been made. As a Virginian he would help pull the southern colonies along with New England into the common effort. As noted before, Washington was of commanding appearance and dignified presence. He was six feet two inches tall, weighed nearly 200 pounds, was a magnificent horseman, and possessed great endurance and steadfastness. His judgment was sound, and he could come to decisions in time to act. His impressive character and integrity held the army and cause together, and Washington saw clearly that the Continental army *was* the revolution. He was the best-known military man of high reputation throughout the colonies because of his long experience since early manhood in the wars against French and Indians, although he had not commanded large numbers of troops. This masterful figure was the one indispensable man—possibly the only one who could have won the Revolution—and one of the great figures in human history. He accepted every responsibility thrust upon him and fulfilled it.[12]

The army of some fourteen thousand men that Washington commanded about Boston was fearfully deficient in almost everything that soldiers required, and he devoted his talents and energies to achieve some level of efficiency. Nor were many of the local Massachusetts people overly cooperative. Washington cried out, "Such a dearth of public spirit, and want of virtue, such stock-jobbing, and fertility in all the low arts to obtain advantages of one kind or another . . . I never saw before, and pray God I may never be witness to again." But while easily perceiving the shortcomings of the people, the army, and the nation—and readily criticizing them—Washington sensed and quickly grasped their inherent and slowly developing strengths. In his words, he was acutely aware that "the fate of unborn millions will now depend, under God, on the Courage and Conduct of this Army."[13]

Still fresh in the minds of the provincials, however, was the fear of standing armies as a menace to liberty and freedom. Therefore, to ensure early civilian supremacy over the military, Congress insisted that General Washington report regularly to them and acknowledge the supremacy of Congress in the selection of his chief of staff and line officers. He was instructed to consult his principal officers in councils of war for decisions on major matters. The master of Mount Vernon set a shining example in doing this and assured military subordination to civilian authority. That sublime example has shone down the centuries as a standard of model soldierly deportment against which to measure all men in uniform serving the republic.[14]

While the siege of Boston dragged on into the fall and winter of 1775, an

American expedition was launched against powerful Quebec. Benedict Arnold, leading a force via the Kennebec River in Maine, reached the St. Lawrence at Quebec after incredible hardships. Another patriot force, moving upon the same point by way of Montreal, was commanded by the man who had just replaced the seemingly lethargic Gen. Philip J. Schuyler—forty-three-year-old Richard Montgomery, a very capable officer, born in Ireland and the son of a member of Parliament. Entering the British army at seventeen, Montgomery served under Amherst at Crown Point and Ticonderoga and married into the Livingston family of New York. He was a tall man—purposeful, energetic, yet studious. This fine American general was faithful to duty, aggressive, and cool in his judgments. Opposing Arnold and Montgomery at Quebec was Sir Guy Carleton, a vigorous general of fifty-one and certainly one of Britain's ablest commanders in the war.[15]

Learning that the terms of enlistment of most of their soldiers would expire on the last day of the year, Montgomery and Arnold were obliged to deliver what they knew to be a premature attack on the night of 30 December 1775 against the lower and upper town of Quebec—an assault that was launched in a snowstorm. There were perhaps 975 American effectives pitted against a smaller enemy force within the strongest fortification in North America. After slight initial gains in the lower town, and despite the desperate courage of the tall former teamster Daniel Morgan, who led several attacks, and Arnold and Montgomery, the British, skillfully led by Carleton, finally repelled the assaults. Montgomery was slain while leading a charge on a blockhouse, and Arnold was shot in the leg. As against just 20 enemy casualties, the colonists lost approximately 100 killed and wounded and 400 prisoners. Congress sent some reinforcements; Arnold, confined to his hospital cot, managed to maintain a semisiege. Although the venture ended in tactical failure, it helped deflect many British reinforcements from England to Canada instead of against Washington at New York. Arnold raised the siege of Quebec on 4 May 1776 and fell back via Montreal and Lake Champlain to the area around Ticonderoga.[16]

In the early months of 1776 Washington pushed the siege of Boston relentlessly. These efforts finally bore fruit when Sir William Howe evacuated Boston on St. Patrick's Day (17 March 1776) with his 170 ships, troops, and 1,000 British loyalists. The force moved to Nova Scotia where he settled the tories and awaited supplies and reinforcements. Some 250 British cannon were left in the hands of the Bostonians. It was a splendid triumph, revealing Washington's perseverance and his troops' fidelity in a long and monotonous siege.[17]

Another consequential triumph was secured farther south along the coast. Lord George Germain dispatched Lord Charles Cornwallis and troops from England, accompanied by a naval force under Vice Adm. Sir Peter Parker. This force was to join a detachment from Howe, under Clinton, off the mouth of Cape Fear River, North Carolina, and the entire armada was to move upon Charleston, South Carolina. This city of 12,000 people was defended by 6,000 soldiers under the command of Charles Lee and by batteries erected by Col. William Moultrie. Some of their 100 guns were emplaced in a rude palmetto log fort, bearing Moultrie's name, on Sullivan's Island. Relations were strained between Clinton and Parker; nor were they improved when Parker had his breeches blown off in the June 1776 bombardment of ten hours in which the British force participated. In the hard fought engagement the superior American gunnery repelled the attack, a number of enemy ships were destroyed or damaged, and the British sustained casualties of 225 redcoats and sailors.[18]

While Howe was gathering a force of 32,000 effectives to strike at New York City in the late summer of 1776, Arnold and his remnants retreated from Quebec to the south end of Lake Champlain. Here he boldly built sixteen small vessels and manned them with soldiers. Sir Guy Carleton, in his least skillfully waged campaign of the war, reinforced to some 10,000 troops consisting of Burgoyne's redcoats, Hessians, Canadians, and Indians, moved with a flotilla upon the Americans. In a bruising seven-hour battle off Valcour Island on 11 October 1776 Arnold lost two of his poorly constructed vessels but beat off the enemy. Two days later Carleton bettered Arnold in a running battle, and the rebels lost all their craft. For once Carleton was shaken by the ferocity of the contest; though he took Crown Point, he decided not to besiege Fort Ticonderoga. On 4 November, much to the ambitious Burgoyne's chagrin, Carleton withdrew his army to Montreal. Though a tactical defeat, Arnold's valiant fight at Valcour Island was a strategic success of inestimable value.[19]

In August 1776 what seemed to be a forest of masts appeared at the Narrows. General Howe, accompanied by his brother, Adm. Richard Howe, sailed into the magnificent harbor of New York with 30 warships, 400 transports, and 32,000 troops—the greatest armed force that Great Britain had ever dispatched to the New World. Be it said, however, that the Howes campaigned indifferently, seeming to expect eventual American acquiescence in their proffered armistice. Washington, with a total paper force of 19,000 soldiers (actually closer to 14,000 effectives), was ordered by the Congress to defend New York, as difficult as this task was, so as to encourage the patriots who were, here or in New Jersey or elsewhere, perhaps at least equally balanced by tories. The rebel troops were largely untrained and undisciplined, and Washington soon saw that he could not assume that such well-meaning but severely limited subordinates as Putnam could carry through on his orders.

In an adroit operation, Howe outgeneraled Washington and his colleagues, defeated the Americans at Brooklyn Heights on Long Island, and forced them—with John Glover's Marbleheaders performing a key action—to withdraw to Manhattan Island. The rebels suffered some 1,400 losses compared to enemy casualties of under 400. Washington was saved by his powerful artillery on Governor's Island and at the Battery at the tip of Manhattan, by sunken impediments in the water, and by winds unfavorable to Adm. Howe's penetration of the East River. Nonetheless, despite sharp delaying actions at Kip's Bay, Harlem Heights, Pell's Point, and White Plains, the Continentals lost Manhattan and suffered a severe setback and losses at Forts Washington and Lee on the Hudson River. It was a disheartening defeat, eased only by Howe's indolence in pursuit. By mid-November Washington's disintegrating army was in full flight, and New Jersey was threatened by the victorious British and Hessians.[20]

To make matters worse, reinforcements failed to arrive to succor

Washington's army. Charles Lee, advancing reluctantly, was ignominiously captured by the British in the middle of the night in a tavern and unceremoniously hustled off while still dressed in an elaborate flannel bathrobe. Congress had fled from Philadelphia to Baltimore. Howe and Cornwallis were convinced that Washington's army would be unable to continue the contest and that the war would soon be over. The terms of enlistment of all but 1,400 of Washington's soldiers would expire on 31 December, while there were no less than 12,000 enemy troops in the vicinity of Trenton, Princeton, and nearby points. It was the darkest hour of the war for the American cause.[21]

It seems incredible today, across the span of two centuries, that at this crucial moment Washington was actually planning to take the offensive—but it was true. The American commander, determined to strike before most of his tiny army melted away, crossed the ice-filled Delaware on Christmas night to bring about a surpassing feat of arms. Though disappointed by the failure of two of his subordinates to get their columns across, Washington marched through a sleet storm and fell upon and routed Col. Johann Rall's unsuspecting Hessians at Trenton, with enemy losses of over 900 (mostly prisoners) at a cost of only 4 slightly wounded Americans. Thus Washington won the crucial battle of the American Revolution—the one the Americans could not have afforded to lose. Historian George Bancroft declared, "Until that hour, the life of the United States flickered like a dying flame." Washington fell back to safety again on the Pennsylvania side of the Delaware.[22]

But the Continental commander soon recrossed the river near Trenton, on 31 December 1776, determined to prove that his triumph at Trenton was no mere lucky accident and that the tide of battle had really turned, at least for the time being, in his favor. He had a total force of some 5,000, many of them raw recruits, against 8,000 British under Cornwallis. Realizing that he could not fight the large enemy army at Trenton, Washington left his campfires burning to deceive the British on the night of 2 January 1777, and swooped down on three enemy regiments at Princeton. A British bayonet charge began to hurl the provincials back in near rout. But with defeat seemingly inevitable, Washington rode onto the field and courageously rallied his faltering troops, daring to ride within thirty yards of the blazing British line. By a miracle he passed along unscathed, and his stirring example pulled his soldiers into a swift counterattack that drove the foe from the field and achieved yet another striking victory. Some 35 men were killed, but Washington inflicted 300 casualties on the enemy. He then moved the Continental army into winter quarters at Morristown in the New Jersey highlands.[23]

Washington's victories in the Trenton-Princeton campaign not only saved Philadelphia and the patriots' cause but they also prompted Robert Morris—not knowing what the general's conduct throughout the remaining seven long years of war and eight more distinguished years as president of the United States would be—to declare, "He is the greatest man on earth." And perhaps he was. Cornwallis would say to Washington upon surrendering to him at Yorktown in 1781, "Fame will gather your brightest laurels from the banks of the Delaware rather than from the Chesapeake."[24]

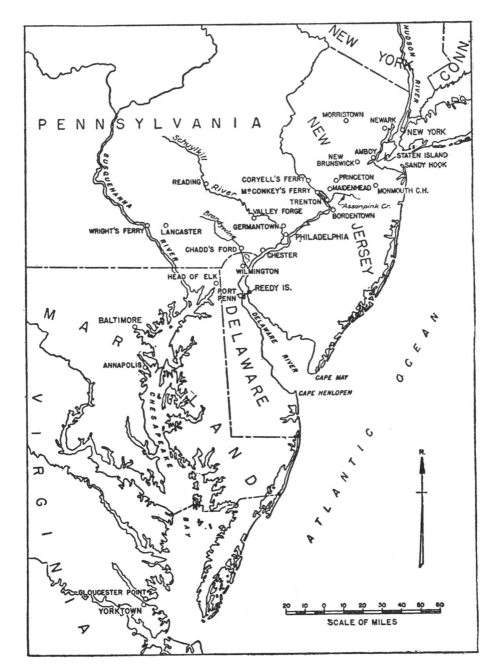

FIG. 2.2. THE MIDDLE COLONIES

THE BRITISH PLAN of grand strategy for 1777 was drawn up in London by the rather befuddled Lord George Germain, with kibitzing from Howe and Burgoyne, the latter again back in England. Burgoyne, who succeeded Carleton whom Germain disliked and retained only as Governor of Canada, was to move with 7,000 men (and many women) southward from Montreal down the classic invasion route of Lake Champlain and the Hudson to Albany, there to meet a force under Col. Barry St. Leger coming in from the west from Lake Ontario via the Mohawk River. Howe was to hold New York City and Newport and cooperate by making available 3,000 troops from New York to go up the Hudson to assist Burgoyne in cutting off New England from the rest of the colonies. Howe's main assignment was to move 11,000 men by sea from New York to capture Philadelphia. Unfortunately for the British, Germain typically failed to coordinate the several prongs of the operation.[25]

All did not go according to plan. Burgoyne started southward from Montreal on 15 June 1777. Splendid picnics and banquets along the shores did little to speed his advance. But the Americans were also beset with problems. The mediocre Schuyler had to be eased out of command, to be replaced by Horatio Gates. The latter was no godsend. Born in England, Gates entered the British army at twenty-seven and participated in operations at Martinique and under Braddock. Here he had become known to Washington, who probably recommended him for high command in the Continental army. He was named adjutant general in 1775. Gates was distinctly unmilitary in appearance— bespectacled, with florid complexion, thinning gray hair, heavy features, and heavy-lidded eyes. Yet he was a hard worker and good administrator, knew how to move paper work along, and was an effective lobbyist in Congress. But his character was marred by excessive ambition and he could be a calculating intriguer. Burgoyne is said to have termed Gates an "old midwife," and his later operations in the war fitted that description.[26]

Burgoyne's force moved slowly southward, capturing Crown Point and Fort Ticonderoga on the way. Somewhat alarmed at the steady progress of the invaders, Washington, with his keen sense of strategic priorities, sent Benedict Arnold, Benjamin Lincoln, and Daniel Morgan northward with reinforcements. And the going got sticky for Burgoyne after his initial success. He sent some of his Hessians to seize Bennington, where needed horses and supplies were said to be located. There, in two battles fought on 16 August, the 1,190 mercenaries were thrashed with a loss of over 200 killed and 700 prisoners by approximately 1,500 New Hampshiremen (who lost but 30 killed and 40 wounded) under the command of Brig. Gen. John Stark, a natural leader of men who had served in the French and Indian War with Rogers's Rangers. This brave and experienced soldier-farmer had already fought well at Bunker Hill, Quebec, Trenton, and Princeton. Burgoyne reached Saratoga, near Albany; hampered by rains and low supplies, he could go no farther and looked for help from Howe and St. Leger.[27]

But Gentleman Johnny Burgoyne was to be cruelly disappointed. Howe sent Clinton up the Hudson River a few miles north from New York City in a perfunctory move that soon returned these British troops to the comforts of

Manhattan. St. Leger, too, came a cropper. Augmented by some Indians and tories, he took Fort Oswego in mid-July and pressed on toward old Fort Stanwix (renamed Fort Schuyler—now Rome, New York). To the aid of the fort came 800 men under the command of a local landholder and son of a German immigrant, Nicholas Herkimer, but these provincials ran into an ambush at Oriskany, set by the educated Mohawk, Joseph Brant. Bloody hand-to-hand fighting cost him half of his men; Herkimer broke out of the trap, but he could not reach the fort. Fortunately for the Americans, and just in time, Arnold and a thousand volunteers rushed to the relief of Fort Schuyler. The pompous St. Leger was deserted by droves of his Indian and loyalist allies and retreated to Oswego, leaving Burgoyne on his own, alone, at Saratoga.[28]

In the final two battles in the autumn of 1777 at Stillwater, near Saratoga, Burgoyne had about 5,200 troops facing approximately 7,000 Americans in his front plus some 2,500 gathered in his rear that increased in the final days of the campaign. Gates's position was at Bemis Heights, just south of Saratoga, where the Polish engineer, Baron Thaddeus Kosciuszko, had erected fortifications. Burgoyne moved forward in attack formation and Arnold was allowed, belatedly, to advance to meet him on 19 September at Freeman's Farm. In a hotly fought engagement Arnold drove his troops between two enemy units, but Gates refused his appeal for a second group of reinforcements and Arnold was obliged to break off the action. Arnold was so angry at Gates that the latter relieved him of his command for insubordination. Actually Gates's hesitancy had prevented a more decisive success. Almost 600 British and Hessian soldiers were casualties as compared to patriot losses of 320.

The Battle of Saratoga was resumed on 7 October when Burgoyne advanced to attack the American position on Bemis Heights. When the British and Hessians paused in a long line on open ground, Gates ordered attacks against both their flanks, although he stayed well behind at headquarters. Arnold, unable to stand hearing musketry or being absent from the strife, spurred forward to lead the American charge despite Gates's efforts to have him recalled. Inspired by the dashing, magnetic Arnold, who carelessly exposed himself to enemy fire, the provincials were aided effectively by Daniel Morgan and his riflemen and drove the foe back from several redoubts in furious fighting. The entire enemy position might have been carried but for Gates's failure to commit reserves; he was so far in the rear that he could not see the valuable advantages gained. Arnold's horse was killed and the general's leg broken, and the momentum of the rebel attack was lost. Only 150 American casualties were suffered, but Burgoyne's actions around Freeman's Farm and Bemis Heights had cost him nearly 1,000 men. He fell back to the north to Saratoga (now Schuylerville, New York) and was hemmed in by increasing numbers of local soldiers. On 13 October 1777 Gentleman Johnny asked Gates for surrender terms. In the negotiations Gates caved in to such an extent that the capitulated British troops had only to yield their arms and were permitted to march off to a port where they simply released other redcoats for active service. But Saratoga was the turning point of the American Revolution, paving the way as it did for an invaluable alliance with France.[29]

While Burgoyne was en route to catastrophe along the classic invasion route, Howe in July and August of 1777 left Clinton with 7,200 men in New York City and moved some 14,000 troops by water up the Chesapeake Bay to Head of Elk (Elkton, Maryland) to seize the Continentals' capital of Philadelphia. Washington had anticipated this move and was able to confront the British commander at Brandywine Creek with about 11,000 soldiers. Battle was joined on 11 September. Despite Washington's warning, John Sullivan on the American right wing allowed Cornwallis to swing well around his flank and shatter his position. Only swift action by Nathanael Greene, who rushed his troops up from Chad's Ford, checked the British advance so that the Continental army could retreat to Chester. Here they came to a temporary halt when a nineteen-year-old Frenchman, the Marquis de Lafayette, helped Washington and Greene rally the rebels even though he was suffering from a leg wound. The British at the battle of Brandywine lost 90 killed and nearly 500 wounded; the patriots lost 300 killed and possibly 600 wounded, with 400 more made prisoner. On 20 September Anthony Wayne's hoped-for ambush to the west of Philadelphia at Paoli was revealed to the British by loyalists, and he suffered a sharp setback (the "Paoli Massacre") with some 250 casualties and 71 prisoners. Howe entered Philadelphia on 26 September, and the Congress fled to York.[30]

Washington made one last desperate effort to fall upon a segment of Howe's army at Germantown to the north of the city, before it could settle in for the winter. The American commander ordered his 11,000 troops to move southward in attack along four roads converging upon Howe's 9,000 men at Germantown. Surprised on the early foggy morning of 4 October by this attack, the British were saved from possible defeat. In the heavy mists some patriots under the drunken Adam Stephen (who was court-martialed and cashiered) fired into other colonists by mistake. Nonetheless Greene's main attack broke through the foe's lines and thrust into town, where vicious house-to-house fighting ensued. But with no pressure on the British flanks, caused in part by John Armstrong's turning back too easily, reinforcements under Cornwallis dashed out of Philadelphia and penetrated between two colonial units. Thus the confused rebels suddenly began to retreat. In this disheartening reversal, Washington's army lost 152 killed, 521 wounded, and 400 captured, while the British casualties amounted to 100 killed and 420 wounded. The Continental army moved to nearby Valley Forge to spend the winter of 1777–1778. After costly but successful combats on the lower Delaware River at Forts Mifflin and Mercer in November, Howe was secure in Philadelphia with his gambling cronies and his mistress.[31]

While the winter of the encampment at Valley Forge was not more severe than several others of the war, the American soldiers were never more poorly clothed, shod, or fed. Their pay was in arrears, and it was a remarkable feat for Washington and his officers to hold the army together after the disappointments around Philadelphia. But by extraordinarily good fortune they were assisted at Valley Forge in their training and regularizing of the army by the appearance of a capable forty-seven-year-old Prussian soldier who offered his services without pay, asking only for his expenses (Washington, too, throughout the Revolution, accepted no salary, taking just his minutely kept costs). This man, calling himself Baron Frederick Von Steuben, was well built, with thinning light brown hair, heavy eyebrows, and high forehead. He was unusually affable even though he did not speak English. Von Steuben was not the baron he claimed to be; he had been merely a captain and not a lieutenant general in Frederick the Great's army. However he possessed priceless talents as an organizer, drillmaster, and administrator.[32]

While Washington tried to clothe, feed, supply, and equip his army and bury the 2,500 soldiers who perished at Valley Forge, Von Steuben drew up a drill book of instructions for the Continental army. He wisely adopted only those parts of the Prussian drill manual that could be applied to irregular soldiers in the conditions prevalent in the North American wilderness, and he was thorough in his work. Thus the remnants of Washington's army that marched out of Valley Forge soon proved that they were regulars who could stand up in open line of battle against the best of the British "lobsterbacks."[33]

THE FRENCH ALLIANCE of 1778, of unparalleled significance, was engineered in great measure by the diplomatic efforts of Benjamin Franklin in Paris. France, burning for revenge because of her defeats in the previous wars in North America including her great loss of Canada to the British, was receptive to a modus operandi worked out between wily old Franklin, Vergennes, and King Louis XVI. The terms of the alliance, the only entangling alliance America would contract until the North Atlantic Treaty Organization (NATO) of 1949, provided for important French army and navy aid to the colonists and stipulated that neither country would lay down its arms until America won independence. In return for the continuing French and Spanish aid in arms, the Americans pledged not to make a separate peace with England and to assist the French in their acquisition of British sugar islands in the Caribbean (an unrealistic provision). In short, it was a mutually advantageous alliance.[34]

General Clinton, Howe's successor as supreme commander, was ordered to evacuate Philadelphia and decided to march his army from Philadelphia to New York City instead of moving it by sea. Washington correctly determined to strike the redcoats on the march and in doing so brought on the hard fought battle at Monmouth Court House, New Jersey, on the blistering hot day of 28 June 1778. Lee, directed by Washington to assail the enemy, neglected to prepare his attack properly and failed to coordinate it well. Nonetheless several of the piecemeal assaults were advancing when Lee, for reasons still unknown, suddenly called off his advance and retreated. Clinton pressed a counterattack that was only checked by the arrival of Washington personally and some reinforcements that restored the American lines and repulsed the enemy. Riding up to Lee, who had certainly showed some lack of internal stamina, Washington denounced him and ordered him off the field. The British, who lost more men at Monmouth than had the Continentals, reached New York safely.[35]

Policy decisions during the war reflected the long-voiced fear of Americans against standing armies, conscription, and military dictatorships. As early as 14 October 1774 the First Continental Congress declared that standing armies were permitted in each province only with that colony's consent. On 12 June 1776 Congress established a Board of War and Ordinance composed of six civilians, and this group acted as a war department until a secretary at war was named later in the conflict. By 1777 several military officers were included on the Board of War, and in 1781 Gen. Benjamin Lincoln was appointed secretary at war.

On 14 June 1775 Congress authorized the raising of troops for one year only. While these short-term enlistments were unwise, the measure at least created the Continental Army. But the unfortunate lesson of Bunker Hill persuaded the locals that a regular army was not essential. Washington exhorted the colonists to put aside particularism and merge all soldiers and efforts into a truly national American endeavor. However, the dread of standing armies and the belief that this would be a short war deterred Congress from making the Continental army a permanent establishment. Washington saw early that in a long war patriotism would not keep the ranks filled, and he fought a lengthy, hard battle against great odds to hold his army together. He was successful, although it required a superhuman effort. Bounties and eventually a draft were resorted to in order to supply the cannon fodder. To bolster the Continentals still more, Washington urged land grants for the soldiers.

And Washington came into new temporary authority. The crisis of late December 1776 induced Congress to give Washington dictatorial powers for six months, a practice that was repeated on another critical occasion. The general exercised these vast powers with great restraint and typical responsibility.[36]

Seeing that all other inducements were insufficient to maintain the Continental army, Congress called upon the colonies on 6 February 1777 to conscript men for nine months' service until enough three-year volunteers turned out. The provinces, however, were lax in enforcing these draft calls. Washington had the good sense to place the new recruits in old units, but recruiting was hampered by news of the suffering of the men at Valley Forge. Congress then permitted the states to fill their draft quotas by any means they saw fit and to retain the $200 bounty. The states, however, continued to hold back in administering their allotments.[37]

England's strategy to shift the emphasis of the war to the Southern colonies would involve the capture of a major port along the Atlantic coast to land British troops and supplies and encourage active loyalists in that region. The city of Savannah, with a population of 3,500, was selected as the objective of Lt. Col. Archibald Campbell's invasion force of 3,500 redcoats, coming from New York City. In late November 1778 American Gen. Robert Howe sought to defend Savannah with 700 regulars and 150 militia. His positions were struck by a joint flank and frontal assault and the patriots' defenses caved in and the city yielded with a loss of 83 rebels killed and 453 prisoners. Campbell proceeded to occupy Augusta in January 1779.[38]

After their fine repulse of the British attack in late 1776, the citizens of the proud port of Charleston allowed their fortifications to deteriorate, and Lincoln had only 6,000 troops of differing caliber to defend the important city. Clinton moved against it in February and March 1780, by land and water with 9,500 troops, and bombarded Benjamin Lincoln's defenses in April. Clinton was assisted by one of Britain's ablest young subordinate generals, the twenty-five-year-old Lord Francis Rawdon whose friendly and winning mien attracted many to him despite his reputation as "the ugliest man in England." In due time Charleston was surrounded and after another bombardment the still-resistant Lincoln was petitioned by the mercurial citizens to give up. He capitulated on 12 May 1780, and the loss by capture of 6,000 troops set a record as the largest number of American soldiers so taken until over 12,000 Union troops were surrendered to Stonewall Jackson at Harper's Ferry in September 1862. It was one of Britain's most striking victories of the war, with three American warships and some 300 cannon among the booty captured.[39]

In the backcountry of the South a particularly vicious, bushwhacking type of warfare ensued, with patriot pitted against loyalist neighbor. Burning, rape, murder, and pillaging were common; little quarter was asked or given. The American patriots in the South had their effective partisan rangers, and some of them were well led. One of the foremost of these leaders was Thomas Sumter, the forty-six-year-old "Gamecock" of South Carolina, who operated effectively in the northern and western part of that province. Though a former Continental army officer, this feudal grandee was living quietly on his plantation. But when it was burned by Tarleton's legion, Sumter became a partisan commander. Of imperious countenance, he was not as scrupulous as Marion, nor was he a particularly good strategist in that he did not coordinate his raids well with Continental authorities. The proud Gamecock was uncommunicative and self-important—"all sweat and fury," as one compatriot commented. Yet he lived to be ninety-eight. Sumter's was a great fighting spirit, and his intrepid sweeps kept the British and their tories constantly perplexed over his whereabouts.[40]

Perhaps Francis Marion, the forty-eight-year-old "Swamp Fox," had finer personal qualities. He, like Sumter, was also an ex-Continental officer who failed to coordinate his partisan raids with American officials. Marion was small in size but durable and courageous. He was quiet and impassive in expression. A good, fertile-minded strategist, he was not rash yet he acted vigorously and rapidly. This "Robin Hood of the Revolution," as some termed him, was abstemious in his personal habits, but he was a strict disciplinarian with his rangers. His raids were capably conducted between the Santee and Pee Dee Rivers in eastern South Carolina. Like Sumter, the Swamp Fox proved to be a constant thorn in the flank of the British lion.[41]

The third of the Southern triumvirate of partisan American leaders was the forty-three-year-old Andrew Pickens, a veteran of the colonial war against the Indians. This devout elder of the Presbyterian church was dour, seldom smiled, and never laughed. Vigorous but less successful than Sumter or Marion, Pickens had trounced a big band of tories in 1779 at Kettle Creek, but then had turned loyalist himself for a while after the fall of Charleston and the town of Ninety-six. When pro-British bushwhackers plundered his estate, this silent and unspectacular soldier took to partisan warfare. He coordinated his raids with Continental authorities better than did the Gamecock and Swamp Fox, and he personified another menace that tied down enemy troops and their commanders' attention.[42]

In the trans-Appalachian war, the name George Rogers Clark looms

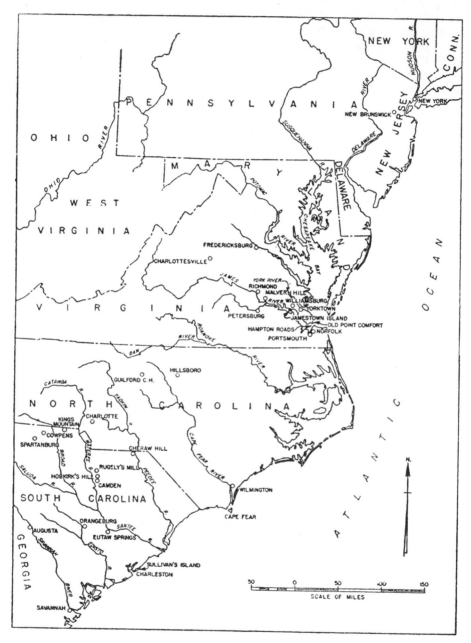

FIG. 2.3. THE SOUTHERN COLONIES

large. Twenty-five years old in 1778, this six-foot, black-eyed redhead was born near Charlottesville. While receiving little formal education, Clark did read in history, geography, and natural history while working on his father's farm, and then became a surveyor. His work, hunting, and exploring took him down the Ohio River into Kentucky, where his ability to gain friends and supporters did not go unnoticed. He served in 1774 in Dunmore's War as a captain of militia.[43]

Clark interested Gov. Patrick Henry and the Virginia assembly in his project and was authorized to move against the British and their Indian allies to the west. In June 1778 he moved with 175 troops down the Ohio and across southern Illinois to seize Kaskaskia on 4 July from the small enemy garrison. He informed the French settlers of the alliance between America and France and won over the allegiance of many. On 20 July he captured the important post at Vincennes. A British counteroffensive by the able Henry Hamilton, British lieutenant governor at Detroit, recaptured Vincennes on 17 December. But Clark in early 1779, with 172 men, marched 180 miles through flooded countryside, suffered severe hardships, and finally regained Vincennes, capturing Hamilton and 79 troops. However, Clark's plan to move from Kaskaskia upon Detroit had to be canceled when an insufficient number of soldiers turned out. Certainly his remarkable achievements helped make possible the inclusion within the boundaries of the new nation the great area from the Appalachians to the Mississippi River in the peace terms ending the war.[44]

Meanwhile operations continued to the east. Because Washington was unable to dispatch soldiers from his Continental army that faced the main British army, loyalist rangers and Iroquois Indian allies wreaked havoc upon the nearly helpless patriot frontier settlements in Pennsylvania and New York. These raiding tory bands operated out of Fort Niagara as a base and were led by British Maj. John Butler and by his son, Capt. Walter Butler, both formerly of St. Leger's army. Sweeping into Pennsylvania's Wyoming Valley on the upper Susquehanna River, the Butlers' force of 110 loyalist rangers and almost 500 Indians pounced upon Forty Fort, near present-day Wilkes-Barre, captured it on 4 July 1778, and butchered the American wounded. Walter Butler and 200 of his rangers, joined by 442 Mohawk Indians under Joseph Brant, swooped down upon Cherry Valley across the border in New York. In a cold rain on 11 November they burned houses and slaughtered at least 31 settlers. The excesses of these loyalists in Pennsylvania and New York later made these states untenable for them after the final American victory in the war.[45]

To avenge these massacres, John Sullivan was detached by Washington to wage a relentless punitive campaign against the Iroquois with a force of 4,200 troops. Though known as a hard-luck general, and at times tending toward rashness, the thirty-nine-year-old Sullivan developed one of the finest operations of the war. Born in New Hampshire, he became a lawyer, delegate to the First Continental Congress, and soldier in the Continental army, beginning with the siege of Boston. Brave and overly generous, Sullivan was also hypersensitive, hotheaded, and ostentatious.

He began his campaign into the Wyoming Valley from Easton in May 1779, destroying Indian villages along the way. On 29 August he roundly defeated a force of 1,200 rangers and Indians under the two Butlers and Brant near modern Elmira, New York. Further destruction was wrought by Sullivan's command at the head of Seneca Lake at Geneseo (near present Cuylerville) and along Cayuga Lake. The force returned to Easton in the autumn and in early November rejoined Washington's main army. Sullivan in his famous raid leveled forty-one Indian villages and lost only 41 soldiers. He became so ill that he had to resign his commission, but he broke the Indians' offensive power for the time being. Sullivan was later elected to Congress from New Hampshire and eventually became its governor.[46]

In May 1779 Spain entered the war against England, but she was not a welcome ally of the Americans along the southern border of the colonies. Also, the rebels were committed to fight until Gibralter was wrested from England and given to Spain. Despite her unpopularity, Spain contributed something to the American war effort against Britain. An unusually energetic Spanish official—the twenty-three-year-old Governor of New Orleans, Bernardo de Galvez—had previously opened thé port of New Orleans to Americans, loaned them money, and sold them munitions; now he seized the British posts of Natchez, Baton Rouge, and Manchac in September 1779 and Mobile in March 1780. This action helped abort a threatened enemy thrust from Fort Mackinac against the Illinois country and St. Louis and another one from Detroit against Kentucky. A result was that American settlers continued to pour across the mountains and through Cumberland Gap into the "dark and bloody ground."[47]

MIXED FORTUNES greeted the patriots' naval efforts during their war for independence. Even before Washington chartered and armed a few vessels to harass Britain's water lines of supply and communication, Rhode Island resolved on 26 August 1775 that the Continental Congress construct its own fleet of warships. The first real exploit of the Continental navy occurred in the spring of 1776. Eight American warships under the command of Esek Hopkins descended upon Nassau in the Bahamas and with the aid of the new Marine Corps (its first combat) under Samuel Nicholas, a Philadelphia tavern keeper, they captured some valuable munitions.[48]

However, the foray of the Massachusetts navy under Dudley Saltonstall in 1779 against Penobscot Bay, Maine, with Paul Revere as artillery chief, was disastrous. This expedition was mounted without consulting Washington and came to grief when the 900 militiamen stormed the fort unsupported by Saltonstall's nineteen men-of-war, which were lost anyway upon the arrival of a British squadron. It resulted in the failure of the land assault, the termination of the Massachusetts navy, the deletion of its merchant fleet, and the futile expenditure of £750,000.[49]

The American navy was early geared to commerce raiding (*guerre-de-course*) and to the frigate tradition instead of to ships-of-the-line, capital ships, and the command-of-the-sea school. Her frigates, or cruisers, though hastily developed, were actually well designed and some were well built. It would be the beginning of a small force of increasingly splendid frigates that would make a surpassing reputation for the infant navy from 1798 to 1800 and in the War of 1812.[50]

Of a number of intrepid and significant American naval commanders, four stand out above the others. One of these was a Marylander, Lambert Wickes, who was probably forty years old when the Revolution commenced. He had the distinction of commanding the first American warship, the *Reprisal,* after independence had been proclaimed and the honor of carrying Ben Franklin safely to France. Wickes captured many enemy prize vessels, but he lost his life when his ship foundered off Newfoundland. Another Marylander, Joshua Barney, went to sea at thirteen and commanded a ship at fifteen. He was just seventeen years old at the start of the Revolutionary War but was entrusted to carry secret dispatches to Franklin in Paris. He served as first mate on such famous American men-of-war as *Hornet, Wasp,* and *Saratoga.* Barney captured a number of British merchantmen and in a memorable fight as captain of *Hyder-Ally* he defeated *General Monk.* But Barney's most notable exploits would have to await the War of 1812.[51]

John Barry, who is sometimes called the father of the American navy and whose statue stands in front of Independence Hall, was born in Ireland and was thirty when the revolution began. In command of *Lexington*, he made the first capture in battle of an enemy warship for the newborn navy of the colonists. Barry fought in the Continental army at Trenton before he returned to the navy and captured other British prizes. He was also chosen to take Lafayette and American envoys to France.[52]

Most famous of all American naval heroes in the Revolution was John Paul Jones, born John Paul, in Scotland. He went to sea at twelve and commanded a ship at twenty-two. He was something of a martinet and ran into trouble when he had a seaman flogged to death and when he fatally sworded a mutineer. Seeking obscurity in Fredericksburg, Virginia, at his brother's home, he added the name Jones and joined the American navy upon the outbreak of revolt. He was a magnificent seaman, naval fighter, and student. This fiery, indomitable leader's writings on naval matters were of the highest order. His two most noteworthy feats were his fruitful cruise in 1777–1778 in *Ranger* around the British Isles, where he put a landing party ashore in Scotland on a daring raid, and his courageous and memorable fight in the leaky old East Indiaman, *Bonhomme Richard,* in which he finally defeated H.M.S. *Serapis.* Jones set the highest traditions for the infant navy, but his postwar career, including service in the navy of the Empress of Russia, was a checkered and not too happy one.[53]

On land, Washington's main Continental army waged no major campaigns for a year after July 1778. It was stretched in an arc across the Hudson, with the general's headquarters at West Point. The forts at the Point were strengthened and the soldiers were drilled under Von Steuben's arms manual. Clinton was also inactive, except for his push up the Hudson to King's Ferry and seizure of fortified Stony Point. Washington, however, judiciously refused to be baited into a hasty, ill-advised countermovement; yet he was determined to recapture Stony Point.[54]

The man selected to accomplish this objective was the rebel General

"Mad Anthony" Wayne, who had 1,360 light infantrymen available for the mission. The thirty-four-year-old Wayne was born in Waynesboro, Pennsylvania, and attended an academy in Philadelphia. He worked as a surveyor for a time and operated a tannery. When rebellion threatened, he played a leading role in his county's association with the Continental Congress. Wayne was of moderate height and had a handsome, well-proportioned face with a high forehead and slightly aquiline nose. Although he was quite young and lacked formal military training, Wayne proved to be a competent commander even though he suffered several bitter setbacks (as at Paoli). Though he could be impetuous, he was intelligent, self-possessed, and courageous.[55]

Wayne reconnoitered Stony Point carefully and supplied his colonels with accurate maps. One column of patriots approached the stronghold from the west while the other two attacked from the southern and northern slopes. Only the former column was allowed to use loaded muskets; the others were to employ only the cold steel of the bayonet. Wayne's brilliant assault began at midnight on 15 July 1779 and, after a bloody fight, the fortress was captured. The British lost 63 killed and 73 wounded, and the remainder of the 680-man garrison surrendered. Wayne's casualties amounted to 15 killed and 83 wounded, the general being among the latter. A store of arms and equipment was seized and the value of Von Steuben's training was confirmed by the excellent combat qualities displayed by the well-led Continentals.[56]

MEANWHILE in France Lafayette's and Franklin's efforts finally bore fruit. The king and Foreign Minister Vergennes agreed to provide the American rebels five French frigates and seven ships-of-the-line as well as an initial contingent of 5,000 French troops under the command of the fifty-five-year-old Comte de Rochambeau. Fortunately this veteran of the Seven Years War was neither jealous nor hypersensitive. Like General Washington, whom he admired, Rochambeau was gracious, dignified, and moderate. The French expedition arrived at Newport on 11 July 1780, and Rochambeau swiftly grasped the problems confronting Washington.[57]

The year 1780 was marred for Washington by Benedict Arnold's treason at West Point. Although he had been shamefully treated by Gates and was unappreciated by many members of Congress, Arnold did not inspire confidence by his thin-skinned and sulky attitude or his careless or indifferent use of captured equipment and supplies. He was appointed commander of the American garrison in Philadelphia and soon incurred heavy debts by high living and his marriage to vivacious young Peggy Shippen—expensive baggage herself. He reached the depths of dishonor when he requested a transfer to West Point as commander of that strategic post in order to open negotiations with Clinton. In these protracted dickerings, Arnold asked a steep price to sell out vital West Point, its garrison, and fortifications. When his treachery was discovered at the last moment, Arnold fled to the enemy and became a major general in the British army. None of his later campaigns with the English, however, were marked by a fraction of the ability he had shown on the patriots' side. He died in England after the war, scorned and embittered.[58]

To redeem the ominous developments in South Carolina, Congress, without consulting the commander in chief, named Horatio Gates to semi-independent command in the Southern theater—a choice that distressed Washington immensely. Normally a cautious general, Gates suddenly and inexplicably became rash in his foolhardy attempts to redeem the situation. In command of 3,000 effectives, he engaged Cornwallis's 2,200 at Camden in a sharp battle on 16 August 1780. Largely because of Gates's poor generalship, the colonists were thoroughly whipped and Baron Johann DeKalb was among the 750 American casualties. The British lost 68 killed and 245 wounded. Gates fled so swiftly to the rear that he was soon sixty-five miles from his shattered remnants. It was a disaster that the rebels could barely absorb.[59]

Two events redeemed the desperate plight of the provincials in the South. One was a sudden, surprising, and overwhelming triumph scored over 1,000 tories under Maj. Patrick Ferguson on 7 October 1780 at the Battle of King's Mountain by some 900 American backwater men or overmountain men from Tennessee and Kentucky under the command of such leaders as John Sevier, Isaac Shelby, William Campbell, and William Cleveland. This striking victory some thirty miles west of Charlotte cost the loyalists approximately 300 killed (including Ferguson) and wounded and almost 700 prisoners—practically their total force—as compared to American casualties of 28 killed and 62 wounded. This astonishing success came at the time most needed to keep alive the battle for independence in the South.[60]

The other necessary event required to bolster the patriots' cause in the Carolinas was the appointment by Washington of Nathanael Greene to replace the discredited Gates as commander in the Southern theater. Now thirty-eight years old, Greene was born at Potowomut, Rhode Island, and worked in his earlier years in his father's iron business. For several years he was deputy to the general assembly of Rhode Island, all the while reading and studying military literature. Brought up a Quaker, Greene was ousted from that faith when he was caught attending a military parade.

Greene entered the Continental army as quartermaster and became a troop leader. His many talents were only slightly diminished by his hypersensitivity (his gimpy knee perhaps made him resentful of insults) and his abrasiveness with Congress; by 1780 he was calmer and more judicious than he had been earlier in the conflict. He was not a brilliant tactician in maneuvering troops on the battlefield, but he was a careful yet bold strategist in planning larger operations. Greene could work amicably with partisans, contractors, governors, assemblymen, and other diverse types in the South, and he was a true nationalist and patriot who won Washington's approbation. Intelligent and energetic, patient, prudent yet enterprising, this resolute man, although not a dynamic troop leader nor especially lucky, was able to win the Southern campaign strategically while losing most of his battles tactically. He read Cornwallis's character and intentions like a book and was able to baffle him to the degree that he helped set up the British debacle at Yorktown.[61]

Although the Americans were outnumbered 4,000 to 2,700 by the British and their loyalists, the year 1781 opened auspiciously for them. In early January a group of raiding tories was smashed by Morgan near Ninety-six.

Morgan soon followed up this minor success by a masterly victory in northern South Carolina over the redoubtable Tarleton. This victory on 17 January at the Cowpens (a well-used local grazing area containing corrals) involved 1,040 rebel troops against 1,100 foes. Morgan conducted a deft double envelopment of the enemy forces. At a cost of 12 rebels killed and 60 wounded, Morgan inflicted casualties on Tarleton of 110 killed, 229 wounded, and almost 700 captured. As a result Cornwallis, who was playing a losing cat-and-mouse game with Greene, now began moving out of South Carolina and into North Carolina and Virginia. His overall strategy had been ruined unless he could redeem it by even greater efforts.[62]

Greene's army was reinforced by some 4,400 men; 1,500 were Continental regulars but only 630 of these were seasoned soldiers. Outnumbering Cornwallis now more than two to one, Greene determined to risk a stand-up battle on 15 March 1781 near Guilford Court House, North Carolina, not far from the Virginia border. In a desperate, seesaw engagement, the British came out a little ahead only after Cornwallis ordered his artillery to fire into the confused mass of fighting soldiery, killing some of his own men in the process but gaining time to regroup. Tarleton had three fingers blown off his hand. Not knowing how badly off the enemy was and wishing to ensure that his main field army remained intact and operable in the field, Greene pulled away, thereby giving the British a tactical success. This was a near-Pyrrhic victory for the outnumbered English; Cornwallis lost 93 killed and 183 wounded, although many of the North Carolina militia were missing from the ranks briefly after the battle.[63]

Cornwallis at last perceived that he had been hoodwinked and staggered back 175 miles southeastwardly to Wilmington to be resupplied by ship. North Carolina was left open and undefended and Greene soon headed southward through North Carolina toward Camden, South Carolina. Later Clinton might comment sardonically of Cornwallis's North Carolina campaign:

> After forcing the passage of several great rivers, fighting a bloody battle, and running eight hundred and twenty miles over almost every part of the invaded province at the expense of above three thousand men, he accomplished no other purpose but the having exposed by an unnecessary retreat to Wilmington, the two valuable colonies behind him to be overrun and conquered by that very army which he boasts to have completely routed but a week or two before.[64]

With Greene bearing down on Camden from the north with 1,550 soldiers, Lord Francis Rawdon had but 900 there to meet the American thrust. When Greene went into camp at Hobkirk's Hill north of Camden, the able and bold Rawdon sortied out to assail the patriots' position on 25 April 1781. Greene counterattacked and was countercharged in turn. Several errors by subordinate colonial officers and his own skill enabled Rawdon to gain a tactical edge and Greene fell back from a field that should have been a triumph, but wasn't. The Americans lost 19 killed, 115 wounded, and 136 missing as contrasted to British casualties of 38 killed and 220 wounded and prisoners. A swift rebel mop-up of most remaining British posts in South Carolina ensued.[65]

One final operation and battle occurred, although it altered little the declining British situation. Following an inactive summer, Greene, augmented by Sumter, Marion, and Pickens, put his 2,400 militia and Continentals in motion toward the 2,000-man force of Lt. Col. Walter Stewart, who had succeeded Rawdon and marched from Orangeburg to Eutaw Springs. At the latter point Greene attacked on 8 September 1781, bringing on a tenacious battle of three hours. The enemy line was cracked and Stewart was obliged to withdraw toward Charleston. A total American follow-up and victory were foreclosed when Greene's soldiers suddenly took to looting the captured enemy supplies, eating the food, and guzzling down the rum. Still, casualties of 84 killed, 351 wounded, and 257 missing (mostly prisoners) had been inflicted on the redcoats at a cost of 139 Americans killed and 375 wounded. Any further pursuit was frustrated by the departure of the partisan leaders and their contingents. Greene concluded his remarkable Southern campaign by moving forward and encamping outside of Charleston, with the British bottled up therein.[66]

The chagrined Clinton ordered Cornwallis to move to Yorktown, Virginia, and to fortify that place. This Cornwallis did with his 7,500 regular troops after an indecisive brush with Wayne's soldiers on 6 July at Green Spring Farm near Jamestown. His lordship's abortive Virginia offensive had come to an end when he dug in on the York River.[67]

Washington saw the possiblities of a grand American-French combination in the Chesapeake Bay area if Admiral De Grasse's main fleet would but come there. Yet he worried that Cornwallis might possibly send some of his troops from Yorktown to Charleston and some to New York City. There were too many imponderables, including De Grasse's vital intentions, for Washington to choose between an offensive against Manhattan or Yorktown.[68]

Then, to Washington's great joy, word arrived that De Grasse would bring his battle fleet to the Chesapeake; so the American commander planned and executed a magnificent combined operation of two fleets (De Grasse's and Admiral Barras's from Newport with the siege artillery) and two armies (the Continental army and Rochambeau's French army). Leaving sufficient troops to contain Clinton's army in New York, Washington marched toward Yorktown on 17 August 1781 with his own and Rochambeau's armies. His route took him through Pompton, New Brunswick, Trenton, and Philadelphia to Head of Elk, where the forces were transported by ship down the Chesapeake Bay to the vicinity of Yorktown, while Barras's small squadron brought the important siege guns from Newport to the same place. De Grasse's main fleet arrived at the beginning of September. It was all one masterful combination engineered by the American commander in chief.[69]

With the American and French armies moving up to begin the siege of Cornwallis's army at Yorktown, the outcome of the campaign would depend in large measure upon De Grasse's ability to keep Graves's British fleet out of the York River. On 5 September Graves sailed against the French fleet in the Battle of the Virginia Capes, and the British admiral launched a sloppy, bungling attack that De Grasse managed to beat off successfully. With a number of his great ships badly mauled, Graves supinely gave up and sailed away to New York, leaving Cornwallis to his own limited devices.[70]

At Yorktown there were now over 8,000 British redcoats and Hessian mercenaries, 7,800 French troops, 5,700 Continentals, and 3,200 patriot militia. The siege commenced in early October and the bombardment of Cornwallis's positions began on 9 October.[71]

Although almost as indecisive as Clinton, Cornwallis—perhaps bemoaning his stupidity in abandoning the Carolinas—did at least make a stern defense of Yorktown and Gloucester Point across the river. The British were well dug in, with redoubts strengthening their lines. But French engineers, miners, and sappers assisted the Americans in constructing siege parallels and positioning cannon, and Washington soon began a persistent and relentless artillery barrage by 100 guns and mortars. The British situation became desperate. Horses had to be shot as Cornwallis's own troops and loyalist refugees consumed the food; then smallpox broke out. Two advanced British redoubts were successfully stormed by French and American troops, including those led by young Lt. Col. Alexander Hamilton, on the night of 14 October. Cornwallis tried a final gallant but forlorn sortie before dawn on 16 October; while initially successful, the redcoats had to fall back and Washington resumed the terrific pounding from his siege ordnance.[72]

On 17 October 1781, the precise day that Clinton and Graves dropped down New York harbor on their belated cruise to try to save the British army at Yorktown, it was all over. A drummer and a flag of truce appeared over the British ramparts at Yorktown. An appropriately terse message was delivered under the white flag to Washington. It read: "Propose a cessation of hostilities . . . to settle terms for the surrender. . . . Cornwallis." Washington wisely rejected Cornwallis's demand that the British army be permitted to go home on parole, as Gates had permitted Burgoyne's men when the sly redcoat duped Gates at Saratoga. So as the band played "The World Turned Upside Down," the 8,000 British and Hessian troops and sailors came out in the bright sunshine to "surrender field" on 18 October and laid down their arms as prisoners of war to the undaunted patriot commander in chief, probably the only man who could have won the Revolution for the colonies.[73]

Peace was now at hand for the belligerents. Benjamin Franklin's skillful diplomacy led Britain to conclude a provisional peace treaty that was ratified by Congress on 19 April 1783, exactly eight years to the day after Lexington and Concord, and a final treaty of peace that was signed on 3 September 1783.[74]

In the meantime, while the peacemaking was slowly proceeding, the shameful treatment of American Continental soldiers by Congress, including serious arrears in pay, led to two near mutinies among officers and men. At Washington's headquarters, officers who were disgruntled with Congress about neglected pay, pensions, and land grants, heeded the anonymously written "Newburgh Addresses" that had been drawn up by troublemaker John Armstrong, and sent their ominous warning to Congress. Washington returned to his headquarters in March 1783 and in a moving scene confronted his dissatisfied officers with a stern countenance. He first somewhat dramatically donned his glasses and remarked that he had not only grown old but almost blind as well in the service of his country. These words and those that followed effectively quelled the threatened uprising. Finally, some nearly mutinous soldiers near Philadelphia presented a "petition on boots" in June by marching into the city. Congress adjourned in haste to Princeton, but Washington suppressed the demonstrators by dispatching Continental troops to the City of Brotherly Love. The men's contempt for the politicians was evident even though they returned to their homes peacefully, and members of Congress in the future would remember with trepidation this supposed threat by the military.[75]

George Washington bid farewell to his officers on 4 December 1783 at Fraunces Tavern in New York City in one of the most poignant scenes in American history. In an emotion-choked atmosphere, with staunch soldiers like Henry Knox and Von Steuben present, the commander in chief toasted them by saying, "With a heart full of love and gratitude, I now take leave of you. I most devoutly wish that your latter days may be as prosperous and happy as your former ones have been glorious and honorable." In the silence that followed, and without a dry eye in the room, each officer in turn was embraced and kissed on the cheek by an unrestrained Washington. Then their honored commander departed by way of Philadelphia for his beloved Mount Vernon.[76]

One final ceremony remained: Washington's resignation of his commission. This took place at the Maryland state house in Annapolis, where Congress was sitting. The galleries were filled for this memorable occasion on 23 December. When the large man entered the chamber, the Congressmen remained seated with their hats on while Washington stood before them, hat in hand. The civilian supremacy over the military would be honored. His hands trembled as he read a brief preamble in which he thanked his comrades in arms, his aides, and Almighty God, and closed with the following words of farewell:

> Having now finished the work assigned me, I retire from the great theatre
> of action; and bidding an Affectionate farewell to this August body under
> whose orders I have so long acted, I here offer my commission, and take
> my leave of all the employments of public life.

It had been over seven tortuous years since these Congressmen had pledged for independence their lives, their fortunes, and their sacred honor; Washington had now redeemed their pledge. The late commander in chief shook hands with all present and rode quietly away to Mount Vernon, where he arrived on Christmas Eve, 1783. Yet it would not be long before he would be beckoned again by the republic for an additional decade of signal public service.[77]

BY WAR'S END approximately 400,000 American soldiers had been mustered into service at one time or another at a cost of about $370,000,000. Casualties in the Continental army, while not accurately known, totaled perhaps 12,000 dead. Had Congress, which unfortunately managed both legislative and executive authority, been less incompetent, one-fourth of this number of troops would have been sufficient; never could Washington gather more than 17,000 men together at one time or place during the war. Too, lack of unity among the American colonies led to frightful failures in the war effort, as did the structure of Congress under the Confederation, which lacked power itself and had to requisition the states for taxes, food, clothing, supplies, and equipment. Inexperienced officers also handicapped the provincials' military efforts.[78]

But certain British weaknesses and the boon of French assistance helped shape the final triumph of the Yankees. The conflict showed that civilians, trained in due time and with guns in their hands, could eventually defeat the best of European professional armies that could be brought against them. The war was won in part by the superb fighting qualities developed by our citizen-soldiers in the ranks, and by the perseverance and ability of a handful of generals from Washington on down through Knox, Greene, Morgan, Arnold for a time, and Wayne. The British were fighting not just an army but a people who simply refused to be conquered. Finally, America had George Washington, an indispensable man for all seasons if ever a leader were that. He was better at the kind of warfare he was obliged to wage than were the English commanders at theirs.

American belief in equality led to somewhat better treatment of the men in the ranks than was the custom abroad, although fear of militarism and a standing peacetime regular army would long remain a cardinal tenet of American military policy; hence the oftentimes unwise overreliance on militia to fight the nation's wars in the future.[79]

Vigilance, unity, and preparedness were the high prices Americans would have to pay to preserve their freedom, and this basic lesson of the American Revolutionary War remains with us today and will probably remain so in the twenty-first century.

CHAPTER THREE

Military Vulnerability

Their deeds of heroism were accepted by the nation and their comrades in arms as merely a part of inescapable duty. Although they won for the republic the range of an empire, the annals of the Northwest are barren of their deeds. Only here and there do forgotten mounds of earth and simple headstones mark the resting places of their moldering bones. In their own day they were looked upon as merely hirelings of the government, grudgingly considered necessary at times but generally distrusted by the majority of the people.

JOHN RIPLEY JACOBS
on soldiers on the frontier
in the 1790s

WHEN THE GUNS fell silent at Yorktown in 1781, peace with Great Britain was still a year and a half away. And when the Treaty of Paris of 1783 was finally signed, military problems for the new nation remained. It had been a costly war in men and money, and the new nation faced its independence with serious financial as well as political and military policies unresolved. Soldiers of the Continental army went unpaid, British soldiers continued to occupy illegally the Northwest posts on American soil, and Congress practically demobilized the army and took steps to sell or give away all of the navy's warships. The English did not evacuate New York City until 26 November 1783, a mere two days before General Washington resigned his commission and retired to private life at Mount Vernon. One of Washington's last actions was to station some six hundred soldiers, under the command of Henry Knox, in New York. But the supremacy of civilian rule over the military was everywhere apparent.[1]

Congress tried to hammer out a viable military policy. Alexander Hamilton, chairman of a congressional committee, asked George Washington on 9 April 1783 for his views on a permanent peacetime military establishment. Ever mindful of his country's well-being, Washington consulted his wartime contemporaries Baron von Steuben, Henry Knox, Rufus Putnam, and others before composing his own "Sentiments on a Peace Establishment" and sending this paper to Hamilton's committee.[2]

4 7

This document reflected some of Washington's most enlightened advice. He argued cogently for seven policies: (1) a regular army of 2,631 troops, mostly to garrison the frontier posts and "to awe the Indians, protect our trade, prevent the encroachments of our Neighbours of Canada and the Florida's, and guard us at least from surprizes"; (2) for "security of our Magazines"; (3) a regular, well-equipped navy without which, in the event of war, "we could neither protect our Commerce, nor yield that Assistance to each other, which, on such an extent of Sea-Coast, our mutual Safety would require"; (4) a well-organized militia based "upon a Plan that will pervade all the States, and introduce similarity in their Establishments"; (5) arsenals for all kinds of military stores and equipment; (6) one or more military academies "for the Instruction of the Art Military; particularly those Branches of it which respect Engineering and Artillery, the knowledge of which, is most difficult to obtain"; and (7) industries capable of manufacturing war goods. Hamilton's committee carefully studied Washington's proposals for five months and then issued to Congress its own report in which it recommended most of Washington's proposals except for a military academy, which it deferred so as not to rile the legislators.[3]

Although timid states' rights advocates were fearful of the strong nationalistic bent of the Continental army, something had to be done to maintain at least a miniscule regular army. After the year's study and in complete disregard for the proposals of Washington, Hamilton, and others, on 2 June 1784 Congress voted the regular (Continental) army out of existence save for eighty soldiers—fifty-five at West Point and twenty-five at Fort Pitt—to guard military stores. The following day the lawmakers agreed to raise a regular army of seven hundred men to serve for one year, one regiment of eight companies of infantry and two companies of artillery, from the militias of Connecticut, New York, Pennsylvania, and New Jersey. A large regular army was impossible at this time because of the conviction of many Congressmen that "standing armies in time of peace are inconsistent with the principles of republican governments, dangerous to the liberties of a free people, and generally converted into destructive engines for establishing despotism." Since Pennsylvania furnished 260 troops of this 700-man force, this state was honored by the appointment of a Philadelphia Main-Liner, Lt. Col. Josiah Harmar, to command the first American regiment. On 1 April 1785 Congress resolved to continue the men in this army for three years' service; thus it became more of a regular army.[4]

In the spring of 1785 Congress named Henry Knox to the vacant post of secretary at war. By June 1786 the portly Knox could report that 640 of the authorized 700 soldiers were recruited. The secretary received a salary of $2,450 per year; his three clerks, $450 each; and a messenger, $150. The generous legislators agreed also to the munificent appropriation of $176 per year to Knox for office expenses, including stationery, fuel, and candles. As secretary at war, Knox was made responsible for Indian affairs; he tried to curtail the demands of northwestern frontiersmen for land cessions from the natives. Knox even went so far as to evict squatters from Indians' lands.[5]

While the secretary labored on his plan to remodel the militia, the Congress had already rejected a proposal put forward by Frederick von Steuben sometime before. The baron's plan had called for a military establishment consisting of one regular army-type legion of 3,000 troops; a corps of artillery of 1,000 men; and seven sublegions of well-disciplined militia of 3,000 each, to be ready at a moment's notice and expandable to 42,000 in a crisis. Von Steuben would train only the younger militiamen for thirty-one days per year. The baron recommended that each 3,000-man sublegion be composed of two small infantry brigades, two batteries of artillery, and a squadron of two troops of cavalry. He thought the military establishment should be decentralized into three geographic departments, each including essential ordnance manufactures, arsenals, and a system of military education.[6]

With von Steuben's plan dead, Knox submitted in March 1786 his own scheme for organizing the nation's militia system. Differing from von Steuben by ignoring regulars in favor of training volunteer militia, Knox divided the militiamen into three age groups, with only the younger ones to receive six weeks' training each year at an annual cost of $750,000. The total potential number of these citizen-soldiers was estimated at 450,000. The secretary argued that in an emergency the younger militiamen could be quickly mobilized into a Continental army organized on a regional basis. These troops would be armed either by the states or initially by themselves. The War Department and professional army officers would provide every state with specimens of each weapon and piece of equipment to be used. Finally, the secretary's plan called for all mariners or seamen to be registered and divided into two age groups, the younger to serve aboard a public warship for three years. But like the other comprehensive plans of Washington, Hamilton, and von Steuben, Knox's plan was not accepted by Congress, which continued to rely solely upon the tiny 700-man regular army.[7]

After the passage of the admirable Land Ordnance of 1785, which was designed to open up frontier lands quickly and systematically, especially in the Northwest, Lt. Col. Josiah Harmar was authorized to advance along the Ohio River to the mouth of the Great Miami, where he built Fort Finney. He later marched to Fort Steuben, some twenty miles above Wheeling. In the summer of 1787 one of Harmar's subordinates, Maj. John Hamtramck, moved to Vincennes along the Wabash River, and the remainder of the regiment pressed on down the Ohio to Muskingham. By late in the year the federal troops stretched from the upper reaches of the Allegheny River to near Louisville, Kentucky. Harmar had much of the small army with him; the only other regular troops were in the East at West Point and Springfield, Massachusetts. So plagued was the army by corrupt and inefficient contractors and an inept military stores commissioner, that Harmar was obliged to take money from his own pocket to feed his men.[8]

There was trouble as well in the Northeast. After Daniel Shays's band of rebels numbering 2,000 had mobbed jail officials and released debtor prisoners in late 1786, troops under Benjamin Lincoln broke up an attack on the Springfield arsenal with several whiffs of grape shot and the so-called rebellion collapsed. As a result of this threat, Congress was finally prevailed upon to increase the regular army to 2,040, with an enlistment period of three years.

Both Knox and Washington were gravely disturbed by Shays's rebellion and warned of the danger of an ineffective government, especially one with little or no executive powers. Finally a call was issued by Congress for a conclave representing the states, and in the summer of 1787 the famous gathering of great talents known as the Constitutional Convention was convened in Philadelphia. Presided over by Washington, the assembled delegates decided to scrap the Articles of Confederation and draw up a wholly new Federal Constitution.[9]

(Having finally decided on a tripartite federal government of three coequal branches, with separation of powers and a system of checks and balances, they struggled to determine the power that they should confer upon the executive branch. They approached with caution the questions of the nature of the military establishment, civilian supremacy over the military, war powers of Congress, and the military authority of the president of the United States. Congress was given the power to declare war, to raise and support armies, to provide and maintain a navy, and to make rules for the government and regulation of the armed forces, among other powers.) Nonetheless the president was made the commander in chief of the armed forces of the United States and of the militia of the states when federalized. There was no elaboration on the chief executive's powers as commander in chief and this omission caused serious misgivings among some who voted for these powers at the Constitutional Convention and at the state ratifying meetings; yet they were designed to ensure civilian supremacy and to provide unity of command. Finally, after a protracted struggle, the Constitution was adopted and went into effect in 1789. George Washington was unanimously chosen as the first president.[10]

On 7 August 1789 Congress created the War Department headed by a secretary of war who was to handle matters pertaining to the army, navy, and Indians, as directed by the president and not by Congress, as before. The secretary's salary was to be $3,000, and he was to be assisted by a chief clerk. By 1792 there were nine other clerks whose annual salaries averaged $460. The six-foot, 280-pound former secretary at war and Revolutionary War artillery chief Henry Knox was forty-two years old when he was named secretary of war. Knox possessed Washington's full confidence (together they had helped found the Society of the Cincinnati), and Knox remained in his position until the end of 1794. Because he was accustomed to high living in the capital, the secretary soon earned the nickname of the Philadelphia Nabob. Yet on the whole he performed quite well as secretary. Pressured to respond to ominous Indian activities on the frontier, Congress reluctantly passed a law on 29 September 1789 adopting as the regular army the 840 men authorized by the legislation of 3 October 1787, although only some 672 of these soldiers were actually in the ranks.[11]

Secretary Knox took Washington's earlier thoughts, as well as his own previous study, and grafted them onto a new militia plan that he laid before Congress on 21 January 1790. He recommended the universal obligation of military service for all free men, including a naval militia for mariner types. He suggested a regular army, or legion, of 2,033 plus "a small corps of well-disciplined and well-informed artillerists and engineers." He urged that this slender force be bolstered by "an energetic national militia" drawn from a reservoir of men between eighteen and sixty, the younger men to train for thirty days per year. The cost to each citizen of the republic to support such a militia force of 325,000 would amount to one-eighth of a dollar. In contending that the government should be able to control events vigorously, "instead of being convulsed or subverted by them," Knox unfortunately termed the militia the "strong corrective arm" of the authorities, and this frightened the timid men in Congress.[12]

Opposition to Knox's plan quickly developed in the press and elsewhere, and on 26 April 1790 the plan was withdrawn from the committee of the whole house and referred to a committee named to study and bring in a bill for the nation's defense needs. Military historian James Ripley Jacobs has commented that these state militia forces, stubbornly retained, were "hypothetical soldiers assigned to imaginary brigades and divisions. They were admirable as a political machine, but for uses in battle they were utterly futile. They were dominated by an epauletted hierarchy that bulged with fat and ignorance."[13]

RELATIONS with the Indians to the north remained threatening. Massacres of whites were frequent, and it was estimated that 1,500 settlers in and bound for Kentucky alone had thus perished, not to mention other similar outrages. Washington's administration had bent every effort to secure peace, but in vain. Northwest Territory Gov. Arthur St. Clair had persuaded some chiefs of the Senecas, Delawares, and Wyandots (outstanding among them was Cornplanter) to sign the Treaty of Fort Harmar on 9 June 1789 that reemphasized the previous boundaries of the Indian country and contained other terms to regulate affairs more amicably between whites and red men. St. Clair contributed $3,000 worth of goods as gifts, but the Indian raids and scalping parties continued almost unabated.[14]

Josiah Harmar's campaign against the Indians suffered a cruel fate, though little fault could be laid directly at the door of the thirty-one-year-old commander. He seemed like a solid sort. Harmar grew up among affluent Philadelphians, received good schooling, and served patriotically in the Continental army during the Revolution, attaining the rank of lieutenant colonel. His good reputation and contact with important people helped him accrue a satisfactory income. He was entrusted by Congress to bear the ratified treaty to the United States minister in Paris at the end of the war. Soon after, he married and received the frontier troop command previously mentioned. Harmar in August 1790 was at Fort Washington, and with St. Clair's full support, was being lectured in writing to prepare and conduct his important expedition with care, thoroughness, speed, and decisiveness; the secretary urged Harmar to take precautions against being surprised by the Indians.[15]

Harmar could do little to improve his force of tattered soldiers who had signed up for short-term service. Because of inadequate training time, these rustics were ill equipped, poorly disciplined, badly led, untrained, and low in morale. In order to train this raw and inexperienced force, Harmar's marches, encampments, and battle deployments were always rigidly routine and unvarying. Perhaps he did not give sufficient attention to terrain, use of reserves, and unpredictable Indian characteristics; yet he could do only so much with such ill-prepared officers and soldiers.[16]

Moving in September and October 1790, Harmar's force of 1,133 green militia and 320 regulars found the Indian villages abandoned and burned by the Maumee. Disobeying repeated orders to remain concentrated, parties of thirty or forty soldiers scattered out in all directions to plunder. Luckily none were ambushed at this time, and Harmar's main body arrived on 17 October. Five villages were put to the torch, including 184 cabins, and a lot of growing corn was destroyed in the field.[17]

Harmar ordered a reconnoitering party under the cowardly Col. James Trotter to scout out the area, but they soon returned to camp. So Harmar ordered out a second force of 210, but nearly half of this band lurked shamefully in the rear. Its commander rashly pressed forward and failed to heed warning shots fired by Indians ahead. Suddenly the remaining column was engulfed by hostile fire from all directions from perhaps 130 Indians. Most of the troops fled to the rear in terror; only the 30 regulars and 9 militiamen stood firm and fought to the last. They were cut to ribbons; only 6 or 7 escaped alive by their own herculean exertions. John Hardin's whole force retreated, pursued for awhile by an encouraged foe.[18]

With a third of his pack horses lost or dead through their guards' neglect, and convinced by the defeats of his detachments that further offensive action was impossible, Harmar realistically withdrew his demoralized army on 23 October toward Fort Washington. The militiamen would not obey orders and were beyond control for most of the march. When Harmar finally gave mild punishment to one offender, he was harshly denounced as incompetent to conduct operations against the Indians by a number of blundering militia officers. The army limped into Fort Washington on 3 November 1790, where the militiamen were quickly discharged. Instead of criticizing their conduct, Harmar gave a banquet to all of his field officers and friendships were restored. His defeat in terms of casualties showed that of the 320 regulars, 75 were killed and 3 wounded, and of the 1,133 militiamen, 108 were killed and 28 wounded. In addition, rations and equipment were lost, destroyed, or stolen.[19]

Harmar considered resigning, but the purple prose of James Wilkinson convinced him not to. Such resignation, Wilkinson boomed, would be "unphilosophical, petulant and boyish," and must be shunned like "plague, pestilence and famine." A court of inquiry, the pompous Wilkinson argued, would "refute the calumnies which the envenomed tongue of slander and detractions have let fly at you without mercy." Harmar reluctantly acquiesced, and the court began its hearings on 15 September 1791 at the southeast blockhouse of Fort Washington. After nine days it brought in a verdict that exonerated him completely and hailed his conduct of the campaign as worthy of "high approbation." But Harmar could never explain satisfactorily why he had permitted his depleted detachments to go forth.[20]

One result of Harmar's defeat was congressional authorization on 3 March 1791 of an additional regiment of 912 troops, thereby bringing the regular army total up to 2,128. The act also empowered the president in an emergency to raise a further force of 2,000 levies. These were to be volunteers as distinct from militia and began a practice that would allow the president to name their officers.[21]

A significant figure helped draw up the law of 3 March 1791. He was Arthur St. Clair, who journeyed to the East after Harmar's defeat. Born in Scotland, St. Clair studied medicine in London and with his mother's money bought a commission in the British army and came to America with Boscawen. He served at Louisbourg under Amherst and at Quebec with Wolfe. St. Clair settled in western Pennsylvania after resigning his commission in 1762. He married a half-sister of the governor of Massachusetts, and purchased extensive lands in western Pennsylvania. St. Clair joined the American cause in the Revolution, and rose to the rank of major general by 1777. Though not always victorious, he gained Washington's commendation for his participation at Ticonderoga, Trenton, Princeton, Brandywine, and Yorktown. He became a Congressman, and in 1787 was elected president of Congress. A year later he was named governor of the Northwest Territory. St. Clair had been negotiating with the Indians of the Northwest since 1789. It was assumed that he was an authority on the Indians, and that he could combine military and civil duties successfully. On 4 March 1791 he was appointed a major general, thus giving him two high posts and two salaries.[22]

Problems quickly arose. At Fort Washington St. Clair failed to receive the requisite support from the settlers who thought he did not understand their problems and regarded him as incompetent to conduct a major expedition against the Indians. Although more troops were needed, they came in slowly; many were held needlessly at Fort Pitt until the last of August. The governor learned that instead of the planned 3,000, he would have but 2,500 men and that he would have to supplement his numbers by local recruits. With many of his officers demonstrably incompetent, St. Clair faced the dilemmas of trying to train, feed, supply, and discipline his men in a short time. Even Secretary of War Knox was dilatory about speeding essential items to St. Clair's army, and Alexander Hamilton's economies in the Treasury Department were made at times at the expense of supplies for this force.[23]

Five weeks behind schedule, St. Clair finally moved the six miles from Fort Washington to Ludlow's Station with 2,300 troops on 7 August, although desertions were already occurring. President Washington beseeched the general to employ "decisive measures," and, by "every principle that is sacred," to move as swiftly as possible. But the army needed three days to hack its way eighteen miles through swamps and heavy forest to arrive at the Great Miami River on 19 September. Here, the large Fort Hamilton was constructed in two weeks of back-breaking labor. Fortunately, no Indian attacks took place.[24]

The ill-clad army lurched northward again on 4 October, with scouts well to the fore and rear. Extreme caution was exercised at predawn, the favorite time for hostile assault. The force averaged only five miles per day for the next ten days. New arrivals of recruits possibly balanced desertions. The army was accompanied by dozens of male and female camp followers, as well as some wives or washerwomen, some even carrying babies. A few of these women would actually fight the Indians. It cannot be overstressed how hampered St. Clair was by his inept officers and soldiers, and by short supplies, especially food, that had been forwarded in inadequate amounts by the venal contractor.[25]

Bickering over a suitable campsite on 3 November dampened the troops' already dejected spirits. This fateful camp, near the east bank of the upper Wabash River (fifty miles from the later city of Fort Wayne), was some ninety-seven miles north of Fort Washington. The camp, facing west, had low and marshy ground on both flanks and to the rear, and the whole site was covered with trees. In front was the twenty-yard-wide Wabash, which could be waded. Higher ground was situated to the west. The Indians, numbering several hundred, knew the terrain intimately—and were lurking in the vicinity. They could sneak through the cover of timber undetected. St. Clair decided against throwing up hasty breastworks when he arrived because his men were dead tired, and he refrained from this vital task.[26]

Thirty minutes before dawn, while soldiers were cooking breakfast, the Indians suddenly launched their onslaught with fearful yelps. The Kentucky militiamen, to the front across the Wabash, fired a few shots and immediately abandoned their naturally strong position and fled panic-stricken back across the river and through the two American lines, spreading terror and confusion. Other Indians assailed the rear of the camp, on the east. Some of the fugitive militia were scalped while racing to the rear. Repulsed by Richard Butler's regulars in the front line, the Indians swung to the left and right and shot down the outguards on the flanks and surrounded the camp. The approximately 1,000 Indians, skillfully led by Little Turtle and Simon Girty, fired from cover into the milling soldiers with deadly effect. St. Clair's artillery opened fire, ineffectively, as did his musketeers.[27]

The old governor, ignoring his crippling gout in the crisis of the moment, courageously joined the collapsing troops on the left and personally led their counterattack that drove the Indians back. Part of the American second line charged across the Wabash but could not hold its gains and fell back, and soon the Shawnees and Delawares counterattacked. Several other brave counter-charges by the regular Second Regiment and other units drove back the enemy, but the soldiers were forced to retreat in turn, minus their increased casualties. Most artillerymen were shot down as the Indians closed in, and Butler and others were mortally wounded. St. Clair's uniform was perforated by nine bullets, but he remained unscathed.[28]

The panic spread. Most officers were slain, and the heavy losses led to the senseless wandering of terror-stricken, demoralized fugitives. Some women fought well and, with the few determined officers remaining, shamed some of the skulking militia into action. Perhaps only three women escaped alive. St. Clair realized that it was retreat or annihilation; he moved to the right, and ordered an immediate withdrawal, abandoning everything. The general led a charge to the rear that broke through the Indian line that was attempting to block a retreat. Thus over 200 soldiers escaped. After pursuing some three miles, the Indians gave up the chase and returned to camp to torture their helpless victims. St. Clair forced some fleeing, fainthearted militia to form rear guards in the retrograde movement to Fort Jefferson, but many of the fugitives threw away arms and equipment and fled pell-mell. Some of the more courageous performed heroic deeds in the retreat.[29]

The army returned to Cincinnati on 9 November and St. Clair took stock of his casualties. There were approximately 35 officers killed, 622 enlisted men killed, 29 officers wounded, and 242 men in the ranks wounded. These totaled 918, plus perhaps 30 women casualties. Theodore Roosevelt observed that "the only regular regiment present lost every officer killed or wounded."[30]

The report of the sorry affair did not reach the president until 19 December 1791. Knox delivered the bad news in person to Washington's door; the chief executive left his dinner guests to receive it. Washington remained calm throughout dinner and until he had ushered his guests from the presidential mansion. Then his olympian temper erupted and he damned St. Clair for permitting the one thing he had warned against to happen—to be surprised by the Indians. Yes, Washington roared, St. Clair had permitted his army "to be cut to pieces, hacked, butchered, tomahawked, by a surprise. . . . He is worse than a murderer! How can he answer to his country?" Then the president, regained his control and after a brief silence promised that "General St. Clair shall have justice—I will hear him without prejudice; he shall have full justice!"[31]

When the defeated governor arrived in Philadelphia in January 1792 the commander in chief received him amiably but demanded his immediate resignation, pending the outcome of a congressional investigation. A committee of the House of Representatives examined documents and interviewed witnesses for a month and submitted its report to the House on 8 May 1792, where it lay without action until November. Finally on 15 February 1793 the House handed down its verdict that completely exonerated St. Clair and criticized Knox and Quartermaster Hodgdon. They admitted that Congress itself was partly to blame by its delay in passing legislation that would authorize a larger force of soldiers.[32]

It is true that Congress was criminally negligent, despite Washington's repeated warnings beginning as early as 8 December 1790, for its delays and evasions of responsibilities. But Knox and St. Clair had procrastinated badly, especially over supplies; and Quartermaster Hodgdon was a poor choice for his job. Yet Arthur St. Clair was loyal and conspicuously courageous, and he consistently strove to carry out the directions of his superiors. He calmly accepted his share of censure and, in a dignified way, refused to blame his unreliable subordinates. Although no longer a major general, he was allowed to stay on as governor of the Northwest Territory.[33]

The first session of the Second Congress convened in Philadelphia on 24 October 1791. Congress debated St. Clair's defeat and whether it was possible or wise to try to rectify the situation. After protracted discussion, the famous (or infamous) Militia Act of 1792 became law. This notorious legislation, far from providing the well-organized and disciplined militia urged by Washington, Knox, and von Steuben, paid mere lip service to the idea of the citizens' military obligation. It piously provided that every free, white, able-bodied male between eighteen and forty-five be registered on the local militia rolls. However, and this was the rub, within six months of such enrollment, the militiaman was required to supply himself with arms, ammunition, and equipment! Thus Congress abdicated its constitutional duty to arm and equip the militia, and thrust these responsibilities upon the shoulders of the individual citizen.[34]

Despite some opposition in Congress and elsewhere to maintaining the struggle against the Indians of the Northwest and against increasing the regular army, the legislators took action in March 1792 to provide a regular force sufficient to deal more effectively with the Indians and to impress the British who were still garrisoning the Northwest posts. The regular army was to be increased by adding 960 enlisted men to each of the two existing regiments to bring them up to full strength, and three more regiments for three years' service were to be added. In addition, four troops of light dragoons might be called up, if needed. This produced a total regular army of 5,000; it was designated the Legion of the United States (until 1796), and the chief executive was authorized to name its four brigadier generals.[35]

Commander in Chief Washington's main problem was to find a competent successor to St. Clair to command of the Legion and lead a third and crucial campaign to chastise the northwestern Indians who had so badly defeated that general and Harmar. Washington thought long and hard about the qualities of nine generals—men like Charles Cotesworth Pinckney, Baron von Steuben, Benjamin Lincoln, and William Moultrie—but rejected them for certain shortcomings that might again spell disaster. Washington's personal preference was "Light Horse Harry" Lee, but this was opposed because Virginia already had many men in high government positions, and because Lee had been only a lieutenant colonel during the Revolutionary War.[36]

Then the name of General Anthony Wayne was put forward. The president knew of Mad Anthony's liabilities. He was, said Washington, "more active and enterprising than Judicious and cautious. No economist it is feared:— open to flattery—vain—easily imposed upon and liable to be drawn into scrapes. Too indulgent (the effect perhaps of some of the causes just mentioned) to his officers and men.—Whether sober—or little addicted to the bottle" the chief executive did not know. Aware of the critical nature of this appointment, Washington probably overstated Wayne's defects, which, if true in that degree, might have been disastrous in a commanding general.[37]

But the president also knew of Wayne's surpassing service for eight years in the Revolution, and his many fine qualities were firmly established in Washington's mind. Born in Chester County, Pennsylvania, on 1 January 1745, Wayne was educated at a private academy in Philadelphia. He became a surveyor and in 1766 was married to Mary Penrose, daughter of a Philadelphia merchant. The Waynes had two children. In due time this animated man took over and operated his father's profitable tannery. Wayne was a man of medium height, with dark hair, penetrating brown eyes, high forehead, handsome face, and a slightly aquiline nose. At the outset of the Revolution, he was an impetuous person and active in early Pennsylvania protests against British practices. During the war he fought and led with conspicuous ability at

Quebec, Fort Ticonderoga, Paoli, Germantown, Valley Forge, Monmouth, Stony Point (where his brilliant surprise attack brought him over 500 prisoners, fifteen guns, and military supplies), West Point (which he had saved by his prompt action after Benedict Arnold's treason), and in Greene's campaign that culminated in the victory at Yorktown.[38]

Commander in Chief Washington perceived that Wayne's dominant characteristic was an unswerving determination, not possessed by anyone else available, to close with the enemy and destroy him. On balance, Washington regarded Wayne as the "most eligible," despite his shortcomings, and Wayne was confirmed by the Senate on 5 March 1792, though some of the lawmakers hesitated to do so.[39] At the time of Wayne's appointment the regular army, or Legion of the United States, numbered 5,120 men. Wayne's stern but fair-minded training of his force and employment of high standards that were realistic began to mold the riff-raff into a healthy, spirited, and effective force.[40]

While Wayne was building his army near Pittsburgh, his second in command, Brig. Gen. James Wilkinson and several hundred of St. Clair's remnants were stationed at Fort Washington. Wilkinson's minor 1791 forays against the Indians, plus his relaxed and engaging personality and bountiful hospitality, won over many of these rough-hewn frontiersmen. These traits had also won over the Spaniards, in whose pay Wilkinson had flourished for some twenty years. He was a man of easy principles and as changeable as a chameleon. But he could not delegate authority and immersed himself in minor and insignificant details that should have been handled by subordinates. Nor was he a competent strategist or tactician.[41]

Word soon arrived in the capital of renewed Indian raids, accompanied by rumors of the aggressive intentions of the British and Spanish. The secretary of war, therefore, authorized Wayne to move his force of 2,643 soldiers down the Ohio. Wayne and his army floated down the broad river in April 1793 and arrived at Cincinnati in early May to the delight of citizens and troops already there. A military camp, called Hobson's Choice, was set up a mile west of Fort Washington, where Wayne's men remained until autumn. Training was slow and plagued by petty squabbles among officers and men over discipline, and by irreconcilable hostility between Wayne, who was irritable, vindictive, dogmatic, and overbearing, and Wilkinson, who was loose-tongued, deceitful, and disloyal. Despite his lack of personal popularity among the troops and officers, Wayne was thorough and generally skillful in his training, and he succeeded in creating a respectable force for the coming military operations.[42]

On 7 October 1793 Wayne's Legion marched out of Hobson's Choice to the north, with strong distant and close-in reconnaissances maintained. His disciplined force moved twice as fast as had St. Clair's along the route where the well-stocked forts were twenty-five miles apart. The Indians were disconcerted by this well-planned and conducted march. By 14 October Wayne reached a point six miles north of Fort Jefferson near the southwestern branch of the Maumee River. Here, he determined to winter; bad weather was setting in and his lines of supply and communications were often harassed by the enemy. The new stockade built there was called Fort Greenville. Illness and shortages of rations and supplies hampered Wayne's plans for offensive operations in the spring of 1794, and the general angrily demanded that the sluggish contractors secure more transportation. Added to his problems was Wayne's realization that a few of his officers were still unreliable and that he could not trust Wilkinson at all. Wayne watched him closely while otherwise ignoring his advice, a reaction that Wilkinson disliked and resented.[43]

On 24 December 1793 Wayne and eight companies of troops moved to the site of St. Clair's defeat, where they built Fort Recovery. Fortunately the Indians were powerless at that moment to prevent it, although the British in Canada encouraged the Indians to resist the Americans. The redcoats built a strong new fort on American soil along the Maumee and sold arms and ammunition to the Indians. Wayne, aware of the developing good qualities of his soldiers and his fine regulars, was prepared when the Indians, led by Little Turtle, Blue Jacket, and Simon Girty, launched heavy attacks upon Fort Recovery at the end of June 1794. All of these assaults by some 1,750 braves were repulsed by the troops, even though they were outnumbered almost ten to one. The Indians suffered heavy losses when compared to just 22 soldiers killed and 30 wounded.[44]

Reinforced at Fort Greenville by Maj. Gen. Charles Scott's 1,500 mounted volunteers, Wayne set out on 28 July 1794 with 3,500 soldiers under his command on this decisive campaign. Twelve days later, after a hot, hard march, the force arrived at the confluence of the Auglaize and Maumee. Wayne remained here a week to build Fort Defiance and reconnoiter. On 15 August he crossed the Maumee and three days later approached within ten miles of the British-held Fort Miami. The Indians tried to buy time to collect warriors by a sudden but unsuccessful profession of peace. Wayne threw up a hasty, crude fieldwork, the citadel, to house nonessential stores and equipment and began his advance on 20 August, a clear, hot day, with Hamtramck on the left and Wilkinson on the right flank.[45]

At about 10:00 A.M., while five miles out on the march, Wayne's advance elements were attacked and driven back by the Indians. Possibly some 1,300 hostiles were present, with 60 Canadian militia and 400 Indians forming the core of the enemy formation. They were supplied by the nearby British fort and were ensconced in an area of trees knocked down years before by a tornado. Wayne galloped to the front, called up his reinforcements, and ordered a charge that was instantly and powerfully delivered. The Indians were flushed from their natural breastworks and retreated from the forest out onto the prairie, where they were pursued for two miles. A total American victory might have been secured had Scott's mounted volunteers encircled the right flank of the enemy. On the left flank, however, the troopers of R. M. Campbell cut the enemy to pieces in the chase that they pursued right up to the British fort.[46]

The Battle of Fallen Timbers was over in three-quarters of an hour. In the actual combat, some 500 Indians were pitted against perhaps 1,000 of Wayne's Legion. The general listed his casualties as 33 killed and 100 wounded. Exact Indian losses were unknown, ranging upward in estimates from 19 killed and 2 wounded, although most sources admit that a number of chiefs were slain. The gates of the British fort were closed to Indians seeking refuge. The ruthless Americans burned the Indians' crops and obliterated other Indian, British, and Canadian installations. The natives perceived the futility, at least for the present, of checking Wayne's skillful advance, and temporarily renounced the counsels of their own warmongers. They were angered, too, at the British for their failure to support them after the British had incited the tribes to go on the warpath.[47]

Wayne remained a year longer in the area, negotiating with the Indians who respected him as an unrelenting enemy. In accordance with Jay's Treaty, the British finally abandoned their forts on American soil. Negotiations between Wayne and the Indians, begun in early 1795, continued into the summer. Finally the Treaty of Greenville was signed on 3 August; the Indians, in return for money and supplies, relinquished their claims to most of Ohio and eastern Indiana.[48]

On 14 December 1795 Wayne left the Northwest after issuing an order expressing his appreciation to his troops. James Wilkinson assumed command two days later and promptly issued a bombastic statement that denounced Wayne and his methods and congratulated himself on his virtues. Wayne journeyed to Philadelphia in the hope that he might succeed Henry Knox as secretary of war and prevent Congress from further severe reductions in the army. He arrived at the capital on 6 February 1796 and was given a hero's welcome. With army strength retained at the same level, at least for the moment, Wayne returned to Fort Washington and Greenville, where he allowed Wilkinson to depart for the East. Wayne proceeded via Fort Defiance to the battlefield at Fallen Timbers, then on to Fort Miami, Lake Erie, and finally Detroit. Here he became quite ill and remained three months, issuing the orders to occupy and garrison the evacuated British forts and warning off the recalcitrant Spanish on lands opposite the mouth of the Ohio River. The report that Wilkinson, typically, was trying to discredit him back East hastened Wayne's departure from Detroit on 13 November; as he set forth, he was honored by soldiers and citizens alike. Five days later at Presque Isle his condition worsened, and he succumbed on 15 December 1796. With his death, one of the military greats of the new republic was gone forever.[49]

On 22 September 1796 Wilkinson, generously paid and employed by Spain since 1791, wrote the Spanish Governor of Louisiana that he was going to Philadelphia to "keep down the [United States] military establishment, to disgrace my commander [Wayne], and secure myself command of the Army." Indeed, Wilkinson was soon named to the top army command, although the new secretary of war, James McHenry, refused his request for a court of inquiry to look into criticisms aimed, as Wilkinson phrased it, at his "aspersed reputation." Wilkinson was, in the judgment of James Ripley Jacobs, "probably the most voluble and egotistical high ranking officer. Few trusted him; many hated him; more doubted his honesty and military ability. He was essentially a political opportunist with a military sheen." Frederick Jackson Turner considered him "the most consummate artist in treason that the nation ever possessed"—probably too harsh an assessment.[50]

Meanwhile, although much attention had been paid to Indian affairs in the Old Northwest, events that concerned "pale-faced" rebels near Pittsburgh culminated in 1794 in the so-called Whiskey Rebellion. The defiant reaction of locals to Alexander Hamilton's excise tax on spirits forced the president to act. Washington soon realized that only force would suffice, despite Albert Gallatin's useful negotiations that continued near the forks of the Ohio. The president firmly exercised for the first time his power to call forth the militia to suppress domestic insurrection, and some 13,000 militiamen from Pennsylvania, Virginia, Maryland, and New Jersey turned out. Washington rode from Philadelphia to Carlisle Barracks and on to Fort Bedford to assume personal command of these troops if necessary. He found his trusted comrade-in-arms of the Revolution, Light Horse Harry Lee, governor of Virginia, present to lead. Satisfied, Washington returned to the capital. The Whiskey rebels were quickly suppressed by the militiamen, practically without bloodshed, and their rebellion was soon snuffed out.[51]

ON 20 MAY 1796 Congress dropped the term, Legion of the United States, and reorganized the regular army into four infantry regiments, two companies of light dragoons, and the corps of artillerists and engineers. One major general and two brigadier generals were authorized. During most of the 1790s the army was deliberately officered largely by Federalists, and Washington, Hamilton, and to a lesser extent John Adams concurred in this policy. A shift in focus in foreign policy was caused by the federalist administration's reaction to the wars of the French Revolution that began in 1793. The Federalists moved away from their former French allies and found themselves in closer alliance with their old enemy, England. Meanwhile, Thomas Jefferson and the Democratic-Republicans drew closer to the French connection than Washington or Adams or Hamilton would tolerate. And the chief executive foresaw correctly that foreign relations would have a profound impact on America's military policy.[52]

President Washington, in reaction to the wars abroad, warned:

> Peace has been the order of the day with me since the disturbances in Europe first commenced. My policy has been, and will continue to be . . . to be upon friendly terms with, but independent of, all the nations of the earth; to share in the broils of none; to fulfill our own engagements; to supply the wants and be carrier for them all; being thoroughly convinced that it is our policy and interest so to do. Nothing short of self-respect, and that justice which is essential to a national character, ought to involve us in war; for sure I am, if this country is preserved in tranquility twenty years longer, it may bid defiance in a just cause to any power whatever; such in that time will be its population, wealth and resources.[53]

Washington and his successors were able until the War of 1812 to accomplish this critical objective. On the subject of national defense for the United States, the president on 3 December 1793 advised both houses of Congress thusly:

I cannot recommend to your notice measures for the fulfillment of *our* duties to the rest of the world, without again pressing upon you the necessity of placing ourselves in the condition of a complete defence, and of exacting from *them* the fulfillment of *their* duties towards *us*. The United States ought not to indulge a persuasion that, contrary to the order of human events, they will forever keep at a distance those painful appeals to arms, with which the history of every other nation abounds. There is a rank due to these United States among nations, which will be withheld, if not absolutely lost, by the reputation of weakness. If we desire to avoid insult, we must be able to repel it; if we desire to secure peace, one of the most powerful instruments of our rising prosperity, it must be known, that we are at all times ready for war.

However, the commander in chief added that the country was not that well prepared primarily because of the inadequacies of the Militia Act of 1792.[54]

The European war led to unrelenting attacks on American shipping. Washington's successor, President John Adams, urged a policy of deterrence that would build up the inadequate defenses of the country, especially the navy and the coastal defenses. He also urged an increase in the regular cavalry and artillery and recommended a system to call up, if necessary, a provisional army.[55]

Several of Adams's suggestions bore fruit. The Naval Act of 27 March 1794 included not only provisions for building warships but also provided for the construction of coastal fortifications, four arsenals, and several armories and foundaries. The War Department, by purchase or cession from the states, secured sites for these forts, while seaport citizens contributed part of the essential labor and material. By the outbreak of the War of 1812, twenty-four Vauban-type, star-shaped earth-and-masonry forts, such as Fort McHenry in Baltimore harbor, had been erected along the Atlantic seaboard and mounted a total of 750 guns, including 32 major batteries. Even though the corps of artillerists had been increased by 764 men by act of 9 May 1794, there never were half enough gunners to serve these seacoast fortifications until the second war with Britain.[56]

On 16 May 1797 President Adams angrily informed Congress of his ire over France's expulsion of minister C. C. Pinckney and of his determination to counter such a rebuff forcefully. Congress responded to Adams's appeal with an appropriation of $115,000 for harbor fortifications on 23 June. When on 3 April 1798 the president reported to Congress the continued poor treatment of our envoys and repeated insolent conduct toward the American government by France, Congress responded by approving privateering by Americans against French vessels in the Caribbean. Although some American raiders were lost, a total of eighty-four French ships had been seized or destroyed by 1800. Furthermore, on 27 April 1798 Congress increased the regular army by a regiment of engineers and artillerists at the same time that funds were appropriated for the purchase of small arms and cannon. In the event that the undeclared war with France would mushroom, Congress authorized Adams to call up 10,000 men for no more than three years' service.

A bounty of $10 for enlistment was approved, $600,000 in additional monies was allocated for arms and equipment, and a lieutenant general was to command the army. Yet these 10,000 soldiers were never raised. Instead, the regular army was increased as of 16 July 1798 by adding 9 officers, 8 sergeants, 8 corporals, 184 privates, and 4 musicians to each regiment. The troops' pay was increased one dollar per month and the food ration was augmented. The president was also authorized to recruit twelve infantry regiments and six troops of light dragoons for the duration of the undeclared war. But Adams did not regard the situation as threatening enough to warrant raising this force.[57]

In early 1798 the well-meaning but largely ineffective secretary of war, James McHenry, had passed along to the president Hamilton's recommendation for a regular army of twenty thousand and a provisional army of thirty thousand men. While Adams regarded Hamilton as an alarmist and leaned more toward a larger navy, Hamilton controlled the Federalist party to a greater degree than did the chief executive. In 1799 congress authorized Adams to call up thirty thousand troops in the event of war or a threatened French invasion. On 7 July 1798 Congress confirmed Adams's nomination of Washington as lieutenant general, although the former president did not actually have to take the field. When it was learned that the major generals under Washington would be, in order of rank, Hamilton, C. C. Pinckney, and Henry Knox, heated discussion and feverish maneuvering for these and other subordinate positions followed. Despite Adams's reluctance because of his distrust of Hamilton, Washington pushed hard and successfully to have Hamilton named second in command. Despite the crash program, poor conditions and many supply shortages prevailed at most army posts.[58]

With the reorganization of the army in 1800 and the discharge of the temporary forces, Wilkinson was the only general officer left. He was recalled to the new capital of Washington, D.C., and arrived, via Cuba (possibly to consult with his Spanish employers?), in early July of that year.[59]

In May 1800 when the new secretary of war, Samuel Dexter, did not immediately come to Washington, Wilkinson performed some of the secretary's duties, remaining in the capital until December. Wilkinson played up to the Republicans, especially Jefferson whom the general tried to interest in the trans-Mississippi West. While Wilkinson was sorting out ex-Secretary McHenry's papers, the War Department building mysteriously burned down on 8 November 1800, destroying most of these papers. In January 1801 the Treasury Department building was consumed by another arcane fire. On 14 May 1800 Congress added to the army's anguish by reducing the establishment to the general staff, four infantry regiments, two regiments of artillery and engineers, and two troops of light dragoons—a total of 5,437 men. By 19 December 1801 the Jefferson-dominated legislature reduced the army to 4,501 because of a brief truce in the Napoleonic Wars brought about by the Treaty of Amiens.[60]

Open, declared war with France had been prevented, not by the hasty legislation that set up on paper a larger army, but by the small, growing, and daring new United States Navy, whose exploits from 1798 to 1800 commanded the praise of Americans and even the grudging admiration of the enemy. Naval growth was also stimulated by troubles in the Mediterranean with the Barbary pirates of North Africa. Although warships were costly, Washington had called for a moderate and ready naval force to protect us "from insult or aggression" by bellicose powers.[61]

Secretary of War Henry Knox had tried in vain to obtain warships, but even during Washington's second term Congress preferred to appropriate money to pay ransom (tribute) to Morocco and Algeria rather than build warships. Not until 27 March 1794 did the lawmakers pass a bill providing for four 44-gun frigates and two 36-gun frigates, and some 2,060 sailors. The signing of a peace treaty with the Moslems in early 1796 threatened to terminate work on these superb vessels. Washington delayed executing the provisions of this law, saying the public would lose heavily if work was suspended. A compromise resulted, and work on three of the frigates, *Constitution* (44 guns), *United States* (44 guns), and *Constellation* (36 guns) continued, although construction on the other three was interrupted. Fortunately, building was resumed on these latter ships in the summer of 1797 as hostilities with France seemed imminent.[62]

In his annual message to Congress on 22 November 1797, the president initiated action that would lead to the establishment of a separate navy department. Congress concurred after strenuous debate, and on 30 April 1798 created the Navy Department. The republic was fortunate in the choice of Benjamin Stoddert of Maryland as its secretary. On 11 July Congress officially established the already existing Marine Corps, and placed it under the Navy Department. The legislators provided that the president, at his discretion, could order the marines to service ashore as well as to sea duty.[63]

In the actual naval battles of the Undeclared War with France (1798–1800), the infant American navy was blessed with several magnificent frigates constructed under the talented supervision of such shipbuilders as William Doughty, Josiah Fox, and Joshua Humphreys. Clean in design beneath the waterline as well as above, sturdily constructed, and mounted with powerful batteries for frigates, these beautiful warships could outshoot anything they could not outsail. This was as true of our 36-gun *Constellation* as it was of the surpassing 44s. In the two most famous ship-to-ship duels of the war, *Constellation*, under the command of the brilliant Capt. Thomas Truxtun, shattered the French frigate *Insurgente* (36 guns) in 1799 and *Vengeance* (40 guns) in 1800.[64]

In reply to Secretary Stoddert's well-reasoned call on 29 December 1798 for massive naval expansion, Congress on 25 February 1799 authorized the construction of six 74-gun, two-deck ships-of-the-line; two docks for the repair of warships; $200,000 to buy timbers or timber lands; and subsidies to manufacturers of copper and canvas items and hemp growers. By April 1801 Stoddert had also bought sites for navy yards for $135,000 that were large enough to build properly the 74s. But this encouraging genesis of the navy was reversed by Congress early in 1801 when peace was restored with France: the legislature proceeded to authorize on 3 March the sale of all men-of-war except thirteen, six to remain in commission and the other seven to be laid up in ordinary. It was all quite discouraging for the fledgling service.[65]

On 4 March 1801 in his first inaugural address, Thomas Jefferson revealed his political acumen, his states' rights views, his belief in government economy, and his dim view of the Federalist-created army and navy. He called for virtual disarmament, reechoed Washington's views of civilian supremacy over the military, and contended that the tiny regular army (4,051 men) could be augmented by a well-disciplined militia. But he was totally unrealistic in his assumption that the small regular army, scattered in garrisons along the coasts and all over the western frontier, could be quickly collected to support the militia in the early stages of an enemy invasion—a situation that actually occurred in the War of 1812.[66]

In addition, the chief executive wanted to lay up in ordinary at the nearby Washington navy yard all of the navy's larger warships, but he was prevented from doing this by the outbreak of the Tripolitan War three months after his inauguration. He therefore reluctantly agreed to keep in commission a small naval force and to dispatch several of its vessels to the Mediterranean. In this war of 1801–1805, the navy, under Edward Preble, more than held its own in operations against the harbor of Tripoli—including Stephen Decatur's feat in burning the grounded *Philadelphia*. But a polyglot army commanded by a civilian, William Eaton, which included a few United States Marines, achieved only limited success at Derna, to the east of Tripoli. Yet Jefferson set aside continued construction of coastal forts and was dubious about continuing other naval building.[67]

The secretary of war for eight years under Jefferson was Maj. Gen. Henry Dearborn, a fifty-year-old six-footer with gray hair and blue eyes who made an impressive appearance. Dearborn left his medical practice at the start of the Revolutionary War to raise a company of troops. He compiled a good war record, participating in the military operations at Bunker Hill, Quebec, Valley Forge, Saratoga, in Sullivan's campaign, and at Yorktown. After the war he became a major general of Massachusetts militia and a United States marshal for Maine. The religious Dearborn was a staunch Jeffersonian Republican. As secretary of war he would be thrifty, practical, and fairly competent, but he was neither well traveled nor widely read. He had less influence on the chief executive than had James Madison and Albert Gallatin, although he was trusted by Jefferson. Dearborn, in turn, was loyal to the president and worked to carry out Jefferson's military policies.[68]

On 16 March 1802 Congress cut the regular army back to two regiments of infantry and one of artillery—a total of 3,042 men. By this law the Quartermaster Department was relegated to the spoils system instead of being operated by trained military men. Under the rubric of a corps of engineers, this legislation did establish the United States Military Academy at West Point, New York, initially comprising 7 faculty officers and 10 cadets. Congress cut the number of marines in July 1801 to 31 officers and 400 men, while the number of regular naval personnel was lowered to 1,000 men.[69]

Jefferson's successful negotiation for the purchase of the Louisiana Territory from France increased American territory by 140 percent and led to its transfer to the United States late in 1803. The transfer coincided with the renewal of the Napoleonic wars in Europe, however, and Jefferson appeared unconcerned about any defense of this vast new American area. By 4 February 1805 the regular army would consist of 2,579 officers and men who were ill prepared and whose morale was low. The navy had only two 44s and five smaller men-of-war in the Mediterranean; thus when the frigate *Philadelphia* fell into the hands of the Tripolitans, she was replaced by the two 18-gun sloops *Wasp* and *Hornet*.[70]

Two years earlier Congress had authorized the construction of four 16-gun warships for service in the Mediterranean, and fifteen small gunboats. Jefferson's pet gunboats were to be scattered, according to the president's wishes, around the seaports where Jefferson ordered that they "be manned by the seamen and militia of the place in which they are wanting." The commander in chief urged Congress to build more of these nearly worthless little gunboats so that the safety of American harbors "shall be secured," though the regular army was not to be increased. Although the president finally perceived by December 1805 that military preparations were needed, he wanted only the mounting of some seacoast guns and the building of more tiny gunboats. In April 1806 Jefferson finally recommended that several 74s be built. However, in Congress John Randolph of Roanoke was instrumental in eliminating these big ships-of-the-line.[71]

The regular army played a pivotal role in western exploration of the huge new Louisiana Purchase territory and beyond. Jefferson, who started arrangements *before* the Louisiana Purchase had been consumated, dispatched an expedition under regular army officers to explore the area. Congress appropriated $2,500 for the expedition that was directed to find locations for forts to protect settlers and permit trade with the Indians and to secure detailed information about the flora, fauna, and geography of this enormous trans-Mississippi region. Jefferson chose his private secretary, Capt. Meriwether Lewis, and a former army officer, Lt. William Clark (younger brother of George Rogers Clark) to lead this famous expedition. Both were highly competent leaders and they worked well together. Lewis was tall, dignified, and soldierly in appearance. On the expedition, he handled complex mathematical problems and kept massive and invaluable written accounts. Clark, at thirty-three an experienced woodsman, Indian fighter, and topographical engineer, devoted most of his time on the trip to an effective handling of the Indians and the soldiers. While possessing little formal education, Clark was enthusiastic; although a mere second lieutenant, his men called him captain, and Lewis always treated him as coequal.[72]

The expedition, organized under orders of Dearborn and the War Department, was kept secret at first. Lewis and Clark came together at Louisville, where they selected the members of their expedition—nine young Kentuckians and fourteen enlisted soldiers from garrisons at Kaskaskia, Fort Massac, and Southwest Point, plus nine voyageurs, a hunter, a French interpreter, Clark's

Negro servant, and seven other soldiers who would escort them as far as the villages of the Mandan Indians.[73]

The winter of 1803–1804 was spent organizing and training on the east bank of the Mississippi River near St. Louis. The Lewis and Clark expedition pushed off on its epic two and one-half year trip on 14 May 1804. The force ascended the Missouri River to the Mandan villages (later, Bismarck, North Dakota). In the winter of 1804–1805 the expedition remained five months at Fort Mandan, reorganizing and resupplying their wants by hunting parties. Lewis wrote detailed reports and the two leaders attempted to gather as much information as possible about the aborigines and terrain ahead.

The river ice melted by April and the expedition pressed on up the Missouri to the mouth of the Yellowstone River, where more data was collected and compiled. The three forks of the Missouri, named the Jefferson, the Madison, and the Gallatin, were reached by 25 April, and their sources were explored. After a terrible struggle through the high mountain ranges, Clark and Lewis reached the shores of the Pacific Ocean on 7 November 1805. These splendid men, under strict military discipline, suffered but one casualty. Upon their return, their enthusiastic welcome at St. Louis on 23 September 1806 was certainly merited. They covered over 6,000 miles and blazed a well-marked trail to the mighty Pacific. Moreover, they gathered a huge amount of valuable information from which Clark prepared a mammoth report that was finally published in 1814.[74]

When Captain Lewis resigned his commission after reporting to the president in Washington, Jefferson appointed him governor of Louisiana Territory, and he made an excellent executive. Unfortunately, his melancholy temperament developed into mental illness and in 1809 en route to Washington, he was either murdered at a cabin inn along the route, or else he committed suicide there. Clark resigned his commission on 27 February 1807 and became a brigadier general in the militia of Louisiana and Superintendent of Indian Affairs at St. Louis. He was named governor of Louisiana Territory in 1813.[75]

General Wilkinson ordered a foray into another part of the country that was commanded by twenty-six-year-old 1st Lt. Zebulon Montgomery Pike, a short, blue-eyed, light-haired officer who was sober and reliable, served as a cadet around 1794 in his father's army company, and was promoted to ensign and then lieutenant in 1799. Pike's orders from the Washington officials were to find the source of the Mississippi River, to note the terrain on his trek, to observe and work harmoniously with the Indians, and to locate possible sites for forts.[76]

Pike's expedition to explore the area of the northern Mississippi was a very creditable operation. The lieutenant, a sergeant, two corporals, and seventeen privates left St. Louis in a keel boat on 9 August 1805, and by 21 September they were at the mouth of the Minnesota River. Pike acquired 100,000 acres of land from the Sioux for $2,000, including the sites of St. Paul and Minneapolis. On 16 October the expedition reached the mouth of the Swan River, where the men wintered in a fort that they built. The lieutenant, a corporal, and a few of his soldiers explored northward in the blizzards, reaching the post of the British Northwest Company at Sandy Lake on 8 January 1806, and the company's post at Leech Lake that Pike erroneously thought was the source of the Mississippi. The lieutenant laid down the law to the British factors forbidding their use of American soil for the sale of British goods, flying the British flag, or dealing with the Indians, to which the company agents agreed. On 18 February 1806 Pike started the march back, after scoring these significant achievements in the Land of Sky Blue Waters.[77]

Zebulon M. Pike's most famous exploring expedition was ordered by General Wilkinson, this time to the Southwest. Pike was to escort some Indians to their home areas; impress, confer, present gifts, and pacify warring plains Indians; and explore and observe the physical conditions of the Southwest (New Spain). He was also to find the sources of the Arkansas and Red Rivers. Pike, who hoped to familiarize himself with western Louisiana lands so that he might work there in the future, accepted the mission and was ready to depart in the summer of 1806. He was accompanied by 2nd Lt. James Biddle Wilkinson (the son of the general, who asked Pike to go easy on the boy), a volunteer surgeon, two sergeants, a corporal, sixteen privates, an interpreter, and the fifty-one Pawnees and Osages they were escorting.[78]

Pike and his soldiers—seventeen of whom had been with him on his earlier expedition up the Mississippi—journeyed up the Missouri and the Osage River (in what would later be Vernon County, Missouri), where they dropped off the troublesome Osages. Pike treated with the Pawnees at their main village on the Republican River where it crossed the later Kansas-Nebraska border. Here he learned of the nearness of a hostile Spanish force. After conferences with the Pawnees, Pike moved southward in early October 1806 through Kansas to the great bend of the Arkansas River. Part of his force under the inept Lieutenant Wilkinson turned southward to descend the Arkansas River, while Pike headed westward with the remaining troops.[79]

Pike and his party wandered around in Colorado looking for the source of the Red River, and suffering terribly in the winter of 1806 before they were finally captured by Mexican forces from New Mexico. Pike, despite his disclaimers, was on Mexican land at the time. He was taken to Mexico, well treated, and finally released. Pike arrived on American soil on 1 July 1807. He published his account of the trip, against the advice of General Wilkinson, and gained instant fame.[80]

The final event of this chapter in American military affairs is a tawdry one. Almost inevitably it involved General Wilkinson, the blundering American governor of Upper Louisiana at St. Louis, who was finally losing the support of his officers and the citizens of the city. On 16 May 1806 Wilkinson was ordered to move quickly to New Orleans because Spanish forces there were acting hostile and threatening to cross the Sabine River. Moving with his customary glacial speed, the "Tarnished Warrior" did not arrive in New Orleans until 7 September, though he was able to check the Spanish advance.[81]

While near New Orleans Wilkinson received former Vice-President Burr's letter of 29 July 1806 that described his amazing and treacherous plan to move his followers down the Mississippi to New Orleans, detach certain states from the Union, and possibly loot and conquer Mexico. Burr invited Wilkinson to join him in this fantastic scheme. Instead, for his own personal gain, the general turned against Burr and exposed his plan in a letter to President Jefferson in October. The chief executive gave Wilkinson wide powers to meet this threat, but the Mexican viceroy and governors at Mobile and Pensacola, though they thanked Wilkinson, extended none of the requested monies for this purpose.

Nonetheless Wilkinson at New Orleans, using summary and illegal methods, arrested and handled Burr's followers roughly. When Burr, accompanied by sixty men, came down the river, Wilkinson's troops caught and arrested him on 19 February 1807. Burr was sent East and tried; despite Wilkinson's testimony against him, he escaped conviction for treason, although he was ruined. Wilkinson also lost prestige through his dubious connections with the Spanish and his highhanded actions against Burr's supporters. Thus the general was obliged to remain in Washington until the end of January, 1809. Unfortunately for the United States, Wilkinson continued to serve as a high-ranking officer in the army well into the War of 1812 era.[82]

In one of his militarily prophetic documents, in a lifetime of martial achievement and statesmanship, George Washington recommended in his "Sentiments on a Peace Establishment" not only the format but also the requisite priorities for military forces and their support. Similar wise suggestions for peacetime forces and structure by Henry Knox and Baron von Steuben were likewise ignored by Congress and the public. This was equally true for the regular army, militia, and navy, to the republic's detriment. Part of this inattention to military affairs reflected the lack of power of the central government under the Articles of Confederation. This situation was markedly improved by the adoption of the federal Constitution that realistically and effectively allotted military powers and responsibilities between the executive branch and Congress. But the terse commander in chief clause of the constitution designating civilian control over the military would be questioned occasionally by the military from the time of its creation.

The country was fortunate in having as its first president and commander in chief under the Constitution the tested and true Washington, almost an indispensable man in that time. While the early years of the War Department were often weak and shaky ones, that department was guided with skill by its first secretary, Henry Knox. While the members of Congress wrangled endlessly, the Washington administration, too, had its share of frustrations in quelling the raids of the redoubtable Indians of the Northwest. This was vital because the British lingered on in the posts there. In turn Josiah Harmar and Arthur St. Clair's expeditions were defeated in the early 1790s, and it was only when the president turned to the fiery and capable Anthony Wayne, who was thoroughly prepared to march against the Indians, that victory was attained at Fallen Timbers in 1794. This was the year that Washington successfully tested the power of the chief executive to call forth the militia to suppress the Whiskey Rebellion with temporary citizen-soldiers.

George Washington closed out his magisterial administration with accurate warnings about the wars then under way in Europe as well as cautioning about America's weak defense posture, including an almost nonexistent navy. He had been able at least to coax from Congress a few warships; but his successor, John Adams, faced an undeclared but nonetheless shooting war on the high seas with France. Secretary of War McHenry was less effective than Knox, but he was able to get some forts built, and a larger army was raised for the 1798–1800 emergency. In this crisis Alexander Hamilton played an arcane role, and even Washington was recalled from private life to active duty for a time. Several of our infant navy's warships scored well in battle against French men-of-war. The country was blessed by the appointment of Benjamin Stoddert as the efficient first secretary of the navy. Throughout this period of both Federalist and Republican administrations, the devious James Wilkinson, a man of cunning and duplicity, moved erratically but without success on and off the stage.

The elevation to the White House of the peace-loving Thomas Jefferson endangered the existence not only of the larger ships of the navy, but also of the regular army. As commander in chief he was unrealistic in his heavy reliance upon little gunboats and the militia. The purchase of Louisiana and the troubles with the Barbary pirates forced him, however, to maintain some men-of-war and to employ at least the services of a small standing army. Invaluable explorations by the army under Zebulon M. Pike and especially under Lewis and Clark were performed handsomely. Jefferson also approved the establishment of a military academy at West Point. In all this, the president was assisted by the mediocre but otherwise solid Henry Dearborn as secretary of war.

In the alternating periods of halting progress and unfortunate regression between Yorktown and the events leading up to the War of 1812, the inescapable conclusion is that the splendid foundation, grasp, and appreciation of military affairs by George Washington and his many successes in the field were perhaps almost counterbalanced by the oftentimes wise but occasionally inept John Adams and the militarily naive Thomas Jefferson. Knox was a better secretary of war than either Dearborn or McHenry. Stoddert and Thomas Truxtun performed ably, but the highly competent Wayne's triumphs have to be compared with the previous setbacks of Harmar and St. Clair, and with Wilkinson's machinations.

All in all, the indifference and stubborn provincialism of Congress and the public ensured a small and weak regular army and navy. The American military establishment was in no way ready for the shock of arms with Britain and Canada in 1812. Perhaps the legislators and American people deserved that shock, given their reluctance and suspicions of things military.

CHAPTER FOUR

Stalemate with Britain, 1812–1815

Our soldiers can beat their soldiers in fighting, but their generals beat our's [sic] *in management.*

UNKNOWN AMERICAN SOLDIER
IN THE RANKS, WAR OF 1812

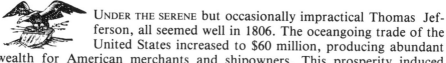 UNDER THE SERENE but occasionally impractical Thomas Jefferson, all seemed well in 1806. The oceangoing trade of the United States increased to $60 million, producing abundant wealth for American merchants and shipowners. This prosperity induced British seamen, including tars aboard warships flying the Union Jack, to desert to the American merchant marine and its higher pay and better living conditions. Britain, enmeshed in a life and death struggle with Napoleon and in dire need of crews for men-of-war, began impressing American sailors, a practice denounced and protested in vain by the president. On 21 November 1806 Napoleon responded with his Berlin Decree that set up a blockade of the British Isles. This "Continental System" was answered by England's Order in Council of 7 January 1807, designed to prevent neutrals from trading with the French-controlled continent.

On 21 June 1807 the new American frigate *Chesapeake* (36 guns) sailed out of Norfolk bound for the Mediterranean. The ship had few of its guns mounted, and her crew had only been mustered three times. No sooner had she cleared the three-mile limit than H.M.S. *Leopard* (38 guns), hailed and demanded the right to inspect her for four sailors who had allegedly deserted nearby British warships. When Commodore James Barron refused, the *Leopard* opened fire on the helpless *Chesapeake* and bombarded her for fifteen minutes before Barron struck his colors. The four British sailors were impressed into his majesty's royal navy, and the *Chesapeake* limped back to Norfolk for repairs.

In response, President Jefferson inaugurated his pet embargo that prohibited all trade into or out of American ports. Hard times ensued, especially in New England coastal towns, and some American sailors even joined the British navy voluntarily. Actually, the embargo did not hurt England or France too critically, and the hostile opposition to Jefferson's Republican Party asserted itself when his hand-picked successor, James Madison, was elected to the presidency with only 122 electoral votes as compared to Jefferson's 162 in 1804. With the country near economic stagnation, the dubious embargo was repealed on 27 February 1808.

Madison's administration began inauspiciously when the Erskine Agreement, supported by the president and claiming that the repugnant British Orders in Council were about to be withdrawn, was repudiated by the government in London. In the slow, almost imperceptible drift toward war, the American commander in chief could note at the end of January 1810 that his regular army numbered only 6,954, which was about 3,000 under its authorized strength of 9,921. The navy was also tiny, but on 16 May 1811 it redeemed the *Chesapeake's* disgrace. The American frigate *President* (44 guns) sighted a strange ship off the Virginia capes that fled when Commodore John Rodgers spoke her. A shot was fired, and a general exchange of gunfire at sunset resulted in severe damage to the other vessel, later found to be sloop-of-war *Little Belt* (18 guns). Newspapers in both countries exchanged vitriolic tirades. Certainly the question of neutral rights on the high seas and the differing interpretations thereof were now resulting in shooting and a lessening of the chances for settling these serious disputes amicably.[1]

But other irritants between the United States on the one hand and Canada and Great Britain on the other were festering in the forests of the Old Northwest, and they too would play a role in the coming of hostilities. The greed of land-hungry American frontiersmen for the unsettled Ontario peninsula, and the formation of an Indian confederation by the stalwart Shawnee leader Tecumseh and his brother Elkswatawa, led to the authorization in 1811 of Gov. William Henry Harrison of Indiana Territory to lead an expedition against the Indians, especially when massacres of white settlers multiplied.[2]

Tecumseh was an Indian chief of great dignity and high personal courage. But his brother, better known as the Prophet, was a drunkard whose single eye added to his frightening appearance. Yet he was an impassioned and effective orator. Under the contrasting but efficient leadership of these two men a model Indian village had been set up on Tippecanoe Creek at its confluence with the Wabash River. Harrison moved some 900 troops (250 were regulars of the Fourth Infantry) from Vincennes in September and October 1811 and camped on an oak-covered knoll about a mile from the Prophet's village. Harrison refrained from entrenching his position, although the brief negotiations with the Indians were fruitless.[3]

Just before dawn on 7 November, young braves, whipped to a frenzy by the Prophet's fiery exhortations, put on war paint and attacked Harrison's encamped army in a surprise assault that almost overran the American position. But Harrison maintained control and his troops, especially his riflemen, finally beat off the enemy in a sharp combat. American casualties totaled 188; Indian losses were perhaps 200 warriors. Harrison was well on his way to becoming a great folk hero of the West. But what changed the glee of the frontiersmen to white-hot anger was the discovery of British-supplied firearms in the Indian town at Tippecanoe. Here was supposed proof that the English and Canadians were inciting war by supplying guns to natives.[4]

Before the Battle of Tippecanoe, President Madison recommended the filling up of the regular army regiments, the arming and equipping by the states of 100,000 militia, and the recruiting of 20,000 volunteers. But he was ambivalent; at the same time the chief executive allowed Secretary of the Treasury Albert Gallatin to cut the army and navy budgets in half, and Congress did nothing to redress the balance. By 1812 the regular army had merely 6,744 of its authorized 10,000 soldiers.[5]

Nor were the nation's ground forces invincible. "The army of that day," declared young Capt. Winfield Scott, "presented no pleasing aspect. The old officers had very generally sunk into either sloth, ignorance, or habits of intemperate drinking. . . . Many of the appointments were positively bad, and a majority of the remainder indifferent."[6] Furthermore, in early 1812 the United States Navy possessed no ships-of-the-line, and, because of inadequate funds, care, and attention, several of the fine frigates were out of commission.

All the information Madison received indicated that England remained intransigent over impressment and neutral rights. In May 1812 Napoleon formally rescinded his Berlin and Milan Decrees, thus inviting Britain to withdraw her noxious Orders in Council, but English action was not immediately forthcoming. So Congress, supported chiefly by members from the South and West, declared war on 18 June 1812 in response to the president's appeal. Actually on 16 June British Foreign Minister Lord Castlereagh announced the repeal of the Orders in Council, but news traveling by ship arrived too late to prevent hostilities.[7]

The American high civilian and military commands left much to be desired at the start of the war. The sixty-one-year-old James Madison's previous career had been exemplary as a Virginia revolutionist, a brilliant political scientist, and—if anyone was entitled to the term—the Father of the Constitution. But as wartime commander in chief, he did not cut a good figure. "Mr. Madison seemed very little fitted for the scene," Justice Joseph Story remarked.[8]

The slender, wizened president was only five feet six inches tall, and his face looked perpetually perplexed. He was always dressed in black and wore old-style knee breeches. Washington Irving contemptuously called him "a withered little applejohn." An obstinate man and at times an ineffective politician, the chief executive clung stubbornly to his own views even when they were obviously wrong. He was inept at selecting cabinet officers and field commanders. "As commander in chief," declared historian Leonard D. White, "the President was irresolute, weak in his judgment of men, unaware of his proper function, and incapable of giving direction to the course of events." Although well meaning and aiming to please, Madison made himself slightly ridiculous at the start of the war when he visited all the offices of the War Department wearing "his little round hat and huge cockade" and tried to arouse these functionaries to action. Subjected as he was to fearful abuse and invective, Madison remained fairly tolerant of his domestic foes and never panicked when disasters in the field occurred.[9]

Madison's secretary of war was a pathetic appointment. Fifty-nine-year-old Dr. William Eustis's only experience with the army had been as a surgeon in the Revolutionary War. Thereafter he practiced medicine in Boston and demonstrated an active interest in Jeffersonian politics. He served in the

House from 1800 to 1805. This New Englander was selected to head the War Department in order to give geographical balance to the cabinet. He was totally unfit for the onerous position. Hardly anyone, even in his own Republican Party, had any confidence in Eustis. He was a poor judge of generals and was certainly less able than his predecessor, Henry Dearborn. His narrow penny-pinching attitude, even when the republic was fighting for its life, cost the nation dearly.[10]

Like the president, the secretary of war was not a leader, and he could not provide direction. He could be so small that a refused handshake by a general once led to a challenge to a duel! It is difficult to reject James R. Jacob's assessment of Eustis that "He was essentially a military tinker. . . . He concerned himself with details so much that he lost track of missions and principles. . . . He had only a second-rate mind that dwelt on petty things. . . . He had . . . no real ability," and "always consulted the oracles of his party before making any military decision. . . . As secretary of war, he was incompetent."[11]

When hostilities began in June 1812 the War Department consisted of the secretary and a few clerks. Not until the war was nearly a year old did Congress see fit to authorize the secretary of war to create a so-called general staff that was to handle army management, but not operations. Within the 1813 general staff were the following positions: the quartermaster general; the inspector general and his two immediate assistants; the adjutant general and the assistant adjutant general; the commissary general of ordnance, two deputy commissaries of ordnance, and the assistant commissary of ordnance; the paymaster; and the assistant topographical engineer. The members named to this general staff by Eustis and Madison ranged from the mediocre to the incompetent. "For God's sake," blurted William H. Crawford to Albert Gallatin, "endeavor to rid the army of old women and blockheads, at least on the general staff."[12]

When war was declared, Congress increased the authorized strength of the regular army to just 35,603, although only some 7,000 were actually enrolled. In addition to the two authorized major generals (Henry Dearborn, sixty-two years of age, and Thomas Pinckney, sixty-three years old), seven brigadier generals were approved; all the Americans with stars on their shoulders averaged sixty years of age. The Congress adjourned on 6 July without voting the money needed to conduct the war![13]

Because of widespread state opposition, militia were not forthcoming from all of the states. Despite the call up of some fifty thousand men in 1812, only a few thousand actually got to the front. Though after proper training they performed well later in the war, the American militia early in the war often refused to obey orders or to advance into Canada. On the enemy side, with less than five thousand British regulars in all of Canada, the governor general, Lt. Gen. Sir George Prevost, ordered a draft of two thousand militia. Some of these men mutinied, and other troubles developed; yet they would be of some service before the conflict ended.[14]

A month and a half after the war began, Jefferson, in retirement at Monticello, bragged that "the acquisition of Canada this year, as far as the neighborhood of Quebec, will be a mere matter of marching.'' Never was a prognostication more erroneous. But most American frontiersmen in the Old Northwest agreed with him, and, with the dearth of British regulars in Canada, there seemed to be ample reason for this optimism. In terms of grand strategy, Madison and the senior major general, Dearborn, divined that the key enemy position was Montreal, even though American forces were kept badly scattered. There the main blow should be struck, with subsidiary advances to be launched from Sackett's Harbor, the Niagara River front, and Detroit.[15]

The great Maj. Gen. Sir Isaac Brock, the forty-three-year-old governor of Upper Canada, was one of England's most distinguished soldiers and provided a spendid example of manhood. Born in Guernsey of a military family, he entered the army at fifteen and saw heavy and extensive combat in the Netherlands in 1799 and at Copenhagen in 1801. He came to North America in 1802 as commander of the forces in Upper Canada. Brock was at the peak of his powers in 1812, and he possessed a dignified, vigorous, and commanding bearing, an engaging personality, and a keen, penetrating, analytical mind. He was indeed a superb leader of high character, with great personal and moral courage, dash, and unconquerable spirit. Henry Adams truly said of Isaac Brock, ''He stood alone in his superiority as a soldier.'' On the American side, such military qualities were sadly lacking among commanders in 1812.[16]

At first glance it might seem that the British and Canadians were overmatched. In terms of population, some 7,250,000 Americans were pitted against 500,000 Canadians. The 7,000 United States regulars and 400,000 (theoretically) available militiamen were opposed at first by only 4,500 British and 4,000 Canadian regulars, 4,000 Canadian militia, and 3,500 Indians. Upper Canada, with only 70,000 people, appeared particularly vulnerable. But lacking naval power, the American incursion into the beautiful but forbidding Canadian wilderness proved extremely difficult. An invading army would require control of the vital waterways of the St. Lawrence River, Lake Ontario, Lake Erie, and Lake Champlain, as well as the border land bridges at Plattsburg, Sackett's Harbor, Niagara, Detroit, and Mackinac. So strong was Quebec that the United States high command ignored it; but the other key point, Montreal, was largely neglected in the uncoordinated American attacks on other fronts.[17]

Lacking a general in chief, the bungling Madison-Eustis leadership permitted a looseness in command that proved devastating. The president's close friend, the senior major general, Henry Dearborn, was stationed at Plattsburg on Lake Champlain, the classic invasion route. He was placed in command of the northern frontier except for Detroit; but he was not told (or did not remember) that the troops on the Niagara, who were to make a diversion, were a part of his command! The general named to command on the Detroit front, fifty-nine-year-old William Hull, was not informed by his government that war had been declared until 2 July, and when he was, the enemy captured a copy of his orders.[18]

Hull was a distinct liability for the Americans in 1812. A graduate of Yale, he served with distinction as a young officer in the Revolution, winning

FIG. 4.1. WAR OF 1812, NORTHERN THEATER

encomiums from George Washington. He practiced law and for seven years prior to 1812 he was governor of Michigan Territory. He was described in 1812 by an eyewitness as a "short, corpulent, good natured old gentlemen, who bore the marks of good eating and drinking." He was a fine speaker, patriotic, and well meaning. But Hull in command in the field soon revealed his lack of moral courage and resolution. He oscillated between extreme optimism and pessimism. He was aging, hesitant, and afraid to fight a pitched battle. In short, Hull was not competent to handle the trying operations he confronted.[19]

As early as 3 April 1809 and again on 15 June 1811 and 6 March 1812 Hull called for construction of American warships on Lake Erie to gain control of that body of water so vital to land supply and communications, but his advice was ignored. Instead, Madison directed Hull to move his force of approximately 1,500 raw Ohioans some 200 miles from Cincinnati via Dayton to Detroit. After a hard march, the general reached Detroit, a post of about 800 people, on 5 July 1812.[20]

Assuming the offensive, Hull crossed the Detroit River into Canada on 12 July and occupied Sandwich. He moved a detachment close to Fort Malden, but he was obsessively fearful of his supply lines and procrastinated. By this delay he missed a chance to capture Fort Malden and its weak garrison that was about to evacuate the stronghold. On 3 August news reached Hull of the surrender of the American Fort Michilimackinac on 17 July and the massacre that followed. Hull was unnerved because he had predicted that such an occurrence would unloose hordes of hostile Indians upon him; so he hurriedly fell back to Detroit on 8 August.[21]

While Hull vacillated, General Sir Issac Brock acted decisively. He quickly suppressed the defeatist elements in Upper Canada, sent Col. Henry Procter to Fort Malden, gathered a force of militia, and soon followed. Brock told Prevost that he should advance on Detroit, and Prevost proceeded to do so promptly. Brock, skillfully playing upon Hull's many fears, preemptively demanded the surrender of Detroit and its garrison. He hinted that if this were not forthcoming, he could not guarantee control of his Indian allies, whose numbers he exaggerated to be almost 5,000 and whose revenge would be savage.[22]

Hull's situation at Detroit was difficult but not impossible, though several of his relief expeditions for additional supplies had fared badly. Brock's batteries opened fire, but they were not decisive. Hull was unduly shaken. Although the Americans outnumbered the enemy almost two to one, Hull did not return the fire. Instead, he supinely surrendered his garrison and Detroit to Brock. That a man of Hull's weak character would make this craven decision did not surprise the men around him. He was near collapse from the pressure; in the hours before he finally capitulated he sat, tobacco juice drooling down his beard to his vest, seemingly immobile. "Hull's surrender," declared historian Harry L. Coles, "was one of the most disgraceful episodes in the military history of the United States." Neither Eustis nor Madison—nor indeed Jefferson—gave any indication that their reduction of the army in numbers and equipment might bear some responsibility for the debacle at Detroit.[23]

The tragic news of the fall of Detroit was compounded by the defeat of Capt. Nathan Heald's 54-man garrison of Fort Dearborn (Chicago) on 15 August 1812 by some 500 Potawatomis, including the deaths of half of the soldiers and the massacre of about two dozen civilian men, women, and children. The president and cabinet reacted positively; they determined to recapture Detroit and build more warships on Lakes Erie and Ontario. But while Hull and the others were futilely struggling on the northwestern front, Madison and Eustis failed to take the pressure off these forces by simultaneous offensives on the Niagara and Lake Champlain fronts, or even on one of them.[24]

Not much was going on at the Niagara River front; only a few small raids took place on Lake Ontario and the upper St. Lawrence. Dearborn, the overall American commander, and Maj. Gen. Stephen Van Rensselaer, of the New

York state militia and actual commander at the front, were fearful in early September 1812 about the weaknesses of the American forces and the increase in British and Canadian strength on the Niagara. General Van Rensselaer, a Federalist, was educated at Princeton and Harvard and through his Dutch patroon ancestry owned vast landholdings in New York. This patriotic citizen-soldier recognized his own lack of military experience and turned to his nephew, Col. Solomon Van Rensselaer, whose Revolutionary War and regular army experience (he had been severely wounded at Fallen Timbers) he hoped to use. Stephen Van Rensselaer was a man of valor, high moral character, and energy, and in his brief sojourn in command he developed a common-sense approach that served him well.[25]

Dearborn sent Van Rensselaer some reinforcements under regular army Brig. Gen. Alexander Smyth. This force at Buffalo was to attack in the rear of Fort George on the Canadian side of the Niagara. But the unreliable Smyth, unable to confront a mere militia major general as his superior, disobeyed orders to report in person to Van Rensselaer. American numbers totalled at least 6,300 as opposed to 2,200 British. When Van Rensselaer's troops threatened to go home if he did not launch an attack from Lewiston across the Niagara and capture Queenston Heights, he was obliged to do just that.[26]

The first crossing, during a downpour of rain against the background roar of the great falls, began at 3:00 A.M. on 10 October 1812. But it failed when one of the boatmen deserted with all of the oars for the other craft. The British did not take this opera bouffe affair seriously, thinking it merely a feint while the real assault would be made on Fort George. A second crossing attempt was made by Van Rensselaer at 3:00 A.M. on 13 October. This was more successful, although Solomon Van Rensselaer was wounded, leaving capable twenty-three-year-old Capt. John E. Wool, commissioned directly from civilian life just seven months before, in command of the assault upon the difficult, steep slope of the heights that faced the river.[27]

Brock immediately rushed down from Fort George upon hearing of the American crossing and counterattacked. A series of assaults and counter-assaults ensued, and the courageous Brock, leading a charge in person, was shot through the chest at short range and died almost instantly. The Americans had the better of the fierce engagement until the moment the militiamen on the New York side of the river refused to cross to aid their hard-pressed brethren. The British, substantially reinforced by Brock's successor, the competent Maj. Gen. Roger Sheaffe, finally defeated the soldiers of the now wounded John E. Wool and his able young successor, Lt. Col. Winfield Scott. Some 958 Americans were captured, while 90 were killed and 100 wounded, as contrasted to enemy losses of 14 killed, 84 wounded, and 15 missing. Dearborn, without knowing the facts of the battle at Queenston Heights, bitterly denounced Van Rensselaer and directed him to turn over his command to Smyth.[28]

A Virginian of Irish birth, Alexander Smyth was a respected member of the bar and state legislature in the Old Dominion. He entered the regular army in 1808 as colonel of a new rifle regiment and was made inspector general, a post that he filled incompetently. Winfield Scott thought Smyth "showed no talent for command, and made himself ridiculous on the Niagara frontier.'' Smyth sneered at Van Rensselaer's alleged "imbecility" and "relentless malice," and claimed Van Rensselaer's militia had "disgraced the nation." He went on to comment about his own troops in a bombastic fashion:

> They are men accustomed to obedience, silence, and steadiness. They will conquer, or they will die. . . . Has the race degenerated? . . . Shall I imitate the officers of the British king, and suffer our ungathered laurels to be tarnished? Shame, where is thy blush! No. . . . Have you not a wish for Fame? . . . Yes![29]

There were some 4,500 troops available to Smyth, but dysentery, measles, and arrears in pay had lowered morale almost to the point of mutiny. His soldiers were deployed at Black Rock, north of Buffalo, and across from Fort Erie. Smyth made no effort to conceal his moves, and the British, thus tipped off, countered by positioning 1,000 soldiers to entertain him. In a crossing attempt on the night of 28 November 1812, Smyth's advance elements bravely attained the Canadian side of the Niagara in a sleet storm, but were unsupported and captured or forced back. Smyth himself lurked in the rear and was not seen with or by his men. As a result, some of his troops deserted.[30]

Another crossing was ordered for the night of 30 November, primed by Smyth's florid proclamation, "Neither rain, snow, or frost will prevent the embarkation. While embarking, the music will play martial airs. Yankee Doodle will be the signal to get underway. . . . Hearts of War! Tomorrow will be memorable in the annals of the United States." Only 865 regulars, 506 twelve-month volunteers, and 100 militiamen were ready for the crossing. The men were ordered into and then out of the boats. Smyth himself was nowhere to be seen. A hastily called council of war, convened by regular officers, cancelled the crossing and the assault and declared the campaign over, with regulars going into camp and volunteers going home. Discipline among the soldiers broke, weapons were discharged—several shots going in Smyth's direction—and pandemonium reigned. The general fought a bloodless duel and retired to Virginia, where he was reelected to Congress.[31]

Henry Dearborn, the American commander at Plattsburg, was in wretched health, and his military qualities "appeared to have evaporated with age and long disuse." Although Winfield Scott spoke of Dearborn as "a fine old soldier" with "high moral worth . . . patriotism [and] valor," Monroe said of him after a year of war, "he was advanced in years, infirm, and had given no proof of activity or military talent during the year." Both assessments were accurate.[32]

Having moved his headquarters from Albany to Plattsburg on the western shore of Lake Champlain, Dearborn tried in mid-November 1812 to launch an expedition toward Montreal with his 5,737 raw troops. Some 1,900 enemy soldiers, later increased to 3,000, moved southward to defend the Canadian border against this threat. The American advance reached a spot near Rouse's Point about two miles from the boundary, where Col. Zebulon M. Pike's regulars seized an evacuated blockhouse at La Colle Mill. When some United

States militiamen approached their brother regulars in the gray dawn, both forces mistook the other for the enemy and opened fire, with some 50 casualties resulting. Dearborn and 8 of his officers realized that all desire to fight had been drained from their green troops, especially from the insubordinate militia. The only thing to do was return to winter quarters at Plattsburg, and the general so ordered. Dearborn manfully offered to be relieved of his command if the administration could find someone with greater popularity and ability, but the government could not at that moment come up with anyone meeting those qualifications.[33]

By the end of the year 1812 the records show that against the 3,000 British regulars and 3,000 Canadian militia, plus hundreds of Indians, the Americans mustered 15,000 regulars and 49,187 militia. Of course these forces were widely scattered, and the British and Canadians concentrated their men better than did the Americans. The opposition Federalists made political capital of the Madison administration's mistakes, and the chief executive impelled the ineffectual Dr. Eustis to resign as secretary of war.[34] Unfortunately for the United States, his successor would also prove a failure.

John Armstrong of Carlisle, Pennsylvania, was named secretary of war, although he disliked the Virginians and had castigated the administration's conduct of the war. The president admitted that he had neither confidence in nor respect for Armstrong, who was barely confirmed by the Senate and who was bitterly opposed by Secretary of State Monroe, who warned Madison against his appointment. Unlike Eustis, the lamb, Armstrong came into the cabinet like the proverbial lion, "rather as a master than a servant," observed Henry Adams. He was not only detested by many in government, but there were those who thought the president feared him.[35]

In his earlier career, Armstrong fought courageously in the Revolution at Trenton and Princeton; probably wrote, as Horatio Gates's aide, the infamous "Newburgh Address"; studied law after the war; and pursued an erratic political career as a Federalist. He became a protégé of the powerful Livingston clan of New York state by his marriage to a sister of Edward and Robert R. Livingston, a DeWitt Clinton Republican; a surprise supporter of Madison's reelection; and an ineffective diplomat in Paris. Finally, he became a brigadier general in the army, charged with the defense of New York City.[36]

As secretary of war, Armstrong compromised and wavered, and he spent much of his time and energy in an intrigue to supplant the Virginia dynasty in the federal government with a New York–Pennsylvania one, headed by himself. Adams thought Armstrong "a man capable of using power for personal objects, and not easily to be prevented from using it as he pleased." Moreover, the new secretary had an "absence of conventional morals," according to Adams. "Something in his character always created distrust . . . and . . . he suffered from the reputation of indolence and intrigue." In addition he was "negligent of detail" and "he never took unnecessary trouble." His chief accomplishments, though they were few in number, were to energize the department and the army and to gradually replace the superannuated generals with younger, abler, and more vigorous ones.[37]

MADISON's first secretary of the navy was no better than his first two war secretaries. The fifty-one-year-old Paul Hamilton was a South Carolina slaveholder and rice planter who knew practically nothing about naval affairs and learned little while secretary. The French minister, Louis G. Serurier, charged that Hamilton was often drunk by noon. Congressman Nathaniel Macon characterized him as "about as fit for his place as the Indian Prophet would be for Emperor of Europe." Early in the conflict the secretary directed his chief clerk to economize, even as the war mushroomed in size, scope, and intensity, and to "watch well the behavior of our officers; attend also to the Navy Yard at Washington; 'tis a sink of all that needs correction."[38]

It was not until seven months after war began that Congress approved the construction of new ships: four ships-of-the-line (capital ships known as 74s, for the 74 guns they carried), six frigates (44s), and two additional months were to elapse before they voted six sloops (often rated as 18s). So far as naval strategy and the building of warships were concerned, some men at the time as well as such later authoritative naval historians as Alfred Thayer Mahan and Theodore Roosevelt thought that a greater number of larger vessels, ships-of-the-line and frigates, should have been constructed. These ships would have kept at least some sea lanes open and encouraged potential allies in Europe.[39]

When war erupted in 1812, the United States Navy possessed no battleships. The pride of the service afloat was its seven magnificent frigates, vessels that the London *Times* characterized derisively as a "few fir-built frigates with strips of bunting, manned by sons of bitches and outlaws." The *Times* and the English would soon sing a different tune as these finest frigates in the world repeatedly trounced their British counterparts. Three of the American frigates—*Constitution, President,* and *United States*—were rated as 44s, although they often carried as many as 50 to 54 guns and carronades. They were 43 feet abeam and ranged from 175 to 155 feet in length, making them larger than the corresponding British 38. So strongly were they built, including 24-foot planking, that the most famous of these frigates was nicknamed "Old Ironsides" because nonpoint-blank–range cannonballs often bounced off her sides. The other three of the American frigates—*Constellation, Congress,* and *Chesapeake*—were originally rated at 36 guns and later at 38, but in the War of 1812 they too usually carried more guns (often 46) and were also larger than frigates of the same rating of other powers. The smallest frigate in the United States Navy was *Essex,* rated as a 32, but actually carrying 46 guns and carronades. She, too, was bigger than enemy frigates of similar rating. The British Royal Navy, in comparison, numbered perhaps 650 warships in commission, including 120 ships-of-the-line and 116 frigates. Only 3 of the capital ships and 23 frigates, plus 53 sloops, brigs, and schooners were in western Atlantic waters.[40]

But the Yankees did well. Single American frigates achieved astonishing successes against the "spoiled children of Trafalgar." Captain Isaac Hull, nephew of the general who had shamefully surrendered Detroit to Brock, left port in *Constitution* (44) and at daybreak on 12 July 1812 suddenly found himself surrounded and seemingly trapped by four British frigates under Capt.

Philip Broke. Fortunately all vessels were becalmed and *Constitution* finally escaped by the back-breaking rowing of its boat crew and by kedging the ship. Although this was a negative success, Isaac Hull and *Constitution* achieved a striking victory when Old Ironsides on 9 August 1812 met *Guerriere* (38), Capt. James Dacres, and shot her to pieces with 79 casualties compared to American losses of 14. In other noteworthy naval actions, the American sloop *Wasp* (18), Capt. Jacob Jones, on 18 October encountered *Frolic* (18), Capt. Thomas Whingates, north of Bermuda. In a closely fought, evenly matched battle of forty minutes, *Wasp* demolished the enemy vessel with a loss of 90 men out of a crew of 105 compared to 10 American casualties. However, Jones no sooner captured *Frolic* than the damaged *Wasp* had to yield to the British 74-gun ship-of-the-line *Poictiers*.[41]

On 25 October, *United States* (44), under the command of the legendary Stephen Decatur, engaged *Macedonian* (38), Capt. John S. Carden, near Madeira, perforated her 100 times, and compelled her to strike her colors with a loss of 96 killed and wounded contrasted to Decatur's 11 casualties. Finally, Capt. William Bainbridge, sailing from Boston on 26 October in *Constitution*, engaged *Java* (38) off Brazil on 15 December. Old Ironsides's volleys forced Capt. Henry Lambert to capitulate with losses of 161 as against Bainbridge's casualties of 34 killed or wounded. The United States Navy destroyed or captured 4,330 tons of British warships in 1812 and lost only 820 tons of its own. The American navy also brought safely into port forty-six prizes. In addition, United States privateers compiled an enviable record.[42]

Fortunately for the service afloat Hamilton was ousted as secretary of the navy, to be replaced by the energetic and able William Jones of Philadelphia. Jones served in the Revolutionary War, was engaged in the China trade as a merchant who was knowledgeable about ships, and was a former member of Congress who knew the ways of politicians. He would give a very creditable performance in his new and trying position.[43]

RENEWED LAND OPERATIONS were demanded by western areas of Ohio and Kentucky, and they were certain they had found their leader in William Henry Harrison, the Hero of Tippecanoe. Born at Berkeley plantation on the James River near Richmond, Virginia, the son of a governor of the Old Dominion and signer of the Declaration of Independence, young Harrison attended Hampden-Sidney College and studied medicine under Dr. Benjamin Rush. He entered the army in 1791 as an aide to Anthony Wayne in the Indian campaigns in the Northwest Territory. Resigning from the army in 1798, Harrison became territorial secretary and served as its first delegate in Congress, and in 1800 he was named governor of Indiana Territory. He gained further attention in 1811 at the Battle of Tippecanoe and seemed earmarked for important commands in the future.[44]

Thirty-nine years old in the winter of 1812, Harrison was a man of proven courage and martial bearing. Confident of his own abilities, he was flexible in adapting to conditions and obstacles confronting him. He readily shared privations in the field with his miserably equipped and ill-trained militiamen, and with his oratorical talent he could appeal directly to their interests and instincts. Clad in hunting garb, he travelled extensively among the camps, and the raw troops soon became convinced that Harrison not only understood their problems but that he would champion them in high circles.[45]

Perhaps against his better judgment, pressured by western insistence and increased Indian raids in the fall of 1812, plus his anger at the loss of Michigan territory to the enemy under Henry Procter, Harrison agreed to Madison's order to move past the dreaded Black Swamp with 10,000 men to win back Detroit and penetrate Canada. But by mid-December he had only 6,500 green soldiers whom he planned to advance in three columns: one toward Sandusky, one to the rapids of the Maumee River (above the present-day city of Toledo), and one to Fort Defiance higher up the river. Procter was able to muster initially just 2,600 men to oppose the Americans. By January 1813 after incredible hardships and difficulty, the three columns reached their initial objectives. Harrison resumed the advance and reached Maumee Rapids. Half of his 1,800 troops were scheduled to return home in February 1813; so Harrison in the meantime put them to work building Fort Meigs just downstream while he awaited the arrival of new soldiers.[46]

Procter finally advanced upon the strong and well-built Fort Meigs and bombarded it on 1 May 1813. Rallying the defenders, Harrison asked them rhetorically,

> Can the citizens of a free country . . . think of submitting to an army composed of mercenary soldiers, reluctant Canadians, goaded to the field by the bayonet, and of wretched, naked savages? . . . Yes, fellow-citizens, your general sees your countenances beam with the same fire that he witnessed on that glorious occasion [of Fallen Timbers].

Harrison counterattacked and captured a British battery; but the undisciplined American troops pushed too far and were ambushed by the Indians and cut to pieces, 630 of the 800 being killed or captured. Another Harrison counter-assault captured two British batteries and enabled the overextended Americans to fall back safely into the fort. The fainthearted Procter, having suffered about 105 casualties, retreated swiftly to Amherstburg. By his indifference he allowed his Indians, despite Tecumseh's efforts to constrain them, to scalp perhaps 20 of the American prisoners at the nearby former British Fort Miami. Procter withdrew again, this time to Fort Malden, though he still retained Detroit. The American frontiersmen finally realized they had pushed Harrison into a premature campaign, and that further land action against Detroit and Canada would have to await naval control of Lake Erie.[47]

But Lake Ontario was not being neglected. The rival naval commanders there were seasoned, competent, cautious officers. Capt. Isaac Chauncey, forty, the American commander, was a large man who had gone to sea as a mere lad, commanded a ship at nineteen, served under Thomas Truxtun in the quasi war with France and with Edward Preble in the Tripolitan War, and won a number of commendations and command of the New York navyyard by the outbreak of the War of 1812. He was placed in command of all American naval resources on Lakes Erie and Ontario and arrived at Sackett's Harbor on Lake Ontario in October 1812.

Chauncey's counterpart, Commodore Sir James Lucas Yeo, thirty-nine, had been at sea since the age of ten, and had wide experience in naval combat and command in many parts of the world. As circumspect as Chauncey, Yeo was named commander in chief of British and Canadian warships on the American lakes and reached Kingston on Lake Ontario in May 1812. Although Yeo was not well supported by George Prevost, he was, like Chauncey, inexplicably inactive at critical moments on these crucial northern lakes where naval control often decided the outcome on land in the operations of the struggling armies.[48]

There were no pitched naval battles worthy of the name fought on Lake Ontario. Chauncey at Sackett's Harbor and Yeo at Kingston simply tried to outbuild rather than outfight each other, and a log-chopping contest or shipbuilder's war resulted. When Chauncey completed a larger warship than Yeo possessed, he would sail over to Kingston to fight. But Yeo would remain within the harbor under the protection of shore batteries while he constructed a still larger vessel, where upon Chauncey would retire to Sackett's to build yet a bigger man-of-war, while Yeo hovered outside the anchorage. And so it went. By the end of the war, the rival commanders on Lake Ontario were at work on three-deck, 120-gun ships-of-the-line.[49]

An American expedition was ordered in the spring of 1813 against York (Toronto) by Armstrong and Dearborn. The force of 1,700 troops sailed from Sackett's Harbor in Chauncey's fleet of fourteen transports plus warships on 25 April 1813. Dearborn accompanied the force but was so ill that he was confined to his cabin and turned actual command of the men over to thirty-four-year-old Brig. Gen Zebulon Montgomery Pike, the noted explorer, who trained his men well in the time available. The flotilla arrived off York (a town of 625 people) on 27 April and immediately engaged British Maj. Gen. Sir Roger H. Sheaffe's 800 troops in sharp combat. Chauncey's squadron assisted by bombarding Fort York, and Sheaffe retreated with his remnants by land toward Kingston. But the detonation of a huge British mine, or powder magazine, killed and wounded many Americans (and a few Canadian militiamen); the brave Pike perished when his chest was crushed by a large stone that was dislodged by the explosion. Dearborn staggered ashore and assumed command, but it was too late to prevent the angry Americans from pillaging and probably setting fire to the two brick Parliament buildings of the government of Upper Canada in defiance of Dearborn's orders. The Americans lost 66 killed and 220 wounded; the British, 60 killed, 89 wounded, and 290 prisoners.[50]

Fort George was Dearborn's next objective along with the 1,900-man garrison mostly made up of unreliable militiamen under the command of Brig. Gen. John Vincent. Dearborn was so sick that he was forced to watch through a telescope from a warship, and the next senior officer, Brig. Gen. Morgan Lewis, exercised only nominal command. Assisted by Chauncey's naval bombardment of Newark, Winfield Scott's 4,000 troops were landed in choppy water from boats directed by Commander Oliver Hazard Perry. In a spirited contest the British lines were broken, and Vincent ordered a retreat to the west toward Beaver Dam and Burlington Heights near the western end of Lake Ontario. Colonel Scott, in the midst of the heaviest fighting, was wounded and broke his collarbone when blown off his horse by the explosion of a powder magazine. Not only did Fort George and many munitions and supplies fall into American hands, but Vincent also ordered the abandonment of Forts Erie and Chippewa. American casualties were 40 killed and 100 wounded; enemy losses ran to some 50 killed and over 500 wounded, missing, or taken prisoner. Immediate pursuit of Vincent did not take place because of Lewis's vacillation and the wounding of Scott.[51]

When Prevost learned that Dearborn's troops and Chauncey's warships were at the western end of Lake Ontario campaigning against Fort George, he and Yeo seized their chance to attack the vital base at Sackett's Harbor. They loaded 1,200 soldiers (including 800 regulars) onto forty boats, and, accompanied by Yeo's warships, landed near Sackett's and began their assault on 29 May 1813. Defending was a thirty-eight-year-old militia brigadier general, Jacob Brown, who had just 400 regulars, augmented by some volunteers and militia, many of whom were untrained, unequipped, and unreliable. Brown put the militia in front, and when assailed they broke even before expected. But Brown's second line of regulars threw back the British with loss while Brown rallied some of the militia fugitives and with them harassed the enemy flank. The apprehensive Prevost, thinking the returning American militiamen were regulars, ordered a retreat to the boats and thereby gave up the campaign. The British lost 260 killed and wounded in the battle and the Americans about 160. While some historians think Prevost withdrew too hastily from Sackett's Harbor, others are convinced that had he not done so he would have lost his army there.[52]

The United States at last had a legitimate army hero on the Niagara front. Jacob Jennings Brown was a Quaker born in Bucks County, Pennsylvania. To support himself he taught school and did surveying in Ohio. In the process he had acquired several thousand acres of land on the shore of Lake Ontario and prospered in farming and real estate. He located in New York not far from Sackett's Harbor and in 1809 received the command of a militia regiment. By 1811 he was a militia brigadier general and was stationed at Ogdensburg when war began in 1812. Brown's military knowledge of tactics and organization was limited, but he was a zealous, energetic, determined officer, and a natural leader of men—especially militiamen, whom he understood. Scott described him as "an unostentatious Christian—honest, and as obstinately brave as any Puritan in Cromwell's time." Brown's entire career in the War of 1812 could be looked upon by Americans with satisfaction—something that could not be said of most of our generals in that conflict.[53]

Henry Dearborn finally asked to be relieved of his command. He was so ill that he was in bed almost as much as he was afoot, and he suffered from pains and fever and possibly from mortification for his failure to achieve more decisive results with his numerically superior forces. Moreover, Armstrong played a shoddy and devious role in falsely informing Dearborn that the ill president wanted his resignation. The general's request to step down was eventually accepted by the secretary of war and the president on 6 July 1813, and Dearborn was later named to the inactive command of New York City.[54]

MEANWHILE the United States Navy Department was beginning to stir under the able and imaginative direction of William Jones. The new secretary was innovative, vigorous, and adaptable, and he quickly mastered the details of arming, provisioning, supplying, manning, and giving strategic direction to the republic's small naval forces. The president proclaimed him "the fittest Minister who had ever been charged with the Navy Department," though little credit was due the president for whatever improvements came about. Jones recommended the building of a fleet of ships-of-the-line and called for standardization in the construction and equipment of warships, including interchangeability of parts. The secretary urged the maintenance of foundaries, armories, smitheries, and dockyards, and recommended the early gathering and aging of timbers. He strongly suggested the establishment of a permanent career naval service and the creation of a naval academy. Jones wanted compulsory service in the navy, and held that the service afloat should have a board of inspectors made up of three naval officers and two competent civilians to advise the secretary.[55]

In the meantime the British enemy was not inactive. Their naval commander of the North American Station, Admiral Sir John Borlase Warren, selected the vulnerable Chesapeake Bay area in 1813 as the arena in which to bring home to the inhabitants the realities and penalties of making war on Great Britain. Warren's total fleet was being built up to thirty frigates and fifty sloops. To lead the expedition into the Chesapeake and its tributaries, Warren chose Rear Adm. Sir George Cockburn, forty-one, a weather-beaten, hard-bitten veteran.[56]

Cockburn arrived in Hampton Roads in February 1813 with four 74s, lesser men-of-war, and 1,800 troops. An initial bombardment of Lewes, Delaware, by one of Cockburn's detachments on 6 April was repelled without doing much damage, although Cockburn's other forces did terrorize the countryside around Lynnhaven Bay near the strong American naval base at Norfolk. When Warren was unable to approach closer than twenty-five miles to Washington, D.C., he sent Cockburn to the head of Chesapeake Bay. Here, after a sharp combat, Cockburn burned Frenchtown and some vessels on 28 April. This was followed on 3 May by a surprise and successful attack on Havre de Grace, near the mouth of the Susquehanna River; despite the famous one-man fight by John O'Neill and his cannon, Cockburn put forty of the sixty houses of the village to the torch. Then the admiral looted and burned Fredericktown a few days later, and returned to Lynnhaven Bay on 12 May.[57]

Cockburn was joined by his superior, Warren, and the British mustered the largest fleet assembled up to that time in the war: eight ships-of-the-line, twelve frigates, many smaller men-of-war, and 5,000 troops. But this massive force was unable in its heavy attack on the key position of Craney Island near Norfolk on 21 June 1813 to smother Brig. Gen. Robert B. Taylor's staunch troops and accurate artillerists—some from *Constellation* that was blockaded in Norfolk—and the British lost perhaps 200 men in their repulse. After a movement toward Washington, Annapolis, and Baltimore indicated that these places could not be assaulted with easy success, Cockburn departed the Chesapeake Bay and concentrated his marauding on the coasts of the Carolinas and Georgia.[58]

American fortunes varied in the war on the high seas in 1813. Action commenced auspiciously for the American cause when the 18-gun sloop-of-war *Hornet* under Capt. James Lawrence, who had been at sea since fourteen, had participated in the Tripoli War at eighteen, and had commanded a number of vessels, encountered the British brig *Peacock* (18) on 24 February 1813 off San Salvador. After fifteen minutes of furious close-range fighting, the superior seamanship and tactics of Lawrence won the day and the enemy struck her colors. Six British were killed and ninety wounded compared to American losses of three.[59]

The brave but overconfident Lawrence got his comeuppance when he assumed command of the ill-starred *Chesapeake* and its bad-humored, near-mutinous crew. Baited into a duel on 1 June by Capt. Philip Broke of the crack frigate *Shannon* before he and his crew were ready, Lawrence put up a heroic fight before being defeated and mortally wounded. His memorable charge, "Don't give up the ship!" achieved a lasting immortality in the annals of naval history. More fortunate was Lt. William Burrows, whose brig *Enterprise* (14) trounced the British *Boxer* (14) in forty minutes on 1 September off the coast of Maine. Even more spectacular was the famous long cruise of David Porter's frigate *Essex* (32), the first American warship to enter the Pacific. Going halfway across the largest ocean, Porter captured fifteen prizes and practically destroyed the British whaling industry. *Essex,* damaged in a squall and minus her topmast, was finally brought to book in a battle off Valparaiso with *Phoebe* (36) and *Cherub* (20) on 28 March 1814. Porter had to strike his colors with only three guns workable. By the end of this period, most American warships were bottled up in port.[60]

THE UNHAPPY WINTER of 1812–1813 on the northwestern front was accompanied by an American determination to recapture Detroit before the new year ended. However, everyone, from William Henry Harrison to John Armstrong to the citizens, was finally convinced that a victorious land campaign to regain this key post would have to await a naval triumph and control of Lake Erie. Failure to retain command of the lakes was perhaps the greatest strategic British blunder of the war, and it would cost them dearly. The outcome depended now upon the performance of America's brilliant twenty-seven-year-old naval officer on Lake Erie, Master Commandant Oliver Hazard Perry.[61]

Perry's family was steeped in the tradition of service afloat. His father, five brothers, and two brothers-in-law were officers in the navy. Perry began his naval service at the age of fourteen. By seventeen he became a lieutenant, and at twenty he was a schooner captain in the navy's Mediterranean squadron. Early in the War of 1812 he was put in command of a gunboat flotilla at Newport, Rhode Island. Ordered to report to Chauncey at Sackett's Harbor in February 1813, Perry had an amiable meeting with his superior that did not indicate the somewhat strained relations that would develop later between the two. Although often ill, the dedicated Perry could and often did tap his deep reservoirs of energy and determination to accomplish his mission.[62]

Several of Perry's warships were being built at Black Rock on the Niagara River; he journeyed to Presque Isle (Erie), Pennsylvania, to push the construction of others. Both his British counterpart, the able, thirty-two-year-old Capt. Robert H. Barclay at Amherstburg, and Perry had enormous supply difficulties. Green timber was plentiful on the shores, but other equipment, stores, and armaments had to be hauled in from considerable distances. Perry was a hard driver and Pittsburgh mills and merchants provided most of what was needed. Barclay had an even longer and more tenuous supply line to maintain. Veteran seamen and gunners came from some of the blockaded men-of-war on the Atlantic coast, though Chauncey, like Yeo, often siphoned off some of the better seamen before they could reach Lake Erie. Perry had benefitted by the Dearborn-Chauncey raid on York in April 1813; several warships and ordnance and stores earmarked for Barclay's fleet were captured or destroyed. In addition, the American capture of Fort George led to the enemy evacuation of Fort Erie, which permitted Perry to get his warships out of Black Rock and the Niagara River and enabled them to join his other vessels at Presque Isle.[63]

Perry, augmented by one hundred Kentucky riflemen serving as marines, conferred with General Harrison, who had eight thousand troops at Seneca, and moved his fleet to Put-in Bay (at what is now Port Clinton, Ohio) near the western end of Lake Erie. He had the following warships: the brig *Lawrence* (20-gun flagship); brig *Niagara* (20); and seven small schooners that totaled 54 guns, most of them short-range carronades. Barclay's fleet consisted of *Detroit* (21-gun flagship); *Queen Charlotte* (18); *Lady Prevost* (14); *Hunter* (10); and two small vessels that in aggregate amounted to 63 guns, most of them long-range. From 10 August 1813 for an entire month Perry's fleet cruised on the lake and trained in seamanship and gunnery. The experience probably proved decisive in the forthcoming clash.[64]

The consistent and famous Perry luck held when a spy in Fort Malden revealed how Barclay intended to deploy his ships. At a council of war on 9 September, Perry directed that his ships fight in close order, halfcable apart. On the following day, the British squadron appeared off Put-in Bay, and battle was joined about 11:45 A.M. in beautiful, clear weather. Once again Perry was fortunate—the wind shifted in his favor just as the rival fleets deployed for action. Perry handled his ship expertly, but *Lawrence* got the worst of it, with the vessel shattered and her crew suffering severely. Nor was he assisted by Lt. Jesse D. Elliott in *Niagara,* who failed to come to his aid. Perry, in desperation, pulled off a remarkable feat and transferred himself and his flag by boat to *Niagara* and continued direction of the seemingly hopeless struggle. Gradually the tide turned in the American favor as Elliott, now in *Somers,* and the other small warships entered the contest. Perry twice broke through the British line and battered the enemy unmercifully. Barclay was badly wounded and *Detroit* was impelled to strike her colors, soon followed by the other British men-of-war. It was a complete victory, Perry wrote on the back of an old letter to Harrison, "We have met the enemy and they are ours." The Battle of Lake Erie, or Put-in Bay, proved decisive for the outcome of the struggle by the armies on its shores.[65]

GENERAL HARRISON was poised between Port Clinton and Sandusky Bay to follow up Perry's spectacular success by launching an expedition to recapture Detroit and invade Upper Canada. The army gathered there by Harrison (with little help from Secretary Armstrong) consisted of approximately forty-five hundred effectives and included some new regulars and one thousand talented Kentucky riflemen commanded by Col. Richard M. Johnson. This force on 20 September 1813 was put aboard Perry's fleet of nine warships and eighty other vessels. It was an awe-inspiring spectacle: the force constituted the largest American armada assembled to that time. On 27 September the expedition landed near the mouth of the Detroit River.[66]

British Gen. Henry Procter tried to defend Canadian soil with an army low in morale and numbers, and he soon saw that immediate retreat was essential. Thus Harrison occupied Amherstburg and Fort Malden, and reached Sandwich on 29 September 1813. On 30 September Detroit fell to the Americans. Neglecting to burn the bridges in his rear or to impede Harrison's advance, Procter fell back some seventeen miles along the Thames River to make a stand near Chatham, several miles west of Moraviantown, making sure first that his own family and property were removed from harm's way.[67]

The day of the Battle of the Thames, 5 October, found Procter's 830 regulars and 500 Indians manning a 500-yard line from the river northward through several swamps. Harrison authorized Johnson's mounted Kentucky riflemen to charge, and they smashed through the enemy line, inflicting casualties and compelling most of the British to surrender. The forty-four-year-old Tecumseh was slain in the fighting, and the Indians who were not shot or captured scattered. The engagement lasted just twenty minutes, and cost Harrison 15 killed and 30 wounded as against enemy losses of 55 killed and 36 wounded, plus some 600 prisoners. The Battle of the Thames was decisive, and the performance of the citizen-soldiers was exemplary. Detroit was retained by the Americans. For the duration of the war enemy resistance was negligible in the Northwest, and the British were able to retain only the tiny, remote Fort Michilimackinac.[68]

Harrison returned to Detroit on 7 October 1813, garrisoned it, and discharged his Kentucky volunteers on 14 October. By the end of the month the general and his regulars were shifted to the Niagara front. The discouraged British governor general, Prevost, wanted to withdraw all the way to Kingston, but Gen. John Vincent convinced him to hold onto Burlington Heights and York. Harrison hoped to attack the British there, but could get no naval support. Consequently he moved eleven hundred men on Chauncey's ships to Sackett's Harbor. Harrison travelled to Albany, New York City, and Washington; but Armstrong, who had criticized him unfairly and bypassed him in the chain of command by sending orders directly to his subordinates, forced Harrison to resign and go home. Madison, ill at times, refused to reverse Armstrong's action. Thus the Americans lost for the rest of the war one of their abler commanders.[69]

Instead, they got that "acquitted felon," Gen. James Wilkinson, who had served with Armstrong in the Revolutionary War. Wilkinson was ordered to take command at Sackett's Harbor. He conferred for two weeks with Armstrong in Washington, D.C., but no campaign plan was worked out. The often ill Wilkinson proceeded to Sackett's and arrived in August 1813.[70]

Capable of conspiratorial mischief and bearing an unsavory reputation, Wilkinson, although senior general in the army until 1812, was viewed with contempt or antipathy by almost every respectable officer. Winfield Scott thought him an "unprincipled imbecile," and his lack of military ability soon became all too apparent. Wilkinson repaid Madison and Armstrong, who supported him and named him to high rank against almost universal opposition, by heaping abuse upon them.[71]

Directed to play a supposedly cooperative role with Wilkinson on the northern frontier was his arch-enemy, Gen. Wade Hampton, who in July 1813 was thoughtlessly named to the command at Plattsburg on Lake Champlain. Born in 1751 in Halifax County, Virginia, Hampton resided in South Carolina when the Revolution began. He served effectively in that war, especially at the Battle of Eutaw Springs, and became a planter, state legislator, justice of the peace, sheriff, and member of Congress. Hampton showed marked limitations and serious shortcomings in the War of 1812, although he was energetic and well meaning. Winfield Scott, who knew him well, thought Hampton "in mind vigorous, prompt, intrepid, sagacious; but of irritable nerves; consequently often harsh, and sometimes unjust," although he would later try to make amends. According to Henry Adams, the sixty-two-year-old Hampton "was rendered wholly intractable wherever Wilkinson was concerned, by [a] long-standing feud." Yet these two American generals were supposed to cooperate in a difficult, two-pronged operation of considerable complexity.[72]

Hampton accepted the command on Lake Champlain with the explicit understanding from Armstrong that his was a separate and distinct command, free from the orders of Wilkinson, even though the latter was the senior officer. When Wilkinson tested this arrangement by actually trying to issue orders to Hampton, the latter threatened to resign but was saved by Armstrong's pledge that he would not allow this to happen. With the palsied hand of the commander in chief stilled in part by illness or inclination, Armstrong was allowed by Madison to journey northward with Wilkinson to mediate between the two quarreling generals and to try belatedly to work out a plan of campaign. But the moment Armstrong arrived at Sackett's Harbor, Wilkinson cautioned his superior on 24 August 1813 against meddling "with my arrangements," saying that "two heads on the same shoulders make a monster." The campaign was assuredly getting off to a wretched beginning![73]

Wilkinson and Armstrong argued at length over the campaign plans at Sackett's Harbor, and the general seemed to oppose anything the secretary suggested. Armstrong eventually agreed to Wilkinson's asinine plan: a movement on Montreal in two columns—Wilkinson's from Sackett's to the St. Lawrence River and on to Montreal, and Hampton's from Plattsburg toward Montreal. The two were to converge in a final push for the Canadian city; then the Americans were to turn around and capture Kingston. After meddling for over two months at Sackett's, the secretary of war abandoned the generals and the army and returned to Washington, probably telling the president little if anything of what had transpired and failing to secure Madison's approval for his actions. All in all, it was a shabby performance by Armstrong.[74]

Unfortunately, Wilkinson waited until November before he finally moved his 7,000 troops toward the western end of the St. Lawrence. Delays occurred because of rain and wind, then cold weather and snow. The ailing Wilkinson moved down the St. Lawrence and reached Chrysler's Farm. Battle was joined at Chrysler's on 11 November, the 2,000 Americans engaged were checked and forced back by a mere 800 British troops. Wilkinson's casualties were 102 killed, 237 wounded, and 100 prisoners; the enemy lost 22 killed, 148 wounded, and 9 missing. Realizing that Hampton could not or would not cooperate, Wilkinson went into winter quarters at French Mills on the Salmon River, just within the United States border.[75]

While Wilkinson stumbled into unfortunate action, Wade Hampton on Lake Champlain conducted his own futile campaign, hampered by the governors of several New England states who were loath to have their troops remain in Hampton's army. Nonetheless the general pushed his 4,000 raw effectives northward. Drought soon forced him to turn southward and then westward along the Chateaugay River past Chateaugay Four Corners to Spears. Here on 25 October 1813 he encountered British Col. Charles de Salaberry's 1,000 militiamen in prepared positions. Although the first enemy line was overrun, Hampton's men were duped by de Salaberry's intentional ruse of bugles sounded at distant points. The American general thought they indicated mammoth numbers of British redcoats, although actually only 300 of de Salaberry's men were involved. Without an attempt to ascertain their enemy's numbers, a council of officers and the inept Hampton hurriedly ordered an immediate retreat—a decision encouraged by the news that Armstrong had established winter quarters. This of course implied to the general that the secretary had no intention of supporting a campaign into the winter. The dithering Prevost, who arrived after the engagement was over, supinely allowed Hampton to escape. Losses at the ill-fated Battle of Chateaugay totalled 25 British and 50 American. Hampton soon retired from the army.[76]

The aftermath of Armstrong's personal intervention and the operations of the incompetent Wilkinson and Hampton was melancholy indeed. Armstrong and Wilkinson blamed Hampton for the failure of the campaign. Armstrong belabored Wilkinson for giving up the campaign. And Wilkinson and Hampton denounced Armstrong as the chief malefactor in the fiasco. It was all a tragically sorry affair.[77]

At the end of March 1814 Wilkinson ventured one more advance toward Montreal, this time with 4,000 soldiers. He got several miles beyond Rouse's Point and into Canada where he was halted in a combat at La Colle Mill by just 200 enemy troops, later reinforced by perhaps 300 more, and three tiny warships. He lost 154 men; the British, 61. Wilkinson retreated ignominiously, was cashiered from the army by Armstrong, and hailed before a court martial by the secretary on charges of neglect of duty and unofficerlike conduct. Wilkinson as usual was eventually exonerated but was ousted from the army after thirty-seven years of dubious service to the nation whose uniform he wore.[78]

Meanwhile, disaster struck the Americans on the Niagara front. On 10 December 1813 the British flushed the few remaining troops out of Fort George, which Brig. Gen. George McClure had blown up. McClure, seemingly berserk, without authority burned the Canadian towns of Newark and Queenston and turned the citizens out in zero weather. He was condemned by Americans as well as Canadians. In addition, McClure had been criminally negligent in his failure to safeguard Fort Niagara on the American side. The able British General Sir Gordon Drummond with one thousand troops (including Indians) took revenge and attacked and captured Fort Erie on 18 December. Drummond's troops, unrestrained, burned Buffalo, Lewiston, Black Rock, Schlosser, Manchester, and Tuscarora. Supplies were put to the torch, as were five warships, and twenty-seven cannon were captured. A number of American soldiers and civilians were deliberately slaughtered by the Indians.[79]

When the year 1813 mercifully came to an end, the Americans had 19,036 regulars and 130,112 militia under arms, plus some volunteers and rangers. The authorized level of the regular army reached 62,274, the highest it would be until 1898; however, by September 1814 the regular army actually had 38,000 in the ranks, a number approximated by the volunteers.[80]

THE WAR saw vicious hostilities erupt in the South and old Southwest. In Alabama the Creek Indians were peaceful until whipped into a war fever by Tecumseh, fresh from his stellar role in the capture of Detroit, and the Prophet. There were some 4,000 disaffected Creeks, but they were poorly armed. A half-breed, Peter McQueen, was their leader. By 1813 they began to receive arms and ammunition from Britain's ally, Spain, at Pensacola, and undertook scalping raids. On the scorching hot day of 30 August 1813, over 1,000 Creek warriors under the command of another half-breed, William Weathersford, attacked and captured Fort Mims on the Alabama River just north of the Florida border and butchered some 400 of the 553 soldiers and civilians, including women and children. This paved the way for the advent of "Old Hickory" onto the scene.[81]

Andrew Jackson was born in the rude frontier settlement of Waxhaw, South Carolina, in 1767. He lost his mother and two brothers in the Revolution. Though merely a lad in his early teens, he fought in the Revolution at the Battle of Hanging Rock (or Sand's House), was captured, struck by a British sword, and imprisoned for a time. After the war he studied law and moved to Nashville, Tennessee. He aspired to the status of a gentleman, fought several duels, and successfully engaged in land speculation and cotton cultivation at his plantation, The Hermitage. He served in both houses of the United States

Congress, was a superior judge, and in 1802 became major general of the Tennessee militia. Tall, lean, and angular, with high forehead and stiff, erect hair, he had piercing blue eyes that were as quick as his temper. Limited by implacable prejudices, he was nonetheless of good judgment and fine common sense in his military actions and the hero of thousands of Westerners.[82]

While acclaimed in Tennessee when war came in 1812, Jackson's characteristically outspoken denunciations of Jefferson and Dearborn and his disregard for Madison made him unpopular with Washington officialdom, and his offer to serve on the Canadian border was spurned. Armstrong obtusely failed to recognize Old Hickory's abilities. In December 1812 Jackson was placed in command of two thousand men at Nashville with the mission of invading Florida. However, Wilkinson, in command at New Orleans, ordered him to remain in Tennessee, and Jackson had to disband his army.

In January 1814 Old Hickory's force was buttressed by 900 Tennesseans. With them, he moved upon the Creeks and trounced them at Emotochopco Creek, near Emuckfaw, slaying 189 Indians with a loss of 20 of his own killed and 75 wounded. By 6 February Jackson had a total of 5,000 troops, including some friendly Choctaws. The general learned that over 900 Creek warriors (and 300 Indian children and squaws) were in a fortified position at Tohopeka (or Horseshoe Bend), on the Tallapoosa River. Jackson moved against them in March, placing garrisons along his line of communications. This left him 2,000 effective soldiers for the assault that he delivered on 27 March. The fortified position was carried in sharp fighting. When the Creeks refused to surrender, the Americans were ordered by Jackson to slaughter many of them, including some women and children. Over 700 of the 900 Indians were killed, while Jackson lost 32 killed and 99 wounded, plus some 48 casualties among his Indian allies. The Battle of Horseshoe Bend was decisive in crushing the opposition of the Creek nation, and the treaty that Old Hickory wrung from them finalized the cession to the United States of some 20 million acres of land.[83]

ALLIED ARMIES entered Paris on 31 March 1814 and the Madison administration soon learned that fourteen veteran British regiments from Wellington's Peninsula army would be sent to reinforce Canada. Consequently Americans needed to strike hard before the redcoats arrived or face the consequences.[84]

To get ready to assume the offensive, Winfield Scott, with Jacob Brown's blessing, diligently trained his new regular troops in the Buffalo area in a style reminiscent of Baron von Steuben. The soldiers were drilled ten hours a day for three months in linear tactics similar to the British system and not very different from those delineated in William Duane's *Hand Book for Infantry*. Scott could justly boast of the results of his training, and these improvements would be amply demonstrated in the coming summer operations.[85]

As early as 30 April 1814 Armstrong urged Madison to approve an offensive against Fort Erie; because of differences within the cabinet, the president did not authorize a strategic plan of operations until 7 June. Priceless time was lost as fourteen thousand British redcoats were readied for embarkation from

England for Canada. The ambitious American plan now proposed that Brown with eight thousand men cross the Niagara and recapture Fort Erie and Fort George (and Fort Niagara on the American side). He was then to take Burlington Heights, and, with Chauncey's aid, seize York and Kingston. As it evolved, Chauncey's help was minimal because of the destruction of some of his supplies by a British raid on Oswego. [86]

The British general, Gordon Drummond, meanwhile had no easy task. He had a reserve of eighteen hundred soldiers at York and Burlington and twenty-eight hundred under an Irish brigadier of dubious ability, Maj. Gen. Phineas Riall, scattered in garrisons from Fort Erie to Burlington. Facing Riall was Brown's vastly improved army of three thousand five hundred, comprising Peter B. Porter's eager brigade of militia and Indians, the two regular brigades of Scott, and the able but hypercautious Elazar Ripley.[87]

The campaign opened with the American attack on Fort Erie on 3 July 1814. Although Scott was almost drowned in crossing the Niagara River, and despite Ripley's sluggishness, Scott easily captured the lightly held fort and its nearly 200 defenders. To counter this threat, Riall marched southward from Fort George with 2,100 soldiers to confront Brown and deployed into position on the plain near Chippewa. Brown moved northward along the Canadian side of the Niagara. The two armies clashed in a vicious battle at Chippewa on 5 July. Scott was holding a review of his troops when the British moved upon him. With Brown's cooperation, Scott quickly deployed under fire and attacked. Thinking he was to face only militia, the nonplussed Riall, seeing the steadiness and good order of Scott's soldiers, exclaimed in dismay, "Those are Regulars, by God!" The charges by Maj. Henry Leavenworth and John McNeil drove the British from the field with 148 killed and 321 wounded, while Brown lost 60 killed, and 235 wounded. It was a splendid, badly needed victory by the Americans.[88]

Brown withdrew to Chippewa on 24 July and ordered Scott forward (northward) to threaten Queenston. Riall was reinforced by about three thousand, while Drummond left Kingston to assume personal command. In the war's hardest fought battle on 25 July, two thousand Americans clashed with three thousand British in the area where Lundy's Lane crossed a low hill just to the west of Niagara Falls. While Scott's brigade struck the center of Drummond's line, Maj. Thomas Jesup brilliantly gained the enemy's flank. The heavy action continued into the night. Brown arrived with Ripley's brigade and ordered Col. James Miller, a veteran of Harrison's campaign, to capture the cannons in the enemy's center. "I'll try, Sir," was Miller's famous reply; in one of the most gallant actions of the war, he succeeded. Brown, Scott, Drummond, and Riall were wounded. Brown's subsequent actions were hard to explain. Perhaps his mental abilities were affected by his wound, or else he suffered from some inexplicable aberration. Brown ordered Ripley to march his brigade off the battlefield and back to Chippewa for rest, reorganization, and food, even though the British army was still fighting. They were then to return to the field. By the time Ripley got back to Lundy's Lane the enemy had naturally regained the guns captured by Miller and were still essentially holding their positions. Each side lost approximately nine hundred men in this bruising engagement. Although barely a drawn battle, Lundy's Lane was creditable to the Americans, even though strategically it was a British success because the invaders' will to push further into Canada tapered off.[89]

Drummond, reinforced at Lundy's Lane, now had perhaps 3,000 troops. Striving to seize the initiative, he moved upon Black Rock and Buffalo but was repelled by Morgan's rifles on 4 August with a loss of 32 men. Drummond marched against Fort Erie, besieged and bombarded it, and finally attacked on 15 August. Despite a lodgment in the fortification, the British suffered severe losses in hand-to-hand fighting and were hurled back by Edmund Gaines who was wounded in the combat. At a total loss of 84, the Americans inflicted staggering casualties on the British: 57 killed, 307 wounded, and 538 captured or missing.[90]

By autumn an atmosphere of calmness settled on the Niagara front; both Brown's and Drummond's armies were battered into silence. On the American side, Brig. Gen. George Izard, in command at Plattsburg with five to six thousand troops, fortified his position. This able thirty-eight-year-old officer— born near London of a prominent South Carolina planter, patriot, and diplomat who was temporarily residing there—received a military education in Germany, England, and France, and served as a subaltern in the United States army several years in the late 1790s before resigning.[91]

Secretary Armstrong blindly ignored the menacing threat of Prevost's heavily reinforced army north of Lake Champlain and stupidly ordered Izard and four thousand of his troops to march from Plattsburg to Sackett's Harbor. He was directed to operate against either Kingston or proceed to Niagara to buttress Brown at Fort Erie, even though Brown had not requested Izard's soldiers. Izard arrived at Niagara on 5 October and replaced Brown in command. Izard realized that the British force was still resolutely present and that Chauncey would not offer the needed naval support; so he contented himself with raids that netted his forces two hundred bushels of wheat in all. Soon Izard was ordered to evacuate Canada. So he blew up Fort Erie on 5 November and withdrew to American soil. His offer to turn over his command to Brown was refused.[92]

Massive British troop reinforcements reached Canada at last, and a four-pronged plan of grand strategy evolved that called for offensives on the Niagara front (which had been checked already), the Lake Champlain front, New Orleans, and the Chesapeake Bay area. The effort in the Chesapeake region encompassed no less than the capture of the capital of the republic, Washington, and the major port city of Baltimore. By late summer of 1814 the British force available for this purpose in the Chesapeake comprised Vice Admiral Sir Alexander F. I. Cochrane's fleet of four ships-of-the line and twenty frigates and sloops, plus Maj. Gen. Robert Ross's army of some forty-six hundred troops.[93]

Despite the British presence at Hampton Roads and Cockburn's extensive raids of 1813, the Madison administration scandalously neglected this vital area in 1814, although in May the president asked Armstrong to examine defensive measures for the safety of the capital. The secretary dismissed the idea that the town of Washington (population 8,000) was in danger, exclaiming, "No, no! Baltimore is the place, sir; that is of much more consequence," and stubbornly refused to fortify the capital.[94]

The president selected Brig. Gen. William H. Winder to command the district around the capital for no other apparent reason than that Winder was related to the Federalist governor of Maryland. Unfortunately, the chief executive made a poor choice. Thirty-nine years old in 1814, Winder was born in Somerset County, Maryland, where he had practiced law since 1802. He served on the northern front after the war began, was captured at Stoney Creek, exchanged, and remained without an important command until named to the Washington post. Though patriotic and well intentioned, Winder was a military dud. Henry Adams best summed him up with his comment that no general

> showed such incapacity as Winder either to organize, fortify, fight, or escape. When he might have prepared defenses, he acted as scout; when he might have fought, he still scouted; when he retreated, he retreated in the wrong direction; when he fought, he thought only of retreat; and whether scouting, retreating, or fighting, he never betrayed an idea.

Angered by Madison's choice, Armstrong washed his hands of any significant role in the defense of Washington.[95]

While alerting the nearby states of the possible need of their 93,500 militiamen, Winder was forbidden to call up more than 6,000 until a definite British march upon Washington had been detected. Frustrated and lacking an adequate staff, the general exhausted himself physically and mentally by riding around the countryside from 9 July to 27 July to examine the terrain. Winder chose Bladensburg, a village just northeast of Washington, as a rendezvous point; but hardly any equipment or supplies were there by 23 July, and as of 1 August not a single fieldwork had been constructed. Only when word reached Madison on 18 August that the British fleet and transports were in the nearby Patuxent River did the president call for all available regulars and militia.[96]

To oppose the overbearing British fleet were twenty-six barge gunboats commanded by the navy's Commodore Joshua Barney, fifty-five years old. A native of Baltimore County, Barney went to sea at twelve and commanded a ship at sixteen. In the Revolutionary war he had served meritoriously aboard such warships as *Hornet, Wasp,* and *Saratoga.* After a brief civilian business career, he commanded French ships that preyed upon British commerce in the 1790s. When he returned to the United States early in the War of 1812, he engaged in privateering. But now he could do little against Cochrane's powerful squadron. After initially successful counterattacks, Barney was obliged to destroy his flotilla, thereby opening the back door to the capital, while he escaped on foot with five cannon and over four hundred sailors and marines.[97]

Cochrane's fleet landed Robert Ross's army of forty-six hundred at Benedict, twenty miles up the Patuxent. Ross was accompanied by Admiral Cockburn, whose extensive raids in 1813 had made him famliar with the countryside. Winder, still riding aimlessly about, fell into a ditch, wrenched his shoulder, and sprained an ankle. Shadowing the British army on 19 and 20 August was a small group of American dragoons commanded by Secretary of

State Monroe. When citizens of the District of Columbia offered to build fieldworks at Bladensburg at their own expense, Winder accepted.[98]

The enemy, in continuing hot and humid weather, reached Upper Marlboro on 22 August. The following day President Madison and some cabinet members reviewed troops at Battalion Old Fields, and then the commander in chief tagged along with Winder in his wanderings. Only Barney's disrespectful and vigorous protests moved Secretary of the Navy Jones to intervene and allow the commodore and his men and guns to join the others at Bladensburg.[99]

At daybreak on 24 August 1814 Winder's request for advice brought Madison and some cabinet members to his side, although Armstrong arrived later. As they were arguing at length over what course the British might take, word arrived that Ross was marching in force upon Bladensburg, located to the northeast of Washington where a key bridge crossed the eastern branch of the Potomac River. The group of American civilian and military leaders was galvanized into action. Monroe said he would ride to Bladensburg to see to the troops' disposition on the field and galloped off. Winder led his column toward the same crucial place. Madison and Armstrong, the latter declining to offer suggestions and predicting catastrophe, pluckily rode toward Bladensburg, accompanied by the attorney general and the secretary of the navy. The secretary of the treasury gave the president a pair of dueling pistols, but some miscreant would steal them in the course of the day.[100]

The key terrain feature at Bladensburg was Lowndes Hill, to the east of the village where the road passed by, and this position was initially occupied by militia Brig. Gen. Tobias Stansbury's two Baltimore regiments. However, he disobeyed orders and left this hill, crossed the stream, and took position across the main road on the hill beyond. He was buttressed by six guns, and cavalry were posted on the left. A second line of infantry was stationed four hundred yards in the rear on the slope of another hill. Some one thousand yards farther to the rear on the crest was the remainder of the American army.[101]

All was not well. Unfortunately, these forces were not within close supporting distance of each other. Though Winder had some sixty-five hundred troops in the region compared to Ross's forty-six hundred, not all were in position. Moreover, Monroe arrived on the field before the action commenced and, without telling anyone in authority, redeployed some of Stansbury's soldiers to less effective positions. Winder himself did little.[102]

Presently the president of the United States rode onto the field, accompanied by several cabinet members. Armstrong did nothing, although he tried without success to get the president to put him in command of the field. Madison bravely proceeded ahead of the troops and almost blundered across the bridge and into the enemy's lines. Only a scout's warning at the last moment prevented a tragedy. The presidential party rode back into Washington and soon fled into the Virginia woods. Neither the chief executive, the secretary of war, the secretary of state, nor General Winder performed his proper function. Had it not been such a fearfully grave situation, the affair would have been ludicrous.[103]

Without delaying for a lengthy reconnaissance, Ross boldly, even recklessly, attacked with just his forward elements. But he was thrown back, as was a second assault, by the Americans, Stansbury's men, including the Baltimore Fifth Regiment, fighting especially well. Yet British flanking movements soon had the raw militiamen fleeing to the rear, their flight accelerated by the nearly harmless enemy Concreve rockets. Winder did not even use his reserves before giving up the contest. Then Ross came upon Barney's nearly 500 sailors and marines and their five large cannon in the second line. Barney repelled the heavy British attacks at a loss to the invaders. Only when both of his flanks were turned and he was wounded and captured along with most of his men did Barney yield his position. At this point Winder's troops fled to the rear, but toward Georgetown instead of falling back upon Washington. British casualties totalled at least 249, and some Englishmen place them as high as 500, as compared to American losses of just 71 shot and over 100 captured. Winder's performance as field commander had been pathetic.[104]

Accompanied by Admiral Cockburn, who seemed to relish such scorched-earth tactics, Ross and his troops entered Washington, burned the capitol, executive mansion, and several other public buildings, and ate a still warm supper on the White House dining table. The conflagration was said to have been in revenge for the burning by Americans of the government buildings at York and to avenge some shooting by Washingtonians of the British troops as they entered the city. Furthermore, some redcoats got out of hand. The fires were extinguished by a rainstorm, although greater destruction was visited upon the unhappy city by a tornado on the following day. The capture of the republic's capital by a small force with such feeble resistance and light casualties, in the heart of a nation of ten million citizens, is almost without parallel in history and stands as one of the darkest days in the annals of America.[105]

Immediately after the "Bladensburg races" on 24 August, the sixty-three-year-old president, who had been riding since 8:00 A.M.., exited the White House at 3:00 P.M., crossed the Potomac in a boat, and spent the remainder of the afternoon and evening riding in a carriage. That night and the next day during the tornado the commander in chief remained at a tavern in the Virginia woods, where he was reviled and cursed to his face by some American fugitives who thought they had been betrayed by the chief executive. On 29 August, after the British evacuated Washington and American government leaders returned, Madison confronted Armstrong and rebuked him sharply. Troops around the capital refused to obey Armstrong's orders; so the secretary of war decided to leave Washington and retire, which he did on 4 September. He was succeeded by James Monroe, who had really preferred a high field command.[106]

But if the safeguarding of the nation's capital had been a fiasco, the defense of Baltimore against the powerful foe was superb. Guarding the northwest branch of the Patapsco River and the port was Fort McHenry. It was not a huge installation, but it was strong and was ably defended by Maj. George Armistead and his garrison of approximately one thousand regular soldiers, sailors, and volunteer artillerymen. A total of thirteen hundred troops were scattered about the Baltimore area.[107]

The country was fortunate in its choice of Maj. Gen. Samuel Smith for the overall command of the Baltimore militia. Smith was born in Carlisle, Pennsylvania, but moved to Baltimore and became a wealthy merchant and Revolutionary war activist. He fought meritoriously at Monmouth, Fort Mifflin, Long Island, White Plains, and Brandywine, and after the war prospered as a land speculator and merchant in Baltimore. Smith also served in the United States Senate and House of Representatives. Tall, with a commanding presence, he was proud and imperious, tough and shrewd, industrious and intelligent. Above all, he was trusted as were few civil or military leaders of his day. Smith refused to allow Winder the command at Baltimore; he was sustained and Winder served under Smith honorably. Also present and assisting with small gunboats, batteries, and fortifications, were such naval worthies as John Rodgers, Oliver Hazard Perry, and David Porter.[108]

On 11 September 1814 Cochrane's large British fleet of some fifty ships was spotted coming up the Patapsco. About 2:00 A.M. on 12 September Ross's 5,000 troops were disembarked at North Point. General Smith, who thought the enemy numbered from 7,000 to 8,000, ordered militia Brig. Gen. John Stricker and his City Brigade of 3,185 soldiers to move forward to try to slow them down. Stricker formed his men in three lines of battle astride the North Point Road, some fourteen miles east-southeast of Baltimore.[109]

Ross, again accompanied on the field by Admiral Cockburn, attacked without hesitation, but Stricker's militia threw him back several times in sharp fighting at Godly Wood. Ross was struck by a bullet that penetrated his right arm and plunged into his chest. The bullet was probably fired by one of two young Baltimoreans, either Daniel Wells or Henry G. McComas, who soon lost their lives. Ross died while being rushed to the rear after lying for some time unnoticed. Only when Ross's successor, Col. Arthur Brooke, put some 4,000 veteran Wellington redcoats into combat were the Marylanders forced to fall back. They did so gradually and compelled the baffled British to halt their advance and go into bivouac. The Battle of North Point cost the enemy 319 casualties, while the Americans lost 213 men in all.[110]

With their army hesitating, it was now up to Cochrane's fleet to subdue the tenacious Baltimoreans, but again Sam Smith's defenses held. A twenty-five-hour bombardment by the British navy of Fort McHenry on 13 and 14 September involved approximately fifteen hundred enemy projectiles fired, but the British failed to shake Armistead's staunch defenders, and they repulsed with loss a British landing force attempting to seize nearby Fort Covington. The Americans suffered 4 killed and 24 wounded during the bombardment of McHenry. (It was at this time that Francis Scott Key composed the words of the "Star-Spangled Banner.") With the navy repelled, Brooke's army attempted two probes against Smith's well-fortified lines on Hampstead (Loudenslager's) Hill, just east-northeast of the city; with Winder's assistance, the defenders contained them. Cochrane and Brooke agreed that Smith's defenses were too formidable to breach, so the redcoats marched down to North Point, reembarked, and the British fleet sailed away. The local citizen-soldiers' defense of Baltimore was as outstanding as that of Washington had been pitiful.[111]

At the same time the enemy was at the gates of Washington and Baltimore, another more threatening British bid for victory was launched against Lake Champlain on 3 September 1814 from Montreal down the classic invasion route. Sir George Prevost's massive army of 11,300 Wellington veterans, backed by a reserve of 3,700, was the finest ground force that Britain ever sent to the North American shores. Defending against this juggernaut was Alexander Macomb, thirty-two, who had over 4,000 troops of all descriptions at Plattsburg, including raw recruits, militia, and convalescents, in fortified lines near the Saranac River.[112]

Macomb, born in Detroit and educated at an academy in Newark, New Jersey, enrolled at sixteen in a New York militia company and was awarded a regular army commission in 1799. His skills in organization and administration had been learned from Alexander Hamilton. From 1807 to 1812 he worked first on building forts along the Carolina and Georgia coast and then became adjutant general in Washington. Macomb was in command at Sackett's Harbor in the winter of 1812–1813 and took part in the capture of Fort George in the spring of 1813. He was promoted to brigadier general in 1814. All in all, he was an able and useful officer. From Plattsburg he boldly sent out a harassing force under Maj. John E. Wool, of Queenston Heights fame, who waged a brilliant delaying action.[113]

By 6 September Prevost's mighty force reached the Saranac River and began probing Macomb's Plattsburg defenses. Prevost saw there an American flotilla of warships, and he determined to await the arrival of the experienced navy Capt. George Downie and his British squadron.[114]

The American fleet at Plattsburg was commanded by Master Commandant Thomas Macdonough who was but thirty years old. Born at The Trapp, Delaware, the son of a physician, Macdonough entered the navy at sixteen as a midshipman. He served in the quasi war with France and in the Tripolitan War with Decatur when *Philadelphia* was burned. He then helped build gunboats; cruised in *Wasp,* 1807–1808, and enforced the embargo in the Atlantic; and sailed in the southwest Pacific while on furlough. When war came in 1812, Macdonough was aboard *Constellation* but was soon placed in command of the naval station at Portland, Maine. He arrived on Lake Champlain in October 1812, and commenced building a fleet. He was a keen student of naval warfare, was thorough, bold yet judicious, and was destined to play a pivotal role in the war.[115]

The rival squadrons of Macdonough and Downie were evenly matched. The Americans had the frigate *Saratoga* (flagship, 26 guns); the brig *Eagle* (20); the schooner *Ticonderoga* (17); the sloop *Preble* (7); and ten gunboats carrying a total of 16 guns. The British flotilla comprised the frigate *Confiance* (flagship, 37 guns); the brig *Linnet* (16); the sloop *Chubb* (11); the sloop *Finch* (10); and twelve gunboats mounting a total of 16 guns. Macdonough's 45 long guns could throw 759 pounds of metal; his 41 carronades, 1,274 pounds. Downie's 60 long guns could throw 1,128 pounds of shot; his 30 carronades, 736 pounds. Because of this configuration of armament, Macdonough wisely determined to engage on his own terms with spring lines and kedge anchors close to shore in Plattsburg Bay. His intelligent forethought provided for any conceivable mode of enemy attack.[116]

The crucial naval battle of Lake Champlain was fought on 11 September

1814. Downie's squadron rounded Cumberland Head by 8:30 A.M., and the action was joined immediately. Macdonough aimed a number of his pieces himself. Although the *Confiance* was bigger and more powerful than Macdonough's *Saratoga,* the former was not quite completed or well prepared for combat. The battle was close and unrelenting. Within fifteen minutes, Downie was killed instantly when an American projectile hurled a British cannon on his groin. At one point it seemed that the engagement was going badly for Macdonough, who was knocked down and unconscious several times, once by the severed head of one of his midshipmen. But in these desperate straits the American commander wound his ships and brought their heretofore unemployed broadsides to bear; *Confiance* attempted the same turning maneuver, fouled her lines, absorbed terrible punishment, and had to strike her colors. Most of the other British men-of-war had to follow suit and the battle was over by 10:30 A.M. Even though the severely damaged *Saratoga* had to be scuttled, Macdonough captured all of the enemy vessels and inflicted over 200 casualties while he suffered 110 of his own. His masterful strategy and fighting tactics won for America a critical victory—one that the republic could not have afforded to lose.[117]

Alexander Macomb, with his seemingly overmatched ground forces, did more than could have been reasonably expected of him. When the naval battle commenced, Prevost opened a heavy bombardment of Macomb's lines. Then he attacked in three columns. Two of these were blown back by American fire and were unable to get across the Saranac River. The third column successfully forded the river and forced back some New York militiamen, but Macomb threw in some Vermonters to stabilize his lines and the New Yorkers rallied. Also steadying the Americans was word of Macdonough's triumph. Perceiving the difficulties of his troops, although outnumbering Macomb's three to one, the disheartened Prevost supinely gave up the whole operation and invasion and retreated to Canada, minus much of his supplies. He lost at least 382 men compared to Macomb's 100.[118]

THE FOURTH and final phase of the British plan of grand strategy unfolded in late December of 1814. The army of the deceased General Ross was taken by Admiral Cochrane from the Chesapeake to Jamaica. The British government hoped for assistance from France and Spain; this might be secured if the Royal Navy and the army could capture New Orleans.[119]

Not until 2 December did the ailing Andrew Jackson arrive at New Orleans, and then he delayed building defenses to study the terrain first. On 13 December the British expedition of some ten thousand troops aboard Cochrane's fleet of fifty ships arrived at Cat Island, eighty miles east of New Orleans.[120]

The Crescent City, New Orleans, located some miles up the Mississippi River from the delta mouth, was capable of approach from a number of directions. Yet it was also defensible, guarded as it was by Lake Pontchartrain on the north, Lake Borgne on the east, and bayous all around. Finally buoyed to dynamic action, Jackson would perform splendidly.[121] Maj. Gen John Keane,

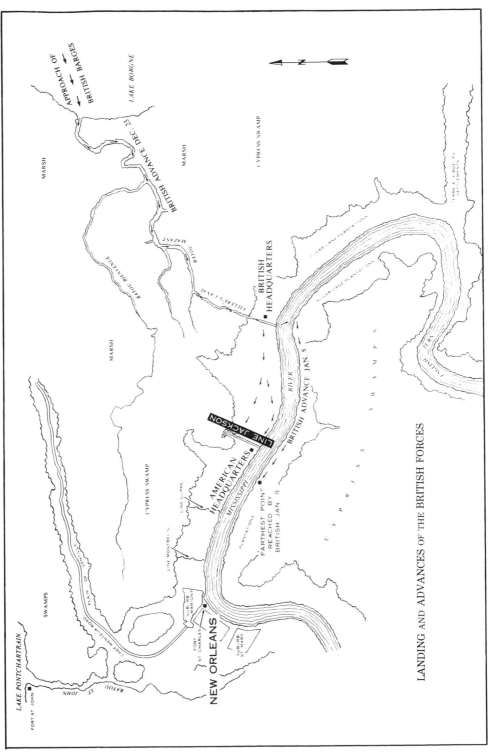

FIG. 4.2 NEW ORLEANS AND VICINITY, 1814–1815 *(Courtesy National Park Service).*

the tall, young black-bearded Irishman of Napoleonic war experience, was in temporary command. By 22 December he led 2,400 redcoats across Lake Borgne, up the undefended and unobstructed Bayou Bienvenue, and along the canal to the Villeré plantation on the east bank of the Mississippi, about ten miles below New Orleans. Jackson at first was unaware of this threat. The British cautiously inched their way ahead. After a personal interview with the Baratarian, Jean Laffite, Old Hickory permitted the buccaneer to add his force of one thousand to the city's defenders. Jackson's breastworks and fifteen cannon, facing southward, were behind the four-foot deep and twenty-foot-wide Rodriguez Canal on the Macarté plantation some ten miles below New Orleans. His right flank was anchored on the Mississippi and his left on the nearly impassable cypress swamps.[122]

General Jackson was almost caught flat-footed. From 1,600 to 1,800 of the advance British elements moved up close to the American position by 23 December 1814. Surprised, Jackson roared into action after dark on 23 December at La Ronde plantation, south of the canal, while the American 14-gun schooner *Carolina* destructively bombarded the enemy camp. Then Old Hickory withdrew behind his canal entrenchments. The defenders won an advantage in this so-called First Battle of New Orleans. The British lost a total of 267 troops while American casualties aggregated 213 men.[123]

Dampened British ardor revived when reinforcements arrived on 25 December, which brought their overall available force to some 10,000 veteran soldiers under the personal command of the new supreme commander, Lt. Gen. Sir Edward Pakenham, accompanied by Maj. Gen. Sir Samuel Gibbs. By 28 December Pakenham had 8,000 of his troops in jump-off positions to attack. When the fog lifted on the morning of 28 December, a striking martial pageant presented itself with the British deployed into two large columns of attack commanded by Gibbs on the right and Keane on the left. The redcoats surged forward only to have their left column fearfully cut up by the American gunboat *Louisiana,* which in seven hours fired some 800 devastating rounds at the splendid British formations, and they were obliged to fall back. The enemy column striving to penetrate Jackson's left wing at the cypress swamps was slowed and finally withdrawn. Pakenham then ordered a general retirement. He lost 150 men compared to Jackson's 17.[124]

By New Year's Day, 1815, at the suggestion of Cochrane, Pakenham laboriously hauled into position twenty-four big 18- and 24-pounders from the navy. One battery was laid to fire at *Louisiana* and the Americans on the right bank of the Mississippi, and three half-moon artillery emplacements were erected within 600 yards of Jackson's main canal line. On 1 January the British guns opened an inaccurate fire that was answered with destructive effect by Jackson's artillery, including *Louisiana*'s, and most of the British guns were destroyed. When the enemy advanced against the American left flank in the cypress swamps, they were repelled by an alert John Coffee, and Pakenham again withdrew from the field to lick his wounds. He had lost 67 men to Jackson's 34.[125] As the fog lifted in the early dawn, the main enemy force, in magnificent array, advanced frontally across Chalmette plain against Jackson's canal line. Gibbs was on the right and Keane was on the left of the assaulting column, though the fascines and ladders were unaccountably too far in the rear. The American artillery opened a decimating fire. Pakenham had a horse shot out from under him and was wounded in the left hand but remounted and remained on the field in open view. Jackson's riflemen hurled murderous volleys into the red lines that melted away under the hail of lead. As the slaughter continued, Gibbs was killed and Keane seriously wounded. The gallant Pakenham received a severe wound and, as he was being led from the battlefield, a grape shot struck him in the thigh, severing an artery, and he quickly bled to death. Maj. Gen. Sir John Lambert, leading the British reserve, assumed command. Although Thornton across the river had defeated Morgan, all Lambert could do in the main contest was to order all surviving attackers to retire at 8:30 A.M. The campaign for New Orleans was over. British losses in the bloody repulse of 8 January reached the staggering total of some 2,000; Jackson lost just 13 killed, 13 wounded, and 19 missing. Pakenham's corpse was returned to his wife and Admiral Cochrane in a cask of rum. This was perhaps a fitting though bizarre conclusion to this incredible war.[126]

The conflict was over. The climax of the Battle of New Orleans came after the peace treaty had been signed at Ghent, Belgium, reasserting the status quo ante bellum. Ships bringing the news of the end of the war arrived of course too late to prevent the holocaust at Chalmette. It was high time for the Madison administration to bring the stalemated war to a conclusion, despite the increased patriotic and nationalistic spirit of the people. Of the regular army of sixty-two thousand authorized for five years' service, only thirty-four thousand had been raised by September 1814, despite tripling the bounties.[127]

CERTAIN CONSEQUENCES of the War of 1812 were evident. So inefficient was the Madison administration, and so lacking was the country in an adequate military policy, that a total of 527,654 troops had to be called up at one time or another, for which the American taxpayer continued to pay until 31 December 1940. The total cost of the war to the United States was at least $80 million— some say $105 million—to which must be added the $46,217,150.57 paid out in pensions, aids to widows, and the like. The actual battle casualties to the nation were not much over five thousand killed and wounded.[128]

The War of 1812 revealed the United States as still unready to accept even a moderate-sized standing army, nor was she prepared to significantly reform the militia system. But the war did stimulate scientific engineering in the country. No fortification built by a West Point engineer was captured by the enemy in the course of the conflict. In combat, American gunnery, time and again on land or water, with cannon or shoulder rifle, showed its superiority to that of the foe, as it had in the Revolution.

The War of 1812 confirmed glaring shortcomings in the American high command, and especially of many of the individuals comprising it. James Madison was, in the main, an ineffective commander in chief, despite his good intentions and patriotism; his many talents lay elsewhere. Among his numerous minuses was his inability or lack of desire to control his secretary of war. John Armstrong, after the brief sojourn of the hapless William Eustis in the post, was a model of how not to handle the office; he was in most ways a fearful handicap to the competent prosecution of the contest.

The senior generals, early in the war at least and with the exception of the capable William Henry Harrison, left a great deal to be desired. It was only after the departure from command of such earnest but ineffectual commanders as Henry Dearborn, William Hull, Alexander Smyth, James Wilkinson, and Wade Hampton, that such younger and more talented generals as Jacob Brown, Winfield Scott, Alexander Macomb, and Andrew Jackson could come to the fore and show their mettle. American naval commanders, almost without exception, were excellent. Although a militant people in some respects, the Americans were shown by the war to be still highly individualistic and antimilitaristic, with their main reliance on the militia or perhaps the volunteer. As one of the troops in the ranks put it, "Our soldiers can beat their soldiers in fighting, but their generals beat our's [sic] in management."[129]

The War of 1812 should have taught the republic and its government that there are no short or easy routes to an adequate national defense; Americans won engagements and campaigns only when convinced that they had to put their whole heart and soul into the effort. At other times the futility of a democratic army was often revealed in its wasted enterprises, money, and lives, although that at times may be the price of liberty and freedom. Consequently, foreign powers, like Britain from 1812 to 1815, assumed that the United States was too ill prepared to fight and tested America again, severely, in 1917, 1941, and 1950, to their own regret.[130]

But the next military ventures would be closer to home against the redoubtable Indians who would prove *their* mettle for the rest of the century.

CHAPTER FIVE

Calhoun, Seminoles, and Black Hawk

[The Second Seminole War] leaves one, as military history so often does, with a sense of wonder at the stamina of the men—even the militiamen—who could go through such operations under the primitive ideas concerning rations, hygiene and medical care which prevailed in that day.

WALTER MILLIS

WHEN NEWS of the Treaty of Ghent reached the United States, heralding the official end of the War of 1812, thoughtful Americans concerned with our permanent peacetime military establishment looked at the balance sheet. What they found was a curious mixture of failures and accomplishments, and no one could say for the future whether lessons would be learned from the past.

"The lessons of the war [of 1812] are so obvious," wrote Emory Upton after the Civil War, "that they need not be stated. Nearly all the blunders committed were repetitious in an aggravated form of the same blunders in the Revolution, and like them had their origin either in the mistakes or omissions of military legislation." In the War for American Independence, the thirteen colonies were practically bankrupt at the end of five years of struggle, with a public debt of $200 million. In the War of 1812, in two and one-half years of fighting, a debt of almost equal magnitude was incurred. Despite the brilliant frigate victories early in the war, the United States navy and our shipping had been largely bottled up in port. Also, as Upton remarks,

In the first war, notwithstanding the steady decline of our military strength two British armies of more than 6,000 men each, were made captive; in the other [war], less than 5,000 men, for the period of two years brought war and devastation into our territory, and successfully withstood the misapplied power of 7,000,000 people.

Certain of our early land and water commanders, men like W. Hull, Smyth, Dearborn, and perhaps Chauncey, proved to be ineffective. In addition, the insistence upon using short-term militiamen was incredible. These had all been embarrassing failures to sensitive Americans.[1]

But redeeming successes had been scored, too, in the recent conflict with the British and Canadians. There had been the land victories of Harrison at the Thames, of Brown and Scott at Chippewa (and the drawn fight at Lundy's Lane), of Smith at Baltimore, and of Jackson at New Orleans. And there had been the hard won naval triumphs of Perry on Lake Erie, of Macdonough on Lake Champlain, and the repulse of the British fleet at Fort McHenry. These went far to help counterbalance the humiliating setbacks of Hull at Detroit, Dearborn and others on the Niagara and Plattsburg fronts, and Winder at Bladensburg.

Then, too, the role of the few graduates of the infant United States Military Academy at West Point—established, it will be remembered, in 1802—was of vital significance. Only 120 officers had been graduated from West Point by the end of the War of 1812, of whom approximately 100 served in junior grades during this conflict. About 25 percent of these young men had been killed or wounded. Especially valuable to the army's operations was the contribution of the academy's engineers. "This branch of the military service," writes Henry Adams in his classic *History of the United States,*

> owed its efficiency and almost its existence to the military school at West Point. . . . At the outbreak of the war the corps of engineers was already efficient. . . . None of the works constructed by a graduate of West Point was captured by the enemy. . . . During the critical campaign of 1814, the West Point engineers doubled the capacity of the little American army for resistance, and introduced a new and scientific character into American life.

These were indeed accomplishments of distinction for the young republic and for the budding professional school of military science, whose further development will be treated subsequently.[2]

But with the termination of the war, the urgent need was comprehensive legislation for the army, and this came in a law passed by Congress on 3 March 1815 that defined the peacetime military establishment, for the time being, at least. This act reduced the regular army to no more than ten thousand men, which was a substantial force-in-being in time of peace. It divided the country into a Northern Division of five departments, commanded by Maj. Gen. Jacob Brown, and a Southern Division of four departments, headed by Maj. Gen. Andrew Jackson. The two generals were coequal, and there was unfortunately no general-in-chief over them to coordinate authority. This power, as in the War of 1812, could pass to the secretary of war, and channels of command could be bypassed. The reorganization authorized by this law of Congress was still defective in that it suppressed the Topographical and Adjutant-General's Departments, and abolished the Quartermaster-General's Department and the Inspector-General's Department.[3]

The law of 3 March 1815 provided for no commander, or general in chief, of the entire army. John Armstrong, the incompetent secretary of war during the conflict of 1812–1815, had truculently bypassed the chain of command by issuing orders directly to subordinate officers without sending copies of the directives or even notifying their superiors of these instructions. After the end of hostilities with the British, acting war secretary George Graham continued this practice on occasion, excusing it on the basis of slow communications and the desire to save time and trouble. Trouble with this pernicious practice came to a head in 1817. General Jackson learned through the newspapers that one of his subordinate officers had been transferred to New York. When the president failed to respond promptly to Jackson's protests, the general directed that none of his officers obey War Department orders unless these came through his headquarters. When a test case occurred, Jackson offered to stand trial before a court-martial. But by then, John C. Calhoun, one of the nation's ablest secretaries of war, had taken office, and he backed Jackson by ordering that the bypassing of superior officers cease.[4]

One final matter of reorganization bears notice before examining ensuing operations of the military forces of the United States. The comprehensive act of 3 March 1815 provided for a so-called General Staff. Supposedly, experts were to be placed in charge of the several departments in Washington. But persons filling these jobs were "drawn indiscriminately from the line and from civil life," and it was seen that a change was necessary. Under the aegis of Secretary Calhoun, Congress responded with legislation in April 1818 that added a surgeon-general and a judge advocate general to the staff, which also included an adjutant-general, a quartermaster-general, an inspector-general, and a commissary-general. The annual salary of these General Staff heads was $2,500. In addition, those officers holding brevet rank were now given the emoluments and pay of the higher grade if they had a command commensurate with it.[5]

THE MILITARY CENTER of attention now shifted from Washington reorganization paperwork to action along the Georgia-Florida border. Trouble with the Seminole Indians and Spaniards led to a great hue and cry, bloodshed, an international crisis, and the enhancing of General Jackson's reputation to such a degree that his name was mentioned with increasing frequency for the presidency. Spain owned Florida, but her hold on the empty, moss-festooned forests and Everglades was as tenuous as the quicksand that menaced any invader of those gloomy swamps. With much of Spain's Latin-American empire crumbling, the United States had taken nibbles out of West Florida in the area south of Mississippi in 1810 and 1813, and the feeble Spaniards had been unable to thwart this. Actually, Spanish authority scarcely extended outside of the three fortified posts of St. Augustine, St. Marks, and Pensacola. There were also in East Florida a few encampments of runaway slaves from Georgia—fugitives called Maroons—in locations such as the so-called Negro Fort (later known as Fort Gadsden) on the Appalachicola River and some scattered Seminole villages.[6]

The Seminoles (meaning separatist), an eastern branch of the Creek Indians, came from Natchez-Muskogean linguistic stock. During the War of 1812 they had been more than friendly with the British. Lieutenant Colonel Edward Nicholls, the British commander in Florida during that war, stayed on at the Negro Fort along the Appalachicola for some months after hostilities ceased. He not only provided the Seminoles with muskets and powder, but deliberately misled them into believing that the 1814 treaty that Jackson had exacted from them, calling for their removal west of the Mississippi, had been voided by the Treaty of Ghent. When Nicholls returned to England in the summer of 1815, his government disavowed his actions. But the British, in a friendly gesture to the Seminoles, presented one of them, Hillis Hago, with a scarlet coat and a brigadier general's commission. When Spanish authorities in Florida failed to disband the Maroon garrison at the menacing Negro Fort near Georgia, an American gunboat and two companies of the Fourth Infantry from Fort Scott blew up the magazine of the Negro Fort and most of the fugitive garrison with it.[7]

But as Gen. Edmund Gaines at Fort Scott pushed construction of forts in Georgia near the Florida border, Seminole forays into Georgia mushroomed in number and intensity. President Monroe vacillated painfully. These raids culminated in the massacre by Indians under Chief Himollemico of some 47 peaceful men and women. By a treaty in 1795, Spain had agreed that she would "not suffer her Indians to attack the citizens of the United States nor the Indians inhabiting their territory," but repeated appeals to the Spanish governor were fruitless. The difficulties were compounded by two British subjects who insinuated themselves into the touchy situation. One of these, a seventy-year-old Scot named Alexander Arbuthnot, traded with the Seminoles at St. Marks and, like Nicholls, told them that Jackson's Creek treaty of 1814 had been abrogated. The other Britisher was young Robert Ambrister, an adventurer and former officer of Nicholls' command, who worked for Arbuthnot for a while before transferring business to Chief Billy Bowlegs on the Suwanee River, where he could also reap a handsome profit from pirates like McGregor on the east coast at Amelia Island.[8]

So Andrew Jackson was directed by the War Department to "be prepared to concentrate [his] forces, and to adopt the necessary measures to terminate [the] conflict. . . ." along the Georgia-Florida border. Jackson and Gaines both exceeded their authority when they raised forces of almost twenty-five hundred men directly. Old Hickory marched 450 miles to Fort Scott, attended by incredible hardships. As Jackson approached, Hillis Hago and Himollemico fled to St. Marks.[9]

On 7 April 1818 Jackson surged into St. Marks and, against the outcries of indignation of the Spanish governor, hauled down the Spanish flag. Arbuthnot and the two Seminole chiefs were captured. The latter were hanged without benefit of a trial and Arbuthnot, after a hearing, suffered a like fate from the yardarm of his own schooner. Jackson pressed eastward through the morasses in order to surprise Billy Bowlegs on the Suwanee. But the beaten Indians, warned by Arbuthnot of the general's approach, escaped into the Everglades of central Florida. However the furious American leader did capture Ambrister at Suwanee, and the dashing British adventurer and accomplice soon fell face forward before Jackson's firing squad. Returning westward via St. Marks and Fort Gadsden, Old Hickory seized the Spanish capital of Pensacola. When the Spanish governor took refuge at nearby Fort Barrancas, Jackson bombarded the post for two days, captured it, and temporarily garrisoned it with American troops.[10]

While these energetic operations ended the war they did not terminate the trouble into which Andrew Jackson had projected himself. The British press was furious at the summary treatment of Arbuthnot and Ambrister, and the Spanish, though too weak for much of a protest, were quite unhappy. A Senate committee reported as follows concerning the high-handed troop-raising activities of Gaines and Jackson: "The committee find the melancholy fact before them, that military officers, even at this early stage of this Republic, have, without the shadow of authority, raised an army of at least 2,500 men and mustered them into the service of the United States." President Monroe, firmly supported by Secretary of State John Quincy Adams, not only defied the Senate but also rejected Secretary of War Calhoun's hostile efforts to have Jackson chastised and ruined, militarily and politically. Not only was Old Hickory spared to be acclaimed as the hero of the West and pushed toward the White House, but the First Seminole War led in February 1819 to the cession of Florida to the United States by the hapless Spaniards. Such were the fruits of the excursion into the trackless land of the Seminoles by the dashing, semidisciplined occupant of the Tennessee Hermitage. But a second Florida war would be required before the tenacious inhabitants of the Everglades could be quieted.[11]

MEANWHILE, even before the First Florida War, plans were being discussed to bring to the militia a tighter discipline, system, and organization, and the war against the Seminoles was expected to act as a tonic that would solve this and other War Department problems.

It was an opportune time for a great secretary of war to grapple with many of these and other thorny matters that harassed the army. John C. Calhoun of South Carolina was only thirty-five years of age in 1817 when he became President Monroe's third secretary of war. An ardent nationalist in this early period of his life, in contrast to his later parochial Southern sectionalism, Calhoun had been one of the rabid "War Hawks" in 1812. The new secretary entered upon his onerous duties with vigor and determination. He sought advice from civilian experts and military officers, studied department records, and worked fourteen to fifteen hours a day. Calhoun soon had a practical mastery of his duties and the problems facing him, and this in spite of the chronic inadequacies of office space and personnel.[12]

One of Calhoun's finest administrative achievements was perfecting a system whereby almost thirty thousand claims for veterans' pensions were handled in his first year in office, with 60 percent of the applications for the Congressional largess accepted on a merit basis under the new rules and procedures of the War Department. Another question concerned the department's unsettled accounts amounting to some $45 million, which had been amassed largely during the War of 1812. Calhoun successfully handled this by earmarking small yearly amounts from the War Department's annual budget to pay off the debts. However, in his recommendation for a second military academy to benefit the southern and western parts of the country, the secretary failed to receive sufficient congressional support. There was a division of opinion on construction of fortifications; President Monroe favored coastal works, while

Calhoun opted for frontier ones, especially in the Northwest, where he felt they should be built up the Missouri as far as the Yellowstone River. While few coastal works were erected, the secretary did get some approved in the East, South, and West. These forts were built by private contractors under the supervision of the Army Corps of Engineers.[13]

To improve army supply and communications in various parts of the country, the South Carolinian proposed the construction of a network of roads and canals connecting existing avenues of transportation and vital bases. But little was accomplished here, some congressmen stressing that these routes could be used by an invading enemy from Canada. And Calhoun's idea of linking up various bays and estuaries to form a protected inside passage from Massachusetts to Georgia was far too advanced for his times. However, the secretary's forthright action did correct another evil that had been permitted to prevail far too long. The army's system of supply, up to this time, had been in the hands of private contractors who were not responsible to the post commanders whom they were to provision with food, uniforms, horses, and the like. Calhoun changed this practice so that the purchases were made directly by the army's commissary general.[14]

Monroe's war secretary was fair and foreseeing in his dealings with the Indians. Realizing that the advance of the frontiersmen and settlers ever westward was irresistible, Calhoun strove nonetheless to safeguard the rights of the Indians. This he sought to do by urging that the tribes be settled on reservations that were to be inviolable. He hoped that respectable government Indian agents would deal squarely with the Indians, and that their trade would be licensed under a superintendent of Indian affairs who would be responsible to the secretary of war. Again, Calhoun's wise counsels went largely unheeded during his lifetime. But the secretary initiated scientific study by army expeditions and inaugurated the invaluable daily weather records that were to be kept by surgeons at all army posts.[15]

Perhaps Calhoun's greatest achievement was his famous expansible army concept. This proposal came in answer to a House resolution of 11 May 1820 that asked the secretary to provide for Congress's expected reduction of the regular army to 6,000 men. Calhoun consulted a number of high-ranking officers, especially Generals Brown and Scott. In December 1820, in one of his ablest state papers, Calhoun propounded a plan whereby the army could be expanded in time of national emergency from 6,000 to 19,000, or higher. This scheme contemplated that when Congress halved the army, they would retain the officer and noncom staff at full strength and make no change in the number of companies, battalions, and regiments. If Congress insisted—which it did—on reducing the size of the army, it could be done merely by reducing the number of privates in each company by half. In time of war, the army's strength could be quickly increased by adding enlisted personnel to the extant companies, and, if more numbers were desired, by dividing the expanded companies in two. The regular army was to be used to wage campaigns, Calhoun averred, while forts were to held more lightly. Washington and Knox had urged something like this before, and Calhoun's expansible army concept was sound in most particulars. But Congress ignored the principal features of the plan; they were not to be adopted by the United States until the twentieth century. By an act passed on 2 March 1821, Congress cut the army from 12,664 men to 6,183.[16]

Finally, the work of this highly competent war secretary climaxed in March 1821, when Calhoun's testy general, Andrew Jackson, retired from the army. Congress passed legislation that belatedly ended the embarrassing situation of retaining two quarreling, coequal major generals. The post of general in chief was given to Jacob Brown, who was superior to the Eastern Department commander, Winfield Scott, and the Western Department head, Edmund P. Gaines. All in all, allowing for public apathy and congressional foot-dragging, John C. Calhoun had performed well in his stubborn efforts in the War Department to give the army and the country the foundation for a sound military policy.[17]

THE SO-CALLED Black Hawk War of 1832 was of such short duration and limited scope that neither the regular army nor the state militias involved were put to a rigorous test. General Jackson was in the White House, and this dyed-in-the-wool westerner pursued relentlessly Jefferson's idea of removing the Indians to the west of the Mississippi. Ninety-four Indian treaties were concluded by his administration between 1829 and 1837, several million acres of land obtained, and thousands of Indians moved more or less forcibly west of the great river. But one Indian who objected strenuously to this policy was the Sac chief, Ma-ka-tai-me-she-kia-kiak (Black Sparrow Hawk), better known simply as Black Hawk. He was an inveterate foe of the white Americans and had fought with a separate group of the Sacs on the British-Canadian side in the War of 1812.[18]

An 1804 treaty signed by some Sac and Fox chiefs provided for Indian withdrawal west of the Mississippi. Black Hawk denied the legality of this compact that would lead to the alienation of the tribal ancestral seats in Illinois and Wisconsin. Even though Black Hawk was impelled in 1816 to confirm the terms of the treaty, he temporarily crossed the Mississippi to the east bank in 1831 with some of his tribe. When he recrossed to the west bank, internecine warfare erupted among the Sac, Fox, Winnebagoes, Sioux, and Chippewas. When the frequent efforts to bring a peaceful end to these hostilities proved futile, the governor of Illinois called out the militia and asked General Gaines for aid. Black Hawk was involved also at this time in efforts to create a new Indian confederacy along the lines of Tecumseh's or Pontiac's, and he thought he had received encouragement of British aid.[19]

On 1 April 1832 the war department ordered Col. Henry Atkinson to move elements of the Sixth Infantry from Jefferson Barracks, St. Louis, up the Mississippi to end the intertribal warfare. Soon after Atkinson placed his troops in motion he was informed that Black Hawk had again crossed to the east bank of the river with five hundred warriors and fifteen hundred women and children. The reason for the chief's action was the peaceful one of finding an empty prairie in which to plant a corn crop. Despite efforts to dissuade him, Black Hawk announced his determination to remain on the east bank. In May, when an undisciplined force of Illinois militiamen shamefully fired upon an Indian flag of truce, killing two Indians, they were in turn routed by the Indians and persuaded to disband and go home. Atkinson's Sixth Infantry, moving up the Rock River, was augmented by local post garrisons and by elements of Col. Zachary Taylor's First Infantry. About a thousand mounted militiamen tried to assist Atkinson, but only a few of these men, under Colonels James D. Henry and Henry Dodge, were effective.[20]

Atkinson had ample force to dispatch Black Hawk's braves. The rowdy Illinois volunteeers caught up with the northward-moving Indians on 21 July 1832 and soundly whipped them at the Battle of Wisconsin Bluffs, not far from the present-day city of Madison. Finally, Atkinson's augmented force delivered the coup de grace at the Battle of Bad Axe, where the Indians were defeated at the juncture of that river with the Mississippi, halfway between La Crosse and Prairie du Chien. The palefaces in these two engagements lost 30 men out of a force of 900 militiamen and 400 regulars. The Indian loss is variously estimated at between 150 and 300, including some women and children who were brutally slaughtered while trying to ford the river. The remnant of the tribe was then permitted to cross to the west side of the Mississippi.[21]

The one redeeming act of this entire war was the decent treatment of Black Hawk, who was captured in the operations by Lt. Jefferson Davis. Nominally under arrest, the Indian chief was taken East, where he met President Jackson and was shown marked attention and kindness. Despite a brief sojourn in confinement at Fortress Monroe, Black Hawk's hostility toward the Americans was erased. When released, he spent the remainder of his days peacefully in Iowa. The entire Black Hawk War was not one of the more ennobling pages in the iliad of the American frontier.[22]

IF THE 1832 war against Black Hawk on the northwestern frontier proved to be a short and comparatively easy one, the Second Florida War of 1835–1842 against the Seminoles on the southeastern frontier turned out to be long and frustrating. The country in which it was fought was not at all hospitable to the white man. An officer wrote of the campaign:

> The undergrowth is almost impenetrable, consisting of scrub oak, palmetto, and grapevines, so thick that a passage can only be made with the assistance of an ax, cutting a footpath as through a wall. At the distance of 10 feet an individual is totally obscured. The wet hummocks are more formidable but less frequented. In most of them the water stands the year around from 4 to 6 inches deep, with a thick undergrowth, intermixed with cypress stumps and trees. The cypress swamps are generally filled with water from 1 to 3 feet deep. The trees are covered with a heavy, dark-green moss, festooned from tree to tree like drapery, totally obscuring the sun, almost the light of day. A green scum floats upon the surface and when disturbed by footmen, the atmosphere becomes impregnated with a noxious effluvium.[23]

For their services in this country of quicksand and resourceful natives, privates serving in the United States Army were paid five dollars a month.

Affairs with the Seminoles had never been fully settled since the First Seminole War of 1817–1818. And now that Gen. Andrew Jackson, the principal participant in the first Florida war, was in the White House, his pet policy of Indian removal was pursued. As a consequence, several of the lesser Seminole chiefs were induced to sign the Treaty of Payne's Landing on 9 May 1832 that provided for the tribe to be moved west of the Mississippi within three years. This period of time was markedly shortened by the Treaty of Fort Gibson, which was cunningly extracted from some of the Seminoles on 28 May 1833. The greatest of the chiefs, Osceola, objected strenuously to these treaties. When Indian agent Wiley Thompson (formerly a major general of Georgia militia) called him and several other Seminole leaders together on 22 April 1835 to acknowledge the treaties, the other chiefs silently refused to sign the paper, while Osceola is reputed to have plunged his great knife into the document in a gesture of defiance. No doubt Osceola's disposition had not been sweetened when his young wife had been seized as a slave. The war department now realized that the Indians simply refused to be moved peacefully out of Florida.[24]

The explosion came on 28 December when Capt. Francis L. Dade and 109 other soldiers were assaulted by Seminoles at Wahoo Swamp, midway between Fort Brooke (Tampa Bay)and Fort King (Ocala), and massacred almost to a man. On the same day, Osceola and a war party of 60 braves ambushed General Thompson and another officer about one mile from Fort King. The Seminoles pumped fifteen bullets into Thompson and then scalped him. Reacting swiftly, Col. Duncan Lamont Clinch moved on the Indians from Fort King with some 200 regulars, assisted by 30 (out of more than 100 available) volunteers. On the last day of the year he caught up with the Indians at the Withlacoochee River and defeated them with the loss of 57 of his regulars, the Seminoles losing perhaps 50 warriors.[25]

An officer of experience, stature, and ability was needed to try to bring the war to a swift end; so the commander of the Eastern Department, General Scott, was ordered on 9 January 1836 to proceed at once to the scene of hostilities. With some 500 regulars and 4,000 militiamen in hand, Scott hoped by March to converge upon the Seminoles in three columns and crush them in one campaign. But Scott's plans were frustrated. General Gaines, in command of the Western Department, without authorization from Washington, sailed from New Orleans on 3 February for Tampa with a mixed force of 1,140 volunteers and regulars. He arrived at Fort King on 22 February with his supplies practically exhausted. These were replenished by appropriating almost all of the rations and forage at Fort Doane that Scott had amassed for his own operations. Resuming his march, Gaines reached the Withlacoochee on 27 February and was attacked and besieged by the Semioles. Gaines suffered 51 casualties and his men were reduced to eating horseflesh before they were rescued by Clinch's force on 6 March. The Western Department commander turned over the command to Clinch and abruptly returned to his own headquarters. Gaines's dubious action thwarted Scott's plan of operations, much to the latter's chagrin. Not until 14 April 1836 could Scott move, but when he did his martial array was so formidable that the Seminoles refused battle and simply melted away into the interior.[26]

Scott turned over his command to Clinch and, assisted by Gen. Thomas S. Jesup, went to Georgia and Alabama to put down a Creek uprising. This was done successfully, despite grave shortages in equipment. From there, Scott was ordered to return to Washington "in order that an inquiry be had into the unaccountable delay in prosecuting the Creek war and the failure of the campaign in Florida." The court of inquiry completely exonerated the Eastern Department commander.[27]

Meanwhile in Florida, from June to November 1836, there was, in William Addleman Ganoe's words,

> a succession of small actions . . . wherever any Indians could be induced to appear. In the meantime the savage was carrying on raids of extermination on every white man, woman and child who could be seized. . . . A massacre would occur in one place while the troops were at another. Seldom was the meager force in that wide country able to catch up with a foe that was capable of rapid disappearance.

When Clinch resigned, he was succeeded by Gov. Richard K. Call who, in turn, was replaced by Jesup on 8 December. Jesup complained to the secretary of war in December that Southern militiamen refused to perform manual labor on roads, bridges, camps, and the like, and that he was forced to call upon the regulars to do this back-breaking work.[28]

Jesup reported on 21 October that since assuming command, his troops had killed 30 Seminoles and captured 500. One of those taken in October was Osceola, whom Jesup ordered seized while under a white flag of truce. Finally, in December of 1837, Col. Zachary Taylor took a column of 870 men and pressed southward relentlessly into the Everglades. He eventually caught up with the Indians at Lake Okeechobee and in sawgrass five feet high and knee-deep mud and water fought a victorious three-hour battle on Christmas Day. Both sides lost approximately 140 men, but the Seminoles, although keeping up a guerrilla warfare, were unable again to stand and fight a full-scale pitched battle.[29]

Jesup was relieved at his own request on 15 May 1838 and succeeded by Taylor. He in turn, at his own asking, was ordered by the general in chief, Alexander Macomb, to be replaced in the summer of 1840 by Brig. Gen. Walker K. Armistead, the third graduate of the Military Academy in 1803. With most of the temporary troops discharged, Congress in 1838 authorized a new regiment, the Eighth Infantry. The last change in command in Florida occurred late in May 1841 when Col. William S. Worth of the Eighth was named to succeed Armistead in command of the whole army fighting the Seminoles.[30]

While the previous commanders were competent men, the elevation of Worth to the top command was a wise appointment. "Haughty Bill," as this efficient officer was fondly called while Commandant of Cadets at West Point from 1820 to 1828, immediately announced that he would conduct continuous operations the year round, despite doubts about the effectiveness of campaigning in the torrid summer months. Worth's searing year-round tactics finally prevailed. Although the five thousand American troops present suffered sixteen thousand cases of illness between June 1841 and February 1842, they destroyed Indian crops and dwellings wherever found. Being constantly prodded and forced to move back onto remote and unhealthy ground, the Seminoles were unable to harvest crops, and without this subsistence, they were forced to surrender in the summer of 1842.[31]

The costs of this seven-year-long war in Florida were proportionately high. A total number of 60,691 militiamen, volunteers, and regulars served as against the 1,200 Seminole warriors. In terms of casualties, the regulars, from a maximum strength of 4,191, lost 1,466 officers and men during the war—a total of 41 percent. In calculating the total financial costs of the Second Seminole War, it must be remembered that a respectable part of these costs were incurred by the United States Navy, which played an important role in transporting men and supplies to Florida. The Treasury Department, therefore, paid out no less than $115,032,335.88 of the taxpayers' money.[32]

The aftermath of this second war against the Seminoles was a curious one. Actually the main reason for fighting the war—to effect the removal of the Seminoles west of the Mississippi—was not accomplished. Most of the remnants of Osceola's tribe remained in Florida. They were first granted a temporary reservation south of Pease Creek, where they stayed so peaceful that Worth was impelled to write as follows to the adjutant general in November 1843:

> Since the pacification of August, 1842, these people have observed perfect good faith and strictly fulfilled their engagements; not an instance of rudeness toward the whites has yet occurred. They plant and hunt diligently, and take their game and skins to Fort Brooke, procure the necessaries they desire, and return quietly to their grounds.

The descendents of these Seminoles are still there. Thus the question of who really won the war is a moot one.[33]

NINE DAYS after the end of the Second Seminole War Congress reduced the regular army from a total of 12,539 to 8,613 officers and men. It was against this unsympathetic tide of congressional and public apathy that the highly competent secretary of war, Joel R. Poinsett, was determined to do battle. Poinsett had some military experience as a special agent and advisor in Chile in 1812–1814 and, according to J. Fred Rippy, was "Long a student of military affairs and [was] wholeheartedly devoted to the subject. . . ." As Martin Van Buren's secretary of war, Poinsett was able to broaden the curricula and enlarge the physical plant at West Point, improve the artillery of the army, and move some forty thousand Indians west of the Mississippi River.[34]

What Congress had been doing—and it was continued as sort of an intended substitute for a plan of Poinsett's—was to appropriate approximately one million dollars annually for harbor and coastal fortifications. This was considered good politics at the local level for many sections of the country and provided many jobs over a long period of time. However, incredibly small amounts of money were appropriated by Congress for armaments for the forts, with the result that ordnance production fell eighteen years behind fort construction. Poinsett reported in 1839 that many coastal works were as yet unfinished and unarmed; therefore most harbors and cities were in reality undefended. Of course the change from wooden to masonry forts allowed hostile politicians to contend that such defensive works were too expensive and would soon became obsolete.[35]

ONE of the truly significant episodes in American military history in the first half of the nineteenth century was the establishment of the United States Military Academy at West Point, New York, and its early struggles for existence, near demise, and rebirth under Sylvanus Thayer.

Although inclined toward pacifism, President Thomas Jefferson supported Washington's early call for a military academy. On 16 March 1802 Congress passed a law creating a military academy at West Point. The faculty was to be composed of seven engineering officers, there were to be ten cadets, and the senior engineering officer was to be superintendent of the institution. "The West Point site," historian Sidney Forman comments, "was singled out for its economy and convenience: its buildings had been preserved and a small garrison was maintained there after independence was won." The first superintendent of the military academy was fifty-two-year-old Lt. Col. Jonathan Williams, a nephew of Benjamin Franklin and a talented man who traveled widely in Europe and studied subjects such as fortifications, law, medicine, and mathematics. Although an obese man, Williams led these first cadets in surveying teams around the grounds at West Point and delivered lectures on fortifications. One cadet, John Lillie, was only 10½ years of age. In a few short months, on 12 October 1802, the academy graduated its first cadets as second lieutenants: Joseph G. Swift and Simon M. Levy.[36]

Conditions at the academy at West Point were compared to "a foundling, barely existing among the mountains." The cadets slept on dirty mattresses on the floor of the Long Barrack, a rambling building famous since the days of the Revolution. By 1807 cadets were allowed to eat and sleep away from the academy buildings, if they could afford it. Theoretically the schedule called for drill from 5 to 6 A.M.; mathematics from 8 to 11 A.M.; drawing or French from 11 A.M. to 1 P.M.; a study period from 2 to 4 P.M., followed by practical field work in surveying, gunnery, or engineering. But often this schedule was not followed. The laxity that was prevalent allowed plenty of time for chess or loitering.[37]

Perhaps Williams's greatest achievement—and he had few to show for his tenure as first superintendent, although the fault was scarcely his—was his creation of the United States Military Philosophical Society in November 1802, with President Jefferson as its chief patron. This organization helped to broaden the academy's curriculum and build up its library into the best collection of technical books in America. The society made West Point a national center of scientific investigation and study, and it numbered among its distinguished members such men as Jefferson, Madison, Monroe, John Quincy Adams, Benjamin Latrobe, Eli Whitney, Robert Fulton, John Marshall, DeWitt Clinton, Joel Barlow, Bushrod Washington, Isaac Hull, Stephen Decatur, William Bainbridge, and many scholars, professors, and professional men. The West Point cadets were automatically members and sat in on the presentation of learned papers. In many ways the academy and the philosophical society became almost indistinguishable in their operation and educational objectives.[38]

The War of 1812 was almost disastrous for West Point in several ways. When hostilities began in June, Jonathan Williams asked for the command of Castle William in the harbor of New York. When this was refused, the superintendent resigned from the army on 31 July 1812 and joined the armed forces of Pennsylvania. The Military Philosophical Society foundered the following year, with only the vote of one Captain Sylvanus Thayer arrayed against dissolution (although Joseph Swift said that he was unhappy at its breakup).[39]

The substantial contributions of the few West Point graduates in the War of 1812 have been previously noted. When the conflict erupted, there were only eighty-nine academy graduates, of whom sixty-five were still in the army. One-sixth of the West Point graduates who engaged the enemy in the war were killed in action; one-fourth were killed or wounded; one-fifth of the survivors were awarded one or more brevets for meritorious service.[40]

Next to the law passed in 1802 establishing the academy, the act of 29 April 1812 was perhaps the most important legislation regarding West Point in the century. "The cadets," writes Forman, "who previously had been granted warrants as cadets for the regiments of cavalry, artillery, infantry or riflemen, were now directly appointed to the Military Academy under the Corps of Engineers. Their number was increased to 250." The Corps of Engineers was enlarged by the addition of 6 officers and by a "Company of Bombardiers, Sappers, and Miners"—the latter group numbering 94 enlisted men. The staff of the academy was increased, with professors of mathematics and astronomy, natural and experimental philosophy, engineering, drawing, and French. The 1812 law also put cadets under discipline of academy regulations. They were to be organized into companies by the superintendent and given a three-month encampment. The only admission requirements, however, were that cadets be "well versed in reading, writing, and arithmetic." In addition, they were to "receive a regular degree from an academical staff."[41]

The academy was in the process of reorganization under the new act during the war years, 1812–1815. The Corps of Engineers and the academy were headed in this period by Col. Joseph G. Swift, the institution's first cadet graduate. So as to know better how to run the school, Swift consulted with experienced educators at Harvard and elsewhere. But any plans that he might have formulated were thwarted; like Jonathan Williams, he was often absent from West Point on fort-building duties. In his absence, Swift delegated his authority to Capt. Alden Partridge (known as "Old Pewter"). Partridge had been graduated from the academy in 1806 and had stayed on as professor of mathematics and engineering. Although by 1810 he often performed the duties of superintendent, he was not officially named to that position until January 1815.[42]

And Alden Partridge, serving under Superintendent Swift's advice, directed the academy for a time. Old Pewter was austere in appearance and brusque in manner, although basically he was diffident, even shy. He was expert in artillery and infantry exercises, including the manual of arms. A good and vigorous drillmaster under Swift, Partridge had each cadet rotate as officer of the day and, when the Company of Bombardiers departed in 1814, participate in a cadet-mounted guard. Mess procedures were worked out, and regulations drawn up for bands, drills, parades, and a daily routine. Old Pewter presided over a curriculum including history, geography, philosophy, mathematics, French, military science, and field experiments. Of course he had the advantage in assuming de facto control at West Point; he was always stationed there without having to be away, as was customary for many of the staff on detached duty elsewhere.[43]

However, when he became superintendent in his own right, from 3 January 1815 to 28 July 1817, Partridge's domineering personality led increasingly to poor judgment and fearful abuses that almost wrecked the academy. First of all, Old Pewter played favorites extensively, and his policy of nepotism led to a number of his relatives being placed in significant and lucrative jobs at West Point. It was claimed that he lined his own pockets from the sale of wood from government lands. The public stores were ransacked several times, and the Bombardiers were pitifully disciplined by the man who had the ability so to do if he wished. It was contended that Partridge disregarded the law of 1812 defining the operations of the academy, and that his overbearing attitude toward his faculty as well as the cadets was intolerable. There were seldom admittance examinations; classes were not held regularly, order books not kept, faculty opinions rejected out of hand, cadets permitted to graduate and receive commissions without proper examinations or diploma, and the Bombardiers were allowed to accept pay from Old Pewter's uncle outside of duty hours.[44]

This was bad enough, but even more alarming irregularities were discovered. Some cadets accepted were so young (one was eleven) and under-sized that they could not handle the regular musket, and special small, light ones had to be manufactured for them. Yet at least one cadet was said to be thirty-two years old and married, and another was forty-one; one cadet had only one arm. Undoubtedly cadets were hazed and molested unmercifully by the enlisted men whom they actually outranked. Special privileges could be secured from Partridge, who alternated between periods of great laxity and harsh punishments. He would not delegate authority to others and often failed to back up his own faculty members. Chairs and other objects were thrown from windows. No records were kept of the cadets' scholastic standing, and often the faculty was not apprised of which were to be graduated. To add humiliating insult to outrageous injury, Old Pewter imported a flock of unkempt sheep. The cadets alleged that the only mutton they received was from diseased animals of the flock. The sheep were permitted to wander over the yards and barracks areas of the academy and kept the footpaths befouled.[45]

So it was no wonder when President Monroe visited West Point in June 1817 that he was handed a document of complaint signed by every faculty member of the academy except the superintendent. (Previously, Partridge had been chastised on several particulars by an 1816 court of inquiry). Now, so bitter and specific were the denunciations of personal misrule by the superintendent that Monroe was alarmed and ordered a court-martial for Old Pewter. Shortly thereafter, Bvt. Maj. Sylvanus Thayer, just returned from study abroad, received orders on 17 July 1817 naming him to the superintendency of the academy.[46]

Thayer was born in Braintree, Massachusetts, and was graduated from Dartmouth College in 1807. He entered the military academy that year, and graduated in 1808. During the War of 1812 he saw action on the northern front and at Norfolk, Virginia. While on a two-year tour in France, arranged at his own request by President Madison and Secretary of War Monroe, Thayer not only studied military schools and fortifications, but also purchased and shipped back to the West Point library some 500 maps and charts and 1,000 technical books on mathematics and military art and engineering.[47]

So at the age of thirty-two Thayer arrived at the academy on 28 July 1817 to assume command. Present at the Point were 240 cadets, 15 faculty members, 12 officers, and the company of some 130 Bombardiers. The new superintendent was rudely received by Partridge, who departed the night Thayer arrived. Thayer, astonished to find some of the faculty under arrest, was appalled at the chaos. In addition to the irregularities already noted, he perceived that far too many cadets were absent on special leave or vacation; that Partridge had failed to comply with the regulation permitting admittance only in September; that regular classes therefore could not be held; that extravagance was encouraged by the outgoing superintendent to the extent that cadets were in the habit of borrowing money before payday; that many were graduated without a knowledge of French (the language in which most of the untranslated works on military science and fortification were written); and that studies in general had been sadly neglected. Fortunately the new superintendent was a man of stern fiber. He commenced immediately the necessary reorganization and streamlining of the institution. "I had a solemn duty to perform," he wrote upon assuming the command, " and was determined to perform it whatever were the personal consequences to myself."[48]

It was a monumental task. In the judgment of E. D. J. Waugh, "Everything was to be done, everything to be undone." Gradually Thayer won the respect of the faculty and the implicit obedience of the officers on the post. He ordered all absent cadets to return by the first of September. At the end of August Alden Partridge suddenly reappeared and was greeted by the wild cheers of those cadets who "did not relish restriction after unbridled liberty, or justice where they had before basked in favoritism." Bursting in upon the new superintendent, Old Pewter, without the slightest authority, brusquely demanded that his quarters be returned to him. When Thayer sternly refused, Partridge arbitrarily assumed command. Without the support yet of the cadet body, many of whom reveled in the return of their lax former superintendent, Thayer departed briefly for New York. But within two days he returned with armed guards and orders from the Chief of Engineers, General Swift, not only reinstating Thayer as superintendent but directing the arrest of Partridge and his detention for court martial. Old Pewter departed from West Point on 10 September 1817, escorted by friendly officers and cadets, to the accompaniment of music.[49]

In the first few weeks of his superintendency, Thayer found that Partridge had not properly disciplined the enlisted men of the Company of Bombardiers, Sappers, and Miners, who, he asserted, deported themselves as if they were "composed of fugitives from justice and the refuse of society." The new superintendent solved this problem by steadily replacing the Bombardiers with married enlisted men or local men who were better laborers and more responsible individuals. Noting that some cadets were hardly able to read and write, Thayer discharged "Uncle Sam's bad bargains," as they were called. The corps was organized into two companies—one of tall and the other of shorter cadets—officered by their own members. To instill soldierly discipline and provide competent tactical instruction, Thayer named an army officer at the post to be Commandant of Cadets. A merit system was installed, and a scheme of weekly reports on cadet classroom performance worked out. A standard grading system was inaugurated that was copied from the model set by well-established colleges. The superintendent emphasized daily recitation and practical instruction in small classes. Vacations were abolished (although cadets could secure a leave by furlough upon their parents' request), but some summer encampment was retained. The sheep were banished, and chess and the reading of fiction prohibited.[50]

Major Thayer arranged the cadets in four annual classes, and worked hard to organize an effective curriculum. The first-year cadets (also called the Fourth, or Plebe Class) served as privates in the corps. The subjects they pursued were algebra, geometry, trigonometry, the mensuration of solids and planes, and French. The second-year (Third Class) courses included, again, quite a bit of mathematics, French, and drawing. The third-year (Second Class) studied chemistry, natural philosophy (which included statics, dynamics, hydrostatics, and hydrodynamics), and landscape and topographical drawing. More directly professional were the courses given the fourth-year (First Class) cadets. These included engineering (largely civil engineering, but also encompassing fortification, organization and composition of armies, and principles of strategy), minerology, rhetoric, and moral and political science. Cadets were given sixteen dollars a month and an allowance of two rations a day. Printed regulations governed life at the Point. The bugle and drum dispatched the cadet on his round of military exercises and studies. Housing was in a barracks, with two or three cadets per room. Mattresses sufficed for bedding until 1838, when bedsteads came in. There were no private eating clubs, secret societies, or Greek letter fraternities.[51]

Yet it was in the establishment of invaluable new traditions and the "Spirit of West Point," intangibles difficult to measure but certainly as significant as any of his more specific achievements, that Thayer left an imperishable heritage that still remains on the plain in the highlands of the Hudson. "[Major] Thayer," wrote an 1826 cadet,

> was one of the most remarkable men in the Army. His comprehensive mind embraced principles and details more strongly than any man I ever knew. The students seemed to feel that his eye was ever on them, both in their rooms and abroad, both in their studies and on parade. His object was to make them gentlemen and soldiers. And he illustrated in his own person the great object he sought to accomplish.

An 1829 graduate remembered that "[Major] Thayer was rigid in discipline, but was impartial and just. Was regarded with awe mingled with respect, and considered as the *Father of the Institution.*" In 1833 the superintendent was promoted to brevet colonel.[52]

Thayer's long and honorable career at West Point was cut short during Andrew Jackson's second term as president. Old Hickory had encouraged his nephew, A. J. Donelson, to act as one of the ringleaders in the disorderly protest against military discipline and subordination shortly after Thayer's arrival as superintendent. After his ouster, Donelson became aide-de-camp and then private secretary to Jackson and easily influenced him against Thayer and West Point. Actually the president resented the seemingly aristocratic nature of the Academy. While in the White House, Jackson denigrated the superintendent and staff of the school by often reinstating cadets who had been dismissed or even court-martialed.[53]

Refusing to accede to the introduction of political favoritism and the spoils system at the academy, Sylvanus Thayer submitted his resignation and, at the conclusion of the June examinations, departed forever from West Point. When Jackson was no longer president, Secretary of War Poinsett tried to persuade Thayer to return as superintendent, but to no avail. The "father of the military academy," however, served meritoriously in the army for three more decades. He was appointed to many boards and commissions, was in charge of the construction of numerous coastal fortifications, traveled again in Europe, commanded the Corps of Engineers in 1857–1858, and was breveted brigadier general in 1863, the year of his retirement. General Thayer was a member of a number of professional associations and received honorary degrees from Harvard and Dartmouth. In 1867 he personally endowed the Thayer School of Engineering at his alma mater, Dartmouth, carefully drew up its entrance requirements and curriculum, and appointed its first director—a West Point graduate. He died in 1872 in the town of his birth, Braintree, at the age of eighty-seven. In the Valhalla of American military titans, certainly none deserves a higher niche than that reserved for Sylvanus Thayer, the man who instilled the ineffable West Point tradition upon the military academy and the army itself.[54]

For the United States Navy, the War of 1812 had been one of glory and limited achievement. Although its matchless fir-built frigates emerged triumphant in the famous ship-to-ship duels with their British counterparts, and even though spectacular victories had been gained on Lakes Erie and Champlain, most of its warships and privateers were subsequently bottled up in port by the vastly superior numbers and ships-of-the-line of the enemy. Whether lessons would be learned from the war remained to be seen.

Congress reacted with unusual alacrity shortly after hostilities ceased when it called upon the secretary of the navy to report on how to build up the naval service over a period of years. While Benjamin Crowninshield, the able new secretary, was studying this problem, Congress set up the Board of Navy Commissioners on 7 February 1815. The board was to be composed of three experienced naval captains who were to advise the secretary on administrative, technical, and policy matters. Crowninshield's December 1815 report called for a respectable and permanent naval establishment to free the nation from economic dependence abroad and to protect the growing carrying trade. The secretary recommended an annual increase for the navy of one 74-gun ship-of-the-line, two 44-gun frigates, and two sloops of war (generally carrying 18 guns).[55]

The legislators responded in 1816 by approving the expenditure of $1 million annually for eight years to construct a total of nine 74s and twelve 44s and to erect harbor defenses. This legislation committed the United States to acquire capital ships in peacetime comparable to those of European fleets. In major units, the United States Navy in 1816 possessed five 74s and four 44s. By comparison, in 1842 the navy had one 120-gun three-deck monster, ten 74s, and fourteen 44s. This increase in the number of fighting ships helped the United States achieve the Rush-Bagot Treaty of 1818, which provided for virtual disarmament on the lakes between Canada and the United States. Finally, the enlarged navy was a factor in the promulgation of the Monroe Doctrine in 1823.[56]

The duties of the navy in the decades after the War of 1812 were many and varied. It was to cooperate with the British Navy in the suppression of the African slave trade. Another persistently difficult duty was to safeguard American ships from Caribbean pirates. These buccaneers operated brazenly out of scores of remote little bases in the West Indies stretching from the Bahamas to the coasts of Central and South America, and they were a nuisance and menace. Closely allied with this was the role of the navy in protecting American travelers and businessmen in revolution-torn Latin America. Occasionally peace broke out there, but more often than not our sailors, marines, and warships had to rescue our citizens from numerous delicate embroglios. Then there were the fishing Americans who needed protection in the North Atlantic and North Pacific oceans from their not-too-friendly Canadian and Japanese competitors. In addition, Americans involved in the lucrative China trade and other business enterprises in eastern Asia required naval support, as did our citizens engaged in commerce in the Mediterranean against the hostility and occasional depredations from Algerian freebooters. Finally, of course, navy men and ships performed the usual river and harbor survey work. In short, down to the eruption of war with Mexico, there were many activities to take the time and try the skill, patience, and ingenuity of American sailors.[57]

These various duties required a number of semipermanent squadrons after 1815. The first to be established was the Mediterranean Squadron in 1815, whose function was to overawe the Barbary corsairs. Around 1822 two more squadrons were set up: the West Indian, to police the Caribbean and Gulf of Mexico against raids by the pirates based in these beautiful semitropical islands; and the Pacific Squadron, to protect the widespread commerce and business interests of Americans in that greatest of oceans. In 1826 the South Atlantic, or Brazil, Squadron was created to guard against violence in strife-torn South America, and, because of the increased carrying trade in the Western Pacific, the East Indian Squadron was established in 1835. Finally, the so-called Home Squadron was formed in 1841 to safeguard American interests along the North Atlantic seaboard; and in 1843 a regular slave-trade patrol or African Squadron was instituted. The slowly but steadily expanding navy succeeded in gaining for the young republic a measure of respect abroad, despite jealousies and trepidation on the part of nations that feared America's eventual rise as a naval power.[58]

Yet the navy was beset with some problems that were discouraging. Its officers were often underranked, and, on foreign or home station, were embarrassed and humiliated by the mere presence of their foreign counterparts who generally were a grade or two ahead of them. Also, despite urgings, there was no United States Naval Academy until 1845 (it was charged that all the clamor for a naval academy was due only to a desire to "foster a military class whose members would monopolize all the higher positions in the Navy, contrary to the spirit of democracy").[59]

There was one way, however, to cope with local political issues regarding the navy, and that was to find employment for laborers up and down the coasts. The log-rolling gimmick was the construction and maintenance of docks, shipyards, and bases, and these were built in large numbers in the years after the second war with England. In 1842 the Board of Navy Commissioners was replaced by the bureau system in the department. There were some obvious advantages to having these bureaus of Navy Yards and Docks; Provisions and Clothing; Construction, Equipment, and Repairs; Medicine and Surgery; and Ordnance and Hydrography; but without the board, the secretary of the navy was without a group of experts to help him develop naval policy and grand strategy.[60]

Thus by 1845 the United States Navy was ready to fight a full-scale war against a third-rate naval nation, Mexico.

CHAPTER SIX

From Palo Alto to the
Halls of Montezuma

*The slaughter of the tiny garrison defending the
Alamo in early March, 1836, and the subsequent
burning of their oil-soaked bodies, stacked like
cordwood outside the mission, sent a shudder of
horror through the American public which not
even their pride in the desperate heroism of the
defenders could restrain.*

OTIS SINGLETARY

 IT CAME as no surprise when Texans revolted from Mexican
rule in 1836. Having cast off the yoke of Spain, Mexico encouraged American settlers to migrate to Texas in the 1820s
and 1830s. They gave generous impresario privileges, including the use of
slaves, to men like Moses and Stephen F. Austin if they would settle families
west of the Sabine River. But increasing friction between Mexicans and Texans
climaxed in 1835 when President Antonio Lopez de Santa Anna proclaimed a
unified constitution that ended states' rights.[1]

The Texans' reaction was to establish a provisional government in
November 1835; name Sam Houston commander of a regular Texas army yet
to be recruited; and allow a volunteer army that had trounced a force of 150
Mexicans at Gonzales, to drive other Mexican soldiers out of San Antonio de
Béxar and its crumbling, partly fortified old mission, the Alamo. This was
done in early December. With the Second Seminole War about to erupt in
Florida, the only United States response was to move Gen. Edmund Gaines to
western Louisiana with discretionary authority to cross into Texas in pursuit
of Indians, and to request militiamen from nearby territories, if needed.[2]

But all eyes—American, Texan, and Mexican—were soon riveted on the
charming but decaying outpost town of San Antonio. By the end of 1835 the
Mexican strong man, Santa Anna, began his move with a large army toward
the Rio Grande to redeem the situation. After ordering James Bowie to blow
up the Alamo in San Antonio, Houston traveled northward on furlough to
conclude a treaty with the Cherokees to at least keep them neutral.[3]

Santa Anna's counterpart, Sam Houston, had lived among the Cherokee

1 2 4

and served effectively under Andrew Jackson at Horseshoe Bend in 1814, where he had been wounded. He had been a member of the national House of Representatives and a capable governor of Tennessee. Known as "The Raven" or "The Big Drunk," he was six feet two inches in height and had keen gray eyes. Divorced from his wife, he moved back among the Cherokee, whom he championed and with whom he did business. His interest in Texas at first was incidental, and he probably did not play a leading role in initiating the movement for Texan independence. The vigorous Houston had a talent for dramatic contrasts in dress and speech. He was a masterful stump speaker and had dignified and charming manners. His commanding presence and capacity for getting a difficult job done well aroused enthusiasm and confidence. In short, even with far fewer troops, he was in the end more than a match for Santa Anna.[4]

The man whom Houston had ordered to San Antonio to destroy the Alamo, Jim Bowie, was also a colorful character. Standing a good six feet tall, erect and well proportioned, with sandy hair and small blue eyes, this native Georgian had achieved a reputation for courage, strength, and fighting skill, especially with the famous knife that he and his brother developed. He had prospered, it was said, in the slave-smuggling business. A land-hungry speculator—some of his activities bordered on fraud—he had come to Texas in 1828 in search of gold and silver. He arrived in San Antonio and married—a union that ended with the death of his family in 1832 that literally drove Bowie to drink. Quiet, unobtrusive, and cool, he was almost a legend in his own time. He helped persons in distress, was gentle to some, polished and smooth, and could be courtly with the ladies. Arriving at the Alamo in January 1836, Bowie was soon drinking heavily in a vain attempt to check a developing and fatal case of typhoid-pneumonia. Perhaps because of his extensive holdings of some one million acres of Texas land, and his own independent attitude, the forty-year-old Bowie decided on 2 February to disobey Houston's order to blow up the Alamo and remove the cannon to Gonzales and Goliad. It was a fateful decision by a man who seemed destined for a violent end.[5]

On the same day that Bowie made his momentous decision to spare the Alamo, a strong supporter of the Texas War Party arrived on the scene. This was Lt. Col. William Barret Travis, who had contended with Bowie over the top command but supported him in the decision to retain the Alamo as a key defense between Santa Anna's advancing army and the makeshift army of Texans that Houston would soon be mustering and trying to organize. For a time Bowie and Travis shared the command at San Antonio, each leading his own men in the polyglot little force, until Bowie's rapidly sinking health enabled Travis to assume full and sole command.[6]

Although he could not command as much loyalty from the troops in the Alamo as Bowie, the twenty-seven-year-old Travis manifested many useful qualities. Six feet tall, auburn haired, with penetrating gray blue eyes, Travis easily stood out in his white hat and red pantaloons. Born in South Carolina, he eventually trained as a lawyer. But an unsuccessful marriage led to his move to Texas in 1831, where he soon became a leader against the Mexicans. Very intense, austere, and easily offended, he was nonetheless, in the view of those who observed him, energetic, honorable, and gallant—a man who asked much of others and more of himself.[7]

On 8 February 1836 twelve mounted Tennessee volunteers, commanded by a striking fifty-year-old stalwart wearing a coonskin cap, arrived at the Alamo. This was, of course, David Crockett of Tennessee, a crack shot and a great hunter who had fought under Jackson at Horseshoe Bend. Though he had failed as a farmer, as a younger man he had been elected to Congress because of his homespun wit, good nature, and self-confidence. He went to Texas to make a fortune and with his shrewd simplicity and spellbinding eloquence soon won over most Texans. Those inside the Alamo found him to be honest, fair-minded, and a true soldier. In the running battle between Travis and Bowie for top command, Crockett played an ameliorating role.[8]

After a grinding forced march, Santa Anna and several thousand Mexican troops reached the Rio Grande, where they rested for four days. Meanwhile, a Texan force of some 400 under Col. James W. Fannin retired to Goliad where, despite Houston's orders, he remained too long before attempting to reinforce the Alamo. When at last Fannin did start it was too late, and he and his soldiers suffered a ghastly fate. On 16 February Santa Anna moved out from Laredo. By George Washington's birthday he had reached San Antonio, where he promptly besieged the Alamo, whose defiant defenders were to make an epic thirteen-day stand.[9]

As the Mexicans approached, Travis sent out several messages calling for assistance; but Fannin remained too long at Goliad and Houston simply could not ready his small army to come to their rescue. While Santa Anna's exact numbers in Béxar are unknown, the figure possibly approximates 2,400, and some authorities place it much higher. The Texan numbers within the Alamo's crumbling walls are better known—they probably totaled 183 soldiers. Against these fearful odds the defenders battled skillfully and heroically. Bowie was mortally ill and bedridden in a room of the Alamo; all he could do was lend moral support. Crockett's and especially commander Travis's conduct was superb, and their gallant troops responded with surpassing courage. On 24 February, the second day of the siege, the hopelessness of their situation was apparent; thus Travis sent a resourceful messenger with a final noble appeal for reinforcement, concluding with these words:

> the enemy has demanded a surrender at discretion, otherwise, the garrison are to be put to the sword, if the fort is taken. I have answered the demand with a cannon shot, & our flag still waves proudly from the walls. *I shall never surrender or retreat.* Then, I call on you in the name of Liberty, of patriotism, & everything dear to the American character, to come to our aid, with all dispatch. . . . If this call is neglected, I am determined to sustain myself as long as possible & die like a soldier who never forgets what is due to his own honor & that of his country—VICTORY OR DEATH![10]

Thwarted day after day by the brilliant, dedicated stand of the handful of Texans, Santa Anna, after several more repulses, was finally able to batter down the walls of the Alamo and overwhelm the garrison on 6 March 1836.

Travis, Bowie, and Crockett were slain, along with the other 180 defenders. Those Texans who were wounded and helpless were brutally slaughtered by Santa Anna's orders. In the end these 183 individuals exacted a terrible toll of Mexican soldiers, probably some 600 being killed and wounded. The enemy heaped the American corpses in a pile and burned them. Santa Anna completed his seemingly triumphant crushing of the Texan independence movement by shooting down in cold blood some 400 men of Fannin's force who had already surrendered near Goliad on Palm Sunday, 26 March.[11]

The Mexican "high tide" in the war had been reached. Reconfirmed as commander in chief on 4 March, Sam Houston assumed command of some 400 men at Gonzales a week later. Learning of the fall of the Alamo, Houston began a retreat that was continued on 26 March with the news of Fannin's catastrophe. Each precious day of time bought by Travis at San Antonio was vital while the Raven kept his army together, resolved quarrels, and bided his time by withdrawing in the face of Santa Anna's confident advance. Finally on 21 April 1836 in an ilex grove near the present-day city that bears his name, Houston's 783 men, shouting "Remember the Alamo!" fell upon some 1,200 Mexicans and annihilated them in the crucial Battle of San Jacinto and settled the destiny of Texas. Houston was slightly wounded but spared the life of the captured Santa Anna, who later and typically broke his pledge of friendship and assistance. Nonetheless, Texan independence had been won. Finally, in the closing hours of the administration of John Tyler, Texas was annexed by the United States, and this action so incensed Mexico as to exacerbate still further the growing enmity between greaser and gringo, as they called each other.[12]

THE IMMEDIATE FACTOR that triggered hostilities was Polk's determination to push matters with Mexico to the brink of war, if necessary, and Mexico was not loath to join the issue. In January 1846 Polk sent an emissary, John Slidell, to Mexico City; but the José Herrera and then the Mariano Paredes governments refused to receive him or to negotiate the differences between the two countries. Polk took the fateful step: he directed his secretary of war, William L. Marcy, to instruct Bvt. Brig. Gen. Zachary Taylor to move a force down to the north bank of the Rio Grande. By late March 1846 Taylor and his small army of under 4,000 men, in position at Point Isabel and Fort Brown, were confronted by a Mexican army of twice its size across the Rio Grande at Matamoros. On 25 April Gen. Mariano Arista ordered a strong force of 1,600 cavalrymen across the river where they clashed with some 60 of Taylor's dragoons under the command of Capt. Seth B. Thornton. This resulted in the death of several Americans and the capitulation of the others. Polk could charge that Mexicans had caused the shedding of American blood on allegedly American soil. Thus he asked for and received from Congress a declaration of war.[13]

Many Americans were extremely overconfident about the efforts and the resources that would be needed to conquer Mexico—a state of rugged terrain and vast distances. The strength of the United States regular army at the out-

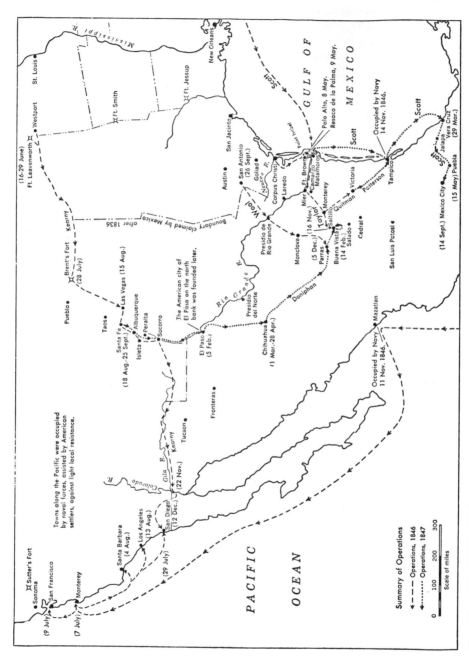

PACIFIC OCEAN

Sonoma •
☒ Sutter's Fort
• San Francisco
(9 July)
Monterey (7 July)
Santa Barbara (4 Aug.)
Los Angeles (13 Aug.)
San Diego (12 Dec.)
(29 July)

Colorado R.
Gila R.
Kearny (22 Nov.)
Tucson •
Fronteras •

Pueblo •
Brent's Fort
(28 July)
Kearny
Taos •
Las Vegas (15 Aug.)
Santa Fe (18 Aug.–25 Sept.)
Albuquerque
Isleta • Peralta
Socorro •
El Paso (5 Feb.)
Presidio del Norte
Chihuahua 1 Mar.–28 Apr.
Doniphan

The American city of El Paso on the north bank was founded later.

Rio Grande R.
Presidio de Rio Grande
Boundary claimed by Mexico after 1836

Towns along the Pacific were occupied by naval forces, assisted by American settlers, against light local resistance.

☒ Ft. Leavenworth (16–29 June)
☒ Westport
• St. Louis
Mississippi R.
☒ Ft. Smith
☒ Ft. Jessup
New Orleans

Austin •
San Antonio (26 Sept.)
Goliad •
San Jacinto
Nueces R.
Corpus Christi
Laredo •
Mier (5 Dec.)
Matamoros
Ft. Brown
Palo Alto, 8 May.
Resaca de la Palma, 9 May.
Point Isabel
Camargo
Occupied by Navy 14 Nov. 1846.

GULF OF MEXICO

Scott
Monclova
Monterey (16 Nov.)
Saltillo
Parras
Buena Vista (14 Feb.)
Salado
Cedral •
Wool
Taylor
Quitman
Victoria •
Patterson
Tampico
Scott
San Luis Potosí •

Mazatlan •
Occupied by Navy 11 Nov. 1846.

Scott
Jalapa
Vera Cruz (29 Mar.)
Puebla (15 May)
Mexico City (14 Sept.)

Summary of Operations
– – – Operations, 1846
• • • • Operations, 1847

Scale of miles
0   100   200   300

FIG. 6.1.   THE MEXICAN WAR

break of war was a little over eight thousand officers and men who were widely scattered in scores of posts across the country. Over 1.5 million militiamen were on the rosters, but there were only fifteen thousand muskets for them. Other deficiencies in uniforms and equipment existed. Unlike earlier wars, in the Mexican War the government called for volunteers, not militia. Soon there were inequities in the geographic sources of volunteers: Texas and the Mississippi Valley supplied some forty-nine thousand volunteers, while the original thirteen states provided thirteen thousand. At first the volunteers had to supply themselves; only later were they reimbursed. A munificent Congress finally voted $10 million for defense and authorized the raising of fifty thousand volunteers, but only for a year's service—too short a time. To strengthen Taylor in this precarious situation, the overly zealous Bvt. Maj. Gen. Edmund P. Gaines in New Orleans called to the colors illegally approximately twelve thousand volunteers and was fired for his trouble.[14]

Although operating more effectively than in the War of 1812, the American high command left much to be desired during the struggle with Mexico. At the apex was the angular, grizzled commander in chief, Pres. James K. Polk. Born in North Carolina in 1795, Polk moved in 1806 to Tennessee and was graduated from the University of North Carolina in 1818. After practicing law in Tennessee, he served in the state legislature, as a Congressman and Speaker of the United States House of Representatives, and as governor in Nashville. The Democrat Polk defeated the Whig, Henry Clay, for the presidency in 1844, and came to office an acknowledged annexationist.[15]

Polk was superior to James Madison as commander in chief and displayed a number of praiseworthy characteristics in this difficult post. Though his was probably a mediocre mind, he was capable of prodigious labor (even serving as his own secretary of war when his appointee fled Washington to escape the summer heat). Polk was determined to be a strong commander in chief and achieved a dominance over Congress in running the war. He kept a close eye on his civilian and uniformed subordinates, and he oversaw even the smallest detail of strategy, organization, and mobilization. Although he insisted on having his own way, the president did at times consult his cabinet and general in chief about the formulation of grand strategy and other war-related matters.[16]

But these positive traits, often useful, were certainly marred and perhaps counterbalanced by several unpleasant, weak characteristics. Polk was a narrow-visioned, obstinate man who was engulfed by his own relentless and violent partisan political passions and prejudices. He often refused to listen to others or take expert advice; yet the chief executive was untutored in military matters, unable to delegate authority properly, and often got bogged down in picayunish details that should have been the concern of subordinates such as the secretary of war, general-in-chief, or lesser officials. So severe and unrestrained were his anti-Whig biases that the president even suggested that the militarily inept and aged politician, Thomas Hart Benton, be elevated to lieutenant general and made supreme commander. Polk was often overly suspicious, petty, vindictive, and unfair, especially in his dealings with his two top generals, and he was slow to grasp realities or learn from experience.

Despite these and other grave shortcomings, he proved to be the first American president who could run a war in a strong and successful way.[17]

The secretary of war, sixty-year-old William L. Marcy, was certainly no outstanding asset to the hardworking, omnipresent commander in chief. Born in Massachusetts, Marcy was educated at Brown University, moved to New York state, and became a successful lawyer. Light service in the War of 1812 was followed by his rise in the Democratic party to a judgeship on the state supreme court, to a seat in the United States Senate, and to three terms as governor of the Empire State. (He was later to serve as Franklin Pierce's secretary of state). As Polk's war secretary Marcy was well-meaning, honest, and forthright, with some administrative skills, but he also had a number of failings. His best work was done at home in his bathrobe, where he imbibed snuff and read voraciously. Tall, square shouldered, and heavy, Marcy was at once genial and yet forbidding and gruff in manner. His quizzical, even fierce countenance could make subordinates quake. Marcy's health was not as robust as it appeared to be, and he renounced Washington's summer heat for cooler climes. This put a further burden on the president and generals, as did the secretary's unfamiliarity with military matters and procedures. Marcy was a forceful writer; however, he often acted as little more than a clerk, passing along messages from the chief executive to the military commanders and returning their replies to Polk for final action. In short, Marcy's performance, while better than that of Armstrong, added little luster to the good reputation he had gained up to 1845 and would retain afterwards.[18]

The general in chief, or commanding general, of the United States Army was the magnificent soldier, Maj. Gen. Winfield Scott. Since his first interest was the law, this Virginia-born giant (he was six feet five inches in height, and weighed close to 300 pounds) did not attend West Point; but he was commissioned a captain in the army in 1808. Scott served illustriously in the War of 1812 on the Niagara front in the hard-fought battles of Chippewa and Lundy's Lane, where he was wounded. He became a department commander, and served in the Black Hawk War and in the conflict with the Seminoles in Florida, as well as on a number of sensitive diplomatic enterprises. Known as "Old Fuss and Feathers," Scott was already sixty years of age in mid-1846, but he was active and vigorous. He could be irascible and a difficult subordinate, but on the whole he was generous, chivalric, and openhearted. A fussy gourmet and walking dress parade in his fancy uniforms, Scott nonetheless had superb soldierly instincts and attainments. A widely read military scholar, he did not lack imagination and was a masterful organizer, tactician, and strategist. Certainly he was the ablest military commander the United States produced between George Washington and the Civil War group of generals.[19]

The first general to cross swords with the foe in the Mexican War was, as has been seen, Zachary Taylor. Like Scott, Taylor was a native Virginian, and he, too, rose through the lower army commissioned grades without benefit of a West Point pedigree. Taylor gained fame as a peerless Indian fighter in the years after his minor services in the War of 1812, his high point coming in the victory over the Seminoles at Lake Okeechobee on Christmas Day, 1837. He acquired a plantation in Louisiana in the early 1840s but was soon ordered by

Polk to the Rio Grande for the opening clashes of the Mexican War in April 1846. Known as "Old Rough and Ready," the sixty-one-year-old Taylor was a useful if somewhat limited officer. Heavy, well-proportioned, and grizzled, he had a commanding air about him. The rustically dressed soldier often wore a hunting shirt and a nonregulation wide-brimmed hat. He was an inspiring troop leader and was a skilled tactician with soldiers that were within his field of vision. But he could not make war on the map, and he was not a good strategist. If he was not a great organizer, logistician, or administrator, Taylor was at least adept in finding subordinates who were competent to perform these duties. Almost as hypersensitive as his immediate superior, Scott, Polk goaded him fearfully and he became a chestnut burr under the President's saddle, although the fault was chiefly Polk's. Certainly the Whig Taylor proved more than adequate for the forthcoming operations on the northern front of the war.[20]

Santa Anna was the best of the batch of Mexican generals, though this one-legged adventurer left something to be desired. Distinguished by restless and brilliant eyes, a head that bulged at the top, a swarthy complexion, and cordial manners, he was nonetheless a charlatan lacking in great military skill and statesmanship and was easily seduced by flattery. Although on occasion capable of improvisation, he was not a deep thinker or student of a problem. Intellectually, his mind was untrained and undisciplined, and he was an inveterate gambler. He misunderstood Americans (as he did Mexicans), and thought a single defeat would be all that was needed to end the war. He was not a good strategist and was a worse tactician.[21]

On the American side, the struggle in the high command to hammer out a plan of grand strategy for the war and organize and prepare troops for the field got intermingled with nasty personality clashes involving the civilian superiors and the top generals. Polk tried hard to energize the bureau chiefs of the War Department's so-called General Staff, several of whom were old mossbacks though certainly not disloyal, as the intemperate president charged. The commander in chief played a leading role in arriving at specific budget estimates for the Navy and War Departments. He also personally oversaw army supply efforts. But Polk's insistence on calling for volunteers for only a year's service, instead of for the duration, or instead of increasing the regular army sufficiently, was a serious mistake.[22]

The president's immediate concern in the field of military operations was to quickly improvise a plan of grand strategy. Lack of preparation by the administration was painfully evident. In consultation with Marcy and Scott, Polk ordered the navy to blockade Vera Cruz and the Gulf coast of Mexico, while two army columns were to penetrate Mexico's northern provinces: one southward toward Monterrey, Saltillo, and San Luis Potosí, and the other southwestward from Fort Leavenworth toward Santa Fe, Chihuahua, and Southern California. While unenthusiastic about Scott, the commander in chief reluctantly named him to command the American land forces. Quite unreasonably he urged him to depart his post at Washington, D.C., and head for the front.[23]

Aware of the president's increasing hostility and partiality for Democrats in high army rank and position, Old Fuss and Feathers exploded to Marcy, in one of his perceptive but contentious letters:

> I am too old a soldier . . . not to feel the infinite importance of securing myself against danger . . . in my rear, before advancing upon the public enemy. . . . I do not desire to place myself in the most perilous of all positions— a fire upon my rear, from Washington, and the fire, in front, from the Mexicans.

Polk confided to his diary that Scott's "bitter hostility toward the administration is such that I could not trust him" to lead the army, "and will not do so." The chief executive threatened to supersede him.[24]

But attention soon shifted to news from Taylor's fighting front along the Rio Grande. At the end of April 1846 Mexican General Arista's army crossed into Texas. Taylor, leaving some five hundred troops under Jacob Brown in the fort bearing the major's name, fell back to strengthen the defenses of his base at Point Isabel on the coast. Brown withstood a bombardment of his fort, although it cost him his life. Old Rough and Ready hastened back to relieve the fort, dragging a long suppy train of over two hundred wagons with him.[25]

On 8 May Taylor ran into the enemy at the watering spot of Palo Alto. Here, in a sharp engagement highlighted by a severe grass fire, Taylor's threatened flanks were relieved by the decimating fire of his so-called Flying Artillery under Samuel Ringgold and James Duncan, whose salvos shattered the advancing Mexican columns and impelled their retreat. In the Battle of Palo Alto, 2,000 Americans, regulars mostly, suffered casualties of 9 killed and 44 wounded, while Arista's 6,000 Mexicans lost over 200 men.[26]

The enemy fell back a few miles along the road from Palo Alto toward Fort Brown to a largely dry arroyo known as Resaca de la Guerrero, where Arista made a stand. Taylor brought the American army forward, after he vetoed any proposals of retreat by several of his top officers, to Resaca de la Palma to confront the enemy, and a battle took place on 9 May that was heavier than the one the day before. The Mexican position was a strong one in the natural trench of the river bed, with secure flanks and abundant chaparral that negated the superior American artillery and compelled a frontal assault. Taylor, who was highly revered by his confident regulars, was seated aboard Old Whitey near the front lines, one leg swung over the pommel of his saddle, when he ordered the attack in mid-afternoon. American infantry forces, usually in separate bodies, inched their way forward in hand-to-hand fighting through the brush toward the Mexican position. A smashing, successful dragoon attack was made by Capt. Charles May that broke through the enemy line and, with the aid of the foot soldiers, captured several cannon. Meanwhile Arista refused to believe that the severe combat was more than a skirmish and remained inside his headquarters tent attending to paper work. After some two hours of hot action the Mexican force was routed and fell back across the river toward Matamoros, Arista barely escaping capture. The gunners inside Fort Brown punished the foe with enfilading fire as they rushed by. Almost 1,200 Mexicans were casualties at Resaca de la Palma as contrasted with a total

American loss of less than 150 men. Taylor occupied Matamoros on 18 May when Arista abandoned it.[27]

Arista, at Linares with his shaken army, was soon replaced in command by the devious Pedro de Ampudia. The Mexicans retreated to Monterrey, where some substantial fortifications were constructed. Taylor's army in Matamoros were the first American forces to experience foreign occupation duty. Adding to Old Zack's heady wine of success was talk of his possible nomination for the presidency that was beginning to circulate among the citizens in the United States. The jealous Polk didn't like this at all. Taylor, exhilarated by this adulation, querulously complained to the administration about supply delays and personnel matters. The president thought that Taylor was "brave but does not seem to have resources or grasp of mind enough to conduct a campaign. . . . I think him unfit for command." With his lack of talent for inspired strategic movements, and perhaps his failure to appreciate the completeness of his victories and the temporary demoralization of the enemy, Old Rough and Ready did not pursue the Mexicans very far.[28]

Informed from Washington that his force would be increased considerably over time, Taylor was told that Monterrey, a city of almost 15,000 located near the stategic Rinconada pass on the vital road to Saltillo, should be his first objective. Cooperating with him, and under his overall control, would be John E. Wool's separate column of three thousand, which was to move upon Chihuahua from San Antonio. Old Rough and Ready determined, therefore, to march a half-regular force some 120 miles up the Rio Grande to Camargo, and thence to approach Monterrey via the San Juan and Santa Catarina rivers. Before the end of the summer he had more than enough troops and supplies at unhealthy Camargo for his southward lunge toward Monterrey.[29]

Taylor moved in late summer with approximately sixty-two hundred men via Cerralvo, after an uneventful march through harsh country, and neared the stone-built city of Monterrey, defended by Ampudia with about seventy-two hundred troops and forty cannon. Reconnaissances by American engineers revealed that the approaches were covered by rugged fortified strong points. September equinoctial rains plagued the determined invaders so that Taylor decided on the risky plan of dividing his army in the face of the more numerous foe. "Haughty Bill" Worth, with one-third of the American army, was to conduct a turning movement to the northward against the western part of Monterrey and seize the important Saltillo road. Taylor, with the rest of the army, was to drive into the city from the northeast.[30]

The pincer movement of the two forces was not well coordinated by Taylor. But Worth performed splendidly. His flanking column cut the Saltillo road, the enemy's lifeline, and in hard fighting captured several fortified heights. Taylor's somewhat aimless attacks at the other end of town were at first repelled with loss. Worth, however, resumed his advance, and Taylor was now able to fight his way into the streets of the city. With Worth pressing also into the town, severe house-to-house and rooftop fighting at close quarters resulted, with Ampudia forced into the area around the plaza. With his own food and ammunition running dangerously low, Old Rough and Ready agreed to Ampudia's appeal for terms. The city and all public property were yielded to the Americans, and the Mexican troops, with full honors of war, evacuated Monterrey and withdrew beyond Rinconada Pass. In addition, Taylor granted an eight-week armistice, the understanding being that either government could terminate it as it saw fit. Taylor lost a total of nearly five hundred casualties in the three-day battle, while Mexican losses were a trifle lower. Because of victory, Taylor's star was now in full ascendency.[31]

But the more victories Old Zack scored, the less praise and more condemnation he received from Washington. The president was especially angered over the armistice that Taylor had approved. "He had the enemy in his grasp," exclaimed Polk, "and should have taken them prisoners. . . . It was a great mistake. . . ." Marcy was instructed to direct the general to end the truce. Taylor, increasingly aware of his enhanced presidential chances, lashed back angrily at the administration in his dispatches. Though ordered not to proceed farther south than Monterrey, Old Rough and Ready moved down to Saltillo anyway. Worth also reached that point on 16 November 1846. Nor could the president extract any requested suggestions from Taylor as to what strategic plan to adopt next. The old general, never much of a strategist, refused to reply specifically and continued to exchange barbed communiqués with Washington.[32]

In consultations with his cabinet and General in Chief Scott, Polk determined on the thrust from the East—a landing at Vera Cruz on Mexico's Gulf coast and a push inland toward the capital, Mexico City. The petty-minded president, however, would not allow the Whig, Taylor, whom he characterized as a "narrow-minded, bigotted partisan" who had been "made giddy with the hope of the presidency," to lead this new expedition. After a futile attempt to place Benton or some other Democrat in this command, the commander in chief turned reluctantly to another Whig, Scott, to head this venture. Many of Taylor's soldiers would be taken from him and added to Scott's force.[33]

Accepting with alacrity, Old Fuss and Feathers journeyed to the Rio Grande to confer with Taylor and to try to soothe his injured pride. Taylor, in a huff and unreasonably angry with Scott, deliberately absented himself from the arranged conference with his general in chief. The rift was complete all around: between the two leading generals, and between each of them and the administration. Such a sad situation did not bode well for Taylor's critical defensive battle in the offing, or Scott's complex campaign for Mexico City.[34]

Then came what was in many ways the climax of the Mexican War—the campaign and battle that the Americans could not have afforded to lose. Santa Anna left Mexico City on 28 September 1846 for San Luis Potosí, where, in perhaps his greatest accomplishment of the war, he energetically and skillfully raised an army of some 25,000 men. An intercepted message from Scott to Taylor fell into his hands that divulged not only the plan for the American descent upon Vera Cruz, but also the dwarfed size of Taylor's depleted force. The Mexican strong man correctly decided to swoop down on Taylor in overwhelming force and crush him and then turn to defend the capital against Scott. With that in mind, Santa Anna and his large army began to move northward out of San Luis Potosí on 2 February 1847. It was a difficult forced march through desolate country, and it took a fearful toll of the wiry Mexican troops.[35]

Taylor initially gave little credence to reports of Santa Anna's rapid advance. Finally, as a result of Texas Ranger Ben McCulloch's invaluable personal reconnaissance, Taylor deployed most of his forty-eight hundred soldiers in position near the Angostura, or Narrows, just south of the Buena Vista ranch, protecting his important base of Saltillo just to the north. Wool was in immediate command on the fingerlike, ravined plateaus to the east of the main road at the Angostura, while Old Rough and Ready, with a few reserves at the hacienda of Buena Vista, guarded the route to Saltillo.[36]

Santa Anna, with between 15,000 and 20,000 men, surged forward and made a strong attack. His blows, all on the east of the road, were indecisive in the late afternoon of 22 February. The main battle was joined on 23 February, and desperate Mexican assaults initially drove the Americans back on their left and critically threatened Wool's position. Only the brilliant service of the flying artillery batteries of Braxton Bragg, Thomas W. Sherman, John M. Washington, and John Paul Jones O'Brien saved the day. At the crisis in this savage engagement, Old Zack rode onto the field and hurled his last reserves into action. Among other troops, valuable counterattacks were delivered by Jefferson Davis's First Mississippi Rifles, which helped check the Mexican onslaught. Some of the fighting was hand-to-hand. Hindered by a tremendous rainstorm and an abortive American charge, Taylor managed to repulse a final enemy assault on his center. This compelled Santa Anna to recall his decimated legions, retreat from the field, and pull back southward for the defense of his capital. In the Battle of Buena Vista the Americans lost 264 killed, 456 wounded, and 23 missing—a total of 746 casualties; the Mexican loss was at least 3,700 men. Taylor and his excited soldiers were so exuberant at their victory over the numerically superior foe that the staid American commander grasped Wool in an impromptu embrace.[37]

But if Old Rough and Ready had any hopes that his spectacular victory would bring praise from the president, he was grievously disappointed. Quite the contrary, Polk was characteristically unhappy with the old Whig general. Angered at Taylor's mushrooming popularity with the public, the commander in chief reasoned that had the general followed directions, he would never have had to fight the engagement in the first place. Feeling that the soldiers had saved the befuddled Taylor from defeat, Polk charged that "our troops, regulars and volunteers, will obtain victories wherever they meet the enemy. This they would do if they were without officers to command them higher than lieutenants. It is an injustice to award the generals all the credit." Nor would the chief executive permit an army salute to the triumph at Buena Vista. Returning home on leave an acclaimed hero, the disgruntled Taylor vented his spleen against the administration, claiming that "Polk, Marcy and Co." had "been more anxious to break me down than to defeat Santa Anna." A great number of citizens were convinced that this was true.[38]

While Scott was planning and preparing his Vera Cruz-Mexico City expedition, events came to a head in New Mexico, Chihuahua, and especially in California, the main plum to be plucked by expansionist Polk. The state of

California was loosely and lightly held by Mexico, and an expedition against it from Ft. Leavenworth was fitted out and placed under the able command of Col. Stephen Watts Kearny, soon to be promoted to brigadier general. Born in 1794 in Newark, New Jersey, Kearny left Columbia University to fight meritoriously as a subaltern in the War of 1812, and was wounded at Queenstown Heights. Remaining in the regular army, he served chiefly on the prairies and plains. This frontier officer had energy, courage, and ability. He was a man of inflexible will and discipline and was stern—even harsh—in manner; but he was every inch a soldier and commander, one who could be relied upon to carry out his mission regardless of consequences.[39]

Kearny and his so-called Army of the West captured Santa Fe on 16 August 1846 with about sixteen hundred troops, after a hard march of over one thousand miles without a skirmish, and hoisted the American flag. He freed the people from Mexican rule, declared them citizens of the United States, and guaranteed their religion, property, and persons. He assisted in setting up a code of laws, made several wise appointments, and ordered Alexander W. Doniphan, a lawyer from Missouri, to take some nine hundred of the soldiers on an expedition against El Paso and Chihuahua. On 25 September Kearny resumed the march toward California with about three hundred men.[40]

Meanwhile, events were swiftly changing the fabric of California itself. One strand led to the American consul in Monterey, Thomas O. Larkin, a Massachusetts-born merchant and confidential government agent who had warned Washington of possible British or French incursions into California affairs. He was instructed to encourage any tendencies toward independence on the part of the Spanish-speaking Californians and commenced an effective propaganda campaign toward that end.[41]

Another strand in the California fabric centered on Commodore John D. Sloat, the aging, infirm commander of the American squadron on the Pacific coast. This native New Yorker, who had served in the naval war with France in 1800 and in the War of 1812, was instructed by the secretary of navy, George Bancroft, should hostilities erupt between Mexico and the United States, to "blockade San Francisco, and blockade or occupy such other ports" as his force would allow.[42]

Arriving on 2 July 1846 in Monterey with his warships, Sloat hesitated five days before landing a force, raising the American flag over the customs house, and proclaiming possession of California in the name of his country. He dispatched men to occupy San Francisco and soon held all of California north of Santa Barbara. Sloat, in failing health, turned over his command to Commodore Robert F. Stockton and returned to the East Coast, where his conduct was praised by the secretary.[43]

Stockton was born in Princeton, New Jersey, in 1795, the son of a United States senator and grandson of a signer of the Declaration of Independence. He attended Princeton, served in the navy in the War of 1812, and declined the secretaryship of the navy proffered him by President Tyler. Taking over from Sloat, the capable Stockton soon revealed personal traits of self-confidence, loyalty, and vanity. But Stockton would have to share honors with two others in the struggle for the Golden State.[44]

Another strand in the California fabric belonged to Bvt. Capt. John C. Frémont, the handsome, precocious, thirty-three-year-old Georgian and husband of Sen. Thomas Hart Benton's vivacious daughter, Jessie. Frémont, a magnetic personality, had led several extensive exploration trips to the West and was in California in 1846 on a paramilitary expedition that was being palmed off as a "scientific" one. When war developed, Frémont helped arm and lead the so-called California Battalion of pro-American Californians. After some hesitation, he cooperated with the forces of Stockton, the overall commander, in the capture of Los Angeles on 13 August, following the "Bear Flag Revolt." Frémont then went north to recruit. Having control of the coast south from San Pedro to San Diego, Stockton issued a proclamation claiming California as a territory of the United States. Then Kearny arrived on the scene and immediately became embroiled in protracted debate with Stockton over supreme command. "Pathfinder" Frémont returned and sided with the naval officer. Unable to bear the substitution of American for Mexican domination, some Californians seized Los Angeles, only to see it recaptured after several sharp skirmishes by Kearny, Frémont, and Stockton. Eventually final orders arrived from Washington naming Kearny to top command. He placed Frémont under virtual arrest and returned him to the East, where a court-martial found the Pathmarker guilty of disobedience and mutiny. The sentence was remitted by Polk, although Frémont resigned in a huff from the army. Thus a rich, magnificent empire, soon to become the giant state of California, was added to the United States at comparatively little cost in lives by a small number of men led by army and navy officers with strong personalities and wide talents.[45]

While Kearny was pressing westward from Santa Fe toward California and Scott was preparing to launch his thrust from the East toward Mexico City, Alexander Doniphan, with 856 ragged, ununiformed men of his First Missouri Regiment, was undertaking a peripheral campaign from Santa Fe and Valverde toward Chihuahua. The thirty-eight-year-old attorney, Doniphan, had been born in Kentucky, but had moved to Missouri, where he had gained an enviable reputation throughout the state as a trial lawyer. His personality and qualities of leadership were taxed to the limit in conducting this remarkable operation—aimed first at the capture of El Paso—which began in mid-December 1846. His troops not only lacked a commissary officer, quartermaster, and paymaster, and suffered shortages of tents and uniforms, but they were without military discipline. Nonetheless Doniphan and his men did splendidly. The Missourians encountered some 1,200 Mexicans at Brazito, just north of El Paso, held their fire until the last moment, and repelled with two musketry volleys a courageous but rash enemy charge. In the thirty-minute action, Doniphan inflicted casualties of at least 43 Mexicans killed and 150 wounded, with the loss of just 7 of his own troops slightly wounded. On 27 December he marched into El Paso.

As they pressed on to the south, the Missouri counselor needed to inspire his men to cope with the harsh, arid insect- and reptile-ridden country. At the Sacramento River, fifteen miles from Chihuahua, Doniphan met some 2,700 Mexican soldiers, supported by about 1,000 armed rancheros, who were drawn up in a naturally formidable defensive position. On 27 February 1847 the

Americans approached by way of the dried Arroyo Seco and struck the weakest part of the strong enemy position. In a desperate combat they finally drove the Mexicans back in disorder. At a cost of 2 killed and 7 wounded, Doniphan's men had killed over 300 Mexicans, wounded at least as many more, and captured 40 prisoners and large amounts of equipment. Chihuahua was entered on 2 March, after which Doniphan hiked another 600 miles to Monterrey, arriving in late May after a march totaling some thirty-six hundred miles. His competent campaign terminated when Doniphan and his troops were shipped back to New Orleans and mustered out of service in St. Louis in early July. This operation was largely a sideshow and not significant in the outcome of the war, since the Polk administration quickly determined not to hold Chihuahua. But Doniphan and his Missourians had made one of the greatest marches in North American military history, covering about six thousand miles in all by land and water.[46]

WHILE the naval role in Scott's expedition was not decisive and certainly did not win the war, it enabled the war to be won by providing for Scott's safe debarkation and thrust inland. The commander of the Gulf flotilla of the Home Squadron was Commodore David Conner, a fifty-four-year-old native of Harrisburg, Pennsylvania, who had served with distinction in the War of 1812 aboard U.S.S. *Hornet* and had been a Naval Commissioner and bureau head. Historian Justin H. Smith evaluates him thusly:

> Conner was a brave, able, accomplished, excellent man. . . . But his constitution had never been robust, and the effects of an old wound, thirty years of service in a southern climate and the torture of neuralgia had now made him a confirmed invalid, worn and wasted. . . . His powers both of thought and of execution were impaired. Naturally such a man did not wish to risk either men or ships; and, lacking the vigor for quick decisions and powerful action, he could not wisely involve himself in dangerous complications. On the outbreak of war he should have been retired.[47]

Conner's ships successfully occupied Tampico but twice failed to capture Alvarado. The American warships effectively blockaded the Gulf coast of Mexico, despite uncharted reefs, rough seas, and several shipwrecks. And Conner, ably seconded midway through the operation by his relief, Commodore Matthew C. ("Old Bruin") Perry, did land Scott's army and assist in the capture of Vera Cruz, with harmonious relations between army and navy prevailing most of the time.[48]

By October 1846 Polk determined on a landing of an army force at Vera Cruz followed by a push along the national highway (the "High Road") that Cortés had taken three centuries before to Mexico City. The president, in ambiguous and vague orders through Marcy, grudgingly gave the command of the expedition to Scott, who left his Lobos Island staging area with some 10,000 troops aboard Conner's ships on 2 March 1847. Santa Anna was at this point mustering some 36,000 soldiers for the defense of Mexico City. The Americans landed a week later via surf boats some three miles below the powerful forts at Vera Cruz. Scott's soldiers, under Haughty Bill Worth (the "Murat" of the American army), the profane David Twiggs (the "Bengal Tiger"), and the notoriously inefficient Robert Patterson, were assisted by a naval bombardment. They succeeded by a semisiege to force the Mexicans to yield the city on 29 March. Scott suffered 19 killed, the Mexicans perhaps 80. In view of the later Civil War it is interesting to speculate about what might have happened in the future had Mexican projectiles struck a small scouting boat and killed the following occupants thereof: Scott, Robert E. Lee, George G. Meade, P. G. T. Beauregard, and Joseph E. Johnston.[49]

Old Fuss and Feathers did not want to remain long in the city of Vera Cruz. He wished to evade the dreaded malaria and yellow fever so prevalent at the lower altitudes. Also, despite efforts to maintain order, some American troops occupying Vera Cruz, chiefly volunteers, broke discipline and behaved badly.[50]

Pressing westward toward Jalapa along the national highway, the American army encountered the Mexican forces at Cerro Gordo pass in the Sierra Madre Mountains. Santa Anna had some 12,200 troops available against Scott's 8,500 effectives. The enemy position was formidable, with its right resting on the Rio Del Plan, its center near the high road protected by artillery on bluffs, and its left anchored on two high spurs, Telegraph Hill and La Atalaya. After a thorough personal reconnaissance and others conducted by his ubiquitous engineers, Scott determined to feint against the Mexican center and especially the right. Meanwhile, he would launch his main attack on 18 April along a rough and circuitous path toward Santa Anna's left. Such later Civil War luminaries as George B. McClellan, U. S. Grant, and Robert E. Lee performed brilliantly as young subalterns at Cerro Gordo. Against staunch Mexican resistance, and in severe fighting, the Americans' coordinated attack succeeded; the Mexican left was enveloped, its rear threatened, and the whole enemy force driven headlong from the pass. At a cost of 63 killed and 337 wounded Americans, Scott inflicted heavy casualties on the Mexicans. Perhaps 1,000 were killed and wounded; 3,000 were captured, including 5 generals; 43 guns and 4,000 muskets were seized; and Santa Anna's personal effects, including possibly one of his wooden legs, were taken and the Mexican commander himself almost captured. The beautiful city of Jalapa was occupied on 19 April, and Puebla on 6 May.[51]

Before Scott could advance into the Valley of Mexico and approach the capital city, he had to allow a large segment of his army with expiring enlistment terms to go home. These twelve-month volunteers, many of whom were participants in the battles of Monterrey, Vera Cruz, and Cerro Gordo, and who had "seen the elephant" were unmoved by Scott's personal pleas or by offers of bounties and insisted on departure. Thus Robert Patterson escorted some three thousand of them back down the High Road to the Gulf coast. This left General Scott deep inside enemy territory with only a little over six thousand soldiers. While awaiting reinforcements, Scott was obliged to remain in Puebla from April to August 1847, a difficult period for the Americans in the hot, dry weather.[52]

Nor was Scott's situation eased by the appearance on the scene of the preposterous-looking chief clerk of the State Department, Nicholas P. Trist. This forty-seven-year-old Virginian attended West Point (though he did not graduate); studied law under Thomas Jefferson, whose granddaughter he married; was private secretary to Andrew Jackson; and served as American consul in Havana before becoming the number two man in the State Depart: ment. Polk had instructed Trist to try to negotiate a peace with Mexico, and Trist bore a sealed letter to be forwarded directly to enemy authorities. Scott was miffed at being bypassed and angered by the unfortunate tone of a message sent him by Trist just before the chief clerk joined the army. Hostile letters were exchanged by the two men. This initial enmity was overcome by Scott and Trist, and they soon became fast friends. Yet the army commander was dubious about possible limitations on his freedom of action against Santa Anna's army by Trist's wish for a truce at a later time.[53]

The march toward the Halls of the Montezumas was resumed on 7 August. After a stiff hike over ten thousand–foot mountain passes, the Americans could gaze at the magnificent Valley of Mexico. Outnumbered three-to-one by enemy forces waiting behind impressive fortifications, the invaders seemed to face a hopeless task. "Scott is lost," exclaimed the Hero of Waterloo, the Duke of Wellington. "He cannot capture the city and he cannot fall back upon his base."[54]

Practically surrounded by lakes and marshes, Mexico City, numbering some two hundred thousand inhabitants, was difficult to reach along its several causeways. However, American reconnaissances in mid-August proved invaluable for Scott and enabled him to bypass, by a southerly route, the powerful forts at El Penon, located to the east of the capital at the southern end of Lake Texcoco. Scott, in a crucial and correct decision, moved south of Lakes Chalco and Xochimilco to San Augustin, south-southeast of Mexico City. In a daring scouting foray, Robert E. Lee discovered a route across the rough lava field known as the Pedregal that would enable Scott to attack at Contreras, just west of the lava bed. A brilliant, decisive stroke was delivered. In a sharp, seventeen-minute battle fought at Contreras early on 20 August the Mexicans were roundly beaten and routed from the field with a loss of 700 killed, a great many wounded, and 813 prisoners, in addition to the American seizure of 700 pack mules, 22 cannon, and vast amounts of other supplies. In contrast, Scott lost only 60 of his own men killed and wounded.[55]

Santa Anna, whose orders had been disobeyed by a subordinate at Contreras, deployed his forces around the convent and church at Churubusco, to the northwest of Contreras. Scott was aware that a portion of his forces to the east under Worth was still not reunited with the main American army and decided to attack Churubusco before assaulting the capital city. A hard-fought combat ensued on that same afternoon of 20 August, with Mexican snipers and artillery operated by the notorious batch of American deserters known as the San Patricio Battalion inflicting severe casualties on Scott's forces. Only a determined American bayonet charge won the day against the enemy, who outnumbered Old Fuss and Feathers two to one. Not only was Santa Anna's force driven back into the inner defenses of the capital, but the Mexicans suffered enormous losses in the twin battles of Contreras and Churubusco; some

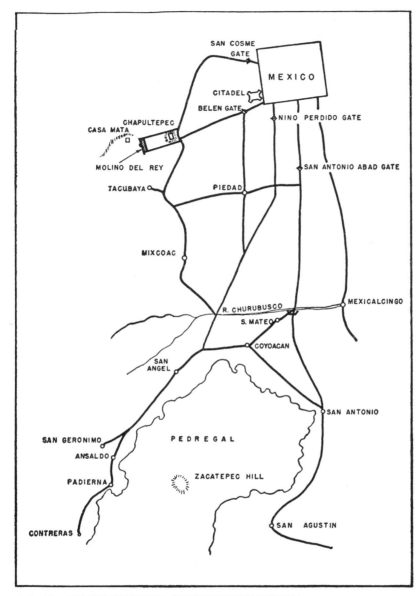

FIG. 6.2. VALLEY OF MEXICO, SOUTHWESTERN SECTION

4,300 killed and wounded; over 2,600 prisoners, including 8 generals; and perhaps 3,000 missing—about one-third of the Mexican army—whereas Scott's casualties in the two engagements totaled 137 killed, 879 wounded, and 40 missing.[56]

Scott, in a genuine peace effort, cooperated with Trist who was still accompanying his army, and agreed to a three-week armistice; but the truce was merely used by Santa Anna as a ploy to buy time to reorganize his shattered army and ready his inner defenses for a desperate stand to save his capital. Scott finally had to repudiate the abortive armistice and began moving his army northward on 7 September against the East, strong Mexican fortifications to the southwest of the city.[57]

The first of these strong points reconnoitered by the American engineers was El Molino del Rey, a cluster of fortified heavy stone mill and foundry buildings that Scott thought he had to seize quickly before more cannon could be made there; and the other, atop a high hill, was the castle of former viceroys and buildings of Chapultepec, then the site of the Mexican military academy. In perhaps his only major mistaken judgment in an otherwise masterful campaign, Scott erred in anticipating little resistance at Molino del Rey.[58]

That bloody battle on 8 September was won late in the day by the Americans only after repeated repulses by the enemy and heavy casualties. It took all-out efforts by Scott's infantry, artillery, and cavalry—skillfully handled by Worth—to accomplish this victory. American losses of 117 killed, 653 wounded, and 18 missing were exceeded by some 2,000 Mexicans killed and wounded and about 700 taken prisoner by Scott. It was a costly success for the invaders, but it enabled the American commander to turn his attention to Chapultepec.[59]

With 7,180 effectives remaining, Scott faced the formidable task of overcoming Santa Anna's 15,000 troops (and another 4,000 back-up soldiers nearby), who were firmly ensconced atop Chapultepec and at the city end of the causeways at Belen Gate and San Cosme Gate. Again, after the usual, valuable reconnaissances by his engineers, Scott planned a masterly two-pronged assault. This attack on the defenses of Chapultepec on 13 September, preceded the day before by a massive artillery bombardment, was marred somewhat by the blunders of several of Scott's subordinate generals.[60]

In the morning Twiggs's demonstration from the south distracted Santa Anna. Gideon Pillow, supported from the west by Worth, charged up the southwestern slope. Quitman attacked from the south. Despite a dogged defense by the Mexicans that included a courageous stand by the youthful cadets of the military academy, Chapultepec was captured and the enemy routed. Some United States Marines participated in the engagement.[61]

John A. Quitman, in one of the most gallant episodes in American military annals, was forced to dash forward along the narrow causeways in the face of galling Mexican fire to storm Belen Gate by 1:30 P.M., while Worth seized San Cosme Gate by 6:00 P.M. American losses of 130 killed, 703 wounded, and 29 missing were greatly surpassed by Santa Anna's 1,800 total losses at Chapultepec in the morning (Mexican losses at the gates in the afternoon are unknown). The enemy dictator fled the capital during the night with the small remnant of his shattered army, and Scott triumphantly entered the City of the Montezumas on 14 September 1847.[62]

The aftermath of the capture of Mexico City was triumph alloyed with calumny. The Yankee occupation of the enemy capital was highly successful. The city and its population were pacified in a magnanimous and enlightened manner, despite some hostilities started by the citizens. Meanwhile, Scott's diplomatic crony, Trist, was ordered home by President Polk on 6 October, but the recall order did not reach him in Mexico City until mid-November. Trist ignored these instructions and concluded the Treaty of Guadalupe-Hidalgo on 2 February 1848. By its terms the Mexicans confirmed the previous annexation of Texas and that of California, in addition to ceding to the United States the vast territories of New Mexico and Utah for the sum of $15 million. Polk quickly accepted the treaty, which was ratified, after a struggle, by the Senate.[63]

The president's outrageous treatment of the victorious Scott, who had conducted a magnificent campaign, crushed Santa Anna's large armies, captured Mexico City, forced the enemy to capitulation, and terminated the war, was far less honorable. Such officers under Scott as Quitman and Pillow were monuments of incompetency, and Worth, while a capable officer, was ruled by an ungovernable temper. Soon after the fall of Mexico City, when Pillow and Worth had become so insubordinate that Old Fuss and Feathers had had to place them under arrest, Polk not only dismissed the charges against these two men but ordered Scott home to face a court of inquiry. The chief executive denounced Scott's alleged "bad temper, dictatorial spirit, and extreme Jealousy." Robert E. Lee commented that when the American commander had done his duty and defeated the enemy, he was "turned out as an old horse to die." Scott was properly cleared by the court in the summer of 1848. He chastised Polk's "cunning," "hypocrisy," and "odious temper;" in 1852, the year he received the Whig nomination for the Presidency, his unaffected military career was capped by his being brevetted a lieutenant general.[64]

While Polk demonstrated that a president could direct a full-blown foreign war as commander in chief, his narrow, bitter, partisanship greatly hampered the military effort, especially the generals' operations in the field. "The President showed himself a small man." The true heroes of the War with Mexico were the American soldiers in the ranks, their officers, Zachary Taylor, and especially Winfield Scott. Although sharply criticizing Taylor on a number of valid points, and praising Scott highly, Old Rough and Ready was not totally rebuked by any means by the foremost authority on the Mexican War, historian Justin H. Smith. According to Smith,

> Scott possessed all the military qualities of Taylor, and all Taylor lacked. . . . Both complained of the government, but Scott had reason to do so. Both disregarded instructions; but while Taylor aimed to gratify himself, Scott's aim was to benefit his country. . . . Both were remarkable. Taylor was a distinguished plebeian, Scott a distinguished patrician; the first a superb captain, the second a superb general; and each a great man.[65]

FOR THE UNITED STATES NAVY after the Mexican War, progress was slow and limited. Some steam-powered warships were built, but no ironclads. Some fatuous citizens even believed that merchantmen in an emergency could be converted into capital ships. And the main appeal for an enlargement of the Marine Corps was made on the basis that since so many foreigners composed the crews of our warships, more marines were needed aboard as guards.[66]

In the early navy there was a prejudice against training sailors anywhere but at sea. The need for more intensive and systematic education and training ashore for the aspiring young naval officer had been seen since the days of John Paul Jones. Before the Mexican War, the hit-or-miss method had been to give a smattering of training aboard receiving ships and cruising vessels at sea or at naval stations. Three informal naval schools were set up in the 1820s at Boston, New York, and Norfolk to give casual instruction between cruises to midshipmen volunteers, and a fourth school was established at Philadelphia in 1839.

The need for a larger and more comprehensive and technical school was realized after 1839 when the first funds were authorized for steam warships and after the notorious *Somers* affair in 1842. Shortly after the famous historian and experienced educator, George Bancroft, became secretary of the navy in 1845, he moved effectively to establish a naval academy. He asked for a report from four of the professors at the navy school in Philadelphia on their procedures and instruction, and received another more detailed survey from Samuel Marcy and Henry H. Lockwood on how the Military Academy at West Point operated. In August 1845 Bancroft secured the transfer from the army to the navy of Fort Severn, at Annapolis, Maryland, an old fortification, including nine buildings.

Commander Franklin Buchanan was appointed its first superintendent, and he soon drew up a plan for its operation. The United States Naval Academy was formally opened on 10 October 1845 with seven professors and a group of midshipmen ranging in age from thirteen to twenty-eight. The original plan was to give the middies a year's instruction at Annapolis and send them to sea for three years; then they would come back to the Academy for their promotion examinations. Among the courses taken were mathematics, navigation, English, geography, Spanish or French, ordnance, gunnery, steam mechanics, chemistry, natural philosophy, optics, and astronomy.

By the end of the Mexican War the smoothly operating academy had produced ninety officers. It was reorganized after hostilities, and in 1851 a four-year program of instruction was instituted. Summer cruises were begun—a custom that still remains. As with West Point, so too the Naval Academy would supply many of the officers of the Union and Confederate services afloat in the Civil War.[67]

More spectacular was the opening of Japan to western trade in 1853–1854 by Commodore Matthew C. Perry, possibly the most important semidiplomatic mission ever given an American naval officer. By threatening the use of the superior force of his warships, yet maintaining patience, flexibility, and an open mind, Perry brilliantly accomplished this sensitive and significant assignment.[68]

THE UNITED STATES ARMY, in the period between the Mexican and Civil Wars, suffered the customary peacetime frustrations of inadequate funding by a suspicious and parsimonious Congress. In 1850, for example, Congress authorized a force of 12,927; actually, there were but 10,763 troops scattered across the country in some one hundred posts. Nor were the native Americans easily pacified. There were no less than twenty-two Indian wars during the 1850s. Also, the army in the West was hampered by having to make do with an inferior mounted infantry instead of being allowed true cavalry.[69]

One of America's ablest peacetime secretaries of war was Jefferson Davis, who held the position for four years during the administration of President Franklin Pierce. Born in Kentucky, Davis graduated twenty-third in the West Point 1828 class of thirty-three and was humane in his treatment of Chief Black Hawk in the Indian war of 1832. He resigned from the army in 1835 and became a member of the United States House of Representatives, then a Mississippi planter, and colonel in command of the First Mississippi Rifles regiment in the Mexican War. Davis won signal honors in this war and was wounded at Buena Vista. In 1847 he was appointed to the United States Senate and became chairman of the Committee on Military Affairs before he later accepted the post of secretary of war in the Pierce cabinet in 1853. Davis was a capable man, courtly in manner, with a strong sense of duty. Yet to all but a small coterie of close friends, he often appeared cold, unbending, a marblelike figure, reserved and unapproachable.[70]

As secretary, Davis not only pushed the army's survey of railroad routes, but boldly experimented with the use of camels in the southwest. Undeterred by lack of conspicuous success in this venture, he helped engineer the Gadsden Purchase of 1854, which gave the United States the Mesilla Valley, an oblong square of land containing some 20 million acres in what is now the southern part of New Mexico and Arizona.[71]

Davis was interested in more effective western patrols and pressed, unsuccessfully, for true light cavalry, for a regular army of 27,818, and for new weapons; but he had to settle in 1855 for an authorized force of 17,867 troops and for the mounted infantry. In addition, he supported the impressive construction work being done by Capt. Montgomery C. Meigs on the great dome and wings of the Capitol building in Washington and in building the Washington aqueduct.[72]

Perhaps Davis's most significant action as secretary was to send an American mission to observe the Crimean War in Europe. One member, young George B. McClellan, remained in Europe for some months after observing the siege of Sevastopol and wrote a comprehensive, invaluable study of European military arts, institutions, weapons, fortifications, and practices.[73]

However, the secretary was less successful in his relations with General in Chief Scott. Both these leaders behaved in a jealous and petty way toward each other. Determined to retain his superior position over Scott, Davis wrote Old Fuss and Feathers: "Your petulance, characteristic egotism and recklessness of accusation have imposed on me the task of unveiling some of your deformities," which, he charged, included "querulousness, insubordination, greed of lucre and want of truth." Never one to recoil from such goading, Scott replied in kind: "My silence, under the new provocation, has been the result, first, of pity, and next forgetfulness. Compassion is always due to an enraged imbecile, who lays about him in blows which hurt only himself. . . ." Nonetheless, Davis's many strong points as secretary of war far outweighed his few minor lapses, and he left the office stronger and the army better off than when he accepted the post.[74]

Before the decade ended, a final contretemps occurred in the West, this time a near-war in 1857–1858 against the Mormons. Under the firm, dynamic leadership of men like Brigham Young, the Mormons established a viable settlement at Salt Lake, in Utah Territory. Certain of their customs, particularly polygamy, ran counter to the laws of the United States, and a military force was ordered to move there to impel them to modify their practices. A remarkable march through terrible weather and against discouraging physical conditions was made by ultimately some 3,000 troops. They were under the inspired leadership of Bvt. Brig. Gen. Albert Sidney Johnston, who was graduated eighth of forty-one cadets in the West Point class of 1826 that included the later Civil War Generals Silas Casey and Samuel P. Heintzelman. Johnston had served in the Black Hawk and Mexican Wars, and had been secretary of war for the Republic of Texas. Zachary Taylor called Johnston "the best soldier I ever commanded," and he was described by Winfield Scott as "a godsend to the army and the country."

Despite Mormon raids and intense opposition, Johnston moved from Fort Leavenworth via Fort Kearny, Fort Laramie, and South Pass before encamping at Fort Bridger and finally entering Salt Lake City. Valuable assistance was rendered to Johnston by the capable governor, Alfred Cumming, who had been Indian affairs superintendent on the upper Missouri, and by a Pennsylvania lawyer, Thomas L. Kane, who knew the Mormons from previous associations with them. A settlement was finally arrived at between the antagonists. While Young remained head of the Church of the Latter Day Saints, the civil governor was respected, as were the laws. This wise, though delayed settlement enabled wagon trains, mails, and settlers to resume peacefully their treks from the Missouri. Now, westward the course of empire could thrust its way to the shores of the Pacific.[75]

THE PERIOD in American military affairs from 1845 to the outbreak of the Civil War was not merely the heyday of the colorful and socially significant militia organizations like the Zouaves, who attracted attention with their precise marching and picturesque Oriental-type uniforms. It also marked the coming of age of the regular army and navy so far as standardized procedures, weapons, techniques, and officers' duties were concerned. These seemingly dull and routine achievements, despite many disappointments and temporary setbacks, paid off in the nation's successful war against Mexico and in the other activities that demanded the time and attention of civilian leaders and men in officers' uniform. That the war south of the border would be a rehearsal for deadly civil conflict in the 1860s could hardly have been anticipated by many citizens or brothers-in-arms in the 1840s. Yet the great war for the Union would stamp American martial prowess upon the republic for all time. It would be hailed not only as the most dramatic and significant happening in the history of the United States as an independent nation, but would be described by no less a statesman and wartime leader than Winston Churchill as one of the most dignified and ennobling events in the history of the English-speaking peoples.

A Search for Generals

I had no opportunity to test my machinery; to move it around and see whether it would work smoothly or not. There was not a man there who had ever maneuvered troops in large bodies. . . . I wanted very much, a little time; all of us wanted it, we did not have a bit of it.

IRVIN McDOWELL

 STORM CENTER was at staid, sleepy, moss-festooned, Charleston, South Carolina. When Robert Anderson's small garrison of some seventy-seven soldiers occupied Fort Sumter in the center of the harbor on the evening of 26 December 1860, these Federals found a five-sided, two-and-one-half-story brick fortification not yet completed. As the secession winter of 1860–1861 moved toward spring, seven states of the deep South were already out of the Union and most other national forts and property located in the South were in Confederate hands. Fort Sumter and, to a much lesser extent, the neutralized Fort Pickens at Pensacola, Florida, became a vital symbol in the struggle for moral ascendency between Abraham Lincoln's Union government and Jefferson Davis's Confederacy.[1]

Lincoln, in his magnificent first inaugural address, offered the South an olive branch, as had James Buchanan in his last weeks in office. Lincoln stated he would continue "to hold, occupy, and possess [he did not say repossess] the property and places belonging to the [federal] government." But when the Confederate government at Montgomery, Alabama, demanded the surrender of Fort Sumter, Lincoln determined not only to resist but to send a relief expedition to Charleston harbor. The president in Washington did not maneuver the South into firing the first shot at Sumter, but he was determined to preserve the Union at any hazard and made certain that if a first shot were to come, the Confederates would fire it. After a thirty-four-hour bloodless bombardment beginning on 12 April 1861 by some fifty-five hundred Confederate troops under Pierre Gustave Toutant Beauregard, Anderson capitulated and marched out of Sumter with full honors of war. Both sections issued calls for troops, and the states of Virginia, North Carolina, Tennessee, and Arkansas seceded from the Union and joined the Confederacy.[2]

With total war the policy of both sections, the qualifications of the two rival presidents and commanders in chief came into sharper focus. Of the two, the Southerner seemed to have more impressive credentials based on his creditable military experiences before 1861; the best that many of Lincoln's friends hoped for was a mediocre administration.[3]

Unlike many presidents of the United States, the tall, brooding man who came out of the prairies to save the Union was essentially inexperienced in military matters. He had been elected captain of an Illinois militia company during the Black Hawk War of 1832, but his few weeks on campaign had been ill starred. He was placed under arrest in one instance for discharging a weapon in camp, and on another occasion he was arrested and impelled to wear an enormous wooden sword—a badge of derision—for allowing his undisciplined men to go off on a drinking spree. At no time had he seen action or the enemy. Lincoln always belittled his brief career as a soldier. Nor had his reputation been heightened by his surreptitious arrival in Washington like a thief in the night for his inauguration. Although untutored in military matters, as chief executive Lincoln, though occasionally slow to learn from experience early in the war, had by patience, observation, and fine common sense become a consummate war director by 1863.[4]

On the other hand, Confederate President Davis was a West Point graduate, a hero of the Mexican War, an able secretary of war in the 1850s, and an influential United States senator from Mississippi. Davis thought himself a peerless commander in chief. He made the mistake of trusting others so little that he felt compelled to handle too many petty details when he should have delegated authority. Although he had five different men at one time or another as Confederate secretaries of war, Davis was really his own secretary much of the time. And he was his own general in chief, too, not naming anyone to that vital position until the final few weeks of the war. In short, Davis was never able to erect a suitable Confederate high command structure. Despite undeniable and praiseworthy characteristics and talents, he was flawed by his impatience with contradiction; his lack of perception, tact, and inner harmony; his excessive pride; and by his hypersensitivity to criticism. As commander in chief of the gray-clad hosts, he failed in several ways.[5]

At the secretary-of-war level, Lincoln was served by two men during the war: one largely incompetent; the other, useful in some ways, but limited and a liability in others. The president's first secretary of war, the sixty-one-year-old Simon Cameron of Pennsylvania, was strictly a political appointment. This native of Lancaster County had been newspaper editor, state printer, contractor, wealthy ironmonger and banker, Indian Commissioner, United States senator, and political machine boss in his home state. As war secretary from March 1861 to his ouster in January 1862 he managed badly. Although he stayed out of strategic matters, he dispensed military and civil positions and army contracts in a lavish and notorious fashion, and fraud and corruption became widespread. Cameron did not line his own pockets, but he could not or would not prevent others from so doing, and shoddy military equipment was purchased at outrageously high prices. It was little wonder that before his removal by Lincoln, Cameron was formally censured by the United States House of Representatives.[6]

Edwin M. Stanton, former attorney general in Buchanan's cabinet, replaced Cameron and was retained by Lincoln as secretary of war throughout the conflict. Born in Steubenville, Ohio, on 19 December 1814, Stanton attended Kenyon College and became an able and well-known lawyer. His great energy and capacity for sustained mental labor brought more businesslike methods to the war department and greater supervision of contracts. A man of passionate devotion to the Union and abolition causes, Stanton eliminated graft and scandal. "Old Mars," as Lincoln called him, moved quickly to surmount any delays and obstructions in the war effort. He took most of his meals at the War Department, where he also slept. On rare occasions the "Black Terrier" could be entertaining and companionable, and it is likely that his extraordinary exertions as secretary of war led to his comparatively early death in 1869.[7]

But these useful characteristics were perhaps more than balanced by a number of disagreeable and unfortunate traits. Stanton often made snap judgments without sufficient evidence and clung to them with grim tenacity even when shown to be wrong. He knew not how to apologize for obvious errors and injustices and was coarse and brusque in his dealings with the patient president. He was capable of monstrous prejudice and vindictiveness, and disliked professional army officers, especially West Pointers. He was grossly ignorant and contemptuous of military science and could be impatient, arrogant, and irascible. He was an implacable intriguer of great deviousness and duplicity. By nature an intimidator, he was basically a timid man, and only rarely could he be made to back down by men of strong will power and character, such as George B. McClellan, Ethan Allen Hitchcock, and Gideon Welles. Stanton's quest for vast and often unnecessary powers was insatiable. He knew nothing of strategy and grand strategy and never came to understand their nature. A more self-righteous and militarily untalented superior to the top generals in blue would have been difficult to find; yet he remained in office until well after Appomattox.[8]

Of the five men who successively held the position of secretary of war in Davis's cabinet, the first two—Leroy Pope Walker and Judah P. Benjamin— were largely incompetent, although Benjamin did perform with some distinction as attorney general. The third, George W. Randolph, who had some combat military experience early in the war as a brigadier general, was fairly able, although not appreciated at the time. James A. Seddon of Virginia, who succeeded Randolph and served as secretary of war from November 1862 until February 1865, possessed considerable ability. He urged concentration of Confederate forces and gave the trans-Appalachian western theater of operations its full due. But of course Jefferson Davis was largely his own war secretary, except for fairly routine office matters. The successor to Seddon, Maj. Gen. John C. Breckinridge, showed moderate capacity, but he served for only the final few weeks of the war.[9]

In the naval high command, Lincoln had a trusted and able cabinet member in Connecticut's Gideon Welles, who served as secretary of the navy throughout Old Abe's and Andrew Johnson's administrations. Born in 1802, Welles attended Norwich Academy and became part owner and editor of the

Hartford Times. A Jacksonian Democrat, he served in the Connecticut legislature, as a postmaster, and as Chief of the Bureau of Provisions and Clothing in the Navy Department. He became a moderate Republican and was the New England man in Lincoln's cabinet. Out of touch with naval matters for many years, Welles swiftly got on top of his job and was aided throughout by a capable assistant, Gustavus Vasa Fox. Welles was an uncanny judge of men, steady and resolute, and a tower of strength in the Lincoln administration. The president consulted him increasingly on matters other than naval. Welles never hesitated to seek expert advice from naval officers or from Fox, but these men soon saw that Welles was master of the department. He was bald but wore a wig, and his white beard reached down to his chest. He was known as "Father Neptune" or "The Old Man of the Sea." Although somewhat self-righteous, Welles was honest, straightforward, and competent. Before his death in 1878 he returned to the Democratic fold.[10]

Jefferson Davis's secretary of the navy was the talented Stephen R. Mallory of Florida, forty-eight years old, who had been interested in ships and maritime matters since his early boyhood in Key West. A customs inspector and lawyer there, Mallory had been sent to the United States Senate in 1851, where he became chairman of the Naval Affairs Committee. On the whole this Confederate secretary of the navy got along well with Davis (who knew little of naval affairs), who consulted him on other matters. Not a genius, but a man of common sense, the reliable Mallory had self-confidence, a wide breadth of view, and grew with his responsibilities.[11]

While Davis had no Confederate general in chief until Robert E. Lee was named to that post near the end of the war, Lincoln inherited in that federal position the seventy-five-year-old Winfield Scott, the "Giant of Three Wars," who was older than the capital itself. This magnificent soldier from Virginia had served masterfully in the War of 1812 and the Mexican War, as well as on a number of sensitive semidiplomatic and political missions. He had a few petty foibles, such as being a fussy gourmet and a fastidious dresser, but these were on the surface and insignificant. While keen in mind in 1861, Scott was infirm in body, and he still carried two British bullets within his 350-pound frame of six feet five inches. He was practically incapacitated by gout, vertigo, and dropsy; a derrick was required to hoist him onto the back of a horse, which he was now unable to ride, to witness reviews. He often had to rest on an office sofa and occasionally fell asleep while conferring with people. Yet he developed the so-called Anaconda Plan of grand strategy to defeat the Confederacy by strangulation. This invaluable officer's days as Union general in chief were numbered, and on 1 November 1861 he would retire in favor of young George B. McClellan, and go to West Point, where he died in 1866, revered by all.[12]

THE TERRAIN over which the contending armies would move was largely wooded, poor for large-scale cavalry charges or for massed artillery. With a few exceptions, such as Gettysburg, Antietam, and Fredericksburg, most of the great battles of the Civil War were fought in heavily forested arenas. The Appalachian Mountains effectively divided military campaigns into eastern and western theaters of operations. As they were in the Colonial and Revolutionary wars, so too from 1861 to 1865 strategic planning and army movements were based often on use and control of great water avenues of advance such as the Mississippi, Cumberland, Tennessee, and Potomac Rivers, and on the capture or holding of such great river ports and posts as Nashville, Louisville, Chattanooga, Vicksburg, Harper's Ferry, Fredericksburg, Henry, Donelson, Pittsburg Landing, or Port Hudson. In short, the North had to conquer a vast empire—a challenge that had defeated the British in the American Revolutionary War.[13]

In comparing the two rival sections, one should note that there were twenty-three Union states pitted against eleven Confederate; that there were 22 million people in the North and just 9 million (including 3.5 million Negro slaves) in the South; that the Federal states had heavy advantages in railroad mileage, a merchant marine, and industrial and financial resources; and that Lincoln brought into the field some 1,556,000 troops (based on the normal three-year standard term of enlistment) as contrasted to the approximately 800,000 that Davis could bring under arms. Despite these Northern advantages, the South was not predestined to defeat; other peoples had won independence against even greater odds. The Confederates possessed the advantages of interior lines, a coastline of some 3,500 miles that seemed to defy blockade, a staunch military tradition that had bulked large in the earlier history of the United States, good generals in high command from the start, the expectation of foreign aid and intervention, and the powerful intangible of fighting for their homes against the invader and for white supremacy.[14]

In weapons and systems to deploy them more effectively, the Civil War was a transitional conflict that ushered in the modern era. It was the first in which a practical machine gun was seen; the first where repeating rifles were used; the first to use railroads as a major means of transporting supplies and large bodies of troops; the first to employ mobile siege artillery mounted on railway cars; the first where extensive trenches and field fortifications were routinely dug and later protected by wire entanglements; the first to use land and naval mines on a large scale; the first where ironclad warships clashed, and the first in which a multimanned submarine sank an enemy warship; the first where widespread organized use was made of military signal service and the telegraph; the first where hospital trains were widely employed; the first where extensive use was made of manned balloons for military reconnaissance; the first where conscription was used on a grand scale, and where voting by servicemen in the field took place in a national election; and the first in which the income tax was levied, and in which combat photography was extensively used.[15]

As war was declared, Washington, D.C., was temporarily isolated by the Confederates who cut telegraph lines and railroads, and troops were desperately needed to guard the federal capital. But this was not easily accomplished. On 19 April 1861 the armed Sixth Massachusetts and the unarmed Twenty-seventh Pennsylvania regiments tried to cross the Baltimore waterfront from one railroad station to another but were attacked by bricks and pistol shots propelled by a secessionist mob. The Massachusetts militiamen were obliged to open fire upon their assailants in self-defense. With the help of the Baltimore police, commanded in person by Mayor George W. Brown (a Southern sympathizer), the citizen-soldiers from the North managed to reach Camden station and entrain for the national capital, after some four of their number and perhaps a dozen of the mob had been killed and others wounded.[16]

Only when political general Benjamin Franklin Butler, in one of his few effective military actions of the war, occupied Annapolis on 22 April and seized control of Baltimore on 13 May was Washington opened up fully to unfettered transportation and communication use by the Federals. Although powerful Fort Monroe, at Old Point Comfort on the tip of the historic peninsula where the York and James Rivers flow into Hampton Roads at the mouth of Chesapeake Bay, was retained by the Union, the extensive Norfolk navy yard across the water was perhaps prematurely evacuated on 20 April and was seized by the Confederates. Two days before, Virginia troops under Thomas

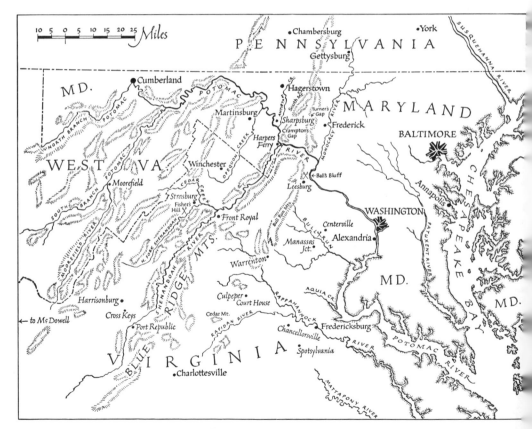

FIG. 7.1. WASHINGTON AND VICINITY

Jonathan Jackson occupied Harper's Ferry, where the Shenandoah River joins the Potomac, and took over the Union's armory and arsenal there.[17]

To assume the strategic offensive and devise a plan of operations that would crush the Confederacy were duties met by Union General in Chief Scott. In a series of telegraphic exchanges on 27 April, 3 May, and 21 May 1861 with George B. McClellan at Cincinnati, in command of Ohio, Indiana, and Illinois troops, Scott evolved the Anaconda Plan. It called for strangulation of the South, with the least possible loss of life and expenditure of money, by a complete naval blockade of the coastline of the Confederacy and a powerful thrust by land and water down the Mississippi River where cordons would be set up. The general in chief was convinced also that it would take at least 300,000 Federal soldiers, three years of grim warfare, and a general of the ability of a James Wolfe to defeat the determined Southerners. While Scott's Anaconda Plan was not formally adopted as a master blueprint, the war was finally won by the North when it fell, willy-nilly, into Old Fuss and Feather's plan of grand strategy.[18]

Although the Confederates were committed to the strategic defensive in overall grand strategy, this would not forestall Davis from approving several "spoiling" forays by gray-clad forces into Northern territory. But the Unionists—largely dominated by the Napoleonic idea of several smashing offensives that would crush the enemy's armies and will to continue the war—felt compelled, by the example of British failure in 1775–1781, to continue and sustain advances into the Confederacy regardless of casualties and consequences. There were few departures by either side from this procedure.

WHILE blue and gray forces were gathering in northern Virginia between Washington and the new Confederate capital of Richmond, one hundred and ten miles apart, the first sustained land operations took place in northwestern Virginia. Young George Brinton McClellan, with approval from Washington but on his own initiative, launched Federal troops to secure that important pro-Union part of the Old Dominion. Born in Philadelphia in 1826, the son of a prominent surgeon, McClellan graduated second in the West Point class of 1846 and won two brevets in the Mexican War. He was sent as an observer to the Crimean War, and his voluminous report on European military practices and institutions won for him a high reputation in the army that was echoed by Scott. McClellan retired from the army in 1857 and became a railway president before he volunteered for service in the Union army when war came. A handsome, blue-eyed man, five feet eight inches in height and muscular in build, McClellan had regular features, dark auburn hair, mustache and goatee, and he was a magnificent horseman.[19]

The general's character has baffled many observers and historians. "McClellan is to me one of the mysteries of the war," declared U. S. Grant after Appomattox. Cautious and circumspect as a commander, "Little Mac" was a perfectionist and often magnified his own difficulties without making allowances for similar problems facing his opponents. Yet he had vast military and administrative knowledge and skill, was an unexcelled organizer and molder of armies, and had a sure grasp of strategic probabilities. McClellan was occasionally tactless with his superiors and sometimes failed to appreciate the political necessities of the moment. However, he was a first-rate engineer and artillery officer and had few peers as a defensive fighter. He was one of the most popular generals ever to command American troops and was respected by his Confederate counterparts, especially Robert E. Lee.[20]

The countryside in northwestern Virginia into which McClellan vigorously projected his forces—some 10,000 men in all—was wooded and mountainous, with numerous streams coursing through the brush. His strategic plan was simply to close with the enemy, wherever found, and defeat him. At the covered bridge at Philippi on 3 June 1861, in the first land battle of the war, McClellan surprised the Confederates in a small engagement and sent them reeling backward so swiftly that the affair became known as the "Philippi races." On 11 July in the main battle of the campaign at Rich Mountain, Little Mac hesitated momentarily but threw William S. Rosecrans in a turning movement against the enemy flank and rear. Defeated, with the loss of 553 captured against only 46 total Federal casualties, the Southerners who escaped fell back in rout to Carrick's Ford. There, the gray commander, Robert Garnett, fell mortally wounded in a futile effort to extricate his rear guard, and the Confederates were again trounced by McClellan on 13 July with another 80 casualties.[21]

Although there would be a few minor operations later, McClellan's energetic campaign and three victories paved the way for the creation of the new state of West Virginia, which entered the Union in 1863. The general's triumphs elicited from Scott, his immediate superior, this encomium: "The General-in-Chief, and what is more, the Cabinet, including the President, are charmed with your activity, valor, and consequent success. . . . We do not doubt that you will in due time sweep the rebels from Virginia, but we do not mean to precipitate you as you are fast enough." McClellan would soon be called from the West Virginia mountains to the nation's capital to confront a more dangerous situation.[22]

When Fort Sumter was bombarded, Lincoln, Cameron, and Scott sought a field commander for the main Union army in the East that was about to gather around Washington. They offered the command to Col. Robert E. Lee; in an agonizing personal decision, Lee felt obliged to turn down the tempting proffer. After considering a neutral role, Lee accepted command of all Virginia armed forces and still later was made a four-star general in the Confederate army and named military adviser (but not general in chief) to Davis, on duty in the Confederate War Department in Richmond.[23]

The son of "Light Horse Harry" Lee, Robert E. Lee was fifty-four years old in 1861 and already had a distinguished military career. Brilliant as a cadet at West Point, one of Scott's ablest subordinates in the War with Mexico, superintendent of the military academy at West Point, he excelled in every assignment ever given him. Imbued with the ideas of Jomini, as were most leaders on both sides, Lee was bolder than most. Almost saintly in character and a man of exceptional personal traits, the splendid-looking Lee was an outstanding leader. But he was also a hard-nosed realist who had a brilliant yet practical mind. He made few mistakes during the Civil War. His high reputation has survived across the span of more than a century, and he remains one of the most revered of Americans.[24]

On 6 May 1861 Lee ordered a small force to Manassas Junction, some twenty-six miles west-southwest of Washington, where the Orange and Alexandria Railroad was joined by the Manassas Gap Railroad from the Shenandoah Valley. This force, soon to be commanded by Beauregard, was augmented and took up a position along the Bull Run, a few miles north of Manassas. Although President Davis was determined to remain generally on the defensive, perhaps the Confederacy's best chance to win would have been to assume an early offensive. The graycoats would still be standing on the defensive at Manassas in July 1861 when blue-clad Federals would appear from the north to challenge them.[25]

If Scott had very limited influence in helping shape Union grand strategy concerning the forts in South Carolina, the general who was named to command the main Northern field army in the east had even less. This individual, Irvin McDowell, was humorless and conscientious but had a rough temper and gargantuan appetite that attracted unfavorable attention. The forty-two-year-old soldier who assumed command of the Union forces around Washington on 27 May 1861 had only one minor line command in his previous military career; most of his other army assignments after West Point had been staff appointments, and he had been Scott's assistant adjutant general just prior to receiving the important field position. The general in chief was a little reluctant to name McDowell to this command but was encouraged to do so partly through an intrigue by the secretary of the treasury, Salmon P. Chase, who, like McDowell, was an Ohio man.[26]

Directed to advance in mid-July with about thirty thousand men against what would be a slightly smaller Confederate force at Bull Run, "General McDowell spread his maps on the table, and demonstrated his plan with . . . clearness and precision." As actually carried out, McDowell would attempt to envelop the enemy's left flank while conducting a holding operation in front. "General McDowell," boomed Scott, "that is as good a plan of battle as I ever saw upon paper." It now remained for the Federal field commander to translate the design into successful action.[27]

Contending forces in the Shenandoah Valley to the west were part and parcel of the main contest near Manassas. The incompetent, elderly Robert Patterson, who finally reoccupied Harper's Ferry, was in command of some eighteen thousand Federals in the northern valley near Martinsburg and was clearly instructed by Scott to apply heavy pressure on Joseph E. Johnston's nine thousand Confederates to prevent the graycoats from slipping away and joining Beauregard along the Bull Run. But the addle-headed septuagenarian was simply not up to this task, although he blatantly proclaimed to the general in chief that he was "fixing" Johnston's Southerners near Winchester by feints and demonstrations. In reality, he was doing nothing effective, and Johnston easily bluffed an attack, gave Patterson the slip on 18 July, and moved his force to Manassas just in time to cooperate with Beauregard in checking McDowell's advance. As military historian R. M. Johnston avers,

"A critique of Patterson's generalship belongs less to the domain of military art than to that of musical comedy."[28]

McDowell pushed off reluctantly from Washington and Alexandria on 16 July in warm and sunny weather. Two days were taken by the straggling, raw troops to cover the twenty-six miles to Bull Run where Beauregard had judiciously stationed his Southerners. There on 18 July a Union probe at Blackburn's Ford on the Confederate right was repulsed by James Longstreet. McDowell squandered two precious days in overly elaborate reconnaissances, thereby giving Johnston's troops time to arrive from the valley. Had the Federal commander been able to bring himself to attack on either 19 or 20 July, he would probably have been successful. As it was, his initial assaults on the morning of 21 July against Beauregard's left wing gained ground and threatened the Confederate position. But a stand by Stonewall Jackson on the Henry House Hill, the loss of two Union regular artillery batteries coupled with the exhaustion of the blue soldiers, and the timely arrival at the eleventh hour of the last of Johnston's troops directly on the Union right flank led to the breakdown of McDowell's offensive and the withdrawal of his forces by midafternoon. Unfortunately, their retreat back to Washington developed into a partial rout. The total Union loss in the First Battle of Bull Run (or Manassas) was 2,708 killed, wounded, and missing (including prisoners), while the Confederates suffered aggregate losses of 1,981 men.[29]

On the Union side, "The wonder . . . is not that [McDowell] should not have done more," declared *New York Times* war correspondent William Swinton, "but that he did so much; and the spirit of forbearance and alacrity with which he entered upon and carried through his trying task, entitles him to great credit." This is shown in his official report, which military historian R. M. Johnston reports, "is on the whole a straightforward and honest confession of failure, very little colored or distorted in an endeavor to evade responsibility" at the moment. "As a general," Johnston goes on, "he proved faithful to his duty, courageous, painstaking; but it cannot be said that his abilities extended further." McDowell was soon superseded in command by McClellan.[30]

WHEN it was perceived that the conflict would last longer than anticipated, both the Federal and Confederate governments turned to raising the massive volunteer armies that were to fight the war for the next four years. Local citizens of prominence and means organized regiments that were initially equipped by the states and then mustered into the service of the Union or Confederate government. As the war dragged on and casualties mounted fearfully, both sides resorted to the draft to fill the ranks. The first Confederate conscription law was passed on 16 April 1862, making liable for military service all white men between the ages of eighteen and thirty-five (later, seventeen to fifty). The Washington government, because of Secretary of War Stanton's shortsightedness, did not pass its first draft law until 7 July 1862 and this was so ineffective that it had to be supplanted with another one on 3 March 1863. White males (soon also Negroes) up to forty-five years of age were liable, although one could evade military service by hiring a substitute or paying a commutation fee. Along with this policy that allowed men to buy their way out of the draft, another evil, that of paying bounties, with all their abuses, was never overcome. The Lincoln government did not make proper use of the regular army as cadre, and only in the last few weeks of the war did the Confederate government finally agree to permit blacks to serve in its armies. In short, both contending parties had grave difficulties in coping with the excessive growth of mobilization on a grand scale.[31]

While Joseph E. Johnston organized the Confederate army of some fifty thousand at Manassas and Centerville, McClellan worked eighteen hours a day the remainder of the summer and the fall and winter of 1861 to bring order out of chaos around Washington. Unlike Johnston, who soon fell into disputes with Davis, McClellan got along well with the administration and the Congress at first. Little Mac was a brilliant organizer, administrator, drillmaster, and disciplinarian, and his molding of the truly superb Army of the Potomac won for him encomiums from that day to this. In addition, he constructed some thirty-three miles of powerful fortifications on both sides of the Potomac to defend the Federal capital. But he would not be stampeded into an advance against the enemy army and Richmond until he was ready; thus strained relations began to develop between McClellan and the administration, including the general in chief.[32]

In the fall of 1861 misfortune befell the Federals, just as many newspapers and politicians were again chanting, "On to Richmond." McClellan authorized a reconnaissance in force up the Potomac River under the overall supervision of Charles P. Stone. The latter was ill served when one of his subordinates, the gallant Edward Baker, rashly crossed the river at Ball's Bluff, near Leesburg, on 21 October to scout out the Confederate forces on the south bank. Counterattacked by a superior number of graycoats under Nathan G. ("Shanks") Evans, Baker was mortally wounded and 921 of his men were casualties when pushed into the Potomac at the bluff. The Radical Republicans in Congress were especially outraged because Baker, a political appointee in rank, had served in the Senate. The Ball's Bluff fiasco set in motion investigations by the Joint Congressional Committee on the Conduct of the War, which not only made the capable Stone the scapegoat by throwing him into prison for 189 days, but would continue to hale generals before it and encourage the denunciation of conservative Democratic generals like McClellan, Buell, and Meade and promote pro-Radical tenets. The committee seriously hampered Lincoln, his leading commanders, and the Union war effort.[33]

The minor military debacle at Ball's Bluff showed a certain looseness in the Federal command and that officers were inexperienced in handling units. It probably influenced McClellan to postpone until the following spring any major invasion of Virginia by his Army of the Potomac.[34]

During the summer and autumn of 1861 McClellan had increasing trouble with his superior, General in Chief Scott. Some of it was caused by Little Mac's tactlessness, but a great deal came from Scott's hypersensitivity, punctiliousness, and insistence that the young general clear matters pertaining to his

Department of the Potomac through the commanding general. During the summer of 1861 Scott tried twice, unsuccessfully, to retire; finally on 1 November Lincoln agreed reluctantly that the magnificent old soldier might step down. Scott hoped Henry W. Halleck would succeed him; instead, Lincoln named the thirty-five-year-old McClellan to the onerous post of general in chief, in addition to his command of the Army of the Potomac. On 3 November McClellan saw Old Fuss and Feathers off for his retirement home at West Point at 4:00 A.M. at the Washington railroad station and was moved to write his wife: ". . . it may be that some distant day I, too, shall totter away from Washington, a worn-out soldier, with naught to do but make my peace with God. The sight of this morning was a lesson to me which I hope not soon to forget."[35]

Now highly involved in grand strategy planning, McClellan directed Halleck at St. Louis to tighten up administration of that department, previously commanded by John C. Frémont, and to prepare for operations down the Mississippi. The new general in chief, pressured by Lincoln's concern for the pro-Union folk of eastern Tennessee and his desire to keep the border states in line, instructed Don Carlos Buell, in command in Kentucky, to ready his army to move toward Knoxville to aid these nonslaveholding pro-Union elements. Buell, a stern, cold, competent but cautious West Pointer and Mexican War veteran from Ohio, explained that inadequate transportation would make it well nigh impossible for him to plunge into eastern Tennessee. Instead, he wisely urged that his army be permitted to advance toward Nashville in the center of the state, while Halleck's forces moved up the Tennessee and Cumberland rivers. In addition to the armies of Halleck and Buell, McClellan sought to coordinate the movements of other Union armies, including his own and those of Benjamin F. Butler and Thomas W. Sherman, in order to advance almost simultaneously against the enemy.[36]

Meanwhile, across the Appalachians, Jefferson Davis had given Confederate supreme command to a first-rate soldier, Albert Sidney Johnston, who was in Kentucky with some forty thousand troops trying to hold a long line running eastward from Columbus on the Mississippi River through Bowling Green to a point near Cumberland Gap on the east. Fifty-eight years old in early 1862, Johnston was a man of strong physique, magnetic personality, commanding presence, and wide experience. After graduating from West Point he served as commander of Texan forces and later as secretary of war of the Republic of Texas. He served on the fringes of the Mexican War, received the colonelcy of the Second Cavalry in 1855, and won distinction in the pacification of the Mormons in the late 1850s. The Civil War found him in a command post on the Pacific coast. Before he resigned his commission to join the Confederacy, he scrupulously returned to the United States government all posts and equipment under his command as well as all soldiers remaining loyal to the Union.[37]

But Johnston faced an impossible assignment against heavy odds once the Federals moved in force. He could only remain on the strategic defensive. On the Union side, General in Chief McClellan was finally able to get some action from Buell and Halleck. Buell advanced George H. Thomas, a Virginia-born Mexican War veteran of cautious but hard-fighting instincts, into eastern

FIG. 7.2. THE MISSISSIPPI THEATER

Kentucky, and in January 1862, near Cumberland Gap, his men defeated a Confederate force. In the interim Halleck directed his subordinate, Ulysses S. Grant, to move up the Tennessee and Cumberland rivers where, with the help of the navy under Flag Officer Andrew H. Foote, Forts Henry and Donelson were captured in February. Hampered by a divided command at Fort Donelson, the Confederate commander, Simon Bolivar Buckner, who had been Grant's West Point roommate, actually broke out of the encircling Federal lines but felt impelled to fall back into the fort to secure neglected supplies. He was again bottled up and, after losing about 2,000 battle casualties, felt obliged to surrender unconditionally his remaining 15,000 troops to Grant, who had lost approximately 2,832 men out of about 27,000 available.[38]

Meanwhile in the trans-Mississippi Southwest, gold, silver, and the desire for a Southern California port for supplies and a haven for sea raiders were the lures that beckoned the Confederates into the ill-starred invasion of the Union's Department of New Mexico in the winter of 1861–1862. Defending this vast area for the Union, with a total of 3,810 troops, was Edward R. S. Canby, forty-four years old and a native of Kentucky, assisted by the legendary Kit Carson. A former subordinate of Canby's, Henry Hopkins Sibley, a thirty-five-year-old Louisianan who invented the tent that still bears his name, was the leader of Confederate forces. Initially some 3,700 men mainly from Texas, the Confederates were severely reduced in numbers by pneumonia and smallpox. The ailing (psychosomatic?) Sibley moved up the Rio Grande from Fort Bliss (El Paso) and on 21 February 1862 fought and defeated in battle at Valverde, near Fort Craig, some of Canby's soldiers. Approximately 263 Federals were casualties as against Southern losses of 196. Sibley captured Albuquerque and Santa Fe shortly thereafter and near the end of March engaged the Union garrison of nearby Fort Union at places known variously as Pigeon's Ranch, Johnson's Ranch, Apache Canyon, and La Glorieta Pass, with the Federals coming out ahead. Having lost most of his train of supply wagons, Sibley was obliged to retreat all the way back to San Antonio, pursued part way in a leisurely fashion by Canby, who said he could not supply and feed large numbers of prisoners. Sibley lost some 1,700 men and had left only 7 of his original 337 supply wagons. It was a total fiasco for the Confederates, and they were not able to mount another serious invasion of the Southwest during the war.[39]

Back on the Washington front, Union affairs were proceeding less smoothly than west of the Appalachians. Beginning in January and running into March 1862, General in Chief McClellan became involved in increasingly strenuous debates with Lincoln and with the hostile Stanton over what route of advance the Army of the Potomac should take in its campaign against the Confederate force under Johnston defending Richmond. Little Mac wished to delay an advance until his army was prepared for a sustained invasion, and he wanted to move by water via the Potomac River and Chesapeake Bay to a point near Fort Monroe in order to capitalize on a short land advance toward the enemy capital. The president and secretary of war held out for an immediate advance, regardless of whether the army was ready or not, along the so-called overland route through Manassas or Fredericksburg toward Rich-

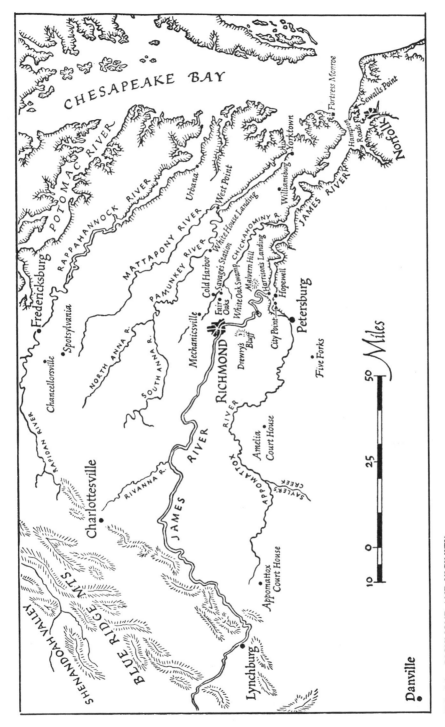

FIG. 7.3. RICHMOND AND VICINITY

mond. Although finally allowing McClellan his water route, the commander in chief abruptly relieved him as general in chief (no one else was named to that vital post for four months), cut by one-third the size of his invading army, and insisted that the offensive begin in March 1862. Suddenly on 8 and 9 March, Johnston, possibly through unintentional leaks in information from Washington, withdrew the Confederate Army of Northern Virginia from its forward places at Centreville and Manassas to positions behind the Rappahannock River, where it would be in a better location to move swiftly to defend Richmond.[40]

McClellan's Peninsula campaign was a close thing. Moving with about ninety-five thousand men, he captured Yorktown on 4 May after a month's siege and then slogged up through the mud and heaviest rains in twenty years to a point some four miles from Richmond, after having shaken the enemy loose from their redoubts in the Confederate delaying action at Williamsburg on 5 May. All the while McClellan was engaged in a sharp, running battle with Lincoln and Stanton over details of movements, reinforcements, and coordination with other Federal forces scampering about the countryside of northern Virginia.[41]

Joe Johnston and his army on the Confederate side were surmounting a number of thorny problems brought on in part by the strained relations between the general and President Davis. In command of some 74,000 troops and aware that the nearly 100,000 Federals were split by the swollen Chickahominy River near Richmond, Johnston maneuvered twenty-three of his twenty-seven brigades against McClellan's left wing and attacked heavily on 31 May in the Battle of Fair Oaks or Seven Pines. The Union left wing was hurled back almost a mile. McClellan, suffering badly from malaria and neuralgia, arose from his sick bed and threw in timely reinforcements that finally checked the Confederate advance that day. Johnston was severely wounded by a shell fragment in his chest, and Robert E. Lee was trotted out from his desk in Richmond to assume command of the Army of Northern Virginia, a command he would handle masterfully until the end at Appomattox. The battle was resumed the following day on 1 June, with McClellan's counterattacks throwing back the graycoats to points near their starting place. Lee withdrew the Southern army into the environs and fortifications of the capital. The Confederates at Fair Oaks had lost a total of 6,134 men as compared to 5,031 Northern casualties. McClellan thus maintained his position and inched forward slowly toward Richmond in June.[42]

As the Union commander closed in on Richmond's defenses, he called long and loudly for McDowell's corps at Fredericksburg to be sent posthaste. Lincoln and Stanton finally granted his request and ordered McDowell to begin his march toward the Confederate capital while at the same time staying between the enemy and Washington. On 17 May 1862 the secretary of war sent McClellan an order of momentous import: "[McDowell] is ordered . . . so to operate as to place his left wing in communication with your right wing, and you are instructed to cooperate, so as to establish this communication as soon as possible, by extending your right wing to the north of Richmond." This directive compelled McClellan to expose his right wing northeast of the treacherous Chickahominy, while the administration's insistence on an early advance impelled him at the same time to throw his left wing across that river to the southwest side so as to move against Richmond.[43]

Then Stonewall Jackson appeared in the Shenandoah in his classic Valley campaign. Surging northward, Jackson threatened Harper's Ferry as well as a crossing of the Potomac River. One of the main goals of the Southerners was to menace Washington sufficiently to cause the Lincoln administration to prevent McDowell from joining McClellan, and the president and secretary of war played directly into the hands of the Confederates by panicking and ordering McDowell to halt his movement toward Richmond and move instantly in what proved to be a futile operation to cut off Stonewall's withdrawal southward up the Shenandoah Valley. McClellan correctly appraised the Confederate plan and telegraphed Lincoln on 25 May, "The object of the [enemy] movement is probably to prevent reinforcements being sent me." McClellan's right wing to the northeast of Richmond was anchored in that exposed position by the unrevoked order of his superiors. Jackson defeated and eluded the several small Federal armies, including McDowell's, trying to trap him and marched to join Lee's main army at Richmond, swelling Confederate numbers there to some ninety thousand (the largest force Lee ever commanded and a figure approximated by McClellan).[44]

By the last week of June 1862 all of McClellan's army was on the Richmond (southwest) side of the Chickahominy except for Fitz John Porter's Fifth Corps, which was fixed in its vulnerable position by the orders from Washington. A raid by the dashing Confederate cavalryman, Jeb Stuart, revealed the precarious state of McClellan's right flank and his great supply base at White House on the Pamunkey River. The national commander began sending off some supplies by water to the James River in the event that he might have to change his base to that stream.[45]

Lee seized the initiative from McClellan by attacking the Union right wing at Mechanicsville on 26 June in the start of the great Seven Days Battle. Hurled back there with loss, the Confederates renewed the attack the next day at Gaines's Mill and won their only tactical success in the entire operation. McClellan felt unable to advance toward Richmond with his left wing. Changing his base under extreme pressure in a way that made the movement look like a retreat, the Union commander repulsed the Southern assaults over the next several days at such places at Golding's, Garnett's, Savage's Station, White Oak Swamp, Allen's Farm, and Glendale. And on 1 July at Malvern Hill near the James River, McClellan administered to Lee one of the gray chieftain's worst defeats when the Federals repelled the final bloody and desperate Confederate charges. In his skillful operation, McClellan inflicted 20,614 casualties on Lee while he suffered 15,849 of his own. The Northern army then moved to its supplies at Harrison's Landing.[46]

The Seven Days combat was the greatest series of battles that had ever been fought in the Western Hemisphere up to that time. Lee saved the capital of the Confederacy, but he failed to annihilate McClellan's army or to budge it from the neighborhood of Richmond. "Under ordinary circumstances," Lee admitted in his official report, "the Federal army should have been destroyed." Confederate Gen. D. H. Hill acknowledged that "throughout this campaign we attacked just when and where the enemy wished us to attack." However, while all this and more can be said to McClellan's credit, historian John Codman Ropes asserts that "the moral and political effect of the whole series of movements and battles was entirely to the advantage of the Confederates. . . . The abrupt change of the part played by the Federal general from the role of the invader to that of the retreating and pursued enemy was too dramatic not to arrest general attention."[47]

McClellan urged that his army be reinforced so that it might resume the advance against Richmond. However, following a presidential visit to Harrison's Bar beginning on 7 July, the withdrawal of the Army of the Potomac from the peninsula was ordered—against the strenuous protests of McClellan and all but one of his top generals—on 3 August by Lincoln and by the newly appointed general in chief of the Union armies, Henry Wager Halleck.[48]

ON THE SURFACE Halleck's attainments seemed impressive. After graduation from West Point in 1839, he saw little action in the Mexican War. But he was appointed engineering professor at Harvard (declined), practiced law, wrote books on military science, bitumen, and international law, drew up the state constitution of California, and was head of a railroad and a mining company. Forty-seven years old in 1862, Halleck had an unusually large head and a stoop-shouldered body. He wore chin whiskers and had a double chin, watery eyes, sallow complexion, and a full paunch. He smoked and chewed cigars, was often rude and harsh in manner, and spoke haltingly while he incessantly scratched his elbows. His best talent was converting civilian language into military idiom. Unfortunately for the Federals, "Old Brains" (or as his enemies called him, "Woodenhead") shunned responsibility and was what one might call a moral coward. Lincoln thought him "little more . . . than a first-rate clerk." McClellan called him "the most hopelessly stupid" of men "in high position." Secretary of the Navy Welles's perspicacious summation of Halleck reads as follows: "He has a scholarly intellect and . . . some military acquirements, but his mind is heavy and irresolute. . . . He does not possess originality and . . . he has little real talent. What he has is educational." Welles declared that "Halleck originates nothing, anticipates nothing, to assist others; takes no responsibility, plans nothing, suggests nothing, is good for nothing." Yet Lincoln retained him for a year and a half as general in chief.[49]

While McClellan's Army of the Potomac was withdrawing from the peninsula as swiftly as possible—a necessarily long procedure—a new Union general was named to command the several small forces that had been wandering around in northern Virginia; these had just been amalgamated into what was called the Federal Army of Virginia. This new white hope was Maj. Gen. John Pope, whose father, a judge, had been an acquaintance of Lincoln's. Pope had won two minor victories in the western theater at New Madrid and Island Number Ten and was a friend of Halleck. Erect, soldierly in carriage, with penetrating eyes, Pope's visage was marred somewhat by an often surly and vain expression. He was aggressive, impulsive, and overly confident. This erratic Union commander, according to Henry Villard, had "two very marked failings—first, he talked too much of himself, of what he could do and of what ought to be done; and secondly, he indulged, contrary to good discipline and all propriety, in very free comments upon his superiors and fellow-commanders." Montgomery Blair knew Pope as "a braggart and a liar, with some courage, perhaps, but not much capacity." Welles asserted that "Pope . . . has the reputation among those who know him of being untruthful and wholly unreliable." He also had a rare talent for alienating his subordinate officers.[50]

Pope early revealed alarming ignorance of military probabilities in northern Virginia and reported to the Committee on the Conduct of the War, "I myself doubt very much whether [Lee] will move any of [his] troops in this direction at all." He denounced McClellan and his operations, and said he could march his own army all the way to New Orleans![51]

Once McClellan's army was pulled back from Richmond, which was what Lee wanted, the gray chieftain began his swift move northward to strike Pope before all of McClellan's troops could join him. Splitting his army of some 55,000 into two wings under command of Longstreet and Jackson, Lee directed Stonewall to fall upon Pope's exposed supply base at Manassas Junction and destroy it. This feat was ably accomplished by Jackson on 27 August, who then assumed a strong position near Groveton behind a railroad grading. In a great stew and grossly ignorant of the location of enemy units, Pope, in command of about 70,000 men, launched a series of six rash and inept attacks against Jackson's position on 29 August. All were repulsed with heavy losses. Then Lee with Longstreet's command came onto the field opposite the Union left wing. Refusing to believe the news of this arrival, Pope foolishly attacked again on 30 August only to be repelled. Biding his time, and at the proper moment, Lee hurled Longstreet into a brilliant counterattack against Pope's weakened left wing, and with Jackson also moving forward, drove the Union army from the field. Lee lost 9,197 men at the Battle of Second Manassas as against Pope's 16,054 casualties. The Union army, having lost all confidence in Pope, fell back in near rout toward Washington and showed signs of total disintegration.[52]

Lincoln, Stanton, and Halleck continued to believe in Pope even after his crushing defeat, and to think that McClellan and others of the Army of the Potomac had played false with Pope—a baseless charge. With the Union army in disorganized retreat toward the capital, the president, in one of his finest actions of the war and against the advice of most of his cabinet, restored McClellan to the command. Riding out from Washington toward Fairfax Court House to resume command, McClellan came upon the remnants of Pope's scattered forces, demoralized and in utter chaos. The mere appearance of Little Mac restored the morale of the defeated troops, and McClellan began the truly remarkable task of reorganizing this shattered force and giving it again a fighting edge. Welles noted in his diary that "the defeat of Pope and placing McC[lellan] in command . . . interrupted the intrigue which had been planned for the dismissal of McClellan, and was not only a triumph for him but a severe mortification and disappointment for both Stanton and Chase."[53]

After a brief initial delay caused by lack of food, Lee determined to invade Maryland for military, political, and diplomatic reasons. Feinting a move toward Washington, the Confederate leader pushed his army by early

September 1862 as far as Frederick in western Maryland. Although Lincoln, Stanton, and Halleck refused to give McClellan written authority to pursue Lee, the Union commander doggedly pressed westward from Washington, reorganizing his battered army on the march. But he was plagued by contradictory orders: Lincoln urged him to move even more swiftly after Lee; Halleck directed him to slow down his pursuit and stay closer to Washington. Ignoring these frantic dispatches, McClellan bided his time and, in the decisive battle of South Mountain on 14 September not only defeated the Confederates at three mountain passes, but wrested the vital initiative from Lee. "This victory," declared James Ford Rhodes of South Mountain, "restored the morale of the Union army, and gave heart to the President and the people of the North." Wrote Lincoln to McClellan: "God bless you, and all with you. Destroy the rebel army if possible."[54]

But to "destroy the rebel army" and annihiliate Robert E. Lee was a tall order for anyone. First of all, some 12,500 Union soldiers had been captured at Harper's Ferry by Stonewall Jackson when Halleck, against McClellan's protests, insisted that they remain there in a virtual death trap. It was the greatest surrender of United States troops in history up to that at Corregidor in 1942. Then, pulling his scattered units together at Sharpsburg, Maryland, Lee placed them in a strong though cramped position on the western side of the Antietam Creek. Little Mac deployed his forces on the eastern side of the stream, but spent 15 September in reconnaissance and shifting artillery and infantry units. The Union commander was convinced that Lee had 120,000 men; in reality, the Southerners had no more than 58,000 troops as compared with perhaps 69,000 Union effectives.[55]

The Battle of Antietam, or Sharpsburg, fought on 17 September, was the bloodiest single-day battle of the Civil War. More men in blue and gray were casualities in some fourteen hours of heavy fighting than have ever before or since been experienced in one day by the American people in arms. McClellan's plan of battle called for an attack by his right, soon followed by an assault from his left, with a blow from his center climaxing what he hoped would be an offensive that would drive Lee back into the Potomac in the rear. But Union plans miscarried. "Fighting Joe" Hooker, J. K. F. Mansfield, and Edwin V. Sumner gained some ground on the Union right at the expense of Jackson in the East Woods, Cornfield, and West Woods, and against Longstreet at the Sunken Road ("Bloody Lane"); but inexcusable delays all morning by Ambrose E. Burnside, on McClellan's left wing, allowed the dexterous Lee to shift troops from south to north to finally halt the successful earlier Union advances. With Lee's right wing almost denuded of soldiers, all Burnside had to do was promptly press home his attacks, as McClellan repeatedly ordered. But this was beyond Burnside's meager ability, although in the afternoon he did finally capture the famous stone-arch bridge that bears his name. However, it was too late. Burnside's eventual advance toward Sharpsburg was checked by A. P. Hill's timely arrival and counterattack. McClellan gained some ground but was prevented from smashing Lee's army. The Union commander refrained from resuming the attack the next day, and Lee conducted a safe retreat into Virginia, although he was obliged to leave some of his dead and wounded on the field. Casualties amounted to 12,410 Union and 13,724 Confederate.[56]

Antietam was one of the two battles the North had to win in the Civil War, and while McClellan did little more than gain a draw tactically, he had nevertheless won a strategic success of almost incalculable importance. Only Lee's repulse in Maryland kept the British government from recognizing Confederate independence and intervening decisively in the war. James Ford Rhodes concluded:

> To one who is biassed by the feeling that Lee had by this time shown himself almost invincible, it will be natural to speak well of the general who overcame him in any way on any terms. . . . Let us note the change of feeling at the North from depression before South Mountain to buoyancy after Antietam; let us reflect that a signal Confederate victory in Maryland might have caused the Northern voters at the approaching fall elections to declare for the peace that Jefferson Davis would offer from the head of Lee's victorious army, and that without McClellan's victory the Emancipation Proclamation would have been postponed and might never have been issued!

It was no small accomplishment that Little Mac had achieved.[57]

Soon after the Battle of Antietam, while McClellan was reorganizing the Army of the Potomac, Lincoln visited the general and the army and inspected the battlefields of South Mountain and Antietam. Impressed with what had been achieved, the president pledged that McClellan would be retained in command until the end of the war. The general, however, realistically told Lincoln that this would be impossible politically. When McClellan felt obliged to take additional weeks to mold his army into a force effective enough to undertake a sustained invasion of the enemy's country, Lincoln and Halleck became irked with the delay. Once McClellan did advance into Virginia, he moved skillfully and with celerity. But for alleged military dilatoriness, and especially for a number of political reasons, Lincoln removed McClellan from command, effective 7 November 1862.[58]

Summing up McClellan, Francis W. Palfrey, never a supporter of the Union general's actions, admits that "there are strong grounds for believing that he was the best commander the Army of the Potomac ever had. . . . While the Confederacy was young and fresh and rich, and its armies were numerous, McClellan fought a good, wary, damaging, respectable fight against it." General Francis A. Walker wrote of McClellan: "Let military critics or political enemies say what they will, he who could so move upon the hearts of a great army, as the wind sways long rows of standing corn, was no ordinary man; nor was he who took such heavy toll of Joseph E. Johnston and Robert E. Lee an ordinary soldier." When asked shortly after Appomattox who was the ablest Union general he had faced during the war, Lee, with emphasis and without a moment's hesitation, declared simply, "McClellan by all odds!"[59]

UNFORTUNATELY for the Federals, the man chosen by Lincoln and Halleck (Stanton was now less involved in strategic and command problems) to succeed McClellan was thirty-eight-year-old Ambrose E. Burnside, who had done so poorly as a corps and wing commander at Antietam. A native of Indiana, Burnside was graduated eighteenth in the 1847 West Point class of thirty-eight cadets. He arrived in Mexico too late to participate in the battles, and resigned from the army in 1853 to enter business. At first unsuccessful, he was befriended by the McClellans and developed the carbine that bore his name. He was an ineffective brigade commander at First Bull Run but was victorious in minor operations, won largely by the Union navy, on the North Carolina littoral. Burnside had an open, modest, attractive personality; but he was a procrastinator, unimaginative and obstinate, and unsure of his own ability to command such a large army. In short, he was far beyond his depth.[60]

After painful hesitation about what to do, Burnside swiftly moved his army from near Warrenton to Falmouth, across the Rappahannock River from Confederate-held Fredericksburg. Then Lincoln, Burnside, and Halleck discussed strategic matters at great length. Burnside first recommended one movement up the Rappahannock and then another one down the river. Eventually authorized to cross his army directly in Lee's front at Fredericksburg, but plagued by a careless mix-up between Halleck and himself over delayed pontoons, Burnside surged forward to the attack in mid-December 1862 without having devised a proper plan of battle. Thus far, Lee had anticipated his every move. Burnside had 120,281 men as compared to Confederate numbers of 78,513 soldiers.[61]

December 13 dawned cold and foggy, with a light dusting of snow on the ground. The Union commander was still unsure about which tactical plan he would employ. Palfrey asserted:

> It is a pitiful picture, but is probably a true one, that Burnside passed the evening of the 12th riding about, not quite at his wits' end, but very near it. . . . As far as can be made out, he finally came to the conclusion that he would attempt to do something, he did not quite know what, with his left, and if he succeeded, to do something with his right.[62]

The "something" Burnside did with his left wing was to launch a portion of William B. Franklin's forces, improperly supported, against Jackson's half of the Confederate army, posted in heavy timber. Thus George G. Meade scored only a temporary breakthrough, and that was soon erased. The "something" that Burnside did with his right corps was to hurl them, in some sixteen separate piecemeal attacks, across an open plain, in full view and easy range of Confederate artillery posted atop Marye's Heights, and against Longstreet's densely packed infantry emplaced behind a stone wall along a sunken road. In spite of the desperate courage of the Union soldiers, none came within twenty-five paces of the wall. All assaults were thrown back with fearful loss, and Burnside was reduced to a nearly raving madman. He lost 12,653 men as compared to Lee's casualties of 4,756. Because of the wide river, the Confederate general was unable to follow up his triumph.[63]

After much discussion with his superiors in Washington over strategy, followed by the ill-advised "Mud March" of 20 and 21 January 1863 upstream along the left bank of the Rappahannock—which got nowhere—Burnside was relieved of his command on 25 January, after a final conclave with Lincoln. With Federal soldiers' morale never lower and desertions never higher, the roughly handled Army of the Potomac went into winter quarters at Falmouth while the Army of Northern Virginia did the same across the Rappahannock at Fredericksburg. As for the well-meaning Burnside, Palfrey states, "There probably never was an occasion since the first body of troops was arrayed, when a general did more precisely what his adversary wished him to do than Burnside did at Fredericksburg. "There was," writes Carl Russell Fish, "no such intention to sacrifice but, if stupidity be culpability, few generals of ancient or modern times rank with Burnside in the guilt of manslaughter." Alas for the Union cause, Burnside would be brought back again to command rather large forces of soldiers in blue.[64]

CHAPTER EIGHT

The Road to Appomattox

Virginia and Lee's army is not Tennessee and Bragg's army.

GEORGE G. MEADE

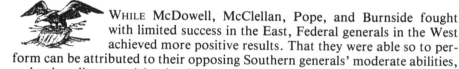 WHILE McDowell, McClellan, Pope, and Burnside fought with limited success in the East, Federal generals in the West achieved more positive results. That they were able so to perform can be attributed to their opposing Southern generals' moderate abilities, and to less direct participation in actual military operations by the Washington high command.

In the key border state of Missouri, affairs began inauspiciously for the Federals. Union commander Nathaniel Lyon, a diminutive, fiery, red-haired Connecticut Yankee, had been a West Pointer, a veteran of the Seminole and Mexican Wars, and had served in California and "Bleeding Kansas." He succeeded in breaking up Confederate Camp Jackson at St. Louis on 10 May 1861 (he was kicked in the stomach by a mule for his trouble!) but soon came a cropper. Pushing southwestwardly with some 5,000 troops, he was brought to battle and defeated at Wilson's Creek on 10 August by 10,000 Confederates under Sterling Price and Benjamin McCulloch. Lyon was mortally wounded in the engagement. John C. Frémont's dubious administration of the Department of the Missouri, with headquarters at St. Louis, was tightened up by Halleck. He replaced Frémont when the latter was ousted by Lincoln for issuing, in effect, his own emancipation proclamation. The Union field army gained revenge, however, and insured the safety of Missouri when its new commander, the steady, reliable Samuel Curtis, advanced with about 11,250 men through the state into northern Arkansas. At the Battle of Pea Ridge (or Elkhorn Tavern), 7–8 March 1862, after an initial setback, Curtis defeated approximately 14,000 Confederates under Earl Van Dorn. Later, in Arkansas, Union soldiers under Frederick Steele marched upon the enemy at Prairie Grove, near Fayetteville, and trounced them on 7 December 1862—a triumph that paved the way for Steele's eventual capture of Little Rock the next September.[1]

After the Union victories at Forts Henry and Donelson, the thirty-nine-year-old Ulysses S. Grant pushed his 40,000 troops incautiously southward along the Tennessee River to Pittsburg Landing on the west bank, hard by

Shiloh church. The Union commander was a singular figure, whose life up to the Civil War had been largely one of failure and frustration. Born in Point Pleasant, Ohio, Grant had stood twenty-first in the 1843 West Point class of thirty-nine. Serving with distinction as a young subaltern in the War with Mexico, Grant received routine assignments, and separation from his family on the West Coast and overcommunication with John Barleycorn forced him to resign his commission. He was unsuccessful as a farmer, real estate agent, and candidate for county engineer, and finally went to work with his brother at a leather-goods store in Galena, Illinois. Grant narrowly missed securing a position on McClellan's staff at the start of the Civil War, which would have meant military oblivion for him, and finally received the colonelcy of an Illinois regiment. Five feet eight inches in height, and habitually dressed in a crusty, battered uniform, Grant was stoop-shouldered and awkward except when mounted. He was grave, silent, and determined. By nature lazy—as he admitted—Grant could perform prodigies of work when necessary and was cool under fire. He was free from political connections at this time. While he could be overly sanguine and careless in an easy situation, he performed best in a crisis or difficult situation. Soldiers and civilians trusted him instinctively, and he understood how a soldier should behave in a republic such as the United States. Capable of growth as he advanced in appointments during the war, Grant lacked Lee's great skill in tactical maneuver but on occasion was superior in strategy. He could see the big picture of the conflict and the role of individual armies and commanders therein.[2]

Grant and his second in command, William T. Sherman, unwisely encamped at Shiloh in early April 1862. They were overconfident and careless in assuming that Albert Sidney Johnston and the Confederates were hopelessly smashed and scattered to the four winds. "There is no enemy nearer than Corinth," intoned Sherman. Grant himself was absent from his army. "I have scarcely the faintest idea of an attack (general one) being made upon us, but will be prepared should such a thing take place," asserted Grant. "There will be no fight at Pittsburg Landing; we will have to go to Corinth, where the Rebels are fortified."[3]

But, in one of the greatest feats of the war, Johnston was preparing to do just this! In a superhuman effort, he gathered together his far-flung, defeated legions. Johnston, with 40,000 men, struck Grant's army at Pittsburg Landing on 6 April 1862, hoping to crush it before Don Carlos Buell could arrive from Nashville with some 20,000 more Federals. Initially, the Confederates seemed brilliantly victorious, and they drove the Unionists back to a point perilously close to the river bluffs. The fighting was of a desperate character. A heroic stand by Benjamin Prentiss at the "Hornet's Nest" helped save the blueclads from total defeat, along with the mortal wounding of Johnston and the arrival later that day of the first reinforcements. Beauregard took over command of the Army of Tennessee, but the Southerners could not hold their gains on 7 April against the heavily augmented Northerners, who counterattacked. Grant lost 13,047 men at Shiloh as against 10,694 Confederate casualties. And he failed to pursue the enemy. The death of Albert Sidney Johnston was a severe loss to Jefferson Davis and the South. Historian Charles P. Roland states:

"Johnston's presence would have been an incalculable asset to the Confederacy in the trying years to come." Halleck assumed command of the mammoth army of 100,000 men, composed of the forces of Grant, Buell, and Pope, and "crawled" at the rate of one mile per day to Corinth, which was evacuated by the outnumbered Beauregard on 30 May 1862.[4]

Meanwhile Buell, another Union commander in the West, was getting the axe. Yet for many months he would offer sage strategic advice to the Lincoln administration and would check a serious Confederate invasion of Kentucky. Like McClellan a conservative Democrat and circumspect commander, Buell was solid if unimaginative, a fine organizer and drillmaster, but a touchy and difficult subordinate. An 1841 graduate of West Point and a meritorious young officer in the Mexican War, the reserved Buell was not overly popular with his troops, but he was a useful if balky officer. In the summer of 1862 after Shiloh and the fall of Corinth to the Union, Buell conducted a slow advance toward Chattanooga. It was only General in Chief Halleck's intercession that kept the president from removing Buell from command.[5]

Beauregard, on the Confederate side, was not well liked by Davis and was soon superseded in command of the Army of Tennessee by Braxton Bragg, a presidential favorite. Bragg had justifiably won distinction as a young subaltern for his brilliant artillery performances in the Mexican War and especially at Buena Vista. Excelling as a drillmaster, disciplinarian, and organizer, Bragg was nevertheless a stern, dyspeptic, unpopular martinet of limited tactical ability.[6]

Leaving twenty-two thousand men under Price and Van Dorn in Mississippi, Bragg, hoping to reconquer Tennessee and carry the war into Kentucky, moved with some thirty thousand gray-clad troops through Chattanooga toward Louisville. Edmund Kirby Smith had about eighteen thousand Southern soldiers at Knoxville. Even while moving back to counter the threat to Louisville, Buell was again almost relieved of his command when Stanton tried to pressure Lincoln into issuing such an order. Again Halleck persuaded the civilian authorities to give Buell a chance to fight Bragg, and the president reluctantly acquiesced.[7]

Bragg was deflected over to Frankfort to install a would-be Confederate governor in the state capital; consequently he was delayed and Buell won the race to safeguard Louisville. The two armies came together southeast of Louisville at Perryville on 8 October 1862, with part of the Union army unengaged at first because of an acoustic shadow that prevented the Union commander from knowing a battle was under way. After an initial Confederate success, prevented from becoming an overwhelming victory by the staunch stand by units such as Philip H. Sheridan's, Buell's troops held on and Bragg was unable to claim a victory. He retreated back into Tennessee. Some 800 Federals were killed at Perryville and 2,800 wounded as against Southern casualties of about 500 killed and 2,600 wounded.[8]

The tall, lonely commander in chief in the White House wanted Buell to pursue Bragg's army, but the Federal general wished to go to Nashville and resume his advance against eastern Tennessee. Buell correctly contended that the best way to do this was via Nashville, but he was warned by Halleck against further delays. When Buell persisted in this strategey, he was removed from command for political and personal reasons by the president on 23 October 1862 and replaced by William S. Rosecrans.[9]

Rosecrans, who won several smallish but important defensive victories over Price and Van Dorn in September and October at Iuka and Corinth in northern Mississippi, was backed for the command by Lincoln, Halleck, and Chase, but had been opposed by Stanton, who preferred George H. Thomas for the position. "Old Rosy" was tall, light-haired, powerful, and temperamental; he could drink and swear with the best of them. After graduating fifth in the class of 1856 at the military academy, he taught at West Point and resigned from the army to become a civil engineer, architect, and refiner of petroleum and coal. As a Union general, Rosecrans was a tireless worker who loved a lengthy discussion of strategy with his superiors, although he was occasionally unable to distinguish between important and unimportant. He lacked the poise and balance of a truly first-class general, but he did nonetheless have good strategical sense and was an offensive-minded commander.[10]

Other army and department commanders came to the fore on the Federal side at this time. Lincoln chose three political generals, Nathaniel P. Banks, Benjamin F. Butler, and John A. McClernand, for important commands. These men turned out to be unfortunate choices, except for the political support they brought the administration. Banks was named to succeed Butler in command of the Department of the Gulf, with headquarters at New Orleans. Although he had treated foreign consuls poorly and had insulted Southern women in the Crescent City, Butler was a fairly competent administrator there. But he was devoid of sufficient military ability to conduct a campaign from that point into Louisiana or toward Vicksburg. Just why Lincoln thought Banks would do better than Butler is a mystery. Banks was equally inept in handling troops in the field.[11]

Lincoln, late in 1862, was only partially satisfied with Rosecrans as Buell's successor. Old Rosy became angry when Halleck told him that Lincoln was so impatient with his reluctance to march that he might be relieved of his command. Rosecrans defiantly replied that he would advance only when ready and that he could not be compelled to move prematurely by intimidation. Halleck tried patiently to explain to Rosecrans the need for an early forward movement.[12]

Rosecrans finally advanced and at the end of December 1862 met the Confederates under Bragg in heavy battle over several days at Stones River, near Murfreesboro, to the southeast of Nashville. Each commander sought to attack the other's flank, but the Southerners struck first and forced part of Rosecrans's army back. But the Union commander and his troops rallied, counterattacked, and regained some of the lost ground. While tactically a draw at best, Rosecrans nevertheless gained a strategic success at Stones River. Bragg withdrew from the field of battle and fell back to the south. Some 12,900 blue casualties were nearly equaled by about 11,700 ones in gray, and

Rosecrans could certainly claim no crushing victory. However, at this same time Burnside suffered a catastrophic defeat at Fredericksburg; so this was a much needed partial success, and Lincoln congratulated Rosecrans.[13]

IN THE EASTERN THEATER, with the rival armies in winter quarters near Fredericksburg, Lincoln named a successor to Burnside to command the Army of the Potomac in January 1863. Appointed was "Fighting Joe" Hooker, a handsome, Massachusetts-born general of forty-eight years of age who had won three brevets in the Mexican War. He resigned his commission but had not fared too well as a farmer near Sonoma, California. Hooker, as an officer in the Civil War, had done extremely well in combat as, successively, a brigade, division, corps, and grand division commander, and he had participated in most of the great battles fought in the East.[14]

Like Lincoln, most people thought highly of Hooker; but a few of the highest ranking generals in the army correctly gauged that Hooker had not the character or intellect to exercise command over this massive force. Despite his undeniable talents as a soldier, Fighting Joe was an intriguer and political Radical who engaged in harsh and unfair backbiting and insubordinate criticism of others, including his superiors. Lincoln knew of some of his less pleasant traits and was obliged to write him the following remarkable letter upon his appointment to the command of the Army of the Potomac in late January 1863:

> I think it best for you to know that there are some things in regard to which I am not quite satisfied with you. . . . I think that during General Burnside's command of the army, you have taken counsel of your ambition, and thwarted him as much as you could, in which you did a great wrong to the country and to a most meritorious and honorable officer. I have heard, in such a way as to believe it, of your recently saying that both the army and the Government needed a dictator. Of course, it was not for this, but in spite of it, that I have given you the command. Only those generals who gain successes can set up dictators. What I now ask of you is military success, and I will risk the dictatorship. . . . And now beware of rashness. Beware of rashness, but with energy and sleepless vigilance go forward and give us victories.

As historian Edward Channing stated, "It was an extraordinary letter to write to one whom a great place has just been given, and seems to carry in itself conclusive reasons why the appointment should not have been made."[15]

After considering crossing the Rappahannock below the Confederate positions at Fredericksburg, Hooker drew up another plan on 11 April whereby the Union cavalry would cross upstream and position itself in Lee's rear. Fighting Joe's main body would cross upstream and hammer the retreating enemy back upon the anvil of the Federal horsemen to the south. Lincoln approved this plan. At the time of his recent visit to the army in camp, the commander in chief was concerned with Hooker's overconfidence and urged him to use all of his troops in the forthcoming battle. When a heavy two-week rain spoiled the cavalry operation, Hooker changed his plans a bit. While still determined to cross the Rappahannock upstream from Fredericksburg with his main body, he now intended to press the Confederates back upon another Union infantry force under John Sedgwick at Fredericksburg.[16]

The Chancellorsville campaign commenced near the end of April 1863 and carried through the first week of May. Hooker initially outmaneuvered Lee with his one hundred thirty-two thousand men pitted against Lee's sixty-two thousand. But the Confederate leader dared to split his force twice, although outnumbered more than two to one. Jackson's force audaciously assailed the Federal right flank under Oliver Otis Howard just to the west of Chancellorsville, some ten miles west of Fredericksburg. In a brilliant feat of arms, Stonewall crumpled the Union flank, although it cost him his life. Hooker uncharacteristically and inexplicably withdrew and refused to take the offensive or use two available fresh corps of his army. Thus gaining the moral ascendency over the bewildered Union commander who had been injured, Lee completely outgeneraled Hooker and forced him back across the river to the former federal position at Falmouth.[17]

Fighting Joe had lost a total of 17,287 men as compared to 12,463 Confederate casualties. Hooker tried, unconvincingly, to explain away his defeat to Lincoln; but the weary president, with ashen face and unalleviated anguish, knew better and could only exclaim in deep despair, "My God, my God, what will the country say! What will the country say!"[18]

Events moved swiftly thereafter. One month after crushing Hooker at Chancellorsville, and buttressed by the return of Longstreet's command, Lee reorganized his army of seventy-five thousand men into three corps commanded by Longstreet, Richard S. Ewell, and A. P. Hill. In order to shift operations away from war-ravaged Virginia into the food-rich Northern states of Maryland and Pennsylvania, and among other reasons to relieve Grant's pressure on Vicksburg, Lee pulled out of the Fredericksburg lines and moved northward via the Shenandoah valley and Frederick to Chambersburg in the Keystone State. Late in June he moved upon York, Harrisburg, and—with Jeb Stuart's ill-advised cavalry sweep—Carlisle.[19]

In the interim the Union commander moved the Army of the Potomac northward, keeping between Lee's army and Washington. Conducting his operations fairly well up to this time, Fighting Joe wisely requested that the Federal garrison at Harper's Ferry be added to his command. When this was refused, Hooker submitted his resignation. Perhaps to his surprise, Lincoln promptly accepted it. The president unsuccessfully sounded out John F. Reynolds for the position and then named George Gordon Meade to the command with the comment that Meade, a Pennsylvanian, would "fight well on his own dunghill."[20]

The forty-seven-year-old Meade had graduated nineteenth in the West Point class of 1835, served meritoriously in the War with Mexico, and compiled a splendid fighting record with the Army of the Potomac. He had been wounded in fighting on the peninsula and had risen from a brigade head in the Pennsylvania Reserves to command of the Fifth Corps. Tall, spare, and slightly balding, the "Old Goggle-eyed Snapping Turtle," as Meade was called, was easily irritated. Yet he was generally an excellent and reliable though not over-ly imaginative officer who had a fine eye for military terrain and was a good judge of men, as well as being a man of upright character and integrity.[21]

Lee's victorious forces were pushing into the heart of Pennsylvania, and with affairs in a dreaded state of uncertainty, Halleck and Lincoln gave Meade control of the Harper's Ferry garrison and assured him that while he must cover Washington with the Army of the Potomac, he was otherwise free to maneuver his army of over 88,000 effectives in the field as he saw fit, free from interference from his superiors in the capital. As historian James G. Randall comments simply, Meade, "accepting extraordinary prerogatives conferred by the President, prepared to fulfill a responsibility unexcelled, unless by [George] Washington, in previous American history."[22]

Nor did Meade fail his country or president in the crisis. With the two ar-mies groping their way along in southern Pennsylvania, elements of both col-lided unexpectedly in an engagement at the small road-hub town of Gettysburg at 8:00 A.M. on 1 July 1863. Neither commander was present on the field on the first day's battle; about 18,000 Federals crossed swords viciously with some 28,000 Confederates. In the initial clash west of town, Union forces of the First Corps under Reynolds (who was killed in combat) and Abner Doubleday were heavily outnumbered and threatened on both flanks but held back the at-tacking Confederates until 4:00 P.M. On the plain north of Gettysburg, O. O. Howard's Eleventh Corps, after strenuous resistance, was crushed and com-pelled to retreat in disorder through the streets of the town to Cemetery Hill and Culp's Hill, south of Gettysburg. The First Corps also fell back later to these points. There the Union withdrawal came to a halt; the Confederates were thus far victorious, although they suffered heavier casualties.

Most remaining men of both armies reached the field during the night; when the battle reopened on 2 July, Lee determined to strike the Union left simultaneously with assaults against Meade's right. But the Nationals were strongly ensconced in a fishhook-shaped line on Cemetery Ridge, and the Con-federates were unable to coordinate their attacks. Longstreet's advance, com-ing about 4:30 P.M., succeeded in driving Daniel Sickles's Third Corps back from the Peach Orchard, the Wheatfield, and the Devil's Den; but the Southern assaults were thrown back at the key area of Little Round Top by Federals who had been rushed there at the last moment by Gouverneur K. Warren. Piecemeal attacks by the Louisiana "Tigers" against East Cemetery Hill at dusk and soon after by Edward Johnson against Culp's Hill were con-tained, although Johnson did manage to occupy breastworks on the partially abandoned lower slopes when Meade boldly shifted troops from his right to meet Longstreet's threat to his left.

The third day's battle opened with Meade seizing the initiative and counterattacking the Confederates on Culp's Hill. Fighting there raged from 4:00 A.M. for seven hours until the Federals had successfully thrown back the enemy. In midafternoon, in what has been called the greatest infantry charge in history, Lee—against Longstreet's contrary advice—hurled nearly 15,000 gallant infantrymen under George E. Pickett across nine-tenths of a mile of open fields against the Union center, held by the indomitable Winfield S. Hancock. The attack had been preceded by nearly two hours of the heaviest artillery bombardment of the war (138 Confederate cannon against 88 Union). Although the graycoats temporarily dented the Northern lines at the angle of a stone wall near a copse of trees, artillery and infantry volleys cut down the attackers, and reinforcements hurled them back with fearful losses. In an attempt to strike the Union rear at the same time that Pickett hit the front, Confederate cavalryman Jeb Stuart and his mounted men, in a desperate engagement three and one-half miles east of town, were checked by Union horsemen under David M. Gregg and George Armstrong Custer and impelled to withdraw. Lee began his retreat from Gettysburg the following day; the greatest and most costly battle ever fought on the shores of the New World resulted in almost 28,000 Confederate casualties as compared to 23,049 Federal.[23]

Even in victory there was contention within the Union high command. When Meade thought it unwise to attack the Confederates before they crossed the Potomac, despite Lincoln's urging him not to "allow" Lee to escape, he was severely criticized by the president. "We had them in our grasp," the chief executive claimed; "we had only to stretch forth our hands and they were ours, and nothing I could say or do could make the army move." And again: "There is bad faith somewhere. . . . What does it mean? . . . Great God! what does it mean?" Meade felt, justifiably, that this blast was undeserved and sent in his resignation, but it was not accepted. Lincoln calmed down and tried to smooth Meade's ruffled feathers. Lee and Meade passed the rest of the summer, fall, and winter of 1863 in indecisive maneuvering in northern Virginia, with no large-scale battles, while both armies lost some of their troops to the Chattanooga area before going into winter quarters.[24]

HOOKER AND MEADE were fighting with differing degrees of success against Lee in the East, and affairs along the Father of Waters in the West seemed to be progressing with maddening slowness, as if the difficulties were insurmountable. Against mounting pressure, Lincoln continued to support Grant, saying that if the general took Vicksburg, then "Grant is my man and I am his the rest of the war." The Union commander in chief's patience paid off. Earlier in the summer of 1862 David G. Farragut had been unsuccessful in approaching Vicksburg by warship from the south. Grant failed utterly in December 1862 in his approach to Vicksburg along the railroad to Jackson, and Earl Van Dorn captured his large supply base at Holly Springs. Grant next tried a series of five so-called "bayou expeditions" to the north, northwest, and northeast of the Confederate fortress, but each of these ended in failure. He was finally succored when David Dixon Porter's ships successfully ran the river batteries of Vicksburg and landed Grant's army south of the stronghold. The Federals were inadvertently aided by the Southern commander at Vicksburg, John C. Pemberton, whose obtuse and literal observance of Jefferson Davis's orders to hold Vicksburg were adhered to by keeping his troops right there. Pemberton also failed to march his troops out to join Joseph E. Johnston's weak force at Jackson to the east. Winning five battles—at Port Gibson, Raymond,

Jackson, Champion's Hill, and Big Black River—Grant conducted a forty-seven-day siege of Vicksburg. Near the end of the campaign, Grant had some seventy-one thousand soldiers as against thirty-one thousand Confederates. Finally on 4 July 1863, the day after the repulse of Pickett's Charge at Gettysburg, Pemberton surrendered his army and Vicksburg.[25]

Complimented by the president "for the almost inestimable service [he had] done the country" at Vicksburg, Grant recommended that he now be permitted to move his army to Mobile, Alabama, and operate from there into the heart of the Confederacy. Lincoln rejected the plan with an eye to sending troops to Banks to invade Texas as a warning to the French in Mexico. Grant agreed to the importance of an advance into Texas.[26]

In central Tennessee increased friction developed between Lincoln and Rosecrans, who had won at least a strategic success at Stones River near Murfreesboro in early January 1863. Old Rosy settled in, demanded more supplies, and asserted that he would require a good deal of time before moving toward Chattanooga.[27]

Furthermore, Rosecrans angrily charged that Stanton was trying to bribe him into making a premature advance by offering him a major generalcy in the regular army. He wired Lincoln that Stanton was not filling supply requisitions promptly, and that he, Rosecrans, should outrank Grant. Lincoln tried to soothe his feelings without agreeing with his charges. While directly criticizing Halleck and Stanton to newspapermen, Rosecrans did resist presidential feelers from the Radicals and urged them to support Lincoln in the coming elections. The chief executive and the general in chief both warned Rosecrans to advance; after further delay, he was finally persuaded to commence his forward movement on 24 June 1863.[28]

After protracted wrangling with his superiors over strategic matters, Rosecrans approached Chattanooga from an unexpected direction with some sixty thousand men and dexterously maneuvered Bragg and his forty-three thousand Confederates out of that key city without a battle. Bragg called loudly to Richmond for reinforcements, and Davis beckoned Lee to the capital to discuss the crisis. Lee favored attacking Meade's army with the full Army of Northern Virginia. Lee's second in command, Longstreet, wanted to take his corps to Tennessee to bolster Bragg's forces so they might counterattack against Rosecrans. The Confederate president ordered that the latter option be tried. Lee expressed some misgivings, but, as Davis noted, "with commendable zeal for the public welfare and characteristic self-denial" promptly started Longstreet and his divisions westward via the Virginia and Tennessee Railroad. Lee urged that Bragg attack Rosecrans without delay. Bragg, who outnumbered the Federals in one of the few times in the war by some sixty-five thousand to sixty thousand, determined to do just that.[29]

Bragg caught Rosecrans off guard at Chickamauga Creek to the southeast of Chattanooga and in a two-day battle, the bloodiest in the western theater, was repulsed in his initial thrusts on 19 September 1863. On the following day a gap in the Union lines, caused by a misunderstanding by Thomas J. Wood of a Rosecrans order, enabled six Confederate divisions under Longstreet to pour through in an irresistible attack that split the Federal army in two. While

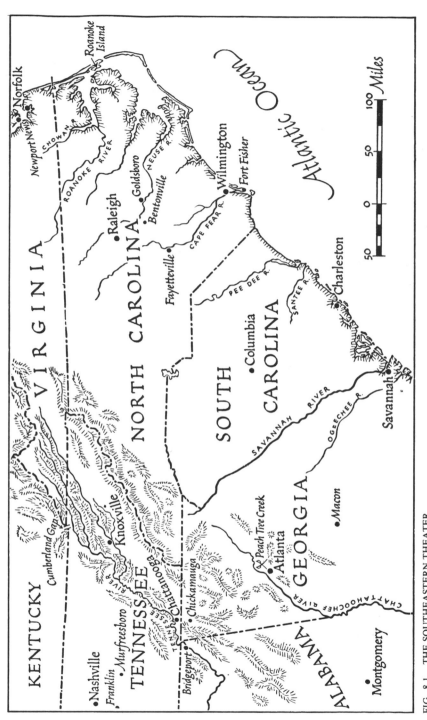

FIG. 8.1. THE SOUTHEASTERN THEATER

George H. Thomas (the "Rock of Chickamauga") made an epic stand for hours on the Union left, Rosecrans and the remainder of the army fell back to Chattanooga and readied their defenses. Then the remnant of the Union army under Thomas retreated to the city. Some sixteen thousand Union and eighteen thousand Confederate casualties were suffered at Chickamauga.[30]

Unwisely detaching Longstreet's command and sending it on a futile siege of Burnside at Knoxville, Bragg with his smaller army moved forward and began his own siege of Rosecrans inside Chattanooga. Lincoln moved to reinforce Rosecrans by rail from Meade's Army of the Potomac with the remnants of Howard's Eleventh Corps and Slocum's Twelfth Corps that were now amalgamated into the new Twentieth Corps under the overall command of Fighting Joe Hooker. Assistant Secretary of War Charles A. Dana in Chattanooga sent dispatches to Washington damning Rosecrans, and eventually Stanton was able to get the general replaced by Thomas. Lincoln lost confidence in Rosecrans as the general began to show signs of emotional disintegration. The president placed Grant in supreme command in the West and told him to go to Chattanooga where he could replace Rosecrans with Thomas if he wished. Grant promptly removed Rosecrans and installed Thomas in his place, and the president approved the decision.[31]

Grant had some sixty thousand troops (counting reinforcements) at Chattanooga as compared to Bragg's forty thousand. The Federals opened new supply routes—the "cracker line"—into the threatened city and massed for an onslaught against the Confederates, who seemed to be firmly ensconced on Lookout Mountain and Missionary Ridge. In a series of sharp, well-planned and executed attacks in the last week of November 1863 Hooker defeated the Southerners on Lookout Mountain. Although Sherman's assaults against Bragg's right at Tunnel Hill were repulsed, the Union attacks in the center succeeded in capturing Missionary Ridge, even though Grant had wanted the attack to halt lower down on the slope. Bragg was forced to order a full retreat, with a loss of sixty-seven hundred men as contrasted with fifty-eight hundred Federal casualties. Confessing failure in himself as army commander, Bragg was soon replaced by Johnston. Lincoln warmly congratulated Grant on his triumph and considered retaining him in the West.[32]

WITH the rival main armies inactive and resting in winter quarters in the early months of 1864, a look at naval matters throughout the war is in order. If Federal naval power did not win the war, it enabled the war to be won. Although blessed with able leaders—Secretary Welles and Assistant Secretary of the Navy Fox—the Northern navy had merely 90 warships, with only 42 in commission, and most of these were on foreign station. To blockade the Confederate coastline of some 3,500 miles, the North had to procure and build warships in a crash program. By late 1863 the blockade became effective, and by the end of the conflict some 671 ships of war were flying the Union flag.[33]

Confederate privateering was successful only during the first year of the war. The Union naval buildup was simply too much for the Confederates, despite actions taken by the able Confederate secretary of the navy, Stephen

Mallory. From some nine thousand seamen at the start of the war, the Union navy numbered fifty-nine thousand sailors by war's end; and naval appropriations increased from $12 million per annum in 1861 to $123 million by 1865.[34]

Technologically, the Civil War had a revolutionary impact on both navies. It was the first war in which a submarine, the Confederate submersible *Hunley,* sank an enemy warship, the blockader U.S.S. *Housatonic,* off Charleston on 17 February 1864. In this operation *Hunley* accidentally destroyed herself. In addition to the increased use of steam power, shell guns, the screw propeller, and rifled ordnance, both sides constructed and used ironclad warships.[35]

The most famous of Civil War ironclads and the first two in history to engage in naval battle were U.S.S. *Monitor,* invented by John Ericsson, and C.S.S. *Virginia,* which was built upon the frame of U.S.S. *Merrimack* that was scuttled when Union forces evacuated the Norfolk navy yard early in the war. *Virginia,* carrying 4 inches of armor and mounting 10 guns, was commanded by Franklin Buchanan, who had helped George Bancroft plan the Naval Academy at Annapolis and had been its superintendent. Buchanan served in the Mexican War, commanded Matthew C. Perry's flagship in his mission to open Japan, and left the federal service to join the Confederacy. *Monitor,* armored with plates ranging from 4½ to 8 inches, had a revolving turret housing two mammoth 11-inch Dahlgren guns.

On 8 March 1862 Buchanan's *Virginia* destroyed U.S.S. *Congress* and U.S.S. *Cumberland* in Hampton Roads, Virginia. The next day *Virginia,* under the command of Catesby ap R. Jones, who succeeded the wounded Buchanan, was about to polish off U.S.S. *Minnesota,* when *Monitor*—that "cheese-box on a raft"—commanded by John Lorimer Worden, appeared on the scene. The two ironclads engaged at very close quarters in a severe but indecisive battle of nearly three hours, with only light damage to both vessels. *Virginia* later had to be blown up by her own crew when McClellan's army advanced up the peninsula, and *Monitor* foundered in a gale off Cape Hatteras at the end of 1862. *Monitor* gave its name generically to a class of Union warships that carried one or two turrets and saw widespread service during the war.[36]

In addition to blockade-runners and privateers, daring Confederate raiders preyed successfully upon Union commerce to such an extent that marine insurance rates became prohibitive, and the serious deterioration of the merchant marine began and has continued down to the present. Among the more auspicious Confederate cruisers were *Sumter,* skippered by the legendary Raphael Semmes, which captured eighteen Union ships early in the war; *Florida,* captained by John Maffit, which seized thirty-seven Northern merchantmen in the North and South Atlantic in 1863; James Waddell's *Shenandoah,* which accounted for thirty-eight Union ships in the Pacific in 1864–1865; and, the most famous of all Confederate cruisers, *Alabama,* under the brilliant Semmes, which captured sixty-nine Union ships while on the prowl for nearly two years in several oceans. *Alabama* was finally destroyed off Cherbourg on 19 June 1864 by the Union warship, U.S.S. *Kearsarge,* commanded by John Winslow.[37]

In addition the Union naval forces fought effectively on the inland rivers, even with "tinclads" and ironclads, and were sometimes assisted by the army's amphibious landings. They also conducted a generally successful series of bombardments of significant Confederate coastal points. A Union naval flotilla under Samuel F. DuPont captured Port Royal, South Carolina, on 7 November 1861, and another squadron under Louis M. Goldsborough assisted Burnside's army in its seizure of Roanoke Island and New Berne, North Carolina, in February and March 1862. In April 1862, without ironclads and aboard his wooden flagship, U.S.S. *Hartford,* David G. Farragut, the most masterly of all Union naval commanders, overwhelmed the Confederate Forts St. Philip and Jackson on the Mississippi River below New Orleans and captured the city, which was then occupied by Ben Butler's army. In April 1862 Quincy A. Gillmore, a talented artillery and engineering officer, aided by the navy, closed Savannah, Georgia, to Confederate blockade-runners by silencing Fort Pulaski, guarding the city.[38]

In their efforts to regain Fort Sumter, defended by Beauregard, Union ironclads were repulsed with loss in April 1863. Even when they were accompanied by Gillmore's army infantry and siege artillery in July and August, they did not succeed. Farragut was more fortunate on 5 August 1864 in Mobile Bay. In the heaviest naval battle of the war, his warships reduced Forts Morgan, Gaines, and Powell, shattered several defending Confederate men-of-war, and closed that port to Southern use. The last Atlantic port to remain open was Wilmington, North Carolina. It successfully withstood a Union naval attack in December 1864 by David Dixon Porter on defending Fort Fisher because Butler's army failed to coordinate its attack properly. It fell the following month to Porter and a capably led army assault by Alfred H. Terry.[39]

In a peripheral campaign of dubious merit, designed in part to capture Confederate cotton, Banks and Porter took some forty-two thousand troops and twenty warships—including thirteen ironclads—up the Red River. The able defense by Richard Taylor and Kirby Smith was unwittingly assisted by Banks's ineptness and led to ignominious failure and retreat by the Federals. Only Galveston, Texas, remained open to Southern use; it did not surrender until 2 June 1865.[40]

In sum, "Uncle Sam's web feet," as Lincoln termed the Union sailors, had been there "at all the watery margins . . . on the deep sea, the broad bay, and the rapid river . . . up the narrow, muddy bayou, and wherever the ground was a little damp, they had been and made their tracks. Thanks to all," said the grateful president.[41]

WITH the re-creation of the three-star rank of lieutenant general, Lincoln called Grant to Washington in March 1864 to replace Halleck as general in chief of all Union armies. Old Brains stepped down to the nonpolicy-making position of chief of staff, under Grant, in the capital. Although Grant had his limitations and shortcomings, he was nonetheless a leader with many strong and positive assets and would make an excellent general in chief.[42]

Arriving in Washington on 8 March 1864, Grant met Lincoln for the first time at a gala White House reception, and the two men conversed, along with Stanton and John G. Nicolay. Grant journeyed to Brandy Station on 10 March and had his first conference with Meade. He determined to retain the Victor of Gettysburg in command of the Army of the Potomac. Grant soon made it clear that he, and not Meade, would direct this army's movements.[43]

Grant later claimed, inaccurately, "The President told me he did not want to know what I proposed to do." "I did not communicate my plans to the President," contended Grant, "nor did I to the Secretary of War or to General Halleck." What the new general in chief meant was that Lincoln did not require him to reveal all the *details* of his grand strategy; the chief executive did continue to scrutinize such matters and insist on knowing the general overall plans that Grant was formulating.[44]

Grant's plan of grand strategy—a good one—called for nearly simultaneous advances by Meade's army against Lee, Butler's Army of the James against Richmond from Fort Monroe, Sherman's army against Atlanta, Franz Sigel's army southward up the Shenandoah Valley toward Staunton and Lynchburg, and Banks's army against Mobile.[45]

Grant's own operations with Meade's Army of the Potomac against Lee in northern Virginia provided that he would cross the Rapidan on 4 May 1864 and plunge southward into the Wilderness with almost 118,000 men. Lee, with 62,000 troops, moved from the west to strike the Federals on their right flank in the forest. Grant was obliged to turn to the right (west) on the Orange Plank Road and the Orange Turnpike to confront the gray leader. The desperate two-day Battle of the Wilderness resulted on 5 and 6 May, with slight initial Union gains that were soon reversed by Longstreet's massive counterattack against Grant's left wing. Although Longstreet was seriously wounded, Lee was able to work his way around both Federal flanks. Aware that he could not bludgeon his way through, Grant pulled away from the field of battle and tried to slip around Lee's right flank. However, Lee anticipated this and moved in time to cover the important crossroads at Spotsylvania Court House to the south. At the Wilderness Lee probably lost at least 8,000 soldiers compared to 17,666 Union casualties.[46]

Grant accomplished little in the complex maneuvering and heavy fighting at Spotsylvania from 8 May through 18 May. Most of his attacks—such as those on 8 May, Emory Upton's well-conceived one on 10 May, and those on 18 May—were repelled with heavy losses. Winfield S. Hancock's brilliant dawn assault on 12 May at the apex of Lee's salient succeeded in capturing some cannon, 4,000 Confederates, and a few yards of ground, but in protracted fighting that day at a slight bend on the western face of the "Mule Shoe," known ever afterwards as the Bloody Angle, the Federals merely held the slight enemy breastworks. Essentially Lee held his main position, losing perhaps 9,000 men in the entire operation as against Grant's losses of 18,399.[47]

Realizing that he could not hammer his way through Lee's lines, Grant abandoned the battlefield and moved several times by his left flank in attempts to slide past Lee's right flank; each time he was unsuccessful. He found Lee in front of him at the North Anna River, at the Totopotomoy, and at Cold Har-

bor, just to the northeast of Richmond, where he partially overlapped Mc-
Clellan's old 1862 battleground of Gaines's Mill. Grant lost 4,000 men in light
fighting at the North Anna and the Totopotomoy. At Cold Harbor his patience and nerves snapped and Grant hurled his troops forward in suicidal
frontal attacks that cost him 12,737 casualties (as compared to very light Confederate losses), and the Union would have lost more men had not Meade
taken the responsibility of calling off the rash assaults. Grant admitted his
blunder in the futile attacks at Cold Harbor on 3 June.[48]

But the tenacious Grant wired back to Washington, "I propose to fight it
out on this line if it takes all summer." It would take him much longer than
"all summer," and he would have to shift to other lines of approach. "I
think," wrote Meade on 5 June, "Grant has had his eyes opened, and is willing to admit that Virginia and Lee's army is not Tennessee and Bragg's
army." The Union general in chief admitted to Halleck, "Without a greater
sacrifice of human life than I am willing to make, all cannot be accomplished
that I had designed" north of Richmond. He had lost almost sixty thousand
men as compared to Lee's twenty thousand, and Northern morale and the will
to continue the struggle sagged dangerously, bolstered only by Federal triumphs elsewhere. Lee definitely had the better of it with Grant.[49]

Finally, for the first time in the whole overland campaign, Grant
outguessed Lee by *again* moving by his left flank and stealing a march on the
Rebels. The Nationals crossed the James River to the southeast of Richmond
and threatened Petersburg, the prime rail-hub south of the Confederate
capital. Bungling of orders by Union high ranking officers, including Grant on
down, enabled Beauregard to put up a bold front and essentially hold off the
Federals to the east of Petersburg until Lee reacted and hurried his main army
there to protect Petersburg and Richmond. Desperate Union attacks at
Petersburg in mid-June, before Lee could strengthen his fortifications, were
hurled back with the heavy loss of about ten thousand Federals.[50]

As the siege of Petersburg became more protracted, with trenches the
order of the day, both sides gradually extended their southern flanks. To
lessen Grant's bulldog grip near Petersburg and Richmond, or to lure him into
a rash attack, Lee shook Jubal Early loose from these cities for a raid down
the Shenandoah Valley in early July 1864. "Old Jube" crossed the Potomac,
was delayed only briefly at the Battle of Monocacy by Lew Wallace, and
descended upon the Union capital to a point just to the northwest of the city's
fortifications that Grant had not had adequately manned. Grant finally
detached some troops stationed near Richmond, and, when Early withdrew
from Washington into the valley, the Federal general in chief, with ill grace,
reluctantly formed a superior army under Philip H. Sheridan. By autumn
these Union forces cleared Early from the valley and inflicted a scorched-earth
campaign foreshadowing the modern total war concept upon the economic
resources of that Confederate breadbasket.[51]

Meanwhile, at Petersburg, Meade and Grant unenthusiastically allowed
Burnside to authorize a dubious mine operation. Since 25 June 1864 Henry
Pleasants's Forty-eighth Pennsylvania had been engaged in tunneling 511 feet
from the Union lines to a point under the Confederate positions and emplacing

some 8,000 pounds of gunpowder. The mine was exploded early on the morning of 30 July; yet despite explicit orders from Grant and especially from Meade, Burnside botched up the attack in a number of ways. The Union troops were permitted to bunch up helplessly in the mine crater that measured 30 feet deep, 80 feet wide, and 170 feet long. The delays allowed the Confederates to hurry up reinforcements, and the Federals were hurled back, after insignificant gains, with over four thousand casualties.[52]

Thereafter until March 1865 Grant and Lee settled down into a trench-type of siege warfare, with Confederate lines stretched thin by Grant's elongated extensions to the south and southwest. However, during these long months Grant could not break through Lee's lines decisively, and the stalemate continued.[53]

ONE of Lincoln and Grant's other top army commanders, William Tecumseh Sherman, was doing better than his general in chief. Poised near Dalton, Georgia, with about one hundred thousand men, and about to engage Joseph E. Johnston's Confederate army of approximately fifty-five thousand in the campaign for Atlanta, Sherman's name had become a household word in the North and South. Interested and informed people knew this red-haired, sharp-eyed, tough-looking soldier by name. Sherman was born in 1820 in Lancaster, Ohio, the son of a judge of the state supreme court. "Cump" graduated sixth in the 1840 class of forty-two at West Point and served in the Seminole and Mexican Wars before resigning from the army in 1853. He worked in banks in San Francisco and New York, became a military school superintendent in Louisiana, and was a railroad president in St. Louis when civil war began. He was easily irritated by the press and by politicians, quick to reply, and occasionally intolerant. Sherman was an animated and excellent conversationalist, and he had a vivid imagination. Though by no means a great battle captain, he excelled in strategic planning, logistics, and conducting long marches.[54]

Sherman, who knew the country better than Johnston, pushed off with his massive force on 7 May 1864, a few days after Grant and Meade began their campaign against Lee. A brilliant series of cat-and-mouse games ensued between Sherman and Johnston, the latter taking up nine successive defensive positions on the road to Atlanta. Sherman would usually put about an equal number of Union troops directly in front of Johnston and then try to swing around one of his flanks to gain his rear (never trying a double envelopment). At seven of the nine positions, the Union commander attempted to turn the Confederate left flank, and in two of them the right flank. But in a masterly exhibition of military prescience, Johnston correctly gauged *each time* which way Sherman would swing and moved in time to counter him. At the sixth position at New Hope Church on 25 to 28 May, and notably at the seventh position at Kenesaw Mountain on 14 June, Sherman's nerves and patience snapped. He delivered frontal attacks that were repulsed by Johnston at Kenesaw Mountain at the cost of some three thousand Federal casualties. Finally, unable to assure Jefferson Davis that the Confederates could stem the Union advance at Peachtree Creek near Atlanta, Johnston was relieved of his command on 17 July just as he had his best chance to counterattack and was about to deliver such a blow at Sherman. Johnston was replaced by John Bell Hood, a maimed, oftentimes rash and incompetent army commander. Attacking in four hasty and ill-advised assaults at the Battles of Peachtree Creek, Atlanta, Ezra Church, and Jonesboro, Hood was defeated in each combat and was obliged to evacuate Atlanta on the night of 31 August–1 September 1864.[55]

When Hood's Confederates threatened to regain the initiative by menacing Alabama and actually invading Tennessee, Sherman recommended an imaginative strategic plan to Grant and Lincoln: Thomas would be sent back to safeguard central Tennessee while Sherman would boldly strike out from Atlanta in a march to the sea to Savannah, destroying all worthwhile Southern economic resources in his path.[56]

Grant passed on Sherman's scheme to the president with only a lukewarm endorsement, insisting that Sherman provide protection for Tennessee and the Union navy provide a base on the coast for Sherman's army. Lincoln, even more reluctant than Grant, finally approved Sherman's design and Grant followed suit.[57] All three Union leaders had a better grasp than did Lee—who adhered more to traditional warfare—of the total war idea of more modern times.

Sherman carried out his plan adroitly. Confronted at first with only William J. ("Old Reliable") Hardee's fifteen thousand Confederates, Sherman spread out his sixty-eight thousand men over a fifty-mile radius and carved out a decimated band of territory to Savannah, which he captured on 21 December 1864. Meanwhile Thomas remained on the defensive at Nashville, ready to withstand Hood's counterthrust into Tennessee.[58]

When it appeared to Lincoln that Thomas, like Rosecrans before him, was stalling over attacking Hood's smaller army, he called it to Grant's attention. Grant, too hastily and with poor judgment, brusquely demanded that Thomas attack Hood at once, an action that Thomas was already preparing with the utmost thoroughness. Forgetting the realities of the difficult situation Thomas faced, complicated by frightful weather conditions, Grant unfairly urged that Lincoln fire Thomas. This the president would not do, although he would permit the general in chief to do so. Grant, with ill humor and indecent haste, moved immediately to remove Thomas. But he was thwarted at the last moment in mid-December, 1864, when the weather moderated, the sheet-ice melted, and Thomas finally launched an all-out assault at Nashville on 15 and 16 December. The Federals, featuring James H. Wilson's brilliant cavalry attack, smashed Hood's army to such an extent that it was virtually useless thereafter.[59]

Once again Lincoln's commonsense insight into generals in the later stages of the war proved to be more accurate than Grant's. When in December 1864 "Beast" Butler bungled an attack on Fort Fisher at Wilmington, North Carolina, Lincoln, still playing an active role in such matters, acceded to Grant's request and in January 1865 removed that incompetent political general. By 1864 Commander in Chief Lincoln had become a consummate war director.[60]

In early April 1865, with Lee's manpower dwindling rapidly, and following the unsuccessful Confederate attack at Fort Stedman on 25 March, Grant succeeded at last in breaking through the Southern lines and forcing Lee to evacuate both Petersburg and Richmond. Grant and Meade now strained every nerve in the eighty-eight-mile pursuit toward Appomattox Court House to cut Lee off and capture his remnants. Lincoln visited Grant and the Army of the Potomac at City Point, and still playing his full role as commander in chief and strategist, pointed out on the maps the positions and movements of the rival armies to guests aboard the *River Queen*. Grant and Sheridan told the president that the enemy would capitulate if the Federal pursuit were pressed. On 7 April 1865, in the last significant military directive of his life Lincoln replied, "Let the *thing* be pressed." Two days later Lee surrendered to Grant at Appomattox Court House.[61]

At the solemn, majestic surrender at the McLean house, Grant, who on the whole performed well as general in chief but had been brought up short many times by Lincoln's overriding control as commander in chief, was permitted by the president to extend his authority as commanding general for the first time during the war. This occurred in Grant's generous terms to Lee and the capitulating Confederates when Grant declared: "Each [Confederate] officer and man will be allowed to return to their homes, *not to be disturbed by United States authority so long as they observe their parole and the laws in force where they may reside.* "[62]

By these words that gave amnesty and pardon to practically everyone in Lee's army, Grant was really assuming presidential and possibly congressional powers; but the magnanimous man from Springfield was so eager to end the war and bloodshed and restore harmony quickly with his former Southern countrymen that he refrained from making an issue over the matter with Grant, and allowed it to stand.[63]

And good news soon came from Sherman. Moving up through the Carolinas he forced Johnston, restored to command by newly appointed Confederate General in Chief Lee, to surrender at Durham Station on 26 April 1865. On 26 May Edmund Kirby Smith in Louisiana yielded the Confederate trans-Mississippi forces to Edward Canby; and, in the final act, Galveston, Texas, capitulated to Union forces on 2 June 1865. During this war some 260,000 Confederate soldiers and about 360,000 Union troops made the supreme sacrifice.[64]

The generals in blue who commanded armies in the field throughout the war had fought with mixed success a long and tenacious battle, not only with the gallant Southerners, but with their own superiors in Washington over matters of strategy and grand strategy and had often seen their plans—as had Confederate generals—scrutinized and frequently altered or countermanded by the president, the secretary of war, or the general in chief. In mid-April 1865 Lincoln was assassinated. The final generous overstep by U. S. Grant, just mentioned, had been overlooked by Abraham Lincoln; but it had been done so deliberately by the towering figure who now belongs to the ages.

IN MANY RESPECTS, the Civil War was the American Iliad. Soldiers in blue and gray fought each other with supreme courage and devotion for the cause each believed just. The fighting qualities of our citizen-soldiers of the 1860s have not yet ceased to astound military men and scholars. Despite some knavery during this "brother's war" of four years, truly noble figures like Abraham Lincoln and Robert E. Lee emerged as did other leaders and soldiers on both sides who closely approached them in character, dedication, and performance.

The leaders of the rival Union and Confederate governments sadly misjudged the length, breadth, and depth of the contest, and they had difficulty in developing grand strategy appropriate to their own resources and objectives. Yet as the grim struggle of attrition continued, a legacy developed that would weld the sundered sections together again after Appomattox—a heritage that encompassed both North and South. Across the span of more than a century Americans would react with pride as they contemplated such masterful military performances as George B. McClellan's in the Seven Days, Albert Sidney Johnston's at Shiloh, Stonewall Jackson's in the Shenandoah Valley, Robert E. Lee's at Chancellorsville, George Gordon Meade's at Gettysburg, U.S. Grant's at Vicksburg, Joseph E. Johnston's on the road to Atlanta, and Nathan Bedford Forrest's at Brice's Crossroads.

So pervasive has the inspiration of the Civil War become to the generations since that day that many of the historic battlefields contested by the blue and gray have been preserved as living memorials to the Republic's sons "who here gave their lives that that nation might live. It is altogether fitting and proper that we should do this."

Sun-Baked Plains and White Ships

> . . . *while these dead* [Indian]*warriors today*
> *ride the plains in tradition taller, swifter, and*
> *stronger than they ever did in life, they do not*
> *ride them alone. They share the sky and the*
> *horizon forever with the United States Cavalry*
> *which fought them, and by so doing made itself*
> *also a part of the legend of a world of bright and*
> *golden courage and endless space.*
>
> RALPH K. ANDRIST

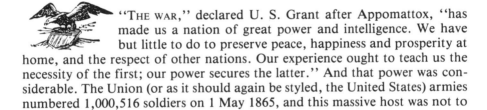 "THE WAR," declared U. S. Grant after Appomattox, "has made us a nation of great power and intelligence. We have but little to do to preserve peace, happiness and prosperity at home, and the respect of other nations. Our experience ought to teach us the necessity of the first; our power secures the latter." And that power was considerable. The Union (or as it should again be styled, the United States) armies numbered 1,000,516 soldiers on 1 May 1865, and this massive host was not to be equaled until the rise of the Prussian army in the late 1860s.[1]

But the mighty blue-clad volunteer armies that saved the Union were soon largely disbanded; this was perhaps natural and understandable, given the attitudes and situation of Americans after a conflict that had claimed some 620,000 lives. The nation's army of over a million men in May 1865 had been reduced to about 200,000 by the end of that year. The country was divided into nineteen military departments and five regional military divisions—the Divisions of the Pacific, the Mississippi, the Gulf, the Tennessee, and the Atlantic. Of the volunteers in the Army of the United States, only 11,043 were left by 1866, of whom 10,000 were Negroes. Even the lure of generous bounties to encourage reenlistments failed to keep sufficient numbers in the army.[2]

During the war, as the Federal armies penetrated the Confederacy, Lincoln appointed civilian military governors, such as Andrew Johnson in Tennessee, to help establish new state governments. Actually, the military department commanders dominated the so-called military governors. Law and order were maintained by the army's provost marshals, who permitted varying local participation by Southerners according to the degree that these inhabitants accepted the loyalty oaths administered to them. After the horrors of the war, only the Federal army's military government prevented anarchy or chaos in the states of the ex-Confederacy.[3]

President Andrew Johnson, Lincoln's successor, had been a tailor in his early adulthood. He was a self-made man who through steady application eventually became a United States senator from Tennessee and vice-president of the United States as Lincoln's running mate in 1864. Essentially Johnson showed little sympathy toward the freedmen. And he was extremely lenient in pardoning ex-Confederates whom he had denied citizenship rights in his plan for Reconstruction and allowed them to reassert their former power and leadership in the provisional governments set up in the South in the months following the end of the war.

Thus emboldened, some of these Southerners took to insulting Federal occupation soldiers. Perceiving little support from Johnson, the army turned per force to Congress and its dominant Radical Republican element. Friction between the legislators and the president began to intensify. Only Johnson's veto of the bill to renew the Freedmen's Bureau was not overridden. Grant, Stanton, and the Congress took action to protect the troops in the South from injustice in local civil courts. Not since the earlier days of the republic had army officers felt obliged to move into partisan politics to such a degree.[4]

To aid the army and the country, Grant and Stanton risked the extreme displeasure of President Johnson by gradually opposing his permissive Southern policies, and the president began to take steps to remove these two leaders from the scene. Getting wind of this action, Congress in March 1867 passed the Tenure of Office Act and the Command of the Army Act over the chief executive's veto.[5]

The Tenure of Office Act was of dubious constitutionality. By this legislation the Radicals sought to prevent Johnson's removal of Stanton or any cabinet member without the consent of the Senate. By the Command of the Army Act, really a rider on an army appropriation bill, Congress meant to diminish the president's powers as commander in chief. The act provided that all orders of the president to the army should be issued through the general in chief (Grant), who could not be removed without the Senate's approval and could not be ordered away from the city of Washington, D.C., by the president. Johnson signed the bill into law so as not to lose the army's appropriations, but he denounced the command of the army section "which," he declared, "virtually deprives the President of his constitutional functions as Commander in Chief of the Army. . . . I . . . protest against the sections. . . ." But he railed in vain.[6]

Beginning in 1867 Congress passed over Johnson's vetoes several so-called Reconstruction Acts, which asserted that in the absence of legal governments in the states of the late Confederacy, they were to be divided into five military districts. Each was to be commanded by a major general of the army who, with his military courts, was to be superior to any civilian official in the South. These men with stars on their shoulders were to enroll eligible voters and make sure that the freedmen were registered and that certain categories of former Confederates were proscribed. General in Chief Grant directed the five generals to follow the instructions of Congress, not the president, in Southern reconstruction. Only the army in the West remained, in effect, under Johnson's orders.[7]

Outraged by these erosions of his powers as commander in chief, the president fired Stanton and installed Grant as secretary of war ad interim. Grant reluctantly accepted the position while remaining commanding general, not out of any love for Johnson but because of his devotion to the army and his belief that its security in the South depended on the Reconstruction policies being projected by Congress. When Congress reconvened, it contended that Johnson's removal of Stanton violated the Tenure of Office Act. Stanton reclaimed his office and Grant yielded it to him. The chief executive held that this act was unconstitutional, refused to accept Stanton as secretary, and tried to supplant him in that position with Adj. Gen. Lorenzo Thomas. Impeachment proceedings were instituted against Johnson and the trial ended in May 1867 with his acquittal by one vote.

Thus the so-called "Rule of the Major Generals" began in the South. With the president unable to get legislation through Congress, and with former Maj. Gen. John M. Schofield serving as a sort of compromise secretary of war, General in Chief Grant exercised almost supreme authority over the army in 1867–1868. Gradually, under the new Radical regimes in the ex-Confederacy, Southern state militias composed chiefly of subservient Negroes took over supervision of elections and other tasks from the undermanned regular army. This black militia was relatively useful until about 1870, when white counterterrorism and the Ku Klux Klan lessened its efficacy. When the Klan became too troublesome, the army was called upon to help suppress it, and this was done by the early 1870s. Certainly, for the army, the Reconstruction years were difficult; those following until 1898 were no rosier.[8]

The army continued to suffer in the matter of numbers. On 3 March 1869 Congress cut the regular army from about 54,000 to 45,000; actually only 41,808 could be obtained because of the long five-year term of enlistment that the army would have to live with for a while. The tiny old War Department building just to the west of the White House did not even provide fire-proof protection for top-secret documents. In 1870 the army was reduced by Congress to 30,000. Except for four-star General in Chief Sherman, the service was permitted only three major generals and six brigadier generals. On 16 June 1874 the army was slashed to 25,000, and it remained at approximately that figure until the Spanish-American War in 1898. In one year (1877), Congress neglected to pass any army appropriation bill, and officers had to borrow money at interest to live. Supply purchases were made on credit, and pay was simply in arrears until the next session of Congress voted the requisite funds.[9]

Moreover, the post-Appomattox decades were not very progressive as far as the introduction of modern weapons was concerned. It will be remembered that the Civil War was fought largely with the single-shot, muzzle-loading shoulder rifle. Congress continued for some time to reject breechloaders, despite Secretary of War Stanton's call for them, on the basis that there was too much muzzle-loading .50 caliber ammunition on hand from the war. Finally in 1869 Congress authorized adoption of the Springfield single-shot breechloader, which was slightly modified in 1873. Some soldiers tried to save their few dollars' pay to purchase repeating breechloaders, inasmuch as many of the hostile Indians possessed such superior rifles. Not until 1892 was the five-shot, .30 caliber, Krag-Jorgenson repeater, burning smokeless powder, adopted.[10]

Nor was the picture any brighter with respect to artillery and the arming of coastal fortifications. Not until 1881 were breech-loading cannon employed. Repair and construction work lagged on the great forts along American coasts, and they were not properly armed with a sufficient number of big guns. In 1885 the Endicott Board recommended that 2,362 artillery pieces be emplaced in these coastal forts, but by 1898 only 151 such guns were in position; hence American cities were largely undefended (except by the navy) against Spanish warships and unreasoning panic developed in certain strategic areas.[11]

The post–Civil War years passed without spectacular developments for the military academy at West Point. Yet there was some progress. The school was removed from the control of the Corps of Engineers; officers of all branches became eligible for the superintendency of the academy; and military training was increased by limiting the dominance of engineering in the curriculum. As a consequence, West Point's reputation for excellence in engineering and science suffered something of a decline. The death of Dennis Hart Mahan in 1871 seemed to usher in a less dynamic era at the academy. The curriculum emphasized narrow technical military instruction in tactics, weapons, and mathematics rather than a wider study of strategy, policy, or military history. While this education was satisfactory for company-level officers, it did little to prepare them for advanced rank and command responsibilities, or develop a broader vision of their profession.[12]

Yet the army did have a singular and influential military thinker in the person of Emory Upton. Born on 27 August 1839 on a farm west of Batavia, New York, Upton attended Oberlin College before entering West Point. Upton graduated eighth in the class of 1861 with a reputation as an excellent student who was something of a firebrand. He went directly from the military academy into the Union army and compiled an outstanding record, rising from second lieutenant to brevet major general in both the volunteer and regular army. Most of his service was with the Army of the Potomac. Upton skillfully commanded artillery, infantry, and cavalry units, and was wounded three times during the war. Perhaps his finest hour was his brilliant attack with twelve picked regiments against the western face of the Confederate salient at Spotsylvania Court House on the morning of 10 May 1864. Much of his post–Civil War career involved instructional assignments, and he was commandant of cadets at West Point from 1870 to 1875. He wrote extensively on military tactics, on *The Military Policy of the United States* from 1775 to 1862, and, after several trips abroad, on *The Armies of Asia and Europe.* Suffering intolerably from migraine headaches and finally a brain tumor, Upton committed suicide at the age of forty-one at the Presidio in San Francisco on 15 March 1881.[13]

But what were Upton's views that have had such a profound impact upon American military policy since he wrote them? Upton esteemed the German army and military system, and in his *Military Policy of the United States,* a scholarly and persuasive military history of America, he damned the civilian high command and the unpreparedness of American ground forces based on too small a regular army and too heavy a reliance on citizen-soldiers as short-term militia or volunteers. Like the German system, the highly proficient United States regular army would be used as a cadre in wartime around which a large conscripted national army would be developed.[14]

Intelligent, humorless, and single minded, Upton pressed his views relentlessly. He especially criticized what he believed to be the excessive and historically ineffective civilian control of the military in the United States, and that included congressional as well as executive interference. Military schools and a general staff were to be based on the German models, and even our national institutions would have to adjust more to military expediency. Years before his book was published in 1904 his ideas had a wide influence on army officers. But the country simply would not believe the times required such rigorous actions as Upton projected, and their relevance to realistic American goals of that era could be questioned despite the logic of many of his contentions.

IN THE FRIGHTFUL Indian wars covering the thirty years after 1865, the United States Army was in the unenviable position of being in the middle of a tragic situation, but its presence was essential to the pacification of the trans–Missouri River West. The agonizing problem had been created by the attitudes and actions of the federal government and the nation's citizens. President Rutherford B. Hayes acknowledged in his annual report of 1877:

> . . . the Indians are certainly entitled to our sympathy and to a conscientious respect on our part for their claims upon our sense of justice. They were the original occupants of the land we now possess. They have been driven from place to place. The purchase money paid to them in some cases for what they called their own has still left them poor. In many instances, when they had settled down upon land assigned to them by compact and begun to support themselves by their own labor, they were rudely jostled off and thrust into the wilderness again. Many, if not most, of our Indian wars have had their origin in broken promises and acts of injustice upon our part. . . .[15]

During this period on the Great Plains and Rocky Mountains there were perhaps 250,000 to 300,000 Indians; possibly 175,000 were organized into specific tribal entities while the others were nomadic and moved up and down the plains with the seasons following the great herds of bison. The Indian wars of the last third of the nineteenth century provided the army with a number of well-trained Indian fighters and were valuable lessons in small-unit handling. Yet the officers and army were not thereby enlightened to the more sophisticated aspects of their profession, nor were they readied to wage a full-scale war against a first-rate military power.[16]

Between 1865 and 1891 there were 13 different campaigns and 1,067 separate engagements fought between the army and the Indians. There was hostility from the press and Easterners whether the army won or lost a battle

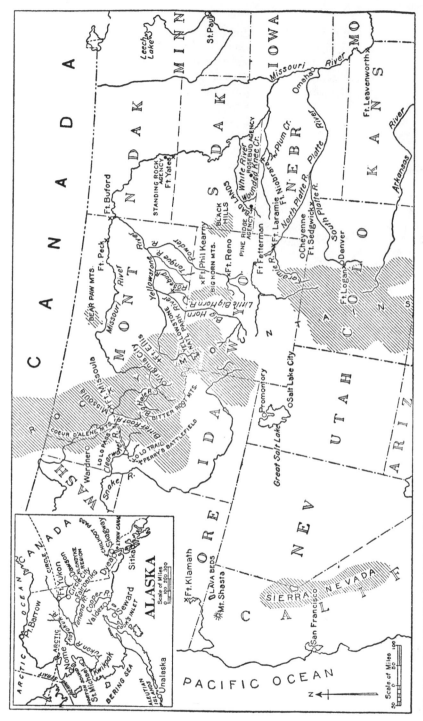

FIG. 9.1. THE NORTHWEST AND ALASKA

against the Indians, and that enmity was inflated in the partisan writings such as those of Helen Hunt Jackson. As a warrior, the Plains Indian was one of the finest light cavalrymen in the world. Most of them respected army leaders as men of honor and integrity, even as they fought them to the death. Various tactics were used, with final success, against the so-called savages; George Crook's single light, swift, pursuing column, or Nelson Miles's converging columns. But whatever way, it was a long, frustrating, and difficult assignment that included privations, horrors, and hardships for the men in blue west of the Mississippi.[17]

When gold was discovered near Virginia City, in what is now Montana, John M. Bozeman constructed a trail, which soon bore his name, from a point northwest of Fort Laramie along the eastern side of the Big Horn Mountain range and across the Yellowstone River to Virginia City. This trail traversed some of the best hunting grounds of the Sioux; so it was decided in 1866 to build forts along the road. Similar forts had successfully pacified Indians in Texas and elsewhere in Montana. However, the Indians regarded the wooden stockades on the Bozeman Trail—like those at Fort Phil Kearny in Wyoming just south of Montana at the eastern foot of the Big Horns—as having an aura of permanency about them. "Building posts in their country," said impulsive but honest Brig. Gen. Edward O. C. Ord, "demoralizes them more than anything else except money and whiskey." Thus it was that Chief Red Cloud of the Oglala Sioux led his braves off the reservation in 1866 and onto the warpath.[18]

When hostile Oglala Sioux attacked in the vicinity of Fort Kearny on 6 December 1866, killing two and wounding five soldiers, Col. Henry B. Carrington decided to chastise them when they again assaulted a wood-gathering wagon train of soldiers from the fort on 21 December. He authorized Capt. William J. Fetterman, a proven though somewhat reckless combat officer, and some 80 cavalrymen and infantrymen to relieve the besieged wagon train. Under no circumstances were they to pursue the Indians far enough away to be ambushed. There were between fifteen hundred and two thousand braves to contend with on the slopes of nearby ridges. Fetterman disregarded these instructions, possibly through circumstances not under his control, and he was ambuscaded and his entire command wiped out to the man, the Indians suffering an indeterminate loss. The corpses of the slain soldiers were found horribly mutilated.[19]

The "Fetterman Massacre" shocked and incensed civilians and the military alike. Many pioneers and soldiers had long held that the only good Indian was a dead Indian, and Sherman telegraphed Grant: "We must act with vindicative [sic] earnestness against the Sioux, even to their extermination, men, women, and children."[20]

The frontier was aflame in 1867 with widespread Indian raids and scalping parties. The commander of the Department of the Platte, the capable Christopher C. Augur, had problems along the Bozeman Trail near Fort Phil Kearny, which was being harassed. Only heavily armed military wagon trains could move along this road. At least 1,500 Indians, mostly Sioux under Red Cloud, moved against the 300 troops commanded by Col. John E. Smith at

Fort Kearny. On 2 August 1867, near the fort at a temporary corral of four-teen wagon-boxes formed for use by woodcutters, the seasoned combat veteran Capt. James W. Powell and 31 men armed with new breech-loading Springfield rifles endured constant sniping and six times repelled the desperate charges of the Indians. In the four-and-one-half-hour "Wagon-Box Fight," the troops inflicted at least 180 casualties on the Indians while suffering losses of 8 of their own. Finally the Indians were dispersed by infantry and howitzer fire provided by a relief column from the fort. But the termination of this im-mediate threat did not bring with it any prolonged peace on the Great Plains—nor in California or Oklahoma, either.[21]

Hostilities continued with the Kiowas, Comanches, Arapahoes, and Cheyennes in Kansas, Oklahoma, and the panhandle of Texas, and army com-mander Phil Sheridan determined to try a winter campaign to bring the intran-sigents in line. Any Indian found off the reservation was to be treated as an outlaw. Sheridan ordered the United States Seventh Cavalry Regiment to move toward the Washita River, northwest of Forts Sill and Cobb, and kill all Indian warriors and hang those captured. All Indian women and children were to be taken prisoner, and all Indian villages, equipment, utensils, and ponies were to be destroyed. These orders were received by Lt. Col. George Arm-strong Custer, who would execute them ruthlessly and efficiently.[22]

One of the most controversial of all army Indian-fighters, Custer was born in 1839 in Ohio and graduated last in the 1861 class at West Point. Although a self-seeking, flamboyant exhibitionist and glory-hunter, Custer was eminently successful in audacious cavalry exploits during the Civil War and rose to division command with the rank of brevet major general of volunteers. His post–Appomattox career was one spent largely on the frontier and much of it in warfare against the Indians. On one occasion he was court-martialed for being absent without leave from his post. Dressed in buckskin and noted for his big mustache and long blondish hair, Custer was a man of slight build, wiry and durable. Bold occasionally to the extent of recklessness, and at times disdaining reconnaissances, Custer in 1868 had been returned to his regular army rank of lieutenant colonel. He could be a headstrong, dif-ficult subordinate, but thus far in his career he had been blessed with what was known widely as "Custer's Luck."[23]

Armed with Spencer seven-shot repeating carbines, Custer's Seventh Cavalry of some eight hundred troopers, accompanied by supply wagons, caught up with the peaceful Chief Black Kettle's not-so-peaceful Cheyennes in the Washita Valley and attacked in four groups in the snow and bitter cold of 27 November 1868. Custer, without proper reconnaissance, caught the Indians by surprise, and in a desperate engagement in which Indian women and young boys fought, carried out Sheridan's orders to the letter. Several dozen Indians were dispatched, including Black Kettle and some of the women and children. Indian squaws had slain in cold blood a captive white woman and her son. Custer's performance was further marred by his failure, although he had been informed several times, to go to the aid of Maj. Joel Elliott and some fifteen troopers who had gotten detached and been assailed by superior numbers of hostiles. Elliott and his men were discovered days later, killed, stripped naked, and butchered. Custer never lived down this abandonment. His losses, including Elliott's, amounted to two officers and nineteen men killed, and three officers (including his brother, Tom Custer) and eleven soldiers wounded. As the army faced continuing Indian wars, the winter experiment at the Washita would demonstrate that perhaps the best way to deal with Indians, as found in the opposite season against the Seminoles, was to campaign against them and their wherewithal to survive, around the calendar year—in short, total war.[24]

The vastness of the area involved in the Indian wars is illustrated by the army's next major encounter with the Indians. This was a campaign against the redoubtable Modocs near the California-Oregon border to the northeast of Mt. Shasta in the vicinity of Lost River and Tule, Clear, and Lower Klamath lakes. The six hundred tough, warlike Modocs, led by Captain Jack, included such wild and dramatically named warriors as Modoc George, Hooker Jim, Black Jim, Scarfaced Charley, Ellen's Man, Boston Charley, Miller's Charley, Curley Headed Doctor, Shacknasty Jim, Bogus Charley, and Steamboat Frank. They had attacked and slaughtered travelers and settlers in their areas and refused to remain on a reservation with the unfriendly Klamath tribe.

The order to attack the Modocs in Captain Jack's stronghold in the Lava Beds south of Lake Tule was issued by the department commander, Brig. Gen. Edward R. S. Canby, the courteous, kindly, accommodating thirty-four-year-old veteran officer who had fought Seminoles, Mexicans, and Southerners with equal ability. Canby had gained fame in the Civil War by repelling Sibley's Confederate invasion of New Mexico, in assailing Mobile, and in receiving the surrender of the Trans-Mississippi Rebel armies.[25]

The Lava Beds comprised a weird assortment of caves, towers, grottoes, turrets, parapets, and ravines, and the whole region looked like rippling seawaves that had instantly congealed. The attack on the 60-odd Modocs in the Lava Beds on 17 January 1873 was made by approximately 330 infantrymen and cavalrymen, supported by artillery. It was beaten back by the Indians who inflicted on the soldiers casualties of 11 killed and 26 wounded. No Modoc had been hit—indeed, none had even been seen by the troops. The usually capable Canby foolishly agreed that he and several Indian commissioners would negotiate with the hostiles, who were divided among themselves over peace or war.

In the famous conference on Good Friday, 11 April 1873, in the midst of the supposedly peaceful powwow, Captain Jack suddenly whipped out a concealed pistol and shot Canby under the eye at point-blank range. Staggering to his feet with the mortal wound, the general was shot with a rifle by Ellen's Man and stabbed by Captain Jack. Several other whites were assaulted at the peace table. Outraged by the murder of the respected and well-liked Canby, the army, under the overall command of the hard-bitten Civil War veteran Jefferson C. Davis, renewed its attack on Jack's stronghold in the Lava Beds in mid-April. After three days of sharp fighting, the troops drove the Modocs out of the stronghold and by mid-May out of the Lava Beds entirely, but at a cost of twenty-five soldiers killed and sixteen wounded. Finally, with the help of some Modocs who had surrendered, the troops captured Captain Jack and his braves in early June. Captain Jack and three others were executed by hanging on 3 October 1873, and their heads were severed and shipped to the Army Medical Museum in Washington, D.C. Some 155 Modoc prisoners were then settled on a reservation in Indian Territory.[26]

FARTHER to the east it took two grim decades before the army could subdue the magnificent fighting warriors of the Plains Indians. The Custer tragedy at the Little Bighorn had its origins, in part, in the reactions of the great Hunkpapa Sioux leader, Sitting Bull, to the continuing relentless pressure of the white man's westward expansion. Nursing an unyielding hatred of the whites and their encroachments, Sitting Bull remained a religious, military, and political chief with significant influence over a number of tribes. His commanding presence, courage, intelligence, and positive judgments made him a leader to be reckoned with. The Treaty of 1868 had delimited the Great Sioux Reservation to that part of present-day South Dakota west of the Missouri River. Not all Indians remained on the agency-controlled reservations, however; thousands retained the traditional hunting urge and migrated in and out of the agencies to the camps of nontreaty chiefs such as Sitting Bull. The winter of 1873–1874 was one of widespread raiding and scalping, even against other Indians who were peaceful, by off-agency hostiles who respected treaty boundaries no better than did the whites.[27]

Complicating the situation was the penetration by the Northern Pacific Railroad up the valley of the Yellowstone that permitted a further influx of whites whose presence threatened the herds of bison. Sitting Bull's Sioux resisted stoutly. An army expedition up the Yellowstone in 1873, commanded by Col. Davis S. Stanley and including ten troops of Custer's Seventh Cavalry, resulted in defeat for the Sioux in two engagements in August: one where the Tongue River empties into the Yellowstone, and the other on the north bank of the Yellowstone below the mouth of the Bighorn River. This was followed by the illegal and immoral incursion by miners and settlers into the Black Hills of southwestern South Dakota, a sanctuary of the Sioux supposedly guaranteed by solemn treaty. To counter Sioux raids in Ord's Platte Department, and aware of possible gold discoveries, Sheridan in 1874 prevailed upon the president and secretaries of war and interior to order Custer to invade the Black Hills. Spending only two months in these mountains, Custer located a likely site for a fort; in his official report, he scarcely mentioned gold. But word leaked out that emphasized the precious metal, and this was whipped up by the press into a full-scale gold rush. President Grant directed the small army to try to keep the stampeding hundreds of gold seekers out of the Black Hills in the summer of 1875, but it was to no avail.[28]

In a difficult winter campaign commencing in early 1876, George Crook with almost nine hundred soldiers pressed northward through the snow and subzero weather along the Bozeman Trail from Fort Fetterman. A third of this force under friendly old Joseph J. Reynolds met some two hundred Cheyennes and Oglala Sioux on 17 March at the Powder River in a combat that favored the Indians and impelled Crook's withdrawal to Fort Fetterman.

Meanwhile, heavy snows and the more westward location of the Indians delayed the Custer expedition then fitting out at Fort Abraham Lincoln (across the Missouri River from Bismarck) under the overall command of Brig. Gen. Alfred H. Terry. A cultured, widely respected, and wealthy bachelor, the Connecticut-born Terry was not a West Pointer and had risen from militia officer to fame in the Civil War. He fought capably at Bull Run, Port Royal, Fort Pulaski, Charleston, Petersburg, and Richmond, but gained his greatest fame by his capture of Fort Fisher at Wilmington, North Carolina. But he, like Hancock before him, was inexperienced in Indian warfare. Once Terry and Custer were ready, they would push westward from Fort Lincoln; John Gibbon would move eastward from Fort Ellis, Montana; and Crook would again march northward from Fort Fetterman on the North Platte, Wyoming.[29]

John Gibbon, operating under Terry's orders, moved first with the Montana column. He left Fort Ellis on 30 March 1876 with some 450 troops, surmounted Bozeman Pass, and patrolled the north bank of the Yellowstone. Custer's column, under Terry's overall command, left Fort Lincoln on 17 May. It almost had to do without the services of "Yellowhair," who was delayed by testifying, successfully, before a committee of Congress in Washington, D.C., against an officer befriended by Grant. The president reluctantly allowed Custer to rejoin his Seventh Cavalry regiment in time for the expedition. Some 700 of the approximately 925 soldiers were from the Seventh. Supplies were carried by 150 wagons and in steamers up the Missouri and Yellowstone Rivers. This Dakota Column plodded through heavy wet weather into eastern Montana.[30]

Meanwhile, on 29 May Crook renewed his march from Fort Fetterman up the Bozeman Trail, his force numbering 1,047 troops plus 262 Crow and Shoshoni Indian scouts and auxiliaries. Although Indians would not often stand and fight against disciplined soldiers, and though game and grass could not sustain large groupings of Indians for long, nonetheless massive hosts of Indians were gathering against Crook, Gibbon, Terry, and Custer—perhaps as many as 15,000 people, and 3,000 to 4,000 braves. These included Sioux, Cheyennes, Arapahoes, Santees, Brulés, Yanktonais, Blackfeet, and Sans Arc. Crossing from the Tongue to the Rosebud, Crook fell into a fierce six-hour battle on 17 June with Crazy Horse's Sioux that took place in the hills, ravines, and ridges and ended in the Indian's favor, with almost 100 casualties on each side. Crook was obliged to retreat. He was neutralized at an unpropitious time and withdrew from the overall operation as far as Gibbon, Terry, and Custer were concerned.[31]

Unaware of the Sioux aggressiveness or of Crook's setback, Terry and Gibbon conferred on 9 June 1876 on the Yellowstone aboard the supply steamer *Far West*. To confirm the reports of scouts that there were no Indians east of the Rosebud, Terry ordered Maj. Marcus A. Reno to reconnoiter the valleys of the Powder and Tongue with six troops of the Seventh Cavalry. Custer, with the rest of the Seventh, stayed at the mouth of the Tongue, while Terry moved his base to the mouth of the Powder. Exceeding his directions, Reno went as far as the Rosebud, where he discovered the trail of Sitting Bull's huge moving village. Reno's sweep—which could have alerted the Sioux to the presence of the troops—angered Terry, who had moved to concentrate his cavalry at the mouth of the Rosebud.[32]

On the *Far West* on the evening of 21 June, Terry, Custer, and Gibbon held a lengthy council of war in which Terry issued detailed instructions on how the Indians were to be cut off. Gibbon was to move southward up the Bighorn River, while Custer was to advance up the Rosebud to its head and then drive northward down the Little Bighorn. Since Gibbon could not reach the mouth of the Little Bighorn before 26 June, Custer was to keep well to the left, or south, of the westward-moving Indians so that the hostiles could not escape to the south. Custer rejected the Gatling guns and reinforcements that Terry offered him. Although Terry phrased the written orders that were immediately drawn up politely, allowing Custer some discretion should different circumstances arise, Custer knew precisely what Terry wanted done.[33]

After a review of the troops, Custer's force pushed off on 22 June. As he was about to depart, Gibbon called out, "Now, Custer, don't be greedy. Wait for us," to which Custer, with his hair now clipped short, retorted gaily, "No, I won't"—a reply that could be taken two ways. Discovering the big Sioux trail heading westward, as Terry predicted he would, Custer perhaps became obsessed with the notion that the Indians were aware of his presence and might escape. Thus he willfully, even high-handedly, disregarded the spirit if not the letter of his superior's orders and barrelled directly along the trail, instead of side-stepping to the south, a full day before he was supposed to on 26 June.[34] Perhaps Custer wanted to win the battle with his own troops, alone, convinced as he was that the Seventh Cavalry could defeat *any* Indian force it encountered.

Atop the Wolf Mountains (known now as the Rosebud Mountains), overlooking the valley of the Little Bighorn and almost in sight of the huge Indian village on the west bank, at noon on the hot Sunday of 25 June 1876 Custer unwisely divided his exhausted command. The senior captain, Frederick Benteen, a splendid, cool, veteran officer of ability and reliability, was to scout to the left with three troops (125 men); Reno, excitable and less stable but seasoned and knowledgeable, with three troops was to drive straight ahead across a line of bluffs overlooking the river and gallop to attack the Indian village from the south on the west bank of the river. Custer promised Reno that "the whole outfit would support" him. Some 130 soldiers were to stay with the ammunition pack train, which would come up in due time, while Custer with five troops totaling 215 troopers would bear to the right and north, keeping on the eastern side of the bluffs. The total force of 582 soldiers was to be confronted by possibly 3,000 warriors.[35]

On the far (western) side of the Little Bighorn River, Reno's attack toward the Southern edge of the tremendous Indian village was met head-on by a vicious counterattack by large numbers of braves. Reno dismounted his men and fought in two positions without success. Then he remounted his troopers, crossed to the east (right) bank of the river, and took up a defensive position atop the line of bluffs. He had suffered heavy casualties. Reno was soon joined by Benteen, who had wisely moved to the right from his scout to help Reno. Here on the bluffs a successful stand was made, although Reno and Benteen lost about half of their force. Seeing a swirling cloud of dust from a likely battle several miles to the north, where Custer was thought to be, some of Reno's troops moved to the north only to be challenged near Weir Point and forced back to their defensive perimeter. Here, they held on tenaciously against renewed attacks later that day and on 26 June.

Since there were no survivors in Custer's own column on the right, only conjecture, based on conflicting Indian testimony given in many cases long after the battle, can be made. Custer probably rode northward along the eastern side of the bluffs, when he was suddenly attacked on a ridge first from the south-southwest by many Indians led by the Hunkpapa chief, Gall, and then from the northwest by Crazy Horse. Hemmed in by many Indians fighting on horseback and many more on foot, Custer could not keep his dismounted command together in the tall grass, gullies, ravines, and hillocks, and a battle-to-the-death lasting perhaps an hour ensued. A small knot of resisting soldiers, perhaps some 50 in all and including Custer, his two brothers, and a nephew, made the famous last stand on a hillside. Custer was killed by a shot in the temple and another in the chest. Some 261 other soldiers' bodies were found; most were stripped naked and many mutilated (Custer's was stripped but not disfigured). Another 53 under Reno and Benteen were wounded. The number of Indians killed was estimated at anywhere from 30 to 300. Custer's was the ultimate responsibility for the disaster at the Little Bighorn because he had encountered hostile forces exactly as Terry had anticipated; essentially he had violated his orders.[36]

Perhaps the affair on the Little Bighorn should have been termed the Indians' Last Stand, for it marked the crest of their success against the army. The Indians who had whipped Custer withdrew upon the approach of Terry and Gibbon on 27 June. Crook followed up with a successful attack of the village of Chief American Horse at Slim Buttes in northwestern South Dakota on 9 September. The Bighorn and Yellowstone campaign was terminated by Sheridan, who organized the Powder River expedition to defeat the Indians in the hard winter months of 1876–1877. Crook marched northward from Fort Fetterman in November 1876 while forces under Col. Nelson A. Miles moved southward from the Yellowstone.

Miles was an intensely ambitious, hard-nosed officer who would become one of the nation's greatest Indian fighters and eventually in 1895 general in chief of the United States army, and finally lieutenant general. Born in 1839 on a farm near Westminster, Massachusetts, Miles had little formal schooling and worked as a clerk in a Boston store. When the Civil War came, he rose from a lieutenant of volunteers in the Union army to brevet major general, was wounded four times while participating in most of the battles of the Army of the Potomac, and won the Medal of Honor for his conduct at Chancellorsville. His unrelenting drive for advancement through almost any means, his disdain for sharing laurels, and his disparagement of the accomplishments of others caused many to dislike him personally while acknowledging his undoubted talents. And Miles's abilities were many and real. He was a superb field officer—audacious, innovative, high-spirited, and willing to adopt new strategies or tactics. Yet he was unyielding in pursuit of his goals. His services now in Montana would be put to excellent use.[37]

On 25 November 1876 Crook's cavalry destroyed the camp of Chief Dull

Knife and drove his Cheyennes northward, where they linked up with Crazy Horse. Miles's initial peace talk with Gall and Sitting Bull's Sioux had ended in combat in October, but he had persuaded many hundreds of Indians to yield and come onto the reservation, while he relentlessly pursued the fugitives in subzero weather. Sitting Bull, Gall, and a few followers sought refuge in Canada, where the former remained in exile until 1881. In January 1877 Miles almost succeeded in capturing the wily Crazy Horse who along with his exhausted warriors had been reduced to a starving condition. But Miles was robbed of his imminent capture of Crazy Horse when Crook, who had a good name among the Indians as an officer who kept his word, persuaded the Indian war leader to come into Camp Robinson in northwestern Nebraska and surrender on 6 May.[38]

The remainder of the dealings with these Indians followed the customary story of unbridled larceny and violated promises. A peace commission, at work since late summer of 1876, again forced by threats and bribery a few reservation chiefs of the Northern Cheyennes, Arapahoes, and Sioux to sign a new agreement whereby one-third of the Great Sioux Reservation (namely, the unceded Powder River country and the Black Hills and adjacent lands) was taken away from the tribes. This violated the solemn pledge made in the Fort Laramie Treaty that only by a vote of three-fourths of the adult males of the tribe could the treaty be altered. Despite trips to Omaha, Chicago, and Washington, D.C., Crook was unable to make good his pledge to Crazy Horse of a reservation for his group in the Powder River country. Further tragedy struck when the great Indian leader surrendered and was bayoneted to death on 5 September 1877 by a soldier who objected to Crazy Horse's resistance to entering the guardhouse. Dispirited, the Sioux allowed Crook to move them peacefully to their new agencies on the reduced reservation. By the end of 1877, it appeared that not a so-called wild Indian or free tribe would be found on the Great Plains.[39]

ALMOST, but not quite. Indians of the Northwest, the Nez Percés, had settled on the constricted Lapwai reservation in Idaho near the eastern corners of Oregon and Washington. The nontreaty Nez Percés, under Chief Joseph and others, took up arms to remain in the northwestern corner of Oregon that the government had shamefully opened up to settlement in 1875 in violation of solemn agreement and in spite of Brig. Gen. Oliver Otis Howard's humanitarian sympathy for these Indians. A persistent legend and stereotype portraying Joseph, chief of the Wallowa band of the Nez Percés, as *the* leader of the tribe and a military genius comparable to Napoleon has developed through the years. In actuality he was more of a political than a military chief and had to share equal and often more authority with such other chiefs as Looking Glass, Toohoolhoolzote, Poker Joe, and White Bird. Although Joseph was not a brilliant strategist or tactician, the Nez Percés collectively demonstrated a high degree of military capability.[40]

Howard untactfully ordered the nontreaty Nez Percés in northwestern Oregon to move to the Lapwai reservation in Idaho. While the chiefs were discussing whether to acquiesce or go on the warpath, three inebriated brethren of the tribe murdered four whites in mid-June 1877, soon followed by some fifteen more slayings. Hostilities ensued.[41]

The first engagement took place to the east at White Bird Canyon, Idaho, where some 60 to 70 keen-eyed Indian effectives on 17 June sharply trounced a force of approximately 112 inexperienced and exhausted soldiers under Capt. David Perry, the troops losing 34 killed as against 3 Indians wounded. The Nez Percé moved their entire village, including some 800 men, women, and children and the warriors, northward and then eastward. They clashed with Howard's troops on 11–12 July at the Clearwater River at the mouth of Cottonwood Creek, some miles northeast of the previous engagement. Here, in a protracted battle, the army, aided by Gatling guns and howitzers, more than held its own and forced the Nez Percés to withdraw. The soldiers inflicted over 12 casualties on the Indians while sustaining losses of 15 killed and 25 wounded.[42]

Continuing their amazing retreat, the entire Nez Percé village picked up camp and crossed the rugged Bitterroot Mountains via Lolo Trail with Howard and some 560 infantrymen and cavalrymen following. Reaching a point just south of Fort Missoula, the Indians turned southward via Stevensville to a campsite on the Big Hole River, where Looking Glass insisted they rest. They were attacked at dawn on 9 August by Gibbon's 206 soldiers from Missoula; after an initial success, they were repulsed with the loss of 24 troops killed and 35 wounded as against Nez Percé casualties of 89 killed. The Indians, with Howard in hesitant pursuit, continued their long withdrawal to the southeast, halting long enough to kill 9 white people. At Camas Meadows, south of Henry's Lake, Idaho, another indecisive combat cost Howard 8 more casualties and the Indians once again escaped.[43]

With tired and discouraged officers and men, Howard paused in agonizing indecision as the Indians moved eastward through Yellowstone National Park. But Sherman brought him up sharply, asserting, "That force of yours should pursue the Nez Percés to the death, lead where they may. . . . If you are tired, give the command to some young energetic officer." Cut to the quick, the regalvanized Howard retorted, "I never flag. . . . Neither you nor General McDowell can doubt my pluck or energy," and resumed the chase.[44]

On 11 September Howard linked up with Col. Samuel D. Sturgis's outmaneuvered detachment from Miles's force near the Tongue River. The Nez Percés raided more settlements and slaughtered more whites. Howard permitted Sturgis on 13 September to attack and bring on the Battle of Canyon Creek, Montana, just north of its juncture with the Yellowstone River. In this engagement Sturgis's assaults were repelled and his movements foiled by the Indians, who again escaped to the north after inflicting 14 casualties on the troopers.[45]

The Nez Percés pounded northward toward the Canadian border and safety; Howard, in desperation, asked Nelson A. Miles to the northeast for help. Miles's instant and positive response was a fresh, spontaneous tonic. With some 375 soldiers, a twelve-pounder Napoleon cannon, and a breech-loading Hotchkiss gun, Miles's swift pursuit was aided by Howard's deliberate slowing down of his own column to induce the Indians to follow Looking Glass's advice to rest a bit after they had crossed the Missouri River. Finally, almost within sight of the Canadian boundary near the Bear Paw Mountains, on 30 September Miles's forces attacked the Nez Percé village. The troops were at first held back with the loss of 24 killed and 42 wounded. The Battle of Bear Paw settled into a siege, with the Nez Percés holding their own. Yet they were finally disheartened by the loss of most of their pony herd, the numbing cold and falling snow, and the absence of any help from Sitting Bull in Canada. Miles treacherously captured Chief Joseph, who was now more influential at the Indian councils, under a white truce flag but had to let him go in exchange for release of a captured army officer.[46]

For five days the siege continued, Howard arriving in the meantime but generously permitting Miles to accept the Nez Percés' long-hoped-for capitulation on 5 October 1877. Miles reacted arrogantly, though with some justification, claiming for himself the Indians' surrender. "I am tired. My heart is sick and sad," said Chief Joseph in surrender. "From where the sun now stands I will fight no more forever." Over 400 of the Nez Percés yielded, some 100 of them warriors; but about 200 women and children and 98 braves reached Sitting Bull's camp in Canada.[47]

Howard and Miles expected that Joseph and his people would be allowed to return to the Lapwai reservation in western Idaho, but many people of the state plus Sherman and Sheridan were opposed. Against Miles's strong protests, the Indians were moved first to Fort Leavenworth and then to the Indian Territory. With Miles's staunch support, Joseph's tireless efforts, and growing sympathy by Americans for their cause, the Nez Percés were finally allowed to return to the Northwest: 118 of White Bird and Looking Glass's people went to the Lapwai reservation, and some 150 of Joseph's group to the Colville reservation in the state of Washington. Despite Joseph's unrelenting efforts, including an 1897 pilgrimage to see Great White Father William McKinley in the White House and Miles's and Howard's continuing help, a shift to the Wallowa Valley in Oregon was disallowed, and Joseph died at Colville on 21 September 1904. Less spectacular developments for the army were its generally successful operations in 1878 and 1879 against the Paiutes, Utes, Sheepeaters, and Bannocks in Washington, Idaho, and Colorado.[48]

The Nez Percé epic, in which the army was again entrapped in a thankless role, involved some eight hundred people who traveled almost seventeen hundred miles in three months. The Indians' endurance and bravery have won admiration from a tearful public ever since those tragic days of 1877 when they outfought and outthought most of the high-ranking officers and the soldiers who finally halted them just miles short of sanctuary in Canada. "The Nez Percés are the boldest men and best marksmen of any Indians I have ever encountered, and Chief Joseph is a man of more sagacity and intelligence than any Indian I have ever met," acknowledged Miles generously, and his words were echoed by Sherman, who owned, "The Indians throughout displayed a courage and skill that elicited universal praise; they abstained from scalping, let captive women go free, did not commit indiscriminate murder of peaceful families which is usual, and fought with almost scientific skill, using advance and rear guards, skirmish-lines and field fortifications."[49]

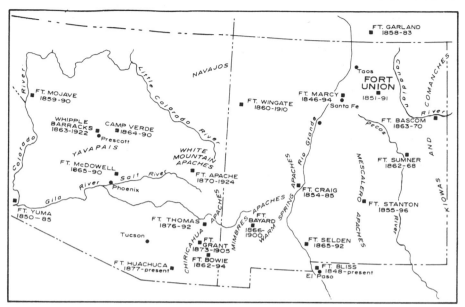

FIG. 9.2.   SOUTHWESTERN DEFENSE SYSTEM AFTER THE CIVIL WAR (*Courtesy National Park Service*).

Less noble were the Apaches and other Indians of the Southwest. For a decade after 1870 there were raids and killings by these hostiles in western Texas, southern New Mexico and Arizona, and in northern Mexico. Except for Col. Benjamin Grierson's campaign conducted with Negro troops, and perhaps those of William R. Shafter and Ranald S. Mackenzie in 1880 against the notorious Apache miscreant, Victorio, little had been done to pacify these Indians or settle them on reservations.[50]

A great deal more had to be done, and much of it revolved around the army's frustrating attempts, over a number of years, to capture and hold the brutal Apache, Geronimo. While not a chief, Geronimo was regarded by some other Indians as a trouble-making renegade. Nevertheless he became the greatest Indian war leader in the Southwest. Undeniably a bloodthirsty savage, if there ever was such, the short, squat Geronimo showed himself to be cunning, vigorous, and resourceful, as his raids and campaigns would prove.[51]

The year 1880 found Geronimo and other Apaches on the San Carlos reservation in what would become southeastern Arizona. The able administration of Capt. Adna R. Chaffee was the only bright spot in an otherwise dismal set of conditions facing the Indians on and around San Carlos reservation. The arrest on 30 August 1881 of an Apache medicine man named Nakaidoklini at Cibicu, some thirty miles northwest of Fort Apache, by Col. Eugene A. Carr's troops precipitated a battle in which the soldiers, not particularly well led by Carr, lost seven killed and two wounded and were fortunate to escape, although the fort was held. On the night of 30 September Geronimo, several other war leaders, and almost seventy-five Chiricahua Apaches bolted the reservation for Mexico, beating off their pursuers at Cedar Springs on 2 October.[52]

Led by Geronimo and others, an Apache war band raided the Gila Valley in mid-April 1882 and slaughtered approximately forty white persons. Pursuing troops lost twelve men killed and wounded at Horseshoe Canyon on the Arizona-New Mexico border on 23 April but pushed the hostiles into Mexico. A week later they were ambuscaded and defeated with the loss of seventy-eight braves by Mexican troops under Col. Lorenzo Garcia. The Indians then slipped away into the rugged Sierra Madre Mountains.[53]

In September 1882 the masterful George Crook assumed command in Arizona. His first achievement was to establish an efficient administration on the San Carlos reservation. A reciprocal crossing treaty, signed by Mexico and the United States on 29 July 1882, would permit Crook to move into Mexico in pursuit of the Chiricahua and Warm Springs Apaches led by Geronimo, who were murderously raiding in northern Mexico. Suddenly Chato's Apaches turned up in southern Arizona and New Mexico in a week's foray in March 1883 and massacred over a dozen persons.[54]

Crook, however, was ready for them. His column included nearly 200 friendly Indian scouts under the competent officers Lt. Charles B. Gatewood and Capt. Emmet Crawford, 45 regulars of the Sixth Cavalry under Chaffee, and 350 packmules. Crossing into Mexico, they trounced some of Chato's warriors on 15 May. Crook's own chase was relentless, and impelled Geronimo, Chato, and other Apache war leaders to negotiate. Geronimo and most of the others, and their followers and families, surrendered in March 1884 and were soon back on the San Carlos agency. Crook's Sierra Madre campaign was a model of how to employ Indian scouts to dig out warring Indians from the mountain fastness, how to gain maximum mobility by use of pack animals, and how to convince the hostiles that he could penetrate their supposedly impregnable strongholds.[55]

The year that followed was one of growing discontent on the San Carlos agency. The chief problems arose over women and drink. Before Crook could intervene, Geronimo, Chihuahua, and other war leaders, plus 134 Apaches, stormed off the reservation on 17 May 1885, with Chihuahua cleverly eluding the pursuing soldiers and raiding in southwestern New Mexico and southeastern Arizona before crossing into Mexico. Crook's two pursuing columns lost the Indians in the wild Sierra Madre Mountains of Mexico and were recalled in October. In early November Chihuahua's brother, Josanie, and a dozen braves rampaged across southern New Mexico and Arizona, murdered thirty-eight Americans, and captured 250 animals before escaping.[56]

In the last weeks of 1885 and in January 1886 Crook determined to subdue the Indians. Employing mostly friendly Indian scouts instead of regulars, he sent forces under Captains Crawford and Wirt Davis in pursuit into Mexico's Sierra Madres. Crawford unearthed the secluded Apache camp on 9 January in a rough and harsh wilderness some 200 miles south of the border. As Geronimo and Chihuahua were about to confer with Crawford, Mexican troops who had also ferreted out the Apaches attacked. After a brush with the American forces, Crawford was killed trying to convince the Indians that he was not party to the resumption of hostilities. Geronimo still indicated he would talk, but only with Crook; so the American troops fell back to Fort Bowie in southeastern Arizona.[57]

In late March 1886 Geronimo and Chihuahua surrendered to Crook; but Geronimo got drunk, went berserk, and fled into the Mexican mountains. When Sheridan angrily interfered with Crook's arrangements, Crook asked on 1 April 1886 to be relieved of his command. Miles was ordered to replace him and to pacify the hostiles. Although claiming to use new strategy and tactics, Miles actually did not markedly change those employed by the brilliant Crook.[58]

On 5 May Miles's column, commanded by Capt. Henry W. Lawton, a hard-drinking, rough-hewn, competent Civil War veteran from Ohio and Harvard who had served under Mackenzie, entered Mexico accompanied by Leonard Wood, a medical officer of later renown. A 2,000-mile, four-month march ensued, although the Apaches could not be brought to battle. Finally, hearing from Gatewood that Miles was shipping all Chiricahua and Warm Springs Apaches from Arizona to Florida, Geronimo surrendered to Miles on 4 September 1886 at Skeleton Canyon, some 65 miles southeast of Fort Bowie in the southeastern corner of Arizona. From there, Geronimo and his followers were put on a train for Florida.[59]

The nineteenth century's final chapter on relations between the army and the Indians was a poignant and heart-rending one. It began when the peaceful Ghost Dance was turned by the Teton Sioux into a dance of active militancy. Angered by the loss of half of the Great Sioux Reservation and hungry as well, the Sioux on the Pine Ridge and Rosebud agencies in southwestern South Dakota, an area controlled by Brig. Gen. John R. Brooke and his five hundred troops, came close to violence in November 1890. Finally in December the Oglala and Brulé Sioux, some six hundred men and their families, defiantly holed themselves up near the White River in the northwestern corner of the Pine Ridge reservation. To prevent other uprisings, Miles ordered the arrest of Sitting Bull and Big Foot. In a skirmish on 15 December 1890 at Standing Rock Agency in northern South Dakota, six Indian policemen and six Ghost Dancers were killed, including Sitting Bull himself.[60]

The Miniconjou leader and pacificator, Big Foot, had been asked by the Oglalas to visit Pine Ridge and restore peace. Eluding the pursuing troops for a time, the pneumonia-ridden chief and his people were intercepted on 28 December by Maj. Samuel M. Whitside and four troops of the Seventh Cavalry, who escorted them as far as Wounded Knee Creek, twelve miles east of Pine Ridge Agency, where they camped. During the night, Col. James W. Forsyth arrived on the scene with Battery E of the First Light Artillery and the remainder of the Seventh Cavalry. Forsyth had been ordered by Brooke to disarm Big Foot's braves in preparation for their entrainment for Omaha, Nebraska.[61]

Daybreak on 29 December 1890 found the Sioux encircled by 500 soldiers and four rapid-firing, breech-loading, Hotchkiss cannon. While 230 Indian women and children packed up for the march, the 120 Indian men—and some of their women—were gathered by Forsyth into a group in front of a heated tent. No one apparently anticipated a battle. Forsyth asked the Indians for their weapons, which included modern Winchester repeating rifles. When the upset Miniconjous refused to yield them, the troops were obliged to go among the Indians to search for these firearms. Yellow Bird, a medicine man, began jumping about, beseeching resistance to the soldiers. Tempers heightened and a rifle went off in a scuffle between a Miniconjou and a trooper. Immediately, the young Sioux braves whipped out their concealed weapons and fired a murderous volley into the closest group of soldiers. A desperate hand-to-hand melee followed, with no quarter asked nor given. The Hotchkiss cannon opened a devastating fire, and those Indians not wounded raced from the arena of combat. But 25 troops had been killed and 39 wounded, as contrasted with over 150 dead Sioux, including Big Foot, Yellow Bird, men, women, and children, with about 50 wounded. But Miles acted with dispatch, ability, and patience; his 3,500 troops surrounded, at a distance, the approximately 900 Indian warriors and their village of 4,000 and convinced the hostiles to surrender on 15 January 1891.[62]

Ironically, or perhaps symbolically, the census of 1890 indicated to historian Frederick Jackson Turner three years later that the frontier had come to an end, and the Dawes Act of 1887 attempted to improve Indian conditions by putting Indian policy in a national frame of reference. The day of the roving, warlike Indian was over, but it had cost the native Americans nearly six thousand casualties and the army two thousand in over one thousand engagements, large and small.[63]

Caught between large numbers of unyielding savage Indians who fought fanatically for what they believed to be theirs, often with just cause, and an unusually ignorant, shortsighted, and untrustworthy government Indian policy, the United States Army in its thankless task had not performed badly. Across the span of a century the army can claim equal stature with their worthy foe for the towering legends that have been taken for gospel by many. Historian Ralph K. Andrist concludes:

> While these dead [Indian] warriors today ride the plains in tradition taller, swifter, and stronger than they ever did in life, they do not ride them alone. They share the sky and the horizon forever with the United States Cavalry which fought them, and by so doing made itself a part of the legend of a world of bright and golden courage and endless space.[64]

IF THE ARMY could show only limited and often frustratingly slow progress on a comparatively small scale in the generation after Appomattox, in this same period the even wider spaces of open blue salt water came to witness an encouragingly greater number of modern white steel warships flying the American ensign. These vessels would chase the westerning sun from Santiago, Cuba, to the magnificent Bay of Manila, halfway around the world, and they would persevere and triumph with a glory undimmed by loss or failure.

American naval policy in the years after 1865 was halting and often reactionary. During the Civil War, in the full flood-tide of Union success, Secretary of the Navy Welles reported that the Union navy numbered almost

700 warships mounting nearly 5,000 guns. A year later the figure was 626 men-of-war, including 65 ironclads and 160 other steamers. But Congress was niggardly with naval appropriations, and Americans were weary of war. Their attention was riveted on Reconstruction in the South and the problems of the westward-moving frontier; so, like the Union armies, the navy too would be startlingly reduced. Despite the claim by President Grant's secretary of the navy, George M. Robeson, that the navy was much better at the end (1877) of his eight years in office than at the start, the direct opposite was true.[65]

How did this unfortunate situation come about? Although Congress was parsimonious about the armed services in this era, it was not unaware of the political implications of this limited policy. Consequently it was considered good politics to maintain a large number of navy yards to service the ancient wooden warships, and millions of dollars were voted to keep the old hulks afloat. Thus after Appomattox the navy was obliged to revert largely to sails and wind for propulsion. The use of full sail power was ordered for all men-of-war, and no steam power was to be employed except in an emergency.[66]

While calling for a big modern navy, such prominent naval figures as Admirals David Dixon Porter and Daniel Ammen strongly opposed a complete switch to steam propulsion, arguing that use of full steam power would take control and command of the ship away from the captain on the bridge and place them in the hands of the marine boiler engineers down in the bowels of the vessel. British naval circles voiced amazement at this head-in-the-clouds attitude of distinguished naval officers with outstanding Civil War records. Compounding American naval woes was the lag in developing armor and new guns. But a significant new beginning on a modern navy would be inaugurated in the administrations of James A. Garfield and especially Chester A. Arthur.[67]

In 1881 the bureau chiefs in the Navy Department were succeeded in some of their few recommendatory powers by the new Naval Advisory Board headed by Adm. John Rodgers. The board promptly called for the construction of forty-three modern steel cruisers. In 1882 Congress, with an alacrity that was both surprising and unusual, authorized two modern, light, steel cruisers but appropriated no money to build them. It was not only opposition from some Democrats who opposed a bigger and modernized navy; there were really no American shipyards equipped to build the new ships. Private contractors were reluctant to build these first steel vessels because new tools and machines would have to be secured and installed and there was no assurance of continued government orders for men-of-war. Nor would the government subsidize shipbuilding, as the British did, and as it did with the building of the railroads. It was all very discouraging.[68]

Finally in 1883 Congress authorized and funded the construction of four new steel warships: *Atlanta, Boston, Chicago,* and *Dolphin.* The latter was merely a small so-called dispatch boat, but the "ABC" ships were fairly respectable protected cruisers, which meant that their decks were armor-plated with 4 inches of steel to protect the vessel's interiors, although their sides were not so protected. They ranged downward from 325-foot-long *Chicago,* of 4,500 tons, carrying a mixture of 8-inch, 6-inch, and 5-inch guns. Two more such light cruisers were approved in 1885. Although they still carried sails and used steam engines, the cruisers making up this so-called Squadron of Evolution or White Squadron had some defects. They were useful chiefly for commerce raiding, although even here they were too slow to catch fast merchantmen or escape swift enemy armored cruisers or battleships. Nevertheless, it was a beginning.[69]

The new naval policy, like that before 1861, was geared to commerce raiding and not to the long line of capital ships, and this cruiser policy was backed by Porter and Ammen, although opposed by Capt. Alfred Thayer Mahan. President Cleveland's secretary of the navy, William C. Whitney, championed faster ships and successfully encouraged the American steel industry to make its own rolled iron and rifled cannon. In their four years in office, Cleveland and Whitney wrung from a somewhat reluctant Congress two second-class battleships (*Maine* and *Texas*), an armored cruiser (*New York*) with steel armor-plated sides as well as decks, six protected cruisers (one of which was the famous *Olympia*), and six nearly worthless coastline monitors— some thirty warships of all types and sizes.[70]

Although the four new steel warships visited European ports, Adm. Stephen B. Luce and others declared that the United States had no first-class battleships and hence really no navy of consequence. Benjamin Harrison, sworn in as president in 1889, was a friend of the navy; his Secretary of the Navy, Benjamin Franklin Tracy, worked unceasingly to build a larger and more efficient force afloat. Tracy urged the construction of no less than twenty first-class battleships. With the end of Southern Reconstruction and with the passing of the frontier about 1890, a new naval consciousness gained momentum in the nation, stimulated by news of naval activities of other first-class powers around the world. Congress in 1890 approved the construction of three first-class battleships (*Oregon, Indiana,* and *Massachusetts*), each of 10,000 tons, carrying four 13-inch guns and eight 8-inch guns, and capable of a speed of approximately sixteen knots. It was high time that the navy was strengthened. In 1891 the so-called *"Baltimore* affair" in Valparaiso ensued with near hostilities and showed that the Chilean navy was superior in a number of categories to that of America.[71]

Warship building continued steadily down to the outbreak of the Spanish-American War. In 1897, a year before the outbreak of that conflict, the United States Navy had completed four first-class battleships, two second-class battleships, two armored cruisers, sixteen light protected cruisers, and fifteen gunboats; under construction were another five first-class battleships, sixteen surface torpedo-boats, and one submarine—a fairly impressive development.[72]

Higher education in the navy centered around the establishment of the Naval War College at Newport, Rhode Island. Long opposed by Congress and the bureau chiefs in the Navy Department, the college was set up by executive order, with the backing of Luce's Naval Board and Secretary of the Navy Chandler. Instruction began in 1886, and the faculty was soon made permanent. Like a general staff, the college worked on the solution of war problems, and its success helped its brother service to gain its Army War College in 1901.[73]

The presence of Capt. Alfred T. Mahan at the Naval War College in its early years gave distinction to that institution. Mahan was born in 1840 at West Point, New York, the son of the army's military educator, Dennis Hart Mahan. Young Mahan graduated second in his class at the Naval Academy at Annapolis in 1859. Over six feet tall and slender, with sandy hair and blue-gray eyes, he was an avid reader and writer, and was brilliant and gracious; yet he was an unyielding disciplinarian and was not overly popular with many of his naval contemporaries. He had a good Civil War record, seeing service at Port Royal on blockade duty and on Adm. John Dahlgren's staff. In 1885 he wrote his first book, *The Gulf and Inland Waters,* dealing with the Civil War. Then followed routine sea duty for twenty years before he was asked to deliver lectures on naval history, strategy, and tactics at Newport.[74]

Mahan's lectures were made into his great book, *The Influence of Sea Power upon History,* which was published in 1890. In it, Mahan argued cogently that the American naval policy of *guerre de course,* or commerce raiding, based on large numbers of cruisers alone, was most unfortunate in that it could only be an indecisive nuisance to an enemy. Instead, Mahan argued for his so-called command-of-the-sea or capital ship theory, and insisted that only command of the oceans of the world with large numbers of battleships able to stand in line of battle against an enemy's capital ships could be decisive. Consequently he asserted that naval bases at strategic points on the globe like those of Great Britain were essential, and he would prefer that they be on colonial territories owned by the United States. This implied that a larger navy and army would be needed to guard the bases. These ports, in turn, would open up remote areas of the earth for religious conversion by missionaries, for extraction and importation of raw materials and natural resources, and for the sale of American manufactured goods. Mahan had something for everyone; he was an imperialist and favored the "large policy.[75]

Mahan was at Newport for only several years; a feud with Secretary of the Navy Whitney forced him out. But he would gain increasing fame at home during and after the war with Spain in 1898. Before that, he would be a prophet with honor in the admiralties abroad.

Maintaining adequate numbers of trained naval personnel for the ships the navy did possess created problems. In 1869 there were only 8,500 enlisted men in the navy, and this situation caused considerable irritation and hardship for warship commanders and the secretary. In 1877 the navy numbered 7,012 men, and in 1882 the figure was approximately 8,000 men along with 1,817 officers to man its thirty-one commissioned ships. Many of the enlisted men could neither speak nor understand English. The secretary remarked in disgust that when the *Trenton,* "our best ship, lately went into commission, as fine a body of Germans, Huns, Gauls, Chinese, and other outside barbarians as one could wish were on board." In 1897, on the eve of the war with Spain, the navy numbered 1,508 officers and 11,000 enlisted men.[76]

The United States Marine Corps, under the authority of the Navy Department, was almost threatened with extinction. It numbered some 2,500 officers and men in 1868, 2,093 in 1893, and a mere 2,600 in 1896, because of the stinginess of Congress.[77]

THE YEARS from 1865 to 1898 might be called the army's "Dark Ages." The parsimony of the politicians and the attractions of industry and the western frontier downgraded soldiering as a popular profession. Low pay, austere living conditions, and increased menial tasks discouraged enlistments as much as did scarcity of funds. The Indian wars, though the army successfully implemented government policy, were fought under trying conditions. Their experiences in the Indian wars neither broadened the officers' knowledge of strategy and tactics, nor readied the ground forces for large-scale war against a great power. Weapons development lagged, as did tactical and strategical doctrines. The shortcomings of the army and the War Department would be all too evident in the "bully" little Spanish-American War.

While still not large in 1898, the United States Navy had made some encouraging progress since the Civil War. The initial reactionary doctrine that retained sails and wooden hulls was modified to permit the construction in the 1880s and 1890s of more modern, respectable, steel warships. Yet the designs of several of the vessels were a bit flawed and emphasis continued too long on cruisers rather than capital ships. Only gradually and almost belatedly did naval concepts shift from emphasis on commerce raiding to Mahan's command-of-the-sea doctrine. And personnel problems continued to plague the service afloat. More heartening was the creation of the Naval War College in the mid-1880s. The belief seemed to be growing as the century drew to a close that the navy was indeed the republic's first line of defense and should remain so.

The "Splendid Little War"

It has been a splendid little war; begun with the highest motives, carried on with magnificent intelligence and spirit favored by that fortune which loves the brave. It is now to be concluded, I hope, with that . . . good nature which is . . . the distinguishing trait of the American character.

JOHN HAY

"THE SUBJUGATION OF A CONTINENT," remarked the *Overland Monthly* in 1898, "was sufficient to keep the American people busy at home for a century. . . . But now that the continent is subdued, we are looking for fresh worlds to conquer. . . ."[1] With the agonies of Reconstruction well in the past, and with the disappearance of the frontier by about 1890, such American imperialists as Alfred T. Mahan, Theodore Roosevelt, Albert J. Beveridge, and Henry Cabot Lodge were pressing for a "large policy" of expansion and colonial acquisition. This white man's burden theory was trumpeted repeatedly by those favoring a large navy, an isthmian canal, a safe field for religious missionary work, commercial markets for American manufactured goods, sources of raw materials and natural resources, and by those who felt that the young men of the country would benefit from fighting in their own little war.

In 1895 another revolt by the Cubans against Spanish rule was played up wildly by the American yellow press, accompanied by many atrocities on both sides that had marked the insurgents' previously unsuccessful rebellion in 1868–1878. On 4 March 1897 the genial William McKinley was sworn in as the twenty-fifth president of the United States. Born in 1843 in Niles, Ohio, McKinley attended Allegheny College in Meadville, Pennsylvania, and when the Civil War began, enlisted in the Union army in Rutherford B. Hayes's Twenty-third Ohio regiment. He served as a sergeant at Antietam and as captain under Philip Sheridan at Kernstown and Cedar Creek in the Shenandoah Valley. He was mustered out with a good army record as a brevet major. McKinley practiced law in Canton and was elected as a Republican to the United States House of Representatives and as governor of Ohio. Under the tutelage of Mark Hanna he built up a reputation in national politics that would win him the Republican nomination and the presidency in 1896.[2]

McKinley somewhat resembled Daniel Webster in appearance, with a cleft chin, eaglelike nose, and shadowed, deep-set eyes. Though out of the army for more than thirty years, and now quite short and obese, the new chief executive had a firm mouth and air of command, stood erect, and was never questioned about his orders as commander in chief. He was formal yet friendly and kind, and he liked to meet people and to ride the Washington trolleys unescorted by guards. He spoke far less than he listened. At times he was maddeningly slow in reaching a decision but he could digest large quantities of facts swiftly and easily maintained the power and dignity of his office. He directed formulation of grand strategy and saw to it that military and naval operations harmonized with political and diplomatic objectives. McKinley exercised great self-control, was usually relaxed in manner, and could readily throw off the cares of the presidency once decisions were made. He had a strong sense of duty and responsibility and regarded some military service as beneficial for young men. The most soldierly chief executive ever to be a wartime commander in chief, McKinley would show when he chose to that he was in complete command of all political, diplomatic, and military situations.[3]

After a riot in the Cuban capital on 12 January 1898 the United States second-class battleship *Maine* was ordered to Havana harbor, where Captain Charles D. Sigsbee, his officers, crew, and ship were well received. "The Spanish officials on every hand gave us all the official courtesy to which we were entitled," Sigsbee related, "and they gave it with the grace of manner that is characteristic of their nation." Designed originally as an armored cruiser, *Maine* was launched in 1890. She displaced 6,650 tons, was 324 feet long with a 57-foot beam, and carried four 10-inch guns, six 6-inch guns, seven 6-pounders, and eight 1-pounders. Although aging a bit, she was still a useful warship.[4]

At about 9:40 P.M. on the hot, overcast, humid night of 15 February 1898, with some 350 of the crew aboard, and while Sigsbee wrote a letter to his wife, *Maine* suffered the hard jolt of a small explosion followed immediately by the tremendous detonation of her magazines that caused the vessel to sink rapidly with the loss of 260 men. Sigsbee and the other members of the crew who were saved were rescued by the Spanish naval forces who risked much from the exploding ammunition aboard the American battleship. Sigsbee cabled Washington about the destruction of his ship and wisely urged that the public avoid hasty conclusions until the facts were known.[5]

Sigsbee was convinced that *Maine's* destruction was caused by an explosive charge placed against the outside hull of his man-of-war which, when detonated, triggered the explosion of his magazines. A Spanish official investigation (done without actually inspecting the hulk) seemed to imply that the ship internally destroyed herself by accident. This seems somewhat unlikely though theoretically possible. An American naval court of inquiry chaired by William T. Sampson was immediately convened, and divers were sent down to examine the twisted wreck on the harbor floor. Their report stated that a smallish external explosive had been placed against the outer hull of *Maine* that when touched off ignited the ship's powder magazines. This finding was essentially corroborated in 1911 when the vessel's remains were hoisted out of the water and inspected.[6]

The hulk was towed out to one of the deepest points in the Atlantic and sunk anew—thus far never to be reexamined. While an accident aboard was conceivable, and while it was remotely possible that a Spanish subaltern ran amok and placed the outside charge, or a mine drifted loose against the hull, it is more likely that Cuban rebels set the external explosive and detonated it so that the Americans would think that Spain had committed the crime—a belief that was held by a great many American citizens immediately after the *Maine* was blown up. Nor was American public opinion calmed when it was discovered that Spanish Ambassador Erique de Lôme in a private letter stolen by a spy and acquired by the Hearst newspaper had excoriated McKinley.

On 11 April after the Spanish government in Madrid had yielded to most of McKinley's ultimatum demanding Spanish withdrawal from Cuba, the president, refusing to continue negotiations, sent his war message to Congress, and war was voted overwhelmingly. Once war was declared, McKinley grasped the reins of commander in chief decisively. He conferred regularly with his cabinet and military chiefs and showed a keen comprehension of complex war problems. His private secretary, George Cortelyou, affirmed that "the dominating force" of the American high command was McKinley. The president set up a war room in a second-floor office of the White House; one entire wall was covered with huge maps festooned with colored pins showing the locations of Spanish and American land and sea forces. A battery of fifteen special telephones and twenty-five telegraph instruments enabled McKinley to contact quickly various bureaus, departments, and distant points. No previous American chief executive had had such a modern communication system.[7]

The civilian head of the United States Navy, fifty-nine-year-old John D. Long of Massachusetts, was a solid though not brilliant secretary. A man who was truly a naval expert, however, was the assistant secretary, the ebullient Theodore Roosevelt. Just thirty-nine years of age when war came, TR had behind him an array of outstanding accomplishments, including graduating Phi Beta Kappa from Harvard; writing *The Naval War of 1812* and a number of other historical, adventure, and travel books; ranching in the Dakotas; serving in the New York State legislature (he had been born in New York City), as a Civil Service commissioner, and as police commissioner of New York City; and finally as Long's talented assistant in the Navy Department. As will be seen, Roosevelt played a crucial role in having George Dewey assigned to the command of the Asiatic Squadron. He spent large sums of appropriated monies in target practice and dispatched a vital cablegram to prime Dewey's force for the attack on the Philippines. Too active to remain behind a desk when hostilities commenced, Teddy would resign his assistant secretaryship to become lieutenant colonel of the Rough Riders and would lead them to fame and glory in the Santiago campaign.[8]

But if the Navy Department was in reasonably good hands, McKinley's War Department was under palsied direction. Russell A. Alger was sixty-two years old in 1898. He was born in a log cabin in the Western Reserve of Ohio and was probably related to Horatio Alger, whose tales of rags to riches might well have included Russell Alger's life story. In 1857 he was admitted to the Ohio bar, and in 1859 he moved to Michigan and entered the lumber business.[9]

When the Civil War came, Alger helped raise a unit of Michigan cavalry, and by 1863 he commanded the Fifth Michigan Cavalry in Custer's brigade. Alger was wounded several times and fought creditably at Gettysburg, the Wilderness, and in the Shenandoah Valley. Colonel of volunteers was his highest actual rank, although he was eventually brevetted major general of volunteers. Illness forced Alger's resignation in 1864; Custer charged him with being absent without leave from his command, a charge that was apparently not valid but left a permanent scar on his Civil War record.[10]

After he left the Union army, Alger returned to his Michigan lumber business and by skill and hard work became quite wealthy and served on the boards of directors of a number of firms. He served one term as Governor of Michigan, and was its favorite-son candidate in the 1888 Republican national convention. After the election and initial consideration, he was rejected by Benjamin Harrison for the post of secretary of war. Alger campaigned for McKinley in 1896, especially among Civil War veterans, and was rewarded with the post he coveted, secretary of war. He had been in office scarcely five months before characteristically asserting that the army was "the best under God's footstool." His preposterous claim that if America were attacked by a major power, "in thirty days we could put millions of fighting men in the field" did not augur well for his future judgment as war secretary.[11]

In 1898 Alger was personally courteous, generous, humane, and gracious. He was still tall, slender, erect, and wore a white mustache and goatee. He was experienced in business, patriotic, devoted to the army and its soldiers, and could occasionally take professional advice. But Alger was a weak appointment, and the job of secretary in wartime was simply too much for him. Despite his Civil War service he lacked experience in large-scale military affairs, and he had not kept himself informed on new military technology, weapons, or tactics. He also lacked experience in government at the federal level. He could be unpredictable, temperamental, and choleric. He imagined insults where none existed and haggled over insignificant matters with his fellow cabinet members and underlings in the War Department. He was selfish, vain, and egotistical; on balance, he was more of a liability than an asset.[12]

The general in chief, the experienced Nelson A. Miles, had been promoted to brigadier general in 1880 and to major general in 1890. He was a forward-looking administrator who had worked on realistic large-scale maneuvers in the field. In 1894 he directed the army force that helped break up the Pullman Strike. In September 1895, as senior major general, he became commanding general of the army and general in chief.[13]

In the late 1890s Miles was still a tall, powerful man of commanding appearance and presence. He loved fancy uniforms and was something of a poseur. He stayed physically fit by riding a bicycle as well as horses, and he kept abreast of tactical changes, was an innovator in weapons and equipment, and remained a superb field commander. Miles's shortcomings have been examined previously, and most of them became apparent in his last years as general in chief. Sensitive about alleged conspiracies and slights to his honor, he was cantankerous, ambitious, and egotistical.[14]

While it had been a large and very strong force in the Civil War, the United States regular army by the 1880s, according to the secretary of war, had become "by far the feeblest in a military sense of all the nations called great." When war came with Spain in 1898, the regular army numbered 28,183, and these soldiers were scattered in seventy-seven army posts. In Congress Representative George B. McClellan, Jr. warned vociferously that the army was of sixteenth-century vintage and totally unfit to fight a war. Most secretaries of war since the 1880s had appealed earnestly to Congress for appropriations to enlarge the army, but in vain.[15]

So unconcerned was the American high command with deteriorating relations with Spain in 1897 that Alger fled the Washington summer heat for a vacation on Lake Champlain. He became ill with typhoid fever and was bedridden until January 1898. Miles journeyed to Europe in the summer of 1897 to observe Balkan military operations in the war between Greece and Turkey and in the autumn attended maneuvers of the armies of the major continental powers. When Alger returned to his office in early 1898, he pushed McKinley to issue an ultimatum to Spain to get out of Cuba. Miles, however, when he returned, questioned the wisdom of pressing a war with Spain and recommended a more circumspect policy. And the unconcerned Secretary of the Navy Long, in an economy measure, planned to put some American warships in mothballs.[16]

On 9 March 1898 Congress appropriated $50 million for national defense with the intention that it be used only for defensive purposes and not for actual mobilization for war. McKinley was slow to indicate how the money was to be divided. Obviously, the navy's mission would be to destroy Spanish fleets and blockade Spanish colonies if war came; but the War Department, confused by McKinley's silence, did not know what kind of a war it might be expected to wage or how big an army it might need. The president finally allocated $29 million to the navy and $19 million to the army because conditions seemed to favor the navy's priorities. With their share of the appropriations, Long and Roosevelt readied fleets in the Atlantic and Pacific, built up stockpiles of fuel and ammunition, and purchased or chartered warships and merchant and passenger vessels for conversion to naval use.[17]

Immediately after Congress declared war on 25 April, Representative John A. T. Hull of Iowa drew up a bill limiting the enlisted force to sixty thousand for wartime expansion of the regular army and including larger volunteer state forces. Miles had already prepared a plan for an expeditionary force of all the regulars plus about forty-five thousand volunteers. Deferring to strong National Guard preferences, the first call was for sixty thousand volunteers for two years' service.[18]

Not completely trusting Alger or Miles, McKinley installed the elderly retired former general in chief and secretary of war, John M. Schofield, in an office in the State, War and Navy Building as his confidential advisor. The president consulted Schofield almost daily for several weeks only to find that he generally reflected Miles's views. McKinley and his principal civilian and military advisers at first inclined toward capture of Havana if an invasion of Cuba were attempted, but warnings of the prevalence of yellow fever and malaria led the president to change his mind several times about an attack on the Cuban capital. Such army operations would have to await the destruction of the Spanish fleet, which on paper looked fairly formidable. And the sailing of Pascual Cervera's squadron to the Portuguese Cape Verde Islands and its safe presence there for a time—final destination unknown—curtailed American freedom of action until Cervera's intentions and actions were revealed.[19]

For the previous two winters the North Atlantic Squadron had avoided any action that might have inflamed the Cuban situation or antagonized Spain and had sacrificed its normal winter drills, maneuvers, and target practice off the west coast of Florida. This resulted in some decline in efficiency and morale. To reinforce the Atlantic fleet, the battleship *Oregon* left Bremerton, Washington, on 7 March on her famous dash around the southern tip of South America and arrived at Key West, Florida, on 26 May. The ailing Rear Adm. Montgomery Sicard was replaced in command of the North Atlantic Fleet on 26 March by Capt. (soon Commodore, then Rear Adm.) William T. Sampson.[20]

Sampson, fifty-eight years of age, was born at Palmyra, New York, of Scots-Irish ancestry, and graduated first in his class at Annapolis in 1861, a year behind Winfield S. Schley. He served early in the Civil War as an instructor at Newport, and was assigned to the monitor *Patapsco* that was blown up by a mine in Charleston harbor. A lieutenant commander in 1866 aboard *Colorado,* he was described by shipmate George Dewey as being one of the handsomest men he had ever seen, as well as possessing "a most brilliant mind and the qualities of a practical and efficient officer on board ship." Then routine duties ashore and afloat followed, capped by Sampson's assignment as superintendent of the naval academy from 1886 to 1890. He was widely known as a scholar keenly interested and expert in the scientific and technological aspects of the naval profession, including ships, guns, ammunition, and equipment. These attainments were shaded a bit by Sampson's cold, austere nature and by his dignified aloofness. Yet on the whole he was an excellent officer.[21]

The fleet Sampson inherited, while not large, had come a long way since the early 1880s and included some good warships. Of the four first-class battleships, *Oregon, Massachusetts,* and *Indiana* were sister ships of 10,288 tons displacement, mounting four 13-inch guns in two turrets, and eight 8-inch guns in four turrets; plus four 6-inch, twenty 6-pounder, and six 1-pounder guns. The other first-class battleship, *Iowa,* had four 12-inch guns, eight 8-inch guns, and six 4-inch, twenty 6-pounder, and four 1-pounder guns. The second-class battleship *Texas* of 6,315 tons carried two 12-inch, six 6-inch, twelve 6-pounder, and six 1-pounder guns.

The two armored cruisers, capable of 21 knots, were formidable vessels of their type. Sampson's flagship, *New York,* displaced 8,200 tons and was armed with four 8-inch guns, two 6-inch guns, twelve 4-inch rapid-firing guns, eight 6-pounders, and two 1-pounders. *Brooklyn* displaced 9,215 tons and carried eight 8-inch guns, twelve 6-pounders, and four 1-pounders. In addition, Sampson's North Atlantic Squadron had six double-turreted monitors fit for sea service if the ocean were smooth; thirteen ancient Civil War–vintage single-turret monitors serviceable only for harbor defense; some dozen smaller protected cruisers; the strange so-called dynamite cruiser *Vesuvius*; eighteen gunboats; ten torpedo boats; and an assortment of lightly-armed revenue cutters and purchased or chartered transports. The Spanish navy, although numerically respectable, was a sorry spectacle of neglect and lack of professionalism, except for its gallant leader, Adm. Pascual Cervera, who would take a squadron to the West Indies.[22]

Yet this pitiful Spanish navy caused unreasoned fear on the East Coast of the United States; bankers and jewelers actually sent their valuables far into the interior for safety. Such precautions seemed plausible at the time. The old Civil War monitors were moved to safeguard these cities' harbors, as were some elderly smoothbore cannon of the same era. In addition, public pressure forced the Navy Department to segment Sampson's fleet, the so-called Flying Squadron being formed at Norfolk under command of Commodore Schley and comprising *Massachusetts, Texas, Brooklyn,* and *New Orleans.*[23]

There was doubt early in the war over whether an American attack upon Havana would be successful. So Sampson established an effective blockade of Havana and several other Cuban ports on the north coast of the island that resulted in the capture of a number of fine Spanish steamers. The small American torpedo boats carried messages to Key West and other points, and some were battered in the rough waters on this essential service. The heavy seas also demonstrated the uselessness of the monitors. Several American lighter warships and commandeered passenger steamers, though not all available ones, patrolled the eastern Caribbean on lookout for the hostile fleet.[24]

MEANWHILE the center of naval action shifted to the western Pacific. The command of the American Asiatic Squadron became vacant in the fall of 1897. Commodore George Dewey, reluctant to use political leverage, was assigned the command because of pressure for his appointment by Sen. Redfield Proctor and especially by the assistant secretary of the navy, Theodore Roosevelt. Before leaving Washington and on his trip across the Pacific on a mail steamer, Dewey read all the books and studied all the charts that could be obtained on the Philippines (the Navy Department had received no official reports on this archipelago since 1876).[25]

The man who assumed command of America's significant Asiatic Squadron had behind him a solid career of achievement in the navy. Born in 1837 in Montpelier, Vermont, Dewey graduated fifth in his class at Annapolis in 1858. As executive officer of *Mississippi* under Farragut, he performed meritoriously in the attack on New Orleans in April 1862 and under Porter in the Union assault on Fort Fisher, Wilmington, North Carolina, near the end of the Civil War. Routine duty afloat and ashore was followed by Dewey's appointment in 1889 as chief of the Bureau of Equipment, and in 1895 he became president of the Board of Inspection and Survey that passed on all new warships being built. He performed in a cool, confident manner, was a strong disciplinarian, expert on all naval matters, and a highly respected professional. Dewey took over his command in Tokyo Bay on 3 January 1898.[26]

It was on Dewey's initiative and awareness that a conflict with Spain and naval action in the Philippines were likely that he chose to lead his squadron to Hong Kong as a better springboard for action in the Philippines rather than to Nagasaki. His fleet arrived in Hong Kong on 17 February 1898 at about the time word was flashed of the destruction of *Maine*. His squadron on 22 April comprised the protected cruisers *Olympia*, flagship (5,870 tons; speed, 21.68 knots; carrying four 8-inch guns, ten 5-inch rapid-fire guns, fourteen 6-pounders, and ten lesser guns); *Baltimore* (4,413 tons; speed, 20.09 knots; armed with four 8-inch guns, six 6-inch guns, four 6-pounders, and ten lesser guns); *Boston* (3,000 tons; speed 15.6 knots; carrying two 8-inch guns, six 6-inch guns, and six lesser guns); *Raleigh* (3,213 tons; speed 19 knots; armed with one 6-inch gun, ten 5-inch rapid-fire guns, eight 6-pounders, and six lesser guns); the light unprotected cruiser *Concord* (1,710 tons; speed, 16.8 knots; carrying six 6-inch guns, two 6-pounders, and seven lesser guns); and the gun-boat *Petrel* (892 tons; speed, 11.79 knots; carrying four 6-inch guns and seven lesser guns). The government should have ordered the two powerful monitors *Monterey* and *Monadnock* to sail at once to the Philippines from California, but this was not done until June. By contrast, in the Philippines, Spanish Adm. Patricio Montojo y Pasaron commanded a pitiful fleet of ten wretched warships.[27]

Guarding the mouth of Manila Bay were seventeen Spanish artillery pieces, nine of which were old muzzle-loaders. Inside the bay, defending the capital city, were 226 additional cannon; 164 were muzzle-loaders, four dating from the 1700s. The enemy batteries in the bay that would actually fire at Dewey's ships included three 9.4-inch guns, two muzzle-loading 6.3-inch guns, two 5.9s, and one 4.7-inch gun. All but the 6.3s were modern breech-loading rifled pieces.[28]

On 25 February 1898 Roosevelt, not without McKinley's acquiescence, sent the following famous cablegram to Dewey: "Keep full of coal. In the event of declaration of war Spain, your duty will be to see that the Spanish Squadron does not leave the Asiatic coast, and then offensive operations in Philippine Islands. . . ." In the time remaining, Dewey prepared and drilled his crews and had his warships in top fighting trim. Much valuable information (though some was not quite accurate) reached Dewey from the American consul in Manila, O. F. Williams, who "remained at his post in spite of threats and warnings that his life was in danger."[29]

With war under way, Dewey was informed by the British that he would have to leave Hong Kong within twenty-four hours; he did so, proceeding to Mirs Bay on the China coast some thirty miles east-northeast of Hong Kong. The friendly British army and navy officers were betting heavily that Dewey would be defeated if he attacked the Spanish at Manila. On 26 April Dewey received orders from Washington: "Proceed at once to Philippine Islands. Commence operations at once, particularly against the Spanish fleet. You must capture vessels or destroy. Use utmost endeavors." The Commodore replied that he would sail immediately from Mirs Bay, which he did, on calm seas, at 2:00 P.M. on 27 April.[30]

Dewey's first task was to locate Montojo's fleet, which possessed a dozen

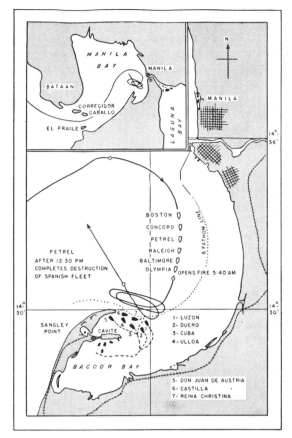

MANILA BAY

BATAAN

CORREGIDOR
CABALLO

EL FRAILE

MANILA

LAGUNA BAY

N

MANILA

14° 36'

BOSTON
CONCORD
PETREL
RALEIGH
BALTIMORE
OLYMPIA OPENS FIRE 5:40 AM

PETREL
AFTER 12:30 PM
COMPLETES DESTRUCTION
OF SPANISH FLEET

6 FATHOM LINE

14° 30'

14° 30'

SANGLEY
POINT

CAVITE

1- LUZON
2- DUERO
3- CUBA
4- ULLOA

BACOOR BAY

5- DON JUAN DE AUSTRIA
6- CASTILLA
7- REINA CHRISTINA

FIG. 10.1. BATTLE OF MANILA
BAY, MAY 1, 1898

harbors of refuge within a day's sail from Manila Bay. The Commodore arrived at Subic Bay on 30 April, peered in, and found no enemy ships. He steamed on toward Manila Bay, timing his arrival to enter the magnificent twenty-mile-wide harbor just before dawn on 1 May. His guns were ready, with the men and ample ammunition near the gun stations. Most lights were extinguished.[31]

Dewey later related that as he neared the mouth of the bay, facing unknown mines and shore batteries, he asked himself what would Farragut have done under similar circumstances and was comforted with the conviction that he was doing exactly what the great Civil War naval hero would have done. Dewey determined to ignore the mines that he suspected might be faulty and that were praised too much by the Spaniards. In his final council of war with his captains aboard *Olympia,* the Commodore's only instructions to them were "you will follow the motions and movements of the flagship, which will lead." All other procedures had been worked out and practiced before.[32]

When the accompanying revenue cutter *McCulloch* was opposite Corregidor in the mouth of Manila Bay, soot in her stack ignited and hurled heavenward a huge plume of sparks and fire. Thus alerted, Spanish batteries opened fire on 1 May at 12:10 A.M., and several of Dewey's ships replied. The firing ceased as the American squadron stood into the large bay. Dewey slowed his speed to arrive off the city of Manila at daybreak. But Montojo's squadron was not there; the Commodore steamed southwestward until a little after 5:00 A.M. and discovered the enemy ships off Cavite. A few wild shots were thrown by Spanish batteries near the capital city. Dewey steamed toward the enemy men-of-war, *Olympia* leading and followed at two hundred yards by *Baltimore, Raleigh, Petrel, Concord,* and *Boston.* Two submarine mines were detonated by the rattled Spaniards some two miles ahead of Dewey's column.[33]

At 5:40 A.M. Dewey said quietly to the captain of *Olympia,* "You may fire when you are ready, Gridley," and at an average range of three thousand yards the American ships, steaming in eliptical courses to starboard and making a total of five broadside passes at the Spanish squadron, opened a heavy but deliberate fire. Smoke obscured the effects of Dewey's cannonading. A false report reached the Commodore at 7:36 A.M. that his ammunition was running low and caused him to break off the battle, send the men to breakfast, and wait for the gunsmoke to lift while he checked out the disturbing report. Finding he had plenty of projectiles, Dewey returned to the fray only to find Montojo's fleet reduced to scrap iron and lumber.

Each Spanish warship at the Battle of Manila Bay was shattered beyond use. Some 381 sons of Spain had been killed or wounded. On the American side only a few light hits were sustained by the ships, no sailors were killed, and only 8 were slightly wounded. Dewey proceeded to bombard the shore batteries at Cavite, silenced them, and forced the enemy to hoist the white flag in capitulation. As the Spanish commandant at the Cavite navy yard acknowledged, "It was not a battle, but a slaughter." At sundown, with the Manila batteries choosing not to engage the American ships, Dewey anchored near the city. Thousands of citizens flocked to the waterfront to stare at the Americans; so the band aboard *Olympia*, "for their benefit," played "La Paloma" and other Spanish airs. The local battery commander put a pistol to his head.[34]

Meanwhile, in the Caribbean arena, the guessing game over where Cervera would make his landfall continued. Thinking that perhaps the Spanish fleet was at San Juan, Puerto Rico, Sampson sailed there from a point off Havana with battleships *Iowa* and *Indiana*, armored cruiser flagship *New York*, light cruiser *Detroit,* and monitors. Heavy seas, the snapping of tow lines on the troublesome monitors, and leaky boilers of *Indiana* caused delays. An American correspondent on one of the accompanying press steamers violated Sampson's confidence and published the objective of the American forces. Cervera touched in at Martinique, learned Sampson's destination, and consequently changed his destination from San Juan to Santiago, Cuba.

On 12 May Sampson overcautiously engaged at a range of about fifteen hundred yards Morro Castle and the other old forts of San Juan that contained forty-one guns. Cervera's squadron was not there, and Sampson, remembering his orders from the Navy Department—"Do not risk so crippling your vessels against fortifications as to prevent from soon afterward successfully fighting Spanish fleet"—drew off from the indecisive action. Damage to the Spanish forts was light, although 13 Spaniards were killed and 100 wounded, mostly civilians. Sampson's *Iowa* was struck twice, with 3 men wounded, and *New York* once, with 1 man killed and 4 wounded. His monitors were shaken by the concussion of their own guns.[35]

While returning to Key West on 16 May, Sampson received word from the Navy Department claiming that Cervera and a load of munitions essential for defense of the Cuban capital was headed either for Havana, or, more likely, for Cienfuegos (where a railroad ran to Havana). Therefore Schley, with *Brooklyn, Massachusetts,* and *Texas*, due to arrive at Key West on 18 May, would be sent to Cienfuegos as swiftly as possible. Sampson was ordered to send one of his armored ships to join Schley and to hasten with his other vessels to join the blockade at Havana. *New York* and *Iowa* arrived at Key West on 18 May, the same day Schley got there with his three men-of-war. *Indiana* reached Key West on 19 May and joined the other ships already there: three protected cruisers, monitors, and lesser ships, including the incredible dynamite cruiser *Vesuvius,* and a transport bearing Huntington's marine battalion.[36]

Schley, who had previously been senior in rank to Sampson but was not so now, came aboard *New York* for a conference. The Navy Department and Schley thought Cervera was bound for Cienfuegos; Sampson, that he was headed for Santiago. But for the only time in the war, Sampson was hesitant and did not insist that his own views prevail over Schley's. *Iowa* was added to Schley's squadron, which was ordered to leave Key West on 19 May to blockade Cienfuegos. Moreover, the welcome news was received that *Oregon* had arrived in good shape at Barbados and would be available to Sampson or Schley.[37]

Winfield Scott Schley had graduated near the bottom of his Annapolis class. Unlike scholar Sampson, Schley was more a man of action with a damn-the-torpedoes-full-speed-ahead attitude. He also differed from Sampson in his wittiness, sociability, outgoingness, and congeniality. Schley had seen combat in the Civil War under Farragut on the lower Mississippi and had managed to find more action in 1871 in faraway Korea, where he participated in the storming of the buccaneers' forts. Schley gained additional fame as leader of the mission sent to rescue Lt. A. W. Greely in the Arctic, and as captain of the cruiser *Baltimore* in the explosive "True Blue Saloon Affair" in Valparaiso where threatened use of naval force had humiliated Chile. Although he lacked Sampson's intellectual abilities and wide-ranging naval expertise, Schley was nonetheless a useful, efficient, and practical officer.[38]

Cervera, slowed by barnacled hulls, low on fuel, and informed of Sampson's proximity to San Juan, took on a little coal at Curaçao and with morale still high among his crews limped into Santiago on 19 May. He wired Havana and Madrid that he would have to remain some days at Santiago to clean his boilers and engines, and that he needed more coal; but he pledged to do his best to assist in the defense of Cuba. At the exact hour Cervera entered Santiago Bay, Schley sailed from Key West for Cienfuegos. Late on 20 May Sampson received firm word at Key West that Cervera was in Santiago. He sent a message to Schley on 21 May to "proceed with all dispatch, but cautiously" to Santiago and blockade the Spanish ships in the bay. Sampson then sailed for Havana.[39]

Schley's squadron arrived off Santiago on 26 May. High bluffs on both sides of the mouth of Santiago Bay and the "narrow and twisting cañon of the entrance" to the harbor prevented the bay—three and one-half miles long and one mile wide—and the ships therein from being seen from the sea. Some Spanish artillery batteries were atop the two-hundred-foot-high eastern bluff at Morro Castle as well as at Socapa on the peak of the eastern cliff, although some of these cannon were ancient muzzle-loaders. Some thirteen mines had been laid by the Spaniards near the mouth of Santiago harbor; Sampson was aware of their presence, but they were as ineffective as the pathetic Spanish artillery batteries emplaced near the harbor entrance.[40]

Having arrived at Key West on 28 May, Sampson received notice that day from the Navy Department that he would soon have to convoy an army expedition of some ten thousand troops aboard nearly twenty transports and disembark them at a point eight miles east of Santiago. The following day the admiral reported that he could occupy Guantanamo, that he was anxious to depart for Santiago with *New York* and *Oregon*, and that *Indiana* would soon be with him. He asked Washington to try to retain Schley's squadron at Santiago. But later on 29 May Sampson heard from Schley that he had just been able to do some coaling and that he would "hold position off Santiago," and the Atlantic fleet commander congratulated Schley on his determination. Later that day the Navy Department approved Sampson's sailing with his own squadron to Santiago and urged him to seize Guantanamo that the department asserted was very weakly held by the enemy. On his way to Santiago, Sampson received word from Schley finally that all of Cervera's warships were definitely in the bay.[41]

Sampson arrived off Santiago on 1 June and assumed command of the combined American fleet. He was alerted that day by the Navy Department of the impending movement of an army force from Tampa, Florida, and was instructed to assist the soldiers' landing near Santiago, but without risk to his crews or armored ships.[42]

That morning Assistant Naval Constructor Richmond Pearson Hobson closely inspected the harbor mouth from a steam launch to determine the feasibility of sinking the collier *Merrimac* across the narrowest part of the channel. In a gallant endeavor, Hobson and six volunteers stood into Santiago's harbor mouth at 3:30 A.M. on 3 June under a full moon. They were detected by the Spaniards who fired at them as Hobson began sinking his ship. An enemy projectile struck and disabled the steering gear, and the collier sank in a wider part of the channel than intended; thus the harbor mouth remained open. Hobson and all of his crew were rescued by Cervera who treated them well. The American effort was courageous, but the Spanish warships could still come out of the bay when they desired.[43]

On 6 June Huntington's battalion of United States Marines sailed from Key West for Guantanamo Bay. On the same day Sampson dispatched

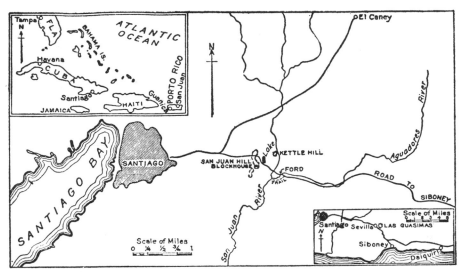

FIG. 10.2. THE WEST INDIES

Marblehead and *Yankee* to "Gitmo" to take and hold the lower part of that magnificent bay until the troops and other ships arrived. While mines in the harbor were reported, the Spanish shore batteries at Guantanamo were pitifully few and were antiquated smoothbore bronze guns. Some six thousand enemy troops were there, but could not communicate with Santiago because of the action of Cuban insurgents.[44]

Marblehead and *Yankee* arrived on 7 June and easily seized and held the lower harbor. The Marines landed and soon had the situation well in hand, although they suffered a few casualties from 11 to 14 June. Their capture of Cuzco Well forced the withdrawal of enemy troops to a point west of Guantanamo Bay, where they erroneously thought the Marines would pass through to Santiago. Sampson wisely rejected a land march from Gitmo to Santiago as impractical.[45]

Sampson unveiled his terror weapon, the strange dynamite-cruiser *Vesuvius,* at Santiago. For a number of nights, this vessel would close to a point near the harbor at precisely 11:00 P.M. and fire pneumatically a total of three shells from her three 15-inch compressed air tubes, each shell containing up to five hundred pounds of wet guncotton. The Spanish soldiers and sailors in Santiago did not retire for the night until *Vesuvius* had come in and performed. The shells burst with terrific concussion. Unfortunately, they hit little, although one shell explosion sent up a tremendous geyser near the torpedo-boat *Furor,* which was "violently shaken," causing her and the cruiser *Maria Teresa* to change their anchorage positions.[46]

The admiral finally received the long-awaited word that the American army expedition to Santiago would leave Tampa on 12 June. Sampson's *New York* on 18 June scouted out Daiquiri Beach, just east of Santiago Bay, as a possible landing place for the American troops who would arrive two days later.[47]

WHILE these American naval activities were slowly evolving, matters relating to the Army of the United States were progressing even more haltingly. On 23 April, instead of calling for the 60,000 volunteers as expected, McKinley appeased the rabid National Guard in many states and requested 125,000 troops from the states, a figure that slightly exceeded the number of National Guardsmen. This was a typical McKinley political response. Miles correctly protested against such an unnecessarily large force that the War Department could not equip, but his objections were overridden by Alger and the president. Now placated, the guardsmen permitted the reorganization of the regular army infantry regiments from ten companies to the more modern three-battalion, twelve-company organization. The new Hull bill, backed now by the National Guard, was signed into law by McKinley on 2 April.[48]

One of the new units mustered in and organized at San Antonio was the First Volunteer Cavalry Regiment commanded by Leonard Wood, an army sawbones who had been McKinley's personal physician, with the publicity-conscious but highly talented Theodore Roosevelt as lieutenant colonel. This famous regiment was known first as the Western Regiment, then the Cowboy Regiment, the Rustler Regiment, and finally as Teddy's Terrors or the Roosevelt Rough Riders. It was to win renown for itself and for its ebullient lieutenant colonel.[49]

General in Chief Miles urged on 26 April that the volunteers be kept thirty days in their initial state mustering camps while the War Department selected their general and staff officers and tried to collect equipment for them. McKinley and Alger agreed on 6 May. Thirty-seven infantry regiments and some artillery and cavalry were ordered to Chickamauga battlefield, near Chattanooga, and twenty-four infantry regiments and some artillery and cavalry to Camp Alger in northern Virginia, near Washington. The regiments were not to leave their home states until they had received their weapons, uniforms, and field equipment. To assist the blockade of Cuba, Alger approved Miles's order of 29 April to gather six thousand regular infantry, artillery, and cavalry at Tampa.[50]

In the meantime in the Far East, Dewey had called officially on 13 May for troops to be sent to Manila Bay. Miles had already worked out a plan to dispatch five thousand troops to seize the capital city of Manila. The Philippine expeditionary force was soon ordered increased, first to ten or twelve thousand, then to twenty thousand; the force was to be designated the Eighth Army Corps. Brig. Gen. Wesley Merritt was named to the command. Merritt, even after talking with the commander in chief, did not know whether McKinley wanted him to capture all of the Philippine Islands or just the city of Manila.[51]

Minority manpower was also something of a problem. The regular army on the eve of the war had two black infantry and two black cavalry regiments. Few Negroes were taken at first among the Spanish War volunteers because most National Guard units did not accept blacks. Some Negroes protested, and McKinley finally took about 9,000 black troops before the end of the war. Several black volunteer regiments had their own Negro officers; one had a colonel, the highest Negro rank to that date. No black volunteers saw combat, although some black regulars fought at San Juan Hill. By the end of the conflict, volunteers of all colors numbered approximately 275,000.[52]

Plaguing American army mobilization were problems at this stage of the war within the War Department lines of command. No one really supervised the whole, although Alger should have done so; but he lacked the energy, ability, knowledge, or inclination. Miles spoke up about strategic planning, but McKinley increasingly ignored him. Alger did little to participate or lead in technology or strategy. In cabinet meetings he usually repeated the views of Miles and the bureau chiefs. The capable adjutant general, Henry C. Corbin, directed the recruitment and mustering of troops; with Miles, he handled assignment and promotions of officers. Another disruptive, though well meaning element was Schofield, whom McKinley at first consulted frequently. But Miles largely disregarded him, as did Alger, and even the president after a while. Schofield departed the capital in June. When the chief executive did consult someone, he often turned to Corbin.[53]

Alger also failed, in the words of Graham Cosmas, "to relate command assignments to the military tasks that had to be performed." Moreover, Miles clashed angrily with the secretary over their respective powers and responsibilities. The department labored strenuously, and, on the whole, honorably to improvise and ready the unprepared army for the unanticipated demands for larger overseas expeditions. So great was the continuing press at the office for favors, commissions, and contracts that Alger stayed at home in the mornings to get his correspondence done without interruption, and he and Corbin still labored at night and on Sundays to finish their administrative work.[54]

Problems of proper and sufficient small arms and artillery were treated with mixed success by Alger. The subsistence department tried to overcome early shortages of food and managed to provide enough food, although the diet was monotonous. There were some bad lots of meat supplied to the army by packers—cans containing gristle scraps, dead maggots, and pieces of rope—but there was no "embalmed beef" given to the soldiers, as was later charged.[55]

Tampa, chosen for the concentration of the Fifth Corps, was closer to Havana than any other viable port. But the city of twenty-six thousand was almost ten miles from Port Tampa, and only a single-track railroad traversed the roadless, sandy countryside between the two points. However, the Bay of Tampa was a good, sheltered, deep anchorage.[56]

To command the forces gathering at Tampa, Alger and McKinley selected Maj. Gen. William Rufus Shafter. Born on 16 October 1835, he was the first white male born in Kalamazoo County, Michigan. Before the Civil War he had worked on his father's farm and taught school. Enlisting in the Union army, Shafter fought at Ball's Bluff and on the peninsula; at Fair Oaks, he won the Medal of Honor. He commanded the Seventeenth United States Colored Infantry, and had participated in the Battle of Nashville. After the war, "Pecos

Bill" had made something of a name for himself fighting Indians in the Southwest, and he was in command of the Department of California, with headquarters at the Presidio in San Francisco, when the war with Spain began.[57]

Shafter was nearly six feet tall and was an enormous man, weighing over 300 pounds. Called by some "a floating tent," he had a large mustache, big hands and head, and a tousled mop of gray hair. When he walked with his short legs he seemed to lumber about like a bear; yet he had an incongruous, high-pitched voice for his intimidating physique. Shafter possessed strength of character, high courage, and an indomitable will; but he was blunt, profane, and rough in manner and speech. Though quick tempered, he was zealous and aggressive and could do difficult things well. Generally, he showed good judgment, common sense, and judicious management. A believer in hard and thorough work and firm discipline, he was without obligations or entanglements, and he entertained no political ambitions.

Shafter was the unanimous choice of Corbin, Miles, and Alger, and McKinley had no objections to him. This officer could bullyrag subordinates, but those who knew him admired his swift decisions and determined action. Though not an administrative genius, he delegated authority to experienced and aggressive regular army staff officers, whom he strongly backed. Col. Herbert H. Sargent, who served under Shafter in Cuba, said of him: "He was sent to Santiago to do a certain thing, and, despite the most unfavourable conditions, he did it. . . . He was successful because he had a clear comprehension of the principles of war; because he had made a study of previous campaigns in the West Indies. . . ." Shafter closely questioned Frederick Funston and others who knew the terrain and conditions in Cuba intimately. Generally, despite some shortcomings and criticisms of him by others, General Shafter was more than adequate for the difficult task entrusted to him.[58]

However, it was beyond the ability of any mortal man to bring instant order out of the frightful chaos that inevitably developed at Tampa. Headquarters was Morton Plant's great, ornate Tampa Bay Hotel, with its wide verandas serving as areas of reunion for gathering officers of the army who had not seen each other for decades. There was a lack of coordination between line and staff officers, and grave shortages of equipment. The single-track railroad was soon backed up for miles with unloaded freight cars. When the raw volunteers arrived, the lack of camp sanitation became a problem, and the soldiers sweated unremittingly in their winter uniforms. War correspondents, including the theatrical Richard Harding Davis, and foreign military observers were present in ample numbers. Although the newspaper reporters often embarrassed and complicated army activities and operations, their presence in large numbers enabled the press for the first time to point out to the American people the difficulties the army had to endure to secure appropriations from Congress for adequate supplies, equipment, and troops.[59]

Transport vessels from New York began arriving at Port Tampa by the end of April, and by 26 May there were some thirty of them present. On 24 May Shafter wisely organized most of his regular regiments into one corps—an efficient force that had been fully schooled in savage warfare with the Indians on rugged terrain.[60]

Since Sampson had convinced himself that his blockading warships could not go into Santiago harbor after Cervera's ships, the Navy Department again urged that Shafter's troops at Tampa, poised for an assault on Havana, be directed to proceed at once to Santiago to flush out the Spanish warships. There was also an increasing feeling that the Americans should move against San Juan, Puerto Rico, to prevent Spain from using that port to reinforce Cervera.[61]

Therefore on 26 May the president convened a White House strategy conference. This conclave decided to abandon temporarily the attack on Havana and strike Santiago instead. This was a victory for Miles, who had urged something like this all along, and he was instructed to draw up plans. Miles's proposal was for Shafter's force to assault Santiago and help the navy crush Cervera. Shafter's army, reinforced from the United States, would then attack Puerto Rico. Finally, going beyond the scope of the president's conference, Miles declared that a still larger army should capture all of Cuba and besiege Havana. Alger and McKinley accepted all of Miles's scheme except the total occupation of Cuba. Some valuable information on the Cuban situation had been brought from the island by the dashing Lt. A. A. Rowan. More intelligence that the Spanish supposedly had forty thousand troops in Santiago province was also received.[62]

Affairs at Tampa were necessarily in a disorganized state, but the pandemonium reached its zenith when Washington on 31 May suddenly ordered Shafter to embark. A mad, disorderly rush ensued of nearly twenty thousand troops and their mountains of supplies, animals, and equipment along the single railroad track from Tampa to Port Tampa. The congestion and confusion were heightened by ill-advised meddling from Washington. Despite the stampede, some sixteen thousand soldiers were miraculously put aboard the thirty-one transports. These transports were small, ill-prepared vessels, and the men were jammed aboard like sardines. Fortunately, the seas were calm. The expedition sailed from Port Tampa on 14 June and was joined off Tortugas by the battleship *Indiana* and other convoying warships. A slow, straggling, uncomfortable journey ensued to the southeastern coast of Cuba. Unfortunately, the Spaniards on Cuba had been tipped off on American strategy by American newspaper reporters who heedlessly published details of the expedition.[63]

As to his campaign plans, the too-modest Shafter merely said, "There was no strategy about it." Fear of malaria and yellow fever in the warm months determined the corpulent general "to rush it." It will be seen, however, that Shafter, given his large degree of discretion from civilian supervision, accomplished all that was expected of him, and more, even if at times he seemed to be acting independently of the navy or not always doing what the service afloat wished him to do.[64]

The American expedition arrived off Santiago on 20 June, and Shafter conferred with Sampson and Cuban rebel leader Garcia. The admiral pressed Shafter to immediately storm the Spanish shore batteries near the mouth of Santiago harbor. The general, however, had been told erroneously by Alger that there were five thousand enemy troops near the Morro but that there were scarcely any Spanish soldiers near the city. Garcia recommended that the army

land at Daiquiri Beach, some fifteen miles east of Santiago, and Shafter agreed
to do so, apparently never seriously considering the navy's urgings to assault
the nearly impregnable high ground and guns at Morro and Socapa. The
general presented Garcia's grateful insurgents with nine thousand food rations.[65]

There was one small pier at Daiquiri; at Siboney, five miles west of Daiquiri, landings could be made only in small open boats. The terrain between
Daiquiri and Santiago comprised steep hills and almost impenetrable jungle,
with several execrable roads connecting these points. The main Spanish defensive position before the city to the east was atop the north-and-south-running
San Juan Heights that terminated on the north in the fortified position of El
Caney.[66]

At daybreak on 22 June Sampson's warships bombarded the coast, and
the few Spaniards fled from Daiquiri Beach. Shafter's landing was aided by
twelve navy steam launches and forty other boats; the naval assistance elicited
praise from Shafter. There was trouble enough getting the troops ashore, but
the only way to land the mules and horses was to throw them overboard; this
was done, and some horses swam out to sea and were lost. By 26 June Shafter
had his force ashore, the first part at Daiquiri and some later troops at
Siboney. Facing the sixteen thousand American troops were approximately
36,000 Spanish soldiers in the province of Santiago, with some 13,096 of them
in and near the city of Santiago. They were well armed with good Mauser
rifles, but did not have many effective cannon. Strong blockhouses and field
entrenchments with barbed wire had been thrown up to contain the
Americans. The actual army movement inland was terribly difficult because of
the miserable roads and trails; only Shafter's wise decision to bring along the
hardy, reliable army mules and seven pack trains enabled them to provide the
minimum supplies, food, and ammunition. Adding to the woe of all were the
hard showers that fell nearly every afternoon.[67]

At the crossroads of Las Guasimas, at 7:30 A.M. on 24 June, "Fighting
Joe" Wheeler's advance struck Spanish rear-guard troops concealed in rifle
pits, stone breastworks, and blockhouses. With Roosevelt and Wood in the
forefront, the American attackers met fierce Spanish resistance for an hour
and a quarter but finally drove the enemy back with perhaps 250 enemy
casualties compared to 16 invaders killed and 52 wounded. Forgetting for a
moment which war he was in, Confederate Civil War veteran Joe Wheeler,
amid the excitement of battle, shouted, "We've got the damn Yankees on the
run!" Shafter informed Sampson on 26 June that he intended to seize El
Caney and attack San Juan Heights from the northeast and east, and he
thanked the admiral cordially "for your assistance."[68]

The army crept through the jungle to Los Mangos and Sevilla and remained there for five days, until 1 July. A foot trail led northwestward to El
Caney; the so-called main road led westward to the San Juan stream, and
beyond was open ground, with Kettle Hill to the right front. Behind was a
shallow lagoon and to the left front was the main San Juan Hill defensive line.
General Shafter's headquarters were to the rear near the El Pozo artillery position. Already some American soldiers were suffering from malaria, typhoid,
and the dreaded yellow fever. They were suffering also from a lack of tobacco

and from their heavy woollen uniforms. The obese Shafter was nearly incapacitated by the heat, and he could only move about on a "stout-hearted white mule." Later a door was taken off its hinges and the general was carried around on it like some oriental potentate. Not only the spreading disease but also the report that an additional eight thousand Spanish troops were on the way encouraged Shafter on 28 June to "rush it."[69]

Hearing that El Caney was lightly held, Henry Lawton convinced Shafter, who had made a partial personal reconnaissance from El Pozo, that El Caney and its 520 troops should be attacked and that he, Lawton, could capture it in just two hours. Following a council of war on 30 June, Shafter's plan of battle was for Lawton to asault El Caney on 1 July while the main attack by S. S. Sumner and J. F. Kent would be made from the east against Kettle Hill and San Juan Hill, with Grimes's battery in action from El Pozo. It was expected that Lawton would quickly take El Caney and come down upon the Spanish left flank on San Juan ridge. Unfortunately, Garcia's rebel troops were next to useless to the north of Santiago, merely firing at long range.[70]

The temperature on 1 July 1898, the thirty-fifth anniversary of the opening of the Battle of Gettysburg, was in the 90s, as it had been each day thus far. Shafter asked Sampson, as a diversion, to bombard the mouth of the harbor. Lawton's force had been on the march for El Caney since 3:30 P.M. the previous day and it found the enemy strongly posted there in four blockhouses and other masonry buildings. Lawton's few light cannon and his infantry opened fire early in the morning. The battle lasted most of the day at El Caney, with the American soldiers pinned down by galling fire from the gallant defenders. Finally, an order to Lawton from Shafter to attack more decisively was carried out by Adna R. Chaffee, and a determined, courageous American charge at last carried El Caney. Lawton moved his exhausted soldiers toward Santiago at about 7:30 P.M. where the main combat of the day was over.[71]

At El Pozo at the rear of the American column in front of San Juan Heights, Grimes's artillery battery opened fire at 8:00 A.M. The black gunpowder sent up white billows of smoke that drew accurate Spanish counterbattery shrapnel fire from modern Krupp guns that inflicted casualties among Shafter's troops and some Cuban rebels who, in the words of Theodore Roosevelt, scattered "like Guinea hens." Forced by the great heat and gout to remain back at an observation post near headquarters, Shafter had to depend on the uncoordinated efforts of his aide, Lt. John H. Miley, and the officers at the front. Despite Shafter's orders, these officers had difficulty in mounting a sustained attack. And the American observation balloon floating above the treetops as it was slowly towed along the road at the front of the column revealed the exact location of the troops to the enemy. The Spanish, according to John J. Pershing who was present, opened an accurate and deadly fire at this point, causing a stampede of part of the Seventy-first New York regiment; otherwise, the soldiers behaved well. Fortunately, the balloon was soon shot down by the Spaniards.[72]

Finally, after much confusion, Shafter's troops organized and launched a forward movement. San Juan Creek was crossed, after losses and a delay, and a relentless attack was launched against San Juan Hill by General Hawkins—

to the left of the road to Santiago with the Sixth and Sixteenth United States Infantry regiments, and to the right of the road against Kettle Hill by the horseless First and Ninth United States Cavalry and Roosevelt's First Volunteer Cavalry (Rough Riders). Both attacks were across largely open fields of high grass and occasional trees, and up steep slopes and through barbed wire in the face of murderous Spanish musketry fire. Both assaults, among the most gallant ever made in warfare, were relentlessly pressed home. Roosevelt and his Rough Riders crossed a lagoon and captured Kettle Hill; Hawkins's men, aided by the timely arrival of Lt. John H. Parker's Gatling guns, drove the enemy from San Juan Hill.[73]

The Spanish retreated westward toward Santiago some five hundred yards to new, strong positions on ridges and kept up a long-range fire into the evening and for the next two days. Of the 15,065 Americans engaged, Shafter suffered casualties of 225 killed and 1,384 wounded (about 10 percent), while Spanish losses were proportionately heavier, amounting to 593 killed and wounded. The care for wounded was handicapped by a paucity of ambulances and the delay in getting the fairly ample quantities of medical supplies ashore.[74]

It now appeared that the American navy's turn had come. The harbor mouth of Santiago was only seventy-six yards wide; so the Spanish warships would have to come out one at a time, enabling the Americans to concentrate their fire successively on each ship as it emerged from the harbor. On the morning of 3 July the battleship *Massachusetts* was absent, coaling, as was *New York,* which had steamed seven miles to the east so that Sampson could confer ashore with Shafter. The day was calm, clear, and sunny, with a smooth sea.[75]

So the Spanish flagship *Maria Teresa,* followed by *Vizcaya, Cristobal Colon,* and *Oquendo,* and the lesser vessels steamed out of the harbor, opened "a frantic fire" at the American ships under Schley's immediate command, and turned to the westward with their best speed. As soon as Sampson saw the sortie of the Spanish ships at 9:35 A.M., he ordered Capt. French Ensor Chadwick to turn *New York* around and head back, but he was never really able to catch up significantly with the westward-running battle; therefore it was Schley who exercised actual command of the American ships. Schley was aware of his superior's standing order to "close and engage as soon as possible, and endeavor to sink the enemy's vessels or force them to run ashore."[76]

It took ten minutes for Schley's ships to get under way, *Brooklyn* almost colliding with *Texas* as the former came about in pursuit of Cervera along the coast to the west. Heavy exchanges of gunfire ensued as one after another of the American battleships joined *Brooklyn* in pounding the enemy vessels as they emerged from the mouth and turned westward. All of Cervera's ships were heavily hit and, shattered and burning fiercely, ran themselves aground to give some of their crews a chance to escape alive. The American ships rescued some Spanish sailors, including the gallant and uninjured Cervera. When some men aboard *Texas* started shouting in triumph over defeat of the enemy, they were admonished by Capt. J. W. Philip, "Don't cheer, boys, the poor devils are dying!"[77]

The American naval victory was complete; all Spanish warships had been destroyed. Cervera lost over five hundred sailors killed and wounded; Schley had one killed and ten wounded. The American ships fired 9,433 shots and scored a total of at least 122 hits on Cervera's armored cruisers and an indeterminate number on the Spanish torpedo boats. Schley's ships were hit about 33 times, largely by smaller caliber shells; little damage was done to them. Unfortunately, when Sampson claimed that he was in command of the American ships, with the inference that the victory at Santiago was his rather than Schley's, a bitter controversy raged between supporters of the two admirals that brought little credit to either. A majority of the court of inquiry in 1901 rapped Schley over the knuckles on a number of counts. Only the president of the court, Admiral Dewey no less, backed Schley on several points. And only Dewey regarded Schley as the officer in command at Santiago and therefore entitled to the credit for the victory, an opinion echoed by General Miles.[78]

On 11 July General in Chief Miles arrived in Cuba, along with reinforcements. This "was like a tonic," and "braced all hands up," reported Leonard Wood. Miles and Shafter conferred with José V. Toral on 12 July over surrender terms; this process was repeated on 13 July under a ceiba tree. On 16 July Toral received permission from Madrid to capitulate and did so with the understanding that the United States would ship the disarmed Spanish troops back to Spain at American expense. President McKinley warmly congratulated Shafter "for the brilliant achievements at Santiago." At high noon on Sunday, 17 July, the formal surrender ceremony took place, and the American flag was run up. With the help of the Spaniards, Sampson immediately removed from the harbor all eleven mines, a number of which were duds.[79]

Shafter's main problem was to evacuate his army, many of whom had tropical fevers, and by 27 July some 3,770 soldiers were ill. Eventually about 427 of this army would die of malaria and yellow fever. The bulk of Shafter's army left Cuba by 25 August, as fast as transports were available. The troops were sent to Camp Wikoff at Montauk Point, Long Island. Despite Shafter's early and repeated warnings, the conditions, plans, and management of Alger and the War Department at Camp Wikoff left much to be desired. These failures were well publicized by the press, and scandal and bitterness followed in their wake and accelerated the decline of the secretary of war's reputation.[80]

Rumors of peace negotiations with Spain expedited Miles's favorite Puerto Rico campaign. By the third week in July Miles had prepared his expedition to sail from Cuba to Puerto Rico; other troops from the United States were to join him shortly thereafter. Moreover, President McKinley ordered the "dilatory" Sampson to send stronger warships with Miles.[81]

The campaign for Puerto Rico was capably conducted. The general's fine eye for terrain and skill at tactical arrangements had not eroded since his Indian-fighting days. He changed his mind and determined to disembark on the southern coast of the island. The landings were successfully made with only light skirmishing at Guanica on 25 July and at Ponce on 28 July. The port of Arroyo, sixty miles east of Ponce, was seized, although a shortage of supplies delayed an advance for a week. Naval cooperation was excellent. Many of the citizens of Puerto Rico greeted the American troops enthusiastically.[82]

Miles faced only small engagements as he pushed his way irresistibly northward in several columns; his total force eventually reached some seventeen thousand well-supplied soldiers as against approximately eight thousand Spanish regulars. The original landing point, Fajardo, was easily occupied by the navy in early August, and Mayaguez was entered on 11 July. When Sampson proposed to get into the act by bombarding San Juan with his fleet, Miles indignantly protested to Alger that this was an army show, and the president ordered Sampson away. Most of the island had been captured by 12 August when the Spanish signed an armistice leading to a cease fire. Miles's campaign was won with the loss of just four Americans killed and some forty wounded.[83]

It will be remembered that in the Far East Dewey's fine naval victory had not given the Americans the city of Manila. The admiral stated that he could seize the city but could not hold it without troops and asked for five thousand. Dewey reported that the Spanish were supposed to have ten thousand soldiers near Manila; Emilio Aguinaldo's rebel army, which nearly surrounded Manila, numbered thirty thousand. In addition to the American cruisers in Manila Bay, there were foreign ones as well. The German squadron assumed a menacing posture, but Dewey's firm attitude and the friendly, pro-American stance of British Commodore Chichester with his warships minimized the Kaiser's threat.[84]

Aguinaldo, according to Dewey, "was not yet thirty, a soft-spoken, unimpressive little man who had enormous prestige with the Filipino people" and "had been at one time a copyist in the Cavite arsenal under the Spanish regime." This rebel leader now began to loom alarmingly as a possibly hostile threat.[85]

The expedition for the Philippines, some 1,200 troops at first, began collecting and fitting out at San Francisco under the temporary direction of the able Brig. Gen. Elwell S. Otis. Named to command the expedition was Maj. Gen. Wesley Merritt, then commander of the Department of the East. Merritt was almost sixty-four years old and had been one of the volunteer "boy generals" on the Union side in the Civil War. Born in New York City, appointed to West Point from Illinois, Merritt graduated halfway down his class at the academy in 1860 and served meritoriously in the cavalry of the Army of the Potomac as a brigade and then as a division commander. After Appomattox, he rose from his regular army rank of lieutenant colonel to two-star general, serving on the frontier against the Indians, as superintendent at West Point, and as commander of various military departments. Unlike many American generals in 1898, he had considerable experience commanding large units. A handsome man, Merritt was agreeable, modest, strong willed, reliable, and competent. He was given some qualified subordinates and staff officers, and many of his volunteer regimental commanders were experienced National Guard officers.[86]

From his headquarters at the Presidio in San Francisco, Merritt organized his Eighth Corps. Field exercises were held outside the city. Each unit that sailed in the several separate expeditions to the Philippines was a self-contained force. Transport vessels were selected with some care and were fairly well fitted out. The first twenty-five hundred troops sailed on 15 June; the second contingent of three thousand departed on 25 June; and the third force of forty-six hundred, including Merritt himself, left San Francisco on 27 and 29 June. In July and August additional soldiers left the Golden Gate for Manila, but not in time to fight there.[87]

The seventy-five-hundred-mile voyage across the Pacific was uneventful except for the peaceful capture of the surprised Spanish on Guam, who did not even know that Spain and the United States were at war. Hot and clear weather prevailed, and generally good health was maintained enroute through the use of fruit, mineral water, and "a good ice machine." The first contingent arrived in Manila Bay on 30 June and, with Dewey's assistance, went into camp at Cavite in an area cleared by the rebels.[88]

The city of Manila numbered 300,000 people in 1898. Its old eighteenth-century walled inner city was surrounded by water on three sides. There were about 13,000 Spanish troops defending the capital, and over one hundred artillery pieces, only four of which were modern breechloaders! To assist Dewey in his bombardment of Manila's defenses and to be able to cope with Camara's squadron with 4,000 Spanish troops aboard, which had reached Suez, the cumbersome monitors *Monterey* and *Monadnock* were ordered to join his squadron. By the end of July the bulk of the American troops had arrived in Manila Bay.[89]

Merritt organized his force in the lines south of Manila into a division (commanded by Brig. Gen. Thomas M. Anderson) of two brigades (commanded by Brig. Gens. Arthur MacArthur and Francis V. Greene). Now military actions were being augmented by diplomatic efforts. The Belgian consul in Manila, M. Edward André, tried to convince Spanish officials to surrender the city and prevent further bloodshed. The governor general initially told André that to yield without a fight would affront Spanish honor and was impossible. At least a semblance of resistance, or a token battle was necessary. On 5 August the governor general was replaced by his second in command, Fermin Jaudenes.[90]

On the same day that Merritt issued a general order defining and restricting his troops' behavior toward the Filipino people, he and Dewey praised Jaudenes in a letter for "his determined and prolonged resistance . . . after the loss of your naval forces, and without hope of succor." Spanish honor had been served and Jaudenes could now capitulate. Merritt's plan provided for a bombardment of the Spanish lines by his and Dewey's guns. The American infantry was to advance, Greene on the left and MacArthur on the right, and Aguinaldo's rebels were to be kept out of the city. Merritt's headquarters and six volunteer infantry companies were aboard one of Dewey's warships; if the Spaniards hoisted the white flag as indicated, these American forces were to enter directly into the inner walled city.[91]

By 11 August, through André, Jaudenes indicated he would follow through with this opera-bouffe "engagement." The scenario called for American ground soldiers to advance only when the Spanish white flag was raised, and the insurgents were to be kept from participating. Therefore, the whole "battle" had been worked out and agreed upon beforehand; so its execution would be largely cut-and-dried and certainly anticlimactic.[92]

The near-sham combat came off according to the arranged format on 13

August 1898. At 9:35 A.M. Merritt's and Dewey's guns spoke. To save honor, Jaudenes returned the fire briefly. A few losses occurred, chiefly because some rebels refused to cooperate. The American infantry advanced a little. The Spanish hoisted the white bunting—seen first by Dewey himself—and Greene, a few of his aides, and some naval officers, followed by Merritt's staff officers from the warship, rode directly into the city of Manila. A few Oregon soldiers began disarming the stoic Spanish troops, and the Stars and Stripes were raised over the port's office. There was no disorder. The total American loss was 5 killed and 44 wounded. Jaudenes signed the formal articles of capitulation on 14 August. Approximately 13,000 Spanish soldiers were captured, along with 22,000 stand of arms and artillery in this strange event in military annals. It signalled the last stand of the enemy in the conflict.[93]

The final peace treaty between the United States and Spain was signed at Paris at 8:50 P.M. on 10 December 1898. The treaty was accepted by McKinley and ratified on the same day (6 February 1899) by the Senate, and by Spain on 19 March 1899. It was proclaimed in effect on 11 April 1899.[94]

Shortly before he became Secretary of State, John Hay wrote to his friend, Lt. Col. Theodore Roosevelt, on 27 July 1898, "It has been a splendid little war; begun with the highest motives, carried on with magnificent intelligence and spirit favored by that fortune which loves the brave. It is now to be concluded, I hope, with that . . . good nature which is . . . the distinguishing trait of the American character." Unfortunately, some of the following repercussions were more melancholy and less good-natured than Hay anticipated.[95]

Strong criticism was heaped upon the hapless secretary of war. "Sweep Alger out of the way first," demanded one newspaper editor. "Remove the polluting influence of Michigan politics and the rest will follow as a matter of course. Algerism is at the bottom of war scandals." In answer to these charges, McKinley promptly set up a commission headed by Grenville M. Dodge to investigate the War Department's conduct of the war. During October, November, and early December, 1898, the commission took voluminous testimony from many civilian and military leaders and lesser figures and visited a number of camps and cities. The commission's report came out on 9 February 1899. It found no significant corruption or deliberate negligence on the part of the War Department, but it did criticize its poor management and planning for the rail problems and transports at Tampa. The Dodge Commission concluded that in terms of Alger's performance "there was lacking in the general administration of the War Department . . . that complete grasp of the situation which was essential to the highest efficiency and discipline of the army." McKinley insisted upon and received, effective 1 August 1899, the secretary's resignation on grounds of political treason and unreliability, not of War Department maladministration.[96]

A DEPRESSING AFTERMATH of the victory over Spain was the Philippine Insurrection of 1899–1902. Immediately after the capture of Manila by the Americans,

General Merritt on 14 August 1898 issued a proclamation pledging to respect "all factions of people in all their rights" and declaring that the Philippine "local laws and courts will continue to function as before the war. Merritt was named military governor of the archipelago, and Elwell Otis became commander of the Eighth Corps when he arrived on 21 August. Merritt and Dewey received the following orders from the commander in chief: "The President directs that there must be no joint occupation with the insurgents. . . . The insurgents and all others must recognize the military occupation and authority of the United States. . . . Use whatever means in your judgment are necessary to this end."[97]

Aguinaldo was furious. What followed is stated succinctly in the report of the United States Philippine Commission:

> After the taking of Manila, the feeling between the Americans and the insurgents grew worse day by day. All manner of abuses were indulged in by the insurgent troops, who committed assaults and robberies and . . . even kidnapped natives who were friendly toward the Americans and carried them off in the mountains or killed them. In the interest of law and order, it became necessary to order the Filipino forces back, and this order made them angry. Aguinaldo removed his seat of government to Malalos [north of Manila], where the so-called Filipino Congress assembled.[98]

On the night of 4 February 1899 the War of the Philippine Insurrection officially began north of Manila when shots were exchanged with the rebels. The first combats were conventional pitched battles north of the capital fought by United States regulars and American Spanish War volunteers, who repeatedly drove the rebels from their fortified lines by skillful and sharp assaults. In the campaigning in the heat and difficult terrain, American troops in retaliation, as they would do later in Vietnam, occasionally looted and committed acts of violence. On the whole, the army would perform ruthlessly and efficiently against the Filipinos.[99]

The war was pressed relentlessly by Generals Elwell S. Otis, Henry Lawton, J. H. Smith, R. P. Hughes, Franklin Bell, S. B. M. Young, M. P. Miller, J. C. Bates, and MacArthur against the determined rebels under Aguinaldo. While pursuing the insurgents north of Manila and capturing Malalos on 31 March, the Americans also captured Iloilo on 11 February 1899, with the help of *Baltimore* and *Petrel* of Dewey's squadron. In March the islands of Panay and Negros came under American domination, as did the Sulu Archipelago between May and August. In early 1900 American forces went ashore on Mindanao, the Visayans, Mindoro, Cebu, Bohol, and Samar, and throughout 1900 and 1901 mop-up operations were pushed there and on Luzon.[100] The conflict had become a guerrilla war for the Filipinos.

On 23 March 1901 Aguinaldo was tricked and captured by a mixed American and native force led by Brig. Gen. Frederick Funston. Casualties for the Americans between 5 May 1900 and 30 June 1901 were 245 killed, 490 wounded, 130 missing (including captured); for the Filipinos, 3,854 killed, 1,193 wounded, 6,572 captured, and 23,095 surrendered. At different times in

1902 the various Filipino guerrilla leaders and their forces surrendered, and the insurrection was considered at an end, although sporadic and spasmodic hostilities erupted from time to time—by the Moros on Mindanao—for several years.[101]

The Boxer Revolt of 1900 was of a different character than the Philippine War. In response to foreign spheres of influence and penetration, young Chinese nationalists, mostly students, sought to oust the "foreign devils." Posing as secret athletic societies, these Boxers gained the upper hand over the Dowager Empress. Aided by some imperial forces, they gained possession of Peking and the territory to the coast, and even part of Manchuria. They slew the German minister in cold blood and proceeded to murder 231 foreigners, including women and children. The diplomatic corps and their families took refuge in the British legation in Peking and called plaintively for help as they were besieged by the Boxers.[102]

An international army of nearly 19,000 troops was quickly formed under the eventual command of a German officer, Count von Waldersee. The American contingent of finally over 5,000 soldiers, mostly from the Philippines, was under the effective command of Adna R. Chaffee. After an initial repulse, the Americans helped storm the walls of Tientsin on 13–14 July 1900, and the international army marched on Peking, arriving on 14 August in time to save the courageous diplomats and missionaries. The defeated Boxers cost China a large indemnity; part of the American share was returned unspent to China by President Theodore Roosevelt to finance the education of Chinese students in America.[103]

The termination of the Boxer Rebellion and the beginning of the end of the Philippine Insurrection would usher in an era of peace for the United States of some fifteen years. This span of time permitted an understanding of the lessons of these turn-of-the-century wars and some modest but significant reform and advancement, despite the customary American peacetime apathy, for the navy and especially for the army under brilliant civilian leadership.

The period of American imperialism around the turn of the century was instructive in a number of particulars. In the War with Spain, the American high command performed capably, on the whole. President McKinley, a master politician who smoothed relations with Congress, was a more effective commander in chief than many historians have indicated. In the main he performed creditably and with considerable success. Navy Secretary Long was at least a fairly competent public official who had the initial advantage of Theodore Roosevelt as his talented assistant. Secretary of War Alger left a great deal to be desired. Good intentions were not sufficient; Alger possessed neither executive skill nor administrative, organizational, or command ability. Fortunately, General in Chief Miles, despite his personal shortcomings, was an experienced, knowledgeable, and aggressive officer who saw the big picture as well as the smaller details.

America's admirals performed well. Dewey's entire action was outstanding; on occasion, his conduct was inspired. He had imagination, innovative talent, and strategic and tactical mastery of his profession. Sampson, too, performed quite well in the higher aspects of his command, despite the few limitations previously noted. Schley, while perhaps a cut below these admirals, was sufficiently capable in action to win handily the naval battle off Santiago.

Among the main field commanders, Shafter, although he suffered from an occasionally hostile press and has not been held in high regard by some historians, did win every skirmish, battle, and campaign; he pressed ahead relentlessly with an ill-equipped and ill-prepared army over difficult terrain. There are few brighter moments in American army annals than the attack at El Caney and the gallant charge at San Juan Hill at Santiago, Cuba. Merritt, with a better trained and accoutered army, was more than adequate for his role in the Manila operation.

After painful initial inadequacies and inefficiencies, the War Department and army gained in skill, training, and efficacy, as did inexperienced civilians and officers in on-the-job training. Certainly the navy and its department were well prepared, as they demonstrated, to fight a successful war—against what turned out to be a third-rate naval power like Spain. Both army and navy would need to be streamlined and prepared in the more sophisticated aspects of strategy and command before they could compete with the first-rate European naval and land powers. That was the next political, administrative, and technical task for the navy and especially for the War Department in the years immediately after America's victorious quest for empire.

Reform and Apathy, 1898–1917

There is now one soldier to every fourteen hundred people in this country—less than one-tenth of one percent. We cannot be asked seriously to argue as to the amount of possible tyranny contained in these figures. The [regular] army as it is now is as small as it can possibly be and serve its purpose as an effective nucleus for the organization, equipment and supply of a volunteer [or conscript] army in time of need.

THEODORE ROOSEVELT

ONE OF THE ABLEST and most influential civilian administrators below the presidential level in American history was Elihu Root, secretary of war under William McKinley and Theodore Roosevelt and also secretary of state under the Rough Rider. He was born in 1845 in Clinton, New York, where his father was a mathematics professor at Hamilton College. A lover of nature all of his life, Elihu grew up in this pastoral setting and graduated from Hamilton in 1864 as class valedictorian.

After finishing law school at New York University, Root formed his own law firm and was soon a successful counselor for railroads, banks, corporations, and municipal agencies of New York City's government. He was a good speaker, witty and balanced, and was clear, concise, and systematic in law cases that reflected his prodigious work and mastery of detail. Root was a conservative New York state Republican who was a friend of President Chester A. Arthur and a legal adviser of Theodore Roosevelt. A dignified and respected figure, senator and international jurist, Root later allowed his name to be placed in nomination for the presidency and, as an admired elder statesman, lived in Gotham until his death within a week of his ninety-second birthday.[1]

When McKinley ousted the ineffectual Russell Alger as secretary of war, he selected Root as his replacement because of his reputation as a leader of the American bar. In his new cabinet position, Root would be called upon to direct the government of the former Spanish islands. The new secretary lacked military knowledge; hence he tended to be relatively free from preconceived ideas about the strengths and weaknesses of his department and developed an objective attitude that would increase his effectiveness as secretary. He immediately began a thorough study of the army and War Department.[2]

Root noted that the report of the Dodge Commission emphasized that for many years "the divided authority and responsibility in the War Department has produced friction, for which, in the interest of the service, a remedy, if possible, should be found." The influential general, William G. H. Carter, declared that the fault was at least partially in the system—one under which a bureau chief could "work along his own lines in ignorance of, and on a different basis from, what other bureau chiefs were doing—a course contrary to every economic and business principle." This general situation and faulty system, according to the *Review of Reviews,* was the inevitable consequence of "the policy that we adopted after the Civil War, which was to do without an army altogether, except as we needed it for detached garrison and guard service, chiefly in the Indian Country."[3]

This dim view of our military system was echoed by several famous Americans. Theodore Roosevelt, governor of New York after his spectacular army service in Cuba, stated with characteristic forthrightness: "There is no head, no management in the War Department. Against a good nation we should be helpless." Senator Henry Cabot Lodge concluded, with truth,

> The [War Department] system stands guilty, and the war being over, reforms are resented by patriots who have so little faith in the republic that they think that a properly organized army of 100,000 men puts it in danger, and by bureau chiefs and their friends in Congress who want no change, for reasons obvious if not public spirited.[4]

Following his first study of the army and War Department, Secretary Root concluded that they were like a great corporation, run, not by a board of directors or a general manager, but by the superintendents of the various departments of the concern. Root realized that he would have to move circumspectly, even gingerly, with the groundwork well prepared if he was going to try to supply a "general manager" for the touchy "superintendents." A General Staff, based upon that of Germany, the secretary perceived, was requisite for the complete reorganization that he contemplated.[5]

Five additional War Department defects existed when Root became secretary: there was no connection between the army proper and the staff bureaus; there was no central planning agency (such as a General Staff); there was a continuing permanent assignment of staff officers to bureau duties; there was a lack of coordination between the several staff bureaus; and there was the wastefulness of a decentralized system of purchase and supply.[6]

With the approval of his president, Root appointed a board of officers on 19 February 1900 that would draft a plan for an Army War College that would control the army service schools and the Division of Military Information (Military Intelligence Division). The board would also draw up a course of instruction for the War College, including instruction to reservists in civilian life. Congress duly appropriated funds so that the Army War College could be formally set up (on Jackson Place, Washington, D.C.) by General Order 155 on 27 November 1901. The establishment of the War College, and the duties imposed upon it, were about as close as Root could get in 1901 to a General Staff.[7]

It was the objective of the secretary and the Army War College that officers would go to the post and the branch schools; the best would move on to the Command and General Staff College at Fort Leavenworth, and from there to the Army War College to study problems of national defense strategy and matters pertaining to military science and high command. Under the presidency of Brig. Gen. Tasker H. Bliss the initial emphasis, as he interpreted his instructions of 27 October 1903, was to develop a schedule of practical lectures that would make this early War College not an institution of higher learning but rather, in its infancy, more of an adjunct of the General Staff that would be created in 1903.[8]

In 1902 Root was ready to put his ideas for a General Staff in written form, and he directed Col. William H. Carter to draw up such a proposal. A bill embodying Root's views was introduced in Congress on 14 February. The bill could not be gotten through the Congress during that session because of the powerful opposition of the influential bureau chiefs and General in Chief Miles. The latter objected on the not unreasonable ground that in the future junior detailed officers, in the name of the General Staff or the chief of staff, might seize control of military operations from senior commanders, although this would not always be unfortunate.[9]

Finally, the Congress passed the General Staff Act on 14 February 1903, and it was readily signed into law by President Roosevelt. The act abolished the separate office of general in chief (or commanding general of the army) and created instead a chief of staff under the secretary of war and the president. The chief of the General Staff was to have supervision of both line troops and bureau chiefs who headed the special staff and supply departments and had formerly reported directly to the secretary of war. The new General Staff was to comprise the chief of staff and forty-four officers, who were relieved of all other duties. The act went into effect on 15 August 1903 when Miles would retire as the republic's last general in chief.[10]

In 1910 Leonard Wood became chief of staff, an appointment generally well received, although there was some criticism of Wood's medical background and limited military and command experience except for the few months in 1898. Born in 1860 in Winchester, New Hampshire, Wood, despite financial handicaps, graduated from Harvard Medical School. But he found private practice in Boston unremunerative and accepted an interim appointment as a contract surgeon in the army. In rigorous campaigning in the Southwest against Geronimo and the Apaches, Wood earned such a fine reputation for endurance, bravery, and leadership that he won the Medal of Honor and a regular commission as a medical officer. In 1898 he and Roosevelt organized the First Volunteer Cavalry Regiment (the Rough Riders) and Wood led it courageously as colonel in the campaign for Santiago, Cuba, where he held also a temporary brigade command. In 1899 Wood was named military governor of Cuba and performed admirably in cleaning up the disease-ridden island and bringing administrative order out of the chaos of war. He was a huge man, charming and sincere, with a keen, retentive mind, shrewd and penetrating insight into human nature, and indefatigable energy. Though never an inspiring speaker, Wood's great determination and other qualities made him one of America's most effective military evangelists.[11]

Trouble developed almost immediately for Wood. The legislators were alarmed when Wood and the secretary of war, Henry L. Stimson, moved to close down certain unneeded army posts. The seething legislators retaliated unsuccessfully by trying to legislate Wood out of his chief of staff post. But Wood received solid backing from Sen. Henry Cabot Lodge and from ex-Secretary Root. Congress then attached a rider to an army appropriation bill that would prevent the president from closing down the army posts. After conferring with Secretary Stimson, William Howard Taft courageously vetoed the bill. Public pressure impelled the lawmakers to redraft the bill minus the objectionable rider. With this out of the way, Wood and Stimson thought the General Staff could now devote its full attention to the creation of an overdue military policy for the nation.[12]

The establishment of the Army War College in 1901 was not the end of the streamlining of the ground forces' school system. In the early days of the army, instruction was given only at the unit level. The military academy had been set up at West Point in 1802, and the War of 1812 pointed up the need for more schools. The result was an Artillery School of Practice that was finally established in April 1824, at Fort Monroe, Virginia. In 1907 the artillery divided into the Coast Artillery, which remained at Fort Monroe (until its demise at the start of World War II, when it was replaced by the Antiaircraft Artillery), and a Field Artillery School, which was established in 1911 at Fort Sill, Oklahoma. In 1950 the two artilleries would be reunited into one arm. Later, a branch of antiaircraft and guided missiles was set up at Fort Bliss, near El Paso, Texas.[13]

A school for the training of the infantry began when the Third and Sixth Infantry Regiments were ordered in 1826 to establish an Infantry School at Jefferson Barracks, St. Louis, Missouri, but this school was abandoned two years later. Not until 1881 was the infantry school reestablished, at Fort Leavenworth, Kansas, under the cumbersome title, The School of Application for Cavalry and Infantry. In 1882 the school's program provided practical instruction "in everything which pertains to army organization, tactics, discipline, equipment, drill, care of men, care of horses, public property, accountability, etc." In addition, attention was to be given to elementary matters "which ought to precede a commission, but is not always the case," as well as to the practice and science of war.[14]

The name of the school at Fort Leavenworth was changed in 1886 to the United States Infantry and Cavalry School. A board of officers inaugurated a two-year course in 1888 comprising instruction under departments of infantry, cavalry, artillery, military art, engineering, law, and military hygiene. In 1890 the War Department stated that honor graduates of the Fort Leavenworth school would be so designated on the Army Register. In 1891 graduates were exempted for five years from the promotional examinations in professional subjects, and a year later a mathematics course was added to the curriculum. In 1897 the new departments of tactics and strategy were added and those of infantry, artillery, and cavalry were incorporated into that of military art. Although an infantry school was established at Fort Benning, Georgia, in the World War II era, the Fort Leavenworth school continued to expand its role, influence, and prestige. A law was passed declaring that, in addition to being able to set up instruction in "the Common English branches of education," the president could also appoint an army officer to serve as professor, superintendent, or president of a college or university requesting the same. In 1890 the War Department issued a directive saying that graduates of the Fort Leavenworth infantry and cavalry school were to be given preference as Reserve Officers Training Corps (ROTC) instructors. In 1893 the secretary of war recommended junior ROTCs for large city high schools. By 1895 a total of 104 army officers were giving military instruction in over one hundred college and university ROTCs, with constant efforts being made to improve the instruction.[15]

Deciding that infantry and cavalry training were too much for the Fort Leavenworth school to handle well, the War Department established the Cavalry School at Fort Riley, Kansas, in 1891, with instruction also in light artillery. In the same year a School for the Instruction of the Signal Corps was founded. An engineer school had been created in 1867, and it became the United States Engineer School in 1890. This institution was moved to Washington, D.C., in 1901, and its title was again altered to the Engineer School of Application. In the early 1890s a school for the Hospital Corps was founded at Fort Riley. This was then reopened as the Army Medical School in 1893 in Washington, D.C.[16]

After Roosevelt entered the White House and Elihu Root became secretary of war, the procedures of the army school system were more regularized. An officer went from his branch service school to the prestigious Command and General Staff College (as it would be renamed) at Fort Leavenworth, with the cream of the crop going on to the Army War College that after World War II was relocated from Washington to Carlisle Barracks, Pennsylvania.[17]

Commenting on the priceless value of the Command and General Staff College and the Army War College, General of the Armies John J. Pershing declared:

> During the [First] World War the graduates of Leavenworth and the War College held the most responsible positions in our armies, and I should like to make it of record that in my opinion, had it not been for the able and loyal assistance of the officers trained at these schools, the tremendous problems of combat, supply and transportation could not have been solved.[18]

After World War II, the armed forces' school system would comprise, in addition to the many army institutions just noted, the navy with its Naval Academy at Annapolis, its several special technical schools, the Navy Post-Graduate School at Monterey, California, and the Naval War College at Newport, Rhode Island. The United States Marines' advanced schools were at Quantico, Virginia. The United States Air Force would have in addition to its special technical schools the Air Force Academy at Colorado Springs, and, at Maxwell Air Force Base near Montgomery, Alabama, the Air University, composed of the Air Force Command and Staff College and the Air War College. After the reorganization of the armed services in the late 1940s, the

Armed Forces Staff College at Norfolk, Virginia, was founded to provide joint training and study programs. Finally, for some graduates of the several war colleges or the Armed Forces Staff College, there was the last step up to one of the two new schools at Fort McNair, Washington, D.C.—the National War College or the Industrial College of the Armed Forces.[19]

Another of Root's contributions was to reorganize the militia so that the National Guard was strengthened. Unusually responsive and cooperative, Congress rallied to assist the secretary. On 1 January 1903 an act named for Representative Charles W. Dick, of Ohio, wisely divided the militia into two elements: one class was the organized militia, or National Guard, and the other class was made up of the remainder of the able-bodied men between the ages of eighteen and forty-five. The National Guard was directed to conform more to regular army practices. Moreover, the Dick Act provided for regular army inspection of Guard units, fixed pay and allowances, and joint maneuvers. The act also heralded the future federal volunteer service.

Unfortunately, the legislation lacked the compulsory service clause of the 1792 law. It retained the provision that the militia could be called up only through the governors of the states, thereby risking their rejection (although many thought the Constitution empowered the president to call forth the militia directly). It limited the commander in chief to using the National Guard for only nine months' service, and then in the United States only. Finally, it provided inadequate enforcement machinery. On balance, however, the Dick Act was an improvement over the hoary old 1792 legislation.[20]

Some progress came in command and control when the Militia Act of 1908 authorized the president to call up the Guard for more than nine months and permitted its use outside the continental United States. A Division of Militia Affairs was also established by this act, comprising five active National Guard officers who were to consult on organized militia problems with the secretary of war. This group was succeeded, in turn, by the National Guard Bureau.[21]

Perhaps the greatest single issue of controversy, military or political, between the Spanish-American War and the First World War was that of military preparedness. As early as 1908 Leonard Wood started beating the tom-toms for increased preparedness in a series of persuasively argued magazine articles. Shortly after he became chief of staff on 19 July 1910 he began calling for a reserve of trained soldiers nurtured by short-term enlistments on active duty in the regular army and then placed on a reserve status, thereby keeping the army from becoming one of older men. He denounced criticism of his ideas that were voiced by some in the National Guard and regular army. Wood preferred a year of training but would settle for six months for young men just out of high school or college.[22]

When Congress asked the secretary of war in 1911 for an evaluation of the army's preparedness, the Army War College reported the shocking inadequacy of the regular army in weapons, munitions, and manpower. "It is apparent," said the report, "that we are almost wholly unprepared for war . . . , that the things we need most will take the longest to supply."[23]

One of Wood's problems was that even though theoretically the chief of staff was powerful, he functioned in an advisory rather than an operational capacity because of the latent opposition among the bureau chiefs and others to the general staff concept. These opponents would lead Congress to believe that the General Staff was a sinister body. Consequently, many legislators viewed the General Staff as a threat to America's free institutions and by 1912 Congress reduced the strength of the General Staff from 45 to 35 officers. By 1916 this whittling process had cut it back to just 19 officers. By contrast, the German General Staff at that time numbered 650![24]

Meanwhile, Wood was trying to hammer out a permanent peacetime military policy. In 1911 he directed John McAuley Palmer to draw up a plan for the organization of all land forces of the United States. The scheme that Palmer proposed, instead of expanding a standing army, would mobilize a preexisting citizen army. He did perceive, however, that such a massive volunteer system would not succeed in the event of a large-scale war. This latter view was neither a novel idea, nor was it hidden from the pubic view by the army.[25]

The General Staff was directed by the secretary of war to draw up a plan of its own to organize American land forces. This comprehensive report was known as the Stimson Plan and reflected Upton's views that were based on the traditional American practice of having a nucleus of a small regular army to be augmented by citizen-soldiers in time of war. But now these civilian soldiers would have to have received some previous peacetime military training to be able to meet in battle the mammoth armies of trained men that almost all the great powers could deploy. The Stimson Plan recommended an enlistment period of six years in the regular army—three years on active duty and three years in the reserves. During crises some of the reserves would be employed to bring companies of the regular army to full strength instead of using raw recruits for this purpose, and the rest of the reserves would comprise a pool of replacements. In addition, the Stimson Plan urged expanding West Point, improving the national militia program, and inaugurating a reserve officers program. In the event of United States involvement in a great war requiring masses of soldiery, volunteers would be organized under prearranged plans handled through the machinery of the National Guard and regular army.[26]

Then came a pacifist as president of the United States and commander in chief of its armed forces. Thomas Woodrow Wilson was born in 1856 in Staunton, Virginia, the son of a Presbyterian minister. Some of his earliest recollections were of Civil War military operations and the scorched earth tactics in the Shenandoah Valley, which made an indelible mark on his impressionable young mind. After graduating from Princeton, he attended the law school of the University of Virginia. But he did not like law practice nor was he successful. So he entered the Johns Hopkins University, from which he received the Ph.D. in 1886 in History and Political Science. After several other teaching jobs, he accepted a professorship at Princeton, all the while writing a number of competent books on American history and government. He became president of Princeton and then governor of New Jersey.

As president of the United States, Wilson soon revealed to observant persons mixed traits comprising both strengths and weaknesses. He was highly intelligent, with a quick, keen, and analytical mind. He grasped things swiftly, and was impatient with the slower witted. He was clean and high minded, idealistic, and strongly supported Progressive reform measures. Wilson was a strong executive, courageous in standing up for his views, and was a champion of the underprivileged of the earth. But he was also arrogant, obstinate, and self-righteous, and he brooked no opposition to his views. He was generally ignorant of military affairs and was contemptuous of them. The pacifist president's stubbornness in opposing increased preparedness for America would be difficult to surmount and would cost the nation dearly when hostilities came.[27]

Although Wilson and the Democratic platform on which he had run had scarcely mentioned military matters, the chief executive, strangely or perhaps through ignorance of the individual, named a strong propreparedness man, the forty-eight-year-old Lindley M. Garrison, as his secretary of war. From Camden, New Jersey, Garrison attended Phillips Exeter Academy and Harvard before graduating from the University of Pennsylvania Law School. He soon established himself as a flourishing lawyer, first in Philadelphia and then in Jersey City, and was generally recognized as a leader of the state bar. As secretary of war, Garrison completely understood the intricacies of the army, the war department, and military affairs. He was a skilled administrator and brilliant in his expositions to Congress. Probably without knowing it, though, he was somewhat patronizing, overbearing, and condescending in his manner to the Congressmen, and a personal antipathy developed toward him in some of the legislators. Furthermore, the secretary would be too strong a man for Wilson to tolerate.[28]

At the beginning of his tenure, Garrison, like his chief of staff, Wood, was a preparedness stalwart who believed in enlarging the land forces of the country without greatly increasing the regular army. In 1913 Wood urged the development of trained reserves and recommended that young men out of high school or college be given a chance to sign up for a year's military training. Consequently the chief of staff set up two such experimental camps in the summer of 1913 for these students. This experiment was deemed a success even though only 245 young men attended these two citizens' training camps at Gettysburg and Monterey.[29]

The crisis with Mexico, to be discussed later, impelled Congress to pass reluctantly the so-called Volunteer Bill of April 1914 that directed the president to call up volunteers when authorized by Congress. It also provided that if 75 percent of the units of the National Guard volunteered their services they were to be accepted before any other volunteers and put under federal control. But even this was not sufficiently realistic or viable in preparing the republic for total war; the volunteer system would have to be abandoned in 1917 when the United States entered the First World War. In short, Congress and especially the Wilson administration failed to supply the leadership needed to ready the nation for a likely war on a grand scale. Apathy by the president and Congress killed any chance that the regular army might reach its authorized strength of 100,000; appropriations were so low that they provided for an army of just 85,000 men.[30]

Then an unfriendly and overt act was committed south of the border in

Tampico. The trouble was triggered by the civil war that raged after the revolution of 1911 that had overthrown the longtime dictator, Porfirio Diaz. Some of the crew members of the U.S.S. *Dolphin* were arrested by Mexican authorities on 9 April 1914. In due time the prisoners were released, but the Mexicans refused to deliver a twenty-one-gun salute, which was not mandatory. Wilson, with congressional approval, ordered the navy to retaliate by seizing Vera Cruz. After bombardment from the *San Francisco, Chester,* and *Prairie,* Vera Cruz was stormed by seamen and United States Marines. After sharp fighting and the loss of fifteen "leathernecks" killed and fifty-six wounded, the marines soon had the situation well in hand. Only successful mediation by the "ABC Powers" (Argentina, Brazil, and Chile) bailed the president out of the embarrassing embroglio. But the commander in chief did order our warships to remain off the coast of Mexico until November 1914.[31]

As late as this same month, Wilson's closest personal adviser and confidant, Col. Edward M. House, found the president still adamant about mounting a preparedness program even though several months had elapsed since the outbreak of the First World War. To House's painful astonishment, the chief executive contended that there would be ample time to prepare for war after or if America entered it. Therefore Wilson refused to act although he acknowledged the need for a reserve to buttress the small regular army. The only thing the president would do at this time was to go along with a congressional bill to establish a Council of National Defense to examine the military needs of the country. The confused president owned that he might support the contrary idea of universal military training *"on a voluntary basis"*! Wilson also admitted that the United States would never be prepared for war so long as the nation adhered to its present political principles.[32]

When Wood was chief of staff, he set up summer camps at which military training was given to college students who paid for it. In 1915, while commander of the Department of the East, Wood established a similar camp at Plattsburg, New York, for professional and businessmen. Its expenses were paid by private contributions. Volunteers for the Plattsburg camp were assured by the momentum of the preparedness movement. These influential citizen-volunteers would leave the camp, not only with basic military training, but also with renewed enthusiasm for the preparedness campaign. The "Plattsburg Idea" grew to the extent that other similar camps were opened. During the First World War sixteen camps based on the Plattsburg model were authorized by the National Defense Act of 1916. They were set up and run by the War Department from 15 May to 11 August 1917, and over 27,000 officers were duly commissioned.[33]

As the armies and navies of the warring nations struggled bloodily but indecisively in Europe, Africa, and the Far East, the drumbeat for increased American military preparedness was heightened in 1915, with more compulsion being brought to bear on the obstinate president and Congress to arm America in the name of her very existence. This unremitting pressure on Wilson and his party in Congress was led by such stalwarts as ex-President Roosevelt. Also in 1915 and 1916 several cogently argued and influential books were published: Leonard Wood's *The Military Obligation of Citizenship* and *Our Military History, Its Facts and Fallacies,* and especially Frederic L. Huidekoper's *The Military Unpreparedness of the United States.* Secretary of War Garrison spoke and wrote supporting army reorganization and enlargement. But Wilson shrank from even a modest increase of American land forces; essentially he wished to avoid any confrontation with Kaiser Wilhem II that might lead to war. It apparently never occurred to the president that Germany might be more reasonable if the United States had available sufficient military force to support Wilson's demands for German "accountability."[34]

But the chief executive's hand was finally forced to raise itself in support of preparedness. The secretary of war asked the Army War College to draw up a comprehensive plan that would swiftly and effectively augment the land forces in wartime. On 21 July 1915 Wilson came around to the extent that he asked Garrison to prepare a program reflecting what the army and War Department thought necessary for adequate national defense. Garrison wanted, if possible, both the General Staff and Congress to be able to agree on an overall military policy plan supported by detailed studies of particulars of the program.[35]

The comprehensive War College Plan was ready in September 1915. It recommended a force of 500,000 trained and organized ready troops made up of a regular army of 281,000 and a reserve to bring the total to half a million. Another 500,000 troops were to be available within three months. In addition, the plan urged a system to produce at least another 500,000 as replacements. This latter force—the so-called Continental Army—was really a federalized militia whose men would receive two months training per year for three years. Because of what the architects of the plan thought to be Constitutional limitations, no provision was included for augmenting the National Guard. The War College calculated that it would require eight years for this program to reach fruition.[36]

Hoping to make the program acceptable to Congress, the secretary of war reworked the War College scheme. The resulting Garrison Plan suggested that the regular army be increased to 141,843 soldiers. A citizen army (or Continental Army) of 400,000 should be established, organized, equipped, and intensively trained for brief periods of two months. Garrison recommended that the National Guard should number 129,000, and that it should have increased federal support. Little was said about the reserves or how they were to evolve. The 400,000-man citizen army was to be composed of annual groups of 133,000 enlisted for three years on active duty and three years in the reserves. This scheme was similar in some ways to the 1783 ideas of George Washington. Garrison thought his plan the best possible one short of universal military training, an option he disliked because he feared that its administration would require too many federal officials.[37]

The National Guard Association and the influential *Army and Navy Journal* opposed Garrison's plan on the grounds that it was allegedly a political and not a military scheme and that it would weaken the National Guard and regular army. Surprisingly, the president backed the plan, and

Chief of Staff Hugh Scott thought it had enough public support to get through Congress. Even the persistent foe of the military in the House, James Hay, agreed to carry it through his committee; but the congressman soon did a quick about-face and endorsed a militia bill. Belatedly, Wilson wrote a letter to Hay, strongly backing Garrison's plan. The chief executive even made a propreparedness speaking tour, one that ended on 3 February 1916.[38]

Suddenly—and the reasons for the turnabout have never been satisfactorily explained—Wilson concluded that Garrison's presentation of his plan to Congress had been intolerant, impolitic, and peremptory toward the solons. The president abruptly reversed himself and backed away from support of the secretary's program which a few days earlier he had strenuously supported.[39]

Garrison naturally asked Wilson whether the president was now backing the secretary's plan or Hay's militia bill. Wilson hedged and rebuked Garrison for testifying before the House committee that universal military training was the only viable alternative to the secretary's continental army plan. The result was that Garrison resigned that same day (10 February 1916) as secretary of war. The chief of staff greatly regretted losing the Garrison Plan in Congress and voiced fears for the entire preparedness program. Scott did not hesitate privately to denounce the president's lack of support. But Wilson wandered blithely along without any qualms about the damage to the preparedness cause resulting from Garrison's departure. Without effective leadership from the executive branch, the uncertain Congress now essayed the development of military policy on its own.[40]

The slow glide toward a comprehensive piece of legislation for the army and War Department was accelerated by the Punitive Expedition into Mexico, then under way. The coup by Gen. Victoriano Huerta against President Francisco Madero sparked a civil war that alarmed Americans on the north bank of the Rio Grande. Stimson assured President Taft that strong forces could swiftly augment the army's border patrols. The secretary on 24 February 1913 ordered the Second Division's mobilization under Brig. Gen. Frederick Funston at Galveston and Texas City. After the Vera Cruz affair of the navy and marines, Funston and the Second Division's Fifth Brigade were sent to that unhappy city, the force totaling some eight thousand men. Although Wilson soon withdrew this force, the Vera Cruz event angered many Mexicans. It was used as an excuse by Francisco ("Pancho") Villa, one of those struggling for power in Mexico, to stage raids across the Rio Grande into the United States. On 9 March 1916 Villa's band murdered a number of Americans in Columbus, New Mexico.[41]

In a few days Brig. Gen. John J. Pershing was ordered by the War Department to cross the Rio Grande in pursuit of Villa. On 12 April 1916 a skirmish was fought with pro-Carranza troops at Parral. But Villa countered with a raid upon Glen Springs, Texas. War between the two nations seemed inevitable, and the War Department called out the National Guard of Arizona, New Mexico, and Texas on 9 May. But this action did not appear to be sufficient, and the crisis helped resolve the battle in Congress over the pending National Defense Act of 1916 in favor of a stronger bill.[42]

Although Villa escaped capture, Pershing did lead a vigorous chase of the

Mexican bandit and dispersed his bands. Pershing was handicapped by a lack of shells and artillery, supply difficulties involving motor transport and railroads, and an insufficient number of machine guns. And the speed and effectiveness of the mobilization of elements of the regular army and especially of the National Guard left a great deal to be desired. Fortunately neither the more powerful Mexican leaders nor Wilson wanted war, and the president was able to recall Pershing and his force in early 1917.[43]

Domestic political issues and foreign diplomatic and military factors made possible the passage on 3 June 1916 by Congress of the National Defense Act, the republic's first comprehensive legislation for national security. The act defined four classes of ground soldiers in the United States: the regular army, the army reserves, the National Guard, and the volunteer army (the last to be raised only in wartime). The act increased the regular army to 175,000, but only over a five-year period; set the National Guard at approximately 457,000; established a reserve corps of officers and enlisted men and reinforced the ROTCs; took the coast artillery and mobile army divisions away from the General Staff that was limited to three generals and fifty-two other officers of whom only twenty-six could be on duty in Washington, D.C.; and tried to establish a federalized National Guard made up of all men eighteen to forty-five. The act provided that "said Militia shall be divided into three classes, the National Guard, the Naval Militia, and the Unorganized Militia." The men of the National Guard would have terms of enlistment of six years: three years on active service and three in the reserves. The congressmen, however, did not provide any program for the unorganized militia.[44]

Despite its several useful provisions, the National Defense Act of 1916 did not realistically face up to America's vital interests in the desperate world situation. The regular army was still much too small, the volunteer principle was obsolete, and the wartime defense of the nation was left primarily to the National Guard. The act and its ideas were quickly denounced by the new incoming secretary of war, Newton D. Baker, by former Secretaries Stimson, Garrison, and Wright, by the ex-assistant secretary, Henry Breckinridge, and by Chief of Staff Scott.

Up to the time of his appointment as secretary of war, the liberal Baker had been an even more ardent pacifist than his Johns Hopkins classmate, Woodrow Wilson. Baker was born in Martinsburg, West Virginia, in 1871, the son of a physician who had served in the Confederate army. After graduation from Hopkins, Baker got his law degree in 1894 at Washington and Lee University. He practiced law in Martinsburg and then in Cleveland, where he became city solicitor. In 1911 he was elected a reform-type mayor of Cleveland, and was reelected two years later. Small, thin, bespectacled, quiet, and self-effacing, Baker developed into an able wartime secretary, even though he lacked Garrison's ability, grasp, and administrative skill. It was ironic that Baker, like Wilson—both dedicated pacifists—would be obliged to preside over the largest military buildup in the nation's history up to that time.[45]

Baker urged the president to support a bill containing the War College Plan for universal military training. With the backing now of Wilson, Congress passed the Selective Service Act on 18 May 1917, six weeks *after* war had been declared. The bill required all men between twenty-one and thirty (later, eighteen to forty-five) to register for the draft, and some 24,000,000 did so. This wise though belated policy would result in the wartime army of the United States inducting 2,180,296 men, while voluntary enlistments would swell the ranks of the regular army, National Guard, navy, Marine Corps, and Coast Guard to the extent that some 4,000,000 Americans would be under arms at the peak of the First World War effort.[46]

THE UNITED STATES NAVY in the post-Spanish-American War period was ripe for naval expansion, not only because of the public sympathy for its problems and triumphs aroused in the conflict of 1898, but also from its recent acquisition of a far-flung empire of insular possessions. The new president, Theodore Roosevelt, an ex-assistant secretary of the navy and author of a book on the naval war of 1812, was truly an expert on naval matters as well as a champion of a larger and more powerful fleet. In addition, Britain's recall of her capital ships from North America to home waters to check the rising German navy caused the United States to look more to its own naval defenses as well as to look after British interests in the Caribbean because of England's support of the United States in the Panama and isthmian canal affairs. Nor could a modern battle fleet be quickly improvised if a large-scale war erupted with a major naval power, even though the United States had done so, in part, during the recent war with Spain, by using auxiliaries.[47]

In 1900 the General Board of the Navy was created by the McKinley administration. This board was composed of professional naval officers, and its chief purpose was to advise the secretary of the navy and supervise the departmental bureau chiefs. The General Board, which would work toward construction of the astronomical number of forty-eight battleships, would play an increasingly significant role in determining future naval policy. Congress in 1898 approved the construction of three battleships (each carrying a main armament of four 12-inch guns); in 1899, three battleships were approved (each with four 12-inch guns); and in 1900, two battleships (four 12-inch guns) and three armored cruisers. But in 1901 Congress authorized no large warships, although the Navy Department recommended several. As late as 1899 United States capital ships were still termed "coastline battleships." The ignorance of many Congressmen about naval matters remained one of the navy's most aggravating problems.[48]

But Theodore Roosevelt, a disciple of Alfred Thayer Mahan, would set an enviable record as president in building up the United States Navy. In his first five years in office he pressured Congress into adding fifty new combat ships, with thirty-one more authorized or under construction. Naval enlisted personnel in this period increased by more than 50 percent, while the Marine Corps jumped from 7,032 to 9,049. The navy had 21,433 as of 30 June 1902 and 32,163 four years later. In the period 1901–1905 TR obtained ten battleships (most with four 12-inch guns, but with eight 12-inch guns on the 1905 ships) and four armored cruisers. This gave the United States ten armored cruisers of

1898 vintage or later, but even these were immediately rendered obsolescent by 1908–1909 when the British battle-cruiser type appeared. By 1905 America had or would have a total of twenty-eight battleships and twelve armored cruisers, second only to the navies of Britain and France.[49]

Then in December 1906 came one of the truly revolutionary events in world naval history—the launching of H.M.S. *Dreadnought*—the first modern all-big-gun battleship, so large, swift, and powerful that it immediately rendered obsolete every capital ship afloat. It would give its name generically to all post-1906 battleships of its type. In the preceding decade, first-class battleships had as their main armament four large caliber guns (11- to 13-inch) and a larger number of medium guns (8- to 9-inch). But *Dreadnought* had a battery that consisted entirely of large 12-inch guns, ten in number.[50]

American naval designers were not completely unaware of this British development. The United States had installed a main armament of eight 12-inch guns on its two battleships authorized in 1905, but these men-of-war would take over four years to complete, and they were smaller and slower than the British monster. In 1906 the United States laid down her first true dreadnought-type battleship, *Delaware* (ten 12-inch guns), which would be finished only in 1910.[51]

The American yearly standard battleship authorization fell to just one such warship (ten 12-inch guns) in 1907. Partly because of this, partly because of international politics—especially its impact upon the Japanese—and partly because of the technical training it would provide, President Roosevelt sent the American battle fleet of sixteen capital ships on the famous 'round-the-world cruise in 1907. Under the able command of Robley ("Fighting Bob") Evans, the remarkable 46,000-mile trip was skillfully completed and dramatized the need for more naval bases overseas. After the ships had departed on their world cruise, Roosevelt had the audacity to ask Congress in 1908 for four new dreadnoughts. Instead, he got two (ten 12-inch guns), and two more (twelve 12-inch guns) in 1909. The legislators were fearful of stimulating the naval race; this was unrealistic because the United States Navy was still behind Britain and other major powers. Actually, as will be seen, in the eight-year period from 1906 to 1914, the United States Navy would be augmented by just twelve dreadnoughts. Some journalists and others believed that the unilateral slowdown of America's capital ship–building program would entice other great powers to do likewise. But it did not; instead, the other naval powers constructed more battleships and battle cruisers. Although by the end of 1908 the United States was third in total naval tonnage and second only to Britain in first-line battleships, America had only about half as many line officers as Germany, France, and Japan and less than one-third as many as England. President Roosevelt was able to improve somewhat this worrisome situation.[52]

From the beginning of his administration, William Howard Taft backed Roosevelt's naval policies and voiced support for a strong service afloat. But it was only with difficulty and against stiffening congressional opposition that the president obtained two battleships (ten 14-inch guns) in 1910 and two more (ten 14-inch guns) in 1911. And in 1912 the legislators approved just one battleship (twelve 14-inch guns). In 1913 Taft, heavily defeated at the polls for reelection, asked for three battleships because the United States was falling out of the line of march of other great dreadnought powers. But the House, as it had done in 1912, cut down the Senate's higher number and authorized only one battleship (twelve 14-inch guns) for 1913.[53]

The problem of far-flung naval bases remained a sticky one. There was a long delay in building up the base at Guantanamo, Cuba, because some sulking members of Congress were angry at the closing of unneeded bases at New Orleans and Pensacola. In the Philippines the navy used the small Cavite base and tried to build up a base at Subic Bay gradually. Since Subic Bay was far from being a first-rate base, Taft, a joint army-navy board, and Congress agreed in 1909 to build a first-class base at Pearl Harbor in the Hawaiian Islands, but not one in the Philippines or Guam. Some in Congress and elsewhere could not grasp the fact that it would be virtually impossible to defend the Philippines without a superior base in the western Pacific.[54]

President Wilson's secretary of the navy was a somewhat woolly minded Tarheel newspaperman, Josephus Daniels, who had actively backed the Taft administration's naval program. Very early in his tenure Daniels called upon the great powers to limit armaments—a voice in the wilderness unheeded. The General Board of the navy recommended four battleships and a large number of lesser warships, but Daniels asked Congress for only two battleships, eight destroyers, and three submarines. At the same time, the politically minded secretary called for reopening all the government navy yards. Furthermore, Daniels urged setting up government-owned powder, armor plate, and ordnance factories, coal mines, and oil refineries to serve as a model for privately owned industries that were exploiting the government. In addition, the secretary wanted to convert the navy into a "great university" that would supply religious leadership and instruction, and improve the welfare of the navy's enlisted men. Daniels evinced not the slightest concern, in most of his ideas, reports, or recommendations, about the security of the republic or of the interrelationship between naval and foreign policy. However, the Marine Corps was increased on 29 August 1916 by 3,235 leathernecks to a total of 9,921, and the president was authorized to elevate its enlisted strength to 17,400.[55]

Most importantly, the Office of the Chief of Naval Operations was finally established by act of Congress on 3 March 1915. This office and the chief, under the direction of the secretary of the navy, were to command and control fleet operations and develop war plans like a general staff. However, the office was weakened immediately by the lack of subordinates and by the sudden resignation of the chief himself, Rear Adm. Bradley A. Fiske, over the foot-dragging on preparedness by the administration and Congress.[56]

The impact of the great 1916 naval battle of Jutland, and especially the heavy losses of the British, triggered demands for a larger American navy. The navy's General Board recommended for 1916 a navy second to none, to be completed by 1925. The board's specific call was for the following new warships: ten battleships, six battle cruisers, ten light cruisers, fifty destroyers, and eighty lesser men-of-war. In the end, following a battle in Congress, Wilson and Daniels prevailed, their views being reflected in the great and unprecedented Naval Act of 29 August. This legislation provided for the following new warships to be built in three years: ten battleships, six battle cruisers, ten scout cruisers, fifty destroyers, nine fleet submarines, fifty-eight coastal subs, and fourteen lesser vessels. And at the same time the congressmen called for universal disarmament. Furthermore, the Office of the Chief of Naval Operations was enlarged, a flying corps for the navy was established, and increased numbers of officers and men for the navy were provided.[57]

While the service afloat was more nearly ready for war in 1917 than was the army, the navy still had serious shortcomings. These included a lack of viable plans to wage war and delays caused by unpreparedness and drift in implementing effective personnel and management policies. A congressional investigation backed Admiral William S. Sims's charges that at the time the United States declared war on Germany, barely 10 percent of American warships had their full crews and only 34 percent did not need repairs. The Coast Guard, normally under the Treasury in peacetime, came under the jurisdiction of the Navy Department in wartime; thus the navy was strengthened in 1915 when the Life Saving Service and the Revenue Cutter Service were amalgamated to form the Coast Guard.[58]

AFTER CENTURIES of dreaming about flying, America spread its wings after the war with Spain. The saga of flight had come a long but slow way since Leonardo da Vinci had drawn plans in 1483 for a helicopter and declared, "There shall be wings!" Ballooning had come from the Montgolfier brothers through the use of hot-air gasbags in the American Civil War. The first man to fly in such a hot-air balloon was a Frenchman, Jean François Philâtre, on 15 October 1783. On 17 December 1903 the Wright brothers lifted their flyer off the sand dunes of Kill Devil Hill, at Kitty Hawk, North Carolina. And on 1 August 1907 the Army Signal Corps set up an Aeronautical Division to assume "charge of all matters pertaining to military ballooning, air machines, and all kindred subjects."[59]

On 20 July 1908 "Dirigible No. 1," a small nonrigid dirigible balloon that was capable of a speed of 19.61 miles per hour and cost the Signal Corps $5,737.50 was delivered at Fort Myer, Virginia. It was accepted by the army on 28 August and the gasbag was promptly dismantled and sent to Fort Omaha, Nebraska, to be used for training purposes. The first flight by the army's own pilots or "aeronauts," Lts. Benjamin D. Foulois and Frank P. Lahm, took place on 26 May 1909. The motor on this craft was a two-cylinder motorcycle engine made by Glenn H. Curtiss. The "balloon with engines" lasted three years before deteriorating. But the fate of lighter-than-air vehicles, at least in the army, was sealed by the appearance of Curtiss's four-cylinder, water-cooled motor.[60]

But what would in due time transform the glider into the airplane was the high-speed internal combustion engine invented in 1883 by Gottlieb Daimler. One of the first men in the United States to experiment with powered flight as early as 1890 was the secretary of the Smithsonian Institution, Prof. Samuel P. Langley. He did manage, by means of a tiny one and one-half horsepower steam engine geared to twin propellers, to launch from a catapult mounted atop a houseboat a sixteen-foot-long unmanned plane with a thirteen-foot wing, that flew half a mile over the Potomac. This was on 6 May 1896. But Langley's manned flights in 1903 failed at about the time the Wright brothers were succeeding.[61]

The first flying field came into being when the Wrights continued their experiments with newer and larger craft outside a shed they built 8 miles east of Dayton, Ohio, at Simms Station (now Wright-Patterson Air Force Base). By 1905 they recorded a flight of over 6 miles in a pusher-type plane. At first the Wright brothers could not interest the government in their planes or in teaching men to fly. However, President Roosevelt was interested in planes as a possible national defense weapon; so the Signal Corps on 27 December 1907 conferred with the Wrights and was authorized to procure a plane for the army that could convey two men at 40 miles per hour and be able to carry fuel sufficient for a flight of 115 miles.

On 10 February 1908 the Wright brothers got the contract for America's first military plane. On 9 September the aircraft was flown by Orville Wright at Fort Myer for an incredible fifty-seven-minute, thirty-one-second flight. Later that day, Orville took Lieutenant Lahm up—the first army officer to fly in a plane. But a crash on 17 September injured Orville. On 27 July 1909 Orville and Lahm flew for one hour and twelve minutes, a world record for two people. Three days later they flew at 42.5 mph for a distance of ten miles at an altitude of four hundred feet. On 2 August 1909 the Wright "Flyer" was formally accepted by the army. The first two army flyers to solo (at College Park, Maryland, on 26 October) were Lieutenants Lahm and Frederic E. Humphreys, soon followed by Foulois.[62]

In 1912 the secretary of war asked Congress for $2 million for 120 warplanes and for training schools to keep pace with air forces in Europe, but the legislators voted only $125,000. In 1913 funds allowed only the replacement of worn-out planes and barely adequate maintenance. The Signal Corps could not even replace its lone dirigible or continue its activities with balloons. In 1913 the army moved its training facilities from College Park to San Diego, California, where sympathetic private airport owners agreed to let the army use their grounds free of charge. The new San Diego school had seven planes, twelve officers undergoing training, and forty-seven enlisted men. The army had only fifteen planes altogether. In late 1913 the War Department asked for $1 million for its Signal Corps Aviation Section.[63]

However, landlubbers were gaining the ascendency. Both the government and civilian sectors of the country drew back somewhat from an initial enthusiasm for aviation, and the United States was soon lagging behind European nations. Finally on 18 July 1914 Congress passed a bill providing the Signal Corps with its request for $1 million, just as the First World War began.[64]

With wartime developments in aerial combat to observe in Europe, the United States Navy was not backward in experimenting with the design and use of naval planes. Congress approved $10,000 for the naval air arm in 1913. Meanwhile, the secretary of the navy warned against the neglect of military aviation. The expansion of the air war in Europe influenced Congress to appropriate $1 million for aviation, including the creation of eight aero squadrons in 1916, and $3.5 million a year later. The eagle's wings were being strengthened at last.[65]

THE PERIOD from the Spanish-American War to the entry of the United States into the First World War was one in which realistic military reform struggled against congressional and public apathy. It was an era fraught with possible catastrophe for the nation if American army and navy development were to stand still while the world's great powers armed themselves for sustained operations of a magnitude and intensity as yet undreamed of. Fortunately and almost belatedly the United States righted itself in time with last-minute army and air progress and steady naval development. Given the boon of time and distance, the United States was ready to take part in the Great War in Europe and play a decisive role in achieving an Allied victory.

Progress was tortoise paced immediately after the war with Spain. It took all of the considerable talents of Elihu Root and the strong support of William McKinley and Theodore Roosevelt to establish the Army War College, the General Staff, and other long overdue War Department reforms. It also required the reversal of opposition by the bureau chiefs, some members of Congress, and Adj. Gen. Fred C. Ainsworth to solidify these gains. In this period considerable streamlining of the army school system was accomplished that would serve invaluable ends.

On balance, the army and the nation were fortunate in having the imaginative and ebullient Leonard Wood as chief of staff, a man who not only labored strenuously in behalf of the militia and reserves but who was also a persistent and dedicated preparedness champion. In this he was supported by John M. Palmer, Henry Stimson, and William H. Taft. The National Guard became firmly entrenched as an integral part of the country's military institutions albeit playing a somewhat nebulous role in its early existence.

But the preparedness movement received a serious setback when pacifist Woodrow Wilson became president, despite the efforts of Lindley Garrison to ready the republic for eventual participation in World War I. Only slowly, after some vacillating and floundering, was Wilson converted, receiving able assistance from Hugh L. Scott and Newton D. Baker. The strife along the Mexican border seemed to illustrate the nation's needs for greater military efficiency.

America was fortunate in having a strongly pronavy president, Theodore Roosevelt, and he supplied much of the initial impetus for the early twentieth century naval buildup and stamped his high standards on naval matters other than mere warship construction. The president helped stimulate improvements in shipyards, gunnery, personnel policy, and battle fleet formation. He climaxed this activity by acquiring the site for the Panama Canal and beginning its construction during his administration. He dispatched sixteen battleships on the 1907 world cruise and enhanced American naval and diplomatic prestige. President Taft had partial success in continuing the construction of sufficient numbers of men-of-war. Even Wilson's and Josephus Daniels's reluctance was overcome when war erupted in Europe and the United States was obliged to make enormous increases in naval construction in 1916.

The infant air service of the army (and navy) struggled to get off the ground after the Wright brothers' first flight. It was hard going, and the flying service barely survived. The advances were from balloons to dirigibles to the primitive aeroplanes of the Wright era, and the progress was painfully slow because of the doubts and niggardliness of Congress. It was a struggle likewise to develop officers trained in flight, airfields and facilities to further military flying, and the pioneer flights of the uniformed airmen themselves. Only American participation in World War I enabled the eagle to spread its wings significantly.

But it was a familiar refrain: comparatively unprepared for combat when war came, many of the nation's finest young men would rest needlessly beneath white crosses. And it would be distressingly so a generation later.

"Lafayette, We Are Here"

But I doubt whether all the histories that can be written will ever quite convey to the generations who must learn of the war by reading about it, the unity of purpose and the fineness of spirit which our great American democracy developed in that crisis. Only those who lived in its light and felt its strength about them can ever know the full intoxication of being an American when America is at her very best.

NEWTON D. BAKER

PEOPLE IN EUROPE literally danced in the streets and sang from the rooftops as the great powers glided helplessly into war in the summer of 1914. Of course there had been the existence of the noiseless, underlying causes of conflict: the impelling nature of the rival alliance systems; the menacing if muted presence of militarism and navalism, and the dominance of the general staffs; the frantic contest for colonies in Africa and Asia; the blatant claims of nationalism; the two ominous Moroccan crises; the nasty little wars in the Balkans and the competition between Austria-Hungary and Russia as champions of the Slavs, including the yearning for independence of several minority ethnic groups within the Dual Monarchy; and the dynamics of personalities among a number of the leaders of the powers.

But war came in 1914 only when triggered by such immediate causes as the assassination of the Austrian Archduke Franz Ferdinand and his wife in Sarajevo, Bosnia, by members of the Serbian Black Hand organization; Germany's carte blanche to the Dual Monarchy; France and Russia's support of Serbia and each other; Austria's ultimatum to Serbia; the Tsar's crucial step of ordering full general mobilization (which meant war); Germany's declaration of war on France and Russia; and Great Britain's entry into the conflict when Germany invaded Belgium, the "Cockpit of Europe." Among the great powers, Italy and Japan would enter this war in 1915 on the side of the highest bidder, the Allies, while most people in America thought that the United States could remain neutral. Realistically, they should have seen that this would prove impossible no matter how strongly sought.[1]

At first it appeared to many that the war would be a short one. Although in 1914 on the Eastern Front the larger Russian army dealt the Austro-Hungarians some defeats in Galicia, the Tsar's soldiers were severely trounced by the Germans in East Prussia at Tannenberg and the Masurian Lakes, ensuring a longer struggle in Eastern Europe. But on the Western Front the powerful German army pushed steadily through Belgium and in hard fighting defeated Belgian, British, and French troops as the Kaiser's men pressed toward Paris in the counterclockwise Schlieffen wheel. But in September, at the Marne River some thirty-five miles from the French capital, the Germans were halted and fell back to a line along the Aisne River. The trench lines ran from the English Channel to Switzerland, with the defense supreme. All German colonies in Africa but East Africa (where Lettow-Vorbeck held out effectively until 1918) were captured by the Allies. The British naval blockade of Germany was answered by German U-boat activity that would increase in scope and intensity, and Allied shipping losses would soar as the war progressed. In surface ship action in the North Sea the British Grand Fleet seemed dominant, and the German Far Eastern Squadron, after administering a sharp defeat to a British squadron off Chile near the end of 1914, was itself crushed off the Falkland Islands. But the war, with casualties already in the many hundreds of thousands, would run at least into 1915, and this the participants finally perceived.[2]

In 1915 French and British attacks on the Western Front failed dismally. A limited German offensive near Ypres, in which poison chlorine gas was featured, was not exploited. Turkey entered the war on the side of the Central Powers, and French-British naval and land attacks at the Dardanelles and Gallipoli peninsula were checked. But a growing revolt in the desert by the Arabs against the Turks was in the offing and would eventually be triumphant, although 1915 saw British operations in Mesopotamia defeated by the Ottomans at Kut-el-Amara. The fighting seesawed back and forth in Galicia between Russia and Austria-Hungary, but, with German assistance, the Russians were roughly handled in Poland. The Austrians crushed Serbia, with German help, and Allied efforts in Greece did not fare well. Italy entered the war in 1915 on the Allied side; by August 1917 the eleven battles fought along the Isonzo River were all lost strategically by the Italians. By the end of 1915 the warring nations saw that the fearful conflict was stretching into an incredibly bloody and costly one and began to gird themselves for a long war.[3]

The year 1916 was a terrible one for both sides. On the Western Front the Allies had 139 divisions to the Germans' 117. In their assaults against Verdun the Germans not only bled the French army white but sustained enormous casualties themselves with little to show for their months of striving. And the British, under Douglas Haig, in their unimaginative, mammoth attacks at the Somme River, lost tremendous numbers with advances measured only in hundreds of yards. On the first day of the Somme offensive, the British lost more men (nearly 60,000) than have ever been lost in one day before or since in modern warfare. Even the vaunted British navy, under Sir John Jellicoe, experienced a tactical defeat off Jutland at the hands of Reinhardt Scheer's German High Seas Fleet, although the British came out ahead strategically. The Austrians defeated the Italians in the Trentino but were pushed back by

Brusilov's Russian offensive. Both the Austrians and Russians lost approximately 1 million men in this summer operation of 1916—casualties that would decisively weaken both nations. In the Near East the British captured Baghdad. By the end of 1916, only the United States among the great powers had managed to keep out of war, but it was only a matter of months before America would be drawn in.[4]

In 1917 Marshal Joffre was succeeded by Robert G. Nivelle, whose boasting reminds one unpleasantly of Generals John Pope and Joseph Hooker. Nivelle's announced offensive to the northwest of Reims was anticipated by the Germans, who fell back a little in March to the shorter and straighter Hindenburg Line. When the French attack came the following month, it was a ghastly failure, claiming casualties of 120,000 poilus. Henri Philippe Petain replaced Nivelle, but mutinies occurred in the French army that Premier Georges Clemenceau ruthlessly suppressed only with the firing squad. In April 1917 America was finally prodded into entering the war and very likely saved the Allies from defeat and enabled them to gain final victory over the Boches.[5]

Even before the declaration of war in April 1917 a number of Americans had served the Allies in several capacities. Some, such as Ernest Hemingway, were ambulance drivers. Others, such as Herbert C. Hoover, who was Belgian Food Relief Administrator, held civilian positions abroad. But the most famous were those young Americans who served in the storied Lafayette Escadrille of the French army. This aerial squadron included such prominent names as Charles B. Nordhoff, James Norman Hall, Jean Huffer, James R. McConnell, Kenneth Marr, David M. Peterson, Norman Prince, and the greatest American ace before America's entry into the war, Maj. Raoul Gervais Victor Lufbery.[6]

The reasons why the United States entered the First World War are numerous and complex. Almost from the start American public and governmental opinion favored the Allies, and Wilson was quicker to hold Germany to strict accountability than he was Britain or France. American heavy industry soon became geared to the Allied military effort, and these orders helped pull the United States out of an economic recession. It would be nearly ruinous to lose that trade. American political and social institutions and ethnic backgrounds were more closely related to Britain than they were to Germany. British propaganda was more skillful than Germany's, and the Zimmermann Note showed that the Kaiser was trying to stir up trouble between the United States and Mexico. Too, a number of American citizens had lost their lives in the German torpedoing of the *Lusitania* and *Sussex*. It was primarily the resumption of unrestricted submarine warfare by the Germans and the sinking of five more American ships in March 1917 that prompted Wilson to ask Congress for a declaration of war the following month.[7]

While the United States would eventually mobilize some 4,000,000 men, volunteering went slowly before a conscription act was passed; only 32,000 enlisted in the first three weeks. Total mobilization of the nation was essential, not only to support the American armed forces that would be expanded as never before, but also to help supply the battered but still huge war machines of the Allies. Despite many flaws, there had been some value in the mobilization along the Mexican border in 1916 of over 110,000 National Guardsmen, as well as in the establishment of the Plattsburg-type civilian training camps, especially in national morale. Fortunately, the Selective Service Act of 18 May 1917 that called to the colors men between the ages of twenty-one and thirty and then between eighteen and forty-five worked pretty well despite imperfections in its machinery. Its success may also be attributed to the prodigious labors of the provost marshal general, the gruff bachelor Enoch H. Crowder, who was the architect of the system and an effective draft director.[8]

An ominous Allied situation existed when the United States entered the war in the spring of 1917. Nivelle's offensive had been quashed, and the British and French were unable to budge the Germans from their trenches on the Western Front. The Austro-Hungarians were repelling the Italians and holding their own with the Russians, who were being thoroughly trounced by the Germans. Rumania and Serbia were knocked out of the war. So the Allies sent up a cry for fresh American troops. Paul von Hindenburg and Erich Ludendorff discounted the significance of any action that United States ground or naval forces might take, assuming our chief contribution would be funds and supplies; hence Germany's gamble in resuming unrestricted submarine warfare. There was no Allied plan of grand strategy, despite several early conferences, and the French and British missions sent to the United States in late April 1917 were at first only interested in getting more money. Only secondly did they ask Wilson and Baker to dispatch immediately a token force of soldiers to show good faith. No real guidance was given by these military missions on what America's military role or requirements were. So the newly appointed commander of the American Expeditionary Force (AEF) that would be sent to France would have to chart the course his country would take.[9]

The key choice of a high ranking officer in the United States in the war was that of Gen. John Joseph Pershing to head the AEF. The only other plausible choice was Leonard Wood, but Secretary of War Baker discarded Wood when he observed him struggling to climb a hill at Plattsburg. A positive reason why "Black Jack" Pershing was chosen AEF commander was that he had led the Punitive Expedition into Mexico in 1916. Baker wrote that "the force of about ten thousand men, constituting that expedition, was the largest force any American general officer at that time in active service had ever commanded."[10]

Pershing was born near Laclede, Missouri, on 13 September 1860 and was graduated in 1886 from West Point. He served as a cavalry officer in operations against the Indians in the Southwest from 1886 to 1890 and was an ROTC instructor at the University of Nebraska from 1891 to 1895, receiving from that institution in 1893 the LL.B. degree. He was an instructor in tactics at the military academy, 1897–1898 and fought in the Spanish-American War at San Juan Hill. This was followed by outstanding service in the Philippines against the Moros on Mindanao from 1899 to 1903 and again in that archipelago from 1906 to 1913. He was on the army General Staff from 1903 to 1905 and was an observer in the Russo-Japanese War in the latter year. In 1906

President Roosevelt "jumped" him from captain to brigadier general. Pershing commanded the Eighth Cavalry Brigade at the Presidio, San Francisco, and was given the assignment to break up Pancho Villa's raiding force, which he did with distinction in the 1916 foray into Mexico. In 1917 at the age of fifty-six, in excellent physical and mental health, he was chosen by Baker to be commander of the AEF, a mighty host which would number some 2 million men in France.[11]

Throughout his career Pershing excelled in almost everything he undertook. Before the death of his wife and three of his children in a fire at the Presidio, he often revealed good humor; after that tragedy he was a grim and strict, but fair, disciplinarian, totally absorbed in his work. He displayed "unvarying impersonality" in all his tasks, was tough, experienced, and self-confident, and always maintained great poise, presence, and an air of command. According to Douglas MacArthur, he possessed "strength and firmness of character," the ability to make and execute difficult decisions, the will power to carry through under adverse conditions, and the determination to fight and win through to victory under any circumstances. He also had the prized ability of selecting the ablest men and matching their talents to their jobs. Oddly enough, though he demanded unswerving punctuality from others, his most chronic flaw was an inability to keep his own appointments on time, whether with kings, presidents, or premiers, because he was so immersed in concentrating on his mission. In short, he was a superb choice and vindicated every trust placed in him. Russell F. Weigley concludes, "Pershing's ramrod-stiff professional integrity and dedication thoroughly impressed every statesman he ever encountered."[12]

Secretary of War Baker told Pershing he would give him just two orders as AEF commander: "one to go and one to return." As Pershing relates it, his orders from Wilson and Baker gave him

> all the authorities and duties devolved by the laws, regulations, orders, and customs of the United States upon a commander of an Army in the field in time of war and with the authority and duties in like manner devolved upon department commanders in peace and war. . . .[Plus] in general, . . . all necessary authority to carry on the war vigorously in harmony with the spirit of these instructions and toward a victorious conclusion.

And the commander's superior, Secretary Baker, asserted:

> it is eloquent of the foresight and imagination of General Pershing, who from the day he landed in France, seemed to grasp the needs of the situation with surer and larger views than any other person, military or civil, with whom I came into contact either at home or in Europe.[13]

It has been noted that President Wilson was probably bored with, ignorant and even contemptuous of military affairs and officers. As a former dedicated pacifist, he abhorred war; ironically, he was called upon to be commander in chief during the nation's largest military effort to that time. Yet

Wilson almost abdicated his responsibilities in this vital post, delegating his powers to such subordinates as March, Baker, Pershing, Bliss, and Sims, civilian and military leaders whom he faithfully supported in the hope and expectation (usually vindicated) that they would make the critical decisions for him, although many should have been made only by the republic's commander in chief.[14]

Several of the president's shortcomings can be seen in conjunction with his obvious talents. "Wilson's capacity for self-deception was great," writes Harvey A. DeWeerd. "One of his strongest characteristics was his stubborn sense of being 'right' and his lack of patience with views that did not support his own," although he was sympathetic and concerned with the well-being of the young doughboys. Yet Wilson nurtured deep, secret self-doubts. Wilson admitted the "loneliness" of a chief executive "who by no means implicitly trusts his own judgment."[15]

The real "sleeper" in the president's cabinet, and one of America's finest secretaries of war, was the slight, forty-four-year-old Newton D. Baker. He was honest and straightforward and had a keen, retentive, analytical mind. Baker was not afraid to assume the responsibility to act in the absence of direction by Wilson. Despite his gracious and easy mien, Baker could be stern and even ruthless when the occasion warranted. He was a moralist and worked hard to make the American army conform to his moral standards. Pershing, after his first meeting with Baker, commented:

> I was surprised to find him much younger and considerably smaller than I had expected. He looked actually diminutive as he sat behind his desk, doubled up in a rather large office chair, but when he spoke my impression changed immediately. . . . I left Mr. Baker's office with a distinctly favorable impression of the man upon whom . . . would rest the burden of preparing for a great war. . . . He was courteous and pleasant and impressed me as being frank, fair, and businesslike. His conception of the problems seemed broad and comprehensive. From the start he did not hesitate to make definite decisions on the momentous questions involved.

One of the secretary's few imperfections was mentioned by Edward M. Coffman: "Particularly, in the realm of economic mobilization, Baker's delay in reorganizing the army's supply agencies and his opposition to a strong centralized control of the wartime economy impeded an effective solution of the complex problems." The one serious difference arising between Baker and Pershing occurred when Pershing, without consulting the secretary or the president, urged the Supreme Allied War Council to insist upon unconditional surrender by Germany. Baker was for sending the general an official reprimand, but Wilson vetoed this idea, and the contretemps blew over.[16]

Although he admitted to being "old, and heavy and stiff," former President Roosevelt asked for authority to raise and lead a division of troops in France. But Baker and Wilson wanted to play no favorites and also to eliminate the dubious practice of employing political generals, so they rejected the request. Pershing said that TR was a bit too infirm and aged, although he greatly admired the Rough Rider's spirit.[17]

Baker faced a thorny problem in filling the post of chief of staff once

Hugh L. Scott retired. Peyton C. March, who was Pershing's first AEF chief of artillery, was duly named chief of staff, at Pershing's recommendation. It was, in the main, an excellent choice. A West Pointer, March had served gallantly in the Spanish War and in the Philippine Insurrection, as an observer in the Russo-Japanese War, and on the first General Staff. He was efficient, vigorous, and responsible—a large, dynamic man who knew what he was doing, who could innovate and improvise, and who had the courage of his convictions. He fired those he thought unfit and dominated the sometimes balky bureau chiefs. Indeed, his principal fault was his abrasive tactlessness and undiplomatic way of operating. The hardness of the fifty-three-year-old March can be seen in his appraisal of his two predecessors, Scott and Bliss: "They were fine old fellows . . . but neither of them had a certain ruthlessness which disregards accustomed methods and individual likings in striking out along new and untrodden paths."[18]

Some friction would develop between March and Pershing when March occasionally failed to rubber-stamp Pershing's promotion lists. Their chief controversy was whether Pershing should go through March or whether he could (as he sometimes did) deal directly with Baker. In a unitheater war, as it was for the United States until our intervention in Russia, this might be done, though of course March had a strong point in claiming that it should not be done. At one time Baker said all commanders, even Pershing, were subordinate to the chief of staff. But Baker tended to back Pershing and his interpretations more than he did March, and the secretary gave Black Jack most of the credit for winning the war. Generally, Pershing had full sway in doing what he wanted in France.[19]

As Pershing was about to embark in civilian clothes on a transport ship, he was told by Baker in their final meeting, "If you do not make good, they [the American people] will probably hang us both on the first lamp post they can find." Pershing sailed on 28 May 1917 for Europe with a carefully chosen staff and made a thorough examination of the military picture there. On 6 July he cabled his estimate of the situation: a million American soldiers were needed in France, with provision for another million, plus facilities, supplies, and equipment of almost every description. Earlier in 1916 the current chief of staff, Scott, had recommended raising a million-man army, but his suggestion was received with "great hilarity" by a congressional committee. In November 1917 Pershing warned that the United States would have to bend every effort to field American troops to fight in France by the summer of 1918; delay would be fatal. On 15 December 1917 Bliss accurately predicted that a military crisis for the Allies would occur "not later than the end of the next spring," with Germany emerging triumphant unless heavy numbers of American forces were present.[20]

In the minds of the American high command there was no doubt about one thing: the War Department directed Pershing, who was in complete agreement with this order he helped to write, to cooperate with the Allies but to fight the AEF only as an independent army holding its sector of the front. Protracted, persistent, and stubborn but unsuccessful efforts by the French and British to try to grab Pershing's soldiers as replacements ensued, while he tenaciously and courageously held out for independence, except during a grave crisis. Seldom easy to get along with, Pershing could be severe—even harsh—in standing by his orders and principles. And he triumphed in maintaining the independence of the American army, even though there were times when the Allies appealed over his head to the president. Wilson automatically backed the AEF commander so that Wilson would not have to play an active role as commander in chief. Pershing remained in supreme control over the American troops, even though the more conciliatory Bliss once in a great while yielded a few minor concessions to the Allies. Many have thought that Pershing's long battle against amalgamation of our forces with those of the Allies was one of his greatest achievements.[21]

Over 2 million American soldiers were sent to France, half arriving by May 1918, and the other half in the last six months of the war. This effort was accomplished despite shipping shortages and German U-boats. Not one United States army transport vessel was sunk on the loaded eastbound voyage (although several were torpedoed and lost on the empty westbound trip)—a remarkable record unequalled in World War II.[22]

In an attempt to achieve greater unity in military control, the Allied Supreme War Council was established in November, 1917. The War Council acted as a central clearinghouse for military intelligence and oftentimes made sound recommendations to the respective Allied governments. But its advice was only that—unenforceable suggestions. Only during the crisis beginning on 21 March 1918, when the most fully prepared and most powerfully mounted military attack in modern history up to that time struck the British front near where it hinged with the French army and threatened catastrophe did the British, French, and American heads of state act. Ferdinand Foch was named Supreme Allied Commander (but with limitations that will be noted later) on 3 April 1918. Italy, however, never accepted General Foch as strategic director of the Italian army.[23]

WHEN WAR CAME, the Army of the United States numbered some 200,000 men, two-thirds of whom were regulars and one-third National Guardsmen who had been called to the colors for service on the Mexican border. By the end of the conflict this small force had been expanded twenty times to about 4 million men. The army that resulted from the Selective Service Act was made up of regulars, National Guardsmen, and the so-called National Army of draftees. The three components were given approximately equal pay, rights, terms, privileges, and other perquisites. "The willingness with which the American people accepted the universal draft," writes Leonard P. Ayres, "was the most remarkable feature in the history of our preparation for war." Of every six commissioned officers of the 200,000 needed, one had previous military training in the regular army, National Guard, or in the ranks; three came from the officers' training camps; and the other two (mostly physicians, chaplains, or special technical or business types) came from civilian life with little or no prior military training.[24]

The War Department planned to have eighty divisions overseas by July 1919, with one hundred by the end of that year. By the time of the Armistice—11 November 1918—the United States had forty-two divisions in

France, twelve more well advanced in their training, with four more being organized. Each American division numbered twenty-eight thousand, of which number about one thousand were officers. Provisioning the army with clothing, food, and supplies was hindered by the earlier mobilization on the Mexican border that had consumed what reserve supplies America had and exhausted the ordinary capacity of industries normally manufacturing such supplies and equipment. And yet mountains of goods were needed overseas by the AEF. Appropriations for the Quartermaster Department in 1918 totaled $3 billion. Before large numbers of combat troops could be accommodated in France, the Services of Supply (SOS) had to build docks, warehouses, barracks, and hospitals. The SOS strung 100,000 miles of telegraph and telephone wires and constructed 1,125 miles of railroad track. About one in every four soldiers in the AEF was assigned to the SOS.[25]

Among the key top American leaders was the talented vice president of the Pennsylvania Railroad, William W. Atterbury, who was named a brigadier general and appointed by Pershing to command the Transportation Corps of the AEF. "Much to my surprise," affirmed Pershing just after appointing him, "Atterbury seemed to be very familiar with the situation, and his personality, his force, his grasp of the difficulties of the task, and his willingness to undertake it appealed to me at once." He made the transition from civilian to military ways of doing things quickly, and Atterbury skillfully moved the mountains of equipment and supplies over the many miles of railroad that he maintained in France "with remarkable efficiency and dispatch," according to Secretary of War Baker.[26]

Three of Pershing's best planners in the AEF were products of Fort Leavenworth's Staff College, although many division and corps commanders had not had this advantage. Tall, robust Mississippian Fox Conner was the open-minded, highly intelligent chief of operations at General Headquarters. Very professional, though oftentimes frank and sardonic, Conner was keenly interested in military history. He was also praised by Pershing and by Conner's protégé of the 1920s, Dwight D. Eisenhower. The thirty-eight-year-old Hugh Drum was short and handsome, and a highly ambitious officer who had staff experience in the Vera Cruz expedition and in the Mexican border mobilization. Drum became chief of staff of the First Army. Another ambitious though quiet officer was George C. Marshall, thirty-seven-year-old graduate of Virginia Military Institute, who became chief of operations of the First Army under Drum's direction. The self-disciplined, dedicated, but highly strung Marshall would later run around Drum to become army chief of staff. All three of these fine officers left their mark on the AEF and its operations.[27]

THE AMERICAN GENERAL STAFF vindicated itself in the First World War. A congressional act passed on 3 June 1916 unfortunately limited the General Staff to fifty-five officers and provided that only half of them could be "in or near the District of Columbia." Secretary Baker strongly backed the General Staff and directed it to act as a reconciling and coordinating agency as well as one that dealt with staff problems. However, when war was declared the General Staff actually comprised only nineteen officers posted in Washington and twenty-two stationed elsewhere. An act of 12 May 1917 upped the General Staff to ninety-one officers and removed the restriction on the number who could be stationed in the capital. Six days later, Congress authorized the president to increase the number of staff and line officers to whatever was needed for the war. By the armistice, the General Staff had increased to 1,222 officers.[28]

For a thoroughly coordinated effort, Pershing borrowed some concepts from the French and British and created a general staff for the AEF that proved to be most useful. The AEF general staff, plus the General Staff in Washington, proved essential in the tremendous job of logistics, which enabled America to dispatch its 2,086,000 doughboys to France and for them to play a significant role in gaining the final triumph.[29]

WHILE THE ROLE of the United States Navy would not be so huge or far-reaching in World War I as it would be in World War II, nonetheless it would play a significant part in 1917–1918. Unfortunately Josephus Daniels, the secretary of the navy and a former Tarheel newspaperman who often mounted the political stump instead of being solely concerned with Navy Department business, was not a first-class civilian head of the service afloat. Bland, always smiling, he often acted as ambassador between the navy and the public. Yet he was sufficiently lacking in rancor that he could paper the walls of his office with cartoons that lampooned him. As secretary he tried to gag officers; prevent sons of naval officers from attending the naval academy; and in line with his Bible Belt fundamentalism, to prevent the use of alcohol in the service. Daniels also lacked understanding and was tactless and undiplomatic. Much more capable than Daniels was his young assistant, Franklin Delano Roosevelt, who did what he could to harmonize frictions.[30]

Chosen to command American naval forces in European waters was the gifted William Sowden Sims, who was born in 1858 in Port Hope, Ontario, the son of an American civil engineer. He graduated in the middle of his class at Annapolis and was widely read in divergent fields. Sims served on the China Station and as Inspector of Target Practice, hammered hard and successfully for better aiming and range-finding devices and gunnery techniques in the navy, as well as fostering other reforms. He then served as president of the Naval War College. This tall, handsome officer, fifty-eight when the war began, was sharp-tongued, supremely confident, knowledgeable, and usually correct in his recommendations and decisions.[31]

It was determined that Sims and the American naval forces would serve under the crusty but able old British sea-dog, Vice Adm. Lewis Bayly. The first American warships to arrive in British waters were the famous four-stacker destroyers and old torpedo boats brought halfway around the world from the Pacific by Harold Stark. Some of the other individual ship commanders were Chester W. Nimitz, William F. Halsey, and Henry K. Hewitt. Sims and "Uncle Lewis" Bayly worked together harmoniously and effectively. Never before had the navies of two great powers coordinated their operations so well.[32]

A few weeks after America's entry into the war, Admiral Sims arrived in England and conferred with British admiralty leaders. It was a somber discussion. He was told by First Sea Lord, Sir John Jellicoe, that German U-boats had sunk 536,000 tons of shipping in February, 1917; 571,000 tons in March; and the staggering total of 881,000 tons in April. Even at the peak of the Nazi submarine campaign in World War II in November 1942, only 637,000 tons would be sunk. Sims was convinced that American naval help was desperately needed in 1917, and he promptly urged that all available American destroyers be dispatched forthwith to the British Isles. Through June, Sims, joined by United States Ambassador to Britain Walter Hines Page, continued to bombard Washington with urgent cables describing the critical U-boat situation and calling for antisubmarine vessels. By July 1917 there were thirty-four United States destroyers in British waters, and by the Armistice there would be seventy-nine "over there."[33]

In April 1917, 67 percent of all American naval vessels, including one-half of the forty-four new destroyers, needed repairs. It took an average of fifty-six days in shipyards to ready them for combat. In April the United States had 61 shipyards with 213 ways (142 were for steel vessels). By the end of the war there were 1,284 ways for steel ships and 816 for wooden ones, all in 341 yards. In celebration of Independence Day on 4 July 1918, ninety-five ships were launched. By November 1917 Allied losses to U-boats had been reduced to 289,000 tons per month; this decrease, along with new ship construction, was one with which the Allies could live.[34]

Despite opposition from Lord Jellicoe and other British naval authorities, Sims and the former First Lord of the Admiralty, Winston Churchill, urgently recommended adoption of the convoy system. With President Wilson's backing, the convoy system was finally implemented and proved quite successful. To assist the British Grand Fleet in keeping Germany's High Seas Fleet bottled up in port, a division of six American battleships under Rear Adm. Hugh Rodman was stationed in Scotland from late 1917. These coal-burners made no demands upon the limited quantity of Britain's imported oil. Later, three more United States battleships, including two new oil-burners, were stationed in Ireland. Yet the large German warships emerged from their harbors only to surrender at the end of the war.[35]

The war in the Mediterranean also attracted American naval participation, though on a smaller scale than in the North Sea and North Atlantic. Particularly troublesome were Austrian and German submarines that exited from the Adriatic Sea through the forty-mile-wide Strait of Otranto between Greece and Italy. Allied countermeasures succeeded in partially closing this strait, with the Americans providing thirty-six wooden subchasers (the "Splinter Fleet of the Otranto Barrage," as it was called), headed by the irrepressible Capt. Charles P. ("Juggy") Nelson, a rotund man described by Sims as "energetic . . . efficient . . . lovable . . . personally engaging." It is thought that two enemy submarines were sunk in Otranto Strait.[36]

Despite technical protests by the British, Americans persevered in another significant feat. This was the laying of seventy thousand mines between Norway and Scotland to make the passage of enemy submarines more difficult. In this 230-mile-long, 15- to 35-mile-thick North Sea Mine Barrage, the United States Navy laid fifty-six thousand mines, including the new American antenna mine. At least twelve German U-boats were destroyed in this greatest of minefields.[37]

In addition, the navy supplied the AEF with five monster 14-inch artillery tubes emplaced on railway mounts. Manned by naval crews, they were under the command of Rear Adm. Charles P. Plunkett. These great railway guns were frequently in operation after 6 September 1918, firing some 800 rounds—one every seventy seconds—up to ranges of twenty-five miles during the Meuse-Argonne campaign. So severely did they shell the railroad center at Laon that the Germans soon retreated. Equally destructive was the fire of these mammoth guns upon the main enemy railroad by which the Germans could reinforce Sedan. The damage was so great that all rail traffic on this line was stopped for up to ten hours after each shelling.[38]

However, the actual combat physical contact between United States warships and enemy fighting ships was slight. Naval historian Fletcher Pratt summarizes:

> The old armored cruiser *San Diego* sank on a mine . . . and the old battleship *Minnesota* barely made port after hitting another; two armed yachts were torpedoed in the Mediterranean, and in the Channel the destroyer *Jacob Jones* . . . ; destroyers *Fanning* and *Nicholson* sank a sub and captured her people; the armed yacht *Christabel* knocked another about so badly it had to put into a Spanish harbor for internment. . . .[39]

A thorough professional of the Emory Upton school in terms of training, Pershing had authority to commit no American troops to battle until he thought they were properly trained, and he took his time in this matter. Part of the necessary delay was caused by the slow conscription process and the time needed to build training camps. Also, officers and noncoms had to be provided before the draftees could receive instruction. The Plattsburg-type camps yielded 27,341 officers, and other officers training camps were established. For a while the divisions formed their own officers camps, and the four-month program was reduced to three months' training. And Pershing relieved high-ranking officers of command promptly, even ruthlessly, when they failed to measure up to his high standards. These included the early commander of the First Division, Maj. Gen. William L. Sibert (an engineer) and other early division commanders. In the first week of the final campaign, Pershing relieved four infantry brigade commanders, and before the end of October 1918, the Fifth Corps commander (George Cameron) and three division commanders.[40]

Pershing was a perfectionist and insisted on the thorough training of the doughboys in trench warfare and new weapons, and he gladly accepted experienced French and British officers as instructors. But the American commander was determined to train his men in open-field tactics that included quality use of the bayonet and rifle and good marksmanship because he foresaw an eventual end to the static, defensive, trench warfare and a return to an offensive dynamic war of movement. In addition, he wanted his conscripts to develop the bearing and poise of regulars. Black Jack trained the First Division for six months before he would let it occupy a front-line position in the trenches.[41]

ALLIED MILITARY OPERATIONS suffered a number of devastating setbacks that made American participation mandatory in increasingly large numbers. With the French and British unable to force the smaller number of Germans from the Western Front, the autumn of 1917 also saw Italy endure a terrible defeat at Caporetto in October and November, with the loss of some 300,000 men. The Italians called loudly for help, and some British and French troops were sent to their aid. Only a desperate stand along the Piave River north of the great cities kept Italy in the war. On the Riga front, employing the brilliant Hutier tactics of infiltration and bypassing strong-points, the Germans scored a series of striking victories. These, along with the decisive internal weakening caused by the Bolshevik revolution, knocked Russia out of the war that autumn and the Russians suffered a total of some 9 million casualties during the course of the conflict. This great success enabled Hindenburg and Ludendorff, leaving forty second-class German divisions in the Ukraine, to shift fifty-two divisions, not thirty-two, as some Allied leaders thought, to the Western Front. This gave the enemy, for the first time since 1914, a numerical superiority that amounted to 10 percent. Ludendorff trained his shock troops to the peak of their efficiency and planned in March 1918 to strike at the Somme and Oise Rivers, near where the British army hinged with the French.[42]

The first of the five great German drives—one a month beginning in March 1918—was a brilliant tactical success, which even the British acknowledged. Aided by fog and a saturation artillery bombardment, Ludendorff struck on the sixty-one-mile-long Cambrai–St. Quentin front, surprised Haig's men, and carved out remarkable gains of forty miles. Seventy-one German divisions were employed, forty-three of them against the twelve British Expeditionary Forces (BEF) divisions of the Fifth Army. The enemy wheeled into battery 2,508 heavy guns; the British, 976. And the Germans had 730 planes as against 570 British. Ironically, Secretary Baker and the Supreme Allied War Council's executive committee had predicted the German offensive exactly where it occurred. But the British took insufficient precautions because Haig, as usual, was overconfident that he could defeat any enemy assault anywhere.[43]

For his second great drive in April Ludendorff again launched his forces against the British, this time farther north along the Lys River in Flanders, south of Ypres. Although the British had been repeatedly warned, the German assault took Haig by surprise and was highly successful, penetrating the three trench lines for gains up to ten miles before exhaustion overtook the Kaiser's legions. Pershing, reluctantly, consented to send the United States First Division immediately to aid the British near the Lys if Foch thought the matter "urgent"; Foch did not press the issue.[44]

At the time of his third major offensive, May 1918, Ludendorff had 208 divisions on the Western Front as against 170 slightly larger Allied ones. He was determined to knock the French and British armies out of the war before

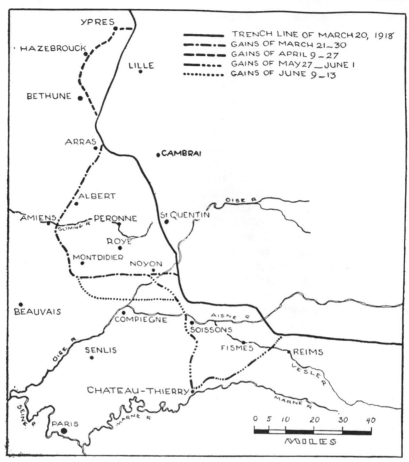

FIG. 12.1.   LUDENDORFF'S FOUR OFFENSIVES IN THE SPRING OF 1918

the Americans could arrive in significant numbers. Following exemplary German preparation, Ludendorff struck the French along the supposedly impregnable Chemin des Dames, a fifteen-mile-long ridge between the Ailette and Aisne Rivers. The drive scored an outstanding success, breaking through the three French lines and gaining thirteen miles the first day. Thus Ludendorff decided to make this his maximum offensive instead of returning to the north against the British in Flanders. Once more the Allies had had warnings of the impending German onslaught. Capt. Samuel T. Hubbard, Jr., a young American intelligence officer, precisely forecast this German attack on the Chemin des Dames, but his report was arrogantly rejected by the French, as were similar predictions by the four recuperating French divisions on this sector. The crisis to the Allied Western Front elicited the following pledge from Pershing, who had been wrangling with the Allies over training time: "At this moment there are no other questions but of fighting," and he generously offered the British and French "Infantry, artillery, aviation, all that we have are yours."[45]

In the apex of the great German Somme salient, just northwest of Montdidier, was the strongly fortified village of Cantigny, standing on high ground. On 28 May, the AEFs First Infantry Division, the "Big Red One," was ordered to capture this important position. A London *Times* war correspondent described what happened:

> The operation began with neutralization fire on the enemies' batteries from our heavies. This lasted one hour and was followed by the combined heavies and light guns for another hour and a half of preparation, diversion and destructive fire. Then, at 6:45 [A.M.] the Americans upon a front of one and one-half miles hopped from their trenches and, under the protection of a well directed rolling barrage from the light guns, with the heavies concentrated upon the distant areas, they advanced in two sturdy waves. They crossed the intervening zone to their objective, a depth of nearly a mile, in exactly 40 minutes, preceded by 12 tanks. There were sharp individual fights in the town of Cantigny. Two hundred and fifty German dead were counted.

The Americans held their gains despite five heavy enemy counterattacks. United States casualties totaled 824 in the offensive phase of the battle and 950 in the defensive.[46]

When the third great German drive reached the Marne, thirty-seven miles from Paris, the Allied situation was desperate. Pétain requested an American division to hold the vital Marne crossings, and Pershing immediately sent the heretofore unbloodied Third Infantry Division, which reached Château-Thiérry on 1 June. Here, in hard fighting, the doughboys repulsed the Germans in their persistent three-day efforts to cross the river. To hold the Château-Thiérry-Paris road a little to the west, Pershing threw into action the Second Division which included the marine brigade, and again the enemy was repelled in furious combat.[47]

To try to tilt the still dangerous Germans off balance, a limited counterattack was staged just to the northwest of Château-Thiérry at Belleau Wood. Here, tenacious enemy troops, skillfully manning cleverly sited machine gun nests, had to be dug out in ferocious close quarter, often hand-to-hand fighting by Pershing's Second Division, including the marine brigade. The American assault, begun on 6 June, required nearly three weeks before the wood was cleared of Germans. The difficulties of the doughboys in Belleau Wood were increased by French disregard for American lives and their failure to help the Yanks with tanks and artillery support. It cost the Americans dearly. The marines lost 52 percent of their numbers engaged in this battle. This compares to a little under 39 percent at Iwo Jima in World War II. In all, thirty thousand marines were to see service overseas in the First World War.[48]

Yet the strategic situation began to erode for the Germans, despite their sizeable gains won in their first three major drives. In his fourth offensive in June 1918, Ludendorff assailed the Allied lines in the Noyen-Montdidier region to the northwest of Soissons. But the Germans for the first time scored no tactical surprise, and their drive was limited to a total of just twelve miles. So despite unfavorable conditions such as an inferiority in numbers, Ludendorff in his fifth and final dying-gasp offensive in July turned against the French both to the east and west of Reims. This brought on the so-called Second Battle of the Marne when the German advance managed to gain eight miles and reach that river's crossings once more. So once again the American Third Division, notably the Thirty-eighth Infantry Regiment (the "Rock of the Marne"), was ordered into action by Pershing and at Château-Thiérry hurled the Germans back from their first bridgeheads on the south bank of the Marne.[49]

In the crisis of the German spring offensives, Ferdinand Foch was finally named supreme allied commander or generalissimo. Yet there were limitations on his power: he could direct the strategic deployment of French, British, and American forces, but Pershing and Haig nonetheless had a veto on exactly how their nations' troops would be fought. In short, Foch was really not supreme.

With large numbers of American soldiers pouring into France, Pershing was able to form the AEF into two corps (and later two armies with the same commanders): the First, commanded by Hunter Liggett, and the Second, led by Robert L. Bullard.

Liggett was an elderly, overweight officer who barely met Pershing's high physical standards. He was born in Reading, Pennsylvania, in 1857, the son of a Pennsylvania legislator. Liggett graduated from West Point in 1879, fought Indians on the Plains, and served in the War with Spain and in the Philippine Insurrection. A solid, reliable man, Liggett kept abreast of military affairs by keen study of the latest trends in his profession. He served on the General Staff and was president of the Army War College. He understood human nature, was trustful and showed shrewd judgment, high moral courage, and loyalty to both superiors and subordinates. This efficient officer, who could be curt when necessary, was nonetheless kindly, calm, good humored, quiet, and charming. A good strategic planner and capable tactician, he proved his worth in battle. Liggett "has no equal in professional ability or noble character among our American generals," said a fellow two-star officer. Air Service hero Billy Mitchell termed Liggett "one of the ablest soldiers I was ever brought in contact with." According to Maj. Gen. Robert Bullard, "Liggett had the valuable faculty of seeing what was important and what not; and he did not waste his time or attention on what was not going to count." Bullard, too, would prove to be a competent corps and army commander, and, to a slightly lesser extent, so would Joseph T. Dickman.[50]

With the Germans having shot their offensive bolt, Foch and the Allies took over the strategic offensive themselves. American forces played an important role in the Aisne-Marne (Soissons) and in the Amiens counteroffensives lasting from 18 July to 6 August 1918 and aimed at both the eastern and western faces of the enemy's Marne salient. Pershing's First and Second Divisions were included in the French Tenth Army that was to make the main assault.

The attack on 18 July caught the weakened enemy by surprise and gained ground over uncratered terrain where there were few trenches. The Germans ordered a withdrawal on 20–21 July. By the time the two United States divisions were relieved they had advanced almost seven miles and suffered eleven thousand casualties but had captured 140 cannon and sixty-five hundred prisoners. A bit to the south the American Third, Twenty-eighth, and Forty-second Divisions, supported by the Fourth and the Third Corps (including the Thirty-second and Twenty-sixth Divisions to the right), advanced to the Vesle and Aisne rivers, spearheading the Allied attack. The value of this advance was that it threw off balance Ludendorff's hopes for a renewed offensive of his own. Meanwhile Haig's British forces struck at the German bulge near Amiens on 8 August, the "Black Day" of the German army. The enemy was surprised and was obliged to fall back to their 1915 line. Near Arras to the north the British attacked on 21 August and drove the German forces out of the Somme salient and back to the Hindenburg Line from which they had sortied in March on their grand offensive.[51]

Pershing demanded the return of all American units that he had loaned to the Allies during the emergency of the German spring offensives. Foch had no alternative but to acquiesce. The American commander stated that his force was now large enough to take over its sector of the front and fight as an independent army. The allied supreme commander assigned to Pershing the southeastern section of the front and charged him with reducing the important St. Mihiel salient that protected the vital German city of Metz and would pose a flankwise threat to any later American offensive in the Argonne Forest and the region to the west of the Meuse River. It took most of August to collect and reassemble American units from along the Western Front and in reserve, but the AEF was ready to open its major attack against the St. Mihiel salient on 12 September.[52]

The American army that launched this assault comprised three corps of fourteen divisions (some 550,000 troops) and 110,000 French soldiers. Of its 3,010 artillery pieces (none of American manufacture), 1,329 were crewed by *poilus*. It had 267 French-made light tanks, 113 of which were manned by the French. Pershing's force also had nearly 1,400 planes, the greatest aerial armada up to that time, under the redoubtable Col. Billy Mitchell's command, but including Maj. Gen. Sir Hugh Trenchard's British Independent Bombing Squadrons and a 600-plane French air division.[53]

The Germans had held the St. Mihiel salient since the autumn of 1914. Not only did it protect the important German Briey coal mines and the great city of Metz, but this bulge hampered Allied lateral communications, especially rail lines from Paris to Lorraine, and threatened the rear of such heavy Allied fortifications as that at Verdun. The plans called for an American advance of six to eight miles to reduce the salient, while *at the same time* Pershing was to begin to deploy large forces for the ensuing and massive Meuse-Argonne offensive.[54]

While the St. Mihiel salient was a naturally strong position and had been carefully fortified with dense barbed-wire entanglements, the Germans had begun on 11 September to remove some heavy equipment, including big guns, in preparation for a slow and gradual withdrawal from the bulge. Pershing directed that a French corps make a secondary attack against the nose of the salient while the two main, nearly simultaneous assaults would be launched by Maj. Gen. George H. Cameron's Fifth Corps against the western face of the bulge and Liggett's First Corps and Dickman's Fourth Corps against the southeastern face.[55]

The commander of the AEF executed his plans admirably. The St. Mihiel battle opened at 1:00 A.M. on 12 September 1918 with a heavy artillery bombardment followed by the infantry attack at 5:00 A.M. All went better than could be wished. So great was the success that all second day objectives were gained by the end of the first day. On the morning of 13 September the First Division, advancing from the south, met the Twenty-sixth Division, moving forward from the west; so all goals of the whole offensive were attained by the end of the second day. Further advances could have been won, but in accordance with plans, the drive was halted to deploy American units for the greater Meuse-Argonne offensive. Some seven thousand doughboys were casualties, but they had captured fifteen thousand prisoners and 257 guns. St. Mihiel was a striking success as the limited offensive it was meant to be. Secretary Baker, on his first visit to France, witnessed the St. Mihiel battle and declared: "Even a layman could understand the perfection with which the operation was executed, and the completeness of its success." For this triumph, Pershing received high praise from Wilson, Foch, and Haig.[56]

MENTION has already been made of the participation of a number of Americans in the Lafayette Escadrille before the United States entered the war. The AEF Signal Corps Air Service soon came under the command of the confident and able thirty-eight-year-old Billy Mitchell. Born in Nice, France, where his parents were temporarily residing, the aggressive and flamboyant lad grew up in Milwaukee and attended Columbian (later George Washington) University. His father was a United States senator. Mitchell enlisted in the Signal Corps of the army during the Spanish-American War, was in Cuba during the occupation, and later served with distinction against Aguinaldo in the Philippines. He received a commission in 1901 and helped establish telegraphic communication with Alaska. Mitchell learned to fly on weekends in 1916 at his own expense. When the Great War seemed imminent, he secured a position as military observer in Spain and went to France when America entered the fray. During the two months before Pershing's arrival, Mitchell journeyed up and down the Western Front, watching and talking with Allied soldiers, flyers, and high officers. He dispatched reports to the States and drew up a program for American aerial participation that the War Department ignored, but he quickly became the AEFs leading air officer in Europe.[57]

A War Department mission of over 100 technical experts, headed by Maj. Raynal C. Bolling, toured Europe for five weeks beginning in June 1917. It worked on aerial collaboration with the Allies, gathered information, and brought back recommendations on types of planes to be produced in the United States. In early 1917 the American Air Service's program, costing $54 million, called for 300 balloonists, 1,850 aviators, 16 balloons, 16 airplane squadrons, and 9 aviation schools. When war was declared, the United States had 55 obsolete planes and 1,200 airmen; thus Congress appropriated funds for the swift expansion of the Aviation Section. The $640 million appropriated for these purposes resulted in expansion to about 10,000 officers and 87,000 enlisted men in the aviation service.[58]

The 103d Pursuit Squadron of the AEF, including members of the Lafayette Escadrille, began operations at the front under French control on 18 February 1918. In mid-March the Ninety-fourth ("Hat in the Ring") Squadron of the First Pursuit Group flew the first flights across enemy lines. During the St. Mihiel offensive, American airmen flew 3,593 hours in aerial combat, ground strafing, bombing, observation, and artillery spotting. Another luminary, along with Maj. Raoul Lufbery, was the undisciplined, impetuous, but brilliant Frank Luke (the "Balloon Buster"), who scored eighteen quick victories before being forced down and killed on the ground while shooting it out with enemy soldiers. But America's greatest ace was the former racing driver and chauffeur with the early Pershing group, Eddie Rickenbacker. For him, the air war was sport and adventure, though he was cautious and seldom reckless in combat. This nerveless, mature, quick-thinking airman scored twenty-five confirmed victories by the armistice—a record that would have been greater had he not been out of action for two months with illness.[59]

During the war United States flyers shot down 755 confirmed German planes and 71 balloons, with American losses totaling 43 balloons and 357 planes. The Air Service took almost 18,000 aerial photographs, flew 35,000 hours over enemy lines, dropped over 250,000 pounds of bombs, and flew 215 bombing missions. In France 35 U.S. balloon companies made 1,642 ascensions, had 3,111 hours in the air, and employed 466 officers and 6,365 enlisted men. It should have been recognized by all observers that the war in the air was significant and would become more so in any future conflict. However, many would assume a head-in-the-sand attitude after 1918.[60]

The United States naval air effort involved 37,409 of its aviators in escorting convoys and troopships and supply vessels, watching for U-boats, and patrolling the coasts. The navy flyers had 695 seaplanes, 262 land planes, 1,170 flying boats, 15 dirigibles, and 10 free balloons. Their work was highly praised by Navy Secretary Daniels. Based in Italy, France, and the British Isles, and without much help from the army aviation people, the naval air arm bombed submarine bases and otherwise assisted in the naval war. By the end of the war there were 17,524 navy flyers overseas. Several of these naval airmen such as David S. Ingalls, Robert A. Lovett, and James V. Forrestal became prominent later in the United States defense establishment.[61]

WITH THE ALLIES on the strategic offensive in the summer and fall of 1918, Foch's prime objective was to gain an Allied victory that year and prevent the Germans from making an orderly withdrawal, taking with them the vast quantities of supplies they had collected in France and Belgium. Such a successful enemy withdrawal depended upon their holding several vital railroad lines and junctions, particularly at Aulnoye and Mézières. Foch, encouraged by Haig's importunities, determined to seize both of these great rail hubs in a pincer movement: a major British drive from the west from Cambrai against Aulnoye, and a major American drive from the south through formidable defenses against Mézières and Sedan, even though this new plan would terminate the promising American advance from St. Mihiel toward Metz. Many, including Bliss and Mitchell, thought this shift in the direction of the principal American effort was a blunder, given the weapons, tactics, and terrain involved. "The art of war had departed," asserted Mitchell. "Attrition, or the gradual killing off of the enemy, was all the ground armies were capable of."[62]

The Allies were partly correct in their criticism of the lack of experience of American unit commanders and their staffs in handling huge numbers of troops and massive logistical problems. This shortcoming could be attributed in part to censorship by the French and British, and in part to America's late entry into the war and American officers' consequent lack of information about the new methods of warfare. Pershing, in the time available, did as much as was possible with staff and other training schools he set up in France. But American staff work was not bad, as evidenced by the complex staff planning in the complicated shift from the St. Mihiel attack to the Meuse-Argonne offensive in which George C. Marshall played an important role. Pershing was as quick to remove staff officers whom he thought were not measuring up as he was to relieve line commanders. While there was some confusion and seeming chaos, 600,000 green American soldiers were moved at night into the area between the Meuse River and the Argonne Forest as 200,000 French exited, and Pershing's forces were ready to jump off on attack day.[63]

The area over which the American attack was to be launched was a difficult one. There was good German observation over the entire region from the heights of the Meuse to the east. The thickly wooded and rugged hills of the Argonne Forest on the west comprised a formidable obstacle and provided excellent observation of the terrain to the east. Between the valley of the Aire River (fordable at only a few points) and the valley of the Meuse (unfordable) ran a commanding north-south ridge. Small villages and woods, mostly fortified as strong points, dotted the generally open zone between the Meuse and Argonne Forest. For over four years the Germans had perfected four main defense lines in this area, although the fourth line was not fully organized.[64]

The strategic plan was for Pershing's First Army to drive the enemy back of the Mézières-Sedan rail line before winter. The French Fourth Army was to attack to the left (west) of the Americans. Stiff German resistance was expected; Mézières and Sedan were absolutely vital to the enemy defense in France. Pershing had three corps available, extending side by side from the Meuse to the Argonne. The main blow was to be struck by Cameron's Fifth Corps in the center, supported on its right by Bullard's Third Corps near the Meuse and on its left by Liggett's First Corps in the Argonne. The nine assault divisions were bolstered by six others in corps and army reserve. Almost 4,000 artillery pieces were present, as were 190 tanks and 820 planes.[65]

Pershing's own hopes were to surprise the Germans and swiftly advance ten miles, thereby penetrating the three main enemy defense lines before

Ludendorff could bring up significant reserves. The American commander appreciated that this might be impossible, but the advance was to be pressed anyway, thereby drawing German divisions into the destructive fire. After the first three defense lines were severed, Pershing would join the French Fourth Army on the left, north of the Argonne Forest, clear the Meuse heights by an attack eastward across the river (and / or by a northward thrust along the east bank), and then drive to the key Mézières-Sedan railway. The AEF would accomplish this mission, long and costly though it would be.[66]

When the American First Army took over command on this front from the French Second Army on 22 September 1918, the doughboys' reconnaissances were carried out in French uniforms to mislead the Germans.[67]

The first phase of the Meuse-Argonne operation, still the largest battle ever waged by Americans in uniform, commenced on 26 September and lasted until 3 October. On 26 September the attack was initiated by an artillery bombardment beginning at 2:30 A.M., followed at 5:30 A.M. by the infantry assault on a front of initially twenty-four miles that was stretched eventually to 90 miles. The Germans were astonished at the scope of the assault, and their first line fell quickly. Most of the southern part of the Argonne and the first two enemy lines were seized in the first several days, but the American advance was brought up short of the third line. Col. George S. Patton, Jr., was wounded here and received the Distinguished Service Cross.

Pershing saw that his hopes for a swift breakthrough of all three lines could not be realized, in part because there were too few tanks available, because many of these ironclad monsters broke down, because the terrain was rough and shell craters pockmarked the fields of the original no-man's-land, because poor roads made resupply difficult, and because of inexperienced soldiers and staffs. Pershing therefore sent in the veteran First, Third, and Thirty-second Divisions to relieve the raw Thirty-fifth, Thirty-seventh, and Seventy-ninth Divisions, and this complicated relief, on congested roads, was accomplished by 1 October. Division and corps commanders, in coping with their own heavy casualties, used MPs to patrol the areas to the rear to round up stragglers and maintain the momentum of the advance in this first phase of the campaign.[68]

The second phase of the Meuse-Argonne offensive extended from 4 to 31 October. It featured a grinding series of necessarily frontal attacks through the third German defense line, and the enemy was reinforced as American casualties mounted. Pershing inaugurated an attack on the east bank of the Meuse, where the Second Army under Bullard was established. Liggett took over Pershing's job as First Army commander, and Pershing became an army group commander. Before the end of October the Germans were driven completely from the Argonne Forest. The slow but steady American advance drew enemy reserves from the French and British parts of the front.[69]

It was during this phase of the battle that several memorable and gallant exploits occurred: of Lt. Col. Charles W. Whittlesey's so-called Lost Battalion of the Seventy-seventh Division, only 194 of the 600 men got back safely to their own lines; Lt. Samuel Woodfill, in the words of Pershing himself, "attacked single-handed a series of German machine gun nests near Cunel and

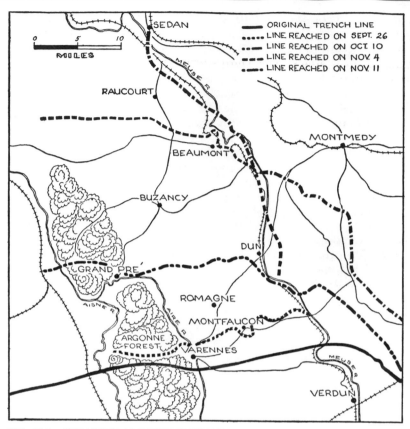

FIG. 12.2.   THE MEUSE-ARGONNE CAMPAIGN

dispatched the crews of each in turn until reduced to the necessity of assaulting the last detachment with a pick''; and Sgt. Alvin C. York captured 4 German officers and 128 men after killing 15 members of a machine gun nest.[70]

Circumstances were more favorable for the AEF at the start of the third phase (1–11 November) of the Meuse-Argonne offensive than prior to the first two phases. The plan was for Charles P. Summerall's Fifth Corps, in the center, to attack northward and cut the fourth and last German line near Barricourt, while to the left the First Corps acted as a link with the French Fourth Army on its left. On the right, the Third Corps was to advance northeastward to force a crossing of the Meuse if the enemy fell back to the east bank; then American and French forces on the east side of the river were to succor the Third Corps by advancing to the north and east.[71]

The attack erupted at dawn on 1 November after a two-hour artillery bombardment. The Fifth Corps in the center swiftly advanced six miles, overrunning German artillery positions and compelling the enemy to order a retreat of the forces facing the First Army west of the Meuse. Summerall's newly developed control of his artillery fire, the "cone of fire," had much to do with this success. The lunge forward continued steadily (with poison gas being used, as before, by both sides), one penetration of five miles being made in an unusual night attack. The Third Corps wrested a crossing of the Meuse south of Dun-sur-Meuse on 4 November. By 7 November the First Division, acting on controversial orders from higher authority, swept across the fronts of the United States First Army and the French Fourth Army to seize the vital high ground commanding Sedan. It was an effective pursuit even if it did disrupt the advance of the two armies. Thus the Germans were denied the use of the crucial Mézières-Sedan railroad; their doom was sealed. American forces east of the Meuse advanced northeastward to secure a good jump-off position from which to launch a coordinated advance toward Montmédy. Mercifully the Armistice at 11:00 A.M. on 11 November ended all further combat operations.[72]

At the peak of the forty-seven-day battle of the Meuse-Argonne, some 1,200,000 American soldiers were involved, and suffered a loss of 120,000 casualties. The offensive had freed 150 villages and captured 16,059 prisoners, 468 guns, 2,864 machine guns, and 177 trench mortars. The AEFs front had widened in the advance from twenty-four to ninety miles. The offensive gained fourteen miles to the northeast and thirty-two miles to the north against 47 German divisions.[73]

In many ways the American advance in the Meuse-Argonne was more significant to Germany's surrender than were the greater French and British advances in easier sectors. Harvey A. DeWeerd declared:

> The American offensive drew one-quarter of the German troops on the western front to the Meuse-Argonne and defeated them there. Tactically the German Army was still in a condition to fight on November 11, but strategically it was unable to extricate itself from the ruin threatening it. General Wilhelm Groener, Ludendorff's successor, paid tribute to the strategic importance of the American attack by saying its consequences "could not be borne."

Pershing analyzed this great final offensive thusly:

> The Meuse-Argonne battle presented numerous difficulties, seemingly insurmountable. The success stands out as one of the great achievements in the history of American arms. Suddenly conceived and hurried in plan and preparation; complicated by close association with a preceding major operation; directed against stubborn defense of the vital point of the Western Front; attended by cold and inclement weather; and fought largely by partially trained troops; this battle was prosecuted with an unselfish and heroic spirit of courage and fortitude which demanded eventual victory.[74]

In the wrap-up operations while the Meuse-Argonne campaign was being fought, the British attacked eastward through the tough Hindenburg Line toward Aulnoye, which was captured, after heavy casualties, on 5 November. Mons, where the BEF fought its first disastrous battle in 1914, was reached by

11 November. Taking part with the British in the assault on the Hindenburg Line were the American Twenty-seventh and Thirtieth Divisions. A regiment of the Twenty-seventh Division lost almost a thousand men killed and wounded on 29 September, the heaviest single day's loss in an American regiment during the war. To the north, the Germans in early September evacuated the Lys salient, which they had carved out in April. This sector was attacked by King Albert's Belgian, French, and British army group beginning 28 September, and, despite a halt caused by the mud in Flanders, the Allies were able to clear the whole coast of Belgium and reach the Escaut south of Ghent by the Armistice. The American Thirty-seventh and Ninety-first Divisions participated in the final ten days of this operation.[75]

Between the Pershing and Haig zones of advance, pressure on the Germans was successfully maintained by two French army groups. For several of these attacks, the American Second and Thirty-sixth Divisions had been loaned to the French. Especially noteworthy was the assault east of Reims on Blanc Mont Ridge on 3 October by the Second Division.[76]

UNITED STATES FORCES were also involved in small numbers in a significant sideshow. The seizure of power in Russia by the Bolsheviks in late 1917, the civil war raging there between the White Russians and the Reds, and the military collapse of that Allied nation led to the conclusion by the Allied Supreme War Council that militarily Russia must be counted out of the war. The secretary of state, Robert Lansing, correctly surmised that many German divisions would be transported from the Eastern to the Western Front, and that the Austro-Hungarians would similarly be able to increase their army fighting the Italians. Bliss felt that our allies' reactions and demands for intervention in Russia with troops to check the Reds were "panicky," though both psychologically and militarily possible. Bliss refused to sign "Joint Note No. 20" of the Supreme War Council on 9 April 1918, which called for immediate military intervention in Siberia. But Pershing, fearing Germany might recruit manpower in Russia, cabled the War Department on 7 June 1918 in support of Allied intervention there.[77]

The AEF commander's civilian superiors in Washington were aware of the grim possibilities of the numbers game. Lansing knew that in the spring of 1918 the Germans on the Western Front had at least 500,000 more troops than did the Allies, not counting any they might pressure defeated Russia to provide. At the same time, the view for Allied intervention in Russia on military grounds was seconded by the British War Office. This attitude was supported also by the French, Foch writing to Wilson directly on the matter. In addition, the French told the president that such intervention would have a good psychological effect upon the French people, and that this was absolutely essential at the moment. The British thought that the re-creation of an Eastern Front in Russia would have a depressing moral impact on the Central Powers. Consequently, Wilson was kept on the defensive in the matter of Allied intervention in Russia against the Bolsheviks, and the British and French so skillfully and persistently played on this theme that intervention came to be practically an accepted fact.[78]

Colonel Edward M. House was not impressed with the argument about the military necessity of intervention in Russia, though he feared the presence of Japanese soldiers in Siberia. This was a similar view to that held by Chief of Staff March, and the latter tried to convince Baker along this line. Lansing urged delay, however, fearing Japanese troops in Siberia and thinking intervention would push Russia into Germany's arms. But six days later, Lansing, seeing that German prisoners might seize control in Siberia, told the president that Japan could not be expected to foreswear the use of her own forces under such circumstances, and he suggested the possibility of joint Allied intervention. But the president refused at this time to reconsider. Lansing thought this stance was caused by the pressures against intervention being exerted on Wilson by his military advisers (except for Pershing). At a cabinet meeting on 29 March 1918, though Secretaries A. S. Burleson and F. K. Lane supported the view that the United States should join Japan in intervention, Lansing and Wilson were opposed.[79]

In June 1918 March, Lansing, and Wilson continued to oppose American military intervention in Siberia because of the cost of such an enterprise, the lack of shipping to the Pacific, the great distances involved, the danger of consequent weakening of the Western Front, and fear of the reaction of the Russian people to an effective force intervening in Russian internal affairs. But hardly anyone wanted to see Japan alone go into Vladivostok. The chief of naval operations, Adm. William S. Benson, also agreed it would be unwise to intervene in Siberia before winning a decision on the Western Front. On 24 June 1918 March concurred and later asserted that Wilson totally agreed. Yet on 17 July 1918 Wilson caved in to the pressure from the Allies and agreed to send an American contingent of troops to join an Allied expedition to Siberia. Under Gen. William S. Graves, nine thousand American soldiers were dispatched there, the Japanese having seventy-two thousand troops in Siberia. Wilson acted because he wanted to cooperate with Pershing and the Allies and desired to check the Japanese. This decision on the president's part antagonized both Russia and Japan.[80]

Urged by the Supreme War Council, the Wilson administration also consented to send an expedition to the Murmansk-Archangel area in northern Russia. The reasons were somewhat similar to those of the Siberian intervention. The 5,000 "Polar Bear" Americans around Archangel, mostly Michigan and Wisconsin conscripts, were under overall British direction. In the skirmishing with the Reds they suffered casualties of 139 killed and 266 wounded. The 9,000 American soldiers in Siberia lost 35 killed and 52 wounded in the lighter action there.[81]

IN ANY SUMMARY and evaluation of the performance of the American Expeditionary Force on the Western Front in France and the few Yanks along the Piave River in Italy, it may be said that on balance, despite a patronizing tendency of some Germans toward the Americans and admission by a few United States officers that our inexperience led to some mistakes that against a less exhausted enemy might have had serious consequences, the enemy, nonetheless, in their official reports indicated their high respect for the doughboys who arrived in the summer of 1918 and showed great dash and courage in their incessant attacks on the slowly retreating German army. Actually the calculations of the German high command were so upset by the appearance and performance of the Yankees that the German generals insisted that their government seek peace.[82]

Any assessment of John J. Pershing should note that he was the only top Allied commander to start and finish the war in his high position. While he delayed a bit in putting the SOS on a firm basis, Pershing was a talented administrator and organizer and is entitled to the great credit he has received for achieving an independent American army in France. He was not an innovator in strategy or tactics, but he did force a return to open-field warfare, thereby enabling the final victory to be won. On the whole, he handled his military operations ably. Pershing would also have considerable influence on the post-1918 staff in Washington. Though somewhat anti-Pershing, the British military historian, Basil H. Liddell Hart, wrote of the AEF commander: "It is sufficient to say that there was perhaps no other man who would or could have built the structure of the American Army on the scale he planned. And without that army the war could hardly have been saved and could not have been won."[83]

Nowhere has a better evaluation of Pershing been made than that penned by the man who perhaps knew him best, Gen. James G. Harbord:

> The Pershing of our time bore himself with distinction in every situation. He set an example always worth following. Thoroughly impersonal in all his official relations, his purpose was as firm and steadfast as a rock. He always knew exactly what he wanted. His force of character, tenacity of purpose, and persistence would have won for him success in any walk of life. An organizer and a leader, a negotiator, and a diplomat of the kind our country needs, we owe him as much for building an integral American Army as we do for the high quality of leadership he gave it after it was created. Not of the era of our Civil War or that of 1870 in Europe, he was a pioneer in directing the management and administration of the tremendous agencies of mechanized modern war. Not the last of the Old, he is one of the first of the New. In the long view of history he will be measured by comparison with those leaders who came after him rather than with those who have gone before.[84]

The casualties for all American armed services in the First World War totaled 53,403 killed and died of wounds and 202,261 wounded. These heavy losses in a brief period of time, along with staggering losses of the other warring nations and the need to bring home to the German people that their army had indeed been defeated in the field, caused Pershing to suggest on 25 October 1918 that no armistice be accepted from the enemy—only unconditional surrender—and that it would be wise to advance into the heart of Germany.[85] But his advice was not taken. Adolf Hitler and the Nazis would drag Europe into a second world war two decades later by claiming that the German army had not been defeated in battle, but that the Fatherland lost the war because the soldiers had been knifed in the back, betrayed by Jews and Socialists on the home front, and Der Fuehrer would be believed. Nor has the bruised world yet recovered from the train of events set in motion by the First World War.

The decisiveness of the entry and the fighting performance by the AEF under Pershing cannot be overemphasized. As late as 2 June 1918 the prime ministers of Britain, France, and Italy cabled President Wilson that "there is a great danger of the war being lost unless the numerical inferiority of the Allies can be remedied as rapidly as possible by the advent of American troops"; in short, it was an admission that they had no more reserves.[86]

Despite the American inexperience in coalition warfare, German Gen. Hermann von Kuhl had to acknowledge:

> The American soldier showed himself full of courage, even if he lacked experience. Fresh, well-fed, and with strong nerves that had known no strain, he advanced against the German Army, which was exhausted by the unprecedented efforts of four years of war. In this and in the great numerical reenforcements which the American brought to our opponents at the decisive moment lies the importance of America's intervention.[87]

The Allies' most formidable opponent, Erich Ludendorff, though always loath to admit his country ever lost the war, summed up in a few words the critical factor tilting the balance against Germany: "America thus became the decisive power in the war."[88]

American Armed Forces in Eclipse

[The First World War was] a conflict so foolishly waged, so monstrously demanding, so obscenely destructive that no man of good will could emerge from it except in a revolutionary frame of mind; unless he had indeed been brutalized into cynicism and apathy.

MAX BELOFF

FOR THE GENERATION of young men who fought with the Allies in the Great War and were overjoyed with the fruits of victory, the aftermath was an appalling disillusionment. Not only did the United States and Great Britain largely surrender to their citizens' demands to demilitarize, but these Western democracies and France, by their international posture of military weakness, would unwittingly encourage the trend toward totalitarianism in the nations of Italy, Germany, and Japan, and within two decades an even greater conflict would occur for the world and its people than the Great War of 1914–1918.

Even before the Armistice the War Department halted the dispatch of troops to France on 1 November 1918, and the Ordnance Department began to dismantle war industries by late October. The Army of the United States (AUS) was to be demobilized by shipping all troops to discharge camps in or near their home states, the separation from the service to be done by military units. The insistence of Congress and the soldiers' families insured that demobilization would be performed swiftly. All nonregular army divisions were out of France by 12 June 1919. By 11 November 1919, 3,236,266 of the 4,086,000 troops had been discharged, and by 1 April 1920 the total demobilization of enlisted personnel was just about completed, the last Americans leaving France on 11 January 1920. But the watch on the Rhine held some doughboys on European soil until 27 January 1923. Several enclaves in Germany were occupied by Allied forces, the American zone being that around Coblenz.[1]

Before they left office, Woodrow Wilson, Newton D. Baker, the Democratic administration, the Congress, and indirectly the American people had to hammer out a peacetime military policy. It remained to be seen whether this time the nation would profit by the costly lessons of the recent Great War.

As a temporary measure, Congress authorized the War Department to reopen enlistments for the regular army. From 1 March 1919 to 1 November 1919 the army got 73,000 one-year recruits and 63,000 three-year ones. In January 1919 Baker asked Congress to inaugurate universal military training (UMT) for a regular army of 500,000; for approval to reorganize the War Department; and for authority to strengthen the General Staff in its direction of the military establishment. But, as might be expected after the "War to End All Wars," the legislators turned a deaf ear, resumed staunch support of the National Guard, and dropped the idea of UMT despite a strong appeal for it by Pershing.[2]

John McAuley Palmer, prominent in the pre–World War I deliberations on military policy, was once again involved in the formulation of a new post–Armistice program for the armed services; he played a leading role in drawing up a fairly sound national defense act. Palmer was a champion of the citizen army rather than of the large professional army that March wanted. This small, frail West Point graduate had ably commanded the Fifty-eighth Infantry Brigade of the Twenty-ninth Division in the Meuse-Argonne offensive. Palmer believed not in the German system but in a military policy that would grow naturally out of the American nation—one that would be an extension of politics rather than a molder of politics. He called for unification of the armed services and a citizen army molded on the Swiss model. Like Pershing, he urged universal military training buttressed by conscription. Citizen-type officers should be added to the professionals on the General Staff, Palmer suggested. He would have none of Emory Upton's expansible army idea (expanding a small regular army that had been previously overofficered). John A. Logan and Thomas Jefferson would have approved.[3]

Palmer's work with the Military Affairs Committee of the Senate was bolstered by Pershing's formidable testimony before both houses of Congress. As a result, there emerged the highly significant National Defense Act of 1920. This piece of legislation stated that the Army of the United States comprised the regular army, the National Guard when federalized, and the organized reserves. The geographical, or territorial, departments were dropped; instead, the country was divided into three tactical armies headquartered at Governors Island, New York; Fort McPherson, Georgia; and the Presidio, San Francisco, California. Grafted onto this system was a network of nine corps areas (for example, the Third Corps Area had its headquarters at Fort Meade, Maryland), each corps area to contain one regular army division, two National Guard divisions, and three organized reserve divisions. The act supposedly fixed the regular army strength at 280,000 enlisted men (including the Philippine Scouts) and 17,000 officers for a total army of 297,000. Included now within the War Department bureaus were the infantry, field artillery, cavalry, and coast artillery headquarters as well as the Air Service, Chemical Warfare Service, and the Finance Department. In addition, the National Defense Act of 1920 created the new War Council, composed of the secretary and assistant secretary of war, the General of the Army (Pershing), and the chief of staff.[4]

This massive piece of legislation provided also for the training of reserve officers, the high school and especially the college ROTCs being most important. The Citizens Military Training Camp was again authorized to qualify personnel as commissioned or noncommissioned officers. The National Guard was given more control over its own affairs, as the act reorganized the Militia Bureau in the War Department, and the Guard was still recognized as being a part of the militia. The act declared that the president could use the Guard, but only when authorized by Congress. The militia of the United States was to comprise the National Guard, the Naval Militia, and the Unorganized Militia. The General Staff was to be made up of the chief of staff, four assistants, and eighty-eight other officers of the rank of captain or above.[5]

Although he did not agree with all particulars, March and most other commentators regarded the National Defense Act of 1920 as sound and one that reflected the experiences of the recent war. But Congress and most American citizens were apathetic; ensuing legislation, or lack thereof, took the teeth out of the act. In the name of economy the regular army was cut to just 150,000 in 1921. This action severely damaged the morale of army officers. In 1922 large numbers of regular army officers were demoted in rank and more than 1,000 were suddenly discharged as surplus. The regular army numbered only 137,000 from 1922 through 1926 and averaged only 118,750 from 1927 to 1935. Pershing was furious. Despite his great prestige and reputation, he was frustrated in his efforts to keep the lawmakers from their drift to a policy of military weakness. Chief of Staff March reminded them that Germany had been limited to a 100,000-man army to make her militarily impotent.[6]

In 1922 and 1923 Pershing grimly cautioned Congress that the regular army was being "cut too much for safety," a warning that the secretary of war, John W. Weeks, echoed forthrightly. But these appeals were in vain. When the army prepared to test its plans for mobilization in 1924, a great outcry arose from church and pacifist groups, governors, and others. Every secretary of war between the two world wars, and every chief of staff from Pershing through Douglas MacArthur to George C. Marshall climbed Capitol Hill to warn against this head-in-the-sand attitude. They also cautioned against manpower shortages, inadequate training, scarcities in materiel, and lags in weapons development. As historian Russell F. Weigley observes:

> . . . the Army during the 1920's and early 1930's may have been less ready to function as a fighting force than at any time in its history. It lacked even the combat capacity that the Indian campaigns had forced on it during the nineteenth century and the pacification of the Philippines had required early in the twentieth century. As anything more than a small school for soldiers the Army scarcely existed.[7]

THE UNITED STATES NAVY was concerned with certain unfinished business after the Armistice. One ugly task was the sweeping of the great North Sea Mine Barrage. Some eighty-nine vessels performed this ten-month assignment successfully, although the cost was eleven men killed and twenty-three ships damaged. In southern European waters an Allied naval mission temporarily supervised affairs in the Adriatic under the terms of the armistice with Austria-Hungary. Almost 300 miles of the Adriatic's eastern coastline were patrolled and administered by American naval forces headed by three admirals. It was a tense situation. The threat of military clashes, heightened by the conflicting aspirations and turbulent political feelings of several nations, was eased largely by the good judgment, tact, and diplomacy of these American naval officers. In 1919 a similar situation around Constantinople led to the appointment of an admiral as American High Commissioner. He remained in this post until 1927 and was effective in establishing a stable climate in the Near East and in protecting American interests throughout the entire region. Finally, American fleets gave support to the Allied intervention in the White Sea until August 1919 and at Vladivostok until April 1920.[8]

During the decades of the twenties and thirties the United States and several of her former wartime allies turned to the dangerous experiment of disarmament and international pacts to outlaw war. These well-intentioned efforts yielded only paper pledges that were eventually found to be unenforceable. On the other hand, German desire for revenge for the harsh Versailles Treaty led her, and Italy and Japan as well, to arm. These attitudes were heightened by the weakness of the League of Nations and by America's nonmembership. Yet many people still had hopes for the League.

The Washington Arms Conference of 1921–1922 had its origins in American weakness in the western Pacific vis-a-vis Japan during and immediately after the Great War, when the attention of the Western Allies was riveted upon Europe. In addition to the ominous naval races that continued after 1918 between Great Britain, the United States, and Japan, there was the potentially menacing Anglo-Japanese Alliance of 1902 that alarmed the British Dominions of Canada, Australia, and New Zealand as well as America. The keen interest in an international conference on arms limitation was supported by such diverse individuals as Sen. William E. Borah of Idaho, Col. Edward M. House, and because Congress would probably not back an adequate postwar army, Generals Pershing and Tasker H. Bliss. So President Warren G. Harding duly issued the invitations and all the great powers (except for Germany and Russia, who were not invited) accepted, Japan reluctantly.[9]

The glittering conference opened on 12 November 1921. Once the delegates and guests were seated, President Harding delivered a brief, emotional but dignified opening address that called for peace, invoking the spirit of the Unknown American Soldier who had been interred the day before at Arlington National Cemetery. Harding received enthusiastic applause as he left the hall.

As the dignitaries at the table settled down for what most thought would be another pro forma address, the distinguished looking American secretary of state, Charles Evans Hughes, arose and loosed a bombshell. Manifesting astounding detailed knowledge of the navies and warships of the great powers, Hughes proceeded to destroy much of the tonnage of the United States, Britain, and Japan with his specific proposals. He said the only way to disarm was to do just that, immediately. He called for a ten-year holiday on capital ship construction, with limits on size and armaments; for the scrapping of many battleships and battle cruisers already built and building, so that the result would be a capital ship ratio of 5:5:3:1.7:1.7, respectively, for Britain, the United States, Japan, France, and Italy. Naval aircraft were to be limited only by the number and size of carriers. Cruisers were to be restricted to 10,000 tons and to 8-inch guns. In all, the secretary prescribed the destruction of sixty-six capital ships totaling 1,878,043 tons—"more," as one British correspondent said, "than all the admirals of the world have sunk in a cycle of centuries." When Hughes sat down after his fifteen-minute tour de force, a painful silence was broken by a crescendo of frenzied applause, more, perhaps, than but a handful of people have ever received throughout history. In most nations, newspapers ran banner headlines and feature stories ushering in what many thought to be the millenium.[10]

With taxpayers groaning in America, Britain, and Japan over financing the construction of warships and especially the great capital ships, there were strong hopes for success as the delegates buckled down to long and hard negotiating following Hughes's proposals. The United States had at Washington the very powerful bargaining lever of possessing by 1924 the impressive total of sixteen superdreadnoughts—post-Jutland capital ships that encompassed the lessons learned from that greatest of naval battles up to that time.[11]

The most important instrument to be signed at Washington was the Five Power Treaty; Britain, the United States, Japan, France, and Italy agreed, respectively, to the 5:5:3:1.7:1.7 ratio (which represented the actual strength of their navies at the time) and to most of Hughes's other naval proposals. Under its terms and in order to achieve this ratio and maintain it in future naval construction, the United States scrapped thirty capital ships built and building, while Britain destroyed nineteen and Japan thirteen. To help Japan save face with its inferior ratio, America and Britain agreed not to strengthen their Pacific fortifications east of Singapore and west of Hawaii (Pearl Harbor), thereby making of the western Pacific a Japanese lake. This proved to be a grave disadvantage to the English-speaking nations. Another inequitable sacrifice by the United States was the scrapping of many battleships—a category in which America was well ahead of Britain and Japan. Yet they were not obliged to destroy surplus cruisers—a class of ship in which they were ahead of the United States. The Five Power Treaty was to remain in effect until 31 December 1936, unless a signatory power gave two years' notice of its determination to renounce the treaty, and the pact would terminate for all contracting powers.[12]

Since the Washington Five Power Treaty dealt only with capital ships, naval races soon developed in cruisers, destroyers, submarines, and the like. The United States did not keep pace with other powers, nor did she build up to her quota of battleships because of the parsimony of Congress and the opposition of the public. President Coolidge's call for another naval conference to impose a 5:5:3 ratio on cruisers resulted in a meeting in 1927 in Geneva. This conclave was an utter failure. But the London Naval Conference of 1930 did yield a six-year treaty that put maximums on all types of warships. The same 5:5:3 ratio remained on capital ships, but Japan was able to increase slightly her position vis-à-vis Britain and the United States by securing at London a 10:10:6 ratio on heavy cruisers and a 10:10:7 ratio on light cruisers and other auxiliary vessels. American naval officials feared they had granted Japan too much if America were really intent on insuring her success in any future naval war in the Pacific.[13]

When Japan invaded Manchuria in 1931, the United States protested vigorously but futilely that this was a violation of the 1922 Nine Power Treaty. In 1934 the Japanese served notice that they were renouncing the Five Power Naval Treaty, which would mean its termination. The complete failure of the naval limitation movement came in London in March 1936 when America, Britain, and France signed a treaty that was not adhered to by Japan. This pact provided some naval limitations, but it also included fatal escape clauses.[14]

In 1928, with the support of the well-intentioned Coolidge, the Kellogg Peace Pact, outlawing war as an instrument of national policy, was signed in Paris. But when Japanese troops invaded Manchuria in 1931, Secretary of State Stimson was unable to activate the Kellogg Pact. Stimson regarded neutrality as an obsolete American idea but he felt the pact provided at least consultative obligations. The deepening crisis in the Far East and increasing tension between Japan and the United States led to an American cabinet discussion on 7 March 1933 of possible war in the western Pacific involving the United States. American naval appropriations in 1921 of $1,019,170,000 had been slashed in 1922 to $536,930,000, and they averaged just $350,000,000 until 1936. The total naval personnel averaged slightly more than ninety thousand. In summary, the words of naval historian Dudley W. Knox ring true:

> It must be confessed that the whole experiment in naval limitation proved disappointing. For the United States the net result was a substantial loss of relative naval power and the complete defeat of her Open Door Policy, paradoxically combined with a growing ill will against her in Japan. These results must be contrasted with the opposite effects of the strong naval policies of President Theodore Roosevelt, and they emphasize the wisdom of President Wilson in striving, after 1916, to create a preeminent American Navy.[15]

THE ARMY AIR SERVICE in the period between the two world wars showed some progress amid white-hot controversy. One of the foremost spokesmen of air power, Brig. Gen. William Mitchell, the prominent high-ranking flying officer in Europe in the Great War, was convinced that because of the performance of the Air Service in the AEF's operations in France, the military, civilian, commercial, and economic futures of nations would be dependent upon the continued development of the airplane.[16]

The irrepressible Mitchell, bordering on the insubordinate and seldom without full newspaper coverage, played the leading role in the fight for air power over sea power and for an independent air corps. He insisted throughout the 1920s and 1930s that new aerial weapons, tactics, and capabilities required a reassessment of the traditional doctrines of the armed forces. Mitchell asserted that in the future air power would dominate both armies and navies, as well as economic endeavors. He called for the creation of an overall Department of National Defense, with independent departments of the Army, Navy, and Air Force. Air power proponents argued that an independent air corps should have separate functions, such as advancing technology in accordance with improvements in aviation science. They held that such an air corps could hit enemy installations beyond the reach of the navy or army, and that it could serve as a middle force in coastal defense between the other two branches.[17]

When the chief of the navy's Bureau of Aeronautics, Rear Adm. William A. Moffett, opposed a separate air force as too expensive and strategically unsound, the debate intensified as Mitchell replied that "the great battleship on the water is as vulnerable to air attack today as was the 'knight in armor' to the footman armed with a musket." Billy insisted that battleships cost too much and that planes were cheaper and more effective. But the public and most government officials, including a majority in Congress, were either unconvinced by Mitchell's arguments or were apathetic or both. Nonetheless he clamored unrelentingly for an aerial test bombing of a real battleship; this would awaken sluggish minds and consciences.[18]

Public clamor intensified and Congress and Secretary of War Baker urged Navy Secretary Daniels to consent to Mitchell's test bombing of modern dreadnoughts. Daniels buckled under the pressure and asked the Army Air Service to join the navy in a joint bombing test. One peripheral but significant result of these maneuvers was the strong push by navy flyers for their own air arm. Consequently, the navy asked and obtained congressional authorization to set up the Bureau of Aeronautics, which commenced operations in August 1921 under the able Moffett—a shrewder, more restrained, and better-paced campaigner than Mitchell, and his implacable foe.[19]

The famous bombing tests in June and July of 1921 off the Virginia Capes were surrounded by such acrimonious controversies that they partly obscured the lessons of the experiments. Mitchell's obstinacy was matched by the stubbornness of Daniels. The Air Service and the navy also bickered hopelessly over what the tests should try to accomplish. With the navy trying to "load" the conditions of the tests in its favor and against Mitchell and his army aviators, and Billy objecting, the Joint Army and Navy Board ruled that the tests were to be conducted under naval procedures and control, but that Mitchell should be provided with a modern battleship for a separate bombing effort by the Air Service. The unfortunate publicity in the November 1920 *Indiana* experiments, in which the old battleship had been severely damaged by the detonation of fixed bombs on the ship, caused the Board to order a full news blackout on the forthcoming tests. The navy insisted on rigid rules and procedures, and Mitchell was obliged to go along with most of them.[20]

The dreadnought given Mitchell was a respectable and modern engine of war. The former German 27,000-ton *Ostfriesland,* built in 1911, was part of the spoils of war. At the Battle of Jutland in 1916 the rugged *Ostfriesland* had struck a mine and been hit by eighteen large shells; so tight were her bulkheads and so strong were her four skins and watertight compartments that she was able to reach port safely for repairs.[21]

In the celebrated test bombings of *Ostfriesland* on 21 and 22 July 1921, Mitchell got the green light on the second day to drop his 2,000-pound bombs against the dreadnought. He was determined to do this in as spectacular a way as possible. Although the navy wanted him to stop the bombing at frequent intervals to allow its architects and construction experts to examine the battleship, Mitchell refused to halt his bombing runs until he had dropped six big bombs. The results were devastating. Bomb hits and especially near-misses sent the mighty *Ostfriesland* to the bottom in just twenty-one minutes. Eyewitness naval officers were openly stunned at the spectacle. Yet the navy contended that the tests were inconclusive and held that a manned dreadnought, underway and firing anti-aircraft guns, might not have been sunk. Mitchell responded that in such a situation, with her magazines filled, *Ostfriesland* would have been an even easier target. And the public and some government officials were highly impressed that a modern dreadnought had been sunk by bombs dropped from planes.[22]

The report of the Joint Board of the Army and Navy admitted that large bombs, carried by shore-based aircraft, could "sink or seriously damage any naval vessel at present constructed," and that no warship could probably be built to withstand such aerial bombs. But the board concluded battleships on the high seas were still viable machines of war. The board urged construction of more aircraft carriers and full development of aviation. It denied Mitchell's contention that air power was a cheap source of national defense and declared that it merely added to the cost and "complexity of naval warfare."[23]

When Charles T. Menoher, head of the Air Service, would not make public Mitchell's report Billy leaked it to the press. Mitchell took little solace from the board's report and claimed his planes could put the entire Atlantic fleet out of action in one attack (ignoring the Air Service's lack of navigational ability over water). Menoher told Secretary of War Weeks that either he (Menoher) or Mitchell would have to go. Weeks, impressed by Mitchell's success in the bombing tests, fired Menoher. Billy, acknowledging that he and his conduct were "a source of irritation within the Air Service," also submitted his resignation, which Weeks refused to accept. But the secretary did not advance Mitchell into Menoher's post as head of the Air Service, giving this top position instead to Maj. Gen. Mason M. Patrick, who promptly slapped Billy down when Mitchell tried to dictate to Patrick about his new duties. And a personal misfortune befell Mitchell at the peak of the *Ostfriesland* controversy in July when his marriage of sixteen years broke up.[24]

Mitchell was acclaimed internationally, and such proponents of air power as Giulio Douhet and Hugh Trenchard were impressed by his accomplishments against a dreadnought with gravity-propelled bombs. One of the reactions of Congress to the sinking of *Ostfriesland* was to agree to convert two battle cruisers into aircraft carriers (*Lexington* and *Saratoga*), instead of authorizing new major warships.[25]

In September Mitchell was authorized to test bomb the old battleship *Alabama,* a predreadnought built in 1900, displacing 11,552 tons, and carrying four 13-inch guns and fourteen 6-inch guns, with an armor belt of 16½ inches, 14 inches on the turrets, and with a 4-inch deck armor. Billy was given carte blanche in the choice of planes and bombs in his aerial attacks on this capital ship.[26]

Alabama was anchored forty-eight miles from Langley Field off Tangier

Island in the Chesapeake Bay near the battered hulks of *Indiana* and *Texas* (the latter having been used as a target back in 1911). The weather on 23 September 1921 was mild and clear. *Alabama* was to be assaulted for several days, first with phosphorus and tear-gas bombs, followed by a nighttime attack, and then the battleship was to be sunk by conventional bombs. In the attacks, even the small phosphorus and 300-pound bombs started fires, and the ship was finished off three days later by 2,000-pound bombs, sinking in thirty seconds. Adm. William M. Fullam, who was on the observation ship with Mitchell, possibly with the belittling attitude of the navy's high command in mind, declared that "it is childish to attempt to discount this result by saying the *Alabama* is an old ship. No modern dreadnought could have survived this attack." The results of these tests were also to have been kept secret from the public, but they leaked out.[27]

Mitchell still sought more tests and publicity to demonstrate air power's capabilities against warships. After nearly two years of fresh appeals he finally secured from the navy in the summer of 1923 two old predreadnought battleships built in 1906, *New Jersey* and *Virginia*, sister ships of 16,094 tons, each mounting four 12-inch, eight 8-inch, and twelve 6-inch guns, and carrying an armor belt of 11 inches, with 3 inches on the deck and from 8 to 12 inches on the turrets. The ships were moored off Cape Hatteras. Mitchell's requests for the vessels to be radio controlled and in motion, for permission to employ 4,000-pound bombs, and for authorization to use the huge trimotored "Owl" bombers were denied. Instead, he had to use the old 2,000-pound bombs left over from the 1921 tests, as well as the old bombers. Four days before the tests, Mitchell was ordered to bomb from 10,000 feet instead of from the planned lower levels.

On 4 September 1923, the day of the tests, a naval transport brought down a clutch of observers, including General Pershing, Glenn Curtis, and the acting secretary of war. Present also were two mine layers loaded with reporters. Mitchell's planes then roared out of the deep blue sky. The air attacks scored five direct hits and some near misses on *New Jersey*, which was finished off with 1,100-pound bombs. Several of the fourteen bombs made direct hits and sank *Virginia* in twenty-six minutes. The navy's rebuttal, uttered strangely enough by Pershing, claimed that these were two "obsolete battleships," and that the tests did not indicate conclusively that such aerial bombs would sink modern manned dreadnoughts able to take defensive measures.[28]

Mitchell followed up his latest successes with unrestrained criticism of what he termed the navy and army bureaucracies' blind opposition to air progress. He flayed a number of his superiors for alleged criminal negligence and would not be quiet or clear his statements with superiors when ordered to do so. This defiance led to his famous court-martial and trial in 1925. Despite the astounding accuracy of many of his predictions about a future Pacific war with Japan and the nature of the early sneak Japanese attacks, he was convicted by the army court, one of whose members was Douglas MacArthur. The latter wrote of his "friend" Mitchell as follows in his *Reminiscences*: "I did what I could in his behalf and I helped save him from dismissal. That he was wrong in the violence of his language is self-evident; that he was right in his thesis is equally true and incontrovertible." But Mitchell resigned from the army in 1926 and continued to make the charge that the United States had "no real military air force" despite the spending of many millions of dollars. He died in 1936. That Billy Mitchell would be vindicated on most of his major points would be amply demonstrated during World War II. In 1942 he was posthumously restored to the service with the rank of major general.[29]

From 1919 to 1926 the average yearly appropriation for the Army Air Service was a little more than $16 million, and that provided for a force of some 10,000 airmen. But even with the paucity of funds, new aerial equipment, tactics, and techniques were evolved at Randolph and Kelly Fields, San Antonio, Texas; Wright Field, Dayton, Ohio; and Langley Field, Virginia. These tests in the 1920s and 1930s included instrument flying, radio experimentation, and nighttime photography. In 1922 the army air arm had 1,681 planes, 13 nonrigid airships, 448 observation balloons, and 55 free balloons.[30]

In 1933 organizational changes were reviewed by a board presided over by Maj. Gen. Hugh A. Drum. It recommended that the Air Corps be removed from command by the regional corps areas and put directly under a General Headquarters (GHQ), Air Force, responsible directly to the General Staff. This would increase the air arm's autonomy. But before the Drum plan could be implemented, President Roosevelt ordered the Army Air Corps to carry the mail. The resulting newsworthy crashes of some of its planes showed that better aircraft, navigation, training, and communications were needed. Still another board, chaired by former Secretary of War Baker, reechoed the need for a GHQ Air Force, not for training and supply, but to control operations in the Air Corps, and on 1 March 1935 this was established. The GHQ Air Force concentrated on developing a strategic heavy bomber. Congress tried to slow this trend, fearing the aggressive nature of heavy bombers, as did the General Staff that was currently interested in developing close ground-support tactical planes. But the Air Corps persisted, and the famous Boeing B-17 four-engine "Flying Fortress" was available, in small numbers, when World War II began.[31]

THE PERIOD between the two world wars was an era in which the armed services were hurt by the polemics and propaganda of pacifist groups made up of well-meaning but unrealistic individuals that believed America would never have to fight again, after the "war to end all wars." One journal that inclined toward pacifism was the *Nation,* which in 1925 characterized the General Staff as allegedly composed of groups of militarists that probably dominated the presidents and "certainly [controlled] Secretaries of War and Congress." The *Nation* charged that the National Defense Act of 1920 would lead to militarizing control by supporting the ROTCs in the schools and colleges, and by allowing too many officers to come into the regular army. In its editorials between 1921 and 1931 the *Nation* plumped for world disarmament and a decrease in America's armed forces. Most criticism was directed against the navy, the number of its warships, men, and bases, and alleged "pork barrel" deals over ship contracts. Attacks were also directed against the army and its Air Corps, and against persons who supported increased appropriations for national defense. The *Nation* claimed the American people disapproved of the congressional military budgets and world armament contests, and it actually urged American disarmament unilaterally in the hope that other great powers would follow suit.[32]

But some clear warnings and thoughtful advice about the republic's dwindling armed forces were sounded; unfortunately, they were largely ignored. *The Outlook* cautioned about rampant pacifism and the failure to provide for adequate manpower, industrial capacity, and strategic resources in the event of a national emergency. Writing in January 1927 the publisher of the *Army and Navy Journal,* Brig. Gen. Henry J. Reilly, revealed clearly the dangerous impact of economizing with the armed services that had especially harmful repercussions on morale, living conditions, training, equipment, and the size of the army. Only the organized officers reserve was up to strength. This unhealthy state of the army was shown in the fourteen thousand desertions in 1926. There were other informed warnings of the serious weaknesses of America's armed forces in the 1920s and 1930s, but these, too, were disregarded by government officials, the public, and Congress.[33]

Nor were the two major political parties of any real help to the armed services. An examination of the Republican and Democratic platforms in the era between the two world wars shows that both called for reduced military appropriations while at the same time they mouthed vague phrases about an adequate national defense. Destructive to morale and recruiting as well as to the feelings of 4 million World War I veterans was the year-and-a-half politically motivated investigation of the War Department and army staged by the Democratic controlled Sixty-sixth Congress, in which the committee reports were scathingly harsh in their criticisms of Baker's War Department. And as late as 1932 Chief of Staff MacArthur emphasized that the army's armored force was fine, except that it lacked one major item—modern tanks—because of the penny-pinching Congress.[34]

Moreover the army's image was damaged by the forced role of a tiny fraction of it in the 1932 Bonus March incident, an unfortunate occurrence that also tarnished the reputation of President Hoover and called into question the conduct of Secretary of War Patrick Hurley and Chief of Staff MacArthur. During the peak of the Great Depression, service veterans—many of them First World War heroes—demanded immediate payment of what would amount to a cash bonus and decided to present a petition on boots in the nation's capital. Some eleven thousand of them, including wives and children, descended upon Washington, D.C. MacArthur merely carried out the instructions of Hoover and Hurley in using force to disperse the bonus army from the front of the Capitol and from the marchers' shantytown temporary lodgings at Anacostia Flats. Although just two lives were lost in this operation, involving at first police action, the army as well as the officials mentioned were given a bad name for roughly handling some of the nation's stalwarts of the First World War.[35]

Meanwhile the country's armed services continued to fight for adequate appropriations in order to remain viable. In 1929 and 1931 plans for an increase in military manpower and mobilization in wartime were rejected in the now familiar name of economy, disarmament, and apathy. In 1933, when FDR and his New Deal administration took power, Chief of Staff MacArthur reported that the United States Army stood seventeenth in size among those of the world.[36]

When MacArthur retired as army chief of staff, he was succeeded on 2 October 1935 by Gen. Malin Craig, a protégé of Pershing, who had been chief of staff of the First Corps in France in the latter months of the war with Germany. After the Armistice, Craig had been chief of cavalry; assistant chief of staff, G-3; a corps commander; and the commandant of the Army War College. As chief of staff, he was interested in furthering the efforts inaugurated by MacArthur for greater realism in logistical, manpower, and war planning. Craig, despite his lower profile than the dramatic MacArthur, accomplished a surprising number of things, aided, finally, by more support from Roosevelt. The chief of staff was both able and farsighted.[37]

Although the National Defense Act of 1920 authorized a regular army of 280,000, Congress's failure to appropriate sufficient funds resulted in an army of only 136,000 in 1933. The War Department hoped the new administration and the legislators would agree to increase it to 165,000. Instead, soon after becoming President, Roosevelt urged the solons to drop 16,000 soldiers from the army and lower the army's budget by $144 million. Such journals as the *Nation* applauded these slices and recommended further cuts, as did such newspapers as the *New York World-Telegram* and the *Baltimore Sun*. Yet some other papers, such as the *New York American* and the *Rochester Democrat and Chronicle*, warned solemnly against weakening the republic's military strength.[38]

When Japan invaded China in 1937, several American warships along with a few marines were engaged in protecting United States citizens and European civilians, and rightfully stood firm despite warnings from the Nipponese to leave the combat zones. The *Augusta* was soon struck by a Japanese shell at Shanghai, and one American sailor was killed and eighteen wounded. In December 1937 the American gunboat *Panay,* clearly marked with huge American flags, was deliberately bombed and sunk by the Japanese while it was evacuating European refugees off Nanking. Two American crewmen were killed and eleven badly wounded. In addition, several United States merchantmen and the British warship *Ladybird* were similarly bombed by the Japanese, who then apologized for these hostile actions. No serious crisis developed.[39]

It took the rise of Adolf Hitler and Fascist aggression in Africa, Europe, and Asia to get even a miniscule increase in the United States Army's strength from 135,684 in 1933 to 138,569 in 1935 and 165,000 in 1936. In contradistinction to his earlier head-in-the-sand attitude toward the country's armed strength, FDR did an abrupt about-face in 1938 and spoke of the "beginning of a vast program of rearmament, owing to a grave international situation and the failure of arms limitations." The president acknowledged that "Our national defense is . . . inadequate for purposes of national security and requires increase for that reason.'' But the chief executive was primarily concerned with naval increases, with only some $17 million more earmarked for the army.[40]

Spurred on finally by the crisis culminating in the Munich Conference, Congress became involved in vigorous debate over defense matters. The neutrality laws certainly did not encourage greater rearmament. At a key conclave at the White House, FDR now urged increases for the military, but chiefly for air power. The commander in chief appealed to Congress on 12 January 1939 for funds for more army warplanes, materiel, and pilot training, saying that American armed forces were utterly inadequate for national defense. With an eye, at last, on the serious international chessboard and the threat of war, the legislators increased military appropriations from about $1 billion in 1938 to $1.631 billion in 1939. But the army benefited little, numbering just 174,079 in July 1939 and scattered in 130 camps and posts, and with no functioning corps or field army forces in the United States.[41]

Only halting progress was made after World War I in army geographical organization. As chief of staff, Douglas MacArthur was concerned that the Emory Upton idea of expansible skeleton units did not provide a deployable force for even minor national emergencies. He hoped to establish in time an instant readiness force. Since the 1920 plan of three tactical armies and their headquarters had never been set up, MacArthur felt obliged to segment the nation into four army areas, the senior corps commander in each being temporary tactical army commander, leaving the nine corps areas' commanders to act primarily as administrative heads. Upon mobilization, each regular army officer would occupy a specific designated slot. But an increase in the army to 165,000 was needed for these instant readiness units, and funds for such an increase were then not forthcoming. However, MacArthur was able at least to get the General Staff more realistically conscious of supply problems.[42]

While a parsimonious Congress, the administration, and public apathy were largely to blame for military shortcomings, the army itself was partly responsible for neglecting the study and development of new offensive and defensive weapons and lessons to be derived from the First World War. Strangely enough, the United States, which was noted for its leadership in adaptations of the internal combustion engine, had lagged in military motor transportation even prior to 1917–1918. Thus the British led the way in the study of theories of armored warfare and in the adoption of tanks. Pershing, never a champion of the tank, did at least see their value on the Western Front and established the American Tank Corps under Col. S. D. Rockenbach. Pershing also set up a tank center at Langres, under the colorful Maj. George S. Patton, Jr. (who later led the 304th Tank Brigade in the AEF's first tank battle at St. Mihiel). There were 23,405 American tanks on order at the time of the Armistice. But the National Defense Act of 1920 put the Tank Corps back under the infantry, and the army retained only 1,115 tanks until 1930.[43]

The size of the army tanks was restricted by the army's seven-and-one-half-ton capacity of standard army bridging equipment; thus the army adhered to light tanks, largely minimizing medium and heavy ones. Unfortunately, the talented tank designer, J. Walter Christie, and his experiments were largely ignored. Only in 1939, after lessons had finally been learned from the Spanish Civil War, did the United States go ahead with a most needed medium tank; but Germany, Russia, and Britain developed better World War II medium and heavy tanks than did America.[44]

Even when the Second World War exploded in Europe on 1 September 1939, the United States did not seem alarmed about its glaring military deficiencies, and little increase took place in American armaments until the fall of France in June 1940. In September 1939 FDR and Congress increased the regular army by only 17,000, bringing it to 227,000. The National Guard was upped by just 35,000 to 235,000. After failing in the spring and summer of 1939 to repeal the Neutrality Acts, Congress finally lifted the embargo on arms in the autumn of that year, authorizing the president to proclaim zones in which American shipping would not be permitted. The Allies were now able to obtain arms and munitions in the United States, but only on a cash-and-carry basis. In mid-May 1940 Roosevelt, alert to the menacing situation, asked Congress for funds of $896 million and fifty thousand warplanes. With the fall of France in several weeks, more requests came from the chief executive, and by 8 October 1940, Congress had passed more than $17 billion in defense appropriations.[45]

Although the National Guard was at less than 40 percent of its authorized strength and lacked modern equipment, FDR asked congressional approval on 31 May 1940 to federalize it; this approval did not come until 27 August of that year. With little initiative from the White House or War Department, but with prodding from a group of public-spirited citizens, the Burke-Wadsworth Selective Service Bill was introduced in Congress on 20 June 1940. Roosevelt supported it only after testing the pulse of the press and Congress. Many influential newspapers, however, were already calling for universal military training.[46]

The conscription bill was finally passed by the legislators and signed into law by the president on 16 September 1940, and some citizens were inducted into the army that same day. The act provided that the Army of the United States was to number 1,400,000. Of this number, 500,000 were to be regular army, 270,000 National Guardsmen, 630,000 draftees, and the rest were reservists. The public overwhelmingly supported these comparatively large numbers. The gigantic task of providing army camps, organization, weapons, equipment, supplies, and training, familiar to those who remembered 1917-1918, again confronted the War Department. But preparation, though scandalously neglected because of lack of money, was better than during the First World War. Staff planning, a more effective National Guard, and a supply of some reservè officers helped. Some 100,000 ROTC officers had been trained between the two wars, and they proved to be invaluable.[47]

The war in the Atlantic involved America in ominous problems concerning convoying, and the Roosevelt leadership was necessarily less than candid with the American people on this topic. Despite pledges to the contrary by the administration, the subject of the convoying of vessels by the United States *was* discussed during the staff conferences held between the United States and Britain. These conferences resulted in the American British Conference-1

(ABC-1) Staff Agreement of 27 March 1941 that stated that the United States navy *would* accept the responsibility for the "organization of a force for escort-of-convoy."[48]

The inevitable incidents occurred as early as 10 April 1941, and the subsequent torpedoing of United States vessels would occur sporadically. By 11 September the president dramatically announced that American warships had been given "shoot on sight" orders if Nazi U-boats were spotted. By 13 November 1941 Congress finally revoked the Neutrality Acts, thereby giving further aid to Britain by allowing American shipping to travel in European waters. This really put the United States, especially the navy, in the war, although vestiges of apathy and isolationist sentiment lingered on in many areas in the country. Fortunately on the eve of America's official entry into World War II the navy was in far better shape than the army despite the scrapping of 928,000 tons of warships since 1921.[49]

The United States had hoped to attain national security by naval disarmament, and for many years it did not build its quota of large warships to replace obsolete ones, as authorized by the Five Power Treaty. Finally in 1933 Congress approved the building of 32 new men-of-war, and in 1934 the construction of 141 new warships up to our treaty limits was authorized. In 1936 FDR asked Congress for a billion dollars to build a two-ocean navy. With 131,485 men in the navy when war came to Europe in 1939, reactivation of many in the naval reserves and on the retired list quickly raised the force to 191,000. Building was begun for fiscal year 1940 on the following new men-of-war: 2 battleships, 2 cruisers, 8 destroyers, 15 submarines, and 4 smaller craft. New construction for fiscal year 1941 included 2 battleships, 1 carrier, 2 cruisers, 8 destroyers, 6 submarines, and 5 smaller vessels.[50]

The sudden fall of France saw not only a marked increase in warship construction but also the acquisition of more merchant ships and their conversion for auxiliary use by the United States Navy. The goal of naval aviation was expanded to 15,000 planes and to some 232,000 personnel. The number of shipyards jumped from 12 to 108, and by June 1941 there were 697 new warships of all types under construction. In the year after June 1940, 2,059 new naval planes were procured, compared to 306 in the preceding year. By the time of the Japanese attack on Pearl Harbor 7 December 1941 the personnel strength of the navy, including the Marine Corps and the Coast Guard, totaled 420,522, up from the 146,198 of 8 September 1939.[51]

The naval air arm was strengthened just two weeks after the Armistice in 1918 when Adm. H. T. Mayo recommended that two aircraft carriers be built. In May 1919 the General Board of the Navy likewise urged increased naval aviation. In the same month, one of four navy NC-4 seaplanes, handled by Cdr. A. C. Read, triumphantly flew the North Atlantic from Newfoundland via the Azores to Lisbon. Especially noteworthy was the work done by Rear Admiral Moffett, chief of the Bureau of Aeronautics from 1921 to 1933. Planes catapulted at sea from American battleships and cruisers in 1923, in a simulated attack on the Panama Canal, dropped "bombs" successfully on the Gatun locks before the defenders could react. In the maneuvers of 1925, *Langley*, a makeshift carrier, did so well that construction was pushed on carriers *Lexington* and *Saratoga*, begun as battle cruisers. Worthy of special attention is the action of *Saratoga* in the 1938 fleet exercises; she launched a surprise air attack on Pearl Harbor from one hundred miles out.[52]

Progress was made also in the development of amphibious techniques. The United States Marines had been in the trenches in the First World War, but after 1918 the leathernecks resumed amphibian training and development. On San Clemente Island, California, and on Culebra Island, off Puerto Rico, large-unit practice landings were made. Transport ships of the fleet began landing exercises after the Fleet Marine Force was established in 1933. A number of problems were tackled: transportation of troops by water, ship-to-shore movements, tactical naval gunfire and air support, assault landings, and evaluation of different types of landing craft. In the practice landing through the surf at San Clemente, live shells were fired from warships. In the 1938 exercises the army and Coast Guard participated. Expanded maneuvers in amphibious warfare were staged in February 1941 and others in August at New River, North Carolina. While there had been excellent progress, many kinks remained to be ironed out. That more hitches in amphibian development did not occur can be attributed to the invaluable procedures drawn up by marine Lt. Col. Earl H. ("Pete") Ellis, who accurately foresaw the island-hopping-type of amphibious operations that would be needed against Japan in the western Pacific in a future war.[53]

IN THE ARMY AIR CORPS the struggle for viability continued in the 1930s. Along with the army ground forces, the service aloft was starved for funds in the early 1930s and ranked a poor fourth behind the air forces of France, Italy, and Great Britain. Not until 1936 did Congress authorize an increase in the number of serviceable planes to 2,320. While appropriations doubled in 1936–1938 over those of 1933–1935, procurement was so slow that there were only 1,600 effective Air Corps planes by the autumn of 1938.[54]

Only the somber Munich Conference and the grim Czechoslovakian crisis of 1938–1939 served to boost American air power. On 16 October 1938 the War Department unrolled a plan to increase markedly the number of Air Corps planes by mass-producing certain standardized types of craft, and to develop new experimental ones. On 11 January 1939 they determined to produce annually some six thousand planes. A day later Roosevelt requested approval of Congress to train twenty thousand civilian pilots per year and for appropriations of $300 million for aircraft procurement. The twenty thousand civilians, between the ages of eighteen and twenty-five, were to be given pilot training at the nation's colleges and universities under the aegis of the Civil Aeronautics Authority.[55]

The president's call for 6,000 planes and for $300 million was approved by congressional legislation on 3 April 1939. The act provided for calling up reserve officers of the Air Corps and for increasing personnel to 3,203 officers and 45,000 enlisted men. The civilian training of the 20,000 pilots was approved by legislation on 27 June 1939. However, with the collapse of France, the Air Corps enlargement program was upgraded. In June 1940 the War

Department said it would train 3,600 navigators and bombardiers and 7,000 pilots yearly; 12,835 planes were to be built by 1 April 1942. But in August 1940 FDR ordered the training of 12,000 pilots, and this figure was increased to 30,000 on 17 December 1940.[56]

This great American air expansion was brought about by the final realization that Germany's striking military victories were due in significant part to the stellar role played in the blitzkrieg by the *Luftwaffe*. In November 1940 Maj. Gen. Henry H. ("Hap") Arnold called for an Army Air Corps second to none.[57]

But progress over these years seemed maddeningly slow. In contrast, the United States Army Air Corps in September 1938 had just 22,000 men; the German Luftwaffe, 1,000,000. The Air Corps had one training center at San Antonio, Texas. There were some 1,000 combat aircraft in 1938, and 2,500 in 1941. The number of officers increased from 2,000 to almost 17,000 and enlisted men from 20,000 to over 180,000. In 1940 and 1941 one expansion after another increased the Air Corps to 30,000 pilots, 10,000 bombardiers and navigators, and 100,000 technicians and mechanics a year to serve eighty-four air groups, the whole program to yield 41,000 officers and 600,000 enlisted men. It was an impressive effort when finally under way.[58]

Although the country was in much better shape militarily and even economically in 1941 than it had been in 1938, it had not been possible to overcome the apathy, deficiencies, and neglect of the two decades since the Germans had walked into Foch's railway car in 1918. Intelligent planning with long lead time was essential to expedite industrial production and create huge, capable, and modern air armadas, naval fleets, and land armies. Once again, as had happened so often in America's past, the United States would be obliged to pay a fearful price in blood and treasure to atone for its military unpreparedness when ruthless, powerful, and victorious enemies would bring the flower of America's youth into battle and test the nation's will and capacity for total war on a scale hitherto undreamed of.

THE PERIOD from the end of World War I to the outbreak of World War II has been well known for its idealistic hopes and unrealistic attitudes toward the military as well as the economic, political, and social problems of the United States. Despite a small force engaged in occupation duty at a tiny enclave in Germany, the four-million-man army was quickly and almost completely demobilized.

In the struggle to hammer out a viable peacetime military policy for the nation, the efforts of John M. Palmer and others resulted in the fairly realistic National Defense Act of 1920. Lack of public and congressional support weakened the act and consequently the armed services as insufficient appropriations led to reductions of the forces beyond a safe point, lags in development and procurement of modern weapons, and inability to keep abreast of strategic and tactical advance, although the army's General Staff was more effectively reorganized.

America played the leading role in the dubious Washington Arms Conference of 1921–1922 that led to the massive scrapping of a great many of our navy's capital ships and a rigid ratio vis-à-vis Britain and Japan. Other agreements at Washington made the western Pacific a Japanese lake. And the eagle's wings remained sharply clipped as prejudice against the fledgling Army Air Service by the navy and ground army curtailed United States military aviators despite the dramatically successful bombing tests and impassioned advocacy of Billy Mitchell. America fell behind her former allies and her future enemies in the development of tanks and mechanized forces. But some advances were scored in tactical training, and warplane evolution went ahead, especially in larger strategic bombers. The navy was in the best shape for hostilities when they came in December 1941, although battleships had been emphasized rather than aircraft carriers, and the marines were pushing ahead on amphibious war techniques.

Nor did public opinion, as partially shaped by the churches, newspapers, and journals, rally behind the armed forces in this intervening period—quite the contrary. After all, the War to End All Wars had been won; hence there would be no future world conflicts, and certainly America would never again enter one if it did occur. Nor was the army's image enhanced by its role in confronting the Bonus Marchers. Some support did come, however, from such lobby groups as the American Legion and the Veterans of Foreign Wars. Nonetheless, the head-in-the-sand attitude of the nation reached its apex in the Neutrality Acts of the 1930s.

Only when the world crisis threatened war in the late 1930s did the United States show some preparedness stirrings, and it was only then that President Roosevelt, after initial delay, could assert the dynamic leadership necessary to get the country ready for another global war. Once America was in the Second World War, he would demonstrate strong and usually effective powers and talents as commander in chief, blessed by an effective Joint Chiefs of Staff and outstanding theater commanders. All of these leaders and millions of GIs would be pressed to the limit to overcome the inaction of the government and people during the twenties and thirties in all things military.

CHAPTER FOURTEEN

World War II Crusade

. . . if we fail, then the whole world, including the
United States, including all that we have known
and cared for, will sink into the abyss of a new
Dark Age, made more sinister, and perhaps more
protracted, by the lights of perverted science.

WINSTON S. CHURCHILL

WHEN THE SONS OF NIPPON sent bombs and torpedoes hurtling from the heavens upon Pearl Harbor at 7:55 A.M. on 7 December 1941, World War II was already two years and three months old. And at first it seemed that the Axis powers—Adolf Hitler's Nazi Germany and Benito Mussolini's Facist Italy, later joined by Japan—would sweep all before them. Invading Poland's flat terrain on 1 September 1939, the powerful German juggernaut of some 1.25 million troops, spearheaded in the new blitzkrieg tactics by panzers augmented by close tactical air support by the Luftwaffe, captured Warsaw. They were aided by a thrust into eastern Poland by Hitler's temporary ally, Josef Stalin's Russia, which overran that hapless country in just four weeks.

Although Great Britain and France instantly declared war on Germany, the Western Front, where France's vaunted Maginot Line and army buttressed by Lord Gort's British Expeditionary Force confronted Hitler's Siegfried Line, remained quiescent for over eight months in the so-called phony war. French Field Marshal Maurice Gamelin, the ineffectual Supreme Allied Commander in the West, and the British generals failed to see that unlike most of World War I, the offensive was once again the queen of the battlefield.

As a hedge against the inevitable day when his alleged partner, Der Fuehrer, would turn Germany's might against Russia, Stalin launched an initially abortive attack upon Finland on 30 November 1939 in an endeavor to push Russia's military frontier as far westward and northward as possible. Repeatedly repulsed by the gallant Finns, superior Soviet manpower finally impelled Finland to yield in March 1940 and the Russians seized the Baltic states of Latvia, Lithuania, and Esthonia. Hitler, using part of his small surface navy and airborne troops, boldly invaded Norway in April 1940 with 150,000 soldiers. A French and British expeditionary force of 30,000, dispatched to Norway to try to retrieve the situation, was defeated and evacuated at Trondheim. As in Poland, German casualties were very light. To cap his spring successes, Hitler invaded and overran Denmark in one day, 9 April 1940, as part of his Norwegian campaign.

France's turn came next. The German plan was to attack northeast of Sedan in May 1940 and knife through the supposedly impenetrable Ardennes Forest to outflank the Maginot Line; then they would crush the Allied left wing by driving westward to the English Channel. This would be followed by an advance southward and then southeastward toward Switzerland, forcing the British and French forces back to the rear of the Maginot Line. The Allies had 119 divisions to the Germans' 122, but the British and French were heavily outnumbered in the air by the Luftwaffe.

The massive German onslaught was brilliantly successful, readily pushing through the weak Dutch and Belgian resistance and pinning the BEF against the Channel at Dunkirk. But in the "Eight-Day Miracle" the British, unveiling the Supermarine Spitfire fighter plane, took some 337,000 troops off the beaches and brought most of them safely back to England, though most of their equipment had to be left at Dunkirk. Astonished and hurt by the sudden and unannounced surrender by King Leopold of the Belgian army, and "stabbed in the back" by Mussolini's attack in the Alps (where the French troops repelled the Italians), France's army was pressed back unrelentingly by the German blitzkrieg and compelled to capitulate on 25 June 1940. A fair-sized area of southeastern France, with a collaborationist government in Vichy headed by Henri Philippe Petain and Pierre Laval, was left unoccupied by Hitler.

Now began the stirring Battle of Britain. The Germans, prior to their planned operation "Sea Lion" (the invasion of the British Isles), had first to win air superiority over England and its Channel. But for the first time the Luftwaffe, built as a tactical and not a strategic air force, failed because of the rallying talents of Britain's great new Prime Minister, Winston S. Churchill; because of Air Marshal Sir Hugh Dowding's sagacious handling of the Royal Air Force's embattled and outnumbered Spitfires and Hawker Hurricanes; and in part because of those planes and their intrepid flyers. Churchill declared, "Never . . . was so much owed by so many to so few." It was indeed Britain's finest hour. By autumn 1940 Hermann Goering's daytime failures impelled him to switch to nighttime bombings of British cities, and the tide in the strategic aerial warfare in the West had turned against Germany, although her ground control over Central and Western Europe seemed complete.

Meanwhile, Hitler's ally, Mussolini, attacked Greece in October 1940, but Il Duce's inept army was checked and thrown back by the Greeks, who counterinvaded Albania. British naval attacks in the Mediterranean, made largely by air, heavily damaged three Italian battleships at Taranto and sank three enemy cruisers at Cape Matapan. Finally in April 1941 Hitler came to the aid of Italy by invading Yugoslavia and Greece and knocking them out of the war. German paratroopers captured Crete in May.

In North Africa an Italian invasion of Egypt from Libya in September 1940 was halted by the British under Field Marshal Sir Archibald Wavell, whose counterattack carried the British across the bulge of Cyrenaica to El Agheila by February 1941. Erwin Rommel's crack German Afrika Korps bolstered the Italians and drove the British (except for the staunch garrison of Tobruk) back to Salum in Egypt by May; many of Wavell's troops had been sent on a futile expedition to Greece. But a reinforced British Eighth Army under Sir Claude Auchinleck counterattacked and drove the Axis forces back to El Agheila by December 1941.

Unable to win a decisive victory in the British Isles or in North Africa, Hitler invaded Russia (against the advice of several of his generals) in operation BARBAROSSA on 22 June 1941. Two and a quarter million German troops, with initial air superiority, were pitted against a similar number of Soviet soldiers, although the Russians were more heavily reinforced in ensuing months. At first the Germans scored impressive gains, capturing Kiev, Sevastopol, and Rostov, and threatening Moscow and Leningrad before the Russians and their severe winter halted the Nazis in December 1941.

In the Far East, Germany and Italy's partner, Japan, successfully invaded Manchuria in 1931, and compounded that victory by attacking China directly in 1937. Over the next several years the seemingly invincible Japanese armies carved out sizable gains along China's eastern and southern coasts and made thrusts well into the interior. The Nipponese also occupied French Indochina in 1941. Finally when the Japanese refused to withdraw from China, because in part of their need for raw materials for the Japanese war machine, the United States, Britain, and the Netherlands government in exile halted shipment of strategic goods to Japan and froze Japanese assets within their countries. Premier Hideki Tojo, who came to power in Tokyo on 17 October 1941, felt obliged to take sterner measures to guarantee Japan's efforts to establish her Greater East Asia Co-Prosperity Sphere. But Americans, the British, and Dutch and their possessions stood in the way.[1]

With abandonment of Japan's rampant nationalistic ambitions unthinkable, the economic sanctions imposed by the United States seemed to leave Japan's leaders with only one alternative: to make herself self-sufficient by military capture of the rich southern resources areas of Malaya and the Dutch East Indies, which contained 65 percent of the world's tin, 85 percent of its rubber, 90 percent of its quinine, and enormous quantities of iron, oil, gold, nickel, bauxite, and manganese. With France and Holland overrun by the Germans, and Britain and Russia fighting for their lives, the time appeared ripe for Japanese aggression. Only the United States and her Pacific Fleet barred the door.[2]

Japan was a formidable military power in 1941. Four and a half years of campaigning in China had given her armed forces training, experience, and toughness, and she began steadily to withdraw some troops from China in mid-1941. The army of Japan numbered some 2.4 million trained soldiers, with 3 million more in partly trained reserves available. The Japanese navy possessed 12 battleships and 9 aircraft carriers by December 1941, plus 209 other warships. Japan had 7,500 warplanes (about half army, half navy), of which 2,675 were frontline aircraft. Some 425 new warplanes were being manufactured monthly, and there were 6,000 trained pilots who were backed by a training program that produced 2,750 more pilots per year. Japan, an island empire, had to import enormous quantities of raw materials to convert to war goods, but her merchant marine was brittle. An additional strength was Japan's interior position in the mandated islands of the western Pacific from which she could strike at Guam, Wake Island, the Aleutians, Hawaii, the Philippines, New Guinea, the Solomon Islands, the Dutch East Indies, Malaya including Singapore, and even Australia.[3]

To oppose this impressive martial array, the British and Dutch had little real strength or military hardware in the Far East; only America could hope to stand up to Japan's conquest of this vast, rich, southern resources area. The United States army garrison in the Hawaiian Islands numbered 59,000, but Lt. Gen. Walter C. Short had many of these troops on training regimen. There were 148 naval and 123 army military combat aircraft available in December 1941, plus some 180 warplanes aboard the carriers *Lexington* and *Enterprise,* then absent from Hawaii. The carrier *Saratoga* was then on the West Coast of the United States. At the great naval base at Pearl Harbor on the island of Oahu was the Pacific Fleet of 9 battleships, the 3 mentioned carriers that were normally at Pearl, 2 heavy cruisers, 18 light cruisers, 54 destroyers, and 22 submarines.

The whole army of the United States in December 1941 numbered over 1.5 million, but only about one-third of these were fully trained. The total navy encompassed seventeen battleships and eight carriers, plus many other units, and a strong and growing merchant marine was another asset. The Army Air Forces possessed 1,157 front-line combat warplanes, of which 159 were four-engine bombers. But this respectable military force was spread quite thin, and, as would be seen, the great distances of the Pacific would require large numbers of all three branches of the armed services to try to hold the far-flung Allied bases on the islands that dotted the vast expanse of the greatest of oceans, plus proficiency in amphibious warfare and in jungle fighting to reoccupy lost territory.[4]

As early as 27 January 1941 the veteran American ambassador to Japan, Joseph C. Grew, passed along to Washington warnings that the Japanese might possibly launch "a surprise mass attack on Pearl Harbor using all their military facilities." By summer of that year, top American officials in Washington were assisted significantly by the breaking of the Japanese code and the ability to intercept and read some of their messages (the so-called Magic procedure). Events moved rapidly as Tojo's militaristic government on 5 November issued its master plan for war operations while their envoys in Washington negotiated with the secretary of state, Cordell Hull. In part, Japan hoped to gain American diplomatic concessions for her continued aggression in the Far East, and in part, she hoped to use the negotiations as a smoke screen in the event that hostilities came.[5]

On 20 November a key Japanese proposal came—an ultimatum so far as they were concerned—stipulating that the United States must resume its shipment of strategic goods to Japan and withdraw American support of China, the Nipponese saying they would then evacuate southern Indochina. The United States rejected this proposal at once and on 26 November offered a counterproposal that called upon Japan to get out of China and Indochina and to cease further aggression. Realizing that Japan would not agree, Hull warned Army Chief of Staff Gen. George C. Marshall, "Those fellows mean to fight and you will have to watch out."[6]

For some time before 7 December, uniformed and civilian leaders in Washington had come to the conclusion that the crisis with Japan could lead to war, and later that hostile attacks would probably come on the weekend of 7 December. Intercepted messages clearly indicated this likelihood. Much, but not all, of this intelligence was sent to warn the two ranking American officers on Oahu, Adm. Husband E. Kimmel and Lt. Gen. Walter Short, but the full crush of urgency was lacking to a degree. Still, as outpost commanders, Short and Kimmel did not take the proper precautions they should have to ready their forces to meet a possible imminent attack.

On Sunday morning, 7 December, Marshall, despite the war warnings for that date, did not vary from his customary horseback ride in the Virginia countryside, and one did not bother the general on such occasions. When he and the chief of naval operations, Harold Stark, were finally informed later that morning of the impending attack, they merely used regular commercial cable facilities to send a final warning to Pearl Harbor. Marshall did not want to risk the use of a direct scrambler telephone to communicate instantly with Oahu; he feared this would tip off the enemy that we had broken their code. So while there was lack of decisive action on the part of Kimmel and Short in the Hawaiian Islands, there was also no urgent action taken in Washington by either Marshall or Stark; and to a lesser extent either by Roosevelt or Hull.[7]

The massive sneak attack on the American fleet at Pearl Harbor was brilliantly executed, but the Japanese were blessed by a remarkably good fortune that enabled the assault to be more effective than it might have been otherwise. Just before dawn on 7 December, some 275 miles northwest of Oahu, the Japanese carriers launched 40 torpedo planes, 135 dive bombers, 104 horizontal bombers, and 81 fighter planes to attack, not the vital major repair and maintenance facilities and oil storage tanks at Pearl Harbor, but chiefly American aircraft on the ground and the eight battleships and the lesser warships of the Pacific Fleet. Most of the battlewagons were anchored in pairs along Ford Island.

Japanese submarines were sighted and reported soon after daybreak at the entrance to Pearl Harbor, but no American action was taken. A radar operator up in the hills, practicing after its closing time on the new instrument, reported shortly after 7:00 A.M. to the aircraft warning information center that a large number of planes were approaching Oahu from the north, some 130 miles distant. The duty officer, inexperienced in radar use and without checking further, told him to "forget it" as they were likely off-course B-17s due in from the mainland, or planes expected from the carrier *Enterprise* on its way back from delivering aircraft to Wake Island.[8]

In perfect weather the first Japanese bombs and torpedoes were loosed at 7:55 A.M., catching the Americans almost totally unready and ill prepared, though some air and antiaircraft opposition was taken that cost the enemy just twenty-five planes and three midget subs. A majority of American planes were destroyed on the ground, many of them at nearby Hickam Field. And the loss and damage to our fleet was frightful. Generally the outboard battleship of the moored pairs at Ford Island suffered heavier damage than its inboard twin. *Arizona* took several hits and was blown up with the loss of most hands. Also a total loss was *Oklahoma,* which took three torpedoes and capsized. *West Virginia* and *California* were heavily struck and sank to the shallow harbor floor, fortunately upright. *Nevada* was also severely wounded. Lighter damage was suffered by *Tennessee, Maryland,* and especially by *Pennsylvania,* which was in drydock. Three light cruisers, three destroyers, and five lesser men-of-war were also sunk or heavily damaged. Had the carriers *Enterprise, Lexington,* and *Saratoga* been at Pearl, they would almost certainly have been sent to the bottom. Some 4,575 Americans were casualties, 3,303 of them killed. It would take many months for most of the stricken battleships to be repaired and put back into service. Pearl Harbor was the most severe naval defeat the United States has ever suffered.[9]

WOULD the American high command meet the test of global war on an even greater scale than that of the First World War? It was not self-evident at the start of the contest. At the apex was the commander in chief, President Franklin Roosevelt. Born with the proverbial silver spoon in his mouth at the family mansion at Hyde Park, New York, on 30 January 1882, this well-to-do country squire studied at Groton, graduated from Harvard in 1904 and then from the Columbia Law School. After practicing law in New York, Roosevelt served as a Democratic state senator from 1911–1913 and became an able assistant secretary of the navy in 1913–1920. He was defeated as presidential candidate James Cox's running mate for the vice-presidency in 1920. A year later, while vacationing at Campobello Island, New Brunswick, Canada, Roosevelt suffered a crippling polio attack. Undaunted, he battled to gain partial use of his legs with the aid of braces. Ever cheerful, optimistic, and friendly to those he liked, with an engaging smile and jaunty-angled cigarette holder, FDR stormed back politically to win the governorship of New York in 1928, a position to which he was reelected two years later. In 1932 he won the presidency overwhelmingly from incumbent Herbert Hoover. The New Dealer was only the third man bearing the Democratic party's standard to gain the White House since before the Civil War, and he had solid Democratic majorities in both houses of Congress.[10]

As wartime president, Roosevelt, while an undisciplined administrator, was nonetheless a strong executive who interpreted the powers of commander in chief broadly and wielded them vigorously and confidently. Unlike Woodrow Wilson, FDR was ever watchful of his prerogatives and was usually unwilling to share his authority. As Secretary of War Stimson, an admirer of Roosevelt, said of the chief executive:

> He has no system. He goes haphazard and he scatters responsibility among a lot of uncoordinated men and consequently things are never done. . . . He has flashes of genius but when it comes to working out a hard problem in a short time with the aid of expert advisers, he just doesn't quite connect and it doesn't work.[11]

Roosevelt did not hesitate on a number of occasions to reject the professional military advice of his Joint Chiefs of Staff. He thought himself a capable strategist and not only liked to be with his military chiefs but thought he could talk with them on equal terms. His personal chief of staff, former Chief of Naval Operations Adm. William D. Leahy, who presided over the meetings of the Joint Chiefs of Staff (JCS) and almost daily briefed the chief executive early in the morning, declared:

> The President kept himself informed minutely on the progress of the war. The maps in the Map Room of the White House were so hung that he would not have to get out of his wheel chair to look at them. There were flags and pins of various colors showing the disposition of our land, naval, and air forces over the entire globe.[12]

Before Pearl Harbor and early in the war Roosevelt often sided with the British in grand strategy planning. He and Churchill worked together closely and usually harmoniously throughout the conflict, and he played a very active and direct role in the debates between his JCS and their British counterparts (together, these officers were known as the Combined Chiefs of Staff or CCS).

But the American commander in chief had another, indirect way of dealing with his military leaders. He was adept at deciding issues by ignoring them, appreciating that in wartime, indecision sometimes decides by default. This technique often led to a degree of negative leadership. Thus FDR frequently did not talk over affairs with his JCS, preferring, it seemed, that they try to read his mind. Roosevelt would accept or reject the results of this process, but he would seldom inform the chiefs of the reasons for his actions. This ploy forced the chiefs to devise policy themselves, to back it unanimously and strongly, and to meet their British counterparts halfway. The American chiefs assumed that since FDR wanted them to act, this was the wisest way to keep him from intervening too often in the details of their actions. Historian William R. Emerson concludes:

> Animated by these powerful though negative motives, Roosevelt was far more sensitive than is generally realized to the political aspects of the war; he performed truly the function of the American Commander in Chief, which is to bind together the varied political and military strands which make up war, keeping each in its proper relation to the whole. If criticism must fall upon his war presidency it probably should fall upon the soundness and realism of his political motives than upon his military actions. . . . More so than appears in the afterlight of victory, World War II was for the Allies a war of narrowly averted disasters, of harsh choices, and of somewhat disheartening possibilities. . . . Historians of the future, sitting in judgment of Franklin Roosevelt's war presidency, may perhaps conclude that what was prevented was more important than what was done and that his leadership of the coalition, given the conditions under which it was exercised, was sounder than his statesmanship.[13]

Vice-Presidents Henry A. Wallace and Harry S. Truman were not employed by the president in the active military prosecution of the war, nor were they kept well informed of strategic developments. Playing a leading role in the greatest total war mobilization in history, though not participating to a great degree in the formulation of strategy and grand strategy, was the dignified secretary of war, Henry L. Stimson. This aging but energetic Republican had been William H. Taft's secretary of war and Hoover's secretary of state. In the First World War he had been a colonel of field artillery in the AEF, and he was governor general of the Philippines from 1927 to 1929. Stimson was liked and respected by those who knew him as an experienced, able, and sagacious administrator. Another Republican, Col. Frank Knox, a former Rough Rider, AEF artillery captain, Chicago newspaper owner, and unsuccessful candidate for vice-president in 1936, proved to be an adequate secretary of the navy. When Knox died in April 1944, he was succeeded by the under secretary, the talented James V. Forrestal, who would later become the nation's first secretary of defense.[14]

Besides the president's chief of staff, Adm. Leahy, the Joint Chiefs of Staff comprised the army chief of staff Gen. George C. Marshall; the Air Force chief, Gen. Henry H. ("Hap") Arnold; and the chief of naval operations, Adm. Harold Stark. A graduate of the Virginia Military Institute, Marshall had served in the AEF with distinction. He pleased those superiors with whom he came in contact, and most of those army men serving under him were impressed with his abilities, character, poise, and tact. Though not a brilliant natural strategist, Marshall was an excellent staff officer who did many things well.[15]

A veteran flyer since 1916 in the early days of the Army Air Service, Hap Arnold was well versed in all phases of air strategy, tactics, and plane development, and he proved to be a competent member of the Joint Chiefs. Admiral Stark served on Sims's staff of the American navy in European waters in the First World War. When success against Nazi U-boats seemed in doubt during World War II, Stark was eased out as chief of naval operations and the skilled though strong-spoken Adm. Ernest J. King replaced him. King had been a midshipman in the 1898 war with Spain; on the Joint Chiefs of Staff he would be an unrelenting champion of pressing the war in the Pacific against Japan.[16]

THE FIRST United States engagement in the war against Germany and Italy was thrust sharply upon her by the U-boat offensive launched off the American East coast by Adm. Karl Doenitz on 12 January 1942. Here the German wolfpacks found a fertile field of endeavor; Allied merchantmen, many of them tankers, sailed northward toward Halifax, Nova Scotia, where large trans-Atlantic convoys were formed. Losses to the U-boats were frightful. There were 82 freighters sunk in the first four months of 1942. When Doenitz shifted his subs to Caribbean waters, 142 merchantmen were lost in May and June 1942. During these six months only 20 German U-boats were destroyed by the Allies, less than the monthly production of new submarines.

Then Ernest J. King succeeded Stark. This hard, grim, determined seaman of forty-one years' experience, who hated publicity and politicians, bore down hard on antisubmarine tactics. This meant pressing more of the smaller escort vessels into service, employing additional Army Air Force and navy patrol planes and blimps, establishing new north-south sea-lane convoys, and eventually using many small escort ("jeep") carriers when they became available. With an average of thirty-one convoys at sea at all times, this was a huge task. Yet it paid off in due time, even when Doenitz shifted his wolfpacks to the South Atlantic and then back to the main North Atlantic convoy routes to Russia and the British Isles. Of all the Latin-American nations, only Brazil—as in 1917-1918—gave the United States any real help. Losses were cut markedly while destruction of U-boats increased noticeably.

The crucial period of the Battle of the Atlantic was from July 1942 to May 1943, and centered on the North Atlantic run to Europe. It was here that the Allies finally triumphed decisively over the U-boat menace with swarms of planes and better protected convoys. The Allies sank large numbers of enemy submarines (forty German and six Italian in 1943 from 1 January to April). Forty-one Axis subs were last in May. Too late came the new German 250-foot, electric-drive, snorkel-type U-boat. Throughout all this dramatic struggle with enemy submarines, Allied troops and equipment and lend-lease supplies continued to cross the Atlantic and set the stage for the first major Allied amphibious offensive against the Axis, the invasion of North Africa.[17]

While Pearl Harbor was being attacked, the British Eighth Army in North Africa under the command of Sir Claude Auchinleck was driving the Italo-German army back from Salum to El Agheila. But Rommel, the "Desert Fox," was made of stern stuff. He launched a smashing counterattack lasting from January to July 1942 which drove the "Great Auk" all the way back to El Alamein, not far west of the British naval base at Alexandria. In this striking drive, near Knightsbridge, Afrika Korps tanks and 88-mm guns destroyed 675 of 740 British tanks, and Tobruk fell to the Axis in June.

But the Germans had run out of steam. Perhaps unfairly, Auchinleck was relieved of his command and replaced by the beret-wearing, nonsmoking, non-cursing, nondrinking master of the set battle piece, Sir Bernard L. Montgomery. With the able Sir Harold Alexander as his superior, Montgomery checked the Axis advance and dug in at El Alamein. Some four hundred Sherman tanks were rushed from the United States to bolster the British. In October and November, 1942, following the greatest artillery bombardment of the war in Africa, "Monty" launched his own great offensive that trounced the Germans and Italians at El Alamein and sent them reeling backwards in retreat across the Cyrenaican bulge, out of Libya, and into Tunisia. Here, the British Eighth Army would link up with Lt. Gen. Dwight D. Eisenhower's American and British invasion forces to crush the enemy and drive him from the continent.[18]

At the Washington conference of June 1942, Roosevelt and Churchill agreed to the invasion of northwestern Africa—the so-called operation TORCH—the Combined Chiefs of Staff starting their plans on 25 July 1942. The State Department had been in contact with anti-Vichy elements in French North Africa, and Maj. Gen. Mark Clark was put ashore from a submarine to confer with and aid Eisenhower in getting Adm. Jean Darlan to order Vichy French forces to cease resisting the Allied landings of 107,000 troops which

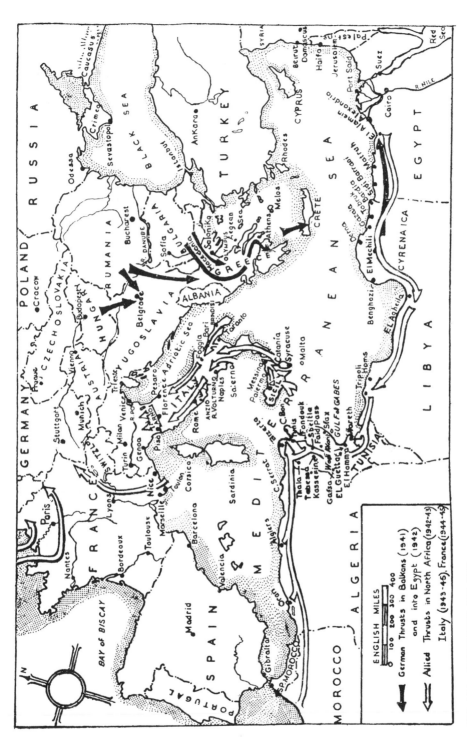

FIG. 14.1. CAMPAIGNS, 1941–1945

took place on 8–11 November 1942 at Algiers, Oran, and Casablanca. As Montgomery pressed into Tunisia from the southeast, Ike's forces did likewise from the west, hampered by rain, poor roads, only one weak railroad from Casablanca, five hundred miles of rugged mountain and desert between Algiers and Tunis, and by 20,000 troops flown by the Germans across the Sicilian straits. This force would be beefed up even more in early 1943. Eventually, the Allied forces would reach 500,000 men.

While Churchill and Roosevelt conferred at Casablanca, Rommel launched a temporarily successful counterattack at Kasserine Pass that drove the Americans back. But it was a last effort; Eisenhower rallied the shaken soldiers capably supported by such rising subordinates as George S. Patton, Jr., and Omar N. Bradley, and the Allies resumed the offensive. With the ill Rommel flown to a hospital in Germany, Gen. J. Von Arnim was pressed into a corner at Bizerte and Cape Bon peninsula by Ike and Monty's forces and was obliged to surrender his remnants on 13 May 1943. Comparatively few Axis soldiers escaped to Sicily; the total prisoner count reached some 248,000. Approximately 350,000 Germans and Italians were casualties in the entire campaign from El Alamein to Northwest Africa, a mammoth operation that guaranteed maintenance of the lifeline to India, the Persian Gulf back-door to Russia, and the Far East.[19]

While the contending armies jousted on the burning sands of Tunisia, a significant conference was held between Roosevelt and Churchill and the CCS from 12 to 25 January 1943 at Casablanca, Morocco. Atop a knoll overlooking the white city, four miles from the azure harbor, the Hotel Anfa and its surrounding villas provided the setting for the conclave. A sharp clash immediately occurred between the more unified British chiefs, headed by Sir Alan Brooke, and the less unified American chiefs. The British chiefs favored using Allied strength in the Mediterranean for the invasion of Sicily and possibly Italy, thus keeping the pressure on the Germans and aiding the Russians. The American chiefs were opposed to diversions that might postpone the gigantic cross-Channel attack on Western Europe (code name ROUNDUP and later changed to OVERLORD) and its military buildup in the British Isles (BOLERO), plus a more aggressive effort in the Pacific against Japan.

After intensive debate, Churchill and FDR compromised to the extent that they agreed upon the attack on Sicily (HUSKY), with a possible invasion of Italy; a delay until 1944 for a main assault on Western France; a stepped-up bomber offensive against the Festung Europa; and the beginning of the reconquest of Burma to reopen the Burma Road into China. Appended to the Casablanca decisions was Roosevelt's still controversial unconditional surrender statement that was to be applied to the capitulation of the Axis powers.[20]

For control of the Mediterranean lifeline, operation HUSKY was a natural. The southern point of Sicily is ninety miles from Tunisia, while the northeastern point of the island is separated from the toe of the Italian boot by the very narrow Strait of Messina. Still under the overall command of Eisenhower (who would soon be sent to England to command OVERLORD), the invasion of Sicily in July 1943 would feature landings of two armies under the direction of Fifteenth Army Group commander, Sir Harold Alexander—

Montgomery's British Eighth Army and the American Seventh Army, led by the colorful George S. Patton, Jr. Patton deserves some attention because of his later prominence.

Tall, long-legged "Georgie" Patton, born in San Gabriel, California, in 1885, came from a Virginia family of wealth, privilege and a high code of honor. He graduated from West Point in 1909 after a year at Virginia Military Institute. Patton was five years older than Eisenhower when these future generals met and became friends while stationed at Camp Meade, Maryland, in 1919. Even then Patton was almost a legend in his own time. The ivory-handled .45 revolvers that he wore on each hip had been used in 1916 during the Villa campaign to kill an enemy in a shoot-out. In the First World War, Patton commanded a tank brigade with distinction at St. Mihiel and in the Meuse-Argonne, where he had been wounded and decorated. He had early called for new tanks of greater range, speed, and reliability. He served on the General Staff from 1935 to 1936. By ability and cutting some corners, he showed up well in the Louisiana army maneuvers before Pearl Harbor.

Patton was a poseur and swaggerer whose fierce expression and slit eyes provided the proper personna for his glorification of war. His rousing speeches to his troops were characterized by personal showmanship, toughness, intensity, and ruthless competitiveness, and were not always in the best taste or timing. These qualities combined with his profanity and occasional obscenity were emphasized because of his conviction that if soldiers were to fight well, they either had to fear or hero-worship their general. His early nickname, the "Green Hornet," was not always one of admiration. He was an impulsive and emotionally tense leader, but he was also capable of tactical flexibility. At times he was unable to control his emotions and was later sternly reprimanded and forced to make a public apology when he brutally slapped two hospitalized soldiers during the Sicilian campaign. Yet Patton was a keen student of warfare and demonstrated great skill as a commander of armored forces and master of the blitzkreig tactics he espoused. However, it would take all the patience and talents of Omar Bradley and especially Eisenhower to handle "Old Blood and Guts" Patton, and his usefulness ceased with the end of hostilities.[21]

For the 10 July 1943 HUSKY landings on the southeastern shores of Sicily, the Allies had available 160,000 troops, 600 tanks, 14,000 other vehicles, 1,800 guns, and some 3,000 ships and landing craft. American strength would reach over 200,000 before the end of the campaign. The Axis had about 200,000 men, but usually only the Germans would offer tough resistance. Deceptive cover plans did divert some German troops toward Sardinia and Greece, though another German division would reinforce the Nazis on Sicily. After the landings, Patton's forces surged westward along the southern coast of Sicily from Licata toward Marsala. They joined more Americans moving northward from Gela—where heavy German counterattacks were finally repelled—toward Palermo, the capital, which was captured on 22 July. Elements of the American Eighty-second Airborne Division jumped in high winds and were scattered over the southeastern area of the island, yet they did assist in driving the enemy back.[22]

The British landed south of Syracuse and pressed northward past strongly held Mt. Etna along the eastern coast toward Messina, the strategic point near the straits on the northeastern tip of Sicily. A race ensued between Patton and Montgomery to reach Messina, while the Germans conducted a skillful withdrawal and got many of their troops across to safety on the toe of Italy despite some Allied naval and air attacks. Some American troops and warships mistakenly fired on their own planes. Old Blood and Guts reached Messina first, followed shortly thereafter by Monty in a campaign that had taken just thirty-eight days. The loss of Sicily and the further disintegration of the Italian army would have significant political and military repercussions.[23]

In reality the Axis collapse in Sicily triggered events that led to the fall of Mussolini and his government on 25 July 1943. King Victor Emmanuel III named Marshal Pietro Badoglio, aging former chief of the General Staff, to head a new government, and Badoglio quickly opened secret negotiations with the Allies not only to take Italy out of the war but to join the Allied side against the Nazis. The Germans, however, reacted quickly by throwing troops into Italy, not only to protect their own soldiers already there, but also to hold the peninsula against likely Allied invasion and occupation. Despite American and British insistence on unconditional surrender, Badoglio accepted their terms and an armistice was signed on 3 September 1943, the date that Montgomery's forces invaded the toe of the Italian boot in operation AVALANCHE. On 8 September the Italian fleet that had suffered heavily from German air attacks, including the sinking of one battleship and the damaging of another, sailed to Malta and surrendered to the British. On that same date two significant events took place: Eisenhower announced that the Italian armistice was in effect; and the American Fifth Army stormed ashore at Salerno, south of Naples, under the command of Mark Wayne Clark.[24]

Born on 1 May 1896 at Madison Barracks (Sacketts Harbor), New York, Clark was graduated in 1917 from West Point, where he knew Eisenhower. He was wounded in the First World War in which he served as a battalion commander. Working his way along and up in the army, he served on the General Staff in 1935–1936, and was chief of staff for the Ground Forces in 1942. Earlier in the war, in operation TORCH, Clark had gone ashore from a British submarine for a daring conference with the French.[25]

Allied leaders expected that the invasion of Italy in September 1943 would pin down some twenty-six German divisions that would otherwise be deployed against the cross-Channel attack or on the Russian front. Montgomery's army landed on the toe of the boot, moved across to and up the eastern side of the peninsula, and captured the important airfields around Foggia. The place where Clark's army landed was determined in part by the range of covering aircraft; so a point twenty-five miles south of Naples, at Salerno, was chosen. Unfortunately the Germans had deduced this and were waiting in the encircling hills. The fighting was furious, and for a time it appeared doubtful that Clark's beachhead could be held—but it was. Assisted by naval and air support, Clark's forces pushed northward and captured Naples by 1 October. A tough enemy defensive line twenty miles north of Naples along the Volturno River was cracked later that month, but the drive was checked by the Germans along the so-called Winter Line, and a little farther to the north at the Gustav Line, based largely on the mountains around Cassino.

To break the stalemate around Cassino in the winter of 1943–1944, an end-run amphibious operation was mounted and a landing made at Anzio, some thirty miles south of Rome on 22 January 1944 by John P. Lucas's Sixth Corps. At the same time vital holding attacks, some of them sustaining heavy casualties, were rightly launched by Clark along the Rapido River. Albert Kesselring reacted like a steel trap, and the Anzio forces were pinned down on the beaches and were unable to break out. A turning movement to be successful must comprise a preponderance of force; simply too few troops were landed at Anzio in comparison to those left near Cassino. Moreover, Lucas hesitated too long in consolidating his beachhead instead of striking out boldly for Rome. Finally, after regrouping, Clark broke through the enemy lines at Cassino on 11 May and into the Liri Valley, while the Anzio forces eventually cut through the encircling cordon. Rome, the Eternal City, fell on 4 June 1944, just two days before the invasion of Normandy.

When Alexander became Mediterranean theater commander, Clark was advanced to Fifteenth Army Group commander, and the talented Lucian K. Truscott moved up to Fifth Army command. Limited by OVERLORD's need for troops, planes, ships, and landing craft, Clark pressed steadily though not swiftly northward toward the Germans' "Gothic Line" behind the Arno River in the northern Apennines, which was attacked in August 1944, though three months of campaigning produced only small gains. Finally in the spring of 1945, despite skillful Nazi defense and delaying tactics, the last German line was penetrated and the Allied armies deployed onto the Po River valley's fertile plains. The less acclaimed and unsensational Italian campaign terminated on 2 May 1945 when the Germans capitulated, five days before they would do the same at Eisenhower's headquarters at Reims.[26]

While the gigantic war on the Eastern Front continued, and while Eisenhower and his subordinates were drawing up plans for the cross-Channel invasion of France, the air war against Festung Europa gained in intensity. Following their failure in the Battle of Britain, the Germans gradually shifted aircraft production from bombers to fighters, while the Royal Air Force's Bomber Command was steadily built up by the construction of four-engine heavies—Stirlings, Halifaxes, and Lancasters. Furthermore, Hitler froze for a time the development of new plane types such as jets in order to build V-1 and V-2 weapons that were comparatively less valuable than new planes. The lower flying British four-engine craft could tote a heavy bomb load, but they were lightly armed and armored and easy to shoot down in daytime raids.

When Ira Eaker's United States Eighth Air Force began arriving in numbers in the British Isles, it was found that its four-motor B-24 Consolidated "Liberators" and especially its famed Boeing B-17 "Flying Fortresses" could perform daylight precision bombing better than could their RAF cousins. Therefore, to undertake around-the-clock bombing of Germany and Nazi-occupied Europe, it was determined that the AAF would bomb by day and the RAF by night.

The first one-thousand-plane Allied air raid of the war was mounted in May 1942 against Cologne. In 1943 the RAF dropped 213,000 tons of bombs on German-held targets as against 123,000 for the AAF. From North Africa and elsewhere in the Mediterranean, the United States Fifteenth Air Force

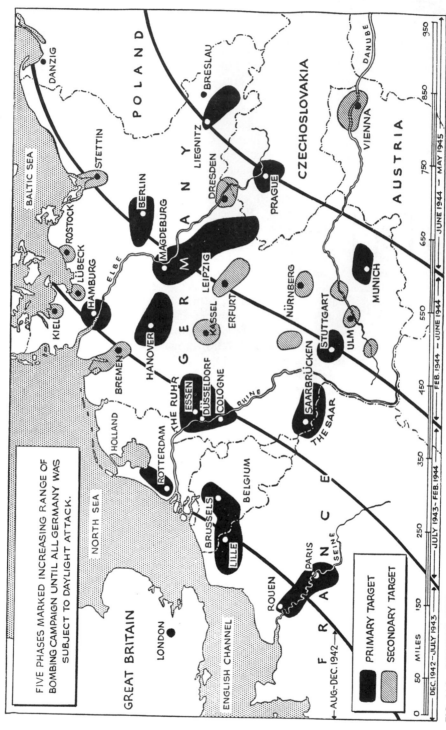

FIVE PHASES MARKED INCREASING RANGE OF
BOMBING CAMPAIGN UNTIL ALL GERMANY WAS
SUBJECT TO DAYLIGHT ATTACK.

PRIMARY TARGET

SECONDARY TARGET

FIG. 14.2.   BOMBERS OVER AXIS INDUSTRY

launched a costly low-level air assault on the rich Ploesti oil fields in Rumania and inflicted some damage in raids that were repeated with more success in April 1944. In 1944, 1,600,000 tons were dropped on Fortress Europe by the Western Allies—900,000 by the AAF and 700,000 by the RAF. In all, 2,700,000 tons were loosed on Nazi-held territory during the war by the British and Americans (the Russians did comparatively little strategic bombing).

In all, some 28,000 warplanes were employed by the Western Allies, and about 1,335,000 airmen were involved, 158,000 of whom never returned. Approximately 57,000 German planes were destroyed during the conflict, 300,000 German civilians were killed, and perhaps another 750,000 wounded. Practically all large Nazi cities were hit from the air, and frightful damage done to many. Although there was tremendous destruction of German war production, the enemy nonetheless, by artful improvisation, managed to keep grinding out more weapons, some in increasing numbers. But the massive American and British air raids were priceless in knocking out German transportation facilities and in blasting enemy petroleum production down to just 5 percent of what it had been. The isolation of the Normandy invasion coast by the relentless and far-ranging attacks against German forces and installations by the RAF and AAF were invaluable. While air power did not win the war, it unquestionably enabled the war to be won.[27]

THE ENORMOUS WAR on the Eastern Front between Germany and Russia demands a few words because American-British grand strategy planning was in part conditioned by the fortunes of war there. When the Nazis invaded Russia on 22 June 1941, their smashing blitzkrieg scored impressive initial gains. By early winter they had neared Leningrad on the northern front and Moscow on the critical central front, while Von Runstedt had adeptly surged into the Ukraine, captured Kiev and the Crimea, including Sevastopol, and reached Rostov on the Don River. Soviet casualties were stunningly high, although the Nazis themselves lost quite a few men. But the Russian winter froze and halted the Wehrmacht, and the Reds counterattacked at selected points.

The spring and summer of 1942 saw Hitler disastrously intervening, as in 1941, in German strategy by insisting that the major drive be into the Caucasus and to Stalingrad at the great bend of the Volga River, instead of the wiser military course of an offensive that would annihilate the Red armies on the Moscow central front. While the Germans again scored striking gains in the Caucasus, including the capture of some oil fields, they eventually exhausted themselves by autumn. At Stalingrad they lost an entire army in a futile effort to wrest that symbolic city from the Soviets. Great quantities of American lend-lease equipment would help the Reds by 1943.

Stalin anticipated another German offensive in the late spring of 1943 and had been calling loudly for the establishment of a second front in Western Europe by the Americans and British, even going so far as to hint at a separate peace with Hitler if this was not done. A very limited German attack at Kursk in June 1943 involved the greatest tank battle in history and was halted almost in its tracks. The Russians took over the strategic offensive for the remainder of 1943 and held it into 1944, and they eventually drove the Nazis out of Russia and into Poland.[28]

Meanwhile, planning in Great Britain for the second front was under way by January 1944 when Dwight David Eisenhower arrived in England as Supreme Allied leader of what would become the greatest integrated military force ever placed under the command of one man. Ike was born in Denison, Texas, on 14 October 1890 and spent his boyhood in Abilene, Kansas. He graduated from West Point in 1916, and during the First World War organized Camp Colt at Gettysburg, Pennsylvania, for the training of tank forces. He rose through the ranks and was warmly praised by John J. Pershing and Fox Conner. Eisenhower graduated first in his class at the Command and General Staff College and was known as one of the army's best brains and an expert on mechanized warfare. He became special assistant in 1933 to Chief of Staff MacArthur, under whom he served from 1935 to 1939 as assistant military adviser to the Philippine Commonwealth. After his return to the United States in 1939, he excelled in the 1941 Louisiana war game maneuvers and was named chief of the War Plans Division in the Office of the Chief of Staff in February 1942. Ike subsequently became chief of the Operations Division, and in June 1942 was named commander of forces for the invasion of North Africa.

Roosevelt and Marshall had chosen well in this man upon whose shoulders the burden and fate of the cross-Channel invasion of Festung Europa would rest. Actually taller than he looked, Eisenhower's thinning light hair was not too evident because of the shape and carriage of his finely formed head. His cold, blue, piercing eyes were more than balanced by his warmth of manner, expressive face, infectious grin, and boyishness. He was charming, articulate, and flexible. His hair-trigger temper was usually controlled, and he showed good emotional balance in working fairly and evenly with all types of military and civilian leaders.

Eisenhower could reach decisions quickly and could be tough, even ruthless on occasion, but generally worked his will by persuasion. His greatest talent was his ability to extract the maximum talents from a highly diverse group of people and shape them to his and the common purpose. Ike would demonstrate a genius for accommodation and compromise and in many ways personified the Allied ideal of unity and teamwork. Few men in history have had such devoted subordinates. While he lacked wide experience in combat situations and in handling large numbers of men, Ike learned quickly and showed fine common sense and judgment. He understood the political, military, economic, and psychological factors of the problems and people with whom he had to deal. He "wore well" and was truly a man for all seasons.[29]

One of the first things that Eisenhower perceived when he arrived in England was the acute shortage of landing craft. Thus the already groaning production lines in the United States and Britain were taxed still more to turn out additional craft. The target date for the D-Day landings in France was accordingly pushed back from early May to early June 1944. The isolation by the air forces of the Normandy beach area where the landings would be made would be decisive to the success of OVERLORD; it would take fifteen weeks,

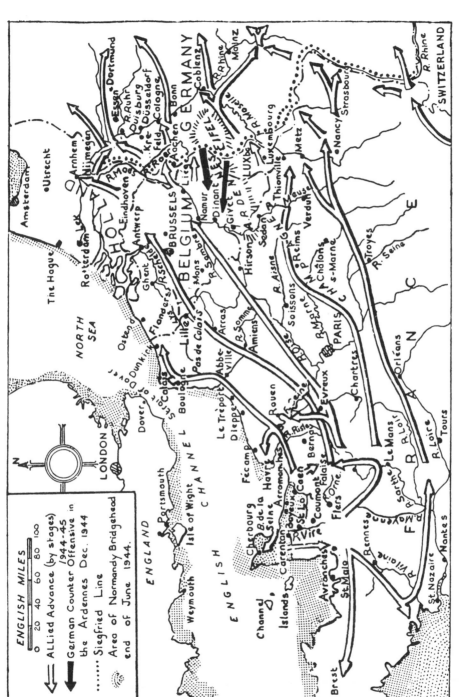

FIG. 14.3. GERMAN AND ALLIED THRUSTS 1944-1945

even with favorable Channel weather, for Eisenhower to land as many tropps as the enemy had available in Belgium and northern France.

American army strength in the United Kingdom would stand at 1,553,000 by D-Day, and the total force under Ike's command would initially be 2,876,000 soldiers, seamen, and airmen. There were 64 million square feet of storage space in the British Isles for the 50,000 military vehicles and other equipment needed. The air forces alone required 163 airfields, 8.5 million square feet for storage, and billets for 450,000 airmen. To handle the shipping, 142 cargo ships were needed, plus 3,780 assault and landing craft. Joint practice exercises were held along the southern coast of England in the spring of 1944 by Allied sea, air, and ground forces. Eisenhower and his planners then studied the strength of the German Atlantic Wall defenses and selected suitable landing beaches over which troops and mountains of supplies could readily be forwarded from their staging and mounting areas in England.[30]

The German Atlantic Wall defenses, running from Norway to Spain, were spotty. They were strong in some places, as the Allies discovered when the Canadians and a few British Commandos and American Rangers were shattered in the raid on Dieppe in August 1942, and weak in others. This was known to Runstedt, supreme German commander in the West with headquarters at Paris, and especially by Rommel, in command along the coast. It was known also to the Allies from intelligence operations and interceptions of the broken German codes. The Nazis had fifty-eight divisions, or 870,000 troops to defend the Atlantic Wall.

In the meticulous planning for OVERLORD, Eisenhower's three top deputies for the amphibian phase of the operation were British officers. He had thirty-nine divisions poised for the great invasion, and an airborne army, plus supporting naval fire from six battleships, two monitors, twenty-two cruisers, and ninety-three destroyers. Eisenhower's presence was in general continuous and all-pervasive, and his two greatest decisions were made solely on his own responsibility. His first decision, taken against the advice of several of his principal advisers, resulted in the successful seizure and retention of the causeways across the flooded areas inland from the beaches (Utah Beach) near the base of the Cherbourg peninsula by airborne troops; the seaborne landings at Utah were only lightly opposed. The second was the vital decision to launch beyond recall the greatest overwater operation in history under doubtful weather conditions. This last decision was taken in the full realization that any delay would mean, because of the moon and tides, a postponement of the mighty endeavor for several weeks or a month, with the consequent decline in morale and loss of the element of surprise. Eisenhower made these decisions courageously and without hesitation, propelling the huge forces toward Normandy on 6 June 1944. Adm. Bertram Ramsay would emphasize Ike's "inspiring leadership, which more perhaps than anything else," would lead to the stunning triumph of the invading forces upon which the victorious outcome of the Allied cause would depend. Fantastically intricate invasion plans were worked and reworked down to what each soldier was to do.[31]

For his cross-Channel tactical plan, Ike deployed his forces as follows: on the left of the American forces as they would cross the water was Lt. Gen.

Miles C. Dempsey's British Second Army, which was to land on Gold, Juno, and Sword beaches between Bayeux and Cayenne; and Lt. Gen. Omar N. Bradley's United States First Army, one of whose components, Maj. Gen. Leonard T. Gerow's Fifth Corps, was to land on Omaha Beach to the right of the British, and the other unit, Maj. Gen. J. Lawton Collins's Seventh was to land on Utah Beach, which was on the east coast of the Cotentin Peninsula. Ike ruthlessly maintained tight security measures.[32] All was set for the unprecedented undertaking; only the imponderables remained.

In Omar Bradley, Eisenhower had a solid, reliable, and highly capable top subordinate. Born in 1893 in Clark, Missouri, Bradley graduated from the military academy in 1915. At the beginning of World War II he was in command of the Infantry School at Fort Benning, Georgia. Well liked by both officers and enlisted men, Bradley was cool, level-headed, and often served as a mediator between more volatile generals, such as Patton and Montgomery. Before the war was over, he would be elevated to an army group commander with four armies under his command, and after the war would rise to army chief of staff and chairman of the Joint Chiefs, with five-star rank.

In the early hours of 6 June the airborne troops were dropped behind the Atlantic Wall and, despite some losses at such places as St. Mere Eglise, these forces accomplished their mission without undue casualties, as Eisenhower had predicted. The weather was adequate for air and naval bombardment of the Normandy coastline and rear areas. The seaborne assault on the fifty miles of beaches commenced at 6:30 A.M. The heaviest opposition was on Omaha Beach. Soldiers of Gerow's Fifth Corps were pinned down by murderous enemy fire and barely maintained themselves until finally they overcame the stubborn German resistance, heaved themselves forward, and secured the beachhead.

Lighter defenses were generally encountered on the other beaches, and the "crust" of the Atlantic Wall had been broken. In response to the German destruction of the ports and to aid the Allies in securing their landings and supplying the buildup of troops, two large artificial ports of concrete caissons were towed across the Channel and sunk off the beaches, where steel bridges linked them to the shore. In this operation MULBERRY a total of fifty-four ships were deliberately sunk to form a breakwater behind each of these artificial ports—one for the British and one for the Americans. Supplies and equipment and men immediately began pouring ashore, preventing the logistical nightmare that would otherwise have ensued. Cooperation between Allied land, sea, and air forces was excellent, and the bombing and strafing of transportation facilities and routes by the air force kept Rommel from concentrating superior forces against the beachhead before sufficient troops could be brought ashore. The D-Day landings and consolidation on the Normandy coast constituted a decisive step in the sequence of events that would end in the destruction of the Nazi forces.[33]

Tenacious hedgerow fighting in the "Bocage" country followed. At first the Allies were unable to break through the determined German defenses, although "Lightning Joe" Collins's Seventh Corps did dash up the peninsula and capture Cherbourg on 27 June. It was particularly heavy going for Montgomery's forces around Caen and west to St. Lo. Breakout operation COBRA was helped by cavalry Sergeant Curtis G. Culin's steel horns designed to help chop through the wiry hedgerows.

On 1 August Bradley's Twelfth Army Group (later designated the Central Group of Armies) became operational, and included Lt. Gen. Courtney H. Hodges's First Army and Patton's Third Army, the total force comprising five armored and thirteen infantry divisions; and Montgomery's Twenty-first Army Group (later styled the Northern Group of Armies), composed of Dempsey's British Second Army and H. D. G. Crerar's Canadian First Army. Eisenhower's forces were augmented by the average daily reinforcement of thirty thousand men.

Finally, General Hodges, preceded by a heavy air attack, was able to break out of Normandy beginning on 25 July at Avranches and St. Lo—a breach exploited by Patton. The Brittany peninsula was cut off and one-hundred thousand Germans were trapped in the Falaise pocket. A southern flank along the Loire River opened the way for Patton's explosive dash eastward to the Seine River, which was reached in late August. This relentless pursuit was skillfully assisted by the Nineteenth Tactical Air Command's close air-to-ground support.[34]

Meanwhile a major blow against the Germans in the south of France (operation DRAGOON) was launched. Landings were made between Cannes and Toulon on 15 August 1944 by Lt. Gen. Alexander M. Patch's United States Seventh Army, headed by Lucian K. Truscott's Sixth Corps, that were soon augmented in strength by the First and Second French Corps under Gen. Lattre de Tassigny. The Germans were unable to cope with this new invasion. Truscott exploited the breakout and Grenoble was seized, as was Nice on 1 September, and a rapid advance northward up the Rhone River valley ensued.

On 15 September Lt. Gen. Jacob L. Devers assumed command of the Sixth Army Group (later known as the Southern Group of Armies), comprising American and French forces. On 17–18 August Hitler finally consented to abandon southern France, though reinforced German garrisons were to defend Toulon and Marseilles to the end. The Germans were barely able to escape the Rhone pocket in their retrograde movement; only an Allied shortage of trucks and long, slow lines of supply permitted their retreat. But the fighting effectiveness of the battered Nazis had been shattered. While some thought these twelve Allied divisions could have been used to better military-political advantage in the Danube area, they provided valuable reinforcements against the Germans when they launched their dying gasp offensive in the Ardennes in December.[35]

While Ike's forces raced across France to the Siegfried Line (West Wall) after the fleeing enemy, the Germans had left behind dogged-fighting garrisons in such ports as Brest, Dieppe, St. Nazaire, St. Malo, Lorient, and Le Havre to deny their use by the Allies. Paris had fallen on 25 August, and the Germans had already lost some 400,000 men, half of them as prisoners of war. By 5 September approximately 2,086,000 Allied soldiers were sweeping eastward. First Army's Seventh Corps crossed the Aisne and pressed on to Mons, where the First Infantry Division cut off five of the retreating enemy divisions. Northwest of Dijon, Patton linked up on 11 September with the Seventh Army pressing up from the south. To the north, the Belgian frontier had been crossed by Hodges on 2 September. Herculean efforts were made, such as the one-way "Red Ball Express" of trucks to supply the swiftly advancing troops. Germany was reached from Luxembourg on 11 September by the First Army.[36]

It was ironic that one of the war's most audacious gambles was proposed by the circumspect Montgomery. His plan, MARKET-GARDEN, was designed to keep the momentum of the Allied offensive rolling by a turning movement around the northwest flank of the fortified German Siegfried Line. This was to be accomplished by crossing the several rivers of Holland and advancing north of the Ruhr Valley onto the north German plain, where they might steamroller into Berlin. Eisenhower gave his approval, having already supplied Monty's Twenty-first Army Group more than Bradley's Twelfth Army Group, so that they might seize Antwerp and its vital Scheldt estuary approaches.

The MARKET part of the operation in mid-September saw the First Airborne Army attempt to capture essential bridges across the waterways of the Maas and Waal Rivers through Eindhoven (Maj. Gen. Maxwell D. Taylor's U.S. 101st Airborne Division), Nijmegen (the U.S. Eighty-second Airborne Division, commanded by Brig. Gen. James M. Gavin), and Arnhem (Maj. Gen. Robert E. Urquhart's British First Airborne Division, the "Red Devils"). Then, in the GARDEN phase of the operation, the British Thirtieth Corps, spearheaded by the Guards Armored Division, was to surge along a road through Eindhoven and Nijmegen to join up with the Red Devils at Arnhem. Although Ike was primarily advancing on a broad front, this MARKET-GARDEN concept was an attempt to annihilate the enemy west of the Rhine. At the time it looked like a good risk.

The two American airborne divisions accomplished most of their objectives, but the hard fighting First British Airborne Division at Arnhem was caught in a death trap when unexpected German armored units reacted strongly and nearly encircled Arnhem. Despite superior efforts, the British armored column was simply unable to blast its way in time along the single vulnerable road into Arnhem. Yet they did arrive close enough to help rally the pitifully few fugitives of the Red Devils, who were able to fight their way out of the trap. It had been a brilliantly planned, courageous, and efficient effort, but fate was against the Allies. At least the Scheldt estuary approaches were finally cleared after harsh fighting by 9 November, and the port of Antwerp was in operation by 27 November. Soon it was handling over 25,000 tons of supplies daily despite a desperate rain of German V weapons. This took the strain off the long supply lines back to Normandy and took out of enemy hands the V weapon sites from which the flying projectiles had been launched, damaging Britain and her morale.[37]

When Roosevelt, Churchill, and the Combined Chiefs of Staff met for a second time in Quebec at the OCTAGON conference, Eisenhower reported a stiffening of German opposition as the formidable Siegfried Line defenses were encountered. Bloody fighting was required to capture Aachen on 21 October. By the end of November the important Metz area had been captured, as had Strasbourg on the Rhine River and the area between Mulhouse and Switzerland, also on the Rhine. Between these points was the Colmar pocket—a large portion of Alsace. With more than 3 million Allied troops on the Continent, and in the worst weather in years, it took bitter fighting—including two attacks on Schmidt—to seize the vital Roer River dams. Heavy casualties were sustained as well as inflicted east of Aachen, where the First Army bludgeoned its way through the bloody Huertgen Forest. And it was only a little easier going to occupy the Roer River plain and to reduce the Colmar pocket, although the Rhine was reached north and south of Dusseldorf by 2 March 1945 as a late autumn–early winter deadlock loomed in the offing.[38]

And then it happened. The Germans, in a last-dying-gasp effort, struck hard in an unexpected counterattack ordered by Hitler, which is known variously as Runstedt's offensive, the Battle of the Bulge, the Ardennes counteroffensive, or the Battle of Bastogne. Despite disclaimers and some warning intelligence, the Allies were surprised and the line of their four divisions between Trier and Monschau was breached on a forty-mile front by eight of Runstedt's ten panzer divisions, assisted by sixteen German infantry divisions.

The well-prepared enemy drive, beginning on 16 December 1944, was aided initially by heavy fog that enabled the Nazis to deploy unseen and rapidly advance through the Ardennes Forest without being hit by Allied air attacks for some time. Aiming at Liege, Namur, and especially Antwerp, the Germans surged ahead for sixty miles in a narrow salient that reached west almost to the Meuse. They seized one vital road and rail communications hub, St. Vith, despite heroic resistance by the U.S. Seventh Armored Division. On the southern shoulder of the bulge, owing to a gallant and successful stand made by the 101st Airborne and elements of the Tenth Armored Division at Bastogne, they were unable to capture that important town and widen the penetration.

By 22 December the tide had begun to turn and the limit of greatest Nazi advance was attained by 26 December. What finally checked the Germans was the clear weather that enabled Allied planes to take to the air; pressure against the southern shoulder of the salient by Patton's Third Army; and, to a lesser extent, pressure by Hodges's First Army to the north. By late January 1945 the bulge was eliminated with a cost to the enemy of 220,000 men, including 110,000 prisoners, and over 1,400 assault guns and tanks. Their losses were fatal for the Germans, as Runstedt had warned, and hastened the end of the war. All that the Nazis had achieved was to win a striking psychological victory in the British and American press, and to delay Eisenhower's main offensive in the north and impel him to take the rest of January to regroup.[39]

Resuming the grand offensive, Patton's tanks reached the Rhine near Coblenz on 9 March and by 11 March Eisenhower's forces held the west bank of the Rhine from Coblenz to Nijmegen. Cologne was captured by the First Army on 7 March. Then a stunning break occurred. Elements of the Ninth Armored Division discovered the Ludendorff railroad bridge at Remagen intact and seized it just before the Germans could blow it up. Ike ordered that a secure bridgehead be carved out on the east bank. This would threaten the heart of the Fatherland and provide a diversion of high significance to the main drive in the Ruhr and the elimination of enemy resistance between the Rhine and Saar Rivers.[40]

Although Eisenhower had planned that Montgomery's carefully nurtured attack across the Rhine north of the Ruhr would be the main Allied invasion of Germany, it was Patton's Fifth Infantry Division that breached the Rhine unopposed on 22 March at Oppenheim, south of Coblenz. Both the Germans and Allies were surprised by Old Blood and Guts's success. Monty's assault crossing of the lower Rhine north of Wesel on 23 March against medium opposition was matched by the Ninth Army's spanning of the Rhine south of Wesel the following day. And in two days the bridgehead was six miles deep and stretched for twenty-five miles along the Rhine. Three days later the advance reached sixteen miles beyond the great river.

With Bradley's armies sweeping around the rear of the major portion of Germany's remaining armed forces above (south of) the Ruhr, the enemy was soon encircled in the so-called Ruhr pocket between the First and Ninth Armies. Almost 350,000 German prisoners were captured in March. The Ruhr pocket was one of the greatest Cannae-like double envelopments in history, and it yielded the Allies another 300,000 prisoners. Elements of eighteen enemy divisions were caught in the net, to be reduced shortly, as Ninth and First Army forces surged forward to the east toward Leipzig. Both armies crossed the Weser River north of Kassel and approached the westward-advancing Russians by the end of the last week of April.[41]

Near defeat, fanatical Nazi propaganda efforts were radioed to try to bolster crushed German morale, implying that a suicide stand would be made in the mountainous Bavarian-Austrian Tyrol. In the absence of guiding political advice or direction from his civilian superiors, Ike, weighing military considerations, determined to hold with his left along the Mulde and Elbe Rivers near Wittenberge while driving to the southeast with his right toward Munich and Linz. The long-heralded meeting of the western Allies with the Soviets occurred on 25 April at Torgau, northeast of Leipzig.[42]

To the north, the British Second Army's advance was at Bremen by mid-April 1945 and was nearing Hamburg, while the Canadians, still farther northward, drove the enemy from the rest of northern and eastern Holland. Patton's Third Army swept into Czechoslovakia on 1 May and pressed on toward the Danube. To the right, the Seventh Army and French forces captured Karlsruhe, the Black Forest, and Stuttgart, and by 1 May they had cleared the enemy from the Swiss border to the west of Lake Constance and had invaded Austria. When Maj. Gen. Matthew B. Ridgway's Eighteenth Corps reached the Baltic on 2 May and linked up with the Russians at Wismar, all German forces in Denmark, Holland, and northwest Germany surrendered on 5 May 1945.

To the far south, Patch's Seventh Army captured Salzburg, Berchtesgaden, and Innsbruck, and drove through the Brenner Pass to establish contact with the Fifth Army at Vitipeno. On 6 May all enemy forces in Austria yielded. Hitler committed suicide in Berlin. Surrounded on all fronts by anarchy as well as by triumphant Allied forces, the German government officially capitulated to Eisenhower on 7 May in a schoolhouse in Reims, surrendering all land, sea, and air forces. The following day was proclaimed V-E Day.[43]

An impressive martial deployment had taken place on the soil of Western Europe. The strength of United States fighting forces under Dwight D. Eisenhower's command totaled 3,065,000 by V-E Day. Of that number, the Americans suffered the following casualties: 133,482 dead, 369,773 wounded; 88,366 missing (most of whom were prisoners of war)—an aggregate loss of 591,621. Of the 1,073,000 British combatants, a total casualty figure of 187,396 was reached. Total Allied losses in Western Europe amounted to 842,294. Aggregate German losses on the Western Front were: 263,000 battle dead, 49,000 permanently disabled, 7,614,794 captured (including 3,404,949 disarmed enemy forces)—total casualties (not counting wounded) were 7,926,794.[44]

Although there may be a strong and protracted debate over Allied grand strategy and the emphasis that should have been given to the Mediterranean Theater, there is little debate that the Allied Forces, with their preponderant air and naval superiority and combat experience under Alexander and especially under Eisenhower, waged a highly effective and conclusive war against Italy and Germany. In the invasion of North Africa and Sicily, despite occasional minor setbacks, Ike, Alexander, Montgomery, Bradley, and Patton handled the operations skillfully, and competent staff know-how was developed. In the Italian campaign the terrain, available forces, and the dexterity of Kesselring often reduced the Allied advance to a slow pace. While some disagree over several of Clark's command decisions in Italy, there is less debate about his technical proficiency or overall ability.

In the great OVERLORD invasion of Normandy, there can be only praise for Eisenhower's performance. This holds true in the main of his command of the sweep across France and into the heart of Germany, although there are still some who argue in favor of Montgomery's "narrow-front" idea in contradistinction to Ike's "broad-front" strategy. While never forgetting the large Russian contribution, the enemy in Western Europe was totally crushed in campaigning that lasted just eleven months. The record speaks for itself; it was an impressive job.

JAPANESE military strategy planners, as noted, had to plan for a short war. After knocking out the American Pacific Fleet, the Nipponese would strive to conquer the extensive and fabulously rich southern resources area of Southeast Asia and the Southwest Pacific. As in the Russo-Japanese War of 1904–1905, which also began with a sneak Japanese attack on the Russian fleet at Port Arthur, the Allies tended to underestimate enemy capabilities.

American strategic planning for war against Japan first centered largely on refinement of the "Rainbow 5" plan, originally drawn up in the 1930s. The United States Navy's version of Rainbow 5 called for the following action in the Far East by the navy and army: destroy Axis sea communications east of

180° (the International Date Line), raid Japanese forces in the Far Eastern and Pacific areas, and protect Allied ocean communications in the Far East and east of Australia.

In January 1941 the joint Anglo-American ABC-1 staff agreement stated that in the event of hostilities with Japan, the Americans and British would fight on the strategic defensive in the Pacific and Far East, except for possible offensive diversionary sweeps by the United States Pacific Fleet. But the Americans thought British naval weakness in the Far East precluded a viable combined, joint plan of strategy, and they urged Roosevelt and the State Department to try through diplomacy to delay war with Japan until they could strengthen their western Pacific forces. Therefore, when war came at Pearl Harbor and elsewhere, the Americans and British had to put into operation their own separate war plans.[45]

When the many Japanese advances began after 7 December 1941, they took place simultaneously, or almost so. Therefore, while they will be discussed separately, it should be remembered that much was going on at the same time.

On 8 December 1941, the Japanese commenced their attack on the outnumbered British garrison of twelve thousand at Hong Kong. With the enemy holding the harbor and the mainland area behind the island of Hong Kong, the fate of this crown colony was sealed, especially when the leasehold of Kowloon on the mainland was seized. The British, after a valorous defense, were impelled to surrender on Christmas day. Rich, oil-producing British North Borneo fell after ineffective resistance to the Japanese shortly after their capture of Hong Kong.[46]

Soon after the Japanese landed farther south than expected on Malaya's east coast on 8 December, Thailand fell. British (Australian) air and ground resistance in Malaya was annoying but ineffective, and the enemy moved to the west coast, where they pushed southward, employing occasional amphibious end runs around successive British defensive lines. The seasoned Japanese troops pressed victoriously through Johore at the bottom of the peninsula by 27 January 1942, a distance of 600 miles, and were soon poised to strike at the island of Singapore. The enemy showed excellent land, sea, and air coordination. Enemy planes caught the British capital ships *Repulse* and *Prince of Wales* without air cover off the east coast of Malaya on 10 December and sent them to the bottom.[47]

Recently arrived Field Marshal Wavell was shocked to see no defenses on the northern part of the island of Singapore and evidence of smug complacency and sloth on the part of some previous commanders and governors. Churchill ordered a defense to the utmost, but there were hundreds of thousands of helpless civilians on the island with no place to find safety, and most of the seventy thousand defending troops were inexperienced. Allied morale was not high. Moreover, the big guns had chiefly armor-piercing shells, not high explosive ones for land fighting. Nor were the Aussies trained in jungle warfare; they fought desperately but could not stem the invasion by waves of Nipponese soldiers, 200,000 in all. Drinking water was almost exhausted, but Wavell ordered fighting to continue until the troops had none

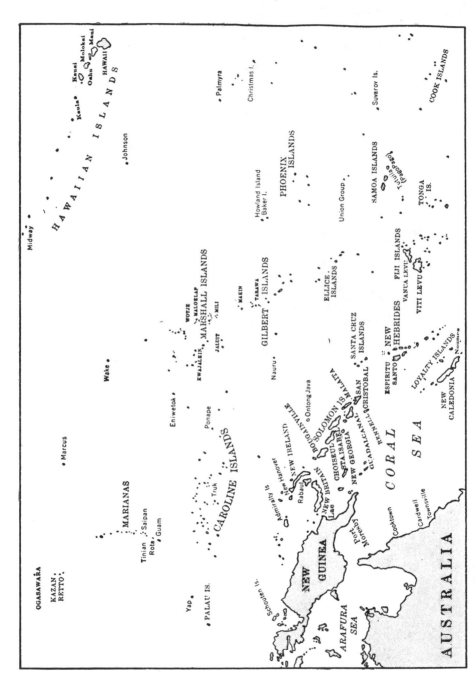

FIG. 14.4. THE SOUTH PACIFIC

left. Nonetheless, capitulation was inevitable and came on 15 February, thirty days sooner than called for by the enemy timetable.[48]

In the China-Burma-India (CBI) theater, a complicated Allied command structure existed. Major General Joseph W. Stilwell had been sent to the Far East as commander of the American army forces in the Chinese theater, but he was also named chief of staff to Supreme Commander Generalissimo Chiang Kai-shek, who also possessed a Chinese chief of staff of his Chinese armies. When Stilwell's forces operated in Burma they would be under Wavell's control. And Stilwell acted as liaison officer between Wavell and the difficult Chiang, as well as being in charge of lend-lease aid to our Allies in the Far East. Stilwell's mission was to keep open the Burma Road and fly supplies into China over the hump of the Himalayas from India. It was a needlessly confused command setup and led to trouble.[49]

Nor was "Vinegar Joe" Stilwell an unalloyed asset, despite his keen mind, knowledge of the Chinese army and language, and considerable soldierly talents. His nickname indicated sourness of temper, but his chestnut-burr-under-the-saddle temperament came largely from impatience with procrastination, corruption, and inefficiency. It had usually been that way since his birth in Florida in 1883 and his graduation from West Point in 1904, where he had later been an instructor. Stilwell served in the Philippines from 1904 to 1906 and from 1911 to 1912, and he was a staff officer at the general headquarters of the AEF in France. He was at Tientsin in 1926-1929, and was military attaché in Peiping, 1935-1939. Before World War II, Vinegar Joe was a brigade, then a division comander. In March 1942 he was appointed (with his superiors' blessings) commander of the Fifth and Sixth Chinese armies in Burma by Chiang. Unfortunately, Stilwell and Chiang could not, or would not, get along amicably with each other; one of the mildest epithets Stilwell called Chiang was "The Peanut." Such a tragic relationship did not augur well for future operations.[50]

The enemy did not keep the Allies waiting long in the CBI theater. From Siam a Japanese army of some eighteen thousand invaded Burma on 10 January 1942. Although the defending forces had almost equal numbers, they were inferior in mobility and tactical ability and were badly dispersed. Moreover, they again underestimated the enemy and were overinvolved in fighting delaying actions. Rangoon and then Mandalay were captured by the enterprising Nipponese. Colonel Claire Chennault's American Volunteer Group (the famed "Flying Tigers") and their Curtis P-40s, under United States command helped out until exhausted. An expeditionary force into Burma comprising two Chinese armies, under the command of Stilwell, was defeated along with the British. So the Allies were obliged to evacuate Burma, via land and air, by May 1942.

Stilwell blamed the debacle on a bad tactical situation, apathy, poor communications and supply, Chiang's interference, and a "stupid, gutless command." The Burma Road was now closed and China completely blockaded. After cutting his way through almost impassable terrain to escape into India, Vinegar Joe frankly acknowledged, "I claim we got a hell of a beating. We got run out of Burma and . . . I think we ought to find out what caused it, go back, and retake it." But it was not until October 1943 that the reconquest of Burma would begin, and it would take until May 1945 to achieve.[51]

The only island in the Marianas not already controlled by Japan was Guam, held by the United States since 1898. Strengthening of fortifications on this strategic island had been forbidden since 1922 by the Washington Conference treaties, but even after Japan renounced these pacts and the situation began to deteriorate in the western Pacific, the American Congress refused appropriations to expand the feeble existing defenses there. On Guam were a naval vessel refueling station, a transoceanic cable relay, a naval radio station, and a stop for Pan American clippers. The United States garrison of 400 naval personnel and 155 marines had no real fortifications behind which to fight. After several air attacks on 8–10 December 1941 the Japanese landed about 6,000 troops on the western shore of the island. The American commander, after early courageous fighting, realized the hopelessness of the situation and swiftly yielded in order to save the lives of the 20,000 civilians on Guam.[52]

Just to the northeast of Australia is the huge island of New Guinea, and northeast of it are the islands of the Bismarck Archipelago. Chief of these is New Britain, and on the northeast coast of this island was Rabaul, which contained one of the very finest natural harbors in the entire southwest Pacific. The Japanese were determined to seize Rabaul and use it as an important base on their planned imperial perimeter. Therefore in December 1941, from their great base at Truk in the Carolines, "Rising-Sun" planes began raids on Rabaul. These culminated on 20 January 1942 in a devastating air raid by 126 planes. On 22 December another heavy strike silenced the Aussie garrison's coastal guns. This was followed by an invasion of 5,300 enemy troops from Guam. The disorganized 1,400-man garrison was defeated, only 400 escaping capture or death, and Rabaul was added to the Japanese column.[53]

Outlying from the Hawaiian Islands, 1,137 miles northwest of Oahu, was Midway, made up of two low, sandy islands encircled by a small atoll. Midway was a transoceanic cable relay station and a Pan American clipper stopover point. The marine detachment defending the island numbered 843; they had six 5-inch and twelve 3-inch guns, thirty .30-caliber and some .50-caliber machine guns. On the night of 7 December 1941 two Japanese destroyers, in a hit-and-run raid, shelled the Midway air base, killing four and doing some damage. But the American garrison was steadily reinforced in ensuing months. Johnston Island, to the south and nearer to Oahu than to Midway, was fired upon in December by Japanese submarines, but with little damage; the American return fire was also ineffective. An enemy sub also lightly shelled Palmyra Island. Japanese forces with little trouble seized Tarawa and Makin islands in the British-controlled Gilberts along the equator, and it would require hellish combat later to regain them.[54]

Due west of Oahu and north of the Marshall Islands was another American bastion, Wake Island, consisting of a coral-surrounded lagoon. The United States belatedly began strengthening Wake's military installations, and there were some one thousand civilian construction workers there, plus five hundred marines (some one hundred of whom initially had no weapons). A dozen ill-equipped Grumman "Wildcat" planes had also just arrived. There was no radar nor any warning devices, and the artillery pieces were only partially emplaced when on 8 December 1941 the Japanese began a series of destructive air raids from the Marshalls. The few patched and repatched marine planes gave a good account of themselves until none was flyable. A naval relief force, ordered forth by Kimmel at Pearl Harbor, headed for Wake but was recalled when the fate of the island appeared sealed.

The Japanese, after capturing Guam, dispatched a surface naval force that bombarded Wake, but Maj. James P. S. Devereux's marines repulsed the enemy, sinking two Japanese destroyers and damaging other vessels. Then Japanese carrier planes joined in the assault on Wake, wreaking heavy destruction. On 23 December, one thousand enemy troops landed, even though the leathernecks sank a destroyer transport and damaged another. After courageous resistance and learning of the turn-about of the American relief force, Devereux and his officers were compelled to surrender after losing one-fifth of their men. But they had killed about seven hundred Japanese before yielding.[55]

Standing tall and unafraid in command in the Philippines was Douglas MacArthur. This remarkable and controversial soldier was born in 1880 in Little Rock, Arkansas, the son of an army officer who would become famous in the Philippine Insurrection and attain three-star rank. Douglas graduated from the military academy first in the class of 1903, and achieved one of the highest records ever scored at West Point. He served in the Philippines, China, Siam, Java, Malaya, Burma, India, Ceylon, and Japan, and as aide-de-camp to President Theodore Roosevelt, followed by service on the General Staff.

In the First World War he commanded the Eighty-fourth Infantry Brigade and the Forty-second (Rainbow) Division, was twice wounded, and was highly decorated. He was named superintendent of West Point in 1919, where he instituted needed reforms; and made brigadier general the following year. MacArthur returned to the Philippines as commander of the Manila District, 1922–1925, was promoted to major general in 1925, and jumped to full general in 1930. He was army chief of staff from 1930 to 1935, when he became director of the Philippine national defense organization. He was named a field marshal in the Philippine army in 1936, and retired the following year from the United States Army. He was recalled as general to active duty on 26 July 1941 as commander of American forces in the Far East.

There have been few more complex figures in history than Douglas MacArthur. His character and personality have baffled many would-be chroniclers. He was highly intelligent, widely read and had a keen, analytical, and retentive mind. He believed in destiny and was almost messianic in outlook. An egotistical man, he could be pompous, bordering on the insubordinate, and narrow-minded. Yet at other times he was warm, even humorous, and gracious. A stauncher American patriot never breathed air. He kept abreast of military developments in tactics as well as in weapons, and was outstanding in mastering complex problems.

MacArthur was tenacious and courageous when fighting on the defensive against overwhelming numbers, and audacious, sagacious, and far-sighted in outguessing an enemy when operating on the offensive. He grasped the big picture as well as the narrower tactical scene, and he would prove adept in actions involving combined arms and joint operations of the land, air, and sea forces of many nations. Most high-ranking officers, including those of the navy and Army Air Forces such as Gen. George C. Kenney and Adm. William F. Halsey, were unstinting in their praise of his fairness, his generalship, and his command abilities. In the early, dark days of Allied defeat in the Far East and southwest Pacific, MacArthur became a symbol of unyielding opposition to the Japanese aggressor and hope for eventual triumph in the vast reaches of the greatest of oceans. These visions would not be disappointed as he would conduct a masterly campaign resulting in final victory over the sons of Nippon.[56]

In the gallant and capable but hopeless defense of the Philippines against overwhelming Japanese forces, which had aerial and naval as well as ground superiority over the weak Allied forces, MacArthur was ably seconded by Maj. Gen. Jonathan M. Wainwright IV, who would have the onerous duty of surrendering the pitiful remnant of American and Filipino troops to the conquering enemy.

For his defense of the Philippines, MacArthur had just 12,000 Philippine Scouts, 19,000 United States Army troops, and 100,000 new levies of partly trained and semiequipped soldiers, concentrated in the main on the island of Luzon. Many of the 250 Allied planes, which included 107 P-40s and 35 B-17s, had been destroyed on the ground by the Japanese sneak air attacks of 8 December against Clark Field and other air bases. This fiasco occurred largely because of the lack of dispersal areas and suitable radar or antiaircraft guns. Japanese landings were made on 10 December on the northern coast of Luzon at Aparri and on the northwestern shore at Vigan, but the main thrust came on 22 December on the west coast at Lingayen Gulf. MacArthur was forced to wage delaying actions while he withdrew his raw and ill-equipped forces onto the Bataan Peninsula, jutting southward into Manila Bay. The capital of Manila was declared an open city, but the enemy bombed and shelled it anyway.

An epic stand was made on Bataan until April 1942, the Japanese attacking with superior land, air, and sea forces. Suffering malnutrition and physical exhaustion from less than half-rations of horse and mule meat, an Allied remnant withdrew to Corregidor, where a brave stand was made into May. After declining several orders to escape to safety to Australia, MacArthur, on personal orders from President Roosevelt, was evacuated to Mindanao by PT-boats commanded by John Bulkeley. MacArthur, his wife and son, and a small staff were flown to Australia, vowing "I shall return!"

The big 12-inch disappearing rifles and other guns on Corregidor did well but were handicapped by being battered in obsolete, unhardened emplacements open to air attack. Finally, overwhelmed by superior enemy forces, Wainwright was obliged to surrender his remnants on 6 May 1942, only to have his men subjected to the infamous "Bataan Death March" to the prison pens. Nonetheless, the five-month stand at Bataan and Corregidor slowed the Japanese a bit; the enemy still underestimated the fighting qualities of the Americans.[57]

THE ONWARD TIDE of Japanese conquest flowed unrelentingly in the winter of 1941–1942 with the dramatic capture of the rich Dutch East Indies. For success, the Japanese had only to await destruction of American air power on Luzon and British naval power at Singapore. Some 60 million people inhabited the Indies, 40 million of them on Java. This vast archipelago of literally thousands of islands and islets stretches nearly thirty-five hundred miles in a huge crescent from Timor, just to the northwest of Darwin, Australia, to Sumatra, which extends to the west of Malaya. These islands constituted a stepping stone almost connecting the continents of Asia and Australia so wealthy in oil, rubber, and tin that they could keep the Japanese war machine running for years.

In spite of a minor Allied naval success in Macassar Strait on 24 January 1942, the enemy swiftly seized Celebes and Borneo. Wavell arrived on Java on 10 January to assume command of the American-British-Dutch-Australian Command (ABDACOM), but he was soon impelled to depart for India on 25 February as the Japanese surge continued in the Indies with persistent air attacks on bases and shipping. A disparate Allied naval squadron was soundly defeated, after some small initial successes, on 27 and 28 February in Sunda Strait and in the Java Sea, with the loss of several cruisers and lesser men-of-war. Sumatra and the Moluccas were taken next by the Nipponese. Then Java and Timor were invaded and captured, the Dutch formally surrendering the entire Netherlands East Indies to the Japanese on 9 March. Australia now was threatened with invasion, if the foe could not be halted somewhere to the north and northeast of Australia in his southward advance.[58]

To stem the tide, the Allied leaders named Adm. Chester W. Nimitz commander of the Pacific Ocean Areas, and Gen. Douglas MacArthur commander of the southwest Pacific theater of operations. The fifty-seven-year-old, silver-haired Nimitz, a native of Texas and an Annapolis graduate in 1905, had been chief of staff of the Atlantic Fleet submarine forces in the First World War and had wide experience in command of several types of major surface warships and squadrons. He made rear admiral in 1938 and was chief of the Bureau of Navigation of the Navy Department from June 1939 to December 1941. He became commander in chief of the Pacific Fleet, with headquarters at Pearl Harbor, and served with distinction throughout the war, making five-star Admiral of the Fleet in 1944. Nimitz was cautious yet enterprising, and he worked well with other high-ranking officers of all branches of the service.

MacArthur and Nimitz were charged with containing the enemy advance and holding Australia and the lines of communication thereto. But theirs seemed a dubious task as the Rising-Sun forces rolled ahead relentlessly. So rapid had been the Japanese conquests that, instead of consolidating and strengthening their defensive perimeter as planned, they were seized with "Victory Disease." They determined to shift their plans to keep the momentum of advance going by throwing forward at once their spearheads to occupy even more territory, looking to a possible early invasion of Australia.[59]

The only bright spot in the otherwise dark Allied situation in the western Pacific in early 1942 was the psychological success scored in the famous 18

April raid upon Tokyo made by Lt. Col. James H. Doolittle's sixteen North American "Mitchell" B-25 Army Air Force medium bombers. Jimmy Doolittle had had a colorful career prior to his assignment to this trying task. Born in Alameda, California, in 1896, he received early education in Nome, Alabama, and in the Los Angeles Junior College, 1914–1916. He graduated from the University of California in 1918, and was a fellow in aeronautical engineering at Massachusetts Institute of Technology in 1924, receiving an M.S. degree that year and a Sc.D. in 1925. He was an army aviator from 1917 to 1930, and manager of the aviation department of Shell Oil Company from 1930 to 1940. In the 1920s and 1930s barnstorming Doolittle was the winner and record holder of many major air races, and in July 1940 he was appointed a major in the Army Air Corps. By 1944 he wore three stars.

Doolittle trained his B-25 crews at Eglin Field, Florida, with practice takeoffs on a runway marked the length and width of an aircraft carrier's flight deck. The daring plan was to strike the Japanese home islands and land behind Chiang Kai-shek's lines in China. Under the command of William F. Halsey, Jr., the small task force was to launch the planes some four hundred miles from Japan. When still over six hundred miles away, Japanese patrol vessels were sighted and the heavily laden B-25's were obliged to take off prematurely but successfully in heavy seas from the carrier *Hornet*. The targets were hit satisfactorily, thirteen of the planes bombing Tokyo and one each hitting Osaka, Kobe, and Nagoya.

The bold raid completely surprised the Japanese, who were baffled by the origin of such comparatively large planes—a mystification that was only deepened by Roosevelt's jocose statement that they had come from "Shangri-La." All sixteen of the B-25s ran out of fuel before they could reach the designated Chinese airfields, but only two crews fell into enemy hands. Doolittle eventually made his way back to England, where he subsequently became commander of the U.S. Eighth Air Force. The news that Tokyo had been bombed electrified the Allied world, despite the relatively small damage wrought by the B-25s, and it was an inducement to the Japanese to expand beyond their original defensive perimeter and acquire additional bases to the east. They now readied forces for a twin attack on the Aleutians and Midway.[60]

Admiral "Bull" Halsey, who commanded the small task force that launched the Doolittle raid, would become one of America's foremost naval heroes in the Pacific. In 1882 he was born in Elizabeth, New Jersey, and in 1904, like his father before him, he graduated from Annapolis, having been the fullback on the Middie football team. In the First World War he was a destroyer commander, and in 1935 he became a naval aviator and captain of the carrier *Saratoga*. A curmudgeon type, he nonetheless worked successfully with MacArthur and George C. Kenney, Fifth Army Air Force commander. On occasion, Halsey could be impetuous, self-assertive, and flamboyant. But he was also physically and morally courageous and had high capacity for hard decision-making. The muscular, 165-pound admiral, with mobile face, bushy eyebrows, square jaw, and piercing eyes, was known for occasional intemperate public statements, a fiery temper, and love of battle as well as for swiftness of movement and boldness of tactics. In the ensuing crucial naval operations, Halsey would prove an invaluable link between the occasionally impatient and seemingly rash F. Jack Fletcher and the steady, cautious but able Raymond A. Spruance.[61]

Meanwhile, the onward rush of victorious Japanese expansion seemed inexorable. The sons of Nippon had seized the Admiralty Islands; the Bismarcks, including Rabaul—which they would build up into a great advanced base—on the northeastern tip of the island of New Britain; and they had invaded several of the Solomon Islands—Bougainville, Choiseul, Vella Lavella, and New Georgia with its important Munda airfield; Rendova; Kolombangara; Guadalcanal, with its useful airstrip; Tulagi; and Florida islands, separated by the Coral Sea, just to the northeast of Australia.

Although the enemy did not reach south of the Solomons to the New Hebrides, where the United States AAF was striving to establish a base at Espiritu Santu for some B-17s, the Japanese were determined to capture Port Moresby. It was here that MacArthur was beginning to develop a major base at his most advanced position remaining in the southwest Pacific. Port Moresby was located on the southwest coast of Papua, in southern New Guinea, which was a huge island extending thirteen hundred miles to the north-northeast of Australia. Capture of Port Moresby by the enemy would not only pave the way for air attacks on Australia and a possible later invasion of that island continent, but it would also enable the Japanese to attack New Caledonia, the Fiji Islands, and Samoa, and interrupt the vital communications and supply line from the United States to Australia.[62]

HOWEVER, the turn of the tide of the Pacific war was about to come, in four pivotal battles. The first was the Battle of the Coral Sea. Having broken the Japanese code, Americans were forewarned that a sizeable enemy task force comprising three aircraft carriers, eleven cruisers, thirteen destroyers and lesser warships coming from Truk around San Cristobal, and five laden troop transports from the northern Solomons were about to enter the Coral Sea in a direct water attack against Port Moresby. Fletcher moved to counter the enemy fleet with a squadron composed of two carriers, *Lexington* and *Yorktown,* and lesser men-of-war.

On 7–8 May 1942, in the first naval battle ever fought in which the opposing surface warships never saw each other or exchanged gunfire, and in which each side committed its share of errors, an exchange of carrier-plane strikes resulted in the loss of *Lexington* and some damage to *Yorktown,* while one Japanese carrier was sunk, a larger one almost destroyed, and the third also suffered some damage. Eighty enemy planes were lost as against American losses of sixty-six. While at best the battle was a draw tactically, the Americans had nonetheless scored a crucial strategic victory, for the foe's task force retired from the Coral Sea and Port Moresby was saved, at least from sea attack. It was the first major check the Japanese navy had suffered in modern times.[63]

The second decisive engagement that helped turn the war around in the

Pacific was Midway. While the loss of *Lexington* meant Nimitz would have one less carrier, the Japanese Adm. Isoroku Yamamoto would have two fewer ones to employ in the massive and daring naval attack he was about to undertake to the north and east. This was no less than a great sweep upon the Midway Islands, with secondary movements against the Aleutians.

Midway, the "Sentry for Hawaii," comprised two islets. Since 1935 one of these had been a touchdown for the Pan American clippers, and since then hundreds of millions of dollars had been spent on building a seaplane base, a large airfield, an artificial harbor, shore defenses, and a ship channel between the two isles into a central lagoon.

So Nimitz determined to fight with all he had when in June 1942 the Japanese approached Midway with a huge armada comprising nine carriers, eleven battleships (including the *Yamato,* a superdreadnought of sixty-four thousand tons that carried nine 18.1-inch guns and belt armor of over 18 inches), eighteen cruisers, fifty-six destroyers, twenty-two submarines, and lesser craft, plus approximately four hundred aircraft and five thousand soldiers aboard transports. What Nimitz had to fight with were just three carriers (*Yorktown, Enterprise,* and *Hornet*), eight cruisers, sixteen destroyers, and nineteen submarines. Code interceptions enabled the Americans to learn enemy intentions.

In the Battle of Midway on 3–4 June 1942, where again surface units did not see each other, Spruance and Fletcher's forces in an exchange of air strikes scored a smashing and essential triumph. With the loss of *Yorktown,* a destroyer, and about 150 planes, the Americans sank four Japanese carriers, one cruiser (another was almost sunk), and caused the loss of approximately 250 enemy planes. The Nipponese air attacks on Midway itself, though destructive, were indecisive; the shattered enemy fleet was compelled to return toward home in humiliating defeat, the greatest it had suffered in three and a half centuries.[64]

In a spin-off, peripheral operation from Yamamoto's main attack upon Midway, the Japanese moved small but sufficient forces against the Aleutian Islands. The American base near the eastern end of the chain, Dutch Harbor, was bombed on 3 and 4 June 1942, the second raid doing considerable damage. The enemy task force comprised two carriers, eight cruisers, fifteen destroyers, and five submarines, against which Rear Adm. Robert A. Theobald could muster only five cruisers, eleven destroyers, and six submarines. What caused the exodus of the Japanese squadron from its position to attack Dutch Harbor were the attacks of American land-based planes against the enemy, although no damage was done to the enemy fleet.

On 6 June the island of Kiska, near the extreme western end of the Aleutians, was occupied by a Nipponese naval landing battalion, and on 7 June Attu was taken by an enemy army battalion. The landings were unseen by the Americans through the fog for four days; by then it was too late to budge the foe from his firmly established beachheads. Because of the usual foul weather, raids and counterraids had to be kept to a minimum. The Japanese bases on Kiska and Attu, their only ones in the Western Hemisphere, hurt only American pride, although the United States would later insist on reconquering them.[65]

The third critical battle that checked the Japanese advance in the southwest Pacific took place in Papua, New Guinea, for control of significant Port Moresby and other points. With climate and terrain among the most inhospitable on earth, Papua featured lowlands replete with mangrove swamps and tropical jungles, and its Owen Stanley mountain range, which runs lengthwise down the Papuan peninsula, parallel to the coasts, was largely covered with moss forests. Until recent times cannibalistic headhunters roamed these jungles.

In March 1942 the Japanese occupied Salamaua and Lae, established bases, and then seized Gona and the Buna mission on the coast across the Owen Stanleys from Port Moresby. Veteran enemy troops began to push from Buna along the Kokoda Trail over the mountains and by 17 September reached a point just thirty-two miles from Port Moresby and only twenty from its airfield. Here, in sharp fighting, MacArthur's Australian troops checked the Japanese advance and threw them back toward Buna-Gona; the enemy leader drowned, and his soldiers were decimated by disease and starvation in the wild countryside. In late July the overconfident Nipponese were repulsed by the Allies in their attempt to seize Milne Bay at the extreme eastern tip of New Guinea and its airport under construction.

The American Thirty-second Infantry Division was airlifted over the Owen Stanleys by George C. Kenney's Fifth Air Force in an attempt to dislodge the enemy, now strongly ensconced in his Buna-Gona stronghold. The fifty-three-year-old Kenney, born in Nova Scotia and a graduate of the Massachusetts Institute of Technology, had been a civilian construction engineer until he became a lieutenant in the Army Air Service in the First World War and worked his way up in that branch. Criticized by MacArthur when he first arrived in the southwest Pacific for less than desirable air results, Kenney staunchly replied that it was scarcely his fault and that the Fifth Air Force would develop quickly, which it did. Kenney and the supreme allied commander got along famously thereafter.

Other equally inexperienced American ground forces moved over the Kokoda Trail and up along the coast from Milne Bay to join the thirty-second in investing Buna-Gona. But they and the exhausted Aussies bogged down in the swamps, were hit by tropical fever, and suffered deficiencies of food and ammunition. The six weeks of ineffectual combat reduced Allied numbers by 50 percent and lowered morale.

It took the arrival on the scene of Lt. Gen. Robert L. Eichelberger to expedite matters. Urbana, Ohio, was the site of his birth in 1886, and he graduated from the military academy in 1909. Eichelberger then served in the Panama Canal Zone and on the Mexican border as well as in Siberia in 1918 and later in China and Japan. Service on the General Staff had been followed by his superintendency of the military academy, 1940–1942, before coming out to New Guinea. He rallied the disheartened troops and resumed the offensive—finally with success. On 9 December 1942 the Australians captured Gona, and on 2 January 1943 the Americans took Buna, all enemy resistance being extinguished in the hotly contested area by 22 January.

Like Coral Sea and Midway, the Papuan campaign was a turning point in the Pacific war. For the first time (the Guadalcanal fighting was still continu-

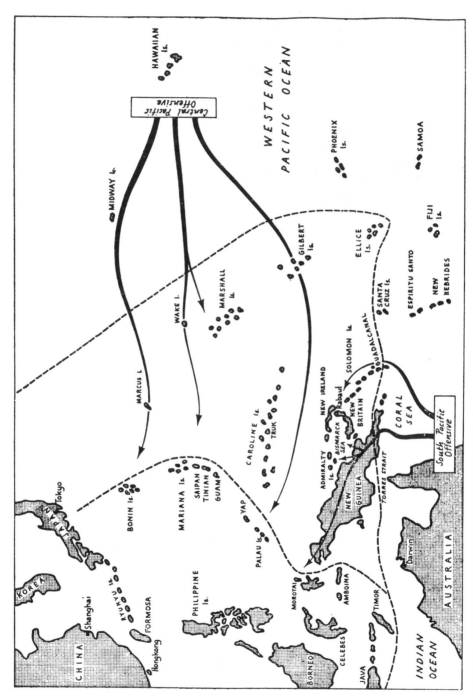

FIG. 14.5. STRATEGY OF THE WESTERN PACIFIC, 1942–1944

ing) experienced enemy ground troops had been bettered by green Allied soldiers and dug out of their strong defenses. In addition, Allied troops were transported and supplied for the first time by air alone. It was not an inconsiderable triumph, but a long and difficult campaign up the northeast coast of New Guinea would be required before Japanese resistance would be smashed there.[66]

The fourth pivotal operation that wrenched the initiative in the Pacific from Japan and marked the reversal of their hitherto seemingly invincible progress was the campaign for the Solomon Island of Guadalcanal, site of an important airstrip soon known as Henderson Field. In July 1942 the Japanese landed on Guadalcanal and worked feverishly on the vital runway. The commander of the South Pacific Command, Adm. R. L. Ghormley (replaced by Admiral Halsey on 18 October), ordered the taking of the airfield as well as the excellent anchorage between Tulagi and Florida islands, some twenty miles northeast of Guadalcanal.

Two assaults were made by the First Marine Division at the same time on Guadalcanal and Tulagi on 7 August 1942. Encountering sharp resistance only on Tulagi, the leathernecks made good progress at first on Guadalcanal and captured Henderson Field. But the Japanese reacted violently, pressaging half a year of heavy land, sea, and air fighting on, over, and around Guadalcanal as the Japanese poured forces, piecemeal, down from Rabaul. The Rising Sun's so-called Tokyo Express made almost nightly runs down the "Slot" between the two chains of islands of the Solomons group, bringing in reinforcements, equipment, and supplies. By September and October of 1942 the situation for the Allies was ominous, even when army units came to the aid of the marines. Fighting in the gloomy jungles and on the ridges was ferocious.

Naval warfare fluctuated, at first in Japan's favor, in the waters around Guadalcanal. In seven distinct naval engagements in which the Japanese showed their prowess in night-fighting, each side lost twenty-four warships; enemy losses included one carrier, two battleships, and one cruiser, while the Allies lost two carriers (*Wasp* and *Hornet*) and eight cruisers. In one action, the Japanese lost eleven troop transports. The biggest of the naval engagements, the Battle of Guadalcanal on 12–15 November 1942, determined who would control the seas around Guadalcanal, and the Nipponese lost sixteen ships, including the two battleships.

By 4 January 1943 the First Marine Division was replaced by the army's Fourteenth Corps, and in a month the last of the enemies' organized soldiers were exterminated, but a few die-hards continued to exist in the boondocks of the island. Of the forty-two thousand enemy troops, two thousand were successfully evacuated; but twenty-four thousand were killed, fifteen thousand died of disease, and five hundred were captured. Aided by the famous civilian "coastwatchers" on several of the Solomon Islands, Halsey coordinated his operations with MacArthur effectively and the seemingly lost situation was redeemed. Allied air, land, and sea forces were capably handled, and the enemy was able to get only some 20 percent of his supplies through safely from Rabaul to Guadalcanal. The Nipponese suffered from lack of food, ammunition, and heavy equipment. Yet the Japanese might have won anyway had they first gathered their forces and then struck en masse instead of striving to take the island by piecemeal efforts.[67]

AT THE Casablanca Conference, the Combined Chiefs of Staff in January 1943 determined to continue the new strategic offensive against Japan within the parameter of the limited means available for the Pacific. MacArthur's drive from the south toward the Philippines and Japan itself would complement another converging drive under Nimitz from the Central Pacific.

Within his own theater, MacArthur now had local air and naval superiority and engineered two converging, simultaneous operations designed to isolate Japan's great base at Rabaul. The southern drive on New Guinea's northeastern coast was commanded by Lt. Gen. Walter Krueger, and the northern drive in the Solomons was led by Halsey.

Krueger was an interesting character. Born in Germany, he attended Cincinati Technical School (1896–1898) and served in the army ranks in Cuba in the Spanish-American War. He became a lieutenant in 1901 and saw combat action in the Philippine Insurrection. He was on the Mexican border in 1916 and in the AEF tank corps in France, 1918–1919. Krueger then became an instructor at the Army War College at Fort Leavenworth, and at the Naval War College. He was the chief of the War Plans Division of the War Department General Staff and member of the Joint Army-Navy Board from 1936–1938. He commanded the Second Division, 1939–1940, the Eighth Corps, 1940–1941, and the Third Army from May 1941 to February 1943.

In June 1943, after the Buna campaign, two regimental combat teams seized Trobriand and Woodlark Islands off the eastern tip of New Guinea. Airfields carved out on these isles enabled MacArthur to advance on Salamaua, which fell on 11 September 1943. The important forward enemy port and air base of Lae was wrested from the Nipponese on 16 September after stubborn fighting. Australian ground forces had been aided by American forces. Employing vigorous air attacks and outguessing the enemy time and again, MacArthur swiftly struck next at Finschhafen, which fell on 2 October. The Huon Peninsula on which Finschhafen is situated was completely in Allied hands by February 1944. Saidor, farther along the coast, had been seized in early January 1944 and an airstrip put in use there. Bypassed enemy garrisons, isolated in the fantastically grim terrain, lacked air cover and were left to wither and die on the vine rather than be dug out of their stout defenses at high cost to the attacking force.[68]

While the New Guinea operation was generally proceeding smoothly, the swing northward through the Solomons was gaining momentum. The seizure of Rendova Island enabled the Fourteenth Corps to emplace artillery with which to bombard the larger island of New Georgia which, with its important airfield at Munda, was captured between 30 June and 5 August 1943. The strongly held island of Kolombangara was bypassed, and Vella Lavella island was taken by the Fourteenth Corps by 9 October.

The Third Marine Division, preceded by diversionary landings in northwestern Choiseul, came ashore in western Bougainville at Empress Augusta

Bay on 1 November after a navy sweep had taken place. Three airfields and a naval base were set up at this point, thereby bringing within easy air range the great Japanese base at Rabaul, some 235 miles away on New Britain in the Bismarcks. This large enemy installation was hammered by Halsey's task force, the remaining Japanese facilities in the Solomons having been neutralized. To gain control of Dampier and Vitiaz Straits and the western part of New Britain, army forces landed at Arawe on 15 September, and marines seized an airdrome to the northwest on nearby Cape Gloucester on 30 September, thus securing the western area of the island. With Allied air and naval superiority evident, the enemy could expect no relief from the relentless advances in the southwest Pacific and elsewhere.[69]

To the north, Japanese occupation of Kiska and Attu in the fogbound Aleutians made the American high command uneasy and they determined to eliminate this remote threat to Alaska and continental United States. In the eleven months after the seizure of these two islands by the enemy, the Americans occupied islands to the east in the chain and constructed airfields. So close was the surveillance by the United States Eleventh Air Force that the Japanese had to run food and supplies by submarine into their garrisons of 5,400 on Kiska and 2,500 on Attu.

In the interim the American Seventh Division underwent desert training in California and amphibious exercises on the northwest coast. In April 1943 it was moved to Cold Bay, east of Dutch Harbor. Finally, after delays caused by miserable weather in the Aleutians, the Seventh Division moved to attack Attu on 11 May, accompanied by the task force of Adm. Thomas C. Kinkaid, a native of Hanover, New Hampshire. It took the 12,000 GIs some three weeks of bitter fighting to annihilate the enemy on Attu, at a cost of 561 Americans killed and 1,136 wounded. The large body of bypassed Japanese on Kiska was evacuated by light vessels in the fog on 29 July. The Americans and some Canadians occupied Kiska on 15 August. In ensuing months United States aircraft would fly from bases in the Aleutians—when the vile weather permitted—to bomb enemy installations in the Kurile Islands to the northeast of the main Japanese home islands.[70]

A movement against the Admiralty Islands, originally scheduled for April 1944, was pushed up at Kenney's suggestion, after MacArthur daringly accompanied advance elements aboard Kinkaid's transports and destroyers that reconnoitered Los Negros Island on 29 February. It was found that there were two airfields and a splendid anchorage, Seeadler ("Sea Eagle") Harbor, between the two main islands of Los Negros and the larger Manus and some islets. This harbor was 260 miles west of Kavieng and 200 miles northeast of New Guinea. Planning coordination was entrusted to Krueger, who chose the reinforced First Cavalry Division for the assault on the Admiralties.

After sluggish initial Japanese resistance, the advance American party beat off sudden, desperate enemy attacks and hung on until the bulk of the main force arrived on 9 March and captured Los Negros. Artillery, planes, and tanks led the way in an invasion of Manus on 15 March and secured the valuable airfields and Seeadler Harbor against occasionally heavy opposition, and isolated Japanese resistance was smothered by 18 May. The expansive harbor became one of the busiest in the Pacific, with major repair facilities for even the largest of warships. Conquest of the Admiralties helped considerably the advances on New Guinea and in the central Pacific that were going on simultaneously.[71]

Nimitz's sweep across the vast central Pacific theater of operations was one of unprecedented scope and distance. With the Japanese occupied by MacArthur's steamroller tactics in the southwest Pacific, Nimitz selected Makin and Tarawa in the Gilbert islands, a former British possession astride the equator some fourteen hundred miles northwest of Samoa and now held by the enemy, as his first main objective (operation GALVANIC) in the westward thrust. Some 2,540 construction workers were still strengthening the islands' defenses, especially on Tarawa. The Japanese had 260 troops on Makin, where there was a seaplane base, and 2,700 on Tarawa, where there was an air base. On Tarawa in particular they were strongly dug into fortified pillboxes and protected by beach obstacles and mines. Admiral Richmond Kelly Turner commanded the overall operation, while marine Maj. Gen. Holland M. ("Howling Mad") Smith led the ground forces. The atolls of Tarawa and Makin were heavily bombarded by warships and by army, navy, and marine planes. The assault landings commenced on 21 November 1943. Makin was easily overrun late on 23 November by a regimental combat team of the army's Twenty-seventh Infantry Division and some 700 enemy soldiers and civilians were killed.

Yet on Betio island on the Tarawa atoll, the Second Marine Division encountered ferocious enemy resistance from formidable fortifications and Japanese artillery that had been only lightly damaged by the preliminary bombardments. Many landing craft got hung up on the coral reefs, and for a day and a night the marines were pinned down on the beach. But the leathernecks finally broke out and in furious fighting mopped up organized resistance by 24 November. While sustaining casualties of 985 slain and 2,193 wounded, the marines killed 4,500 Japanese. Few military prisoners were taken on either island. The Tarawa battle proved the need for amphibious tractors, which in future operations would be invaluable in surmounting the reefs and moving across the beaches.[72]

Admiral Nimitz's next objective was the several atolls in the Marshall Islands, located to the northwest of the Gilberts and to the east-northeast of Truk in the Carolines. Two days of intensive naval bombardment preceded the landings that were made on 31 January 1944. The army's Seventh Infantry Division, veterans of Attu, stormed ashore on the southern isles of Kwajalein atoll while the Fourth Marine Division struck the beaches on the northern edge at Roi and Namur. While not so deadly as on Tarawa, Japanese resistance was strong; by 8 February the enemy was crushed on Kwajalein, the defenders killed almost to a man. Prior to the combat landings on Eniwetok atoll, carrier planes pounded the defenses. On 19 February combat teams of the marines and of the army's Twenty-seventh Infantry Division hit the beaches, and by 22 February effected the capture of the atoll. The mighty Japanese base at Truk was now more open to air assault and interdiction until it could be further isolated.[73]

Since July 1942 the Japanese Combined Fleet had been based at Truk, capital of the Caroline Islands under both German and Japanese mandates, and it provided the best fleet anchorage in any of the enemy islands, as well as an air base. Unlike most atolls, the Truk islands were volcanic and attained elevations of fifteen hundred feet. Although most formidable to direct sea attack, Truk was vulnerable to air strikes from fast carrier forces. Warned on 4 February 1944 by a marine plane that took important air photographs of Truk, the Japanese hurriedly moved most of their men-of-war to the Palaus to the west. Nonetheless, on 17 February Adm. Marc Mitscher's Task Force Fifty-eight struck hard at Truk.

The rugged, beetle-browed Mitscher, born in 1887 in Hillsboro, Wisconsin, graduated from the naval academy in 1910 and had been associated with naval aviation since 1915. He was a pilot on the first navy trans-Atlantic flight in 1919 and had been executive officer of the carriers *Langley* and *Saratoga.* Mitscher was assistant chief of the Bureau of Aeronautics from 1939 to 1941, when he made rear admiral. He had commanded *Hornet* in the Doolittle raid on Tokyo and another carrier in the Battle of Midway. He was naval air commander in the Solomons from April to June, 1943.

In his 17 February 1944 strike on Truk, Mitscher had available the planes of no less than nine carriers in his Task Force Fifty-eight. Thirty Japanese planes were shot down and another forty were destroyed on the ground. Nipponese torpedo planes damaged the carrier *Intrepid,* but an American carrier night air attack—the first of the war—wreaked havoc on enemy ground installations and destruction was increased in follow-up raids the next morning. Some 220,000 tons of Japanese shipping were sunk, including a light cruiser and destroyer in follow-up raids.[74]

In an attempt to possibly bypass Truk as well as pave the way for assaults on the Mariana Islands and the Philippines, the American navy hoped to bring to battle a sizeable portion of the enemy fleet. When a powerful Japanese naval force was reported entering the Philippine Sea, Spruance moved his Fifth Fleet to engage it. In gigantic air battles that raged on 19 June 1944, the Americans shot down 402 of 545 enemy planes sighted, while Americans suffered just 26 lost. On the following day Spruance brought the main enemy fleet units to battle. His planes bagged a Japanese carrier and two tankers, and severely damaged four more carriers, a battleship, a cruiser, and another tanker, while American submarines sank two more enemy carriers. It was a dark day for the Imperial Navy, which retired from the Philippine Sea post haste.[75]

In the meantime MacArthur's forces were wrapping up the long but brilliant New Guinea campaign in preparation for further offensive action to the north. In leapfrog tactics, usually preceded by softening-up air attacks, the Americans, aided by Australian and previously by New Zealand troops, constantly outguessed the enemy and scored an unbroken series of successes over frightful terrain and in inclement weather against still tenacious defenders.

The next jump was one of some 400 miles to Hollandia, where Humboldt Bay proved to be a useful supply and naval base, and where three good airfields existed. At Aitape, 125 miles southeast of Hollandia and within range of land-based fighter plane protection, another airstrip had been built by the Japanese. On 22 April 1944 MacArthur's forces, supported by carrier planes, surprised the enemy's five thousand troops at Hollandia, and by 30 April the airfields were in American hands. Some fifty thousand Nipponese soldiers had been cut off to the southeast. The army's Forty-first Infantry Division landed in May on Biak Island, another 330 miles to the northwest, and by 22 June the eight thousand enemy troops, despite their bitter defense, were overcome and the three airstrips there were in Allied service.

In early July, in another surprise attack supported by paratroopers, a regimental combat team seized Noemfoor Island and its airfields. This enabled MacArthur's forces to practically eliminate enemy air power over New Guinea. Still farther northwest on the Vogelkop Peninsula at the tip of New Guinea, units of the Sixth Division captured more naval and air bases at Sansapor on 30 July 1944, and this additional surprise attack defeated eighteen thousand Nipponese soldiers.

In a little over a year the Allies had come some thirteen hundred miles along New Guinea's coast and had bypassed over 135,000 enemy troops who were left impotent in the rear. Kenney's Army Air Force bombers in the meantime were striking hard at Japanese installations in Java, Celebes, Borneo, and Timor in the Dutch East Indies as the war was pressed ever closer to the enemy homeland.[76]

Instead of assaulting Truk and the Carolines directly, Nimitz decided to bypass them and strike at the Marianas (operation FORAGER). On 15 June 1944 Holland Smith's Fifth Marine Amphibious Corps attacked Saipan, the Second and Fourth Marine Divisions hitting the beaches first, soon followed by the army's Twenty-seventh Infantry Division. Severe fighting of the harshest nature continued for twenty-five days before Saipan was in Allied possession, though several more months were needed to mop up enemy diehards. Some 27,000 Japanese were killed and 2,000 captured, American losses being 3,126 killed, 326 missing, and 13,160 wounded. Army-marine cooperation was marred when marine Gen. Holland Smith abruptly relieved from command army Maj. Gen. Ralph C. Smith. Soon after Saipan had been captured, American Twenty-fourth Corps artillery, assisted by fighter planes of the Seventh Air Force, began pounding Tinian. Elements of the Marine Second and Fourth Divisions struck the island on 24 July and, in sharp combat, wrested it from the foe by 2 August.

Burning to recapture the former American island of Guam in the Marianas, the army's Seventy-seventh Infantry Division, the Third Marine Division, and another marine brigade attacked Guam on 21 July following one of the Pacific war's heaviest and most sustained naval and air bombardments that lasted thirteen days. In savage jungle fighting, the enemy was driven onto the northern end of Guam and was snuffed out by 10 August. About 17,000 Japanese were killed and 485 taken prisoner at a loss of 2,000 Americans killed and 7,000 wounded. Soon planes from Saipan were striking at the Palau, Volcano, and Bonin Islands. On 24 November 1944 huge B-29 bombers began direct and increasingly destructive raids on the Japanese home islands.[77]

Another stepping stone for MacArthur's return to the Philippines was

Morotai, just north of Halmahera (whose large garrisoned island would be bypassed) in the Moluccas, northwest of the Vogelkop Peninsula on New Guinea. Morotai was invaded on 15 September 1944 and captured.[78] On the same day that MacArthur struck at the Moluccas, Nimitz's forces invaded the Palaus, northeast of the Moluccas, due west of Truk, and directly east of Mindanao in the Philippines. It is possible that the Palaus could have been bypassed instead of directly attacked.

Approximately forty thousand Japanese soldiers in the Palaus were assaulted by twenty-four thousand marines and twenty thousand army troops. Halsey commanded the operation. Especially ferocious was the two-and-a-half-month struggle for Peleliu, strongest of the Palaus. Temperatures of 115°F and a shortage of water made the operation more difficult. Nearby Angaur fell in one month's hard combat, and Ulithi to the northeast of Yap was taken without opposition. Unfortunately, the Palau airfields proved to be of less value than anticipated, strengthening Halsey's argument that Peleliu and the other islands of the group should have been passed by. But Ulithi atoll, in the western Carolines, provided a good naval base.[79]

A cordial but firmly argued debate took place between MacArthur and Nimitz over Formosa and an island (Okinawa) in the Ryukyus. Roosevelt, in conference in Hawaii with these two fine theater commanders, was soon convinced as were the Joint Chiefs by MacArthur's reasoning and directed that he keep the faith and redeem his pledge to "return" to the Philippines.

The island of Leyte was chosen for the initial landings, to be followed by the reconquest of Luzon and others of the archipelago. Halsey's task force destroyed nearly two thousand enemy aircraft in the Philippines, Formosa, and the Ryukyus in September 1944. On 20 October, accompanied by MacArthur, personally, the Tenth and Twenty-fourth Corps of Krueger's Sixth Army stormed ashore on Leyte's east coast, a heavy naval bombardment having opened the contest. In reaction, the desperate Japanese determined to risk most of their remaining navy in bringing the American fleet to battle off Leyte, not only to destroy as many United States men-of-war as possible, but also to smash the invading ground forces on the island beaches.[80]

The resulting naval battle for Leyte Gulf was the greatest of the war, fully comparable to Jutland in the First World War. Approaching Leyte in several columns and aided by land-based planes in the Philippines, the enemy had the following formidable fleet available for action on the water to pit against the mighty American armada: nine battleships, four carriers, thirteen heavy cruisers, six light cruisers, and thirty-four destroyers.

In the battle, Halsey's large carrier task force was lured off to the northeast ("Halsey's End Run") in pursuit of Rising-Sun carriers deliberately used as decoys. This risky action exposed American troops on the beaches of Leyte and their supply and supporting vessels to the other enemy naval forces coming at them. Fortunately Rear Adm. Jesse B. Oldendorf was equal to the crisis. His superior, Kinkaid, in command of the strong Seventh Fleet, had available six old battleships (each of which had been badly damaged at Pearl Harbor), sixteen small and slow escort carriers, eleven cruisers, and eighty-eight destroyers.

Thus on 25 October, when the enemy force came through Surigao Strait,

Oldendorf's cruisers and battleships "crossed the T," poured a devastating fire upon the Nipponese and practically destroyed the enemy force, including sinking two battleships. In Halsey's engagement, and in others making up the sprawling Battle of Leyte Gulf, enemy losses were compounded and reached the staggering total of three battleships (one of them the monster sixty-four-thousand-ton *Musashi*, which carried nine 18.1-inch guns), four aircraft carriers, six heavy cruisers, four light cruisers, and nine destroyers against American losses of just one light carrier (*Princeton*), two small "jeep" carriers, and two destroyers. The shattered remnants of the enemy naval forces fled, the Imperial Japanese Navy never able again to challenge the expanding American fleet. By the end of December 1944 the Nipponese were all but crushed in the land fighting on Leyte, Eichelberger's Eighth Army taking over from Krueger's Sixth Army that had significant business elsewhere.[81]

On Luzon were 235,000 Japanese troops, and they were reinforced by many more. Boldly steaming from Leyte through the Sulu and Mindanao Seas, Krueger's Sixth Army, composed of the First and Fourteenth Corps, was preceded by Kenney's heavy aerial softening up of enemy targets on Luzon. These included the transportation facilities to prevent Yamashita from shifting troops to the landing point, Lingayen Gulf on the northwest of the island. Guerrillas cooperated in sabotage activities. Feints toward the southeast coast of Luzon confused the Japanese to the extent that when Krueger's soldiers struck the beaches on 9 January 1945 he was able on the first day to land sixty-eight thousand soldiers on a fifteen-mile beachhead that had become six thousand yards deep. Elements of the Eighth Army landed at Subic Bay on 29 January and promptly drove eastward, cutting off the Bataan Peninsula.

On 31 January the Eighth Army's Eleventh Airborne Division landed unopposed at Nasugbu, south of Manila. Tenacious enemy resistance reduced the capital city to rubble, but it fell to the invaders on 23 February. By the first of March, Corregidor was captured after 4,215 Japanese troops were killed in its fanatical defense. Desperate organized enemy resistance on Luzon continued until August, when only small numbers of Nipponese soldiers remained in the high mountains and jungles. For every American lost, 24 Japanese had been killed.

In February and March American forces landed in western Mindanao and on Palawan as well as on Panay, Negros, Cebu, Jolo, and other islands. The capture of the Philippines was one of MacArthur's greatest victories. At a cost of 10,000 American dead and 50,000 wounded, his forces had slain a total of 317,000 Japanese and had captured 7,236.[82]

MacArthur's masterful three thousand–mile campaign from New Guinea to the Philippines included thirty-nine major amphibious landings, and he consistently outguessed, outmaneuvered, and outfought a tenacious foe defending from behind prepared fortifications. His use of combined land, sea, and air forces constituted one of the greatest campaigns in modern military history and was a masterpiece.[83]

BUT there was fighting in arenas other than the islands of the western Pacific. Just as the Japanese conquest of Burma in 1942 had been cleverly accomplished, so too was Nipponese defense of this rich area skillful, and it took from October 1943 until May 1945 to free Burma. Stilwell's Chinese forces, later aided by a British division, and supplied totally from the air from May to October 1944, had begun the invasion of Burma from the north in October 1943, aided by Brig. Gen. Frank D. "Merrill's Marauders." West from India came British troops under Lt. Gen. William J. Slim, assisted by the "Chindits," British Maj. Gen. Orde "Wingate's Raiders." The important enemy base of Myitkyina fell to the Allies in August 1944. On 19 October Stilwell, whose differences with Chiang were at an impasse, was replaced in command by Lt. Gen. Albert C. Wedemeyer. Lord Louis Mountbatten proved to be an excellent theater commander.

Allied momentum slackened when two Chinese divisions had to be sent back from Burma to China. A new Japanese offensive in the summer of 1944 overran seven United States Fourteenth Air Force bases by April 1945, the enemy drive threatening almost to knock China out of the war. But pressure continued in Burma against the outnumbered Nipponese. In January 1945 Allied forces from Burma, China, and India converged on and captured Wanting; thus the Burma Road as well as the Ledo Road into China were opened, although the big airlift over the hump of the Himalayas continued.

Events moved swiftly toward their conclusion in Burma. A deep drive to the southeast across the Irrawaddy by Slim in mid-February 1945 undermined the entire Japanese position in central Burma. To the north the important city of Mandalay fell to the Allies on 21 March. British airborne soldiers seized Rangoon on the southern coast on 3 May. With only a few enemy soldiers able to escape to the east, the Burma campaign was finally over. One of the most vital side effects was that it strengthened the sagging Chinese morale so that she could remain in the war against the enemy.[84]

Contributing significantly to Allied victory in the Pacific war were the striking achievements of the silent service, the United States Navy's submarines. Convoying had been scorned by the offensive-minded Japanese navy until late in 1943, when losses of merchantmen to American subs led to adoption of this tactic. Losses continued, especially of tankers, and soon the flow of precious oil from the Netherlands East Indies was drastically curtailed. Only for a time in the Sea of Japan was the enemy able to give some protection to its exposed merchant marine, and even this heavily mined body of water was penetrated in 1945 by United States underseas craft equipped with FMS, the new electronic sonar device.

Losses of Nipponese warships to American submarine attacks were staggering. Almost 5 million tons of enemy shipping were destroyed by American submarines, including 1,113 merchant vessels and 201 Japanese men-of-war. Japanese warships sent to the bottom by United States submarines included one battleship, nine carriers, thirteen cruisers, thirty-nine destroyers, and twenty-five subs. The champion American submarine, with twenty-six enemy ships of all kinds sunk, was *Tautog*. And American subs helped tighten the cordon around the Japanese home islands so that actual starvation of the enemy civilian populace loomed on the not-too-distant horizon.[85]

In the reconquest of the Dutch East Indies, many enemy troops were bypassed and left innocuous until the end of the war. But other islands in the great archipelago were captured. On 1 May 1945 Australian and Dutch troops who had been driven from their East Indies made amphibious landings on Tarakan, an oil-rich island off the northeast coast of Borneo, and seized all significant installations there by the end of the month. Brunei Bay in northwest Borneo was captured by the Aussies in June; the prizes included oil fields as well as air fields and naval anchorages. Australian forces also occupied Balikpapan in southeastern Borneo on 1 July, and by the middle of the month the port was in use by Allied shipping.[86]

Because of several damaging Japanese raids from fields on Iwo Jima and the demands from the AAF for a sit-down base between Saipan and Japan, it was decided to assail Iwo Jima (operation DETACHMENT), the only island in the Bonin and Volcano Islands capable of sustaining airstrips and installations for accelerating the B-29 raids on Japan. Only eight square miles in area, dry, inhospitable Iwo Jima was composed of black volcanic ash, sand, and rock. In addition to the natural caves, the enemy had honeycombed the island with underground bunkers and passageways, casemated coastal guns, and automatic weapons in pillboxes that produced a withering crossfire. Including naval personnel, the Japanese garrison numbered some twenty-three thousand.

After weeks of preliminary air bombings and bombardment from six battleships and supporting cruisers and destroyers, the Fifth Marine Amphibious Corps, comprising the Third, Fourth, and Fifth Divisions, stormed ashore on the southern beaches of Iwo on 19 February 1945, supported by Spruance's Fifth Fleet. In violent and protracted fighting, the enemy had to be dug out with flamethrowers, grenades, and small arms fire, heavier bombardment having been indecisive. There was no room to maneuver on the cramped island; only costly frontal attacks could be made. In a moving, poignant scene, the American flag was raised on captured Mt. Suribachi, and the enemy was gradually compressed onto the northern end of Iwo Jima. All organized resistance was ended on 16 March, although mopping up of isolated enemy soldiers took many days. At a cost of 4,503 marines killed and 16,035 wounded, over 21,000 Japanese troops were slain and 212 captured. Many more Nipponese perished in their sealed-up underground shelters.

Was Iwo Jima worth such an effusion of American blood? In the first three months after the capture of the island, over 850 B-29s made emergency landings on Iwo's airfield, thereby saving nine thousand crew members and heightening morale among the flyers on the sixteen-hour round trip from Saipan to Japan. The epic battle of Iwo Jima was imperishably etched on the pages of Marine Corps history.[87]

A final island had to be taken in the last step before the planned invasion of the Japanese home islands could be undertaken. The capture of Okinawa in the Ryukyus had been discussed as early as August 1943 at the QUADRANT conference at Quebec and it was now selected. This island was just 325 miles from Kyushu, 450 miles southeast of Shanghai on the Chinese coast, and 375 miles east-northeast of Formosa. It had been determined that once Okinawa was in American hands, it would be used as a base for an early invasion of the Japanese homeland.

Okinawa was some sixty miles long and—except for a narrow two-mile-wide isthmus—from fifteen to eighteen miles in breadth. It was comparatively flat and had suitable terrain for air and naval bases. It would be fiercely contested by the 130,000 Japanese defenders. Oddly, the campaign for the island was half over before the Americans had an accurate map of Okinawa.

The American forces that on 1 April 1945 struck the southwest coast of Okinawa north of the capital of Naha, in the Pacific war's largest amphibious operation, were the 180,000 troops of the Tenth Army. They were made up of four army and three marine divisions commanded by Lt. Gen. Simon Bolivar Buckner, Jr., *son* of the Confederate general who surrendered Fort Donelson to U. S. Grant in 1862. Because the Japanese had overrun Chennault's air bases in China, our Fourteenth Air Force could not support the landings. A huge naval task force was in support under the overall command of Spruance, with the amphibian forces under Turner's command. Japanese air bases on Kyushu, within striking range of Okinawa, were pounded in late March by Mitscher's Task Force Fifty-eight, which comprised eight fast new battleships, ten large carriers, twenty-two cruisers, and forty-two destroyers, based on Ulithi. Nipponese bases on Formosa were bombed by Kenney's Fifth Air Force, based on Luzon.

After a pulverizing initial bombardment, the American forces landed against light opposition while the enemy bided his time. A Japanese naval force that included the second and last of the superdreadnoughts, *Yamato,* was crushed while attempting to attack United States support ships. Nearly 8,000 enemy planes, a great many of them the suicide kamikazes, were lost; our plane loss was 763. Thirty-eight American ships were sunk, most by the kamikazes, although none was a capital ship.

By 13 April the weakly held northern part of Okinawa was captured. But the southern part of the island, just north of Naha, was bitterly defended by 130,000 enemy soldiers. After repulsing an ill-advised Japanese suicidal counterattack, Buckner's forces penetrated the enemy positions. For the first time the Nipponese began to surrender en masse, and by 20 June all organized resistance had been stamped out. Just two days before the end, Buckner was killed at the front lines by Japanese artillery fire. His troops suffered 39,430 casualties, including 7,374 killed, while the enemy lost his entire large defending garrison killed except for 7,400 prisoners. Soon planes from some twenty-six newly won airstrips on Okinawa and its nearby islets were striking hard at Kyushu and the coast of China. Victory in the Ryukyus was made possible by the enormous supporting naval armada of warships, transports, and supply ships that maintained itself steadfastly, despite the kamikazes, off the coast of Okinawa. The doom of the Japanese empire was at hand.[88]

As in the First World War, the total American mobilization on the home front in World War II was, on the whole, as well done as it was massive, with the huge pyramid of governmental agencies quickly thrown together in a crash program to provide the sinews of global war and supply some 15 million men and women in uniform. The darker side was the relocation of many Pacific coast Japanese-Americans. But far above and beyond provision of guns, ships, planes, tanks, Norden bombsights, rockets, proximity fuses, napalm, and poison gas (never used) was the American development of the atomic bomb, the so-called MANHATTAN project.

Operating under the overall direction of the Office of Scientific Research and Development (OSRD), headed by Vannevar Bush and James B. Conant, scientists working under the grandstand of Stagg Field at the University of Chicago achieved the world's first self-sustaining nuclear reaction in December 1941. The Army Corps of Engineers under the direction of Maj. Gen. Leslie R. Groves built small cities at Oak Ridge, Tennessee, and Hanford, Washington, to make uranium-235 and plutonium. On 16 July 1945, at Alamogordo in the New Mexico desert, under J. Robert Oppenheimer's supervision, a test atomic device was successfully detonated, and two tactically operational atomic bombs were constructed. Oppenheimer was reminded of the passage from the *Bhagavad-Gita*: "I am become Death, the shatterer of worlds."[89]

At the TERMINAL "Big Three" Potsdam conference, Harry S. Truman (who had become president upon FDR's death in April) and Churchill, after conferring with the CCS, issued an ultimatum to Japan on 26 July 1945 to surrender totally, accept at least a temporary occupation of their home islands, and return all their conquests or face "prompt and utter destruction." But Japan rejected this final opportunity to avert catastrophe.[90]

From Potsdam Gen. Carl ("Tooey") Spaatz was given orders to drop the first atomic bomb on industrial installations of one of four selected Japanese cities, from which he could make his own choice according to target and weather anytime after 3 August. Of course several enemy cities, especially Tokyo, had already been desolated from the air by both AAF B-29s and by navy carrier task forces, and the incendiary raids had been particularly destructive. Truman crisply made the decision to drop the atomic bomb, he said, to shorten the war and to save American, Allied, and enemy lives, even though plans were drawn up for the invasion of Japan. MacArthur and most other military leaders foresaw very heavy American casualties if the Japanese home islands were to be conquered. Besides, the moral questions inherent in the use of the bomb were kept from intruding upon the decision-making by lingering and fresh memories of the sneak attack on Pearl Harbor, the Bataan Death March, and other Japanese atrocities.[91]

On 6 August 1945 the B-29 Enola Gay, commanded by Col. Paul W. Tibbets, Jr., took off from Tinian for Japan. Of all the branches of the armed forces of the warring nations, only the air forces could still retain some chivalric tendencies, particularly the fighter pilots and their small, swift planes that penetrated the vastness of the sky. There was little art left to war, except perhaps for the pursuit flyers; science and technology were at the helm. Perhaps the poignant words of an American-born fighter pilot killed early in the war, RAF Pilot Officer John G. Magee in "High Flight," reflect the sublimation of the mission to kill to a glorification of flight that was still possible in those early days of World War II:

> Oh! I have slipped the surly bonds of earth,
> And danced the skies on laughter-silvered wings;

Sunward I've climbed, and joined the tumbling
　mirth of sun-split clouds—
　and done a hundred things
You have not dreamed of—
—wheeled and soared and swung
High in the sunlit silence. Hov'ring there,
　I've chased the shouting wind along,
　—and flung
My eager craft through footless halls of air
Up, Up the long delirious, burning blue
I've topped the wind-swept heights with easy grace,
Where never lark, or even eagle, flew;
And, while with silent, lifting mind I've trod
The high, untrespassed sanctity of space,
　Put out my hand, and touched the face of God.

But the bomber Enola Gay was strictly an artless engine of scientific, technological war that would foreshadow an age of space and atomic energy, and well might its commander, who had been ordered to drop a u-235 bomb nicknamed "Lean Boy," make supplication to the Deity.

The cataclysmic weapon was loosed over Hiroshima from 31,600 feet at 9:15 A.M. with resulting Japanese casualties of eighty thousand killed. Russia then finally entered the war against Japan, and the Red Army advanced rapidly into Manchuria because Japan's Kwantung Army, ordered not to fight, deliberately fell back in anticipation of surrender. When the Japanese failed to yield, a second atomic mechanism ("Fat Boy"), this time a plutonium bomb, was dropped on 9 August over Nagasaki with different and even more terrible blast effects, some thirty-five thousand citizens being liquidated.[92]

After an internal struggle within the Japanese government, with the emperor exerting a more active pacific role, the enemy sued for peace and the Allies agreed to impose something short of unconditional surrender. In a moving ceremony aboard the battleship *Missouri* in Tokyo Bay, presided over by Douglas MacArthur, the Japanese signed the instrument of capitulation. "It is my earnest hope," said MacArthur into the microphones,

and indeed the hope of all mankind that from this solemn occasion a better world shall emerge out of the blood and carnage of the past. . . . A new era is upon us. Even the lesson of victory itself brings with it profound concern, both for our future security and the survival of civilization. The destructiveness of the war potential, through progressive advances in scientific discovery, has in fact now reached a point which revises the traditional concept of war. . . . We have had our last chance. If we do not now devise some greater and more equitable system, Armageddon will be at our door.

To the American people, MacArthur broadcast the following message:

Today the guns are silent. A great tragedy has ended; a great victory has been won. The skies no longer rain death—the seas bear only commerce—men everywhere walk upright in the sunlight. The entire world is quietly at peace. The holy mission has been completed. And in reporting this to you, the people, I speak for the thousands of silent lips, forever stilled among the jungles and the beaches and in the deep waters of the Pacific which marked the way. I speak for the unnamed brave millions homeward bound to take up the challenge of that future which they did so much to salvage from the brink of disaster. . . . They are homeward bound—take care of them.

V-J Day was proclaimed on 2 September 1945, and the greatest war of history was history.[93]

IN ANY SUMMATION of the United States and its role in World War II, it must be said at the outset that the American high command, in the main, performed most creditably. Roosevelt had shown himself, if not the most astute international leader, certainly a commander in chief of power and discernment, and the service secretaries, notably Stimson, operated quite satisfactorily to the degree that FDR allowed them to act.

Assuredly the Joint Chiefs of Staff, both individually and collectively, showed strong yet restrained leadership with their British counterparts in the Combined Chiefs of Staff and with the American theater commanders. And these latter highly capable men, especially Dwight Eisenhower, Douglas MacArthur, and Chester Nimitz, unquestionably performed masterfully in command of huge numbers of armed men of the United States and many Allied nations. With few exceptions, American lower commanders of land, sea, and air units showed to good advantage, as did most of the fighting men of all branches. The war, in general, was strongly backed on the home front by civilian and military leaders and by the American people. But United States involvement in the later two limited conflicts would receive declining support by the home populace.

Aided by the surpassing effort of American industry, by the boon of time in which to sustain initial defeats without losing the war, and by the unremitting will to win demonstrated by the citizens, the tremendous military machine that America had swiftly built up enabled this juggernaut to develop almost limitless global mobility and unequaled power. Behind all this was the silent revelation of enormous logistical competence and capabilities.

And there was a viable civil-military-scientific arrangement and understanding throughout the war. As Vannevar Bush of the OSRD noted:

> It is extremely dangerous to place military decisions fully in the hands of brash amateurs overriding the judgment of professionals, as history has demonstrated; and the worst example of this is Hitler, with his intuition and gyrations. It is equally dangerous to allow scientific principles and trends to be judged by military men without review.[94]

In the ensuing three decades, efforts—not always successful—would continue to keep in balance and in cooperative harmony American civil, military, and scientific endeavor.

CHAPTER FIFTEEN

Armed Forces in Global Commitment

I was incessantly involved in basic decisions, planning, and meeting with Defense and Atomic Energy Commission officials to approve annual increments in the national atomic stockpile and its dispersal in far-flung posts around the globe. My every footstep was followed by a courier carrying a satchel filled with draft war orders to be issued by code number in case of emergency.

PRESIDENT DWIGHT D. EISENHOWER

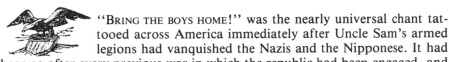 "BRING THE BOYS HOME!" was the nearly universal chant tattooed across America immediately after Uncle Sam's armed legions had vanquished the Nazis and the Nipponese. It had been so after every previous war in which the republic had been engaged, and demobilization and dismantling of the great war machine would be done with such haste that many lessons supposedly learned from past experiences would be ignored again. Only a few unheard voices would cry out that such rapid and ill-advised reductions would damage America's military posture and encourage wide-ranging adventurism from totalitarian powers.[1]

Less than a week after Germany surrendered, and three and one-half months before the Japanese would hoist the white flag, the United States War Department announced that 1.3 million army personnel would be discharged within one year. Demobilization was to be achieved under a point system whereby those who had served longest overseas and those married and with children would be discharged first. It was impossible because of the lack of ships to bring all of the men home as swiftly as demanded, although President Harry S. Truman pledged to get them back as quickly as it could be done. But unrelenting public pressure forced the War Department to abandon the point system later in 1945 and release all men with two years' service.[2]

President Truman on 6 September 1945 urged that conscription be kept and officially asked for universal military training (UMT) on 23 October 1945 for all males eighteen to twenty-five years of age, who would be given a year's basic training, followed by six years in the active reserves, and then go into a "secondary reserve." Truman's plan was backed on the one hand by the *New York Herald-Tribune* and the *New York Times* and opposed by others such as the *San Francisco Chronicle* and the *Salt Lake City Desert News*. On 25 June

1946 Congress temporized on universal military training and extended selective service until 31 March 1947. The army was to be reduced to 1.07 million by 1 July 1947, the navy to 558,000, and the marines to 108,000. A presidential committee on 29 May 1947 strongly recommended UMT.[3]

But Congress bridled at UMT; yet after a bruising contest, the legislators did vote to retain selective service until June 1950. With the outbreak of the Korean War that month, the law was extended until 9 July 1951. In June 1951, despite the loud pleas of the armed services and influential Congressman Carl Vinson, the national legislature again deferred action on UMT, but it did extend the draft until 1955.[4]

Not unrelated to the struggle over UMT was the ugly battle over unification. The United States Army and the Army Air Force declared that World War II showed a future need not only for a closer relationship between military policy and foreign policy, but also for a high degree of coordination— indeed for unification—of the land, sea, and air forces that would save material, energy, and manpower. In 1941 responsibility for the defense of Pearl Harbor had been assigned to six different agencies, each receiving separate orders from a different source. On 16 November 1945 Eisenhower told a Senate committee that another Pearl Harbor could be prevented by one unified defense command and would also yield a 25 percent saving in expenditure and personnel. Ike's view was echoed by Douglas MacArthur and by Gen. Brehon B. Somervell.[5]

While the navy did not throw up a blanket opposition to unification, it did object to some proposals and it feared a submergence of the Marine Corps. An unseemly confrontation resulted. Strenuous opposition to unification, including the use of sharp, unalloyed invective, was resorted to by Forrestal and by such navy and marine high brass as Gen. Alexander A. Vandegrift, Adm. William V. Pratt, and Adm. Ernest J. King. The bitter and caustic clash between the army and navy dragged on into the autumn of 1945.[6]

Then the chief executive intervened. Truman angrily ordered the navy to cease further public agitation or discussion of the issue. He haled the war and navy secretaries to the White House on 13 May 1946 and directed them to compromise on a plan acceptable to both. Finally on 16 January 1947 the army and navy resolved their differences and agreed to jointly recommend the creation of the office and a secretary of national defense and three coequal branches, each with a secretary and each with a military chief. Most newspapers supported the plan, although some wanted more of a merger.[7]

The Gordian Knot was finally cut on 26 July 1947 when Congress passed the National Security Act of 1947 to go into effect on 10 September. Truman named Forrestal as the nation's first secretary of defense with cabinet rank; but the secretaries of the navy, army, and the newly independent air force did not have cabinet status. Each armed service had its own military chief. The Marine Corps was retained under the Navy Department as before. In addition, the act authorized the following groups: the National Security Council, the Central Intelligence Agency, the National Securities Board, the War Council, the Joint Chiefs of Staff (JCS), the Munitions Board, and the Research and Development Board.[8]

On 10 August 1949 the act was amended by Public Law 216, passed by the Eighty-first Congress. Under the modification, the army, navy, and air force were designated military departments instead of executive branches; the secretary of defense was given more authority and responsibility; the setting up of a single military chief of staff over the armed forces and / or an armed forces general staff were banned; and it was made crystal clear that the intent was to provide coordination and unified direction, not a merger of the military departments. Although Truman disliked the Hoover Commission's conclusions and the 1949 act's substitution of the vice-president for the three service secretaries on the National Security Council, he did genuinely like and support the modified National Security Act.[9]

THE NAVY was unhappy in other ways in the post-1945 era. At the end of World War II Forrestal beseeched Congress to maintain a strong navy, but some sixty-eight hundred ships were deactivated and put in the "mothball" reserve fleet. However, despite the Navy's efforts to maintain the reserve fleets in as ready a condition as possible, some deterioration was inevitable because of economy measures. Also serious was the reduction by 1947 from 228 to 5 private ship yards capable of constructing warships. Naval personnel also declined from nearly 3,500,000 at the end of World War II to under 400,000 in 1950. The Naval Reserves by 1947 were at 133,510, just 60 percent of the desired number.[10]

Hardware-in-being is vital to every military service. Even during the latter part of World War II the navy tried to ensure its postwar effectiveness by building more aircraft carriers than would probably be needed to defeat Japan. These included more *Essex*-type carriers and the new forty-five-thousand-ton attack carriers (CVA). The first of these big fast carriers, *Midway* and *Franklin D. Roosevelt*, were launched in the spring of 1945. Although others of this class were scratched near the end of the year, one more, *Coral Sea,* was allowed to be completed in 1946. Striving to get into the role with the air force of carrying atomic bombs, the navy ordered the twin-jet Douglas A3D "Skywarrior" for delivery in March 1949. This plane required carriers larger than the *Essex* class and, the Navy hoped, larger even than the *Midway* class—in other words, very expensive monster supercarriers of some eighty thousand tons. But the air force pointed with justifiable pride to its fleet of 2,132 operational B-29s, and Congress supported such aircraft as atomic bomb transporters. The B-29 would soon be superseded by the gigantic, truly intercontinental six-engine pusher Consolidated-Vultee B-36, a plane aided later by jet-assist engines and by the developing aerial refueling technique.[11]

When Forrestal resigned as secretary of defense on 3 March 1949 he was succeeded by hefty, balding Louis Johnson. The new secretary was a champion of cutting the military not to the bone but to the marrow. Johnson quickly halted work that had begun five days previously on the navy's supercarrier *United States,* a leviathan from whose deck the navy hoped to be allowed to launch planes authorized to carry A-bombs. The air force was not unhappy at this sudden decision because it wanted to retain sole responsibility for strategic delivery of atomic bombs. The navy secretary, John L. Sullivan, resigned in a huff on 26 April 1949, denouncing Johnson and charging him with arbitrarily scrapping a project authorized by Congress and the president. Sullivan contended that navy and marine air would lose out to the air force and that the Marine Corps would have to fight for its very existence.[12]

In September and October 1949 the whole dispute of the B-36 vs. the supercarrier, inaccurately termed the "revolt of the admirals," expanded in scope and intensity into a bitter public spat involving some of the highest ranking officers of the three armed services. Eisenhower hustled down from Columbia University, where he was president, in an attempt to ease tensions between the armed services, as did Herbert Hoover and General Marshall. All three urged unity. But the navy's position and image were damaged some and Truman fired Adm. Louis Denfeld as chief of naval operations and replaced him with Adm. Forrest P. Sherman who was successful in getting work started again on *United States* and restoring some goodwill toward the service afloat.[13]

Meanwhile the cold war intensified between Russia and the West when the Communists engineered a coup in Czechoslovakia that took that nation into the Red orbit in 1948. In this year also the Russians tried unsuccessfully to oust the West from Berlin, only to be thwarted by the American-devised Berlin airlift. Fearing further Soviet expansion and turning to collective security, the North Atlantic Treaty Organization (NATO) was formed on 4 April 1949 by twelve nations, including the United States, and later adhered to by others. Its main provision was a collective security measure; an attack against any one of the signatories would be considered an attack upon all members.

NATO headquarters were established at Paris and General of the Army Eisenhower was called back to active duty as supreme Allied commander. A finer choice could not have been made. His immense and difficult task required all of Ike's considerable talents; quarreling and foot-dragging would pose severe problems. Finally, with a pledge of continued maintenance of British and American ground as well as sea and air forces on the European continent, France approved the admission of West German forces coming into the field to join other NATO forces. (Years later France would in effect pull out of NATO.) Since NATO was formed, an American has always been supreme commander; the United States paid most of the bills and contributed substantial forces to the alliance. Outnumbered by the Russian and Warsaw Pact forces, NATO concentrated on quality and on nuclear weapons and has managed to almost hold its own militarily against Russia to the present.[14]

Other profound events transpired in 1949, among them the defeat of Chiang Kai-shek's Nationalists by the Chinese Communists of Mao Tse-tung. Chiang and the remnants of his armies were forced to flee to Formosa (Taiwan). At about the same time Secretary of Defense Johnson, Secretary of State Acheson, and Chairman David Lilienthal of the Atomic Energy Commission recommended to Truman that the United States produce the awesome hydrogen bomb, a nuclear fusion weapon, not an atomic fission one like the A-bomb. In response, the president directed Johnson and Acheson to reexamine American grand strategy and national objectives as they concerned the developing revolution in national and military policy. The chief executive presented the report to the National Security Council. But in an election year Truman and Johnson and many in Congress wanted to curtail military spending to just $13 billion for fiscal year (FY) 1951. And the chairman of the Joint Chiefs of Staff, Gen. Omar N. Bradley, endorsed the limited military budgets that had been in existence since 1945. Bradley actually opposed even a defense budget of $14.5 billion as one that would threaten the collapse of the American economy.[15]

There was nothing new about severe cuts in defense spending after a war. They were pushed, not so much by Congress as usually was the case, but by Secretary Johnson. He wanted to pare the fat, as he phrased it, from the armed forces budget and cut way back in equipment, facilities, and personnel. Some 64,000 men had already been dropped from the military services in the last six months of 1949. Truman, too, agreed with heavy economies in military spending. His budget request of 9 January 1950 looked to a further reduction in the armed forces of some 190,000 men, to a request for fifty fewer ships for the navy than originally authorized, and to a small forty-eight-group air force.[16]

Moreover the civilian leaders received unusual support in these cuts from military leaders. Johnson, J. Lawton Collins, and Bradley claimed that American military forces were adequate to repel an enemy, even though the United States in early 1950 was spending just 6 percent of its national income on defense as compared to Russia's 25 percent. In other contrasts, the annual warplane production of the Soviet Union was seven thousand, while America's was twelve hundred; Russia's army numbered 2.6 million as compared to the United States' 640,000; and there were nine thousand Soviet warplanes to thirty-three hundred American. A feverish military crash program was undertaken when the Korean War erupted in June 1950. But Johnson's feud with Dean Acheson, and his responsibility—along with Truman's and that of several military chiefs—for an obviously inadequate national defense establishment led not only to Johnson's resignation on 12 September 1950, but caused untold grief to the nation as it attempted with pitifully inadequate forces to check Communist aggression.[17]

THE IMPERTURBABLE Truman, Acheson, and Louis Johnson were terribly shocked when Communist North Korean forces surged across the thirty-eighth parallel and invaded South Korea on 24–25 June 1950. The Reds had been encouraged by Acheson's blunder made in an official statement in January 1950 that Korea was beyond the defense perimeter of the United States, thereby implying that America would not fight to defend South Korea. It amounted to a carte blanche for Communist attack.[18]

As early as 8 December 1949 Douglas MacArthur's headquarters in Tokyo repeatedly warned of the advent in June 1950 of just such a North Korean attack. This aggression and the steel-trap reaction of the United States astonished the world. "The Communists," declared Russell F. Weigley,

> had almost certainly miscalculated by failing to foresee the American response. The Americans had certainly miscalculated by failing to include

small wars on the periphery of the Communist empire within their serious military planning. The Army and the Joint Chiefs themselves were delinquent in neglecting the possibility, though a larger delinquency belonged to the policy makers who gave them no indication that the country would involve itself in such wars.[19]

Unfortunately, at the outbreak of the Korean War, American armed forces were stretched very thinly around the globe and, with the exception of the Strategic Air Command's bombers, were ill prepared to engage in war. Eisenhower, now president of Columbia, voiced his concern to Johnson about the backwardness of Chairman Bradley and the JCS in speaking up on behalf of strategic bombing if war came.[20]

The plan of the North Koreans, who were aided by Soviet advisers, was to launch the surprise assault along the whole thirty-eighth parallel, with the main drive against the South Korean capital of Seoul. Well equipped with Russian military hardware, including some 100 T-34 tanks, the Soviet-trained North Korean army numbered one hundred thousand, with at least that many trained reserves. On the other hand, the South Korean army was devoid of tanks and medium and heavy artillery and was really just a very lightly equipped constabulary force, aided by some five hundred American advisers. It numbered about one hundred thousand men. The South Korean plan was to conduct a delaying action until friendly intervention occurred.[21]

The friendly intervention would come in the form of United States forces. Although understrength and unready for combat because of occupation duty, four American divisions were available in Japan. Moreover, the enemy in Korea could be attacked by United States planes, although not in great number, and his coasts were dominated by American warships, although some of these were aging and many had to be taken out of mothballs. But it was at least some armed force that might help the South Koreans stem the Red tide, if it could be gotten there in time.[22]

This put the chief stress on Harry S. Truman, who had blatantly proclaimed that "the buck stops here" with the president. He was born in Lamar, Missouri, on 8 May 1884 and served as captain of Battery D, 129th Field Artillery, Thirty-fifth Division with the AEF in France in 1918. He had been previously employed on the *Kansas City Star,* as a timekeeper for a railroad contractor, as a bank employee in Kansas City, and as a farmer near Independence. After the war he studied at the Kansas City School of Law from 1923 to 1925 and failed in business as a haberdasher. Affiliated with the notorious Pendergast political machine, Truman was a county commissioner in Jackson County, Missouri, until 1934. In that year he was elected to the United States Senate and was reelected in 1940. He gained national attention as chairman of a special Senate committee investigating the national defense program during World War II. Chosen by Roosevelt as his vice-presidential running mate, Truman was elected to that position in 1944, and became president after Roosevelt's death on 12 April 1945. He courageously made the decision to drop the two atomic bombs on Japan later that year. Although he could be quick-tempered, petty, and vindictive, Truman as president made a

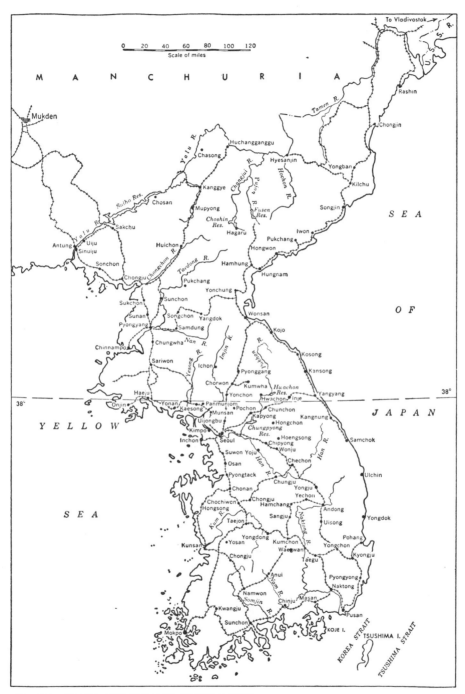

FIG. 15.1.   KOREA: THE THEATER OF OPERATION

number of far-reaching decisions in foreign affairs, especially in Europe, and would demand subordination of military leaders to their commander in chief.

When the North Korean Reds attacked South Korea, the president ordered MacArthur to throw available American air and sea forces into the fray. The United States Seventh Fleet was directed to protect Formosa from the Chinese Communists (and also to keep Chiang from raiding the mainland), and increased military assistance was ordered for the Philippines and French Indochina. On 25 June the United Nations Security Council (the Soviet delegate being absent) branded the North Korean attack "a breach of the peace" and demanded that she halt her aggression. When this was refused, the Security Council two days later called upon U.N. members to provide armed forces to "repel the armed attack and to restore international peace and security in the area."[23]

In response to a request for first-hand information, MacArthur personally inspected the battle front in Korea for eight hours, going right up to the edge of the fighting. By 29 June it was painfully evident that the well-equipped and trained North Korean army could not be halted by the ill-prepared and lightly equipped Republic of Korea (ROK) soldiers from the South or by American air and sea forces alone. So Truman instructed MacArthur to hurl what ground troops he had in Japan into the battle and launch air strikes upon targets in North Korea.

When the United Nations asked America to name a supreme Allied commander, Truman instantly chose MacArthur for that onerous position. The plenitude of the general's powers, his ability and vigorous command presence, and his dominant personality meant unquestioned obedience and maximum effort. He was handicapped in that the rainy season was just commencing in Korea and the four understrength divisions of his Eighth Army in Japan were raw, scattered, ill prepared, and inexperienced. The same was largely true of the other twelve divisions, two of them marine, in the United States (eleven of them understrength). Also, fear of Communist aggression elsewhere in the world pinned down most of these pathetically few divisions.[24]

Nor were the Allies aided by the clumsy high command structure. The Joint Chiefs of Staff sent their directives to the secretary of defense for his approval and then the army chief of staff (because the army was the principal service in the Korean War), Gen. J. Lawton ("Lightning Joe") Collins, issued them to MacArthur. Even after George C. Marshall, whom Truman admired, succeeded Louis Johnson on 12 September 1950, the role of the secretary of defense was nebulous about command and strategy. The secretary passed the directives of the JCS through the chairman, Bradley, to the president for his approval. Some directives were funneled also to the National Security Council. United Nations directives to MacArthur went through the president, and a closer rapport between the State and Defense Departments was attained.

Of the secretary of defense, Weigley states: ". . . his office was not much stronger than the assertive commanding generals of the past would have liked the Secretary of War to be." The same military historian mentions another crucial problem for the United States: "Any strategy other than the now familiar strategy of annihilation proved so frustratingly at variance with the

American conception of war that it upset the balance of judgment of American officers in the field and threatened the psychological balance of the nation itself.''[25]

Meanwhile, the North Korean tide rolled ahead unrelentingly despite heroic efforts south of Seoul at Osan and Taejon by the Twenty-fourth Infantry Division and by sublimely courageous efforts by such officers as Maj. Gen. William F. Dean and Lt. Col. Charles B. Smith. Trading space for time, the weak and heavily outnumbered Eighth Army under the competent Lt. Gen. Walton H. Walker was forced back into a beachhead about the size of Connecticut around the port of Pusan in southeastern Korea. This Pusan perimeter along the Naktong river was successfully held by American forces and South Korean remnants, aided considerably by air force, marine, and navy planes, the latter from two *Essex*-type fast attack carriers, *Valley Forge* and then *Philippine Sea,* the small escort carriers *Badoeng Strait* and *Sicily*, and by the overly long enemy supply lines.[26]

MacArthur steadily built up his defensive forces in the Pusan perimeter and readied a strike force under Maj. Gen. Edward L. Almond's Tenth Corps for one of the boldest and most masterful attacks in warfare—the amphibious assault on Inchon, the west-coast port city near the capital of Seoul. This daring stroke was opposed by most of MacArthur's superiors in Washington, and it was only grudgingly that the Joint Chiefs of Staff permitted him to go ahead. The menacing problems at Inchon were the narrow ship channel, the thirty-three-foot-high tides (highest in the Far East) and their resulting enormous mudbanks, and the need to put troops ashore at nightfall upon a seawall rather than on a beach.

The whole operation, begun on 15 September 1950, was supported by naval air attacks and bombardment and was brilliantly executed—one of the finest actions of MacArthur's long career. Seoul was recaptured on 27 September, and Walker's forces broke out of the Pusan beachhead. The two Allied forces drove the shattered North Korean forces out of South Korea and across the thirty-eighth parallel. On October 7 a U.N. resolution gave the green light to MacArthur to pursue the routed foe into North Korea. President Truman, the JCS, and the National Security Council concurred.[27]

Of the operation, Weigley declares: "But if Inchon was probably Douglas MacArthur's greatest single triumph, it was also his last. It was an immensely successful reapplication of his World War II experience; but after Inchon, the experience of 1941–45 too mechanically reapplied began to play MacArthur false.'' Like Italy, where Mark Clark and the Allies in World War II experienced serious difficulty, Korea was a peninsula with one closed end open to the enemy for communications and supplies from a mainland. MacArthur did not perceive this (as he might have done from his experiences on Bataan peninsula) about Korea, oriented as he was to his previously successful Pacific island strategy of bypassing and annihilation in 1941–1945, where air and naval superiority had helped cut off the enemy ground forces repeatedly.[28]

Triumphantly pursuing the aggressors into North Korea, MacArthur's forces captured the capital of Pyongyang on 9 October 1950. By the end of the month the residue of the crushed and demoralized enemy army fled toward the mountainous border between North Korea and Chinese Communist-dominated Manchuria, an Allied amphibian landing well up the east coast at Wonsan helping to speed the rout.[29]

But there was a problem once MacArthur's forces got beyond the narrow neck of the peninsula. The abrupt widening of the peninsula meant that the U.N. commander would have to advance with his limited forces in two isolated groups beyond the support of each other; namely, Walker's Eighth Army to the right and Almond's Tenth Corps under MacArthur's immediate command to the left. There was no contrary advice to this arrangement from the JCS. Against light opposition, these two separate forces swung northward toward the Yalu River, which formed much of the North Korea–Manchuria boundary.[30]

Then came a politico-military interlude. This was the famous Wake Island conference between Truman and his top subordinates from Washington and MacArthur. As commander in chief in the last months of World War II and in the Korean War, Truman performed in a different, more prosaic way than had Frank Roosevelt. Rather than tossing out some off-the-top-of-the-head decisions as FDR sometimes did, the man from Missouri preferred to work through his regular channels with the secretaries and Joint Chiefs of Staff. Although usually consulting his advisers and capable of being influenced by them, Truman nonetheless often exhibited a stubborn, self-righteous, petty attitude that occasionally marks the self-made man. One crossed him at one's own peril. And while patient with MacArthur up to a point, the president was determined to abide by the constitution and maintain the superiority of the civilian commander in chief over even such a military leader of massive reputation as MacArthur.[31]

At Wake, Truman and MacArthur conferred amicably. They touched briefly on the general's support of administration policies, on domestic politics, supply logistics for Japan, safety of Indochina, prisoners of war, administration in Korea after unification, the Philippine economy, and the efforts to achieve a peace treaty with Japan. When the question of possible Chinese Red intervention in the Korean War came up, MacArthur said (as had the CIA, the JCS, and the State Department previously) that while possible and while his intelligence staff indicated heavy concentrations of Chinese troops in Manchuria, such interposition seemed to be unlikely. But if it occurred, he assumed that he would be permitted to use his unfettered air power to deal crippling blows to the Chinese north as well as south of the Yalu. No one present on Wake Island at that time disagreed with this estimate. MacArthur declared that he had never "flatly and unequivocally predicted that under no circumstances would the Chinese Communists enter the Korean War." The conference lasted just one hour and thirty-six minutes.[32]

As MacArthur's forces neared the Yalu River, he was congratulated on his advance but was forbidden to bomb the power plants *in North Korea* or other targets through which Russian military aid flowed to the North Koreans. Nor did MacArthur's otherwise capable headquarters, intelligence people, or reconnaissance planes perceive the massive numbers of Chinese Red soldiers crossing the Yalu into North Korea, and they repeatedly told him that these forces would not intervene. Although navy carrier planes struck at the ends of the Yalu bridges in North Korean territory, they were unable to interdict and isolate the peninsula as they would have been able to do to a World War II island, especially when the Yalu froze over in winter and could be crossed by Chinese forces almost anywhere.[33]

When the Chinese Communist tide struck on 25 November 1950 in preponderant numbers it overwhelmed the separated forces of the Allies. A few so-called volunteers had been detected in action since the last week of October, but MacArthur's forces were now obliged, in the face of the human tidal wave, to withdraw swiftly in the bitter cold winter weather. Some went directly back down the peninsula into South Korea and some had to be evacuated by sea at Hungnam. In the main the retrograde movement was carried out efficiently and successfully, and a front line was stabilized south of Seoul by mid-January 1951. Lt. Gen. Walton Walker was killed in an unfortunate accident on 23 December 1950, after his jeep was struck and overturned by a ROK truck. His successor in command of the Eighth Army was the highly capable Lt. Gen. Matthew B. Ridgway of World War II airborne fame. Meanwhile, MacArthur was personally praised by Truman on the success of the Allied withdrawal and was complimented earlier by Secretary of State Acheson "for the close cooperation and understanding which you have contributed to our mutual problems." From 25 January through 25 April 1951 MacArthur and Ridgway were able to counterattack skillfully, regain Seoul, and take more ground across the thirty-eighth parallel than the enemy held south of it.[34]

Then it happened. A major upheaval in the U.N. command occurred with stunning suddenness. MacArthur was strongly convinced of the righteousness of his views and was fully cognizant of his power and prerogatives—despite the president's obvious authority over the military—but was unable to go along wholeheartedly with the limited war that he was being compelled to fight. His superiors refused to countenance his recommendations to bomb the Chinese Reds in their Manchurian sanctuary (the Allies had their own sanctuary in Japan to use as a takeoff point for air strikes at North Korean targets), the unleashing of Chiang Kai-shek's Chinese Nationalist forces on Formosa for raids on the Chinese mainland, the imposition of a naval blockade of China, and other actions that Truman and his advisers in Washington feared would bring Russia into the war, trigger World War III, and at the same time exasperate America's Allies, with whom the United States wished to remain united.

Truman's patience was strained beyond its low limit when MacArthur continued to air his views that were obviously at variance with those limited-war ones of the administration in letters to the Veterans of Foreign Wars and to Congresman Joseph Martin, Jr., a conservative Republican. Moreover, the U.N. commander in the Far East antagonized his superiors by offering to negotiate in the field with the enemy commander. Thus Truman relieved MacArthur of his command on 11 April 1951, MacArthur first hearing about it over the radio. The president on 6 April had decided to fire MacArthur and went through the sham of consulting his four most trusted advisers, Marshall, Acheson, Bradley, and Averell Harriman, all of whom agreed with the dismissal. Chairman of the JCS Bradley said extending the conflict to China would be provoking "the wrong war, at the wrong place, at the wrong time, and with the wrong enemy." Although the United States at that time did not as yet have too large a stockpile of atomic bombs and was concerned for the safety of NATO in Europe, Bradley would admit later, "We may have been wrong."[35]

MacArthur returned to the United States for the first time in fifteen years after an emotional farewell in Korea and Japan. In San Francisco he was wildly hailed and in New York City some 6 million, the greatest number ever to greet an American hero, cheered him hysterically during a ticker-tape parade down Broadway. On 19 April MacArthur gave a dramatic address to both houses of Congress. He was a masterful speaker and maintained a dignified composure. The general politely but firmly defended his views and conduct before an enraptured audience that was moved by his eloquence even if many Democrats disagreed with his words. Among his farewell remarks from the rostrum were these:

> I address you with neither rancor nor bitterness in the fading twilight of life, with but one purpose in mind, to serve my country.
>
> The issues are global, and so interlocked that to consider the problems of one sector oblivious to those of another is to court disaster for the whole. While Asia is commonly referred to as the gateway to Europe, it is no less true that Europe is the gateway to Asia, and the broad influence of the one cannot fail to have its impact upon the other.
>
> There are those who claim our strength is inadequate to protect on both fronts, that we cannot divide our effort. I can think of no greater expression of defeatism.
>
> If a potential enemy can divide his strength on two fronts, it is for us to counter his efforts. The Communist threat is a global one. . . .
>
> . . . when Red China intervened with numerically superior ground forces this created a new war and an entirely new situation . . . which called for new decisions in the diplomatic sphere to permit the realistic adjustment of military strategy. Such decisions have not been forthcoming.
>
> While no man in his right mind would advocate sending our ground forces into continental China, and such was never given a thought, the new situation did urgently demand a drastic revision of strategic planning if our political aim was to defeat this new enemy as we had defeated the old. . . .
>
> I called for reinforcements, but was informed that reinforcements were not available. I made clear that if not permitted to destroy the enemy build-up bases north of the Yalu, if not permitted to utilize the friendly Chinese forces of some six hundred thousand men on Formosa, if not permitted to blockade the China coast to prevent the Chinese Reds from getting succor from without, and if there were to be no hope of major reinforcements, the position of the command from the military standpoint forbade victory.
>
> We could hold in Korea by constant maneuver and at an approximate area where our supply-line advantages were in balance with the supply-line disadvantages of the enemy, but we could hope at best for only an indecisive campaign with its terrible and constant attrition upon our forces. . . .

> . . . once war is forced upon us, there is no other alternative than to apply every available means to bring it to a swift end. War's very object is victory, not prolonged indecision.
>
> In war there is no substitute for victory.
>
> There are some who for varying reasons would appease Red China. They are blind to history's clear lesson, for history teaches with unmistakable emphasis that appeasement but begets new and bloodier war. . . .
>
> I am closing my fifty-two years of military service. . . . old soldiers never die; they just fade away.
>
> And like the old soldier of that ballad, I now close my military career and just fade away, an old soldier who tried to do his duty as God gave him the light to see that duty. Good-bye.[36]

These ringing words brooked no acceptance of the doctrine of limited war that the administration felt compelled to live with and that the republic would settle for in coming years. And MacArthur adhered to his views strongly but without rancor in long testimony before investigating congressional committees.[37]

In Korea Ridgway succeeded MacArthur as supreme Allied commander, and the competent Lt. Gen. James A. Van Fleet replaced the deceased Walker as Eighth Army commander. Ridgway and Van Fleet tightened up on discipline, patrolling, and military security and began to get Allied troops out of the valleys and onto the ridges and mountains. Increased and more effective tactical air support was advanced as was more artillery firepower. These measures along with Red Chinese shortcomings and limitations in such areas as transportation, supported Ridgway's more methodical meat-grinder ground tactics rather than mechanized lunges into the valleys.[38]

The air force's use of propeller-driven P-51s and B-26s (the former A-26 Douglas "Invader") as well as jet F-80s (Lockheed "Shooting Stars") and F-84s (Republic "Thunderjets") materially helped the ROKS, Americans, and the handful of other Allied forces to more than hold their own on the ground. This was achieved in spite of the air force's lack of preparation before the war, dearth of planes designed for close tactical support, and absence of joint exercises in air-ground coordination. When increasing numbers of Russian built MiG-15s appeared in the skies over North Korea (only), the new United States Air Force F-86 North American "Sabres" shot them down at a ratio of thirteen enemy planes downed for every American plane lost.

Led by Earle E. Partridge and George E. Stratemeyer, the Fifth Air Force not only repeatedly prevented the enemy from massing troops but also broke up troop and supply concentrations and knocked out enemy bridges and transportation facilities. Yet they still could not keep the Red ground soldiers from being adequately supplied with ammunition and food, half of it by rail. Air force B-29s hit all known strategic targets in North Korea. "If it had not been for the air support," Walker owned, "we should not have been able to stay in Korea." But the prominent champion of air power, Alexander de Seversky, warned that "total war from the air against an undeveloped country or region is well-nigh futile; it is one of the curious features of the most modern weapon that it is especially effective against the most modern types of civilization."[39]

The United States Navy had things pretty much its own way against a practically nonexistent enemy navy. American warships escorted troop and supply ships, and aircraft from a number of carriers, along with marine and air force planes, played an important role in bombing shore targets. Several 45,000-ton battleships of the *Missouri* class were taken out of mothballs, and their 16-inch guns joined the smaller ones of cruisers and destroyers in the bombardment of installations within range on both coasts. But, like American air power, Allied sea power could not by itself defeat the enemy, although it could significantly aid the ground forces in maintaining themselves on the peninsula and preventing an enemy victory.[40]

The Reds launched a spring offensive beginning on 22 April 1951, employing human-sea tactics; but by 22 May this advance had been bloodily halted by Ridgway and Van Fleet. The small amount of ground lost, and more, was regained by an Allied counteroffensive lasting from 22 May 1951 to 18 July. As the war dragged on, with truce talks finally getting under way first at Kaesong and then at Panmunjom, ground action became little more than a stalemate for the Allies, with bloody hill battles being fought with little change in the battle lines. In due time Ridgway and Van Fleet were rotated to other assignments after their creditable tour of duty in Korea. They were replaced respectively by two able and veteran commanders, Mark W. Clark and Maxwell D. Taylor. Clark, like Van Fleet, backed MacArthur's total victory concept although they followed orders and waged the war as directed. Ridgway had accepted the rationale of limited war. Begrudgingly, the enemy acknowledged the impressive fighting capabilities of the Eighth Army. This otherwise frustrating war in Korea at least helped to give the American army a new, stronger, and healthier purpose that could almost be considered a renaissance.[41]

The Korean War stalemate and the Democratic administration's inability to end it acceptably destroyed Truman's reelection chances, and he announced that he would not run again for the presidency. Before he left office, Truman ordered racial integration of the armed forces and this would have marked effects on the makeup of the all-volunteer forces after the Vietnam War. Republican Dwight D. Eisenhower, the five-star former supreme Allied commander in Europe in World War II and recent supreme commander of NATO forces, was triumphant in the presidential election of November 1952. During the political campaign Ike promised, if elected, that he would go to Korea to observe conditions and that he would work to achieve peace there. He kept that pledge during the period he was president-elect.

After being sworn in on 20 January 1953, Eisenhower pushed the Panmunjom armistice talks, threatening at one time to use nuclear weapons and actually shipping to Korea some mammoth 280-mm atomic cannons. Nor was this situation made easier by the refusal of 50,000 of the 132,000 Communist prisoners in Allied stockades to go home. Finally, the Korean War terminated on 27 July 1953 when a truce was signed at Panmunjom. Korea remained divided along the battle lines, roughly near the thirty-eighth parallel, a little more in North Korea than in South Korea, and this frontier (with a supposedly demilitarized buffer zone) exists to this day (1982), with some American forces still there.[42]

THIS ROILING WAR in Korea yielded lessons and legacies as well as frustrations. Except for the ROKS, who fought with increasing efficiency under American tutelage as the war progressed, almost all U.N. forces in the Korean War were American, even though the Allies insisted in participating fully in all decisions and strategy making. Among the best of the U.N. troop contingents were the British Commonwealth unit and a Turkish force. American casualties were over 26,000 killed, 100,000 wounded, and 11,000 missing (including captured). The South Koreans suffered total casualties of almost 257,000, and Communist losses, direct and indirect, are estimated to have aggregated over 2 million. The other Allies lost 13,000 men.[43]

Certain unpalatable lessons of the war in Korea surfaced. These showed that use of combined arms and integrated air-land-sea teamwork were essential. More so than in World War II, the limitations of sea and air power were revealed. Korea was a unit commander's war, where fire, movement, and physical conditioning were musts.

AFTER WORLD WAR II the Anglo-American "Grand Alliance" with Russia broke down largely because of Stalinist expansionism. So the United States turned to collective security and economic and military measures like the Marshall Plan, the Truman Doctrine, NATO, Point Four, Mutual Defense Assistance, Mutual Security Program, United Nations Relief and Rehabilitation Administration (UNRRA), and Bretton Woods agreements. The post-1945 Communist policy of expansion utilized internal subversion, propaganda, espionage, and peripheral war. These limited or "brushfire" wars usually did not involve Russian or (after Korea) Chinese Red troops and were aimed at drawing American military, economic, and financial resources to the breaking point in such areas of confrontation as Greece, Korea, and Indochina. America's response, in a phrase coined by former ambassador to the Soviet Union George F. Kennan, was a policy of containment.[44]

With Robert A. Lovett succeeding General Marshall who had replaced the discredited Louis Johnson as secretary of defense, there was a significant shift from mobilization strategy to a strategy of deterrence, even before the advent in office of Eisenhower and John Foster Dulles. Increased readiness was needed and so were forces in being. To prevent a general enemy attack, America built up its nuclear arsenal and its delivery systems so that sufficient force would be left even after a Red all-out first attack. The air force had 405 Boeing B-47 "Stratojets" by June 1953 and eventually 1,317 of them. These fine planes had a capacity of over five tons and a radius of 2,013 miles at 500 mph. In April 1952 the first prototype of the four-engine Boeing B-52 bomber flew successfully, and in August 1954 the first of these huge craft began rolling off production lines. To deter a Red attack that was less than general, Truman had begun to bolster NATO ready forces, including bringing West German soldiers into the field.[45]

THE NEW PRESIDENT had credentials of a high order. Dwight D. Eisenhower was elected in November 1952 with an overwhelming majority. He had not only an impressive array of high military positions and attainments on his record but possessed a deep and broad base of support of a majority of the American people as well. Yet as commander in chief and president, Ike leaned over backward to avoid any charge of bias in favor of the military, and in this he was successful. However, the nation's armed forces, particularly the army, suffered some from this approach. He tried hard not to be arbitrary or domineering, although his famous quick temper occasionally flashed out. He refrained from putting as many former military men into high office as had Truman.

Eisenhower was the first American peacetime chief executive to confront daily the issues of life and death for the republic that previous presidents had faced only in wartime. Ike described his situation thusly:

> New military developments brought about important changes in the duties that absorbed the urgent and continuous attention of the President. The title Commander in Chief of the armed forces had become something real and critical even in peace. I was incessantly involved in basic decisions, planning, and meeting with Defense and Atomic Energy Commission officials to approve annual increments in the national atomic stockpile and its dispersal in far-flung posts around the globe. My every footstep was followed by a courier carrying a satchel filled with draft war orders to be issued by code number in case of emergency. Our military structure and equipment were changing so rapidly that even the comforting old slogan "Tried and true" was gone. In its place had sprung up a disquieting new one: "If it works, it's obsolete."[46]

Eisenhower and his successors were compelled to peer far into the future and accept more awesome risks with the treasure and lives of the American people than those who had gone before them. So great now was the strain on the president, with his expanding responsibilities and duties, that many were concerned whether the presidency and the office of commander in chief could continue to be efficaciously united in one human being. But Ike demonstrated that in most respects he was a sure-footed commander in chief by his effective handling of such grave international crises as those in Berlin, Lebanon, Suez, and the Formosan Strait.[47]

In 1962–1963 Robert S. McNamara, John F. Kennedy and Lyndon B. Johnson's secretary of defense, reorganized the army so that in addition to the Continental Army Command (CONARC) at Fort Monroe, Virginia, which kept control over training, two other major functional commands were formed, the Combat Developments Command and the Army Matériel Command. Later, there would evolve the Training and Doctrine Command (TRADOC) at Fort Monroe, and the Combined Arms Combat Developments Activity (CACDA) at Fort Leavenworth, Kansas. This reorganization left the army's General Staff devoid of operational functions and returned it to its original role as a policy-making and overall planning body.[48]

The World War II interservice commands led to interservice schools. The Army War College, closed in 1940, reopened only in 1950, first at Fort Leavenworth and then in 1951 at Carlisle Barracks, Pennsylvania. At Fort McNair (formerly known as Washington Barracks), the National War College and the Industrial College of the Armed Forces were established; and the Armed Forces Staff College was set up at Norfolk, Virginia, all three under the control of the JCS. The Naval War College reopened at Newport, Rhode Island. The military academy at West Point and the naval academy at Annapolis continued strong and influential.

The new United States Air Force now had its own academy at Colorado Springs. The faintest murmurings for a separate air academy could be traced to the period immediately after the First World War, but it was not until the creation of the independent United States Air Force in 1947 that heavy pressure was brought to bear to realize this ambition. After much debate in the executive and legislative branches, a bill was finally signed into law in 1954 to establish the United States Air Force Academy. The fledgling school began operations the following year at Lowry Air Force Base outside of Denver, followed soon by the move to its futuristic style permanent buildings near Colorado Springs. The initial founders of the air force academy were mostly West Point graduates, so the new institution largely replicated the military academy way of doing things, with a few aeronautical touches. After some early problems and revision of academic programs, the air force "Falcons" got off the ground with an academy that began to develop some traditions of its own in something of a departure from the "seminary-academy" ones of West Point.

At Maxwell Air Force Base, near Montgomery, Alabama, the Air University was established, comprising the Air Command and Staff College and the Air War College. The army's Command and General Staff College at Fort Leavenworth continued to be the finest and most prestigious advanced school of its kind in the world. The marines had their own well-organized schools at Quantico, Virginia. Branch schools and other specialized ones of all three armed services received increased attention.[49]

The specter of the supreme weapon loomed ominously over the planet after World War II. America's post-1945 atomic and nuclear weapons policy was oftentimes fluctuating and uncertain. Some, like Herbert Hoover, urged retention of our A-bomb knowledge for ourselves alone. But a few like the secretary of commerce, Henry A. Wallace, suggested sharing atomic secrets with the Russians to show America's good faith. Following a cabinet meeting on 21 September 1945 at the White House, Truman told Congress on 3 October that he would refuse to yield atomic information to potentially hostile nations and urged the creation of an atomic energy commission. J. Robert Oppenheimer recommended international control of atomic energy, as did the Association of Los Alamos Scientists. Others, like Supreme Court Justice Owen J. Roberts, urged the abandonment of the U.N. and the creation of a world federal government to prevent atomic war. Albert Einstein suggested establishment of a super international government comprising the United States, Great Britain, and Russia, with each power assigning this government all of its military forces. From several men in Congress came such ideas as outlawing the use of atomic weapons, or having America supply an aerial armada of bombers carrying the A-bomb for the U.N.[50]

At a meeting of the United States, Britain, and the Soviet Union in

Moscow on 27 December 1945, it was agreed to present to the U.N. proposals for the control of atomic energy, and a resolution was passed on 24 January 1946 setting up the U.N. Atomic Energy Commission. On 14 June the generous American Baruch Plan for control of atomic energy was presented to the world body; the United States would surrender all its A-bombs, facilities, and know-how to the U.N. in return for international inspection to guarantee that no power would cheat on the agreement. But the Russians rejected the whole plan. Most responsible Americans thought international inspection essential, because treaties and agreements had often been broken in the past.[51]

Then in 1949 the Western world was shocked to learn that the Soviets had the atomic bomb. It was thought by many that the Russians had been aided and abetted by several Canadian, American, and British citizens who provided the Russians with some of the atomic secrets.[52]

Consequently the United States had to try to develop a political-diplomatic-military policy to cope with its rival's acquisition of the supreme weapon. "After 1945," writes Russell F. Weigley, "a strategy of deterrence would have to become not secondary but uppermost in American military policy. Furthermore . . . the new weapons would make atomic deterrence qualitatively different from any past strategy of deterrence." Henry A. Kissinger noted that for the time being the United States put the atomic bomb in its arsenal but did not ponder its implications at the same time. To American political and military leaders, who were wedded to the concept of all-out war, the atomic bomb was just another weapon in a concept that required total victory.[53]

Lt. Gen. James A. Gavin, at one time head of research and development for the army, said of the atomic bomb: "Military thinking seemed, at the outset, to be paralyzed by its magnitude." However, it was thought that this negative American policy of deterrence might also develop positive goals and programs in the contest to contain Communism. Historically, the United States had conceived of national strategy as the employment of military power for offensive purposes. And in the early 1950s it was asked by some how reliable our policy of deterrence would be in the long run.[54]

A number of individuals in the Eisenhower administration were convinced that it was chiefly the American threat (delivered to the Red Chinese through India) to use atomic weapons that compelled the Communists to agree to end the war in Korea. This strengthened the administration's resolve to provide deterrence—of limited as well as of general wars—chiefly by nuclear weapons. Because of the Korean War, the United States was well ahead of Russia in stockpiling A-bombs, and America had more than 400 B-47s to deliver them from a network of air bases that by 1955 was spread over forty-nine countries on six continents. The Eisenhower-Dulles containment policy was based on a strong deterrent and a willingness to use it—the "New Look"—and to make certain that the enemy was convinced that the United States would use it to punish aggression so severely ("massive retaliation") as to make it suicidal for everyone to risk destruction. The United States would again resort to collective security.[55]

Despite opposition that soon developed to the deemphasis of conventional weapons, many were doubtful that the republic could cut military spending and at the same time have increased or even adequate defense strength. Such sharp critics of the Eisenhower New Look policy as Generals Ridgway, Taylor, and Gavin would not only preach the rebuilding of conventional forces to fight "brushfire" limited wars, but would emphasize their views by resigning from the army. These men and others deemed it too dangerous to touch off a possible total war with the Reds by employing the hydrogen bomb in response to local wars. But Ike would not spend the $46.3 billion recommended by the Truman administration for FY 1954; instead, the figure was reduced to $41.2 billion, largely realized by cutting back the air force goal from 143 wings to 114 wings in FY 1954 and to 120 wings in FY 1955.[56]

Nor had the enemy been idle. It was learned in 1953 that Russia had developed the hydrogen bomb and was beginning to stockpile it, to build bomber forces, and to construct eight-hundred-mile-range ballistic missiles. When French-held Dienbienphu in Indochina fell to the Reds in May 1954, Dulles wanted to use nuclear weapons to retrieve the situation; but he could not get French, Allied, or American congressional support to do this, nor would Eisenhower countenance it.[57]

THE RISE of systems analysis and of the so-called strategy intellectuals coincided with their sharp criticisms of Dulles's massive retaliation doctrine. Such men as William W. Kaufman (a research associate of the Center of International Studies at Princeton University) and Bernard Brodie (of RAND Corporation) voiced grave doubts over the viability of nuclear retaliation in deterring limited wars. Even prior to this, some national figures—such as Chester Bowles, Dean Acheson, and George Kennan—publicly disagreed with massive retaliation.[58]

While Chief of Staff Ridgway reluctantly went along with the reduced military budget for FY 1954, he remonstrated against that for FY 1955, saying the New Look did not provide adequate conventional forces to deter or cope with limited wars. The Eisenhower administration was aware that a return to balanced, nonnuclear, conventional forces that would provide a graduated response to enemy aggression would cost more, and the administration hoped that this would not be necessary. Indeed, the administration announced that the United States no longer insisted on superiority in nuclear weapons, but rather merely on a "sufficient deterrent." Then in 1957 came Sputnik, which showed an American lag in rocket-propelled missiles and led to fear in some quarters in the United States of a "missile gap." But of course America had only begun in the mid-1950s to start real development of rocket-fired missiles.[59]

In January 1959 RAND's Albert J. Wohlstetter startled many by declaring that stability between the two great nuclear powers could not be ensured by the so-called balance of terror because disproportionate strategic superiority could be gained by comparatively small advances in technology by either side. Thus it might encourage one power (Russia) to consider the launching of a preemptive first strike. Futhermore, he warned the United States about its eroding and aging nuclear forces and their capabilities, especially the Strategic Air Command (SAC), but also including its first generation liquid-fueled ballistic missiles.[60]

Late in his eight-year term of office, Eisenhower perceived that he would have to keep much of the army's ground strength that was built up during the Korean War, and that the nuclear deterrent against peripheral, brushfire, limited wars was no more effective than it had been under Truman in the pre-1950 period. So for FY 1959 the Defense Department was obliged to reverse itself and increase the military budget for missile development and halt the reduction in army numbers. At the same time, the secretary of defense was given increased powers.[61]

In the presidential election year 1960, Henry A. Kissinger published a book contending—erroneously, as it turned out—that there would be an unavoidable American missile gap from 1960 to 1965, and most writers on national strategy and policy concurred. The air force, in turn, concerned about the vulnerability of its retaliatory forces, began demanding a "counterforce deterrent"; that is, one that could sustain a first strike by the Soviets and still annihilate the nuclear forces of the enemy. But when the Eisenhower administration continued to adhere largely to its announced "sufficient" and "finite deterrent," the air force appealed to Congress and the public. Thomas Sovereign Gates, Jr., Ike's third secretary of defense, denied that the Russians were building missiles so rapidly as to create an American missile gap. But he could not "blow" the security of American intelligence sources—such as the U-2 flights over Russia—to prove it, and Democrats such as Lyndon B. Johnson refused to believe his statements.[62]

Shortly after John F. Kennedy's close victory for the presidency in November 1960, debate intensified on national military policy. RAND physicist Herman Kahn concluded that some advantages could even be wrung from an all-out nuclear war, although of course he did not advocate such an occurrence. Americans must think about the unthinkable, the possibility of a massive nuclear exchange, said Kahn. They should prepare for it in such a way that they might cushion its worst results and salvage something out of such a holocaust. The United States must harden its nuclear retaliatory forces and build fallout shelters for its people, he declared. Kahn continued to suggest these things through 1965. He claimed that even a general nuclear war could be controlled or limited. "In 1960," writes Weigley,

> John F. Kennedy's seeming promise to encourage Cuban freedom fighters
> and Herman Kahn's scenarios for controlled nuclear war both suggested
> an adjustment to nuclear weapons that was a bit too complacent and a
> wish for a return to positive strategies of action that bordered on the
> reckless.[63]

The confident young man who became president and commander in chief in January 1961 was from a prominent, well-to-do Democratic family of Massachusetts. John F. Kennedy's father was named head of the Securities and Exchange Commission early in the New Deal and then served for a time as ambassador to Great Britain. John graduated from Harvard and served as a PT-boat skipper in the navy in the Pacific in World War II and was credited with saving the life of at least one of his crew after his boat was sheared in two and sunk. He became a United States senator and showed himself to be more of a reader than a talker or listener.[64]

When he became president, Kennedy named Robert S. McNamara his secretary of defense. Formerly head of the Ford Motor Company, McNamara brought into the Defense Department a group of young advisers, not always affectionately known as the "Whiz Kids", who adhered to the premise that problems could be solved by computers, formulae, and cost-effectiveness. Thus it was not necessary to trust too much in mere human beings. While in some ways an efficient office manager in the Pentagon, McNamara's dehumanizing proclivities and his self-righteousness did not make him any too popular with the high brass. And the secretary would make a number of bad misjudgments while in office.[65]

A whirlwind of action soon unfolded. Kennedy and McNamara began reorganizing the armed services, beefing up the army especially in conventional weapons so that the commander in chief would have a greater range and choice of options in responding to hostile threats.[66] The president and secretary soon admitted that there was no missile gap, as Kennedy and others had charged; evidence was secured from new reconnaissance satellites that orbited the planet showing the Soviets were not engaged in a missile building crash program.

While the struggle over military policy went forward, so too did weapons development. In the 1950s and 1960s the United States made impressive strides ahead with the second generation solid-fueled "Minuteman" ICBM (more reliable than the less stable liquid-fueled "Atlas" and "Titan") in harder silos, the goal being one thousand Minutemen. Another successful development was that of the sixteen-missile submarines firing the Polaris from underwater—the *George Washington* launching being the first one in July 1960. The goal was forty-one of these boats. These were no mean accomplishments for which the Eisenhower administration was responsible.[67]

McNamara was soon obliged to retreat from counterforce policy because of intelligence and targeting problems that would be engendered by even a modest Soviet nuclear force enlargement. This, in turn, would require a considerably larger American increase to ensure counterforce capacity. And there was also the problem of the incongruity of American disavowal of launching a preemptive first strike when only such a tactic would guarantee counterforce ability. So the secretary evolved the "assured destruction" concept—an American capability to inflict a degree of "unacceptable" destruction (at least 25 percent of Russia's industry and population) upon the Soviets even after they had launched a total first strike. He thought he could still be discriminating because American retaliation could be aimed only at enemy military forces and installations and hit only in a deliberate and controlled manner Russian industry and cities, hoping that the Soviets would likewise stay away from large population centers in the United States.[68]

Largely because of his mania for cost-effectiveness, McNamara canceled the program to develop the new B-70 intercontinental bomber and snuffed out production of the Nike-Zeus antimissile system. He also compelled the navy and air force to share jointly a new tactical fighter plane, the ill-fated TFX. Rather than actually put the money into the highly publicized policy of flexible response, new funds went into the nuclear retaliatory systems of the secretary's counterforce strategy, chiefly the Minutemen and Polaris. But the 1961 Berlin crisis impelled action on conventional forces and flexible response; so McNamara supported an increase in the army from 875,000 to 1,000,000 men and also an increase in some Reserve and National Guard forces.[69]

In response to his campaign pledge, Kennedy attempted to assume the diplomatic initiative, a "strategy of action" backed by "usable" military power. He embraced the CIA-developed Cuban invasion plan worked out in the last months of the Eisenhower administration and the early weeks of his own. Some 1,000 anti-Castro Cuban refugees, trained and armed by the United States, were to hit the beaches of the Bay of Pigs in the hope that Fidel Castro would be toppled when an expected uprising of the Cuban populace triggered by the invasion would crush Castro's militia force of approximately 200,000.

But subordinate military officers and the CIA failed to provide the JCS with the full information, and the JCS neglected to press the CIA with the proper tough questions. Consequently the JCS went along with the dubious scheme, as did the State Department and the president. Kennedy kept the whole operation covert, in part so as not to antagonize the Latin-American nations. When the unfortunate anti-Castro Cubans landed at the Bay of Pigs in April 1961 Kennedy withheld American air support, without ever really explaining why, and the invaders were crushed. Many captive survivors were brutally murdered by Castro.[70] Kennedy suffered another setback when the Soviets threw up the Berlin Wall without any American response.

The international situation had eroded markedly since Kennedy's presidency and the Bay of Pigs fiasco; he could not afford to suffer another setback in foreign affairs, especially in Cuba. But in October 1962 Kennedy was faced with the Cuban missile crisis. It began when Soviet Premier Nikita Khrushchev, who had been warned a number of times by the United States not to put offensive weapons into Cuba, moved sixteen "soft" launching pads for intermediate ballistic missiles (range up to twenty-two hundred miles) and twenty-four soft launching pads for medium ballistic missiles (range up to one thousand miles) to Cuba and began to assemble Russian IL-28 H-bomb-carrying bombers (range up to seven hundred miles).

At this time the United States was still well ahead in nuclear weapons and their delivery systems: over 600 SAC bombers on fifteen-minute alert vs. about 200 enemy ones; 144 Polaris-submarine missiles; and approximately 225 ICBMs as against perhaps 60 Russian. American U-2 planes discovered the Soviet weapons deploying in Cuba. McNamara was not worried about the enemy missiles there, and President Kennedy was slow to believe the situation in Cuba. However, he and his advisers were finally alarmed and were determined to compel Khrushchev to remove them. A naval blockade of Cuba was quickly instituted and Kennedy warned the Soviet premier that the United States would take whatever steps were necessary, including invasion, to get the missiles out of the island. The Russians backed down from the eyeball-to-eyeball confrontation and turned their ships around. They also removed their bombers and missiles from Cuba and took down their launchers in return for JFK's pledge not to invade Cuba and to dismantle some aging United States missiles in Turkey. At best, this was just a partial victory for Kennedy. Khrushchev realized that America still had a superiority in nuclear capability and in conventional forces very close to Cuba, and this island was far from the Soviet Union.[71]

Soon after Kennedy was elected president, the Vietnamese Reds set up the so-called National Liberation Front in South Vietnam to contest President Ngo Dinh Diem's anti-Communist regime by subversion and guerrilla activity. Kennedy, who was concerned with countering guerrilla threats throughout the world, began pushing the army to expand its Special Forces from fifteen hundred to nine thousand men in a year. The chief executive intended that the Special Forces (the "Green Berets") were to be an elite group, despite the army's longtime suspicion of elite units. Kennedy thought the Green Berets could help local defenders check Communist guerrilla warfare operations in wars of national liberation. The Special Forces were to be trained also in preventive medicine, construction, and leadership in community organization.[72]

The president reacted promptly to this perceived threat; Taylor and Walt W. Rostow were dispatched to South Vietnam in October 1961. After sniffing around, Taylor intimated that the United States might have to pledge to attack the "source of guerrilla aggression in North Vietnam and impose on the Hanoi Government a price for participating in the current war which is commensurate with the damage being inflicted on its neighbors to the south." Taylor thought the chances were slight of such activity mushrooming into a major war on the Asian mainland because, he claimed, North Vietnam was "extremely vulnerable to conventional bombing."[73]

Kennedy initially accepted only Taylor and Rostow's call for air support; he was dubious at first about deploying large numbers of American ground troops in Indochina. The president desired to honor American commitments, made a number of times to South Vietnam since the 1954 Geneva agreements. Because he adhered to the domino theory, he wanted to employ flexible military response to prevent acceleration of Communist-inspired global wars of liberation. So he provided South Vietnam with arms, advisers, planes, and helicopters, and he increased American military personnel there from the eight hundred present when he took office to twenty-three hundred, some two-thirds of whom were United States Army soldiers, by November 1963. "With this American presence," writes Weigley, "Kennedy tied the prestige of the United States to the government in Saigon for all the world to see." But in November 1963 JFK was assassinated. His successor, Lyndon Baines Johnson, after visiting South Vietnam, called for a greater American effort and involvement in Indochina as early as May 1961.[74]

The new president, fifty-five years of age, was born near Stonewall,

Texas, and received a B.S. degree from Southwest Texas State College in San Marcos. From 1930 to 1931 he taught school in Houston and became secretary to Congressman Richard M. Kleberg of Texas from 1931 to 1935. In 1935 he was a student at Georgetown Law School. From 1935 to 1937 Johnson was the state director of the National Youth Administration in Texas and was elected to the Seventy-fifth Congress in 1937 to fill the unexpired term of Congressman James P. Buchanan of Texas's Tenth District. He was reelected to the House from 1938 to 1948. A commander in the United States Naval Reserve, Johnson served on active duty from 1941 to 1942. He was a United States senator (Democrat) from Texas from 1949 to 1961, serving effectively as both minority and majority leader. He was vice-president from 1961 until his accession to the presidency two years later. Soft spoken and a great user of the telephone, he was a voluble talker and listener and not a reader. Johnson was a master at the art of manipulating votes in the Senate and was more knowledgeable on domestic policies and politics than in foreign affairs. Although he lacked poise and polish, he could be especially charming to the ladies and was a power to be reckoned with in his own party. He immediately had nationwide sympathy and support when the cruel hand of the assassin thrust him into the White House.

Upon assuming the presidency, Lyndon Johnson returned to the old concept of not allowing the enemy a sanctuary as America had in the Korean War. He authorized American-sponsored clandestine operations such as bombings, PT-boat attacks, naval commando raids, and sabotage by parachutists to be made directly against North Vietnam. These actions led to clashes between American destroyers and North Vietnamese patrol boats in the Gulf of Tonkin in August 1964. The Gulf of Tonkin Resolution, sought by Johnson and passed overwhelmingly by Congress, gave the commander in chief authority to take whatever measures he deemed essential to repulse attacks on American forces and prevent further successful Red aggression in Southeast Asia. In September the president decided to escalate American participation and bomb North Vietnam directly. Air strikes into North Vietnam were to be made swiftly in retaliation for Viet Cong attacks in South Vietnam.[75]

Lyndon Johnson was easily elected president in his own right in November 1964 over Republican Senator Barry Goldwater, a supposed "hawk." Johnson pledged *not* to expand the war in Vietnam. But in February 1965 the chief executive ordered reprisal attacks on targets in North Vietnam when the enemy assaulted American installations in the South. The commander in chief directed Operation ROLLING THUNDER to be instituted. This called for a sustained American bombing of the North, taking care to stay away from such sensitive areas as Hanoi and its harbor at Haiphong. Next, more army troops and marines were dispatched to protect United States airfields in South Vietnam; the American commander there, Gen. William C. Westmoreland, recommended even more. In the spring of 1965 the GIs were authorized to assume the offensive around their bases, and Johnson sent more marine battalions and approximately nineteen thousand additional support forces.[76]

Westmoreland and the JCS opposed a static policy as America historical-

FIG. 15.2. THE WAR IN SOUTHEAST ASIA

ly had usually done and urged enlarging the offensive to fifty-mile-radius enclaves so that in due time these "ink blots" would touch and overlap. Johnson was not backward in committing more American soldiers in accord with this tactic. The JCS and Westmoreland then recommended a step-up to "search-and-destroy" operations throughout South Vietnam and, eventually, by carrying the war to the enemy, to destroy his forces and crush his ability to continue the conflict. Johnson agreed to increase American troop strength in Vietnam to 194,000 by 30 June 1965. These GIs could now be used, upon the beck of the South Vietnamese, as Westmoreland saw fit. By these new accretions, the general hoped to turn the tide in the South. This included construction activities in the countryside by the end of 1965 and offensive action in 1966, provided more soldiers were sent to him. If the foe continued his fierce resistance, an additional year or year and a half would be required to defeat and destroy the remaining enemy forces and bases.[77]

Despite the Korean experience and the fact that in Indochina the United States was again engaged in a new type of war, the JCS, Westmoreland, and Rostow harkened back to the supposed lessons of World War II. They held that offensive ground action, accompanied by a sustained bombing of North Vietnam, could defeat the enemy once and for all. Yet American intelligence warned that bombing would have little impact on North Vietnam, so primitive and different were its industries and transportation facilities (the latter included the so-called Ho Chi Minh Trail network, part of which ran through supposedly neutral Laos). The concept of limited war that dominated the strategic thinking of the 1950s was now being ignored. The army *had* adjusted weapons and tactics to brushfire wars, but Westmoreland, the JCS, McNamara, Wheeler, and Johnson did not adjust sufficiently. Taylor, in Saigon, opposed in vain the switch from the counterinsurgency enclave policy to the search-and-destroy strategy.[78]

By early 1966 American strength in Vietnam totaled 235,000; by February 1968, it stood at 495,000. Surprisingly, the enemy was able to launch the Tet offensive in February 1968. While the enemy was tactically defeated with enormous casualties, psychologically (with the help, unwitting and otherwise, of a segment of the American media), it shocked and upset America, and Johnson began to have doubts about his policy. Weigley states:

> The Indochina War brought bitter denouement to the long search for a restoration of the use of combat in the service of policy. If the war had been conducted with "a whole new kind of strategy" of counterinsurrectionary war, instead of the old strategies seeking the destruction of the enemy and his logistical systems by means of highly mechanized forces that had a hard time hitting him, conceivably the war might have gone better for the United States. Conceivably, but not probably; counterguerrilla war offers special problems of indecisiveness, and much of the whole larger problem of the use of combat is the persistence in twentieth-century warfare of that inability to produce decisions that overtook war in the nineteenth century, that World War II only superficially appeared to overcome, and that has so painfully reasserted itself in Korea and Indochina.

The Vietnam embroglio led to a return, in the minds of some, to a suggestion that tactical nuclear weapons might be a solution, as these arms improved; but there was always the danger of possible Russian superiority and the danger of escalation into an all-out nuclear holocaust, especially in Europe.[79]

In January 1969 Richard M. Nixon assumed the presidency. He was born in Yorba Linda, California, on 9 January 1913, graduated from Whittier College in 1934, and received a law degree from Duke University in 1937. After practicing law in Whittier and working briefly in Washington in the Office of Price Administration, Nixon served as a naval officer in the Pacific in World War II. He was then a two-term Congressman and served two years in the United States Senate. Nixon became Eisenhower's vice-president for eight years. After defeats for the presidency in 1960 and for the governorship of California in 1962, he became a Wall Street lawyer. He traveled widely abroad and campaigned on behalf of Republican candidates. In 1968 he was rewarded with the Republican nomination and triumphed over Hubert H. Humphrey for the presidency. Suspicious and secretive in his actions, Nixon had some major troubles with his internal and domestic policies that culminated in his threatened impeachment and finally his resignation after the revelations involved in the Watergate affair. But in foreign affairs he showed a sure hand; he finally negotiated an end to the war in Vietnam, and he succeeded in bringing about a rapprochement with Russia and especially with China.

In June 1972, in answer to an enemy land offensive, Nixon authorized a naval bombardment, the mining of Haiphong harbor, and, later, the bombing of Hanoi by B-52s based on Guam and in Thailand, not to mention efforts at interdicting the Ho Chi Minh Trail in Laos and launching raids and an incursion into Cambodia. These partially successful actions did enable Nixon by 1 December 1972 to cut back American strength drastically in Indochina from 565,000 to just 24,000. A cease fire agreement in January 1973 among the involved Vietnamese parties effectively ended American participation in this unhappy war, although the Communists soon broke the armistice and took over all of South Vietnam.[80]

McNamara, who initially supported the Vietnam war, thought the United States could fight two and one-half wars simultaneously (a major war against Russia and another against China, plus a small brushfire war). But the Nixon administration, reflecting American disillusionment with military ventures, said realistically we could fight only one and one-half wars at a time. Moreover, Nixon was the first president, despite the long Cold War, to recognize that world Communism was not a monolithic bloc. But dangerous and unsettled world problems led to a reinstatement of nuclear deterrence as the chief American strategic policy. Nixon declared, as had Secretary Donald A. Quarles back in 1956, that he wanted a "sufficient" deterrent rather than one of "parity" or "superiority." By this the commander in chief meant American ability to inflict on the Soviets as much damage as they could on us, and to prevent any other nuclear nation (especially China) from acquiring the capacity to hurt the United States. Congressional and political pressure in 1967 impelled the dubious McNamara to reluctantly approve the "Sentinel" antiballistic missile (ABM) system. He contended that the ABM was primarily intended to safeguard American cities against Chinese nuclear threats. By a tiny edge, Congress in 1969 approved replacing the Sentinel ABM with the new, yet limited, "Safeguard" program to protect the American deterrent.[81]

What triggered some alarm in the autumn of 1969 was the perception that Russia was surging ahead of the United States in the number of landbased ICBMs. This led not only to the Safeguard ABM decision but also to the determination in 1970 to go ahead with deploying our MIRVs on Minuteman IIIs. Each of these carried three warheads that were independently targetable.[82]

The balance of terror strategy and the continuing likelihood of instability led to the beginning of Strategic Arms Limitation Talks (SALT) between the United States and Russia in the winter of 1969. Finally, in May 1970, amid great fanfare in Moscow, Nixon and the Soviets signed SALT agreements limiting each power to two sites and no more than a total of two hundred ABM launchers. Russia was to keep its one around Moscow and another at a selected missile site; the United States was to deploy one near an air base at Grand Forks, North Dakota. The American site authorized around Washington, D.C., would probably not be set up. The agreement was a significant step away from encouraging one of the two powers to launch a preemptive strike.[83]

In the late 1960s the United States Polaris submarines were fitted out with missile launchers bearing three multiple independently targeted reentry vehicles (MIRVs). For 1973, Nixon projected conversion from Polaris to "Poseidon" missiles with twenty such new subs, each with sixteen missile tubes with ten to fourteen MIRV warheads per missile. This ensured the United States a lead in warheads of fifty-two hundred to twenty-five hundred and later, of nearly eight thousand to under three thousand. America would therefore have sufficiency for five years and beyond, despite the Soviet's undoubted and frenzied efforts to try to close the gap in MIRVs, a process which would be delayed by their need first to test and then deploy them. The United States also retained a superiority in total deliverable megatonnage. It was hoped that in the interval agreements could be reached that would be qualitative as well as quantitative.[84]

SMOLDERING OPPOSITION to the freewheeling employment of military forces in Indochina by Johnson and Nixon had been building up in the Congress, and the legislators made a significant effort to clip the powers of the commander in chief by the controversial War Powers Act of 1973, passed over Nixon's veto. This notorious piece of legislation emphasized that only Congress can declare war, although it admitted that as commander in chief the president could commit American forces to action to the extent that major hostilities could ensue. The resolution required that the chief executive consult Congress and report regularly on the course of such hostilities, and that he might continue combat only with the specific authorization of Congress. It declared that if the Congress directed the removal of American forces from the arena of hostilities, the president must comply.

While Richard Nixon and succeeding chief executives have not agreed with all that the act implies, there has as yet been no Supreme Court test case on its legality. Several members of Congress who voted for the resolution acknowledged that it could destroy an enemy's incentive to reach an early settlement of an international dispute, the foe hoping Congress would compel the president to withdraw American forces. Some think a constitutional amendment is needed to make the resolution binding and that it is too inflexible. Opponents say the act will encourage a president to be less than candid, and that it will encourage him to escalate hostilities, possibly to include nuclear weapons to win a decision within the time limit before he is forced to terminate use of American forces. Here the matter rests at this moment [1982].[85]

ONE of the main goals of the navy, air force, and especially the army, was to restore morale that had plummeted during the Vietnam war. Considerable progress was made, and some also in limiting drug abuse, aided possibly by the all-volunteer force. The brief but lethal recent war in the Middle East between the Arabs and Israel soon gave the armed services much to think about in strategy, tactics, and weapons. The search for a main battle tank (the XMI) for the army and its allies was finally resolved with Chrysler winning out over General Motors and the German "Leopard" tank, but with an interchangeability for the main cannon on the tank. Emphasis seemed to be more on antitank (or antiarmor weapons) and their use. This included progress on such antitank items as the "Tow" and "Dragon," air command planes, night and electronic warfare advances, and such "smart" weapons as wire-, television-, and laser-guided projectiles.[86] Since the main endeavor on the NATO central front was to commit more forces from the United States to forward positions so that not too much of Germany would be sacrificed in a sudden Soviet onslaught, TRADOC hammered away at the theme "Win the first air/land battle." With the severe limitations in such areas as numbers, airlift, and especially sea-lift capacity, this was a most challenging and grave mission.

After Jimmy Carter was sworn in as president in January 1977, it was recognized that the Russians would continue their large-scale efforts to build up their army, air force, weapons stockpiles, and especially their navy, which had gained world-girdling capabilities by the 1970s and posed a threat to American and Allied sea-lanes. The United States Navy struggled to retain authority to man thirteen aircraft carriers and to maintain other ships, some nuclear powered. Carter vetoed continuation of the air force program to develop the new B-1 intercontinental bomber that was designed to replace the aging B-52s, and progress was slow on the new TRIDENT missile and submarine. But the chief executive did give the green light to develop the cruise missile, a highly praised, comparatively inexpensive weapon in which we apparently had a lead over the Soviets.[87]

Carter continued to place emphasis and faith in the SALT talks though progress on them seemed to move at the speed of a glacier. He also submitted for Senate ratification treaties that would end American sovereignty over the Panama Canal and its Zone by the year 2000, with supposedly firm guarantees that the United States would have full access and authority to defend the canal in times of crisis. Although the armed services showed some ill-concealed trepidation, the treaties were passed.

In the ultimately crucial area of American policy on deterrence during the administrations of Nixon, Gerald Ford, and Carter, the Russians sought for their own reasons, whether sincere or an attempt to seduce America into lowering its military guard, to move toward detente with the United States. Henry Kissinger, secretary of state under both Nixon and Ford, was sympathetic. While encouraging detente, the United States remained fairly alert, insisting on "rough equivalence" in strategic nuclear deterrence. As Kissinger phrased it, "The *appearance* of inferiority . . . can have serious political consequences"; for politically significant reasons, both America and Russia had "a high incentive to achieve not only the reality but the appearance of equality."[88] This remained the military posture of the United States as the seventh decade of the twentieth century became history, and the new president, Ronald W. Reagan, moved powerfully to augment America's armed might.

DESPITE global commitments, the need to occupy a number of former enemy territories, and the reaction (such as that of NATO) to Communist expansion, the United States—its citizens, its president, and its Congress—was too complacent during the several years after 1945 in their insistence upon the rapid demobilization of the armed forces to a dangerously low point. This decline was aided and abetted by economy measures pushed by Harry Truman and Louis Johnson.

Even the Red aggression into South Korea in 1950 aroused America only to the extent that she would slowly rebuild her land, sea, and air forces sufficiently to fight a limited war that was little better than a stalemate. Nor was the battle over unification, just before hostilities erupted in Korea, a harbinger of totally effective cooperation between the armed forces during that unhappy conflict, although Americans in uniform fought well.

While Truman's rapid response to the North Korean invasion of the South was worthy, he and the top civilian and military leaders of the administration were fearful of an enlarged war with China in the Far East, possible Russian aggression elsewhere, or World War III. Thus they insisted on fighting a partial and consequently frustrating war on that peninsula—a conflict whose limitations Douglas MacArthur so opposed that he was recalled. This war, fought on extremely rugged terrain and against an under-developed nation, demonstrated to those who would observe the limitations of sea power and especially of air power, despite a generally excellent performance by those armed services.

With the coming of the Dwight Eisenhower administration and the rising costs of weapons and other equipment caused by inflation, an effort was made to curtail American ground forces and to emphasize in the "New Look," massive atomic and nuclear retaliation. But this proved illusory as a response to brushfire wars, and a struggle ensued that involved the retirement or resignation of Matthew Ridgway, Maxwell Taylor, and James Gavin over whether the United States should add to her depleted conventional arms and forces.

Soviet intransigence prevented limitations on nuclear weaponry; so a frightfully expensive and potentially explosive arms race has ensued since the end of World War II, although the SALT talks, undertaken by Richard Nixon, scored a few successes and held out at least a dim hope for the future.

As in other nations belonging to the "nuclear club," protracted and at times acrid debate took place in the United States as to just what the balance should be between the army, navy (and the marines), and air force as well as between nuclear and conventional weapons. New and more frightfully efficient missiles and warheads were being constantly developed.

And America was painfully divided over the war in Vietnam. Held down strictly in numbers and in activities by Eisenhower, American forces in Vietnam were enlarged by Kennedy and were then blown up by Lyndon Johnson to over half a million troops; yet the war could not be won under the gradualist acceleration practiced by Johnson and Robert McNamara and the limited options permitted our commanders in Vietnam. This trying venture was ended by Nixon and Henry Kissinger on what was hoped would be an acceptable basis; but the Communists violated the solemn agreements and ended up with the whole of Indochina. Ford at least regained a little prestige for the nation by his sharp reaction to the *Mayaguez* incident in which he ordered American forces into combat to recapture the ship that had been seized by the North Vietnamese. But the president's wings as commander in chief were seriously clipped by the controversial War Powers Act of 1973, and this issue has not yet been resolved.

As the republic entered the last quarter of the century, the armed forces, with renewed morale, continued their pressure for sufficient support from president and Congress to accomplish their global missions, let alone cope with unexpected crises that could break out at any moment in such powder kegs as the Middle East or Africa.

ACROSS the imperishable canvas of the history of mankind, the United States of America stands as a maturing though still young nation. While it has had, and still has, its share of grim problems—as all industrial nations do—it has also scored some impressive accomplishments, and a number of these have fallen in the area of military affairs.

Though not a militaristic people, Americans have not been unwarlike, and they have been drawn into *every* world war since the 1600s. In addition, her citizens have fought a running battle with the American Indian from 1607 to at least 1891. In time of peace the United States has seldom maintained a large, permanent, regular military establishment, especially an army. We have expanded our forces considerably only in time of war. Yet the American frontier experience chiefly involved struggles with the Indians and impelled Americans to maintain a militia-type establishment capable of meeting sudden local threats.

Americans gained experience in coalition warfare early, or at least as an ally with the mother country in several of the Colonial wars, although the record is spotty on the performance of these hastily gathered soldiers. In the Revolutionary War the raw, untrained, ill-equipped, and poorly disciplined forces did not fare too well against the British at first, especially in stand-up battles in the open. The priceless character and leadership qualities of George Washington and the magnificent staying powers of his few steadfast soldiers kept the colonists in the war. But the Americans excelled at improvisation, as they still do to a certain extent. After decent drill and training, the Yankees performed more creditably, cooperating well with the French in gaining the decisive victory at Yorktown.

In the formulation of a new constitution, most leaders in the United States insisted upon civilian supremacy over the military, and this axiom of polity, given staunch support by Washington, has pervaded our system down to the present with but few contrary ripples on the surface. The father of his country played also a pivotal role in establishing tiny but well-organized land and sea forces during his eight years as president; and, despite the fact that they were too few up until the War of 1812, they could and did prevail when buttressed sufficiently by new accretions.

Ineffective leadership on the part of James Madison, most of his War and Navy Department secretaries, and the superannuated generals led to early defeats in the second war with Britain, although U.S. warships did well. When younger and abler generals were found, and troops seasoned, the United States fared better in the land warfare and ended the war on a rising note. Continued Indian wars until the mid-1840s occupied the attention of the small, scattered regular army, and the navy was dispersed into seven cruising squadrons around the world. After a halting start, West Point developed, under Sylvanus Thayer, into a highly respectable military academy. James Polk showed, in the American victory in the Mexican War, that a president, employing his full commander in chief powers, could administer such a conflict with full plenitude of authority, although he mishandled too many matters to be given a high mark. Zachary Taylor and especially Winfield Scott showed to good advantage in the major field operations, and the halls of the Montezumas were reached.

With the county dividing along sectional lines, the republic just missed being rent asunder by four years of bloody, fratricidal strife. While the Confederate president, Jefferson Davis, did well in a number of matters, it remained for Abraham Lincoln—after a number of false starts and errors—to show what a consummate war director an American president could become. Along with some talented commanders in the field, he sublimely led the Union to a victory that rewelded the sections into a stronger nation than before. The fighting qualities of the massive numbers of soldiers in blue and gray have left a heritage that has not yet ceased to astound people everywhere, even down to our own times.

After 1865 the navy remained backward in warships and in numbers, not beginning to modernize until the 1880s. The army was initially siphoned off into occupation during Reconstruction in the South, then was given the thankless task of pacifying hostile Indians in the vast distances of the West. Both our land and sea forces were adequate to win the short war with Spain in 1898, although this limited war showed the miserably unprepared condition of the army. It remained for Theodore Roosevelt to commence a series of needed army reforms early in the twentieth century—skillfully aided by Elihu Root and others—and to significantly enlarge the navy.

While the United States Navy was deficient in smaller, antisubmarine-type warships, it did play a useful role in helping to defeat the Central Powers in the First World War. The small army was not ready to fight a large-scale war on the European continent, but, under John Pershing's indomitable leadership, once the conscript army had been molded, the doughboys did themselves proud in France. It was a remarkable overseas achievement. Woodrow Wilson's near abdication as commander in chief sat well with the top men in uniform but did not enable America to play a sagacious role in the postwar peace settlement, especially as the United States had not joined the League of Nations.

The 1920s and 1930s saw the same, tattered, sorry tale of the head-in-the-sand attitude regarding the army and its air arm. The navy was better maintained as the first line of defense, although battleships were emphasized more than aircraft carriers. As customary, the nation was caught by surprise when the Japanese struck in December 1941, and an unparalleled mobilization of the country and its military and economic resources was required first to turn the tide against the surging Axis powers and then to roll them back in defeat. Cooperation with British allies was exemplary. Franklin Roosevelt played the part of commander in chief to the hilt, and the United States was blessed by generally excellent performances by those officers in top civilian and uniformed positions—notably by such men as Dwight Eisenhower, Douglas MacArthur, Chester Nimitz, and the other line and staff top brass. By 1945 the great forces of the United States had almost unlimited global mobility. Harry Truman made the momentous decision to drop the only two atomic bombs as yet used in warfare. The will to win through to total victory by the American people was the essential adhesive in this great crusade.

Hesitation and internecine conflict was demonstrated between the armed services after 1945 during the unification struggle, and Harry Truman, Louis Johnson, Congress, and U.S. citizens reduced the military establishment so severely that America was ill prepared when the Korean War came in 1950. The nation was disappointed and dissatisfied with the indecisive nature of this limited war, and—once more—valuable lessons were soon forgotten, if indeed they had been learned at all. Endless squabbling over conventional vs. nuclear weapons was accompanied by the usual and necessary debate over the size of U.S. forces. The nation at first relied on atomic retaliation, retained the nuclear umbrella, and slowly strengthened its conventional weapons and forces.

Then came the Vietnam War that seared the soul of the country and divided its people. Again, somewhat stale limited war techniques were employed, the generals and admirals kept tightly reined in, and final success was eluded. Lyndon Johnson and Robert McNamara could not prevent sagging morale on the home as well as the fighting front, and Richard Nixon was obliged to withdraw from the war, hoping that a decent truce would be honored by the enemy.

It wasn't, and the United States had to regroup its forces and restore its national spirit. Much of this was accomplished, and the reduced but still formidable armed forces modernized to a greater extent than ever before in peacetime. But suspicion of the president's powers and scope of freedom under the commander in chief clause led to Congress's dubious restriction of this authority with the War Powers Act of 1973.

The talent of the United States at improvisation can do only so much in this modern era, and as of 1982 America's military policy was still in a state of flux. Her sons and daughters, with a staggering number of commitments to keep, are thinly stretched in far-flung posts over the globe. All Americans— top civilian and military leaders, the armed forces, and individual citizens— will be tested in the future in as-yet-unknown crises that one can only hope will be met successfully.

Serious reflection on the past achievements and failures in America's military history and affairs and the examples of enlightened leadership in the historical past could be invaluable to today's leaders and citizens, always bearing in mind the need to keep abreast and ahead in new technology and strategies. The price of freedom is eternal vigilance. Can the United States afford to do less?

N O T E S

CHAPTER ONE

1. Peckham, *The Colonial Wars, 1689–1762*, pp. 1–2, 4.
2. Douglas E. Leach, *Arms for Empire*, pp. 11–23; John W. Shy, "A New Look at Colonial Militia," *William and Mary Quarterly*, 3d ser. 20(1963):181–84.
3. Harold L. Peterson, *Arms and Armor in Colonial America;* Michael R. Roberts, *The Military Revolution, 1560–1660;* Hoffman Nickerson, *The Armed Horde*, pp. 19–63.
4. *A Journal of the Proceedings in the Late Expedition to Port Royal* (Boston: Benjamin Harris, 1690), pp. 3–6.
5. Thomas Savage, *An Account of the Late Action of the New Englanders*.
6. E. B. O'Callaghan and Berthold Fernow, eds., *Documents Relative to the Colonial History of the State of New York*, 15 vols. (Albany: Weed, Parsons, 1853–1887), 3:800–805.
7. Peckham, pp. 41–42.
8. Ibid., pp. 49–51; Leach, pp. 106–7.
9. Leach, p. 109; Peckham, pp. 51–53.
10. Charles W. Arnade, *The Siege of St. Augustine in 1702*, pp. 9–10.
11. Francis Parkman, *A Half-Century of Conflict*, 1:chap. 4; Thomas Church, *The History of the Eastern Expeditions of 1689, 1690, 1692, 1696, and 1704 Against the Indians and French* (Boston: Howe & Norton, 1867), pp. 128–81.
12. G. M. Waller, *Samuel Vetch*, pp. 100–119.
13. Ibid., pp. 126, 142, 156; Bruce T. McCully, "Catastrophe in the Wilderness: New Light on the Canada Expedition of 1709," *William and Mary Quarterly* 11(1954):442, 455.
14. Peckham, p. 70; Gerald S. Graham, *Empire of the North Atlantic*, pp. 90–91.
15. Gerald S. Graham, ed., *The Walker Expedition to Quebec, 1711*, p. 269; Leach, pp. 144–49.
16. Peckham, pp. 72–73.
17. Peckham, pp. 74–75.
18. William A. Foote, "The Pennsylvania Men of the American Regiment," *Pennsylvania Magazine of History and Biography* 87(1963):36–37; John W. Fortescue, *A History of the British Army*, 2:62–76.
19. *The Spanish Official Account of the Attack on the Colony of Georgia*, vol. 7. (Savannah: Collections of the Georgia Historical Society), pt. 3; Leach, p. 224.
20. Louis Effingham DeForest, ed., *Louisbourg Journals, 1745* (New York: Society of Colonial Wars, 1932), p. 171.
21. G. A. Rawlyk, *Yankees at Louisbourg*, pp. 35–40.
22. Leach, p. 231; Parkman, *Half-Century of Conflict*.
23. Jack M. Sosin, "Louisburg and the Peace of Aix-la-Chapelle," *William and Mary Quarterly* 14(1957):516–35.
24. William A. Hunter, *Forts on the Pennsylvania Frontier, 1753–1758*, pp. 20–23.
25. Lois Mulkearn, "The English Eye the French in North America," *Pennsylvania History* 21(1954):332–39; Francis Parkman, *Montcalm and Wolfe*, 1:132–42.
26. Parkman, *Montcalm and Wolfe*, 1:333–34.
27. Marcel Trudel, "The Jumonville Affair," *Pennsylvania History* 21(1954):351–81; John C. Fitzpatrick, ed., *The Writings of George Washington*, 1:54–70.
28. Parkman, *Montcalm and Wolfe*, 1:145–62, 2:421–23; Douglas Southall Freeman, *George Washington*, 1:389–412, 548–49.
29. O'Callaghan and Fernow, eds., 6:920–22; Pargellis, ed., pp. 45–48.
30. Lawrence H. Gipson, *The Great War for the Empire*, pp. 71–72, 82–83, 97–98; Fitzpatrick, 1:142–43.

31. Pargellis, pp. 129–30; Freeman, 2:68–82.

32. Peckham, p. 153; John R. Cuneo, *Robert Rogers of the Rangers*, p. 32.

33. *Montcalm and Wolfe*, 1:431–32.

34. Ibid., 2:322, 358–60.

35. Leach, pp. 395, 404; Peckham, pp. 159–60.

36. Owen A. Sherrard, *Lord Chatham*, pp. 284–85.

37. Leach, p. 404.

38. Louis Antoine de Bougainville, *Adventure in the Wilderness*, pp. 152–77.

39. Edward P. Hamilton, *The French and Indian Wars*, pp. 220–23.

40. Parkman, *Montcalm and Wolfe*, 2:184.

41. John S. McLennan, *Louisbourg from Its Foundation to Its Fall*, pp. 236–42, 246–48, 262–63, chaps. 13–15; John C. Webster, ed., *The Journal of Jeffery Amherst*, pp. 46–47, 49, 51, 60–86.

42. Niles Anderson, "The General Chooses a Road: The Forbes Campaign of 1758 to Capture Fort Duquesne," *Western Pennsylvania Historical Magazine* 42(1959):110–14, 120–24; Parkman, *Montcalm and Wolfe*, 2:49, 130–63.

43. Peckham, pp. 179–80: Sigmund Samuel, comp., *The Seven Years War in Canada*, pp. 49–64.

44. On the pivotal Quebec campaign see Arthur G. Doughty, *The Siege of Quebec;* Charles P. Stacey, *Quebec, 1759;* Christopher Lloyd, *The Capture of Quebec;* Christopher Hibbert, *Wolfe at Quebec;* Parkman, *Montcalm and Wolfe*, 2:195–233, 259–99, 436–41.

45. Cuneo, chap. 9; Thomas M. Charland, "The Lake Champlain Army and the Fall of Montreal," *Vermont History*, n.s. 28(1960):296–99.

46. Amherst, *Journal*, pp. 153, 168, 208–9, 227, 232–39, 244; Parkman, *Montcalm and Wolfe*, 2: 361–82.

47. Leach, pp. 500–501; Niles Anderson, "Bushy Run: Decisive Battle in the Wilderness," *Western Pennsylvania Historical Magazine* 41(1963):211–45.

48. See Peckham, pp. 2–3, 214–16.

49. See George Louis Beer, *British Colonial Policy, 1754–1765*, chap. 6; Lawrence H. Gipson, *The Coming of the Revolution*, pp. 55–56.

CHAPTER TWO

1. For the coming of the war see John Shy, *Toward Lexington*.

2. Willard M. Wallace, *Appeal to Arms*, pp. 5–11; John Shy, "Thomas Gage: Weak Link of Empire," George A. Billias, ed., *George Washington's Opponents*, p. 24.

3. Peter Force, ed., *American Archives*, 4th ser., 1:487–550; Allen French, *The Day of Concord and Lexington*.

4. Grindall Reynolds, *Concord Fight, April 19, 1775; Newport Mercury*, Apr. 24, May 8, 1775.

5. Don Higginbotham, *The War of American Independence*, pp. 68–69.

6. Howard H. Peckham, *The War for Independence*, p. 12.

7. Stewart H. Holbrook, *Ethan Allen*.

8. Benson J. Lossing, *The Pictorial Field-Book of the Revolution*, 1:422, 605, 710; Willard M. Wallace, *Traitorous Hero*.

9. Christopher Ward, *The War of the Revolution*, 1:63–72, 405–6; Allen French, *The Taking of Ticonderoga in 1775;* Justin H. Smith, *Our Struggle for the Fourteenth Colony*, 1:110–40.

10. Richard Frothingham, *History of the Siege of Boston*, p. 167; John Cary, *Joseph Warren*.

11. Harold Murdock, *Bunker Hill;* Frothingham, p. 116.

12. Allen French, *The First Years of the American Revolution*, pp. 284–87; on Washington and his role in the Revolution see Douglas Southall Freeman, *George Washington*, vols. 3–5; Thomas G. Frothingham, *Washington, Commander-in-Chief;* and James T. Flexner, *George Washington in the American Revolution*.

13. Ward, 1:chap. 3; John C. Fitzpatrick, ed., *The Writings of George Washington*, 4:124, 5:210, 6:222.

14. Worthington C. Ford, ed., *Journals of the Continental Congress, 1774–1789*, 2:100–101.

15. Smith, *Our Struggle*, 1:320–21, 367–70, 610.

16. Robert M. Hatch, *Thrust for Canada;* John Codman, *Arnold's Expedition to Quebec;* Justin H. Smith, *Arnbold's March from Cambridge to Quebec: Journal of Captain Henry Dearborn in the Quebec Expedition, 1775* (New York: Putnam, 1903).

17. Fitzpatrick, 4:405, 407; R. Frothingham, p. 322.
18. William Moultrie, *Memoirs of the American Revolution*, 1:141; Eric Robson, "The Expedition to the Southern Colonies, 1775-1776," *English Historical Review* 66(1951):535-60; *South Carolina and American General Advertiser*, Aug. 2, 1776.
19. Alfred Thayer Mahan, *The Major Operations of the Navies in the War of American Independence*, pp. 17-25; Force, 4th ser., vol. 4, 5th ser., vol. 1.
20. Bruce Bliven, Jr., *Battle for Manhattan;* Henry P. Johnston, *The Campaign of 1776 Around New York and Brooklyn* (Brooklyn, N.Y.: Long Island Historical Society, 1878), vol. 3; George A. Billias, *General John Glover and His Marblehead Mariners*, pp. 100-123; Ira D. Gruber, "Lord Howe and Lord George Germain," *William and Mary Quarterly* 3d ser., 22(1965):225-43.
21. T. Frothingham, pp. 161-62; John C. Miller, *The Triumph of Freedom, 1775-1783*, p. 148; Ford, Dec. 20, 1776; Ward, 1:285, 290; Edward J. Lowell, *The Hessians and Other German Auxiliaries*, p. 87; Leonard Lundin, *Cockpit of the Revolution*, pp. 148-78.
22. Force, 5th ser., 3:1331, 1342, 1427; George Bancroft, *History of the United States of America*, 9:235; Warren W. Hassler, Jr., "General Washington and the Revolution's Crucial Campaign," *Western Pennsylvania Historical Magazine* 48(1965):249-65; Howard M. Fast, *The Crossing*.
23. Fitzpatrick, 6:447, 449, 470; William S. Stryker, *The Battles of Trenton and Princeton;* Alfred H. Bill, *The Campaign of Princeton;* Lossing, 1:305, 306, 310; Ward, 1:316-24.
24. Bancroft, 9:256; quoted in R. Ernest Dupuy and Trevor N. Dupuy, *The Compact History of the Revolutionary War*, p. 183.
25. William B. Willcox, "Too Many Cooks: British Planning Before Saratoga," *Journal of British Studies* 2(1962-1963):59; Hoffman Nickerson, *The Turning Point of the Revolution*, pp. 83-89.
26. Samuel W. Patterson's *Horatio Gates* is too laudatory. See George A. Billias, ed., *George Washington's Generals*, pp. 79-108.
27. Stryker, *Trenton and Princeton*, p. 350; John Burgoyne, *A State of the Expedition from Canada*, app. xxv-xxvi; Friederike von Riedesel, *Letters and Journals*.
28. William B. Willcox, *Portrait of a General*, pp. 174-96; William L. Stone, *The Campaign of Lieut. Gen. John Burgoyne and the Expedition of Lieut. Col. Barry St. Leger;* Henry B. Dawson, *Battles of the United States*, 1:250-52.
29. Burgoyne, pp. 30, 54, 122; Nickerson; James P. Baxter, *The British Invasion from the North*, pp. 269-70; Don Higginbotham, *Daniel Morgan*, pp. 60-77.
30. W. H. Moomaw, "The Denouement of General Howe's Campaign of 1777," *English Historical Review* 79(1964):498-512; Edward C. Cooch, *The Battle of Cooch's Bridge;* Wallace, *Appeal to Arms*, pp. 136-39, 197.
31. George W. Greene, *The Life of Nathanael Greene*, 1:474-81; Freeman, *George Washington*, 4:485-92.
32. John McAuley Palmer, *General von Steuben*, pp. 3-4, 9, 13, 14.
33. Ibid.; Alfred H. Bill, *Valley Forge;* Joseph R. Riling, *Baron von Steuben and His Regulations for the Order and Discipline of the Troops of the United States*.
34. Elizabeth S. Kite, "French 'Secret Aid' Precursor to the French American Alliance, 1776-1777," *French American Review* 1(1948):143-52; Edward S. Corwin, *French Policy and the American Alliance of 1778*.
35. William S. Stryker, *The Battle of Monmouth;* Fitzpatrick, 12:74-130.
36. Fitzpatrick, 3:309, 6:5-6, 464; Emory Upton, *The Military Policy of the United States*, pp. 21-22.
37. Joseph Bernardo and Eugene H. Bacon, *American Military Policy*, pp. 26, 34-35, 38; Ford, 10:199-203, 13:298-99.
38. Ward, 2:655-64; Kenneth Coleman, *The American Revolution in Georgia*, p. 98; Alexander A. Lawrence, *Storm Over Savannah;* Moultrie, 1:247.
39. *Charleston Gazette*, Jan. 26, 1779; Edward McCrady, *The History of South Carolina in the Revolution* (New York: Macmillan, 1902), pp. 431, 500-510; Lossing, 2:471, 553-61.
40. Banastre Tarleton, *A History of the Campaigns of 1780 and 1781 in the Southern Provinces of North America;* Ward, 2:704-11.
41. Greene, 3:122-27; Henry Lee, *Memoirs of the War in the Southern Department*, pp. 174-75.
42. Lossing, 2:511; Higginbotham, *War of American Independence*, p. 362.
43. *Dictionary of American Biography*, s.v., hereafter cited as *DAB*.

44. John Bakeless, *Background to Glory;* Temple Bodley, *George Rogers Clark;* James A. James, ed., *George Rogers Clark Papers,* 8:97-100, 208-302.
45. Howard Swiggett, *War Out of Niagara,* chaps. 6, 7; Charles Miner, *History of Wyoming,* pp. 225-28.
46. Alexander C. Flick, comp., *The Sullivan-Clinton Campaign of 1779;* Albert H. Wright, comp., *The Sullivan Expedition of 1779.*
47. Lawrence Kinnaird, ed., *Spain in the Mississippi Valley, 1765-1794* (Washington: Government Printing Office, 1949), 2:418; John W. Caughey, *Bernardo de Galvez in Louisiana, 1776-1783,* pp. 85-242.
48. William B. Clark, *George Washington's Navy;* John F. McCusher, "The American Invasion of Nassau in the Bahamas," *American Neptune* 25(1965):189-217.
49. Peckham, pp. 123-24; Higginbotham, *War of American Independence,* p. 338.
50. Howard I. Chapelle, *The History of the American Sailing Navy,* chaps. 1, 2.
51. William B. Clark, *Lambert Wickes;* Ralph D. Paine, *Joshua Barney.*
52. William B. Clark, *Gallant John Barry.*
53. Samuel Eliot Morison, *John Paul Jones;* James Fenimore Cooper, *Lives of Distinguished American Naval Officers,* 2:5-112.
54. Peckham, p. 128.
55. Glenn Tucker, *Mad Anthony Wayne.*
56. Henry P. Johnston, *The Storming of Stony Point;* Henry B. Dawson, *The Assault on Stony Point.*
57. Fitzpatrick, 19:174, 20:103-4; Freeman, 5:296n.
58. James T. Flexner, *The Traitor and the Spy.*
59. *Pennsylvania Journal,* Sept. 20, 1780; Otho H. Williams, "A Narrative of the Campaign of 1780," William Johnson, *Sketches of the Life and Correspondence of Nathanael Greene* (Charleston: A. E. Miller, 1882), 1:App. B, 485-510.
60. Lyman C. Draper, *King's Mountain and Its Heroes.*
61. Russell F. Weigley, *The American Way of War,* chap. 2; George Otto Trevelyan, *The American Revolution,* 4:176-78; Force, 4th ser., 3:1077.
62. Peckham, p. 151; Lee, pp. 226-27; Higginbotham, *Daniel Morgan,* chap. 9; Tarleton, pp. 214-22.
63. Burke Davis, *The Cowpens-Guilford Court House Campaign;* M. F. Treacy, *Prelude to Yorktown.*
64. Peckham, pp. 154-55; W. Stitt Robinson, ed., *Richard Oswald's Memorandum on the Folly of Invading Virginia* (Charlottesville: University of Virginia Press, 1953), pp. 8-9.
65. David Schenck, *North Carolina, 1780-'81,* pp. 400-412; Lee, pp. 334-41; Fortescue, 3:385-87; Tarleton, pp. 474-85.
66. Lossing, 2:492-99; Ward, 2:823-34; Schenck, pp. 444-59; Greene, 3:384-402.
67. William B. Willcox, "The British Road to Yorktown," *American Historical Review* 42 (1946):1-35; Wallace, *Appeal to Arms,* pp. 247, 250; Dawson, *Battles,* 1:701-4.
68. Fitzpatrick, 19:174, 20:103-4.
69. Freeman, 5:chap. 19; Louis Gottschalk, *Lafayette and the Close of the American Revolution,* pp. 189-306.
70. William M. James, *The British Navy in Adversity* (London: Longmans, Green, 1926), pp. 288-94, 444-45.
71. Charles E. Hatch, Jr., *Yorktown and the Siege of 1781.*
72. Henry P. Johnston, *The Yorktown Campaign and the Surrender of Cornwallis;* Donald B. Chidsey, *Victory at Yorktown;* Gottschalk, pp. 307-28.
73. James Thacher, *Military Journal of the American Revolution* (Hartford: Hurlbert, Williams, 1862); Ward, 2:894-95; Lossing, 2:316-18.
74. Richard B. Morris, *The Peacemakers,* pp. 382, 383, 536.
75. Fitzpatrick, 26:227; Richard H. Kohn, "The History of the Newburgh Conspiracy," *William and Mary Quarterly* 3d ser., 27(1970):187-220; Ford, 24:294-97; Upton, pp. 36-43, 62-63.
76. Benjamin Tallmadge, *Memoir of Col. Benjamin Tallmadge* (New York: T. Holman, 1858), pp. 97-98; *New York Gazette,* 6 Dec., 1783; Freeman, 5:466-68.
77. Freeman, 5:475-77; Ford, 25:810, 818-19, 820, 838-39.
78. *American State Papers, Military Affairs,* 1:15-20; Clarence S. Peterson, *Known Military*

Dead during the Revolutionary War, 1775–1783 (Baltimore: C. S. Peterson, 1959); Peckham, p. 200; Bernardo and Bacon, p. 45.

79. Fortescue, 3:chap. 26; Freeman, 5:487–501; Higginbotham, *War of American Independence,* pp. 428–35; Bernardo and Bacon, pp. 44–45.

CHAPTER THREE

1. John C. Miller, *The Triumph of Freedom,* pp. 666–69; C. Joseph Bernardo and Eugene H. Bacon, *American Military Policy,* p. 58; John C. Fitzpatrick, ed., *The Writings of George Washington,* 27:256–57, 278–79; 284–85; Chauncey W. Ford, ed., *The Journals of the Continental Congress,* 27:518.
2. Hamilton to Washington, 9 Apr. 1783, George Washington Papers, Library of Congress, Washington, D.C.; Bernardo and Bacon, p. 48n.
3. Fitzpatrick, 26:375–97; Ford, 25:723–42. An able study of this period is Richard H. Kohn, *Eagle and Sword: The Federalists and the Creation of the Military Establishment in America, 1783–1802.*
4. Bernardo and Bacon, pp. 60–61, 63; Harry M. Ward, *The Department of War, 1781–1789,* p. 42; James Ripley Jacobs, *The Beginning of the U.S. Army, 1783–1812,* p. 14; Russell F. Weigley, *History of the United States Army,* p. 82.
5. J. F. Callan, *The Military Laws of the United States,* p. 78; T. H. S. Hamersly, *Complete Regular Army Register of the United States,* pt. 2, pp. 231–32; Reginald Horsman, "American Indian Policy in the Old Northwest, 1783–1812," *William and Mary Quarterly* 3d ser., 18(1961):35–53; Ward, pp. 60–74.
6. Baron F. von Steuben, "A Letter on the Subject of an Established Militia and Military Arrangements Addressed to the Inhabitants of the United States" (New York: J. McLean, 1784), pp. 3, 7, 11–14, 80, 81; John M. Palmer, *Washington, Lincoln, Wilson,* chap. 5.
7. Henry Knox, "A Plan for the General Arrangement of the Militia of the United States," 18 Mar. 1786, pp. 8, 19, 25, Rare Book Room, Library of Congress; Palmer, *Washington, Lincoln, Wilson,* pp. 90–93; Ford, 33:602–4.
8. "Diary of Erkuries Beatty," *Magazine of American History* 1:313, 380–82, 432–33; B. W. Bond, ed., *The Correspondence of John Cleves Symmes,* pp. 288–90; Erna Risch, *Quartermaster Support of the Army,* pp. 76–81; Raphael P. Thian, *Legislative History of the General Staff,* pp. 190–91, 327–28, 457.
9. Connecticut *Journal,* 6, 27 Nov. 1786; Ward, pp. 75–81; Hamersly, pt. 2, p. 231; Ford, 31:891–92, 32:98–99; *Newport Mercury,* 17 Mar. 1787; Knox, "A Plan," p. 699; Fitzpatrick, 29:52, 121–24; Gaillard Hunt, ed., *The Writings of James Madison,* 2:317.
10. U.S., *Constitution,* art. 1, sec. 8, art. 2, sec. 2; Warren W. Hassler, Jr., *The President as Commander in Chief,* chap. 1.
11. U.S., *Statutes at Large,* 1:49–50, 95; Callan, pp. 85–87; *American State Papers: Military Affairs,* 1:5–6, cited hereafter as *ASPMA; Bulletin of Fort Ticonderoga Museum* (July 1936), pp. 30–31; *Dictionary of American Biography,* s.v., hereafter cited as DAB.
12. *ASPMA,* 1:6–13.
13. See *Boston Gazette and Country Journal,* 22 Feb. 1790; John M. Palmer, *America in Arms,* p. 45; United States *Annals of Congress,* 1st Cong., 2d sess., 26 Apr. 1790, 2:1544; Jacobs, *U.S. Army,* p. 45.
14. Theodore Roosevelt, *The Winning of the West,* 3:72, 77, 80–84; John B. McMaster, *History of the People of the United States,* 1:597; Randolph C. Downes, *Frontier Ohio, 1788–1803,* pp. 10–13, 18–19; *American State Papers: Indian Affairs,* 1:5–7, cited hereafter as *ASPIA.*
15. Josiah Harmar Papers, University of Michigan, Ann Arbor; *DAB,* s.v.; Knox to Harmar, 24 Aug. 1790, Durrett Papers, University of Wisconsin, Madison.
16. *ASPMA,* 1:21, 31–33; Jacobs, *U.S. Army,* pp. 54, 535.
17. *ASPMA,* 1:20–30.
18. Ibid.; James Bachus, 24 Nov. 1790, William Woodbridge Papers, Detroit Public Library.
19. *ASPMA,* 1:23, 35; *ASPIA,* 1:104–6; Francis Paul Prucha, *The Sword of the Republic,* pp. 220–22; Howard H. Peckham, "Josiah Harmar and His Indian Expedition," *Ohio Archeological*

and Historical Quarterly 55(1946):227-41; Emory Upton, *The Military Policy of the United States,* pp. 77-78; Harmar to Knox, 4, 23 Nov. 1790, Harmar Papers; Bond, pp. 132-33.

20. Wilkinson to Harmar, 20 June 1791, Durrett Papers; *ASPMA,* 1:20-30.

21. C. E. Carter, ed., *Territorial Papers of the United States South of the Ohio, 1790 to 1796* (Washington: Government Printing Office, 1936), pp. 102-3; Callan, pp. 90-91; Jacobs, *U.S. Army,* pp. 68-69.

22. *DAB,* s.v.; *American State Papers: Miscellaneous Affairs,* 1:59, cited hereafter as *ASPMisA.*

23. Robert M. McElroy, *Kentucky in the Nation's History,* p. 156; *ASPIA,* 1:171-82; Jacobs, *U.S. Army,* pp. 77-80; *ASPMA,* 1:43.

24. Arthur St. Clair, *Narrative of the Campaign Against the Indians, 1791,* pp. 5, 140, 152-54; *Lexington Kentucky Gazette,* 2, 9 July 1791; William H. Smith, ed., *Arthur St. Clair Papers,* 2: 206-10, 252, 292-93.

25. St. Clair, pp. 29-37, 270-71; Smith, 2:242, 245-47; Winthrop Sargent, "Diary," *Ohio Archeological and Historical Society Publications,* 33:267, 269; Jacobs, *U.S. Army,* pp. 91-93.

26. T. Irwin, "St. Clair's Defeat," *Ohio Archeological and Historical Society Publications,* 10: 378-80; "Military Journal of Major Ebenezer Denny," *Memoirs of the Historical Society of Pennsylvania,* 7:368; Sargent, "Diary," p. 271.

27. "Journal of Denny," p. 258; Sargent, "Diary," p. 259; *New England Historical and Geological Register,* 21:339-40; Irwin, "St. Clair's Defeat," p. 380.

28. St. Clair, pp. 50-51, 220-21; Jacobs, *U.S. Army,* p. 107; Smith, 1:220-21.

29. Sargent, "Diary," p. 269; Smith, 2:261-67; St. Clair, pp. 50-51, 225.

30. Roosevelt, 3:pt. 1, 161, 168-69; Sargent, "Diary," p. 260.

31. Roosevelt, 3:pt. 1, 170-73.

32. U.S., Congress, House, *Journal,* 1st Cong., 1st sess., 1:552, 605, 733; *ASPMA,* 1:38-39, 44; Irving Brant, *James Madison, Father of the Constitution,* p. 367; Bernardo and Bacon, p. 75n.

33. McMaster, 2:11; Jacobs, *U.S. Army,* pp. 118-19, 121-22; Sargent, "Diary," pp. 238-82; *ASPIA,* 1:136-38.

34. T. H. Benton, ed., *Abridgement of the Debates of Congress from 1789 to 1856,* pp. 341-48, 410-14; U.S. Congress, *Annals of Congress,* 2d Cong., pp. 338-55, 418-23, 430-35; U.S., *Statutes at Large,* 1:271-74.

35. See *Boston Independent Chronicle,* 22, 29 Dec. 1791, 7 Jan. 1792; Fitzpatrick, 32:125-26; U.S., *Statutes at Large,* 1:241-43, 246, 264; Callan, pp. 92-93.

36. "Washington's Opinion of General Officers," *Magazine of American History* 3(1879):81-88; Harry E. Wildes, *Anthony Wayne,* pp. 348-49.

37. "Washington's Opinion," pp. 82-83; Jacobs, *U.S. Army,* p. 127.

38. Wildes; *DAB,* s.v.

39. Thomas A. Boyd, *Mad Anthony Wayne,* p. 249; R. Worthington, ed., *Letters and Other Writings of James Madison* (Philadelphia: J. B. Lippincott, 1865), 4:553.

40. *ASPMA,* 1:40-41; Order Book of Anthony Wayne, *Michigan Pioneer and Historical Collections* (Lansing: Wynkoop, Hallenbeck, & Crawford, 1892), vol. 34, 19 Aug., 22 Dec. 1792, 17, 19 Jan., 11 Feb. 1793.

41. James Ripley Jacobs, *The Tarnished Warrior.*

42. *ASPIA,* 1:233, 322, 346; Order Book of Anthony Wayne, 9 May, 6, 21 June, 13 July, 5 Aug., 5, 6 Sept. 1793; Wildes, pp. 382-85, 389; Frazer E. Wilson, *The Peace of Anthony Wayne,* pp. 86-89.

43. Wilson, p. 91; Jacobs, *U.S. Army,* pp. 159-60; A. Wayne to E. Williams and R. Elliott, 16 Oct. 1793, 20 Apr. 1794, Anthony Wayne Papers, vol. 30, Pennsylvania Historical Society, Philadelphia; Order Book of Anthony Wayne, 14 Oct. 1793.

44. Wildes, pp. 408-9, 414-15; Downes, p. 38; Boyd, pp. 270-73.

45. Henry Boyer, "A Journal of Wayne's Campaign," in J. J. Jacobs, *Life of Michael Cresap* (Cincinnati, 1866), pp. 420-21, 424; Ernest A. Cruikshank, ed., *The Correspondence of Lieut. Governor John Graves Simcoe,* 3:7-8; "William Clark's Journal of General Wayne's Campaign," *Mississippi Valley Historical Review* 1:426-28, 16:81-90; Order Book of Anthony Wayne, 19 Aug. 1794.

46. Catharina V. R. Bonney, *A Legacy of Historical Gleanings* (Albany: J. Munsell, 1875), 1:96; Cruikshank, 3:11; A. L. Burt, *The United States, Great Britain, and British North America,* pp.

7-11, 139; *ASPIA*, 1:491-92; "Clark's Journal," p. 429; Henry B. Dawson, *Battles of the United States*, 2:24-26.

47. *ASPIA*, 1:491-92; Cruikshank, 3:7-8, 29-30; Burt, pp. 139-40; Prucha, pp. 28-38; Clarence M. Burton, "Anthony Wayne and the Battle of Fallen Timbers," *Michigan Pioneer and Historical Collections* 31(1901):472-81.

48. *ASPIA*, 1:562-63; Jacobs, *U.S. Army*, pp. 178-81.

49. Wayne, "Order Book," 14, 16 Dec. 1795; Wildes, pp. 448, 453-63.

50. Wilkinson to Baron de Carondelet de Noyelles, 22 Sept. 1796, *Papeles Procedentede Cuba*, Library of Congress; James Wilkinson, *Memoirs of My Own Times*, 2:App., no. 38; Jacobs, *Tarnished Warrior*, p. 152.

51. See Leland Baldwin, *Whiskey Rebels;* J. A. Carroll and M. W. Ashworth, *George Washington*, 7:chap. 7; Jacob E. Cooke, "The Whiskey Insurrection—A Reevaluation," *Pennsylvania History* 30(1963):316-46.

52. Callan, pp. 114-17; Russell F. Weigley, *History of the United States Army*, pp. 102-3; U.S., *Statutes at Large*, 1:483.

53. J. F. C. Fuller, *Decisive Battles of the U.S.A.*, p. vii; *Philadelphia Ladies Magazine*, Apr. 1793, p. 252.

54. James D. Richardson, ed., *A Compilation of the Messages and Papers of the Presidents*, 1: 140.

55. Ibid., 1:237-38, 240.

56. Marshall Smelser, "The Passage of the Naval Act of 1794," *Military Affairs* 22(1958-1959):1-12; Callan, pp. 100-105.

57. Richardson, 1:233-39; Callan, pp. 118-28; U.S., *Statutes at Large*, 1:554-56.

58. B. C. Steiner, *The Life and Correspondence of James McHenry*, pp. 291-95, 311-14; Carlos E. Godfrey, "Organization of the Provisional Army of the United States in the Anticipated War with France, 1798-1800," *Pennsylvania Magazine of History and Biography* 38(1914):129-82; Hamersly, pt. 2, p. 237; Page Smith, *John Adams*, 2:973-74, 980-83; Jacobs, *U.S. Army*, pp. 228-34.

59. Jacobs, *Tarnished Warrior*, pp. 192-93.

60. Ibid., p. 194; *ASPMisA*, 1:247-52; Bernardo and Bacon, pp. 87-88.

61. Richardson, 1:201.

62. Charles O. Paullin, "Early Naval Administration Under the Constitution," *Proceedings of the United States Naval Institute* 32:1002, 1009; U.S., *Statutes at Large*, 1:350-51, 525, 709n; Richardson, 1:192, 193.

63. Richardson, 1:251; U.S., *Statutes at Large*, 1:251, 553-54.

64. E. B. Potter, ed., *The United States and World Sea Power*, pp. 161-62.

65. *Naval Documents Related to the Quasi War Between the United States and France* (Washington: Government Printing Office, 1935), 2:129-31; Paullin, "Early Naval Administration," pp. 1026-29; U.S., *Statutes at Large*, 2:110-11.

66. Richardson, 1:323; Bernardo and Bacon, pp. 93-94.

67. On the Tripolitan War see Glenn Tucker, *Dawn Like Thunder*.

68. H. A. S. Dearborn, "Biography of Henry Dearborn," in manuscript, 7 vols., Maine Historical Society, Portland; *DAB*, s.v.

69. U.S., *Statutes at Large*, 2:132-37; Charles O. Paullin, "Naval Administration Under Secretaries of the Navy Smith, Hamilton, and Jones," *Proceedings of the United States Naval Institute* 33:1302.

70. Henry Adams, *History of the United States*, 2:136, 140.

71. U.S., *Statutes at Large*, 2:206; Richardson, 1:372, 385, 386; Adams, 3:178-80.

72. See Reuben Gold Thwaites, *Original Journals of the Lewis and Clark Expedition*, 1:xxiii-xxx; Jacobs, *U.S. Army*, pp. 316, 321.

73. Thwaites, 1:3-17.

74. Ibid.; Prucha, pp. 81-85; Elliott Coues, ed., *History of the Expedition Under the Command of Lewis and Clark*, 4 vols.

75. *DAB*, s.v.

76. *ASPMisA*, 1:942.

77. Prucha, pp. 88-91; W. Eugene Hollon, *The Lost Pathfinder*.

78. *ASPMisA*, 1:943; Jacobs, *U.S. Army*, pp. 331-32; *American Historical Review* 13(1907-1908):815.

79. *ASPMisA,* 1:19, 20, 39, 50; I. J. Cox, "The Louisiana-Texas Frontier," *Southwestern Historical Quarterly* 17:31; Coues, vol. 2.
80. Coues, vol. 2; William H. Goetzmann, *Army Exploration in the American West, 1803-1863,* pp. 36-39; Prucha, pp. 91-94.
81. Jacobs, *U.S. Army,* pp. 336-37.
82. Jacobs, *Tarnished Warrior,* pp. 209-40.

CHAPTER FOUR

1. *American State Papers: Military Affairs,* 1:249; cited hereafter as *ASPMA;* Benson J. Lossing, *Pictorial Fieldbook of the War of 1812,* p. 184; Harry L. Coles, *The War of 1812,* pp. 2-26.
2. Coles, p. 27; Adams, 4:67-89.
3. On Tecumseh and the Prophet see Glenn Tucker, *Tecumseh;* Adams, 4:67-89.
4. Alfred Pirtle, *The Battle of Tippecanoe* (Louisville: J. P. Morton, 1900); W. H. Harrison to secretary of war, 26 Nov. 1811, Logan Essary, ed., *Messages and Letters of William Henry Harrison* (Indianapolis: Indiana Historical Collections, 1922); 1:637, 651; John K. Mahon, *The War of 1812,* pp. 20-27; Freeman Cleaves, *Old Tippecanoe,* pp. 103-5.
5. James D. Richardson, ed., *A Compilation of the Messages and Papers of the Presidents,* 1:478; Irving Brant, *James Madison, Commander in Chief,* pp. 123-29.
6. Winfield Scott, *Memoirs of Lieut.-General Scott,* 1:31.
7. Beirne, pp. 87-95; Coles, pp. 21-22.
8. William W. Story, *Life and Letters of Joseph H. Story* (Boston: Little, Brown, 1851), 1:196.
9. Walter Lord, *The Dawn's Early Light* (New York: Norton, 1972), p. 21; Adams, 6:229, 398, 7:393; Leonard D. White, *The Jeffersonians,* pp. 36, 219-21.
10. White, p. 217; Adams, 6:168, 206, 392-98; Brant, p. 437; James Ripley Jacobs, *The Beginning of the U.S. Army,* pp. 342-43, 383.
11. Scott, 1:51-52; L. D. Ingersoll, *A History of the War Department of the United States,* pp. 439-40; Jacobs, *U.S. Army,* pp. 363-83.
12. U.S., *Statutes at Large,* 2:732, 816; White, pp. 218-19, 226-32; *ASPMA,* 1:385-88, 432; Gaillard Hunt, ed., *The Writings of James Madison,* 9:278n.
13. U.S., *Statutes at Large,* 2:764, 784-85; *ASPMA,* 1:385-88, 432.
14. Lossing, p. 243; Emory Upton, *The Military Policy of the United States,* pp. 95-97; C. Joseph Bernardo and Eugene H. Bacon, *American Military Policy,* pp. 118-22; J. Mackay Hitsman, *The Incredible War of 1812,* pp. 37, 45.
15. Adams, 6:337, 7:144, 147; Coles, pp. 38-40, 44-55.
16. Scott, 1:67; Louis L. Babcock, *The War of 1812 on the Niagara Frontier,* pp. 38, 48-53, 247; Adams, 6:pp. 316-17.
17. John W. Fortescue, *A History of the British Army,* 9:326-27; Alfred T. Mahan, *Sea Power in Its Relations to the War of 1812,* 1:304; C. P. Stacey, "Another Look at the Battle of Lake Erie," *Canadian Historical Review* 39(1958):42.
18. John Armstrong, *Notices of the War of 1812,* 1:49; Russell F. Weigley, *History of the United States Army,* p. 119.
19. James F. Clarke, *History of the Campaign of 1812 and Surrender of the Post of Detroit,* pp. 425-42; Alec R. Gilpin, *The War of 1812 in the Old Northwest,* p. 24.
20. Clarke, chap. 2, pp. 413-17; Gilpin, pp. 55-60; Beirne, pp. 96-99.
21. Coles, pp. 45-51; Adams, 6:302-14; Gilpin, pp. 88-93, 95-111.
22. Beirne, pp. 102, 103-6; Robert B. McAfee, *History of the Late War in the Western Country,* chap. 2; Lossing, pp. 255-96.
23. Samuel Williams, *The Expedition of Captain Henry Brush* (Cincinnati: R. Clarke, 1870); William Hull, *Report of the Trial of William Hull* (New York: Eastburn, Kirk, 1814); *Niles Register,* 3:92, 266-67; Gilpin, pp. 98-118, 121.
24. Lossing, pp. 303-10; Brant, pp. 73, 74.
25. Beirne, p. 109; Solomon Van Rensselaer, *A Narrative of the Affair at Queenstown in the War of 1812* (New York: Leavitt, Lord, 1836), app., pp. 35, 42.
26. Mahon, p. 76; Lossing, p. 390; Coles, p. 62.
27. Lossing, pp. 392-94; Beirne, pp. 113-14.

28. Scott, 1:56-63, 68; Henry B. Dawson, *Battles of the United States,* 2:chap. 30; Armstrong, 1: 103, 207-12, 253-58; Van Rensselaer, pp. 24-30; R. M. Johnston, *Leading American Soldiers,* p. 114.
29. Scott, 1:54n; *ASPMA,* 1:492-96; *Niles Register,* 3:203.
30. *ASPMA,* 1:493; *Niles Register,* 3:283-85; Beirne, pp. 120-21.
31. Lossing, pp. 427-32; *Niles Register,* 3:264, 282-83; Mahon, pp. 83-85.
32. *Dictionary of American Biography,* s.v., cited hereafter as *DAB;* Scott, 1:88, 93; Adams, 6: 289-90, 397, 7:37.
33. Charles J. Ingersoll, *Historical Sketch of the Second War Between the United States of America and Great Britain,* 1:101; William James, *Full and Correct Account of the Military Occurrences of the Late War Between Great Britain and the United States of America,* 1:129. See Mahon, p. 95.
34. See Beirne, p. 123.
35. Hunt, 2:493, 3:384; Adams, 7:404, 406; White, p. 218; James Wilkinson, *Memoirs of My Own Times,* 1:762.
36. *DAB,* s.v.; Weigley, p. 122; Coles, p. 110.
37. Coles, p. 136; White, p. 218; Ingersoll, *War Department,* pp. 441-45.
38. Coles, p. 109; *DAB,* s.v.; Charles O. Paullin, "Naval Administration under Secretaries of the Navy Smith, Hamilton, and Jones, 1801-1814," *Proceedings of the United States Naval Institute* 32(1906):1307.
39. See Coles, pp. 99-106.
40. Robert G. Albion and Jennie Pope, *Sea Lanes in Wartime* (New York: Norton, 1942), p. 112; Theodore Roosevelt, *The Naval War of 1812,* pp. 39, 48, 51, 62, 176; Howard I. Chapelle, *The History of the American Sailing Navy;* Harold and Margaret Sprout, *The Rise of American Naval Power,* pp. 58-66.
41. Mahan, 1:328-35, 412-15; Roosevelt, pp. 74-89; William James, *The Naval History of Great Britain,* 6:142-57, 159-63.
42. *Niles Register,* 3:253, 410-13, 4:273-74; Mahan, 1:4-7, 416-23; James, *Naval History,* 6: 187-96; George Coggeshall, *History of the American Privateers* (New York: G. Coggeshall, 1856).
43. *DAB,* s.v.; Coles, p. 109.
44. Adams, 6:77; *DAB,* s.v.
45. Howard Lindley, ed., "Captain Cushing in the War of 1812," *Ohio Historical Society Collections* 11(1944); McAfee, pp. 138-45; Richard C. Knopf, *William Henry Harrison and the War of 1812* (Columbus: Ohio Historical Society, 1957), pp. 141-42.
46. *Niles Register,* 3:90; Gilpin, pp. 131-41; Brant, pp. 82-85; Knopf, pp. 35-36.
47. Horace S. Knapp, *History of the Maumee Valley* (Toledo: Blade, 1877), p. 172; Alexander C. Casselman, ed., *Richardson's War of 1812,* pp. 87, 104, 148-80; Adams, 7:104-14; Cleaves, pp. 171-72, 181-82.
48. *DAB,* s.v.; Mahan, 1:362, 2:298-99; Ernest A. Cruikshank, "The Contest for the Command of Lake Ontario in 1812 and 1813," *Transactions of the Royal Society of Canada,* 3d ser., vol. 2, sec. 2.
49. Cruikshank, "Command of Lake Ontario"; C. Winston-Clare, "A Shipbuilder's War," *Mariner's Mirror* July 1943; Scott, 1:113.
50. H. A. Fay, *Collection of the Official Accounts of the Battles During the Years 1812, 13, 14, and 15* (New York: E. Conrad, 1817), pp. 81-86, 98; Lossing, pp. 586-97; Coles, pp. 137-38.
51. Johnston, p. 115; Ernest A. Cruikshank, "The Battle of Fort George," *Niagara Historical Society Transactions* (Niagara, 1896), no. 1; James C. Mills, *Oliver Hazard Perry and the Battle of Lake Erie* (Detroit: J. Phelps, 1913), pp. 64-67.
52. *Niles Register,* 4:241-42, 260; Wilkinson, 1:582-87; James, *Late War,* pp. 167-72; Armstrong, 1:143-46; Dawson, 2:chap. 48.
53. Weigley, p. 130; John S. Jenkins, *The Generals of the Last War with Great Britain* (Auburn: Derby & Miller, 1849), pp. 13-60; Fletcher Pratt, *Eleven Generals: Studies in American Command* (New York: Sloane, 1949), pp. 59-60, 78-79.
54. Coles, p. 143; Brant, p. 203; *Niles Register,* 4:371; Adams, 7:171, 416.
55. Kenneth L. Brown, "Mr. Madison's Secretary of the Navy," *Proceedings of the United States Naval Institute* 73(1947):967-75; White, pp. 271-73.
56. Beirne, pp. 170-71; James, *Naval History,* 6:29.

57. John B. McMaster, *History of the People of the United States,* 4:123; William M. Marine, *The British Invasion of Maryland,* pp. 21–57; Mahon, pp. 115–16.

58. Report of Adm. J. B. Warren, 24 June 1813, London *Gazette,* 10 Aug. 1813.

59. Roosevelt, pp. 141–43; Mahan, 2:9.

60. Beirne, pp. 184–92; James, *Late War,* pp. lix, lxi, 215–32; David Porter, *Journal of a Cruise Made to the Pacific Ocean in the United States Frigate Essex, 1812, 1813, 1814,* 2 vols. (New York: Wiley & Halsted, 1822).

61. Beirne, p. 200; Coles, p. 111.

62. Charles J. Dutton, *Oliver Hazard Perry* (New York: Longmans Green, 1935), pp. 1–72.

63. Adams, 7:116–19; Charles O. Paullin, *The Battle of Lake Erie,* pp. 155–58.

64. Beirne, pp. 203–6; Mahan, 2:63; Paullin, pp. 59–66.

65. Beirne, pp. 207–8; Paullin; Mills, pp. 107–90; Dutton, pp. 105–72.

66. Adams, 7:128; McAfee, p. 414.

67. Casselman, p. 119; McAfee, pp. 308, 313, 316–17.

68. Ernest A. Cruikshank, ed., *The Documentary History of the Campaigns Upon the Niagara Frontier in 1813 and 1814* (Welland: Lundy's Lane Historical Society, *Publications,* 1902–1908), 3:pts. 1–10, 8:168; Bennett H. Young, *The Battle of the Thames* (Louisville: Filson Club Publications, no. 18, 1903).

69. Adams, 7:142; Lossing, pp. 559–63; Cleaves, pp. 209–11, 216–23.

70. Beirne, pp. 221–23; Wilkinson, 3:341–42; Armstrong, 2:23.

71. James R. Jacobs, *Tarnished Warrior; DAB,* s.v.; Thomas R. Hay and M. R. Werner, *The Admirable Trumpeter* (Garden City: Doubleday, 1941).

72. Adams, 7:174–75; Scott, 1:50; *DAB,* s.v.

73. Wilkinson, 3:358, app. 36, 37; Brant, pp. 219–22, 226, 253.

74. *ASPMA,* 1:463, 464, 472; Armstrong, 2:32, 63, 187–210; Wilkinson, 3:70, 190, 193, 197, 353–61, app. 1; Adams, 7:178–86.

75. Lossing, pp. 648–53; Wilkinson, 3:84, 138, 200–214; Mahon, pp. 208–15.

76. Ingersoll, *Second War,* 2:26–27; *ASPMA,* 1:459–60; Hitsman, pp. 164–67.

77. *ASPMA,* 1:478, 480; Wilkinson, 3:362n, app. 5; Armstrong, 2:43.

78. *Niles Register,* 6:131; James, *Late War,* 2:app. 17–19; Wilkinson, 3:2, 16–19, 40, 55, 172–84, 605, 612, 618, 644, 646; Adams, 8:25–27.

79. *ASPMA,* 1:485–87; George McClure, *Causes of the Destruction of Towns on the Niagara Frontier* (Bath, N.Y., 1817), pp. 18, 25; Mahon, pp. 189–91.

80. Callan, pp. 247, 249–52; Upton, pp. 122–23, 133.

81. Beirne, pp. 432–38; H. S. Halbert and T. H. Ball, *The Creek War of 1813 and 1814;* Dawson, 2:chap. 40; Mahon, pp. 234–35.

82. *DAB,* s.v.; Johnston, pp. 83–84; standard biographies include Marquis James, *Andrew Jackson, The Border Captain,* John S. Bassett, *The Life of Andrew Jackson,* and James Parton, *Life of Andrew Jackson.*

83. *Niles Register,* 5:427, 6:130–31, 147–48; James, *Andrew Jackson,* pp. 176–78; *American State Papers: Indian Affairs,* 1:826.

84. Fortescue, 10:125; Beirne, p. 250.

85. Scott, 1:118–21; Charles W. Elliott, *Winfield Scott,* pp. 146–53.

86. Hunt, 3:403; Armstrong, 2:216; Coles, p. 155.

87. Hitsman, p. 194; Coles, pp. 155–56; Beirne, pp. 251–52.

88. Johnston, p. 116; Scott, 1:123–36; James, *Late War,* 2:117–25.

89. Ingersoll, *Second War,* 2:106; Ernest A. Cruikshank, *The Battle of Lundy's Lane* (Welland: Tribune, 1893), pp. 5–43; Scott, 1:chap. 11; Beirne, pp. 256–60.

90. Adams, 8:69–78, 89; *Niles Register,* 6:19–20, 437, 7:19, 21, 101–2.

91. Adams, 8:97–98, 108; *DAB,* s.v.

92. Armstrong, 2:100n, 102–4; Coles, pp. 162–63; *Niles Register,* 7:171–72.

93. Mahon, pp. 247, 281; Coles, pp. 171–72.

94. Hunt, 3:399; *ASPMA,* 1:581.

95. Beirne, pp. 268–70; *DAB,* s.v.; White, p. 220; Adams, 8:153.

96. *ASPMA,* 1:524–99; Lossing, pp. 917–19; Beirne, pp. 270–71.

97. Ralph D. Paine, *Joshua Barney, A Forgotten Hero of Blue Water* (New York: Century, 1924); Hulbert Footner, *Sailor of Fortune: The Life and Adventures of Commodore Barney, U.S.N.* (New York: Harper, 1940), pp. 277–79.

98. Charles G. Muller, *The Darkest Day, 1814,* pp. 42–76; Adams, 8:124–32; Washington *National Intelligencer,* 18 Aug. 1814.
99. White, p. 220; Ingersoll, *Second War,* 2:173; *ASPMA,* 1:554–85, 2:173.
100. Beirne, pp. 277–78.
101. *ASPMA,* 1:552–60; John S. Williams, *History of the Invasion and Capture of Washington* (New York: Harper, 1957), p. 153, app. 1; George R. Gleig, *A Narrative of the Campaign of the British Army at Washington, Baltimore, and New Orleans* (Philadelphia: M. Carey & Son, 1821), pp. 125–27.
102. *ASPMA,* 1:536, 560–61; Armstrong, 2:148; White, p. 221.
103. *ASPMA,* 1:537, 596; Beirne, pp. 279–80; White, pp. 222–23.
104. Weigley, pp. 122, 132; Williams, pp. 179–225, app. 1; Neil H. Swanson, *The Perilous Fight* (New York: Farrar & Rinehart, 1945); Gleig, pp. 109–27.
105. Alan Lloyd, *The Scorching of Washington; Annual Register* (1814), pp. 226–29; Gleig, pp. 125–38, 152–55; Muller, pp. 132–72.
106. Ingersoll, *Second War,* 2:208; Adams, 8:150–52, 160–61; Hunt, 8:300–301.
107. *Niles Register,* 7:40; Beirne, pp. 309–11; Adams, 8:166–67.
108. Coles, pp. 182–83; *DAB,* s.v.; Swanson, pp. 154, 199–211.
109. Gilbert Byron, *The War of 1812 on the Chesapeake Bay* (Baltimore: Maryland Historical Society, 1964), p. 63; Lossing, p. 953.
110. Thomas M. Spaulding, "The Battle of North Point," *Sewanee Review* (1914):319–28; Swanson; Muller, pp. 189–91; Marine, pp. 130–82, 190–94.
111. *Niles Register,* 7:40; Dawson, 2:393–94; Lord, chap. 11.
112. Adams, 8:101–2; Beirne, pp. 291–92; *Niles Register,* 7:60.
113. George H. Richards, *Memoir of Alexander Macomb* (New York: McElrath, Bangs, 1833); *DAB,* s.v.
114. Montreal *Herald,* 24 Sept. 1814; Mahon, pp. 317–19.
115. Rodney Macdonough, *Life of Commodore Macdonough* (Boston: Fort Hill Press, 1909); Coles, p. 164.
116. Mahan, 2:367; Mahon, p. 323.
117. Adams, 8:104–11; Mahan, 2:367–72; James Fenimore Cooper, *History of the Navy of the United States of America* (Philadelphia: Lea & Blanchard, 1839), 2:212–16.
118. Lossing, pp. 859–74; Dawson, 2:chap. 89; C. W. Robinson, "The Expedition to Plattsburg, 1814," *Journal of the Royal United Services Institute* 61(1916):507–18; Armstrong, 2:102–7.
119. See Beirne, pp. 340–41.
120. Parton, 2:25–27, 30; Wilburt S. Brown, *The Amphibious Campaign for West Florida and Louisiana,* pp. 46–64, 186; Samuel Carter III, *Blaze of Glory,* chap. 3.
121. Gleig, pp. 257–59; Donald P. Chidsey, *The Battle of New Orleans.*
122. Lossing, p. 1028; Robin Reilly, *The British at the Gates,* chap. 14; *Annual Register* (1815), pp. 155–57; Charles B. Brooks, *The Siege of New Orleans,* pp. 162–78.
123. *Niles Register,* 7:387; Carter, chap. 11; Gleig, pp. 289–98; A Lacarrière Latour, *Historical Memoir of the War in West Florida and Louisiana in 1814–15,* ed. Rembert W. Patrick, (Gainesville: University of Florida Press, 1964), pp. 58, 88–101, 237–44.
124. Latour, pp. 120–25, app., pp. xlix–1; Brooks, pp. 180–82, 187–95.
125. Reilly, chap. 20; Carter, chap. 15; Brown, pp. 126–27; Latour, pp. 132–35.
126. Gleig, pp. 34–43, 319–31; Latour, app., pp. 132–53; Fortescue, 10:chap. 20; Carter, chaps. 16–18; M. James, pp. 213, 253–70; Brooks, pp. 227–52.
127. Coles, pp. 233–36, 243–46.
128. Upton, pp. 137–42; Beirne, p. 391; Adams, 7:385.
129. Coles, pp. 148, 258, 265; Beirne, p. 390.
130. See Beirne, pp. 389–91.

CHAPTER FIVE

1. Emory Upton, *The Military Policy of the United States,* p. 142.
2. Records of the West Point Alumni Foundation, *Register of Graduates and Former Cadets, United States Military Academy* (1953); Adams, 9:235–36.

3. *American State Papers: Military Affairs,* 1:635, cited hereafter as *ASPMA;* U.S., *Statutes at Large,* 3:426–27.

4. Upton, pp. 129, 145–47; Oliver Lyman Spaulding, *The United States Army in War and Peace,* pp. 148–49; Theodore R. Rodenbough and William L. Haskin, eds., *The Army of the United States* (New York: Maynard, Merrill, 1896), p. 8.

5. Rodenbough and Haskin, 8; C. Joseph Bernardo and Eugene H. Bacon, *American Military Policy,* p. 144; William Addleman Ganoe, *The History of the United States Army,* p. 153.

6. Kendric C. Babcock, *The Rise of American Nationality, 1811–1819* (New York: Harper, 1906), p. 282; Spaulding, p. 149.

7. *American State Papers: Foreign Affairs,* 4:456–60, cited hereafter as *ASPFA;* James Parton, *Life of Andrew Jackson,* 2:399–404.

8. *ASPMA,* 1:739; Ganoe, p. 152; *Treaties and Conventions Concluded Between the United States of America and Other Powers since July 1776* (Washington: Government Printing Office, 1889), p. 1007.

9. *ASPMA,* 1:690; Upton, pp. 148–49.

10. *Niles Register,* 14:334; *ASPMA,* 1:740–41; Parton, 2:chaps. 35, 36.

11. Upton, p. 148; Babcock, pp. 278–85.

12. Charles M. Wiltse, *John C. Calhoun* (Indianapolis: Bobbs-Merrill, 1944), 1:151, 152.

13. U.S., Congress, House, *Annals of Congress,* 16th Cong., 1st sess., p. 854; *ASPMA,* 1:810–13, 834–37; Edgar B. Wesley, *Guarding the Frontier,* chap. 8.

14. Richard K. Crallé, ed., *The Works of John C. Calhoun,* 5:25–54; *American State Papers: Miscellaneous Affairs,* 2:533–37, cited hereafter as *ASPMisA.*

15. *American State Papers: Indian Affairs,* 2:181–85; Crallé, 5:8–24; *Niles Register,* vol. 15, suppl., p. 16.

16. *ASPMA,* 1:452, 2:180, 188–90, 194; Upton, pp. 149–51; Russell F. Weigley, *Towards an American Army,* pp. 30–37; Walter Millis, *Arms and Men,* p. 83; U.S., *Statutes at Large,* 2:615; Wiltse, 1:166; Spaulding, pp. 152–53.

17. *ASPMA,* 2:411; Wiltse, 1:229.

18. Benjamin Drake, *The Life and Adventures of Black Hawk,* p. 64.

19. Reuben Gold Thwaites, *The Story of the Black Hawk War,* p. 7; Grant Foreman, *Advancing the Frontier, 1830–1860* (Norman: University of Oklahoma Press, 1933), p. 111; *ASPMA,* 4:716, 717; Black Hawk, *Autobiography,* p. 89.

20. Frank E. Stevens, *The Black Hawk War,* p. 110; "Expedition Against the Sauk and Fox Indians," *Military and Naval Magazine* (Aug. 1833), pp. 9–10; Thwaites, p. 27; Spaulding, p. 156.

21. Stevens, p. 228; Spaulding, pp. 156–57; Ganoe, p. 172.

22. *Dictionary of American Biography,* s.v., cited hereafter as *DAB.*

23. John T. Sprague, *Origin, Progress and Conclusion of the Florida War,* p. 283.

24. Ibid., pp. 74–76, 80.

25. John K. Mahon, *History of the Second Seminole War,* pp. 104–6; Ganoe, p. 176.

26. Spaulding, p. 161; *ASPMA,* 7:244; Mahon, p. 161; Upton, p. 167.

27. Spaulding, pp. 161–62; *ASPMA,* 7:951.

28. Ganoe, p. 178; Mahon, p. 179; Upton, p. 171; *ASPMA,* 7:821.

29. Upton, p. 173; Spaulding, p. 162; *ASPMA,* 7:987–88; Ganoe, pp. 181–82.

30. Mahon, pp. 274, 276; Upton, pp. 185–86.

31. Sprague, chaps. 5–13; Winfield Scott, *Memoirs of Lieut.-General Scott,* 1:260–65; *National Intelligencer,* 17 Jan. 1942.

32. Upton, pp. 190, 194; U.S., Congress, House, *Congressional Globe,* 25th Cong., 2d sess., app. 3.

33. Mahon, chap. 16; Upton, pp. 187, 194.

34. U.S., *Statutes at Large,* 5:512–13; *DAB,* s.v.

35. U.S., War Department, *Report of the Secretary of War* (1830), p. 81, (1839), p. 42; U.S., Congress, House, *Congressional Globe,* 26th Cong., 2d sess., app., pp. 10–11; Bernardo and Bacon, p. 163.

36. U.S., Congress, *Annals of Congress,* 7th Cong., 1st sess., p. 1312; Sidney Forman, *A History of the United States Military Academy,* pp. 3, 22; *DAB,* s.v.; E. D. J. Waugh, *West Point,* pp. 45, 47; George W. Cullum, *Biographical Register of the Officers and Graduates of the U.S. Military Academy at West Point,* 1:89–91.

37. Thomas J. Fleming, *West Point,* p. 19; James R. Jacobs, *The Beginning of the U.S. Army,* pp. 296–98, 302.

38. Jacobs, pp. 303–4; Forman.

39. Herman Fairchild, *History of the New York Academy of Sciences,* pp. 108–12.

40. Forman, pp. 34–35.

41. Ibid., pp. 36–38.

42. Stephen E. Ambrose, *Duty, Honor, Country,* pp. 40, 46, 60.

43. G. W. Ramsay to G. W. Cullum, 1872, George W. Cullum Papers, Library of Congress, Washington, D.C.; see also Alden Partridge Papers, Norwich University, Norwich, Vt., including a manuscript biography by his son, Henry V. Partridge; Waugh, p. 52.

44. Forman, pp. 40–41; Ambrose, pp. 40–53.

45. Ambrose, pp. 40–53; Waugh, pp. 52, 53, 60, 61, 70.

46. Waugh, p. 63; Forman, p. 41.

47. Cullum, 1:107–8; *DAB,*s.v.; Joseph G. Swift Papers, United States Military Academy Library, West Point, N.Y.

48. Forman, p. 43; Ambrose, pp. 58–59; S. Thayer to his sister and brother-in-law, 17 Oct. 1817, copy by his nephew, J. B. Moulton, in Cullum Papers.

49. Waugh, pp. 67–69; J. G. Swift to S. Thayer, 1 Sept. 1817, Thayer to Swift, 11 Sept. 1817, Swift Papers; Ambrose, pp. 58–60.

50. S. Thayer to J. G. Swift, 28 June 1818, War Department Records, Washington, D.C.; John H. B. Latrobe, *West Point Reminiscences* (n.p. 1887), p. 9.

51. Joseph Ellis and Robert Moore, *School for Soldiers,* p. 32; Forman, pp. 51–59; *ASPMA,* 2: 79; Ambrose, p. 70.

52. G. Woodbridge to G. W. Cullum, 25 Oct. 1872, Cullum Papers.

53. A. Jackson to A. J. Donelson, 28 Dec. 1818, Andrew Jackson Donelson Papers, Library of Congress, Washington, D.C.; A. Jackson to J. Poinsett, 19 Oct. 1837, John S. Bassett, ed., *The Correspondence of Andrew Jackson* (Washington: Carnegie Institute, 1926), 5:516.

54. Engineer Order no. 1, 2 Apr. 1833, United States Military Academy Order Book no. 6, West Point; J. Poinsett to G. Kemble, 15 Nov. 1837, Sylvanus Thayer Papers, United States Military Academy Library, West Point; Cullum, 1:107–8; *DAB,* s.v.

55. *American State Papers: Naval Affairs,* 1:363–65; U.S., *Statutes at Large,* 3:202–3, 231; Charles O. Paullin, "Naval Administration Under the Navy Commissioners, 1815-1842," *Proceedings of the United States Naval Institute* 33:602–6.

56. U.S., *Statutes at Large,* 3:32; Harold and Margaret Sprout, *The Rise of American Naval Power,* pp. 88–91; George T. Davis, *A Navy Second to None,* p. 5; Paullin, pp. 614–16; *ASPFA,* 4:205–6; Richardson, 2:218.

57. Dudley W. Knox, *A History of the United States Navy,* p. 139; Davis, pp. 5–6; Paullin, p. 623.

58. *Report of the Secretary of the Navy* (1825), p. 97; Sprout, pp. 94–95; Paullin, pp. 623–25.

59. Paullin, p. 628; James Russell Soley, *Historical Sketch of the U.S. Naval Academy* (Washington: Government Printing Office, 1876), pp. 7–62; U.S., Congress, *Congressional Globe,* 27th Cong., 2d sess., app. 21.

60. Paullin, pp. 618–21; U.S., *Statutes at Large,* 5:579–81; Charles O. Paullin, "Naval Administration, 1842-1861," pp. 1435–40.

CHAPTER SIX

1. Louis J. Wortham, *A History of Texas,* vol. 1.

2. Nathaniel W. Stephenson, *Texas and the Mexican War,* pp. 34–69; L. Cass to E. Gaines, 23 Jan. 1836, Letters Sent by the Secretary of War, Military Book no. 15, p. 37, Library of Congress, Washington, D.C.

3. Joseph W. Schmitz, *Texan Statecraft, 1836–1845* (San Antonio: Naylor, 1941), pp. 1–9; Wortham, 2:297, 3:68, 135, 139–40, 197–99, 228.

4. *Dictionary of American Biography,* s.v., cited hereafter as *DAB;* Walter Lord, *A Time to Stand,* p. 24; Marquis James, *The Raven.*

5. Lon Tinkle, *13 Days to Glory,* pp. 71-99, 241; Lord, pp. 26-28; *DAB,* s.v.
6. Tinkle, p. 83.
7. Walter F. McCaleb, *William Barrett Travis, DAB,* s.v.; Lord, pp. 33-34; Tinkle, pp. 91-100.
8. James A. Shackford, *David Crockett.*
9. Tinkle, p. 255.
10. Lord, pp. 209-10; Tinkle, p. 89; Stephenson, p. 71.
11. Amelia W. Williams, "A Critical Study of the Siege of the Alamo," (Ph.D. diss., University of Texas, 1931); John M. Myer, *The Alamo;* Lord, p. 209; Tinkle, p. 245; Wortham, 3:239-66.
12. J. F. C. Fuller, *Decisive Battles of the U.S.A.,* pp. 141-45; James, pp. 224-57.
13. Justin H. Smith, *The War with Mexico,* 1:82-101, 138-55; the latest comprehensive study is K. Jack Bauer, *The Mexican War.*
14. Francis B. Heitman, *Historical Register and Dictionary of the United States Army,* 2:626; *Niles Register,* 7 Jan. 1843; C. Joseph Bernardo and Eugene H. Bacon, *American Military Policy,* pp. 175-77.
15. Charles G. Sellers, *James K. Polk,* 1, 2:1-161.
16. Eugene I. McCormac, *James K. Polk.*
17. Warren W. Hassler, Jr., *The President as Commander in Chief,* pp. 51-56; Bernard DeVoto, *The Year of Decision, 1846,* pp. 7-8, 204-5.
18. Ivor D. Spencer, *The Victor and the Spoils;* Smith, 1:193; Robert S. Henry, *The Story of the Mexican War,* p. 48.
19. Charles W. Elliott, *Winfield Scott;* R. M. Johnston, *Leading American Soldiers,* pp. 113-33.
20. On Taylor, see Holman Hamilton, *Zachary Taylor;* Brainerd Dyer, *Zachary Taylor;* Johnston, pp. 97-112.
21. Smith, 1:42, 54, 220, 2:313.
22. Hassler, pp. 51-55.
23. Milo M. Quaife, ed., *The Diary of James K. Polk,* 1:395-401.
24. Elliott, U.S., Congress, *Senate Document 378,* 29th Cong., 1st sess., pp. 5-6; Quaife, 1:407-18.
25. U.S., Congress, *Senate Document 388,* 29th Cong. 2d sess., pp. 31-37; U.S., Congress, *House Executive Document 30,* 30th Cong., 1st sess., pp. 1161-62.
26. *Senate Document 388,* 29th Cong., 1st sess., pp. 2-6; Cadmus M. Wilcox, *History of the Mexican War,* pp. 48-58.
27. Ramon Alcaraz, *The Other Side of the Mexican War,* pp. 50-56; Alfred H. Bill, *Rehearsal for Conflict,* pp. 96-99.
28. Alcaraz, pp. 63-68; Otis A. Singletary, *The Mexican War,* pp. 32-33, 106-7; R. Ernest Dupuy and Trevor N. Dupuy, *Military Heritage of America,* p. 148.
29. Edward J. Nichols, *Zach Taylor's Little Army* (Garden City: Doubleday, 1963), *House Executive Document 60,* 30th Cong., 1st sess., pp. 323-29; Smith, 1:209-12.
30. *House Executive Document 4,* 29th Cong., 2d sess., pp. 76-107; Oliver Lyman Spaulding, *The United States Army in War and Peace,* p. 186.
31. *House Executive Document 60,* 30th Cong., 1st sess., pp. 345-50; Roswell S. Ripley, *The War with Mexico,* 1:chap. 5.
32. Quaife, 2:181; *House Executive Document 60,* 30th Cong., 1st sess., pp. 358-60, 1270-74; Singletary, pp. 43, 107-11.
33. Quaife, 2:219-45; Singletary, p. 111; Winfield Scott, *Memoirs of Lieut.-General Winfield Scott,* 2:397-99.
34. *House Executive Document 60,* 30th Cong., 1st sess., pp. 373-74, 839-59.
35. Alcaraz, pp. 149-54; Smith, 2:7-12.
36. Walter Prescott Webb, *The Texas Rangers,* pp. 112-13.
37. Henry, pp. 245-54; Smith, 1:384-400; Dupuy and Dupuy, pp. 151-57.
38. Singletary, pp. 115-16.
39. Dwight L. Clarke, *Stephen Watts Kearny.*
40. Philip St. George Cooke, *Conquest of New Mexico and California* (New York: Putnam, 1878); Henry, pp. 123-36.
41. *DAB,* s.v.
42. *House Executive Document 4,* 29th Cong., 2d sess., pp. 378, 640; *House Executive Document 60,* 30th Cong., 1st sess., p. 231.
43. E. A. Sherman, *The Life of the Late Rear-Admiral, John Drake Sloat* (Oakland: Carruth & Carruth, 1902); Smith, 1:333-36, 530-31.

44. S. J. Bayard, *A Sketch of the Life of Commodore Robert F. Stockton* (New York: Derby & Jackson, 1856); Smith, 1:336.

45. John C. Fremont, *Memoirs of My Life,* pp. 491–602; Allan Nevins, *Fremont, Pathmarker of the West,* pp. 206–342.

46. John T. Hughes, *Doniphan's Expedition;* William E. Connelly, *Doniphan's Expedition;* DeVoto, pp. 388–420.

47. Smith, 2:196–97; *William H. Parker, Recollections of a Naval Officer,* p. 53.

48. K. Jack Bauer, *Surfboats and Horse Marines;* Samuel Eliot Morison, *"Old Bruin,"* pp. 193–229; Parker, pp. 57–102; P. S. P. Conner, *The Home Squadron.*

49. *House Executive Document 60,* 30th Cong., 1st sess., pp. 362–67; Quaife, 2:198–200, 239–45; Scott, 2:397–99; Henry, pp. 258–71; Conner, p. 64.

50. William Starr Myers, ed., *The Mexican War Diary of George B. McClellan,* p. 91.

51. *Senate Executive Document 1,* 30th Cong., 1st sess., pp. 274–300; Alcaraz, pp. 205–6.

52. *House Executive Document 60,* 30th Cong., 1st sess., pp. 906, 910, 944, 954–57; Raphael Semmes, *Service Afloat and Ashore in the Mexican War,* pp. 208–9.

53. *Senate Executive Document 52,* 30th Cong., 1st sess., pp. 81–89; Elliott, pp. 472–90.

54. Scott, 2:466; Singletary, pp. 82–83.

55. Henry, pp. 322–28; *Senate Executive Document 1,* 30th Cong., 1st sess., pp. 303–8, 322–49; Semmes, pp. 370–77, 389, 393; Smith, 2:101–10, 376–80.

56. Alcaraz, pp. 259–74, 282–99; Smith, 2:110–21, 382–85.

57. Singletary, pp. 92–94, 156–58.

58. Henry, pp. 351–53, 358.

59. *Senate Executive Document 1,* 30th Cong., 1st sess., pp. 354–75, app., pp. 134–66.

60. Ibid., pp. 376–78, 400–401, 426–28.

61. Ibid., pp. 378–418; Elliott, p. 546; Semmes, p. 454.

62. Alcaraz, pp. 366–70; Semmes, pp. 459–60.

63. Edward S. Wallace, "The United States Army in Mexico City," *Military Affairs* 13(1949): 158–66; Quaife, 3:345–50.

64. Singletary, pp. 124–25, 143–44; Quaife, 3:266–67.

65. Smith, 2:314, 315–18.

66. U.S., *Statutes at Large,* 9:187, 10:273; Harold and Margaret Sprout, *The Rise of American Naval Power,* pp. 133–49; Frank Bennett, *The Steam Navy of the United States,* pp. 88–176; *Senate Document 1,* 31st Cong., 1st sess., pp. 370–71.

67. John W. Masland and Laurence I. Radway, *Soldiers and Scholars,* p. 79n; Kendall Banning, *Annapolis Today,* pp. 254–60; U.S., Congress, Senate, *Register of Debates,* 19th Cong., 2d sess., pp. 345–76, 502–24, 1496–1514; James Russell Soley, *Historical Sketch of the United States Naval Academy,* pp. 7–62; Park Benjamin, *The United States Naval Academy,* chap. 10; William D. Puleston, *Anapolis,* chap. 6.

68. Arthur Walworth, *Black Ships Off Japan;* Morison, pp. 261–410.

69. U.S., War Department, *Report of the Secretary of War* (1850), pp. 3, 116, tables in app.; Spaulding, pp. 230–31; Bernardo and Bacon, p. 185.

70. Heitman, 1:358; Hudson Strode, *Jefferson Davis,* 1:245–95; Robert M. McElroy, *Jefferson Davis,* 1:148–73, 407.

71. Will C. Barnes, "Camels on Safari," *Quartermaster Review* 16(1937):7–13, 68–72; James Ford Rhodes, *History of the United States,* 2:7.

72. J. F. Callan, *The Military Laws of the United States,* pp. 435–36; Strode, 1:245–80; Russell F. Weigley, *Quartermaster General of the Union Army,* pp. 65–77.

73. George B. McClellan, *The Armies of Europe* (Philadelphia: J. B. Lippincott, 1861).

74. See Hassler, pp. 57–58.

75. Charles P. Roland, *Albert Sidney Johnston,* pp. 185–237; Norman F. Furniss, *The Mormon Conflict, 1850–1859* (New Haven: Yale University Press, 1960).

CHAPTER SEVEN

1. Robert Underwood Johnson and Clarence Clough Buel, eds., *Battles and Leaders of the Civil War,* 1:26–32, 51–60, cited hereafter as *B & L;* J. G. Randall and David Donald, *The Civil War and Reconstruction,* p. 161.

2. Roy P. Basler, ed., *The Collected Works of Abraham Lincoln,* 4:266; Richard N. Current, *Lincoln and the First Shot;* Samuel Wylie Crawford, *The Genesis of the Civil War.*

3. Charles Francis Adams, *An Autobiography* (Boston: Houghton, Mifflin, 1916), pp. 74–82, 96–97.

4. Benjamin P. Thomas, *Abraham Lincoln,* pp. 31–34, 242–44; John G. Nicolay and John Hay, *Abraham Lincoln,* 3:302–16; Warren W. Hassler, Jr., *The President as Commander in Chief,* pp. 58–70.

5. Rembert W. Patrick, *Jefferson Davis and His Cabinet;* Thomas L. Connelly and Archer Jones, *The Politics of Command.*

6. Erwin S. Bradley, *Simon Cameron;* A. Howard Meneely, *The War Department, 1861;* A. K. McClure, *Abraham Lincoln and Men of War-Times,* pp. 147–68.

7. Charles A. Dana, *Lincoln and His Cabinet,* pp. 20–27; Noah Brooks, *Washington in Lincoln's Time,* pp. 28–29; John T. Morse, Jr., *The Diary of Gideon Welles,* 1:55, 56, 67–69, 127–29; McClure, pp. 155–62.

8. Theodore C. Pease and James G. Randall, eds. (Springfield, Ill.: Illinois State Historical Library, 1925), *The Diary of Orville Hickman Browning,* 1:533–39; Ulysses S. Grant, *Personal Memoirs of U.S. Grant,* 2:105, 123, 506, 536–37; Howard K. Beale, ed., *The Diary of Edward Bates,* pp. 228, 280, 381, 391; Morse, 1:55–69, 127–29, 148–49, 203, 234.

9. Frank E. Vandiver, *Rebel Brass;* Patrick.

10. On Welles see John Niven, *Gideon Welles, Lincoln's Secretary of the Navy;* Richard S. West, Jr., *Gideon Welles, Lincoln's Navy Department.*

11. Joseph T. Durkin, *Stephen Mallory;* Patrick pp. 245–71; Vandiver, pp. 63–74.

12. Charles W. Elliott, *Winfield Scott;* William H. Russell, *My Diary, North and South* (New York: Harper, 1863), p. 148.

13. Albert P. Brigham, *Geographic Influences in American History,* pp. 200–229; Ellen C. Semple and Clarence F. Jones, *American History and Its Geographic Conditions,* pp. 282–309.

14. Allan Nevins, *The War for the Union,* 1:424–26; James Ford Rhodes, *History of the United States,* 5:186; Randall and Donald, pp. 190–92, 529–31.

15. William H. Price, *The Civil War Centennial Handbook,* p. 5; *Facts About the Civil War,* p. 6.

16. George W. Brown, *Baltimore and the Nineteenth of April.*

17. *B & L,* 1:150–56; Comte de Paris, *History of the Civil War in America,* 1:141–52; Douglas Southall Freeman, *R. E. Lee,* 1:473–74.

18. *The War of the Rebellion: A Compilation of the Official Records of the Union and Confederate Armies,* ser. 1, vol. 51, pt. 1, pp. 228–39, ser. 3, vol. 1, pp. 148–49, 177–78, 250, ser. 107, pp. 369–70, 386–87; cited hereafter as *OR,* all references to series 1.

19. *OR,* 2:648, 107:369–87; George W. Cullum, *Biographical Register of the Officers and Graduates of the U.S. Military Academy,* 2:140–41; *B & L,* 1:89.

20. John R. Young, *Around the World with General Grant,* 2:216; Warren W. Hassler, Jr., *General George B. McClellan,* and *Commanders of the Army of the Potomac,* pp. 28–30, 247–49.

21. William Swinton, *Campaigns of the Army of the Potomac,* pp. 36, 39; George B. McClellan, *Report on the Organization and Campaigns of the Army of the Potomac,* pp. 29–34.

22. Randall and Donald, pp. 236–42; *OR,* 2:204.

23. Nicolay and Hay, 4:98; E. D. Townsend, *Anecdotes of the Civil War,* p. 29; Freeman, *R. E. Lee,* 1:462–636, 2:1–74; Rhodes, 3:365n, 380.

24. See Freeman, *R. E. Lee.*

25. *OR,* 2:777, 845, 896; Alfred Roman, *The Military Operations of General Beauregard,* 1:66; Rhodes, 3:376.

26. James Harrison Wilson, *Under the Old Flag,* 1:66; Russell, p. 145; Cullum, 1:559; Townsend, pp. 13–14.

27. Townsend, pp. 55–57; Journal of Samuel P. Heintzelman, 1 Sept. 1861, Library of Congress, Washington, D.C.; *OR,* 2:325–26; J. H. Stine, *History of the Army of the Potomac,* pp. 9–10.

28. *OR,* 2:157–68, 925; R. M. Johnson, *Bull Run, Its Strategy and Tactics* (Boston: Houghton Mifflin, 1913), pp. 29–30, 74; *Report of the Joint Committee on the Conduct of the War* (1863), 2:5, hereafter cited as *CCW.*

29. Journal of Heintzelman, 16–18 July 1862; William C. Davis, *Battle at Bull Run,* chaps. 6, 7; *B & L,* 1:178–87; *OR,* 2:303–31; Johnston; Hassler, *Commanders,* pp. 18–23; Thomas L. Livermore, *Numbers and Losses in the Civil War,* p. 77.

30. Swinton, pp. 43–44; *OR,* 2:323; Johnston, pp. 20, 273.

31. Randall and Donald, pp. 264-69, 310-22.
32. Rhodes, 3:459-60, 493; McClellan, *Report*, pp. 9-10; Hassler, *McClellan*, pp. 23-37.
33. *New York Tribune*, 18 Oct. 1861; *B & L*, 2:123-34; T. Harry Williams, *Lincoln and the Radicals*, chaps. 2-7.
34. Comte de Paris, 1:414-15; *B & L*, 2:114.
35. George B. McClellan, *McClellan's Own Story*, pp. 84-91, 136-37, 170-74; Elliott, pp. 734-39; *OR*, 12:5, 14:4-6, 122:613-14; Beale, p. 200.
36. *McClellan's Own Story*, pp. 207-10; Harvey S. Ford, ed., *Memoirs of a Volunteer*, p. 131; *CCW* (1863), 2:422; McClellan, *Report*, pp. 10, 37-42.
37. Thomas L. Connelly, *Army of the Heartland*, pp. 60-77; Stanley F. Horn, *The Army of Tennessee*, p. 55; Charles P. Roland, *Albert Sidney Johnston*.
38. *OR*, 7:508-11, 568-87; Manning F. Force, *From Fort Henry to Corinth*, pp. 24-65; Grant, 1: 282-315.
39. Martin H. Hall, *Sibley's New Mexico Campaign;* Ray C. Colton, *The Civil War in the Western Territories*, pp. 13-99; *B & L*, 2:103-11.
40. Hassler, *McClellan*, pp. 52-93; *OR*, 5:526-27; *B & L*, 2:121-22.
41. Alexander S. Webb, *The Peninsula*, pp. 35-96; Hassler, *McClellan*, pp. 105-18; McClellan, *Report*, pp. 89-91.
42. *OR*, 12:762-971; Douglas Southall Freeman, *Lee's Lieutenants*, 1:156-73, 201-63; Hassler, *McClellan*, pp. 119-28; Joseph E. Johnston, *Narrative of Military Operations*, pp. 132-46; *B & L*, 2:218-63; Livermore, p. 81.
43. E. M. Stanton to G. B. McClellan, 17 May 1862, George B. McClellan Papers, Library of Congress, Washington, D.C.; *Massachusetts Historical Society Proceedings* 69:106.
44. Robert G. Tanner, *Stonewall in the Valley;* Freeman, *Lee's Lieutenants*, 1:362-469; G. B. McClellan to A. Lincoln, 25 May 1862, Abraham Lincoln Papers, Library of Congress, Washington, D.C.; *CCW* (1863), 1:274, 330; Livermore, p. 86.
45. *OR*, 12:44, 64, 119, 153, 159, 169, 13:19, 193, 228.
46. Hassler, *McClellan*, pp. 141-70; Swinton, p. 164; Livermore, p. 86.
47. *OR*, 13:497; *B & L*, 2:395; John Codman Ropes, *The Story of the Civil War*, 2:208, 209.
48. Journal of Heintzelman, 8, 9 July 1862; Hassler, *McClellan*, pp. 184-204.
49. *New York Tribune*, 31 May 1862; Beale, p. 293; Morse, vol. 1; Wilson, 1:98-99; Pease and Randall, 1:605; *McClellan's Own Story*, p. 137.
50. John R. Boyle, *Soldiers True*, p. 41; *New York Tribune*, 26, 27 June 1862; Jacob D. Cox, *Military Reminiscences of the Civil War*, 1:247-48; Henry Villard, *Memoirs of Henry Villard*, 1:272; Morse, 1:104, 120, 126, 221.
51. *CCW* (1863), 1:276-82.
52. *OR*, 15:330-31, 16:40, 18:523; John Codman Ropes, *The Army Under Pope;* George H. Gordon, *History of the Campaign of the Army of Virginia under John Pope; B & L*, 2:449-541.
53. Williams, pp. 176-79; Cox, 1:243-45; Regis De Trobriand, *Four Years with the Army of the Potomac*, p. 301; *OR*, 12:105; *B & L*, 2:550-51; Morse, 1:109.
54. Freeman, *R. E. Lee*, 2:350-53; Hassler, "The Battle of South Mountain," *Maryland Historical Magazine* 52(1957):39-64; Rhodes, 4:146; *CCW* (1863), 1:489.
55. *B & L*, 2:609-18; Freeman, *Lee's Lieutenants*, 2:193-200; Francis W. Palfrey, *The Antietam and Fredericksburg*, pp. 69-72; Hassler, *McClellan*, pp. 271-73.
56. Palfrey, pp. 42-135; James V. Murfin, *The Gleam of Bayonets;* Hassler, *McClellan*, pp. 263-95; Livermore, pp. 92-94.
57. Thomas A. Bailey, *A Diplomatic History of the American People*, pp. 336-37; Rhodes, 4:154, 156.
58. See Hassler, *McClellan*, pp. 297-323; *B & L*, 3:103.
59. Palfrey, p. 134; Francis A. Walker, *History of the Second Army Corps*, p. 138; Robert E. Lee, [Jr.], *Recollections and Letters of General Robert E. Lee* (New York: Doubleday, Page, 1905), pp. 415-16.
60. Cullum, 2:191; *DAB*, s.v.; Cox, 1:264, 389-90; George Meade, *The Life and Letters of George Gordon Meade*, 1:325; Palfrey, pp. 54-55; *B & L*, 3:106.
61. *OR*, 28:552-54, 31:47-48, 83-99, 180-81, 797-98; G. F. R. Henderson, *The Campaign of Fredericksburg*, p. 37; *CCW* (1863), 1:645-75; Basler, 5:509-14; Palfrey, pp. 141-44; *B & L*, 3:122, 129-30; Livermore, 96.
62. *B & L*, 3:97; Palfrey, p. 151.

63. Vorin E. Whan, *Fiasco at Fredericksburg;* Henderson; Palfrey, pp. 136-90; Freeman, *Lee's Lieutenants,* 2:339-68; *B & L,* 3:70-151.

64. Hassler, *Commanders,* pp. 119-21; Swinton, pp. 252-58; *OR,* 31:998-99; *CCW* (1863) 1: 719-22, (1865) 1:3, 73; Pease and Randall, 1:619; Basler, 6:77n-79n; Villard, 1:348, 375-76; Palfrey, p. 141; Carl Russell Fish, *The American Civil War,* p. 281.

CHAPTER EIGHT

1. John McElroy, *The Struggle for Missouri;* James Peckham, *Gen. Nathaniel Lyon and Missouri in 1861;* Allan Nevins, *The War for the Union,* 1:307-41; William Baxter, *Pea Ridge and Prairie Grove* (Cincinnati: Poe & Hitchcock, 1964).

2. Louis A. Coolidge, *Ulysses S. Grant,* pp. 4, 8-18, 27-35; Lloyd Lewis, *Captain Sam Grant;* Horace Porter, *Campaigning with Grant,* pp. 14-16, 196; George R. Agassiz, ed., *Meade's Headquarters, 1863-1865,* pp. 80-83.

3. Bruce Catton, *Grant Moves South,* pp. 219-20; *War of the Rebellion: A Compilation of the Official Records of the Union and Confederate Armies,* 10:89, 11:93, cited hereafter as *OR;* Manning F. Force, *From Fort Henry to Corinth,* p. 120.

4. On Shiloh see James L. McDonough, *Shiloh;* Wiley Sword, *Shiloh;* Charles P. Roland, *Albert Sidney Johnston,* pp. 298-351; Ulysses S. Grant, *Personal Memoirs of U. S. Grant,* 1:330-81; Robert Underwood Johnson and Clarence Clough Buel, eds., *Battles and Leaders of the Civil War,* 1:465-610, cited hereafter as *B & L.*

5. George W. Cullum, *Biographical Register of the Officers and Graduates of the U.S. Military Academy at West Point,* 2:26; *Dictionary of American Biography,* s.v., cited hereafter as *DAB;* John C. Ropes, *The Story of the Civil War,* 2:3-95; *OR,* 23:314-15, 360.

6. Grady McWhiney, *Braxton Bragg,* vol. 1.

7. Stanley F. Horn, *The Army of Tennessee,* pp. 155-67; *B & L,* 3:1-25; *OR,* 23:538-55, 652.

8. J. G. Randall and David Donald, *The Civil War and Reconstruction,* p. 407; Walter Geer, *Campaigns of the Civil War,* p. 197; Henry M. Cist, *The Army of the Cumberland,* pp. 61-86; Thomas L. Livermore, *Numbers and Losses in the Civil War,* p. 95.

9. *OR,* 23:619-42, 651.

10. Francis Vinton Greene, *The Mississippi,* chap. 2; Freeman Cleaves, *Rock of Chickamauga,* pp. 117-18; Albert Deane Richardson, *The Secret Service,* pp. 335-36; Cullum, 2:42; J. Palmer to L. Trumbull, 11 Jan. 1863, Lyman Trumbull Papers, Library of Congress, Washington, D.C.; William M. Lamers, *The Edge of Glory.*

11. T. Harry Williams, *Lincoln and His Generals,* pp. 187-88.

12. *OR,* 30:117-18, 123-24.

13. Alexander F. Stevenson, *The Battle of Stone's River;* William S. Rosecrans, *Report on the Battle of Murfreesboro;* Roy P. Basler, ed., *The Collected Works of Abraham Lincoln,* 6:39.

14. William F. G. Shanks, *Personal Recollections of Distinguished Generals* (New York: Harper, 1866), pp. 187-91; Cullum, 1:536-37; *DAB,* s.v.; Walter H. Hebert, *Fighting Joe Hooker;* Warren W. Hassler, Jr., *Commanders of the Army of the Potomac,* pp. 127-28.

15. Gameliel Bradford, *Union Portraits,* p. 59; *Harper's Monthly* 31:642; *Scribner's Monthly* 19: 422, 704; Basler, 6:78-79; Edward Channing, *History of the United States* (New York: Macmillan, 1925), 6:477.

16. Basler, 6:161, 169; *B & L,* 3:120; Noah Brooks, *Washington in Lincoln's Time,* pp. 45-57; *OR,* 39:256, 40:236.

17. John Bigelow, Jr., *The Campaign of Chancellorsville;* Hassler, *Commanders,* pp. 137-49; Douglas Southall Freeman, *Lee's Lieutenants,* 2:524-643.

18. Bigelow, pp. 435, 473; *B & L,* 3:237; Brooks, p. 57.

19. Livermore, pp. 102-3; Wilbur S. Nye, *Here Come the Rebels!*

20. *Report of the Joint Committee on the Conduct of the War* (1865), 1:150-51, 173, 292, cited hereafter as *CCW;* Geer, pp. 236-37; George C. Gorham, *Life and Public Services of Edwin M. Stanton* (Boston: Houghton Mifflin, 1889), 2:98-100.

21. Freeman Cleaves, *Meade of Gettysburg;* George H. Gordon, *A War Diary of the Great Rebellion* (Boston: J. R. Osgood, 1882), p. 141; Glenn Tucker, *High Tide at Gettysburg,* p. 74; Bradford, pp. 84-85; Cullum, 1:472-73.

22. *OR,* 43:61; Livermore, p. 102; J. G. Randall, *Lincoln the President,* 2:275.
23. On Gettysburg see Hassler, *Crisis at the Crossroads;* George R. Stewart, *Pickett's Charge* (Boston: Houghton Mifflin, 1959); Edwin B. Coddington, *The Gettysburg Campaign;* Jesse Bowman Young, *The Battle of Gettysburg* (New York: Harper, 1913); John W. Vanderslice, *Gettysburg Then and Now* (New York: G. W. Dillingham, 1899).
24. Hassler, *Commanders,* pp. 187-91; Tyler Dennett, ed., *Lincoln and the Civil War in the Diaries and Letters of John Hay* (New York: Dodd, Mead, 1939), pp. 66-67; *OR,* 43:92-94, 49:361-77; 409-12; Andrew A. Humphreys, *From Gettysburg to the Rapidan* (New York: Scribner, 1883).
25. James F. Rusling, *Men and Things I Saw in Civil War Days,* pp. 16-17; on Vicksburg see Edwin C. Bearss, *Decision in Mississippi,* pp. 66-460; Greene, pp. 55-208; Adolph A. Hoehling, *Vicksburg;* Grant, 1:422-570; John C. Pemberton, *Pemberton, Defender of Vicksburg;* Joseph E. Johnston, *Narrative of Military Operations,* pp. 174-204.
26. Basler, 6:326, 354-75; *OR,* vol. 26, pt. 1, pp. 664-83; Grant to Lincoln, 23 Aug. 1863, Abraham Lincoln Papers, Library of Congress, Washington, D.C.
27. *OR,* 35:31, 33-34, 255-56.
28. Ibid., 95, 111, 138, 146-47, vol. 23, pt. 1, pp. 8, 10, pt. 2, pp. 369, 376, pt. 3, p. 376; Henry Villard, *Memoirs of Henry Villard,* 2:66-68; James A. Gilmore, *Personal Recollections of Abraham Lincoln and the Civil War,* pp. 100-103, 123, 145-47; Basler, 6:236.
29. Williams, pp. 275-78; James Ford Rhodes, *History of the United States,* 4:395-96; *OR,* vol. 29, pt. 2, 709, 720, 726, vol. 51, pt. 2, 761; A. K. McClure, *The Annals of the War,* pp. 443-44; Jefferson Davis, *The Rise and Fall of the Confederate Government,* 2:428; Livermore, pp. 105-6.
30. Glenn Tucker, *Chickamauga;* Archibald Gracie, *The Truth About Chickamauga;* John B. Turchin, *Chickamauga;* Livermore, pp. 105-6.
31. David Homer Bates, *Lincoln in the Telegraph Office* (New York: Century, 1907), pp. 174-75; C. A. Dana to E. M. Stanton, 27, 30 Sept., 12, 17 Oct. 1863, Stanton to Dana, 30 Sept. 1863, Charles A. Dana Papers, Library of Congress, Washington, D.C.; John T. Morse, Jr., *The Diary of Gideon Welles,* 1:447; Cleaves, *Rock of Chickamauga,* pp. 180-83; Basler, 6:475.
32. John Fiske, *The Mississippi Valley in the Civil War,* pp. 303-16; Horn, pp. 275-304; Bragg to Davis, 1 Dec. 1863, Braxton Bragg Papers, Western Reserve Historical Society, Cleveland; J. G. Nicolay's Memorandum, 7 Dec. 1863, John G. Nicolay Papers, Library of Congress, Washington, D.C.; Grant, 2:28-88; *B & L,* 3:676-730.
33. U.S., Congress, *House Executive Document 1,* 37th Cong., 3d sess., 3:24; Charles B. Boynton, *The History of the Navy During the Rebellion,* 1:100, 139; Charles O. Paullin, "A Half Century of Naval Administration," *Proceedings of the United States Naval Institute* 39:165.
34. William M. Robinson, *The Confederate Privateers;* J. Thomas Scharf, *History of the Confederate States Navy,* pp. 53-93; Paullin, 38:1310.
35. Lydel Sims, "The Submarine That Wouldn't Come Up," *American Heritage* 9(1958):110; *American Historical Review* 39:126; James Phinney Baxter, *The Introduction of the Ironclad Warship.*
36. Baxter, p. 265; William C. Whire and Ruth White, *Tin Can on a Shingle;* Robert W. Daly, *How the Merrimac Won; B & L,* 2:264-70.
37. George W. Dalzell, *The Flight from the Flag; Official Records of the Union and Confederate Navies* (Washington: Government Printing Office, 1894-1922), ser. 1, vol. 1, p. 782; Raphael Semmes, *Memoirs of Service Afloat;* James Russell Soley, *The Blockade and the Cruisers.*
38. Alfred Thayer Mahan, *The Gulf and Inland Waters;* John D. Milligan, *Gunboats Down the Mississippi;* Daniel Ammen, *The Atlantic Coast,* pp. 13-45, 163-218; Virgil C. Jones, *The Civil War at Sea,* 1:261-63, 385; Alfred Thayer Mahan, *Admiral Farragut;* Ralston B. Lattimore, *Fort Pulaski.*
39. Samuel Jones, *The Siege of Charleston;* Foxhall A. Parker, *The Battle of Mobile Bay; B & L,* 4:642-62; Richard S. West, Jr., *Mr. Lincoln's Navy,* pp. 288-302.
40. Ludwell H. Johnson, *The Red River Campaign;* Randall and Donald, p. 453.
41. Charles O. Paullin, "President Lincoln and the Navy," *American Historical Review* 14:285.
42. See Hassler, *Commanders,* pp. 195-202, 259.
43. John G. Nicolay and John Hay, *Abraham Lincoln,* 8:339-43; Morse, 1:538-39; George Meade, *The Life and Letters of George Gordon Meade,* 2:177; Grant, 2:117; Agassiz, p. 224.
44. Grant, 2:122-23; Lincoln to Grant, 30 Apr. 1864, Lincoln Papers.
45. Andrew A. Humphreys, *The Virginia Campaign of '64 and '65,* p. 6; *OR,* 59:245-46, 60:794-805, 827-29, 61:8-14, 63; *B & L,* 4:206.

46. On the Wilderness see Edward Steere, *The Wilderness Campaign;* Morris Schaff, *The Battle of the Wilderness;* Hassler, *Commanders,* pp. 208-12; Freeman, *Lee's Lieutenants,* 3:342-73; Livermore, pp. 110-11.

47. For Spotsylvania Court House see Humphreys, pp. 57-118; Grant, 2:217-42; Douglas Southall Freeman, *R. E. Lee,* 3:304-45; *B & L,* 4:170-84; Livermore, p. 112.

48. Hassler, *Commanders,* pp. 216-19; Humphreys, pp. 119-36, 160-93; Grant, 2:243-80.

49. *OR,* 67:4; Meade, 2:201-2; Grant, 2:280n; William Swinton, *Campaigns of the Army of the Potomac,* pp. 491-95.

50. Humphreys, pp. 194-225; Hassler, *Commanders,* pp. 221-22; Livermore, p. 115.

51. *OR,* vol. 37, pt. 1, p. 346; Glenn H. Worthington, *Fighting for Time;* Frank E. Vandiver, *Jubal's Raid;* Hassler, *Commanders,* pp. 225-31; George E. Pond, *The Shenandoah Valley in 1864,* pp. 46-250.

52. Richard J. Sommers, *Richmond Redeemed; CCW* (1865), 1:110-11; Grant, 2:310-12; Humphreys, pp. 247-54; Meade, 2:217; *B & L,* 4:545-67.

53. See Hassler, *Commanders,* pp. 228-32.

54. On Sherman see Cullum, 1:6; *DAB,* s.v.; Lloyd Lewis, *Sherman, Fighting Prophet;* Basil H. Liddell Hart, *Sherman;* Bradford, pp. 131-63.

55. On the Atlanta campaign see Jacob D. Cox, *Atlanta;* Geer, pp. 366-83; Johnston, *Narrative,* pp. 262-370; William T. Sherman, *Personal Memoirs of W. T. Sherman,* 2:5-170; *B & L,* 4:247-344.

56. *OR,* vol. 39, pt. 3, p. 3.

57. Ibid., pp. 63-64, 202, 222, 239, 576, 594.

58. Jacob D. Cox, *The March to the Sea* (New York: Scribner's, 1882); H. V. Boynton, *Sherman's Historical Raid;* George W. Nichols, *The Story of the Great March;* Thomas R. Hay, *Hood's Tennessee Campaign* (New York: Neale, 1929).

59. *OR,* vol. 45, pt. 2, pp. 15-18, 70, 97; Williams, pp. 342-44; Stanley F. Horn, *The Decisive Battle of Nashville.*

60. *OR,* vol. 42, pt. 3, pp. 1087, 1091, vol. 46, pt. 2, pp. 29, 60.

61. Hassler, *Commanders,* pp. 239-40; *Scribner's Magazine* 13(1893):27; Philip H. Sheridan, *Personal Memoirs of P. H. Sheridan,* 2:187; Basler, 8:392.

62. Grant, 2:491-92, italics added.

63. Nicolay and Hay, 10:196.

64. John G. Barrett, *Sherman's March Through the Carolinas; Appleton's Annual Cyclopedia* (1865):74; *B & L,* 4:412; Rhodes, 5:186-88; Randall and Donald, pp. 529-31.

CHAPTER NINE

1. Ulysses S. Grant, *Personal Memoirs of U. S. Grant,* 2:553; U.S. War Department, *Report of the Secretary of War* (1865), 1:19, 21, cited hereafter as *RSW.*

2. *RSW* (1865), 1:19-21; Russell F. Weigley, *History of the United States Army,* p. 262; C. Joseph Bernardo and Eugene H. Bacon, *American Military Policy,* p. 235.

3. Robert F. Futrell, "Federal Military Government in the South, 1861-1865," *Military Affairs* 15(1951):181-91; William P. Moore, "The Provost Marshal Goes to War," *Civil War History* 5 (1959):62-71.

4. James E. Sefton, "The Army and Reconstruction" (Ph.D. diss., University of California, Los Angeles, 1965).

5. Harold M. Hyman, "Johnson, Stanton, and Grant: A Reconsideration of the Army's Role in the Events Leading to Impeachment," *American Historical Review* 66(1960):85-100; U.S., *Statutes at Large,* 14:486-87.

6. Henry Steele Commager, ed., *Documents of American History* (New York: Crofts, 1946), pt. 2, pp. 37-38; James D. Richardson, ed., *A Compilation of the Messages and Papers of the Presidents,* 6:472.

7. *Army and Navy Journal,* 9 Mar. 1867; U.S., *Statutes at Large,* 15:14; Hyman, pp. 96-98; Weigley, p. 260.

8. Eric L. McKitrick, *Andrew Johnson and Reconstruction,* pp. 486-509; Otis A. Singletary, *The Negro Militia and Reconstruction;* Frederick T. Wilson, *Federal Aid in Domestic Disturbances,* chap. 5; William Addleman Ganoe, *The History of the United States Army,* pp. 298-354.

9. *RSW* (1869), pp. 6, 132-51; U.S., *Statutes at Large,* 16:317, 18:72; Ganoe, p. 330; Oliver L. Spaulding, *The United States Army in War and Peace,* p. 369.
10. See I. B. Holley, *Ideas and Weapons,* p. 10; *RSW* (1866), pp. 9-10.
11. Emanuel R. Lewis, *Seacoast Fortifications of the United States,* pp. 66-72; *RSW* (1893), 1:14; Russell A. Alger, *The Spanish-American War,* p. 10.
12. Samuel P. Huntington, *The Soldier and the State,* pp. 237-39; *The Centennial History of the United States Military Academy* (Washington: Government Printing Office, 1904).
13. Peter S. Michie, *The Life and Letters of Emory Upton;* Stephen E. Ambrose, *Upton and the Army.*
14. Michie, pp. 386-87; Ambrose, pp. 85-159; Emory Upton, *The Military Policy of the United States,* pp. 9, 85, 149, 416-17, 426-27.
15. Richardson, 7:475.
16. Ganoe, p. 321; Bernardo and Bacon, p. 242; James C. Malin, *Indian Policy and Westward Expansion* (Lawrence, Kan.: Bulletin of the University of Kansas Humanistic Studies, 1921), vol. 2, no. 3.
17. Helen Hunt Jackson, *A Century of Dishonor;* R. Ernest Dupuy, *Men of West Point,* p. 95; Don Rickey, Jr., *Forty Miles a Day on Beans and Hay.*
18. Ralph K. Andrist, *The Long Death,* pp. 99-101; *RSW* (1879), pp. 4-6; Dee Brown, *Fort Phil Kearny,* U.S., Congress, *Senate Executive Document 13,* 40th Cong., 1st sess., p. 83.
19. Robert M. Utley, *Frontier Regulars,* pp. 98-99; J. W. Vaughn, *Indian Fights,* pp. 32-43; Roy E. Appleman, "The Fetterman Fight," in Potomac Westerners, *Great Western Indian Fights* (Liincoln: University of Nebraska Press, 1960), chap. 10.
20. Robert G. Athearn, *William Tecumseh Sherman and the Settlement of the West,* chap. 7, 8; U.S., Congress, *Senate Executive Document 13,* 40th Cong., 1st sess., pp. 111-14.
21. Robert A. Murray, *Military Posts in the Powder River Country of Wyoming* (Lincoln: University of Nebraska Press, 1968), pp. 86-101; James B. Fry, *Army Sacrifices* (New York: Van Nostrand, 1879), p. 135.
22. Andrist, p. 159; Utley, *Frontier Regulars,* pp. 149-50, 159.
23. The best balanced biography is Jay Monaghan, *Custer: The Life of General George Armstrong Custer* (Boston: Little, Brown, 1959).
24. For the Washita operation see *RSW* (1869), pp. 42-56; George Bird Grinnell, *The Fighting Cheyennes,* chap. 22; George A. Custer, *My Life on the Plains,* chap. 10.
25. The standard work is Max L. Heyman, Jr., *Prudent Soldier: A Biography of Major General E. R. S. Canby* (Glendale: A. H. Clark, 1959).
26. Erwin N. Thompson, *The Modoc War* (Sacramento, Calif.: Argus, 1971); Keith A. Murray, *The Modocs and Their War;* Roy H. Glassley, *Pacific Northwest Indian Wars.*
27. Stanley Vestal, *Sitting Bull,* pp. 91, 113; Utley, *Frontier Regulars,* pp. 237-39; *RSW* (1872), pp. 41-42, (1874), pp. 25, 32-34, 39, (1875), pp. 34-62.
28. U.S., Congress, *House Executive Document 96,* 43d Cong., 3d sess.; Melbourne C. Chandler, *Of Garryowen in Glory,* pp. 38-41; Donald Jackson, *Custer's Gold.*
29. J. W. Vaughn, *The Reynolds Campaign on Powder River; RSW* (1876), pp. 441, 459; Ezra J. Warner, *Generals in Blue,* pp. 497-98; William A. Graham, *The Story of the Little Big Horn,* pp. 53-54.
30. John Gibbon, "Last Summer's Expedition Against the Sioux," and "Hunting Sitting Bull," *American Catholic Quarterly Review* 2(1879):271-304, 665-94; Monaghan, pp. 365-69; Utley, *Frontier Regulars,* pp. 252-53.
31. Jesse W. Vaughn, *With Crook at the Rosebud;* Grinnell, chap. 25.
32. Utley, *Frontier Regulars,* pp. 256-57.
33. Ibid., p. 257; Gibbon, p. 22.
34. Andrist.
35. *RSW* (1876), p. 477; Utley, *Frontier Regulars,* pp. 258-59; Andrist, p. 276.
36. On the battle of the Little Bighorn and Custer's role see Edgar I. Stewart, *Custer's Luck;* Graham; Fred Dustin, *The Custer Tragedy;* Charles Kuhlman, *Legend into History;* Robert M. Utley, *Custer and the Great Controversy;* Joseph Mills Hanson, *The Conquest of the Missouri* (Chicago: McClurg, 1909), pp. 233-300.
37. Warner, pp. 322-24; Virginia Johnson, *The Unregimented General;* Utley, *Frontier Regulars,* pp. 220-89.
38. Andrist, pp. 297-98.

39. Ibid., pp. 298-300.
40. Utley, *Frontier Regulars,* pp. 296-98, 316-17.
41. *RSW* (1877), pp. 589-97; Oliver O. Howard, *My Life and Experiences Among Our Hostile Indians,* chap. 17.
42. Utley, *Frontier Regulars,* p. 320; Andrist, pp. 307-8.
43. *RSW* (1877), pp. 68-72; John Gibbon, "The Battle of the Big Hole," *Harper's Weekly* 39 (1895):1215-16, 1235-36; Utley, *Frontier Regulars,* pp. 307-8.
44. *RSW* (1877), pp. 12-14, 119-31, 585-660; Mark H. Brown, *The Flight of the Nez Percé,* chap. 19.
45. M. Brown, chap. 21; *RSW* (1877), pp. 507-12, 569-72.
46. M. Brown, p. 366; V. Johnson, chaps. 15, 16; Nelson A. Miles, *Personal Recollections and Observations* (Chicago: Werner, 1896), chaps. 20, 21.
47. John P. Turner, *The North-West Mounted Police* (Ottawa: Cloutier, 1950), 1:342.
48. Utley, *Frontier Regulars,* pp. 314-15, 322-43.
49. *RSW* (1877), pp. 15, 529; Merrill D. Beal, *"I Will Fight No More Forever":* *Chief Joseph and the Nez Percé War* (Seattle: University of Washington Press, 1963).
50. Utley, *Frontier Regulars,* chap. 18; *RSW* (1880), pp. 158-63.
51. John G. Bourke, *An Apache Campaign in the Sierra Madre,* p. 108; Jason Betzinez, *I Fought with Geronimo,* p. 58.
52. *RSW* (1880), pp. 206-7, (1881), pp. 140-55; William H. Carter, *The Life of Lieutenant General Chaffee,* chap. 12; Dan L. Thrapp, *The Conquest of Apacheria,* chap. 17; Commissioner of Indian Affairs, *Annual Report* (1881), pp. ix-x.
53. George R. Forsyth, *Thrilling Days in Army Life* (New York: Harper, 1902), pp. 79-121; Betzinez, chaps. 7, 8; Thrapp, chap. 18.
54. Commissioner of Indian Affairs, *Annual Report* (1883), p. 8; U.S., *Statutes at Large,* 20: 934-36; Thrapp, pp. 267-71.
55. *RSW* (1883), pp. 162-63, 173-78; Frank C. Lockwood, *The Apache Indians,* chap. 13; Betzinez, chaps, 12, 13; Thrapp, pp. 272-94.
56. Barry C. Johnson, ed., *Crook's Resumé of Operations Against Apache Indians,* p. 11; Utley, *Frontier Regulars,* pp. 383-84.
57. B. C. Johnson; Thrapp, chaps. 24, 25; Miles, pp. 450-71.
58. U.S., Congress, *Senate Document 88,* 51st Cong., 1st sess.; B. C. Johnson; Miles, pp. 481-84; *RSW* (1886), pp. 72-73, 164-67.
59. *RSW* (1886), pp. 12-15, 73-74, 144-46, 170-81; Miles, pp. 495-517; Thrapp, pp. 354-67; Jack C. Lane, ed., *Chasing Geronimo.*
60. Utley, *Frontier Regulars,* pp. 402-3; *RSW* (1891), pp. 194-99.
61. See Utley, *Frontier Regulars,* pp. 405-6.
62. Ibid., pp. 407-9; Robert M. Utley, *The Last Days of the Sioux Nation,* chap. 7-15; S. L. A. Marshall, *Crimsoned Prairie;* Miles, pp. 241-47; Dee Brown, *Bury My Heart at Wounded Knee.*
63. Joseph P. Peters, ed., *Indian Battles and Skirmishes on the American Frontier.*
64. Andrist, p. 3.
65. U.S., Department of the Navy, *Annual Report of the Secretary of the Navy* (1864), 6:xxiii, (1876), pp. 3-6, cited hereafter as *RSN;* Dudley W. Knox, *A History of the United States Navy,* p. 317; Harold and Margaret Sprout, *The Rise of American Naval Power,* p. 165; *Army and Navy Gazette,* 8 Jan. 1876.
66. Bernardo and Bacon, p. 259; Caspar F. Goodrich, *Rope Yarns from the Old Navy* (New York: Naval History Society, 1931), p. 65; Frank M. Bennett, *The Steam Navy of the United States,* p. 614.
67. David Dixon Porter, "Our Navy," *United Service Magazine* 1(1879):4; Daniel Ammen, "The Purpose of a Navy," ibid., 1(1879):244-55; Bennett, chap. 31; *Army and Navy Journal* 11(1873): 135; Sprout, pp. 170-71.
68. Leon B. Richardson, *William E. Chandler,* pp. 289-90; *RSN* (1883), pp. 89-90; U.S., *Statutes at Large,* 22:291; Sprout, pp. 190-93; Bernardo and Bacon, p. 262.
69. U.S., *Statutes at Large,* 22:472; *Navy Yearbook,* (1917), pp. 29, 738; Benjamin F. Cooling, *Benjamin Franklin Tracy,* p. 53; Sprout, pp. 188, 192-93.
70. *House Executive Document 1,* 43d Cong., 2d sess., pt. 3, 5:209; Mark D. Hirsch, *William C. Whitney,* pp. 298-99; Allan Nevins, *Grover Cleveland,* pp. 217-22.

71. Bernardo and Bacon, p. 263; *RSN* (1889), 1:3, 3:10-12, (1890):3, 11-14, 37; *New York Herald,* 20 Feb. 1889; Cooling; *Navy Yearbook* (1917), pp. 739, 758, 766; Robley D. Evans, *A Sailor's Log,* pp. 259-60.

72. *RSN* (1897), pp. 3-6, 8.

73. Charles O. Paullin, "A Half Century of Naval Administration in America, 1861-1911," *Proceedings of the United States Naval Institute* 36:559-62, 39:1496-97; Bernardo and Bacon, pp. 272-73.

74. Alfred Thayer Mahan, *From Sail to Steam;* Robert Seager, *Alfred Thayer Mahan;* William E. Livezey, *Mahan on Sea Power.*

75. A. T. Mahan, *The Influence of Sea Power upon History,* pp. 26-27, 31, 49, 82-83, 132, 136-38, 539; Sprout, pp. 203-5; Allen Westcott, ed., *Mahan on Naval Warfare* (Boston: Little, Brown, 1941).

76. U.S., *Statutes at Large,* 15:68-72; *RSN* (1868), p. 33, (1869), pp. 23-24, (1870), pp. 157-58, (1877), pp. 6-10, (1888), p. 10, (1893), p. 579, (1896), pp. 34-35, (1897), pp. 36-37.

77. Ibid., (1868), p. 33, (1893), p. 579, (1896), pp. 34-35.

78. Ganoe, title of chap. 9.

CHAPTER TEN

1. *Overland Monthly* 31(1898):177-78; Alfred T. Mahan, "The United States Looking Outward," *Atlantic Monthly* 66(1890):817-23.

2. Standard biographies of McKinley are H. Wayne Morgan, *William McKinley and His America;* Margaret Leech, *In the Days of McKinley.*

3. See Warren W. Hassler, Jr., *The President as Commander in Chief,* pp. 73-74; Russell A. Alger, *The Spanish-American War,* p. 48; John D. Long, *The New American Navy,* 2:149.

4. Charles D. Sigsbee, *The "Maine,"* pp. 1-58, 195-202; John Edward Weems, *The Fate of the "Maine,"* p. 53.

5. Sigsbee, pp. 59-124; Weems, p. 72; Jack Cameron Dierks, *A Leap to Arms,* pp. 18-19; French Ensor Chadwick, *The Relations Between the United States and Spain,* 1:9.

6. Sigsbee, pp. 58, 67, 125-92, 207-12, 231-45; Hyman G. Rickover, *How the Battleship Maine Was Destroyed.*

7. *Papers Relating to the Foreign Relations of the United States* (Washington: Government Printing Office, 1901), pp. 719-49; Hassler, pp. 78-79.

8. Lawrence S. Mayo, ed., *America of Yesteryear as Reflected in the Journal of John Davis Long* (Boston: Atlantic Monthly Press, 1923); Theodore Roosevelt, *An Autobiography.*

9. George W. Hotchkiss, *History of the Lumber and Forest Industry of the Northwest* (Chicago: Hotchkiss, 1898), pp. 75-77; Allen Johnson, ed., *Dictionary of American Biography,* s.v., cited hereafter as *DAB.*

10. James H. Kidd, *Personal Recollections of a Cavalryman* (Ionia, Mich.: Sentinel, 1908); Philip H. Sheridan, *Personal Memoirs of P. H. Sheridan,* 1:140-43, 160-65; Graham A. Cosmas, *An Army for Empire* (Columbia, Mo.: University of Missouri Press, 1971), p. 56.

11. F. Clever Bald, *Michigan in Four Centuries* (New York: Harper, 1954), pp. 297-98; Morgan, pp. 260-61; Leech, pp. 102-4; *New York Times,* 25 Aug. 1897.

12. Leech, p. 102; Mayo, pp. 188, 197; J. F. Weston to J. H. Wilson, 3 Aug. 1899, James H. Wilson Papers, Library of Congress, Washington, D.C.

13. Nelson A. Miles, *Serving the Republic,* pp. 253-60; Virginia W. Johnson, *The Unregimented General,* pp. 261-64, 303-9.

14. Edward Ransom, "'Nelson A. Miles as Commanding General, 1895-1903,'" *Military Affairs* 29:180; Johnson; Cosmas, pp. 61-62.

15. U.S., Department of War, *Report of the Secretary of War* (1887), 1:115-16, (1894), 1:58-63, (1898), 1:5, cited hereafter as *RSW;* Alger, p. 7; *New York Times,* 18 Jan. 1898.

16. Cosmas, pp. 71-72; Leech, pp. 174-75, 184; Miles, pp. 268-69; Harold and Margaret Sprout, *The Rise of American Naval Power,* pp. 224, 228-29.

17. Alger, pp. 8-9; *New York Times,* 8, 9, 10, 16, 24, 25 Mar. 1898; W. M. Goode, *With Sampson Through the War,* pp. 7-13; Long, 1:145-63; Sprout, pp. 229-30.

18. *Washington Post,* 14 Apr. 1898; *Army and Navy Journal,* 9, 16, 23 Apr. 1898.

19. John M. Schofield's undated manuscript memoir, "General Schofield's Experiences in Mc-Kinley's Administration," John M. Schofield Papers, Library of Congress, Washington, D.C.; Alfred Thayer Mahan, *Lessons of the War with Spain,* pp. 42–110.
20. Chadwick, 1:4, 8, 12–16, 18–19.
21. George Dewey, *Autobiography of George Dewey,* p. 139; Long, 1:211; Richard S. West, Jr., *Admirals of American Empire,* pp. 24–26, 53–61, 115–29, 174–93.
22. Herbert W. Wilson, *The Downfall of Spain,* pp. 62–63; Chadwick, 1:28–36.
23. Chadwick, 1:62–63.
24. Herbert H. Sargent, *The Campaign of Santiago de Cuba,* 1:136; Severo Gomez Nunez, *La Guérra Hispanoaméricana,* 3:123–25; Chadwick, 1:64–85, 127–35, 142–51.
25. Dewey, pp. 167–70, 175.
26. Ronald Spector, *Admiral of the New Empire.*
27. Dewey, p. 178; West, pp. 15–18, 65–80, 135–45, 294–96; Chadwick, 1:89–91.
28. Chadwick, 1:163–64, 169; Dewey, p. 203.
29. Dewey, pp. 179–80, 186–87.
30. Ibid., pp. 192, 195–96; Chadwick, 1:156–58.
31. *Proceedings of the United States Naval Institute* 25(1899):269; Dewey, pp. 197–205; *United Service Magazine* (Jan. 1902), p. 25.
32. U.S., Department of the Navy, *Report of the Bureau of Navigation,* (1898), app., p. 100; Dewey, p. 206.
33. Allan Keller, *The Spanish-American War* (New York: Hawthorn, 1969), p. 57; Dewey, pp. 209–15.
34. West, pp. 187–210; Dewey, pp. 214–25; Chadwick, 1:177–205; *Admiral Montojo Before Public Opinion and Before History* (Madrid, 1900), p. 93; Richard H. Titherington, *A History of the Spanish-American War of 1898,* pp. 127–44.
35. Goode, p. 63; Chadick, 1:214–49.
36. Chadwick, 1:245–48.
37. Dierks, pp. 56–57; Chadwick, 1:248–49.
38. Winfield S. Schley, *Forty-Five Years Under the Flag,* pp. 1–255; George E. Graham, *Schley and Santiago,* pp. 21–37; West, pp. 22–24, 46–52, 98–114, 162–73.
39. Victor M. Concas y Palau, *The Squadron of Admiral Cervera* (Washington, D.C.: Office of Naval Intelligence, 1900), pp. 44–50; Pascual Cervera y Topete, *Collection of Documents Relative to the Squadron of Operations in the West Indies* (Washington, D.C.: Office of Naval Intelligence, 1899), pp. 73–77; *Record of Proceedings of a Court of Inquiry in the Case of Rear-Admiral Winfield S. Schley* (Washington: Government Printing Office, 1901), 1:858, cited hereafter as *Court of Inquiry.*
40. *Official Record of Signals, "Brooklyn's" Log, Court of Inquiry,* 1:321; Chadwick, 1:57–58, 300, 318–20.
41. Chadwick, 1:323–25; *Court of Inquiry,* 2:1371.
42. Chadwick, 1:334–36.
43. Ibid., 1:335–36; Richmond Pearson Hobson, *The Sinking of the "Merrimac"* (New York: Century, 1899); Cervera, p. 100.
44. Chadwick, 1:152, 354–56.
45. U.S., Department of the Navy, *Annual Report of the Secretary of the Navy,* (1898), app., p. 451, cited hereafter as *RSN;* Chadwick, 1:373–77.
46. José Muller y Tejeiro, *Battles and Capitulation of Santiago de Cuba,* p. 82; Dierks, p. 113.
47. Chadwick, 1:337n, 377, 384–86, 388.
48. *New York Tribune,* 20, 23, 24 Apr. 1898; *New York Times,* 18–27 Apr. 1898; Miles, p. 270; John A. Hull, "The Hull Army Bill," *The Forum* 25:399.
49. See Keller, pp. 74–75.
50. N. A. Miles to R. A. Alger, 26 Apr., 3, 6 May 1898, *Adjutant General's Office Records,* cited hereafter as *AGOR.*
51. Alger, p. 326; Miles, p. 271; H. C. Corbin to Chief of Ordnance, 11 May 1898, *AGOR; New York Times,* 8, 13, 20 May 1898; War Department, *Correspondence Relating to the War with Spain* (Washington: Government Printing Office, 1902), 2:645–46, cited hereafter as *Correspondence.*
52. *New York Times,* 22–28 June 1898; *Report of the [Grenville M. Dodge] Commission Appointed by the President to Investigate the Conduct of the War Department in the War with Spain*

(Washington: Government Printing Office, 1899), 1:113, 254, cited hereafter as *Dodge Commission;* Alger, pp. 27-28.

53. *Correspondence,* 1:132, 268-69; *Dodge Commission,* 6:2619-20; Charles G. Dawes, *A Journal of the McKinley Years,* pp. 158, 188; Schofield's memoir.

54. Cosmas, pp. 140-48; Alger, pp. 29-33, 39-40; *New York Times,* 27 May, 17 June 1898; *Army and Navy Journal,* 30 Apr. 1898.

55. Cosmas, pp. 155-64, 287-94.

56. *RSW* (1898), 2:591-92; *Dodge Commission,* 3:443, 6:2668; Alger, p. 65.

57. Francis B. Heitman, *Historical Register and Dictionary of the United States Army,* 1:876; *DAB,* s.v.

58. Chadwick, 2:6, 7n; George Kennan, *Campaigning in Cuba,* pp. 246-47; Joseph Wheeler, *The Santiago Campaign,* pp. 6, 196-97; Sargent, 2:7, 162-63.

59. Shafter to Corbin, 7 June 1898, Corbin Papers, Library of Congress, Washington, D.C.; Kennan, p. 49; Alger, pp. 66, 68; John D. Miley, *In Cuba with Shafter,* pp. 22-27, 44; Walter Millis, *The Martial Spirit,* p. 217.

60. Chadwick, 2:12.

61. Ibid., 1:220-318; Alger, pp. 48, 62, 221-26; Mahan, pp. 27-28, 61-99, 138-72; Long, 1:205; Schofield's memoir.

62. Alger, pp. 48-59; *RSW* (1898), 2:583; *Dodge Commission,* 2:885, 3:90, 320, 7:3249; Chadwick, 2:358-59.

63. Miley, pp. 22-24, 27; Theodore Roosevelt, *The Rough Riders,* pp. 57-60; *Dodge Commission,* vols. 5, 6, 7; *RSW* (1898), 1:388, 391, 704, 2:12, 148-49, 592; Chadwick, 2:19-21.

64. Leech, p. 249; Miley, pp. 15-16; Goode, pp. 177-78; Alger, pp. 86-88.

65. Chadwick, 2:21-25; Alger, p. 88; Miley, pp. 58-59.

66. Wheeler, pp. 47, 183-84; Sargent, 2:9-11; *RSW* (1898), 1:406, 2:160, 592-97.

67. *Dodge Commission; RSW* (1898), 1:406; Miley, pp. 26, 76-88; Muller, pp. 32-33, 72; Sargent, 2:49, 102, 130-35; Roosevelt, p. 77.

68. Roosevelt, pp. 77, 82; Sargent, 2:71; Wheeler, p. 242; Dierks, pp. 90-91; Keller, p. 134; Chadwick, 2:48-49, 62.

69. Chadwick, 2:63; Titherington, p. 247; John Black Atkins, *The War in Cuba,* pp. 107-9; *Dodge Commission,* 5:2263; *RSW* (1898), 2:152-53; Wheeler, pp. 262-63.

70. Chadwick, 2:69, 74-75; *Dodge Commission,* 4:946; Sargent, 2:99.

71. Dierks, pp. 97-99; Chadwick, 2:75-83; *Dodge Commission,* 4:901; Frank Freidel, *The Splendid Little War,* p. 139; Keller, pp. 163-64.

72. Roosevelt, p. 118; Titherington, pp. 241-48, 258; Miley, pp. 101, 111; Atkins, pp. 123-25; Keller, pp. 152-53.

73. Richard Harding Davis, *The Cuban and Porto Rican Campaigns,* pp. 206-20; Titherington, p. 247; Roosevelt, p. 128; Miley, p. 118; Dierks, pp. 105-7.

74. Chadwick, 2:97-102; Miley, p. 44; *Dodge Commission,* 8:137-44.

75. Concas, pp. 68-70, 138-39.

76. Ibid., pp. 72-74; "Story of the Captains," *Century Magazine* (May 1899), p. 64; *RSW* (1898), app., p. 526.

77. *Court of Inquiry,* 1:571, 1895; Muller, pp. 103-4; Concas, p. 74; Cervera, pp. 122-33; Keller, p. 194; Chadwick, 2:133-76; Millis, p. 310.

78. Concas, 2:177; Chadwick, 2:165, 177, 184, 409-13; Wilson, pp. 340-42; West, pp. 286-302; A. C. M. Azoy, *Signal 250! The Sea Fight Off Santiago.*

79. L. Wood to his wife, 15 July 1898, Leonard Wood Papers, Library of Congress, Washington, D.C.; Miles, pp. 286-90; Alger, pp. 204-20; Miley, pp. 185-86; Lt. Capehart, "The Mine Defence of Santiago Harbor," *Proceedings of the United States Naval Institute* 24(1898):586.

80. Alger, pp. 269-73; *RSW* (1898), 1:740, 785; Chadwick, 2:261; Cosmas, pp. 251-64.

81. *Correspondence,* 1:154-55, 280-88, 299-303; *RSW* (1898), 2:29.

82. Cosmas, pp. 231-32; Chadwick, 2:284-96; Davis, pp. 325-26.

83. *Dodge Commission,* 7:3255; *RSW* (1898), 1:249-53, 270, 652-57, 2:228; Tanham, "Service Relations Sixty Years Ago," *Military Affairs,* 23:147-48.

84. Chadwick, 2:363-64.

85. Dewey, p. 246.

86. Chadwick, 2:370; Leon Wolff, *Little Brown Brother,* p. 92; Alger, p. 327; *Correspondence,* 2:639-98; *DAB,* s.v.

87. Frederick Funston, *Memories of Two Wars,* pp. 158, 169–70; *RSW* (1898), 1:269, pt. 2, pp. 476–78; *Correspondence,* 2:647, 725, 734–51.
88. Wolff, pp. 97–98; Keller, pp. 221–22; Dewey, p. 248; Chadwick, 2:369.
89. Nunez, 5:118–26; Manila *Official Gazette,* 20 Aug. 1898.
90. *Correspondence,* 1:556; *RSW* (1898), 2:41, 55, 63–66, 678; Frank D. Millet, *The Expedition to the Philippines,* p. 111.
91. Chadwick, 2:406–7; *RSW* (1898), 2:42, 56, 71, 82–83.
92. Dewey, pp. 274–75; William T. Sexton, *Soldiers in the Sun,* p. 38; *Correspondence,* 2:781–82; *RSW* (1898), 2:41–42; Alger, pp. 334–36.
93. Sexton, pp. 43–46; Wolff, p. 125; Millet, pp. 137–53; Dewey, pp. 277–85.
94. Chadwick, 2:471–72.
95. Hay to Roosevelt, 27 July 1898, Theodore Roosevelt Papers, Library of Congress, Washington, D.C.
96. Clipping in 1898 scrapbook, Henry C. Corbin Papers; *Dodge Commission,* 1; Leech, pp. 313–15, 376–78; Alger, pp. 376–77; Morgan, pp. 274, 426–31; *Milwaukee Journal,* 24 Jan. 1907.
97. Manila *Official Gazette,* 20[?] Aug. 1898; Keller, p. 236.
98. *Report of the Philippine Commission,* 1:173; Keller, pp. 236–37.
99. *RSW* (1899), vol. 1, pt. 2, p. 21, pt. 3, pp. 439–46, pt. 4, pp. 175, 365; *Army and Navy Journal,* 22 July 1899; Cosmas, pp. 301–2.
100. U.S., Congress, *House Document 1,* 56th Cong., 1st sess., pt. 2; *RSW* (1901), pt. 7, p. 9; U.S., Congress, *Senate Document 331,* 57th Cong., 1st sess., p. 1606.
101. *RSW* (1901), vol. 1, pt. 4, p. 98, pt. 5, p. 122; Wolff; Uldarico S. Baclagon, *Philippine Campaigns.*
102. U.S., Congress, *Foreign Relations,* 56th Cong., 2d sess., 1900, pp. 161–67.
103. *RSW* (1900), vol. 1, pt. 1, p. 24; C. C. Tan, *The Boxer Catastrophe.*

CHAPTER ELEVEN

1. Richard W. Leopold, *Elihu Root and the Conservative Tradition;* Philip C. Jessup, *Elihu Root.*
2. Jessup, 1:215.
3. *Report of the [Grenville M. Dodge] Commission Appointed by the President to Investigate the Conduct of the War Department in the War with Spain* (Washington: Government Printing Office, 1899), 1:115; William G. H. Carter, *The American Army,* p. 212; *Review of Reviews,* July, 1898.
4. Walter Millis, *The Martial Spirit,* p. 217; Henry Cabot Lodge, *The War with Spain* (New York: Macmillan, 1899), p. 281.
5. Jessup, 1:242, 254.
6. John Dickinson, *The Building of an Army* (New York: Century, 1922), p. 255.
7. E. Root to W. C. Church, 20 Feb. 1900, William C. Church Papers, Library of Congress, Washington, D.C.; Elihu Root, *The Military and Colonial Policy of the United States,* p. 390; U.S., Department of War, *Annual Report of the Secretary of War* (1901), p. 25, cited hereafter as *RSW.*
8. Root, p. 122. Books on the Army War College include George S. Pappas, *Prudens Futuri,* and George P. Ahern, *A Chronicle of the Army War College, 1899–1919.*
9. Otto L. Nelson, Jr., *National Security and the General Staff,* pp. 86–87; N. A. Miles to W. C. Church, 26 Mar. 1902, Church Papers.
10. Philip L. Semsch, "Elihu Root and the General Staff," *Military Affairs* 27(1963–1964):16–27; James E. Hewes, Jr., *From Root to McNamara,* pp. 6–12; Carter, pp. 47–50.
11. *Army and Navy Journal,* 18 Dec. 1909; *New York Evening Post,* 16 Dec. 1909; *Dictionary of American Biography,* s.v., cited hereafter as *DAB;* Hermann Hagedorn, *Leonard Wood;* Russell F. Weigley, *Towards an American Army,* chap. 12.
12. See W. H. Taft to F. E. Warren, 5 June 1912, Taft to H. A. DuPont, 15 June 1912, William Howard Taft Papers, Library of Congress, Washington, D.C.; Hagedorn, 2:123.
13. William A. Ganoe, *The History of the United States Army,* p. 164; C. Joseph Bernardo and Eugene H. Bacon, *American Military Policy,* p. 309.

14. Henry Shindler, *History of the Army Service Schools,* p. 5; H. H. Fuller, "The Development of the Command and General Staff School," *Military Review* 21(1942):5-6.

15. Fuller, pp. 7-8; U.S., *Statutes at Large,* 14:336; *Kansas City Star,* 11 Dec. 1893; *RSW* (1895), pp. 204-5.

16. Ira L. Reeves, *Military Education in the United States,* pp. 255-82.

17. Bernardo and Bacon, p. 312.

18. Fuller, p. 9.

19. John W. Masland and Laurence I. Radway, *Soldiers and Scholars;* Bernardo and Bacon, pp. 312-13.

20. Bernardo and Bacon, pp. 313-14.

21. *RSW* (1908), 1:33-36; U.S., *Statutes at Large,* 35:399-403.

22. L. Wood to W. C. Church, 26 June 1911, Church Papers; Hagedorn, 2:109.

23. *RSW* (1911), pp. 7-10.

24. Bernardo and Bacon, pp. 322-23.

25. John M. Palmer, *America in Arms,* pp. 135-37; Weigley, pp. 225-59; *Infantry Journal* 8 (1911):918.

26. *RSW* (1912), pp. 11-12, 76, 125.

27. The volumes by Arthur S. Link, *Wilson* (Princeton: Princeton University Press, 1947-), comprise the most scholarly biography.

28. David F. Houston, *Eight Years with Wilson's Cabinet;* Arthur S. Link, *Woodrow Wilson and the Progressive Era,* p. 28; *DAB,* s.v.

29. Edward B. Lee, Jr., *Politics of Our Military National Defense,* p. 18; Hagedorn, 2:129-30; Edward H. Brooks, "The National Defense Policy of the Wilson Administration, 1913-1917," 2 vols. (Ph.D. diss., Stanford University, 1950), 1:19-20.

30. U.S., *Statutes at Large,* 38:347-51; Brooks, pp. 97-98; Bernardo and Bacon, pp. 328-29.

31. Dudley W. Knox, *A History of the United States Navy,* pp. 379-80; Bernardo and Bacon, pp. 329-30; Frank O. Hough, *The United States Marine Corps,* pp. 158-59.

32. Charles Seymour, ed., *The Intimate Papers of Colonel House,* 1:298-300; Brooks; *New York Times,* 8 Dec. 1914; *Current Opinion,* June 1916; Ray Stannard Baker and William E. Dodd, eds., *The Public Papers of Woodrow Wilson,* 3:223-27.

33. Ralph Barton Perry, *The Plattsburg Movement;* Hagedorn, 2:159-62, 193-96; Marvin A. Kreidberg and Merton G. Henry, *History of Military Mobilization in the United States Army, 1775-1945,* pp. 281-83; Harold and Margaret Sprout, *The Rise of American Naval Power,* pp. 248-49.

34. Lindley M. Garrison, "The Problem of National Defense," *North American Review* 201 (1915):833-38; John L. Heaton, *Cobb of the World* (New York: Dodd, Mead, 1924), pp. 219-30; Brooks, pp. 125-26.

35. H. P. McCain to H. L. Scott, 22 Mar. 1915, Scott to H. J. Slocum, 30 apr. 1915, L. M. Garrison to the General Staff, 28 July 1915, Hugh L. Scott Papers, Library of Congress, Washington, D.C.; *Army and Navy Journal,* 4 Sept. 1915.

36. United States Army War College, *Statement of a Proper Military Policy for the United States* (Washington: Government Printing Office, 1916), pp. 1-21.

37. Memorandum of L. M. Garrison, 17 Sept. 1915, Scott Papers; Brooks, p. 182.

38. *Army and Navy Journal,* 30 Oct., 6, 13 Nov. 1915; H. L. Scott to R. K. Evans, 1 Nov. 1915, Scott to L. Wood, 1 Dec. 1915, Scott to W. S. Scott, 27 Dec. 1915, Scott Papers; Baker and Dodd, 6:34-35; Frederick Palmer, *Newton D. Baker* (New York: Dodd, Mead, 1931).

39. Brooks, pp. 188-89.

40. *New York Times,* 11 Feb. 1916; H. L. Scott to F. Funston, 11 Feb. 1916, Scott to G. Hutcheson, 14 Feb. 1916, Scott Papers; Brooks, p. 192.

41. Elting E. Morison, *Turmoil and Tradition* (Boston: Houghton Mifflin, 1960), p. 169; Link, *Wilson and the Progressive Era,* pp. 107-36.

42. Link, *Wilson and the Progressive Era,* pp. 137-40, 188; Jim Dan Hill, *The Minute Man in War and Peace,* pp. 221-22.

43. Frank Tompkins, *Chasing Villa;* Roger Batchelder, *Watching and Waiting on the Border;* Walter Millis, *Arms and Men,* pp. 228-32.

44. *RSW* (1916), 1:155-208.

45. Clarence H. Cramer, *Newton D. Baker;* Paler; *DAB,* s.v.

46. N. D. Baker to W. Wilson, 13 Apr. 1917, Woodrow Wilson Papers, Library of Congress, Washington, D.C.; Bernardo and Bacon, p. 349.

47. Carroll S. Alden and Allen Westcott, *The United States Navy*, pp. 327-28; U.S., Department of the Navy, *Annual Report of the Secretary of the Navy* (1902), p. 13, cited hereafter as *RSN*.

48. Charles O. Paullin, "Half Century of Naval Administration," *Proceedings of the United States Naval Institute* 40(1914):111, 116; Bradley A. Fiske, *From Midshipman to Rear Admiral* (New York: Century, 1919), p. 350; *Navy Yearbook, 1917*, pp. 133, 147, 175, 740, 759, 766.

49. *RSN* (1903-1906); Sprout, pp. 259-61.

50. Arthur J. Marder, *From the Dreadnought to Scapa Flow*, 1:13, 43-44, 56-57, 69-70; Sprout, p. 263; *Brassey's Naval Annual, 1907* (New York: Macmillan, 1907), pp. 2, 391.

51. "Ten Years' Development of the Battleship," *Scientific American* 97(1907):408; *Brassey's Naval Annual, 1907*, p. 32; Sprout, pp. 263-64.

52. Sprout, pp. 264-69; Robley D. Evans, *An Admiral's Log* (New York: Appleton, 1910); Richard A. Hart, *The Great White Fleet*; R. J. Miller, *Around the World with the Battleships*; Richard Challener, *Admirals, Generals, and American Foreign Policy*, pp. 40, 181-93, 248-76; *RSN* (1908), p. 11; U.S., *Statutes at Large*, 34:582, 1203, 35:158, 777, 36:1287, 37:354, 911; *Literary Digest*, 2 Mar. 1912; U.S., Department of the Navy, *Annual Reports of the Navy Department* (1908), p. 12.

53. James D. Richardson, ed., *A Compilation of the Messages and Papers of the Presidents*, 15: 7371-72, 7808; *Navy Yearbook, 1917; New York Herald*, 17, 20, 21 Aug. 1912, 3, 4, 5 Mar. 1913; Sprout, pp. 291-92.

54. *Army and Navy Journal* 49(1911):431, 50(1913):1263, 51(1913):1332; Sprout, p. 301; *Harper's Weekly*, 7 June 1913; *Atlantic Monthly*, 107(1911):34.

55. *New York Times*, 6, 9 Mar., 15, 17 June, 14 July 1913, 30, 31 Jan., 6 Feb. 1914; *Annual Reports of the Navy Department* (1912), pp. 63-64, (1913), pp. 5-16, 19-23; U.S., *Statutes at Large*, 38:384, 39:612.

56. U.S., Congress, Senate, *Congressional Record*, 52:2747-48; *Navy Yearbook, 1917*, p. 383; Fiske, pp. 566-71; Alden and Westcott, p. 340.

57. *Annual Reports of the Navy Department* (1915), pp. 77, 80; Sprout, pp. 341-44; *Navy Yearbook, 1917*, p. 400.

58. Alden and Westcott, p. 339; Howard V. L. Bloomfield, *The Compact History of the United States Coast Guard* (New York: Hawthorn, 1966).

59. See F. Stansbury Haydon, *Aeronautics in the Union and Confederate Armies*; Alfred Goldberg, ed., *A History of the United States Air Force*, p. 1; Caroll V. Glines, Jr., *The Compact History of the United States Air Force*, pp. 13-14.

60. Goldberg, pp. 1-2; Glines, pp. 45-46.

61. Glines, pp. 47-49; Goldberg, p. 2.

62. Benjamin F. Foulois, *The Air Power Historian* (Maxwell AFB, Ala.: Air Force Historical Foundation, 1955), pp. 24-25.

63. Glines, pp. 61-62; Goldberg, pp. 7-8.

64. See Arthur Sweetser, *The American Air Service* (New York: Appleton, 1919), pp. 18-19; Glines, p. 63.

65. U.S., *Statutes at Large*, 37:892, 894, 38:930, 39:559; *RSN* (1913), p. 17.

CHAPTER TWELVE

1. On the coming of the First World War see Luigi Albertini, *The Origins of the War of 1914*, 3 vols. (London: Oxford, 1952-1957), although the older studies by Sidney B. Fay and Bernadotte E. Schmitt are also useful.

2. Harvey A. DeWeerd, *President Wilson Fights His War*, chaps. 3, 4; William D. Puleston, *High Command in the World War*, chaps. 9-14.

3. Cyril Falls, *The Great War*, pp. 103-66; Puleston, chaps. 15-22.

4. C. R. M. F. Cruttwell, *A History of the Great War, 1914-1918*, chaps. 15-17, 20.

5. Basil H. Liddell Hart, *A History of the World War, 1914-1918*, p. 388; James E. Edmonds, *A Short History of World War I*, chaps. 19-21.

6. Charles B. Nordhoff and James Norman Hall, *The Lafayette Flying Corps,* 2 vols. (Boston: Houghton Mifflin, 1920); Edward M. Coffman, *The War to End All Wars,* p. 200.

7. See Charles C. Tansill, *America Goes to War* (Boston: Little, Brown, 1938); Charles Seymour, *American Diplomacy during the World War* (Baltimore: Johns Hopkins Press, 1934).

8. U.S., Department of War, *Annual Report of the Secretary of War* (1917), p. 5, cited hereafter as *RSW;* Coffman, pp. 13-15; Enoch H. Crowder, *The Spirit of Selective Service.*

9. Charles Seymour, ed., *The Intimate Papers of Colonel House,* 3:8; Frederick Palmer, *Bliss, Peacemaker,* pp. 145-46.

10. Coffman, p. 43; Thomas G. Frothingham, *The American Reinforcement in the World War,* p. xxi.

11. On Pershing see Frank E. Vandiver, *Black Jack;* Frederick Palmer, *John J. Pershing.*

12. James G. Harbord, *The American Army in France,* pp. 33-47; John J. Pershing, *My Experiences in the World War,* 1:269-70; Coffman, pp. 43-46; Russell F. Weigley, *History of the United States Army,* pp. 377-78, 390.

13. Frederick Palmer, *Newton D. Baker,* p. 180; Pershing, 1:38-40; Frothingham, p. xvi.

14. See Warren W. Hassler, Jr., *The President as Commander in Chief,* pp. 93-104.

15. DeWeerd, p. 9; Coffman, pp. 20, 76; Arthur S. Link, *Wilson,* 3:397.

16. Daniel R. Beaver, *Newton D. Baker and the American War Effort, 1917-1919;* Pershing, 1: 17-18; Coffman, p. 22.

17. Pershing, 1:22-23.

18. Coffman, pp. 162-63; March to Baker, 5 Oct. 1932, Peyton C. March Papers, Library of Congress, Washington, D.C.

19. Harbord, pp. 110-11; Peyton C. March, *The Nation at War* (Garden City: Doubleday, 1932), pp. 49-50; DeWeerd, pp. 228-33.

20. Palmer, *Baker,* 1:180; Palmer, *Bliss,* p. 164; H. L. Scott to *Philadelphia Bulletin,* 4 Jan. 1931, Newton D. Baker Papers, Library of Congress, Washington, D.C.; Ray Stannard Baker, *Woodrow Wilson,* 8:17-18; Pershing, 1:41, 95, 237-50.

21. Baker to Pershing, 26 May 1917, Woodrow Wilson Papers, Library of Congress, Washington, D.C.; Falls, pp. 355-56; Coffman, pp. 168-74.

22. Leonard P. Ayres, *The War with Germany,* pp. 37-38.

23. Charles Seymour, *The Intimate Papers of Colonel House,* 3:271-72; Palmer, *Bliss,* pp. 251-52.

24. Ayres, pp. 16-17, 21; *RSW* (1917), pp. 6, 18.

25. Ayres, pp. 25, 50, 60-61; *RSW* (1917), p. 38; Harbord, pp. 339-404, 486-510; Johnson Hagood, *The Services of Supply.*

26. Pershing, 1:156; *RSW* (1918), p. 34; Frothingham, p. 334.

27. Coffman, pp. 266-67.

28. *RSW* (1916), pp. 49-51; Memorandum, 16 Nov. 1918, James G. Harbord Papers, Library of Congress, Washington, D.C.

29. *RSW* (1918), pp. 67-68; C. Joseph Bernardo and Eugene H. Bacon, *American Military Policy,* p. 369.

30. Fletcher Pratt, *The Navy: A History* (Garden City: Garden City Publishing Co., 1941), pp. 383-85.

31. Carroll S. Alden, and Ralph Earle, *Makers of Naval Tradition* (Boston: Ginn, 1943), chap. 14; Coffman, pp. 93-94.

32. Josephus Daniels, *The Wilson Era,* pp. 69, 73-74; Coffman, pp. 103, 108.

33. *Foreign Relations, 1917,* supp. 2, 1:23-24, 46-47, 106-7, 111-12; William S. Sims and Burton J. Hendrick, *The Victory at Sea,* chap. 1, pp. 374, 401; Baker, *Papers of Colonel House,* 7:34, 121-22.

34. Elting E. Morison, *Admiral Sims and the Modern American Navy,* pp. 355-56; Edward M. Hurley, *The Bridge to France;* Bernardo and Bacon, p. 378n.

35. Llewellyn Woodward, *Great Britain and the War of 1914-1918* (London: Methuen, 1967), pp. 339-46, 491-97; Sims and Hendrick, chap. 3; Morison, pp. 347-53.

36. Coffman, pp. 116-18.

37. Dudley W. Knox, *A History of the United States Navy,* pp. 416-18.

38. Coffman, pp. 99-120; Knox, p. 408.

39. Pratt, p. 398.

40. Pershing, 1:150, 258, 380; Coffman, pp. 141–42, 330–31.

41. Pershing, 1:151–54; Forrest C. Pogue, *George C. Marshall,* chap. 9.

42. T. Dodson Stamps and Vincent J. Esposito, eds., *A Short Military History of World War I* (West Point: U.S. Military Academy, 1954), pp. 204–16, 270–78.

43. James E. Edmonds, *Military Operations, France and Belgium, 1914–1918* (London: Macmillan, 1939), 2:461; Palmer, *Baker,* 2:129; Robert Blake, ed., *The Private Papers of Douglas Haig* (London: Eyre & Spottiswoode, 1952), p. 291.

44. DeWeerd, pp. 277–87; Palmer, *Baker,* 2:154.

45. Coffman, p. 158; Harbord, p. 269; Pershing, 1:305, 352.

46. John B. McMaster, *The United States in the World War, 1918–1920* (New York: Appleton, 1920), p. 88; Robert Bullard, *Personalities and Reminiscences of the War,* chap. 21.

47. Bullard, chap. 22; Shipley Thomas, *History of the A.E.F.* (New York: Doran, 1920), chap. 4; Dale Van Every, *The A.E.F. in Battle* (New York: Appleton, 1928), chaps. 7, 8; Frothingham, p. 275; McMaster, pp. 89–94.

48. *United States Army in the World War, 1917–1919* (Washington, D.C.: Department of the Army, 1948), 4:352; Richard Suskind, *The Battle of Belleau Wood* (New York: Macmillan, 1969); Harbord, pp. 285–99; Lawrence Stallings, *The Doughboys,* chaps. 5, 6; Daniels, pp. 150–52.

49. Barrie Pitt, *1918: The Last Act* (New York: Norton, 1962), pp. 173; Pershing, 2:158–65, 208–11; Van Every, chaps. 9, 10; Thomas, chap. 7.

50. Hunter Liggett, *Commanding an American Army;* Bullard; Joseph T. Dickman, *The Great Crusade.*

51. *Stars and Stripes,* 3, 10 Jan., 14 Feb. 1919; Bullard, chap. 23; Harbord, chap. 19; Stamps and Esposito, pp. 313–18; DeWeerd, pp. 320–28.

52. Pershing, 2:chaps. 41, 42.

53. Ibid., 2:260–63; Alfred T. Hurley, *Billy Mitchell, Crusader for Air Power* (New York: Watts, 1964), p. 35.

54. R. Ernest Dupuy, *Men of West Point,* p. 142; Coffman, pp. 269–73.

55. Pershing, 2:262–63.

56. Gerald L. McEntee, *Military History of the World War,* chap. 72; Frothingham, pp. 299, 309–11; Dickman, p. 137; Van Every, chap. 15.

57. Pershing, 1:162; Hurley; Coffman, pp. 193–94.

58. Coffman, p. 194; *The Official Guide to the Army Air Force* (New York: Simon & Schuster, 1944), pp. 343–44; Ayres, pp. 99–100.

59. *Official Guide,* p. 344; Edward V. Rickenbacker, *Fighting the Flying Circus;* Coffman, pp. 122, 199–203.

60. Arthur Sweetser, *The American Air Service* (New York: Appleton, 1919); Edgar S. Gorrell, *The Measure of America's World War Aeronautical Effort* (Northfield, Mass.: Norwich University Press, 1940); Coffman, chap. 7.

61. Daniels, pp. 121–23.

62. Russell F. Weigley, *The American Way of War,* p. 203; William Mitchell, *Memoirs of World War I* (New York: Random House, 1960), p. 10.

63. Stallings, pp. 156–57, 387; Pogue, pp. 171–79; Van Every, pp. 313–14.

64. Harbord, pp. 432–33; Pershing, 2:282–83.

65. Pershing, 2:280–82, 291–94; Harbord, pp. 433–35.

66. Stamps and Esposito, p. 328.

67. Robert Alexander, *Memories of the World War* (New York: Macmillan, 1931), p. 162.

68. DeWeerd, pp. 339–48; Harbord, pp. 435–44; Bullard, p. 267.

69. Harbord, pp. 444–49; Pershing, 2:320–69.

70. Thomas M. Johnson and Fletcher Pratt, *The Lost Battalion* (Indianapolis: Bobbs-Merrill, 1938); Pershing, 2:324–31, 392; Stallings, pp. 300–303.

71. Stamps and Esposito, pp. 330–32; Harbord, pp. 450–51.

72. Harbord, pp. 452–61; McEntee, chap. 74; Pershing, 2:374–87; Thomas, chap. 12.

73. *United States Army in the World War,* vol. 9, *Meuse-Argonne;* McEntee, p. 535; Bullard, chap. 28.

74. Harbord, pp. 462–64; DeWeerd, pp. 362–63; Pershing, 2:391.

75. Stamps and Esposito, pp. 332–33; DeWeerd, pp. 376–80.

76. See R. Ernest Dupuy and Trevor N. Dupuy, *Military Heritage of America,* p. 393; Stamps and Esposito, pp. 333–34.

77. T. H. Bliss to N. D. Baker, 18 Dec. 1917, Diary of Robert Lansing, 31 Dec. 1917, Report of T. H. Bliss, 6 Feb. 1920, Robert Lansing Papers, Library of Congress, Washington, D.C.; Bliss to Baker, 25 Feb. 1918, Tasker H. Bliss Papers, Library of Congress, Washington, D.C.; Palmer, *Baker,* 2:315-16.

78. Lansing to E. N. Smith, 14 June 1918, Notes of Robert Lansing, 3 Oct. 1921, Lansing Papers; Wilson to E.M. House, 1 May 1918, A. J. Balfour to Lord Reading, 20 June 1918, Edward M. House Papers, Yale University, New Haven, Conn.; Baker, *Papers of Colonel House,* 8:235; Seymour, 3:407.

79. Seymour, 3:391; March, p. 115; Diary of Robert Lansing, 18 Mar. 1918, R. Lansing to W. Wilson, 24 Mar. 1918, Notes of Robert Lansing, 30 Oct. 1921, Lansing Papers; Diary of J. Daniels, 29 Mar. 1918, Josephus Daniels Papers, Library of Congress, Washington, D.C.

80. Diary of Robert Lansing, 12 June 1918, Lansing Papers; Memorandum of W. S. Benson, 22 June 1918, Daniels Papers; March, pp. 116-17, 120; Eugene H. Bacon, "Russian-American Relations, 1917-1921" (Ph.D. diss., Georgetown University, 1951), chap. 5.

81. See Leonid I. Strakhovsky, *The Origins of American Intervention in North Russia* (Princeton: Princeton University Press, 1937); Coffman, pp. 360-61.

82. Paul von Hindenburg, *Out of My Life* (London: Cassell, 1933), p. 284; George C. Marshall, "Profiting by War Experiences," *Infantry Journal* 18(1921):34-37; Russell F. Weigley, *History of the United States Army,* p. 393.

83. DeWeerd, pp. 396-400; Basil H. Liddell Hart, *Reputations Ten Years After* (Boston: Little, Brown, 1928), p. 316.

84. Harbord, p. 575.

85. See Dupuy and Dupuy, p. 402; Pershing, 2:364.

86. Harbord, pp. 464-65.

87. Quoted in R. H. Lutz, *The Causes of the German Collapse in 1918* (Stanford: Stanford University Press, 1934), p. 65.

88. Quoted in Frothingham, p. 17; see also Martin Kitchin, *The Silent Dictatorship* (New York: Holmes & Meier, 1976).

CHAPTER THIRTEEN

1. Benedict Crowell and Robert F. Wilson, *How America Went to War,* pp. 3, 5; U.S., Department of War, *Annual Report of the Secretary of War* (1919), pp. 13, 17, 56, 153, (1920), p. 27, cited hereafter as *RSW;* William A. Ganoe, *The History of the United States Army,* pp. 476-77; John J. Pershing, *Final Report as Commander-in-Chief, American Expeditionary Force,* p. 56.

2. Peyton C. March, *The Nation at War* (Garden City: Doubleday & Doran, 1932), pp. 330-40; U.S., Congress, House, National Defense Hearings, *Historical Documentation Relating to Reorganization Plans of the War Department* (Washington: Government Printing Office, 1927), 1:242, 276-77, 290, 303, 386.

3. John M. Palmer, *America in Arms,* pp. 101-3, 136-41.

4. Frederic L. Paxson, *Postwar Years* (Berkeley: University of California Press, 1948), p. 142; Russell F. Weigley, *Towards an American Army,* pp. 226-41.

5. U.S., *States at Large,* 41:759-812.

6. *RSW* (1921), p. 24; J. J. Pershing to J. G. Harbord, 12 Mar., Harbord to Pershing, 20 Mar. 1921, James G. harbord Papers, Library of Congress, Washington, D.C.; Paxson, p. 141; March, p. 341.

7. Ganoe, pp. 484-86; Paxson, p. 142; Mark S. Watson, *The War Department, Chief of Staff Pre-War Plans and Preparations* (Washington, D.C.: Department of the Army, 1950), pp. 18, 25; Russell F. Weigley, *History of the United States Army,* pp. 402-4.

8. Dudley W. Knox, *A History of the United States Navy,* pp. 422-23.

9. Claudius O. Johnson, *Borah of Idaho* (New York: Longmans, Green, 1936), pp. 262-69; E. B. Potter, ed., *The United States and World Sea Power,* p. 564.

10. Harold and Margaret Sprout, *Toward a New Order of Sea Power,* p. 149.

11. Ibid., pp. 53, 142; Potter, pp. 562-64.

12. Potter, pp. 564-66; Sprout, pp. 266-71; J. C. Vinson, *The Parchment Peace* (Athens: University of Georgia Press, 1956); U.S., Congress, Senate, Conference on the Limitation of Armament, *Senate Document 126,* 67th Cong., 2d sess.

13. C. Joseph Bernardo and Eugene H. Bacon, *American Military Policy*, p. 391; Potter, pp. 567–68.

14. Knox, p. 431; Potter, p. 568.

15. Charles C. Tansill, *Back Door to War* (Chicago: Regnery, 1952), pp. 118, 218; George T. Davis, *A Navy Second to None* (New York: Harcourt, Brace, 1940), pp. 470, 474; Knox, p. 431.

16. William Mitchell, *Our Air Force: Keystone of Defense* (New York: Dutton, 1921), p. 4.

17. *Review of Reviews* 73(1926):314–15.

18. Bernardo and Bacon, p. 393n; *Review of Reviews* 63(1921):273–77; *Official Army Air Force Guide*, pp. 348–50.

19. *New York Times*, 31 Jan. 1921; Alfred F. Hurley, *Billy Mitchell*, p. 61.

20. *New York Times*, 5 Feb., 23 July 1921; Hurley, p. 65.

21. See Burke Davis, *The Billy Mitchell Affair* (New York: Random House, 1967), pp. 100–101.

22. *Official Army Air Force Guide*, pp. 348–50; *New York Times*, 22 July, 28 Aug. 1921; B. Davis, chap. 7.

23. Joint Board 349 (serial no. 159), "Report on Results of Aviation and Ordnance Tests Held during June and July, 1921 and Conclusions Reached," 18 Aug. 1921, pp. 5–7, National Archives, Washington, D.C.

24. Hurley, p. 71; Mason M. Patrick, *The United States in the Air* (Garden City: Doubleday & Doran, 1928), pp. 81–89.

25. Guilio Douhet, *Command of the Air* (New York: Coward-McCann, 1943), p. 31; Andrew Boyle, *Trenchard* (London: Collins, 1962), pp. 471–73; Sprout, pp. 221–28.

26. Memorandum, Mitchell to Chief of the Air Service, "Report on Bombing of Alabama," 15 Oct. 1921, National Archives; B. Davis, p. 121.

27. B. Davis, pp. 124–26.

28. Ibid., pp. 151–55.

29. Bernardo and Bacon, p. 394; Hurley; Douglas MacArthur, *Reminiscences*, pp. 85–86.

30. *Official Army Air Force Guide*, pp. 346–53.

31. R. Earl McClendon, *The Question of Autonomy for the United States Air Arm* (Montgomery, Ala.: Air University, 1954); Historical Studies 6, *The Development of the Heavy Bomber, 1918–1944* (Montgomery, Ala.: Air University, 1955).

32. See *Saturday Evening Post* 197(1925):33; *The Nation* (1921–1928).

33. *The Outlook;* Henry J. Reilly, "Our Crumbling National Defense," *Century Magazine* 113 (1927):273–80; Fox Connor, "The National Defense," *North American Review* 225(1928); Albert W. Atwood, "Why a Navy," *Saturday Evening Post* 205(1933).

34. See *Republican Party Campaign Textbook, 1920*, pp. 3–10; *Democratic Party Campaign Textbook, 1924*, pp. 5–6; N. D. Baker to J. G. Harbord, 17 Mar. 1920, Harbord Papers; March, pp. 352–53; Watson, p. 22.

35. John W. Killigrew, "The Army and the Bonus Incident," *Military Affairs* 26(1962–1963):50–65; Walter W. Waters and William C. White, *B.E.F.: The Whole Story of the Bonus Army* (New York: John Day, 1933).

36. *Literary Digest* 109(1931):8; Watson, p. 401.

37. Marvin A. Kreidberg and Merton G. Henry, *History of Military Mobilization in the United States Army, 1775–1945*, p. 438.

38. Watson, p. 25; Bernardo and Bacon, pp. 402–4; *The Nation* 136(1933):139; *Literary Digest* 115(1933):8.

39. Knox, p. 436.

40. Watson, p. 116; Samuel I. Rosenman, ed., *The Public Papers and Addresses of Franklin D. Roosevelt* (New York: Macmillan , 1941), 7:68–71.

41. *Congressional Digest* 17:67, 90–93; Watson, pp. 87, 126, 148–49; Rosenman, 8:71–72; Charles A. Beard, *American Foreign Policy in the Making, 1932–1940* (New Haven: Yale University Press, 1949), p. 38.

42. Kreidberg and Henry, pp. 424–61; Watson, pp. 26–29, 64.

43. Mildred Harmon Gillie, *Forging the Thunderbolt: A History of the Development of the Armored Force* (Harrisburg: Military Service Publishing Co., 1947), chaps. 1, 2.

44. Ibid., pp. 24, 33–35.

45. Watson, pp. 156–57; Bernardo and Bacon, pp. 407–8; Rosenman, 9:201.

46. U.S., Department of War, *Biennial Report of the Chief of Staff* (1939-1941), p. 4; Rosenman, 9:252; Watson, p. 192; *Washington Star*, 9 June 1940; *Baltimore Sun*, 20 June 1940.

47. U.S., Department of War, *Biennial Report of the Chief of Staff* (1939-1941), pp. 7, 23.

48. Tansill, p. 609.

49. Ibid., p. 645; Bernardo and Bacon, pp. 413-14; Clark H. Woodward, "The Navy's Mission," *Vital Speeches of the Day* 5(1939):438.

50. Bernardo and Bacon, p. 414; Woodward, p. 438; *The Congressional Digest* 18(1938):67-97; U.S., Department of the Navy, Reports of Fleet Admiral Ernest J. King, *United States Navy at War, 1941-1945* (Washington: Government Printing Office, 1946), p. 9; U.S., Department of the Navy, *Annual Report of the Secretary of the Navy* (1940), p. 1, cited hereafter as *RSN*.

51. *RSN* (1941), pp. 2, 3, 9, 14; King, p. 20.

52. Knox, pp. 437-39.

53. Jeter A. Isely and Philip A. Crowl, *The U.S. Marines and Amphibious War* (Princeton: Princeton University Press, 1951); Potter, pp. 576-87; Lynn Montross, "The Mystery of Pete Ellis," *Marine Corps Gazette*, July, 1954, pp. 30-34.

54. *The Aircraft Yearbook for 1933* (New York: Van Nostrand, 1934), p. 61; *Official Army Air Force Guide*, p. 354; Watson, p. 127.

55. *New York Herald-Tribune*, 16 Oct. 1938; Watson, pp. 136-43; *Official Army Air Force Guide*, p. 355; *Pilot Training for University Students* (Washington: Government Printing Office, 1938).

56. *Official Army Air Force Guide*, pp. 355-56; Watson, p. 279.

57. Col. E. M. Benitez, "Conclusions of the European War," *Military Review* 20(1940); Henry H. Arnold, "Air Power in Modern Wars," *Army and Navy Journal*, 30 Nov. 1940.

58. Bernardo and Bacon, p. 419; *The Aircraft Yearbook for 1942*, pp. 42-43.

CHAPTER FOURTEEN

1. Standard accounts of the course of World War II are Henri Michel, *The Second World War* (New York: Praeger, 1974); Peter Calvocoressi and Guy Wint, *Total War: The Story of World War II* (New York: Pantheon, 1972).

2. A. Russell Buchanan, *The United States and World War II*, 1:chap. 2.

3. R. Ernest Dupuy and Trevor N. Dupuy, *Military Heritage of America*, pp. 566-68.

4. Ibid., pp. 568-69.

5. U.S., Congress, Joint Committee on the Investigation of the Pearl Harbor Attack, *Pearl Harbor Attack: Hearings* (Washington: Government Printing Office, 1946), 12:179-81, 14:1042; Cordell Hull, *The Memoirs of Cordell Hull*, 2:985-1096.

6. *Pearl Harbor Attack*, 11:5434-35.

7. Ibid., 3:1513, 10:4662-63, 11:5274, 12:239-45, 27:105-15; Roberta Wohlstetter, *Pearl Harbor*.

8. Samuel Eliot Morison, *History of United States Naval Operations in World War II*, 3:96-97; *Pearl Harbor Attack*, 13:494, 18:2966-68.

9. *Pearl Harbor Attack*, Report, pp. 57-62, 33:1341-43; Morison, 3:98-132; Wesley Frank Craven and James Lea Cate, *The Army Air Forces in World War II*, 1:194-201; Husband E. Kimmel, *Admiral Kimmel's Story*.

10. The most scholarly biography is the as-yet-incomplete one by Frank Freidel, *Franklin D. Roosevelt*, 5 vols. (Boston: Little, Brown, 1952-).

11. Diary of Henry L. Stimson, Library of Congress, Washington, D.C., 2 Apr. & 4 Aug. 1941.

12. William D. Leahy, *I Was There*, p. 99.

13. William D. Emerson, "Franklin Roosevelt as Commander in Chief in World War II," *Military Affairs* 22(1958-1959):206-7; Warren W. Hassler, Jr., *The President as Commander in Chief*, chap. 8.

14. On Stimson see Henry L. Stimson and McGeorge Bundy, *On Active Service in Peace and War* (New York: Harper, 1947); Richard N. Current, *Secretary Stimson: A Study in Statecraft* (Hamden, Archon, 1970).

15. Lord Ismay, *The Memoirs of General Lord Ismay* (New York: Viking, 1960), pp. 251-52; Stimson, pp. 437-38; on Marshall the ablest biography is the one in progress by Forrest C. Pogue, *George C. Marshall*.

16. See Henry H. Arnold, *Global Mission* (New York: Harper, 1949); Ernest J. King and W. M. Whitehill, *Fleet Admiral King* (New York: Norton, 1952).

17. Morison, 1; Karl Doenitz, *Memoirs* (London: Weidenfeld & Nicolson, 1959), chaps. 12, 16, 18, 21.

18. I. S. O. Playfair and C. J. C. Molony, *The Mediterranean and the Middle East* (London: H.M. Stationery Office, 1954), vol. 4; Ronald Lewin, *The Life and Death of the Afrika Korps* (London: B. T. Batsford, 1977).

19. On TORCH and North Africa see George F. Howe, *Northwest Africa;* Winston S. Churchill, *The Hinge of Fate,* chaps. 2, 7, 11-16, 19; Dwight D. Eisenhower, *Crusade in Europe,* chaps. 5-8; Mark W. Clark, *Calculated Risk;* George S. Patton, Jr., *War as I Knew It,* pp. 3-32; Omar N. Bradley, *A Soldier's Story,* chaps. 3-7. Of the spate of books on "Ultra" and its impact, the best to date is Ronald Lewin, *Ultra Goes to War.*

20. Maurice Matloff and Edwin M. Snell, *Strategic Planning for Coalition Warfare, 1941-1942,* pp. 378-80; Maurice Matloff, *Strategic Planning for Coalition Warfare, 1943-1944,* pp. 39-41; Gordon A. Harrison, *Cross-Channel Attack* (Washington, D.C.: Department of the Army, 1951), pp. 38-45; Richard M. Leighton and Robert W. Coakley, *Global Logistics and Strategy, 1940-1943,* pp. 664-86.

21. On Patton see Martin Blumenson, *The Many Faces of George S. Patton, Jr.* (Colorado Springs: U.S. Air Force Academy, 1972); Martin Blumenson, *The Patton Papers* (Boston: Houghton Mifflin, 1972).

22. Morison, 9:28-29, 45-47; Ewen Montagu, *The Man Who Never Was* (Philadelphia: Lippincott, 1954).

23. Howard McGaw Smyth and Albert N. Garland, *Sicily and the Surrender of Italy* (Washington, D.C.: Department of the Army, 1965), chaps. 3-21; Eisenhower, chaps. 9, 10; Bernard L. Montgomery, *The Memoirs of Field-Marshal the Viscount Montgomery* (London: Collins, 1968), chap. 11; Morison, 9:55-147.

24. Clark, pp. 187-88; Smyth and Garland, chaps. 22-29; Elizabeth V. Hassler, "The Surrender of Italy in World War II" (M.A. thesis: Pennsylvania State University, 1961); Norman Kogan, *Italy and the Allies* (Cambridge: Harvard University Press, 1956).

25. On Clark see his memoirs, *Calculated Risk;* Eisenhower, p. 9.

26. For the war in Italy consult Clark; Kogan; Montgomery, chap. 12; Morison, vol. 9; Craven and Cate, 2:488-598; Martin Blumenson, *Salerno to Cassino;* Ernest F. Fisher, Jr., *Cassino to the Alps;* Lucian K. Truscott, *Command Missions.*

27. For the air war see Craven and Cate, vols. 1, 2; *U.S. Strategic Bombing Survey, Overall Report (European War)* (Washington: Government Printing Office, 1945); Charles K. Webster and Noble Frankland, *The Strategic Air Offensive Against Germany, 1939-1945,* 4 vols. (London: H.M. Stationery Office, 1961); Arnold, chaps. 26-29; Anthony Verrier, *The Bomber Offensive* (New York: Macmillan, 1969); Adolf Galland, *The First and the Last: The Rise and Fall of the German Fighter Forces* (New York: Holt, 1954).

28. John Erickson, *The Road to Stalingrad* (New York: Harper & Row, 1975); Albert Seaton, *The Russo-German War, 1941-1945* (New York: Praeger, 1971); Paul Carell, *Hitler's War on Russia* (Boston: Little, Brown, 1965); Alan Clark, *Barbarosa: The Russian-German Conflict, 1941-1945* (New York: Morrow, 1965).

29. On Eisenhower, in addition to his memoirs, *Crusade in Europe,* see Harry C. Butcher, *My Three Years with Eisenhower* (New York: Simon & Schuster, 1946); Walter Bedell Smith, *Eisenhower's Six Great Decisions* (New York: Longmans Green, 1956); Stephen E. Ambrose, *The Supreme Commander.*

30. For pre-D-Day preparations see Leighton and Coakley, chap. 14; Matloff, chap. 18; Eisenhower, chap. 13; Smith, pp. 50-55; Morison, 11:chaps. 2-4; Harrison, chaps. 2, 5; Bradley, chaps. 12-14; Roland G. Ruppenthal, *Logistical Support of the Armies* (Washington: Department of the Army, 1953), 1:chaps. 4-8.

31. Chester Wilmot, *The Struggle for Europe* (New York: Harper, 1952), pp. 221-26; Eisenhower, pp. 211, 223, 249-50; Smith, pp. 50-55; Harrison, pp. 272-74.

32. Bradley, pp. 223-29; Wilmot, p. 213.

33. Harrison, chaps. 8-10; Craven and Cate, 3:chaps. 6, 7; Eisenhower, chap. 14; Morison, 11: chaps. 5-11; Ruppenthal, 1:chap. 10; Cornelius Ryan, *The Longest Day, June 6, 1944* (New York: Simon & Schuster, 1959).

34. Martin Blumenson, *Breakout and Pursuit* (Washington: Department of the Army, 1961), chaps. 4-29; Montgomery, chap. 14; Eisenhower, chap. 15.
35. Truscott, pp. 381-433; Craven and Cate, vol. 3; Eisenhower, chap. 15.
36. Milton Shulman, *Defeat in the West* (New York: Dutton, 1948), pp. 162-77; Eisenhower, chap. 16; Montgomery, chap. 15.
37. Charles B. MacDonald, *The Siegfried Line Campaign* (Washington: Department of the Army, 1963), pp. 119-206; Cornelius Ryan, *A Bridge Too Far* (New York: Simon & Schuster, 1974); Robert E. Urquhart, *Arnhem* (London: Cassell, 1958).
38. MacDonald, *Siegfried Line*, pp. 377-578; Eisenhower, pp. 323-75; Charles B. MacDonald, *The Battle of the Huertgen Forest* (Philadelphia: Lippincott, 1963).
39. John S. D. Eisenhower, *The Bitter Woods* (New York: Putnam, 1969); Eisenhower, chaps. 17, 18; S. L. A. Marshall, *Bastogne;* R. Ernest Dupuy, *St. Vith;* John Toland, *Battle, The Story of the Bulge;* Heinz Guderian, *Panzer Leader;* Craven and Cate, 3:672-701.
40. Ken Hechler, *The Bridge at Remagen* (New York: Ballantine, 1957); Eisenhower, pp. 378-81; Bradley, pp. 510-15; Wilmot, pp. 674-83.
41. Forrest C. Pogue, *The Supreme Command,* pp. 434-47; Morison, 11:317-23; Craven and Cate, 3:769-75; Eisenhower, pp. 387-405; Montgomery, pp. 294-96.
42. Stephen E. Ambrose, *Eisenhower and Berlin;* Eisenhower, pp. 367, 399, 424-25; Pogue, *Supreme Command,* pp. 445-56.
43. Paul Kecskemeti, *Strategic Surrender* (Stanford: Stanford University Press, 1958), pp. 118-54; John Toland, *The Last 100 Days* (New York: Random House, 1965).
44. See T. Dodson Stamps and Vincent J. Esposito, eds., *A Military History of World War II* (West Point: U.S. Military Academy, 1953), 1:607-9.
45. Matloff and Snell, pp. 32-96; S. Woodburn Kirby, *The War Against Japan,* 1:1-88; Louis Morton, *The Fall of the Philippines,* pp. 61-73; *Pearl Harbor Attack,* 15:1423-25, 33:926-85, 995-96.
46. Kirby, 1:107-51, 221-27; Stamps and Esposito, 2:216-19.
47. Churchill, *Hinge of Fate,* pp. 36-59; Lionel Wigmore, *The Japanese Thrust,* pp. 121-283.
48. Wigmore, pp. 202-3, 284-389; Churchill, *Hinge of Fate,* pp. 53, 92-107; Kirby, pp. 375-415.
49. Charles F. Romanus and Riley Sunderland, *Stilwell's Mission to China,* pp. 73-76; Buchanan, 2:469-70.
50. Joseph W. Stilwell, *The Stilwell Papers* (New York: W. Sloane, 1948).
51. Romanus and Sunderland, pp. 81-117, 143, 148; Kirby, 2:1-104.
52. O. R. Lodge, *The Recapture of Guam,* pp. 6-8; Frank O. Hough, et al., *Pearl Harbor to Guadalcanal,* pp. 75-78; Morison, 3:184-86.
53. George H. Gill, *Royal Australian Navy, 1939-1942,* ser. 2, 4:542-44; Wigmore, pp. 392-417.
54. Robert D. Heinl, *Marines at Midway,* pp. 1, 11-22; Hough, 1:78-83.
55. Robert D. Heinl, *The Defense of Wake;* Morison, 3:235-54.
56. On Douglas MacArthur, besides his *Reminiscences,* see D. Clayton James, *The Years of MacArthur;* George C. Kenney, *The MacArthur I Know;* Charles A. Willoughby, *MacArthur, 1941-1951;* Courtney Whitney, *MacArthur;* Frazier Hunt, *The Untold Story of Douglas MacArthur.*
57. Morton; John Toland, *But Not in Shame: The Six Months After Pearl Harbor* (New York: Random House, 1961); Walter D. Edmonds, *They Fought with What They Had* (Boston: Little, Brown, 1951).
58. F. C. Van Oosten, *The Battle of the Java Sea* (Annapolis: Naval Institute Press, 1976).
59. Dupuy and Dupuy, pp. 585-86.
60. Ted W. Lawson, *Thirty Seconds Over Tokyo* (New York: Random House, 1943); Craven and Cate, 1:438-44; Morison, 3:389-98.
61. William F. Halsey and Julian Bryan III, *Admiral Halsey's Story* (New York: Whittlesey House, 1947).
62. See Stamps and Esposito, 2:297-98.
63. E. B. Potter and Chester W. Nimitz, *The Great Sea War,* pp. 219-20; Morison, 4:10-63; Craven and Cate, 1:450-51.
64. Irving Werstein, *The Battle of Midway;* Thaddeus V. Tuleja, *Climax at Midway;* Mitsuo Fuchida and Masataka Okumiya, *Midway, The Battle That Doomed Japan;* Morison, 4:65-159.
65. Craven and Cate, 4:377-86; Morison, 7:22-66.

66. Samuel Milner, *Victory in Papua;* George C. Kenney, *General Kenney Reports;* Robert L. Eichelberger, *Our Jungle Road to Tokyo;* Kirby, 2:286–89.
67. John Miller, Jr., *Guadalcanal;* Walter Lord, *Lonely Vigil, Coastwatchers of the Solomons;* John L. Zimmerman, *The Guadalcanal Campaign;* Richard W. Tregaskis, *Guadalcanal Diary.*
68. George Odgers, *Air War Against Japan, 1943–1945,* pp. 24–29, 262–311; Buchanan, 1:250–58, 262–65.
69. John Miller, Jr., *Cartwheel,* pp. 222–71; John N. Rentz, *Marines in the Central Solomons;* John N. Rentz, *Bougainville and the Northern Solomons.*
70. Morison, 7:22–66; Craven and Cate, 4:377–86.
71. Walter Krueger, *From Down Under to Nippon,* pp. 45–55; Miller, *Cartwheel,* pp. 316–50; Morison, 6:432–48.
72. Philip A. Crowl and Edmund G. Love, *Seizure of the Gilberts and Marshalls,* pp. 1–99; James R. Stockman, *The Battle for Tarawa;* George C. Dyer, *The Amphibians Came to Conquer,* 2: 597–732.
73. Crowl and Love, pp. 199–301; Robert D. Heinl and John A. Crown, *The Marshalls;* Jeter A. Isely and Philip A. Crowl, *The U.S. Marines and Amphibious Warfare,* pp. 252–91.
74. Morison, 7:314–32.
75. Potter and Nimitz, pp. 355–60; Morison, 8:213–321.
76. Robert Ross Smith, *The Approach to the Philippines;* Craven and Cate, 4:575; Morison, 8:59; Eichelberger, pp. 100–122; Krueger, pp. 56–78.
77. Philip A. Crowl, *Campaign in the Marianas;* Carl W. Hoffman, *Saipan;* Carl W. Hoffman, *The Seizure of Tinian;* Lodge, pp. 37–170.
78. Smith, *Approach to the Philippines,* pp. 480–93; Krueger, pp. 122–32; Craven and Cate, 5: 311–14; Morison, 12:19–29.
79. Frank O. Hough, *The Assault on Peleliu;* Morison, 12:36–47; Smith, *Approach to the Philippines,* pp. 494–575.
80. Matloff, pp. 479–89; Leahy, pp. 249–52.
81. Stanley Falk, *Decision at Leyte* (New York: Norton, 1966); C. Vann Woodward, *The Battle for Leyte Gulf* (New York: Macmillan, 1947); M. Hamlin Cannon, *Leyte;* Morison, vols. 12, 13; Craven and Cate, 5:341.
82. MacArthur, pp. 215–54; Robert Ross Smith, *Triumph in the Philippines,* Eichelberger, pp. 188–231; Krueger, pp. 221–329; Craven and Cate, 5:413–64.
83. John Gunther, *The Riddle of MacArthur* (New York: Harper, 1951), pp. 26–42.
84. Lord Louis Mountbatten, *Report to the Combined Chiefs of Staff;* Charles F. Romanus and Riley Sunderland, *Stilwell's Command Problems,* and *Time Runs Out in CBI;* Raymond Callahan, *Burma, 1942–1945.*
85. Theodore Roscoe, *United States Submarine Operations in World War II* (Annapolis: U.S. Naval Institute, 1949); Morison, 14:291–93.
96. Dupuy and Dupuy, p. 620.
87. Whitman S. Bartley, *Iwo Jima;* Holland M. Smith, *Coral and Brass;* Morison, 14.
88. Roy E. Appleman, *Okinawa;* Charles S. Nichols and Henry I. Shaw, Jr., *Okinawa;* Dyer, 2: chap. 24; Halsey.
89. For mobilization on the home front see Eliot Janeway, *The Struggle for Survival;* James Phinney Baxter III, *Scientists Against Time;* Donald M. Nelson, *Arsenal of Democracy;* Frederic C. Lane, *Ships for Victory;* Robert R. Palmer, et al., *The Procurement and Training of Ground Combat Troops;* Leslie R. Groves, *Now It Can Be Told.*
90. Robert J. C. Butow, *Japan's Decision to Surrender* (Stanford: Stanford University Press, 1954), pp. 142–49.
91. Martin Caidin, *A Torch to the Enemy;* Craven and Cate, 5:614–35; Halsey; Harry S. Truman, *Memoirs,* vol. 1; Winston S. Churchill, *Triumph and Tragedy* (Boston: Houghton Mifflin, 1953), pp. 630–46.
92. Merle Miller and Abe Spitzer, *We Dropped the A-Bomb* (New York: Crowell, 1946); *The Effect of the Atomic Bombs on Hiroshima and Nagasaki* (London: H.M. Stationery Office, 1946).
93. Martin J. Sherwin, *A World Destroyed* (New York: Knopf, 1975); Butow; Shigenori Togo, *The Cause of Japan* (New York: Simon & Schuster, 1956); Toshikazu Kase, *Journey to the Missouri* (New Haven: Yale University Press, 1950); Willoughby, chap. 12; MacArthur, pp. 265–77.
94. Vannevar Bush, *Modern Arms and Free Men* (New York: Simon & Schuster, 1949), chap. 7.

CHAPTER FIFTEEN

1. See *New York Herald-Tribune,* 17 Sept. 1945.
2. *Army and Navy Journal,* 12 May 1945; U.S., War Department, *Press Release,* 5 May 1945; *Denver Post,* 3 Sept. 1945; *Chicago Tribune,* 8 Sept. 1945; *New York Daily Worker,* 21 Sept. 1945; *New York Times,* 3, 17 Sept. 1945.
3. *New York Times,* 7 Sept., 24 Oct. 1945, 2 June 1947; C. Joseph Bernardo and Eugene H. Bacon, *American Military Policy,* pp. 447-48; *Facts on File,* 12-18 May 1945.
4. Bernardo and Bacon, pp. 450-52; U.S., *National Military Establishment, First Report of the Secretary of Defense,* 1948, p. 61.
5. *Facts on File,* 31 Oct.-6 Nov., 14-27 Nov., 16, 22 Dec. 1945; *Colliers,* 14 Mar. 1942.
6. *Newsweek,* 17 Sept. 1945; *Facts on File,* 17-30 Oct. 1945; Bernardo and Bacon, p. 456.
7. *Army and Navy Journal,* 20 Apr. 1946, 18 Jan. 1947; Walter Millis and E. S. Duffield, eds., *The Forrestal Diaries,* pp. 228-31.
8. U.S., *Statutes at Large,* vol. 61, pt. 1, pp. 578-92; Millis and Duffield, pp. 295-96.
9. U.S., *Statutes at Large,* vol. 63, pt. 1, pp. 578-92; *New York Times,* 11 Aug. 1949.
10. U.S., Department of the Navy, *Annual Report of the Secretary of the Navy* (1945), p. 1, (1946), p. 35, (1947), pp. 32, 41, (1949), pp. 173, 205-7, 216-17.
11. Vincent Davis, *Postwar Defense Policy and the U.S. Navy, 1943-1946;* Clark G. Reynolds, *The Fast Carriers,* pp. 109-10, 213-35, 324, 351-55, 384-98; Ray Wagner, *American Combat Planes,* pp. 134-43, 357-58.
12. *New York Times,* 24, 27 Apr. 1949.
13. Ibid., 11 Sept.-28 Oct. 1949; Bernardo and Bacon, p. 476.
14. Gordon B. Turner and Richard C. Challener, eds., *National Security in the Nuclear Age* (New York: Praeger, 1960), pp. 143-72.
15. Samuel P. Huntington, *The Common Defense,* pp. 39-53, 278-304; Dean G. Acheson, *Present at the Creation,* pp. 344-49, 374; Henry A. Kissinger, *Nuclear Weapons and Foreign Policy,* pp. 38-39.
16. U.S., Department of Defense, *Semiannual Report of the Secretary of Defense, July 1 to December 1, 1949,* pp. 9, 42, 254, cited hereafter as *RSD; New York Times,* 10 Jan. 1950.
17. Bernardo and Bacon, p. 477.
18. James F. Schnabel, *Policy and Direction,* pp. 1-30; Harry J. Middleton, *The Compact History of the Korean War,* pp. 17-23; David Rees, *Korea,* pp. 7-20.
19. Charles A. Willoughby and John Chamberlain, *MacArthur, 1941-1951,* pp. 350-54; Frazier Hunt, *The Untold Story of Douglas MacArthur,* p. 450; Russell F. Weigley, *History of the United States Army,* pp. 505-6.
20. Huntington, *Common Defense,* p. 519; D. D. Eisenhower to L. Johnson, 3 May 1949, Dwight D. Eisenhower Papers, Eisenhower Library, Abilene, Kan.
21. Douglas MacArthur, *Reminiscences,* pp. 329-30; Schnabel, pp. 31-40; Willoughby and Chamberlain, pp. 355-57.
22. J. Lawton Collins, *War in Peacetime,* chap. 1; Roy E. Appleman, *South to the Naktong, North to the Yalu,* pp. 69-73, 113-14, 180; James A. Field, Jr., *History of United States Naval Operations, Korea,* pp. 39-50, 68-71; Malcolm W. Cagle and Frank A. Manson, *The Sea War in Korea,* pp. 30-33.
23. MacArthur, pp. 330-31; *New York Times,* 28 June 1950; U.S., Department of State Publication 4245, *In Quest of Peace and Security,* pp. 74-75.
24. Appleman, pp. 46-47; MacArthur, pp. 332-35; John W. Spanier, *The Truman-MacArthur Controversy and the Korean War* (Cambridge, Mass.: Belknap, 1959), chap. 5.
25. Weigley, *United States Army,* pp. 512-13; Paul Y. Hammond, *Organizing for Defense,* pp. 248-49; Russell F. Weigley, *The American Way of War,* p. 383.
26. Schnabel, pp. 61-138; MacArthur, pp. 335-45; Appleman, pp. 69-73, 113-14, 176-80; Collins, chaps. 3, 5; Field, pp. 50-121; Robert F. Futrell, et al., *The United States Air Force in Korea* (New York: Duell, Sloan & Pearce, 1961), pp. 23-34.
27. Robert D. Heinl, Jr., *Victory High Tide: The Inchon-Seoul Campaign* (Philadelphia: Lippincott, 1968); MacArthur, pp. 346-56; Schnabel, pp. 139-92; Cagle and Manson, pp. 75-101.
28. Weigley, *Way of War,* pp. 387-89.
29. Schnable, p. 177; Hunt, pp. 473-74; Lynn Montross, *U.S. Marine Operations in Korea,* 3: chaps, 2, 3; MacArthur, pp. 358-60; Appleman, pp. 609-21.

30. Rees, pp. 123–28; Schnable, pp. 215–73; Spanier, chaps. 5–7.
31. See Warren W. Hassler, Jr., *The President as Commander in Chief,* pp. 123–29.
32. MacArthur, pp. 360–63; Hunt, p. 474; Schnabel, pp. 210–14; Willoughby and Chamberlain, pp. 380–83; Rees, pp. 115–22.
33. Willoughby and Chamberlain, pp. 383–85; MacArthur, pp. 364–65; S. L. A. Marshall, *The River and the Gauntlet* (New York: Morrow, 1953); Field, pp. 50–121; Appleman, chaps. 33–35.
34. Allen S. Whiting, *China Crosses the Yalu* (New York: Macmillan, 1960); MacArthur, pp. 365–407; Matthew B. Ridgway, *Soldier,* pp. 192–216.
35. Trumbull Higgins, *Korea and the Fall of MacArthur* (New York: Oxford University Press, 1960); Harry S. Truman, *Memoirs,* 2:436–50; Hunt, pp. 504–16; Omar N. Bradley, "A Soldier's Farewell," *Saturday Evening Post,* 22 Aug. 1953.
36. *New York Times,* 20 Apr. 1951; MacArthur, pp. 399–405.
37. U.S., Congress, Senate, *Hearings Before the Committee on Armed Services and Committee on Foreign Relations, Senate, 82d Congress, 1st Session, to Conduct an Inquiry into the Military Situation in the Far East and Facts Surrounding the Relief of General of the Army Douglas MacArthur* (Washington: Government Printing Office, 1951).
38. S. L. A. Marshall, *Pork Chop Hill* (New York: Morrow, 1956); Weigley, *United States Army,* pp. 521–22.
39. James F. Stewart, *Airpower: The Decisive Force in Korea* (Princeton: Van Nostrand, 1957), pp. 32–50; Futrell; Wagner, pp. 252–63; Alexander P. De Seversky, *Victory Through Air Power,* p. 102; Rees, pp. 370–84.
40. Field; Cagle and Manson.
41. Middleton, pp. 187–95; Ridgway; Mark W. Clark, *From the Danube to the Yalu;* Weigley, *United States Army,* p. 525.
42. Rees, chaps. 17, 22, 23; Hal Vetter, *Mutiny on Koje Island* (Rutland: Tuttle, 1964); Dwight D. Eisenhower, *The White House Years,* chap. 7.
43. Bernardo and Bacon, p. 484; Middleton, p. 230.
44. Halford L. Hoskins, *The Atlantic Pact* (Washington: Public Affairs Press, 1949); James D. Atkinson, "The Communist Revolution in Warfare," *Proceedings of the United States Naval Institute* 79(1953).
45. Wagner, pp. 147–51; Huntington, *Common Defense,* pp. 59, 62, 315–26; Acheson, pp. 482–94, 608–10; 622–27.
46. Eisenhower, *White House Years,* p. 457.
47. Hassler, *President as Commander in Chief,* pp. 129–31.
48. Forrest K. Kleinman and Robert S. Horowitz, *The Modern United States Army* (Princeton: Van Nostrand, 1964), pp. 82–88.
49. John P. Lovell, *Neither Athens Nor Sparta?,* chap. 4; Gene M. Lyons and Louis Morton, *Schools for Strategy.*
50. *Facts on File,* 26 Sep.–2 Oct., 10–16 Oct. 1945; Millis and Duffield, pp. 94–96; *New York Times,* 4, 18 Oct. 1945; *Baltimore Sun,* 9 Sept., 27 Oct. 1945.
51. *New York Times,* 15, 20 June 1946; *Philadelphia Inquirer,* 16 June 1946.
52. Bernardo and Bacon, p. 466.
53. Weigley, *Way of War,* p. 367.
54. James M. Gavin, *War and Peace in the Space Age* (New York: Harper, 1958); Weigley, *Way of War,* p. 398.
55. Eisenhower, *White House Years,* chap. 7; Huntington, *Common Defense,* pp. 62–66; John Foster Dulles, "Policy for Peace and Security," *Department of State Bulletin,* 29 Mar. 1954.
56. William W. Kaufman, ed., *Military Policy and National Security,* pp. 12–38; Ridgway; Maxwell D. Taylor, *The Uncertain Trumpet;* Huntington, *Common Defense,* pp. 70–71.
57. Eisenhower, *White House Years,* pp. 332–57, 455–56; Bernard B. Fall, *Hell in a Very Small Place,* pp. 25–26, 35–52, 293–314.
58. Kaufman, pp. 12–38, 102–36; *The Reporter,* 11(1954):16–21; Morton H. Halperin, *Contemporary Military Strategy* (Boston: Little, Brown, 1967), pp. 48–50.
59. Eisenhower, *White House Years,* pp. 453–55; Huntington, *Common Defense,* pp. 101–2; Urs Schwarz, *American Strategy* (Garden City: Doubleday, 1966), p. 82.
60. Albert J. Wohlstetter, "The Delicate Balance of Terror," *Foreign Affairs* 37(1959):211–34.
61. Gavin, pp. 27, 151; Taylor, *Uncertain Trumpet,* pp. 53–54; Huntington, *Common Defense,* pp. 96–113.

62. Henry A. Kissinger, *The Necessity for Choice* (London: Chatto & Windus, 1967), pp. 15, 26, 35; Huntington, *Common Defense,* pp. 103-5; *New York Times,* 24 Jan. 1960.

63. Herman Kahn, *On Thermonuclear War* (Princeton: Princeton University Press, 1960); Weigley, *Way of War,* p. 440.

64. See Hassler, *President as Commander in Chief,* pp. 131-33.

65. Henry J. Trewhitt, *McNamara* (New York: Harper & Row, 1971); Weigley, *Way of War,* p. 446.

66. *Army* 12(1962):16-20, 26-31, 54-56, 14(1964):28-33.

67. Morton S. Halperin, *Defense Strategies for the Seventies* (Boston: Little, Brown, 1971), p. 49; Trewhitt, pp. 23, 119-24.

68. Glenn H. Snyder, *Deterrence and Defense* (Princeton: Princeton University Press, 1961).

69. James M. Roherty, *Decisions of Robert S. McNamara* (Coral Gables: University of Miami Press, 1970); Trewhitt, pp. 24-25, 111-54, 283-93.

70. Hugh Thomas, *Cuba: The Pursuit of Freedom* (New York: Harper & Row, 1971), chaps. 103, 106; Weigley, *Way of War,* pp. 450-51.

71. Thomas, chaps. 108, 109; Robert A. Divine, ed., *The Cuban Missile Crisis* (Chicago: Quadrangle, 1971); Elie Abel, *The Missile Crisis* (Philadelphia: J. B. Lippincott, 1966).

72. Maxwell D. Taylor, *Swords and Ploughshares* (New York: Norton, 1972), pp. 184, 200-203.

73. Neil Sheean, et al., *The Pentagon Papers,* pp. 99-106, 141-48; Taylor, *Swords and Ploughshares,* pp. 220-44.

74. Roger Hilsman, *To Move a Nation,* pp. 423-523; Weigley, *Way of War,* p. 460; Sheean, p. 128.

75. Sheean, pp. 232-318, 345-77; Eugene Windchy, *Tonkin Gulf* (Garden City: Doubleday, 1971).

76. Chester L. Cooper, *The Lost Crusade,* pp. 259-62, 270-71; Sheean, pp. 382-409, 418-43.

77. Sheean, pp. 402-14, 462-64.

78. J. C. Wylie, *Military Strategy;* Sheean, pp. 404, 475-78.

79. Weigley, *Way of War,* pp. 467-68; *Foreign Affairs,* Apr., 1961; *New York Times,* 8 Jan. 1971.

80. Weigley, *Way of War,* pp. 468-69.

81. *Public Papers of the Presidents of the United States: Richard Nixon* (Washington: Government Printing Office, 1971), p. 19; Herman S. Wolk, "Formulating a National Strategy for the 1970's," *Air University Review* 22(1970):45-50; Trewhitt, pp. 123-321.

82. Alain C. Enthoven and K. Wayne Smith, *How Much Is Enough?* (New York: Harper & Row, 1971).

83. Pierre Gallois, *The Balance of Terror* (Boston: Houghton Mifflin, 1961).

84. *The Military Balance, 1972-1973* (London: International Institute for Strategic Studies, 1972); *New York Times,* 28 May 1972; John Newhouse, *Cold Dawn: The Story of SALT* (New York: Holt, Rinehart, & Winston, 1973).

85. *New York Times,* 8 Nov. 1973.

86. John T. Burke, "Smart Weapons: A Coming Revolution in Tactics,"*Army* vol. 23, no. 2, (1973).

87. See George G. Thomson, *Problems of Strategy in the Pacific and Indian Oceans;* Norman Polmar, *Soviet Naval Power;* Alton H. Quanbeck and Archie L. Frye, *Modernizing the Strategic Bomber Force.*

88. John Erickson, *Soviet Military Power* (Washington: U.S. Strategic Institute, 1973), pp. 2-4; Keith A. Dunn, "Detente and Deterrence: From Kissinger to Carter," *Parameters: Journal of the U.S. Army War College* 7(1977):46-55; U.S., Congress, Senate, Committee on Foreign Relations, *Hearings on United States Relations with Communist Countries,* 93d Cong., 2d sess., pp. 253-54, italics mine.

SELECTED BIBLIOGRAPHY

Acheson, Dean. *Present at the Creation: My Years in the State Department*. New York: Norton, 1969.

Adams, Henry. *History of the United States during the Administrations of Jefferson and Madison*. 9 vols. New York: Scribner's, 1889–1891.

Agassiz, George R. *Meade's Headquarters, 1863–1865: Letters of Colonel Theodore Lyman*. Boston: Atlantic Monthly Press, 1922.

Ahern, George P. *A Chronicle of the Army War College, 1899–1919*. Washington: Government Printing Office, 1919.

Albion, Robert G. *Introduction to Military History*. New York: Appleton-Century-Crofts, 1929.

Alcaraz, Ramon. *The Other Side of the Mexican War*. New York: Wiley, 1850.

Alden, Carroll S., and Earle, Ralph. *Makers of Naval Tradition*. Boston: Ginn, 1943.

Alden, Carroll S., and Westcott, Allen. *The United States Navy*. Phildelphia: Lippincott, 1943.

Alger, Russell A. *The Spanish-American War*. New York: Harper, 1901.

Ambrose, Stephen E. *Upton and the Army*. Baton Rouge: Louisiana State University Press, 1964.

_____. *Duty, Honor, Country: A History of West Point*. Baltimore: Johns Hopkins Press, 1966.

_____. *Eisenhower and Berlin, 1945: The Decision to Halt at the Elbe*. New York: Norton, 1967.

_____. *The Supreme Commander: The War Years of General Dwight D. Eisenhower*. Garden City: Doubleday, 1970.

American State Papers: Foreign Affairs. 6 vols. Washington: Gales & Seaton, 1832–1859.

American State Papers: Indian Affairs. 2 vols. Washington: Gales & Seaton, 1832–1834.

American State Papers: Military Affairs. 7 vols. Washington: Gales & Seaton, 1832–1861.

American State Papers: Miscellaneous Affairs. 2 vols. Washington: Gales & Seaton, 1834.

American State Papers: Naval Affairs. 4 vols. Washington: Gales & Seaton, 1834–1861.

Ammen, Daniel. *The Atlantic Coast*. New York: Scribner's, 1883.

Andrist, Ralph K. *The Long Death: The Last Days of the Plains Indian*. New York: Macmillan, 1964.

Annals of Congress. 42 vols. Washington: Gales & Seaton, 1834–1856.

Appleman, Roy E. *Okinawa: The Last Battle*. Washington: Department of the Army, 1948.

_____. *South to the Naktong, North to the Yalu*. Washington: Department of the Army, 1960.

Armstrong, John. *Notices of the War of 1812*. 2 vols. New York: G. Dearborn, 1836.

Arnade, Charles W. *The Siege of St. Augustine in 1702.* Gainesville: University of Florida Press, 1959.

Athearn, Robert G. *William Tecumseh Sherman and the Settlement of the West.* Norman: University of Oklahoma Press, 1956.

Atkins, John Black. *The War in Cuba.* London: Smith, Elder, 1899.

Ayres, Leonard P. *The War with Germany: A Statistical Summary.* Washington: Government Printing Office, 1919.

Azoy, A. C. M. *Signal 250! The Sea Fight off Santiago.* New York: McKay, 1964.

Babcock, Louis L. *The War of 1812 on the Niagara Frontier.* Buffalo: Buffalo Historical Society, 1927.

Baclagon, Uldarico S. *Philippine Campaigns.* Manila: Graphic House, 1952.

Bailey, Thomas A. *A Diplomatic History of the American People.* New York: Appleton-Century-Crofts, 1964.

_____. *Presidential Greatness.* New York: Appleton, Century, 1966.

Bakeless, John. *Background to Glory: The Life of George Rogers Clark.* Philadelphia: Lippincott, 1957.

Baker, Ray Stannard. *Woodrow Wilson: Life and Letters.* 8 vols. Garden City: Doubleday, Page, 1927–1939.

Baker, Ray Stannard, and Dodd, William E. *The Public Papers of Woodrow Wilson.* 6 vols. New York: Harper, 1925–1927.

Baldwin, Leland. *Whiskey Rebels.* Pittsburgh: University of Pittsburgh Press, 1939.

Bancroft, George. *History of the United States of America.* 10 vols. New York: Appleton, 1887.

Banning, Kendall. *Annapolis Today.* Annapolis: U.S. Naval Institute, 1963.

Bartley, Whitman S. *Iwo Jima: Amphibious Epic.* Washington: Marine Historical Division, 1950.

Basler, Roy P., ed. *The Collected Works of Abraham Lincoln.* 9 vols. New Brunswick, N.J.: Rutgers University Press, 1953.

Bassett, John S. *The Life of Andrew Jackson.* 2 vols. New York: Doubleday, Page, 1911.

Batchelder, Roger. *Watching and Waiting on the Border.* Cambridge: Harvard University Press, 1917.

Bauer, K. Jack. *Surfboats and Horse Marines: U.S. Naval Operations in the Mexican War, 1846–1848.* Annapolis: U.S. Naval Institute, 1969.

_____. *The Mexican War, 1846–1848.* New York: Macmillan, 1974.

Baxter, James Phinney. *The British Invasion from the North.* Albany: J. Munsell, 1887.

_____. *The Introduction of the Ironclad Warship.* Cambridge: Harvard University Press, 1933.

Baxter, James Phinney III. *Scientists Against Time.* Boston: Little, Brown, 1946.

Bearss, Edwin C. *Decision in Mississippi.* Jackson: Commission on the War Between the States, 1962.

Beirne, Francis F. *The War of 1812.* New York: Dutton, 1949.

Beiscleine, John R. *Military Management for National Defense.* New York: Prentice-Hall, 1950.

Benjamin, Park. *The United States Naval Academy.* New York: Putnam, 1900.

Bennett, Frank M. *The Steam Navy of the United States.* Pittsburgh: Warren, 1896.

Berdahl, Clarence A. *War Powers of the Executive in the United States.* Urbana: University of Illinois Press, 1921.

Bernardo, C. Joseph, and Bacon, Eugene H. *American Military Policy: Its Development Since 1775*. Harrisburg: Military Service Publishing Co., 1955.

Betzinez, Jason. *I Fought with Geronimo*. Harrisburg: Stackpole, 1959.

Bigelow, John, Jr. *The Principles of Strategy*. Philadelphia: Lippincott, 1894.

_____. *The Campaign of Chancellorsville: A Strategic and Tactical Study*. New Haven: Yale University Press, 1910.

Bill, Alfred H. *Rehearsal for Conflict: The War with Mexico, 1846-1848*. New York: Knopf, 1947.

_____. *The Campaign of Princeton*. Princeton: Princeton University Press, 1948.

_____. *Valley Forge: The Making of an Army*. New York: Harper, 1952.

Billias, George A. *General John Glover and His Marblehead Mariners*. New York: Holt, 1960.

Billias, George A., ed. *George Washington's Generals*. New York: Morrow, 1964.

_____, ed. *George Washington's Opponents*. New York: Morrow, 1969.

Binkley, William E. *Powers of the President*. Garden City: Doubleday, Doran, 1937.

Black Hawk. *Autobiography*. Rock Island: American Publishing Co., 1833.

Bliven, Bruce, Jr. *Battle for Manhattan*. Baltimore: Penguin, 1956.

Blumenson, Martin. *Salerno to Cassino*. Washington: Department of the Army, 1969.

Bodley, Temple. *George Rogers Clark*. Boston: Houghton Mifflin, 1926.

Bond, B. W., ed. *The Correspondence of John Cleves Symmes*. New York: Macmillan, 1926.

Bougainville, Louis Antoine de. *Adventure in the Wilderness: The American Journals of Louis Antoine de Bougainville, 1756-1776*. Norman: University of Oklahoma Press, 1964.

Bourke, John G. *An Apache Campaign in the Sierra Madre*. New York: Scribner's, 1958.

Boyd, Thomas A. *Mad Anthony Wayne*. New York: Scribner's, 1929.

Boyle, John R. *Soldiers True*. New York: Eaton & Mains, 1903.

Boynton, Charles B. *The Navy during the Rebellion*. 2 vols. New York: Appleton, 1867-1868.

Boynton, H. V. *Sherman's Historical Raid*. Cincinnati: Wilstach, Baldwin, 1875.

Bradford, Gamaliel. *Union Portraits*. Boston: Houghton Mifflin, 1916.

Bradley, Erwin S. *Simon Cameron, Lincoln's Secretary of War: A Political Biography*. Philadelphia: University of Pennsylvania Press, 1966.

Bradley, Omar N. *A Soldier's Story*. New York: Holt, 1951.

Brant, Irving. *James Madison*. 6 vols. Indianapolis: Bobbs-Merrill, 1941-1961.

Brigham, Albert P. *Geographic Influences in American History*. Boston: Ginn, 1903.

Brooks, Charles B. *The Siege of New Orleans*. Seattle: University of Washington Press, 1961.

Brooks, Edward H. "The National Defense Policy of the Wilson Administration, 1913-1917." 2 vols. Ph.D. diss., Stanford University, 1950.

Brooks, Noah. *Washington in Lincoln's Time*. New York: Century, 1895.

Brown, Dee. *Fort Phil Kearny: An American Saga*. New York: Putnam, 1962.

_____. *Bury My Heart at Wounded Knee*. New York: Holt, Rinehart, & Winston, 1971.

Brown, George W. *Baltimore and the Nineteenth of April, 1861*. Baltimore: N. Murray, 1887.

Brown, Mark H. *The Flight of the Nez Percé: A History of the Nez Percé War*. New York: Putnam, 1967.

Brown, Wilburt S. *The Amphibious Campaign for West Florida and Louisiana*. University, Ala.: University of Alabama Press, 1969.

Buchan, Alastair. *War in Modern Society.* New York: Harper & Row, 1968.

Buchanan, A. Russell. *The United States and World War II.* 2 vols. New York: Harper & Row, 1964.

Bullard, Robert Lee. *Personalities and Reminiscences of the War.* Garden City: Doubleday, Page, 1925.

Burgoyne, John. *A State of the Expedition from Canada.* London: J. Almon, 1780.

Burt, A. L. *The United States, Great Britain, and British North America.* New Haven: Yale University Press, 1940.

Cagle, Malcolm W., and Manson, Frank A. *The Sea War in Korea.* Annapolis: U.S. Naval Institute, 1957.

Caidin, Martin. *A Torch to the Enemy.* New York: Ballantine, 1960.

Callahan, Raymond. *Burma, 1942–1945.* London: Davis-Poynter, 1978.

Callan, J. F. *The Military Laws of the United States.* Philadelphia: Childs, 1863.

Cannon, M. Hamlin. *Leyte: The Return to the Philippines.* Washington: Department of the Army, 1954.

Carter, Samuel III. *Blaze of Glory: The Fight for New Orleans.* New York: St. Martin's Press, 1971.

Carter, William G. H. *The American Army.* New York: Bobbs-Merrill, 1905.

Carter, William H. *The Life of Lieutenant General Chaffee.* Chicago: University of Chicago Press, 1917.

Cary, John. *Joseph Warren.* Urbana: University of Illinois Press, 1961.

Casselman, Alexander C., ed. *Richardson's War of 1812.* Toronto: n.p., 1902.

Catton, Bruce. *Grant Moves South.* Boston: Little, Brown, 1960.

Caughey, John W. *Bernardo de Galvez in Louisiana, 1776–1783.* Berkeley: University of California Press, 1934.

Cervera, Pascual y. Topete. *Collection of Documents Relative to the Squadron of Operations in the West Indies.* Washington: Office of Naval Intelligence, 1899.

Chadwick, French Ensor. *The Relations between the United States and Spain: The Spanish-American War.* 2 vols. New York: Scribner's, 1911.

Challener, Richard. *Admirals, Generals, and American Foreign Policy.* Princeton: Princeton University Press, 1973.

Chandler, Melbourne C. *Of Garryowen in Glory: The History of the 7th U.S. Cavalry.* Privately published, 1960.

Chapelle, Howard I. *The History of the American Sailing Navy: The Ships and Their Development.* New York: Norton, 1949.

Chidsey, Donald B. *The Battle of New Orleans.* New York: Crown, 1961.

———. *Victory at Yorktown.* New York: Crown, 1962.

Churchill, Winston S. *The Hinge of Fate.* Boston: Houghton Mifflin, 1950.

Cist, Henry M. *The Army of the Cumberland.* New York: Scribner's, 1882.

Clark, Dwight L. *Stephen Watts Kearny: Soldier of the West.* Norman: University of Oklahoma Press, 1961.

Clark, Mark W. *Calculated Risk.* New York: Harper, 1950.

Clark, William B. *Lambert Wickes: Sea Raider and Diplomat.* New Haven: Yale University Press, 1932.

———. *Gallant John Barry.* New York: Macmillan, 1938.

———. *George Washington's Navy.* Baton Rouge: Louisiana State University Press, 1960.

Clarke, James F. *History of the Campaign of 1812 and Surrender of Detroit.* New York: Appleton, 1848.

Cleaves, Freeman. *Old Tippecanoe: William Henry Harrison and His Time.* New York: Scribner's, 1939.

———. *Rock of Chickamauga: The Life of General George H. Thomas.* Norman: University of Oklahoma Press, 1948.

———. *Meade of Gettysburg.* Norman: University of Oklahoma Press, 1959.

Coddington, Edwin B. *The Gettysburg Campaign: A Study in Command.* New York: Scribner's, 1968.

Codman, John. *Arnold's Expedition to Quebec.* New York: Macmillan, 1902.

Coffman, Edward M. *The War to End All Wars: The American Military Experience in World War I.* New York: Oxford, 1968.

Coleman, Kenneth. *The American Revolution in Georgia.* Athens: University of Georgia Press, 1958.

Coles, Harry L. *The War of 1812.* Chicago: University of Chicago Press, 1965.

Collins, J. Lawton. *War in Peacetime: The History and Lessons of Korea.* Boston: Houghton Mifflin, 1969.

Colton, Ray C. *The Civil War in the Western Territories.* Norman: University of Oklahoma Press, 1959.

Commager, Henry Steele. *Documents of American History.* New York: Croft, 1947.

Comte de Paris. *History of the Civil War in America.* 4 vols. Philadelphia: Porter & Coates, 1875.

Connelly, Thomas L. *Army of the Heartland.* Baton Rouge: Louisiana State University Press, 1967.

Connelly, Thomas L., and Jones, Archer. *The Politics of Command: Factions and Ideas in Confederate Strategy.* Baton Rouge: Louisiana State University Press, 1975.

Connelly, William E. *Doniphan's Expedition: The Conquest of New Mexico and California.* Topeka: Bryant & Douglas, 1907.

Conner, P. S. P. *The Home Squadron in the Mexican War.* Philadelphia: n.p., 1896.

Concas, Victor M. y Palau. *The Squadron of Admiral Cervera.* Washington: Office of Naval Intelligence, 1900.

Cooch, Edward W. *The Battle of Cooch's Bridge.* Wilmington, N.C.: W. N. Cann, 1940.

Coolidge, Louis A. *Ulysses S. Grant.* Boston: Houghton Mifflin, 1917.

Cooling, Benjamin F. *Benjamin Franklin Tracy: Father of the Modern American Navy.* Hamden: Archon, 1973.

Cooper, Chester L. *The Lost Crusade: America in Vietnam.* New York: Dodd, Mead, 1970.

Cooper, James Fenimore. *Lives of Distinguished American Naval Officers.* Auburn, Ala.: J. C. Derby, 1846.

Corwin, Edward S. *French Policy and the American Alliance.* Princeton: Princeton University Press, 1916.

———. *The President: Office and Powers.* New York: New York University Press, 1948.

Coues, Elliott, ed. *History of the Expedition Under the Command of Lewis and Clark.* 4 vols. New York: Harper, 1893.

Cox, Jacob D. *Atlanta.* New York: Scribner's, 1882.

———. *Military Reminiscences of the Civil War.* 2 vols. New York: Scribner's, 1900.

Crallé, Richard K., ed. *The Works of John C. Calhoun.* 10 vols. New York: Appleton, 1854–1857.

Cramer, Clarence H. *Newton D. Baker.* Cleveland: World, 1961.

Craven, Wesley Frank, and Cate, James Lea. *The Army Air Forces in World War II.* 7 vols. Chicago: University of Chicago Press, 1948–1958.

Crawford, Samuel Wylie. *The Genesis of the Civil War.* New York: Webster, 1887.

Crowder, Enoch H. *The Spirit of Selective Service.* New York: Columbia University Press, 1920.

Crowell, Benedict, and Wilson, Robert F. *How America Went to War: Demobilization.* New Haven: Yale University Press, 1921.

Crowl, Philip A. *Campaign in the Marianas.* Washington: Department of the Army, 1960.

Crowl, Philip A., and Love, Edmund G. *Seizure of the Gilberts and Marshalls.* Washington: Department of the Army, 1955.

Cruikshank, Ernest A., ed. *The Correspondence of Lieut. Governor John Graves Simcoe.* Toronto: Ontario Historical Society, 1925.

Cruttwell, C. R. M. F. *A History of the Great War, 1914–1918.* Oxford: Clarendon, 1936.

Cullum, George W. *Biographical Register of the Officers and Graduates of the U.S. Military Academy.* 2 vols. New York: D. Van Nostrand, 1868.

Cuneo, John R. *Robert Rogers of the Rangers.* New York: Oxford, 1959.

Current, Richard N. *Lincoln and the First Shot.* Philadelphia: Lippincott, 1963.

Custer, George A. *My Life on the Plains.* New York: Sheldon, 1874.

Daly, Robert W. *How the Merrimac Won.* New York: Crowell, 1957.

Dalzell, George W. *The Flight from the Flag: The Continuing Effect of the Civil War upon the American Carrying Trade.* Chapel Hill: University of North Carolina Press, 1940.

Dana, Charles A. *Lincoln and His Cabinet.* Cleveland: DeVinne, 1896.

Daniels, Josephus. *The Wilson Era: Years of War and After, 1917–1923.* Chapel Hill: University of North Carolina Press, 1946.

Davis, Burke. *The Cowpens-Guilford Courthouse Campaign.* Philadephia: Lippincott, 1962.

Davis, George T. *A Navy Second to None.* New York: Harcourt, Brace, 1940.

Davis, Jefferson. *The Rise and Fall of the Confederate Government.* 2 vols. New York: Appleton, 1881.

Davis, Richard Harding. *The Cuban and Porto Rican Campaigns.* New York: Scribner's, 1898.

Davis, Vincent. *Postwar Defense Policy and the U.S. Navy, 1943–1946.* Chapel Hill: University of North Carolina Press, 1966.

Davis, William C. *Battle at Bull Run.* Garden City: Doubleday, 1977.

Dawes, Charles G. *A Journal of the McKinley Years.* Chicago: Lakeside Press, 1950.

Dawson, Henry B. *Battles of the United States.* 2 vols. New York: Johnson & Fry, 1858.

_____. *The Assault on Stony Point.* Morrisania: New York Historical Society, 1863.

De Chant, John A. *The Modern United States Marine Corps.* Princeton: Van Nostrand, 1966.

De Seversky, Alexander P. *Victory Through Air Power.* New York: Simon & Schuster, 1942.

De Trobriand, Regis. *Four Years with the Army of the Potomac.* Boston: Ticknor, 1889.

De Voto, Bernard. *The Year of Decision, 1846.* Boston: Houghton Mifflin, 1943.

DeWeerd, Harvey A. *President Wilson Fights His War: World War I and the American Intervention.* New York: Macmillan, 1968.

Dewey, George. *Autobiography of George Dewey: Admiral of the Navy.* New York: Scribner's, 1913.

Dickman, Joseph T. *The Great Crusade.* New York: Appleton, 1927.

Dictionary of American Biography. 20 vols. New York: Scribner's, 1928–1937.

Dierks, Jack Cameron. *A Leap to Arms: The Cuban Campaign of 1898.* Philadelphia: Lippincott, 1970.

Dillon, Richard. *Meriwether Lewis.* New York: Coward-McCann, 1965.

Dorn, Walter L. *Competition for Empire, 1740–1763.* New York: Harper, 1940.

Doughty, Arthur G. *The Siege of Quebec.* 6 vols. Quebec: Dussault & Prouix, 1901.

Douhet, Giulio. *The Command of the Air.* New York: McCann, 1942.

Downes, Randolph C. *Frontier Ohio, 1788–1803.* Columbus: Ohio State Archeological & Historical Society, 1935.

Drake, Benjamin. *The Life and Adventures of Black Hawk.* Cincinnati: G. Conclin, 1849.

Draper, Lyman C. *King's Mountain and Its Heroes.* Cincinnati: P. G. Thomson, 1881.

Dupuy, R. Ernest. *St. Vith: Lion in the Way.* Washington: Combat, 1949.

_____. *Men of West Point.* New York: Sloane, 1951.

Dupuy, R. Ernest, and Dupuy, Trevor N. *Military Heritage of America.* New York: McGraw-Hill, 1956.

_____. *The Compact History of the Revolutionary War.* New York: Hawthorn, 1963.

Durkin, Joseph T. *Stephen R. Mallory: Confederate Navy Chief.* Chapel Hill: University of North Carolina Press, 1954.

Dustin, Fred. *The Custer Tragedy.* Ann Arbor: Edwards, 1939.

Dyer, Brainerd. *Zachary Taylor.* Baton Rouge: Louisiana State University Press, 1946.

Dyer, George C. *The Amphibians Came to Conquer: The Story of Admiral Richmond Kelly Turner.* 2 vols. Washington: Government Printing Office, 1969.

Earle, Edward Mead, ed. *Makers of Modern Strategy.* Princeton: Princeton University Press, 1952.

Edmonds, James E. *A Short History of World War I.* London: Oxford, 1951.

Eichelberger, Robert L. *Our Jungle Road to Tokyo.* New York: Viking, 1950.

Eisenhower, Dwight D. *Crusade in Europe.* New York: Doubleday, 1948.

_____. *The White House Years: Mandate for Change, 1953–1956.* Garden City: Doubleday, 1963.

Elliott, Charles W. *Winfield Scott: The Soldier and the Man.* New York: Macmillan, 1937.

Ellis, Joseph, and Moore, Robert. *School for Soldiers: West Point and the Profession of Arms.* New York: Oxford, 1974.

Evans, Robley D. *A Sailor's Log: Recollections of Forty Years of Naval Life.* New York: Appleton-Century, 1901.

Facts About the Civil War. Washington: Civil War Centennial Commission, 1959.

Fairchild, Herman. *History of the New York Academy of Sciences.* New York: H. L. Fairchild, 1887.

Fall, Bernard B. *Hell in a Very Small Place: The Siege of Dien Bien Phu.* New York: Vintage, 1968.

Falls, Cyril. *The Great War.* New York: Putnam, 1959.

_____. *The Art of War from the Age of Napoleon to the Present Day.* Oxford: Oxford University Press, 1961.

Fast, Howard M. *The Crossing.* New York: Morrow, 1971.

Fiebeger, Gustave J. *Elements of Strategy.* N.p., 1906.

Field, James A., Jr. *History of United States Naval Operations, Korea.* Washington: Government Printing Office, 1962.

Fish, Carl Russell. *The American Civil War.* London: Longmans, Green, 1937.

Fisher, Ernest F., Jr. *Cassino to the Alps.* Washington: Department of the Army, 1977.

Fiske, John. *The Mississippi Valley in the Civil War.* Boston: Houghton Mifflin, 1900.

Fitzpatrick, John C., ed. *The Writings of George Washington.* 39 vols. Washington: Government Printing Office, 1931–1944.

Fleming, Thomas J. *West Point: The Men and Times of the United States Military Academy.* New York: Morrow, 1969.

Flexner, James T. *The Traitor and the Spy.* New York: Harcourt, Brace, 1953.

_____. *George Washington in the American Revolution.* Boston: Little, Brown, 1968.

Flick, Alexander C., comp. *The Sullivan-Clinton Campaign of 1779.* New York: A. C. Flick, 1929.

Force, Manning F. *From Fort Henry to Corinth.* New York: Scribner's, 1881.

Force, Peter, ed. *American Archives.* Washington: Government Printing Office, 1837–1853.

Ford, Harney S., ed. *Memoirs of a Volunteer: 1861–1863.* New York: Norton, 1946.

Ford, Worthington Chauncey, ed. *Journals of the Continental Congress, 1774–1789.* 34 vols. Washington: Government Printing Office, 1934–1937.

Forman, Sidney. *A History of the United States Military Academy.* New York: Columbia University Press, 1950.

Fortescue, John W. *A History of the British Army.* 13 vols. London: Macmillan, 1889–1930.

Freeman, Douglas Southall. *R. E. Lee: A Biography.* New York: Scribner's, 1934.

_____. *Lee's Lieutenants: A Study in Command.* New York: Scribner's, 1942–1944.

_____. *George Washington: A Biography.* 7 vols. New York: Scribner's, 1948–1957.

Freidel, Frank. *The Splendid Little War.* Boston: Little, Brown, 1958.

Fremont, John C. *Memoirs of My Life.* Chicago: Belford, Clarke, 1887.

French, Allen. *The Day of Concord and Lexington.* Boston: Little, Brown, 1925.

_____. *The Taking of Ticonderoga in 1775.* Cambridge: Harvard University Press, 1928.

_____. *The First Years of the American Revolution.* Boston: Houghton Mifflin, 1934.

Frothingham, Richard. *History of the Siege of Boston.* Boston: Little, Brown, 1851.

Frothingham, Thomas G. *A Guide to the Military History of the World War.* Boston: Little, Brown, 1920.

_____. *The American Reinforcement in the World War.* Garden City: Doubleday, Page, 1927.

_____. *Washington, Commander-in-Chief.* Boston: Houghton Mifflin, 1930.

Fry, James B. *Military Miscellanies.* New York: Brentano's, 1889.

Fuchida, Mitsuo, and Okumiya, Masataka. *Midway, The Battle that Doomed Japan.* Annapolis: U.S. Naval Institute, 1955.

Fuller, J. F. C. *Decisive Battles of the U.S.A.* New York: Beechhurst, 1953.

Funston, Frederick. *Memories of Two Wars: Cuban and Philippine Experiences.* New York: Scribner's, 1911.

Ganoe, William Addleman. *The History of the United States Army.* New York: Appleton-Century, 1942.

Geer, Walter. *Campaigns of the Civil War.* New York: Brentano's, 1926.

Gill, George H. *Royal Australian Navy, 1939–1942.* 5 vols. Canberra: Australian War Memorial, 1957.

Gilmore, James A. *Personal Recollections of Abraham Lincoln and the Civil War.* London: J. Macqueen, 1898.

Gilpin, Alec R. *The War of 1812 in the Old Northwest.* East Lansing: Michigan State University Press, 1958.

Gipson, Lawrence H. *Zones of International Friction: North America South of the Great Lakes Region, 1748–1754.* New York: Knopf, 1939.

_____. *The Great War for the Empire: The Years of Defeat, 1754–1957.* New York: Knopf, 1946.

_____. *The Coming of the Revolution.* New York: Harper, 1954.

Glassley, Ray H. *Pacific Northwest Indian Wars.* Portland: Binfords & Mort, 1953.

Glines, Caroll V., Jr. *The Compact History of the United States Air Force.* New York: Hawthorn, 1963.

Goetzmann, William H. *Army Exploration in the American West, 1803–1863.* New Haven: Yale University Press, 1959.

Goldberg, Alfred, ed. *A History of the United States Air Force.* New York: Van Nostrand, 1957.

Goode, W. W. M. *With Sampson Through the War.* New York: Doubleday & McClure, 1899.

Gordon, George H. *History of the Campaign of the Army of Virginia under John Pope.* Boston: Houghton, Osgood, 1880.

Gottschalk, Louis. *Lafayette and the Close of the American Revolution.* Chicago: University of Chicago Press, 1942.

Gracie, Archibald. *The Truth About Chickamauga.* Boston: Houghton Mifflin, 1911.

Graham, George E. *Schley and Santiago.* Chicago: W. B. Conkey, 1902.

Graham, Gerald S. *Empire of the North Atlantic: The Maritime Struggle for North America.* Toronto: Toronto University Press, 1950.

_____. *The Walker Expedition to Quebec, 1711.* Toronto: Toronto University Press, 1953.

Graham, William A. *The Story of the Little Big Horn.* Harrisburg: Stackpole, 1945.

Grant, Ulysses S. *Personal Memoirs of U.S. Grant.* 2 vols. New York: Webster, 1885.

Greene, Francis Vinton. *The Mississippi.* New York: Scribner's, 1882.

Greene, George W. *The Life of Nathanael Greene.* 3 vols. Boston: Little, Brown, 1846.

Grinnell, George Bird. *The Fighting Cheyennes.* Norman: University of Oklahoma Press, 1956.

Groves, Leslie R. *Now It Can Be Told: The Story of the Manhattan Project.* New York: Harper, 1962.

Guderian, Heinz. *Panzer Leader.* London: M. Joseph, 1952.

Hagedorn, Hermann. *Leonard Wood.* 2 vols. New York: Harper, 1931.

Hagood, Johnson. *The Services of Supply.* Cambridge: Harvard University Press, 1927.

Halbert, H. S., and Ball, T. H. *The Creek War of 1813 and 1814.* Chicago: Donohue & Henneberry, 1895.

Hall, Martin H. *Sibley's New Mexico Campaign.* Austin: University of Texas Press, 1960.

Halleck, Henry W. *Elements of Military Art and Science.* New York: Appleton, 1862.

Hamersly, Thomas H. S. *Complete Regular Army Register of the United States.* Washington: Hamersly, 1880.

Hamilton, Edward P. *The French and Indian Wars: The Story of Battles and Forts in the Wilderness*. New York: Doubleday, 1962.

Hamilton, Holman. *Zachary Taylor: Soldier of the Republic*. Indianapolis: Bobbs-Merrill, 1941.

Hammond, Paul Y. *Organizing for Defense: The American Military Establishment in the Twentieth Century*. Princeton: Princeton University Press, 1961.

Harbord, James G. *The American Army in France*. Boston: Little, Brown, 1936.

Hart, Basil H. Liddell. *Sherman: Soldier, Realist, American*. New York: Dodd, Mead, 1929.

_____. *A History of the World War, 1914–1918*. London: Faber & Faber, 1934.

Hart, Richard A. *The Great White Fleet: Its Voyage Around the World, 1907–1909*. Boston: Little, Brown, 1965.

Hassler, Warren W., Jr. *General George B. McClellan: Shield of the Union*. Baton Rouge: Louisiana State University Press, 1957.

_____. *Commanders of the Army of the Potomac*. Baton Rouge: Louisiana State University Press, 1962.

_____. *Crisis at the Crossroads: The First Day at Gettysburg*. University, Ala.: University of Alabama Press, 1970.

_____. *The President as Commander in Chief*. Menlo Park: Addison-Wesley, 1971.

Hatch, Charles E., Jr. *Yorktown and the Siege of 1781*. Washington: Government Printing Office, 1957.

Hatch, Robert M. *Thrust for Canada: The American Attempt on Quebec, 1775–1776*. Boston: Houghton Mifflin, 1979.

Haydon, F. Stansbury. *Aeronautics in the Union and Confederate Armies*. Baltimore: Johns Hopkins Press, 1941.

Hebert, Walter H. *Fighting Joe Hooker*. Indianapolis: Bobbs-Merrill, 1944.

Heinl, Robert D., Jr. *The Defense of Wake*. Washington: Marine Historical Section, 1947.

_____. *The Marines at Midway*. Washington: Marine Historical Section, 1948.

_____. *Soldiers of the Sea: The United States Marine Corps, 1775–1962*. Annapolis: U.S. Naval Institute, 1962.

Heinl, Robert D., and Crown, John A. *The Marshalls: Increasing the Tempo*. Washington: Marine Historical Division, 1954.

Heitman, Francis B. *Historical Register and Dictionary of the United States Army*. 2 vols. Washington: Government Printing Office, 1903.

Hendrick, Burton J. *Statesmen of the Lost Cause: Jefferson Davis and His Cabinet*. New York: Literary Guild, 1939.

Henry, Robert Selph. *The Story of the Mexican War*. Indianapolis: Bobbs-Merrill, 1950.

Hewes, James E., Jr. *From Root to McNamara: Army Organization and Administration, 1900–1963*. Washington: Center of Military History, 1975.

Higginbotham, Don. *Daniel Morgan: Revolutionary Rifleman*. Chapel Hill: University of North Carolina Press, 1961.

_____. *The War of American Independence: Military Attitudes, Policies, and Practice, 1763–1789*. New York: Macmillan, 1971.

Hill, Jim Dan. *The Minute Man in War and Peace: A History of the National Guard*. Harrisburg: Stackpole, 1953.

Hilsman, Roger. *To Move a Nation*. New York: Dell, 1968.

Hirsch, Mark D. *William C. Whitney*. New York: Dodd, Mead, 1948.

Hitsman, J. Mackay. *The Incredible War of 1812: A Military History*. Toronto: University of Toronto Press, 1965.

Hittle, James D. *The Military Staff*. Harrisburg: Military Service Publishing Co., 1949.

Hoehling, Adolph A. *Vicksburg: The 47-Day Siege*. Englewood Cliffs, N.J.: Prentice-Hall, 1969.

Hoffman, Carl W. *Saipan: The Beginning of the End*. Washington: Marine Historical Division, 1950.

_____. *The Seizure of Tinian*. Washington: Marine Historical Division, 1951.

Holbrook, Stewart H. *Ethan Allen*. New York: Macmillan, 1940.

Holley, I. B. *Ideas and Weapons*. New Haven: Yale University Press, 1953.

Hollon, W. Eugene. *The Lost Pathfinder: Zebulon Montgomery Pike*. Norman: University of Oklahoma Press, 1949.

Horn, Stanley F. *The Army of Tennessee*. Indianapolis: Bobbs-Merrill, 1941.

_____. *The Decisive Battle of Nashville*. Baton Rouge: Louisiana State University Press, 1956.

Hough, Frank O. *The Assault on Peleliu*. Washington: Marine Historical Division, 1950.

_____. *The United States Marine Corps*. New York: Hawthorn, 1960.

Hough, Frank O., et al. *Pearl Harbor to Guadalcanal*. Washington: Marine Historical Branch, 1958.

Houston, David F. *Eight Years with Wilson's Cabinet*. Garden City: Doubleday, Page, 1926.

Howard, Michael. *The Theory and Practice of War*. New York: Praeger, 1966.

Howard, Oliver O. *My Life and Experiences Among Our Hostile Indians*. Hartford: A. D. Worthington, 1907.

Howe, George F. *Northwest Africa: Seizing the Initiative in the West*. Washington: Department of the Army, 1957.

Hughes, John T. *Doniphan's Expedition: Containing an Account of the Conquest of New Mexico*. Chicago: Rio Grande Press, 1962.

Huidekoper, Frederic L. *The Military Unpreparedness of the United States*. New York: Macmillan, 1915.

Hull, Cordell. *The Memoirs of Cordell Hull*. 2 vols. New York: Macmillan, 1948.

Hunt, Frazier. *The Untold Story of Douglas MacArthur*. New York: Devin-Adair, 1954.

Hunt, Gaillard, ed. *The Writings of James Madison*. 9 vols. New York: Putnam, 1900–1910.

Hunter, William A. *Forts on the Pennsylvania Frontier, 1753-1758*. Harrisburg: Pennsylvania Historical & Museum Commission, 1960.

Huntington, Samuel P. *The Soldier and the State: The Theory and Politics of Civil-Military Relations*. Cambridge: Harvard University Press, 1957.

_____. *The Common Defense: Strategic Programs in National Politics*. New York: Columbia University Press, 1961.

Hurley, Alfred F. *Billy Mitchell: Crusader for Air Power*. New York: Watts, 1964.

Hurley, Edward N. *The Bridge to France*. Philadelphia: Lippincott, 1927.

Ingersoll, Charles J. *Historical Sketch of the Second War between the United States of America and Great Britain*. Philadelphia: Lea & Blanchard, 1845.

Ingersoll, L. D. *A History of the War Department of the United States*. Washington: F. B. Mohun, 1879.

Isely, Jeter A., and Crowl, Philip A. *The U.S. Marines and Amphibious War*. Princeton: Princeton University Press, 1957.

Jackson, Donald. *Custer's Gold: The United States Cavalry Expedition of 1874*. New Haven: Yale University Press, 1966.

Jackson, Helen Hunt. *A Century of Dishonor*. Boston: Roberts, 1885.

Jacobs, James Ripley. *Tarnished Warrior: Major General James Wilkinson*. New York: Macmillan, 1938.

_____. *The Beginning of the U.S. Army, 1783-1812*. Princeton: Princeton University Press, 1947.

James, D. Clayton. *The Years of MacArthur*. 2 vols. Boston: Houghton Mifflin, 1970-.

James, James A., ed. *George Rogers Clark Papers, 1771-1784*. Springfield: Illinois State Historical Library, *Collections*, vols. 8, 9, 1912, 1926.

James, Marquis. *The Raven: A Biography of Sam Houston*. Indianapolis: Bobbs-Merrill, 1929.

_____. *Andrew Jackson: The Border Captain*. Indianapolis: Bobbs-Merrill, 1933.

James, William. *Full and Correct Account of the Military Occurrences of the Late War between Great Britain and the United States of America*. London: n.p., 1818.

_____. *The Naval History of Great Britain*. Vol. 6. London: R. Bentley, 1826.

Janeway, Eliot. *The Struggle for Survival: A Chronicle of Economic Mobilization in World War II*. New Haven: Yale University Press, 1951.

Janowitz, Morris. *The Professional Soldier*. New York: Free Press, 1964.

Jessup, Philip C. *Elihu Root*. 2 vols. New York: Dodd, Mead, 1938.

Johnson, Robert Underwood, and Buel, Clarence Clough, eds. *Battles and Leaders of the Civil War*. 4 vols. New York: Century, 1887.

Johnson, Barry C., ed. *Crook's Resumé of Operations Against Apache Indians: 1882 to 1886*. London: Johnson-Taunton, 1971.

Johnson, Virginia. *The Unregimented General: A Biography of Nelson A. Miles*. Boston: Houghton Mifflin, 1962.

Johnston, Henry P. *The Storming of Stony Point*. New York: J. T. White, 1900.

_____. *The Yorktown Campaign and the Surrender of Cornwallis*. New York: Harper, 1881.

Johnston, Joseph E. *Narrative of Military Operations*. New York: Appleton, 1874.

Johnston, Robert M. *Leading American Soldiers*. New York: Holt, 1907.

Jones, Archer. *Confederate Strategy from Shiloh to Vicksburg*. Baton Rouge: Louisiana State University Press, 1961.

Jones, Samuel. *The Siege of Charleston*. New York: Neal, 1911.

Jones, Virgil C. *The Civil War at Sea*. 3 vols. New York: Holt, Rinehart, & Winston, 1960-1962.

Kaufman, William W., ed. *Military Policy and National Security*. Princeton: Princeton University Press, 1956.

Kennan, George. *Campaigning in Cuba*. New York: Century, 1899.

Kenney, George C. *General Kenney Reports*. New York: Duell, Sloan, & Pearce, 1949.

_____. *The MacArthur I Know*. New York: Duell, Sloan, & Pearce, 1951.

Kerwin, Jerome G., ed. *Civil-Military Relationship in American Life*. Chicago: University of Chicago Press, 1948.

Kimmel, Husband E. *Admiral Kimmel's Story*. Chicago: Regnery, 1955.

Kirby, S. Woodburn. *The War Against Japan*. London: H. M. Stationery Office, 1957.

Kissinger, Henry A. *Nuclear Weapons and Foreign Policy*. New York: Harper & Row, 1957.

Knox, Dudley W. *A History of the United States Navy*. New York: Putnam, 1948.

Kohn, Richard H. *Eagle and Sword: The Federalists and the Creation of the Military Establishment in America, 1783-1802*. New York: Free Press, 1975.

Kreidberg, Marvin A., and Henry, Merton G. *History of Military Mobilization in the United States Army, 1775-1945*. Washington: Department of the Army, 1955.

Krueger, Walter. *From Down Under to Nippon*. Washington: Combat Forces Press, 1953.

Kuhlman, Charles. *Legend into History: The Custer Mystery*. Harrisburg: Stackpole, 1951.

Lamers, William M. *The Edge of Glory: A Biography of General William S. Rosecrans, U.S.A.* New York: Harcourt, Brace, 1961.

Lane, Frederic C. *Ships for Victory: A History of the United States Maritime Commission*. Baltimore: Johns Hopkins Press, 1951.

Lane, Jack C., ed. *Chasing Geronimo: The Journal of Leonard Wood, May-September, 1886*. Albuquerque: University of New Mexico Press, 1970.

Lattimore, Ralston B. *Fort Pulaski*. Washington: National Park Service, 1954.

Lawrence, Alexander A. *Storm Over Savannah*. Athens: University of Georgia Press, 1951.

Leach, Douglas E. *Arms for Empire: A Military History of the British Colonies in North America, 1607-1763*. New York: Macmillan, 1973.

Leahy, William D. *I Was There*. New York: Whittlesey House, 1950.

Leckie, Robert. *The Wars of America*. New York: Harper & Row, 1968.

Lee, Edward B., Jr. *Politics of Our Military National Defense*. Washington: Government Printing Office, 1940.

Lee, Henry. *Memoirs of the War in the Southern Department*. New York: University Publishing Co., 1869.

Leech, Margaret. *In the Days of McKinley*. New York: Harper, 1959.

Leighton, Richard M., and Coakley, Robert W. *Global Logistics and Strategy, 1940-1943*. Washington: Department of the Army, 1955.

Leopold, Richard W. *Elihu Root and the Conservative Tradition*. Boston: Little, Brown, 1954.

Lewin, Ronald. *Ultra Goes to War*. New York: McGraw-Hill, 1978.

Lewis, Emanuel R. *Seacoast Fortifications of the United States*. Washington: Smithsonian Institution Press, 1970.

Lewis, Lloyd. *Sherman: Fighting Prophet*. New York: Harcourt, Brace, 1932.

_____. *Captain Sam Grant*. Boston: Little, Brown, 1950.

Liddell Hart, Basil H. *Strategy*. New York: Praeger, 1954.

Liggett, Hunter. *Commanding an American Army*. Boston: Houghton Mifflin, 1925.

Link, Arthur S. *Woodrow Wilson and the Progressive Era*. New York: Harper, 1954.

Livermore, Thomas L. *Numbers and Losses in the Civil War in America, 1861-65*. Boston: Houghton Mifflin, 1901.

Livezey, William E. *Mahan on Sea Power*. Norman: University of Oklahoma Press, 1947.

Lloyd, Alan. *The Scorching of Washington: The War of 1812*. Washington: R. B. Luce, 1974.

Lloyd, Christopher. *The Capture of Quebec*. New York: Macmillan, 1959.

Lockwood, Frank C. *The Apache Indians*. New York: Macmillan, 1936.

Lodge, O. R. *The Recapture of Guam*. Washington: Marine Historical Branch, 1954.

Long, John D. *The New American Navy*. 2 vols. New York: Outlook, 1903.

Lord, Walter. *A Time to Stand*. New York: Harper, 1961.

———. *Lonely Vigil: Coastwatchers of the Solomons.* New York: Viking-Penguin, 1976.

Lossing, Benson J. *The Pictorial Field-Book of the Revolution.* 2 vols. New York: Harper, 1860.

———. *The Pictorial Fieldbook of the War of 1812.* New York: Harper, 1869.

Lovell, John P. *Neither Athens Nor Sparta? The American Service Academies in Transition.* Bloomington: Indiana University Press, 1979.

Lowell, Edward J. *The Hessians and Other German Auxiliaries.* New York: Harper, 1884.

Lundin, Leonard. *Cockpit of the Revolution: The War for Independence in New Jersey.* Princeton: Princeton University Press, 1940.

Lyons, Gene M., and Morton, Louis. *Schools for Strategy: Education and Research in National Security Affairs.* New York: Praeger, 1965.

McAfee, Robert V. *History of the Late War in the Western Country.* Bowling Green: Historical Publications Co., 1919.

MacArthur, Douglas. *Reminiscences.* New York: McGraw-Hill, 1964.

McCaleb, Walter F. *William Barrett Travis.* San Antonio: Naylor, 1957.

McClellan, George B. *Report on the Organization and Campaigns of the Army of the Potomac.* New York: Sheldon, 1864.

———. *McClellan's Own Story: The War for the Union.* New York: Webster, 1887.

McClure, Alexander K. *Abraham Lincoln and Men of War-Times.* Philadelphia: Times, 1892.

McCormac, Eugene I. *James K. Polk: A Political Biography.* Berkeley: University of California Press, 1922.

McDonough, James L. *Shiloh.* Knoxville: University of Tennessee Press, 1977.

McElroy, John. *The Struggle for Missouri.* Washington: National Tribune, 1909.

McElroy, Robert M. *Kentucky in the Nation's History.* New York: Moffat, Yard, 1909.

———. *Jefferson Davis: The Unreal and the Real.* 2 vols. New York: Harper, 1937.

McEntee, Gerald L. *Military History of the World War.* New York: Scribner's, 1937.

McKitrick, Eric L. *Andrew Johnson and Reconstruction.* Chicago: University of Chicago Press, 1960.

McLennan, J. S. *Louisbourg from Its Foundation to Its Fall.* London: Macmillan, 1918.

McMaster, John Bach. *A History of the People of the United States.* 8 vols. New York: Appleton, 1883–1913.

McWhiney, Grady. *Braxton Bragg.* 2 vols. New York: Columbia University Press, 1969.

Mahan, Alfred Thayer. *The Gulf and Inland Waters.* New York: Scribner's, 1883.

———. *Lessons of the War with Spain.* Boston: Little, Brown, 1899.

———. *From Sail to Steam.* New York: Harper, 1907.

———. *The Major Operations of the Navies in the War of American Independence.* Boston: Little, Brown, 1913.

———. *Sea Power in Its Relations to the War of 1812.* 2 vols. Boston: Little, Brown, 1919.

Mahan, Dennis Hart. *Advanced-Guard, Outpost . . . with the Essential Principles of Strategy and Grand Tactics.* New York: Wiley, 1863.

Mahon, John K. *History of the Second Seminole War.* Gainesville: University of Florida Press, 1967.

_____. *The War of 1812*. Gainesville: University of Florida Press, 1972.

Marder, Arthur J. *From the Dreadnought to Scapa Flow: The Royal Navy in the Fisher Era, 1904-1919*. 4 vols. London: Oxford University Press, 1961-1969.

Marine, William A. *The British Invasion of Maryland*. Baltimore: Society of the War of 1812, 1913.

Marshall, S. L. A. *Bastogne: The First Eight Days*. Washington: Combat Press, 1946.

_____. *Crimsoned Prairie: The Wars between the United States and the Plains Indians*. New York: Scribner's, 1972.

Masland, John W., and Radway, Lawrence I. *Soldiers and Scholars: Military Education and National Policy*. Princeton: Princeton University Press, 1957.

Massachusetts Historical Society Proceedings. Vol. 69. Boston: Massachusetts Historical Society, 1924.

Matloff, Maurice. *Strategic Planning for Coalition Warfare, 1943-1944*. Washington: Department of the Army, 1959.

Matloff, Maurice, ed. *American Military History*. Washington: Office of the Chief of Military History, 1969.

Matloff, Maurice, and Snell, Edwin M. *Strategic Planning for Coalition Warfare, 1941-1942*. Washington: Department of the Army, 1953.

May, Ernest R., ed. *The Ultimate Decision: The President as Commander in Chief*. New York: Braziller, 1960.

Meade, George. *The Life and Letters of George Gordon Meade*. 2 vols. New York: Scribner's, 1913.

Meneely, A. Howard. *The War Department, 1861: A Study in Mobilization and Administration*. New York: Columbia University Press, 1928.

Michie, Peter S. *The Life and Letters of Emory Upton*. New York: Appleton, 1885.

Middleton, Harry J. *The Compact History of the Korean War*. New York: Hawthorn, 1965.

Miles, Nelson A. *Serving the Republic*. New York: Harper, 1911.

Miley, John D. *In Cuba with Shafter*. New York: Scribner's, 1899.

Miller, John, Jr. *Guadalcanal: The First Offensive*. Washington: Department of the Army, 1949.

_____. *Cartwheel: The Reduction of Rabaul*. Washington: Department of the Army, 1959.

Miller, John C. *The Triumph of Freedom, 1775-1783*. Boston: Little, Brown, 1948.

Miller, R. J. *Around the World with the Battleships*. Chicago: McClurg, 1909.

Milligan, John D. *Gunboats Down the Mississippi*. Annapolis: U.S. Naval Institute, 1965.

Millis, Walter. *The Martial Spirit: A Study of Our War with Spain*. Boston: Houghton Mifflin, 1931.

_____. *Arms and Men: A Study in American Military History*. New York: Putnam, 1966.

Millis, Walter, ed. *American Military Thought*. Indianapolis: Bobbs-Merrill, 1966.

Millis, Walter, and Duffield, E. S., eds. *The Forrestal Diaries*. New York: Viking, 1951.

Milner, Samuel. *Victory in Papua*. Washington: Department of the Army, 1957.

Milton, George Fort. *The Use of Presidential Power*. Boston: Little, Brown, 1944.

Miner, Charles. *History of Wyoming*. Philadelphia: J. Crissy, 1845.

Montross, Lynn. *War Through the Ages*. New York: Harper, 1946.

_____. *U.S. Marine Operations In Korea*. 4 vols. Washington: Marine Historical Branch, 1954-1962.

Morgan, H. Wayne. *William McKinley and His America*. Syracuse: Syracuse University Press, 1963.

Morison, Elting E. *Admiral Sims and the Modern American Navy.* Boston: Houghton Mifflin, 1942.

Morison, Samuel Eliot. *History of United States Naval Operations in World War II.* 15 vols. Boston: Little, Brown, 1947–1965.

————. *John Paul Jones: A Sailor's Biography.* Boston: Little, Brown, 1959.

————. *"Old Bruin": Commodore Matthew C. Perry, 1794–1858.* Boston: Little, Brown, 1967.

Morris, Richard B. *The Peacemakers.* New York: Harper & Row, 1965.

Morse, John T., Jr. *The Diary of Gideon Welles.* 3 vols. Boston: Houghton Mifflin, 1911.

Morton, Louis. *The Fall of the Philippines.* Washington: Department of the Army, 1953.

Moskin, J. Robert. *The U.S. Marine Corps Story.* New York: McGraw-Hill, 1977.

Moultrie, William. *Memoirs of the American Revolution.* 2 vols. New York: D. Longworth, 1802.

Mountbatten, Lord Louis. *Report to the Combined Chiefs of Staff: South-East Asia, 1943–1945.* London: H. M. Stationery Office, 1951.

Muller, Charles G. *The Darkest Day, 1814: The Washington-Baltimore Campaign.* New York: John Day, 1963.

Muller, José y Tejeiro. *Battles and Capitulation of Santiago de Cuba.* Washington: Office of Naval Intelligence, 1899.

Murdock, Harold. *Bunker Hill.* Boston: Houghton Mifflin, 1927.

Murfin, James V. *The Gleam of Bayonets: The Battle of Antietam and the Maryland Campaign of 1862.* New York: Yoseloff, 1965.

Murray, Keith A. *The Modocs and Their War.* Norman: University of Oklahoma Press, 1959.

Myers, John M. *The Alamo.* New York: Dutton, 1948.

Myers, William Starr, ed. *The Mexican War Diary of George B. McClellan.* Princeton: Princeton University Press, 1917.

Nelson, Donald M. *Arsenal of Democracy.* New York: Harcourt, Brace, 1946.

Nelson, Otto L., Jr. *National Security and the General Staff.* Washington: Infantry Journal Press, 1946.

Nevins, Allan. *Grover Cleveland: A Study in Courage.* New York: Dodd, Mead, 1947.

————. *Fremont: Pathmarker of the West.* New York: Longmans, Green, 1955.

————. *The War for the Union.* 4 vols. New York: Scribner's, 1959–1971.

Nichols, Charles S., and Shaw, Henry I., Jr. *Okinawa: Victory in the Pacific.* Washington: Marine Historical Branch, 1955.

Nichols, George W. *The Story of the Great March.* New York: Harper, 1865.

Nichols, Roy F. *The Stakes of Power, 1845–1877.* New York: Hill & Wang, 1961.

Nickerson, Hoffman. *The Turning Point of the Revolution.* Boston: Houghton Mifflin, 1928.

————. *The Armed Horde.* New York: Putman, 1940.

Nicolay, John G., and Hay, John. *Abraham Lincoln: A History.* 10 vols. New York: Century, 1890.

Niven, John. *Gideon Welles: Lincoln's Secretary of the Navy.* New York: Oxford, 1973.

Nunez, Severo Gomez. *La Guerra Hispanoamericana.* 3 vols. Madrid: Imprenta del Cuerpo de Artilleria, 1899.

Nye, Wilbur S. *Here Come the Rebels!* Baton Rouge: Louisiana State University Press, 1965.

O'Connor, Raymond G., ed. *American Defense Policy in Perspective.* New York: Wiley, 1965.

Odgers, George. *Air War Against Japan, 1943–1945.* Canberra: Australian War Memorial, 1957.

Paine, Ralph D. *Joshua Barney: A Forgotten Hero of Blue Water.* New York: Century, 1924.

Palfrey, Francis W. *The Antietam and Fredericksburg.* New York: Scribner's, 1882.

Palmer, Frederick. *Newton D. Baker: America at War.* New York: Dodd, Mead, 1931.

_____. *Bliss, Peacemaker: The Life and Letters of General Tasker Howard Bliss.* New York: Dodd, Mead, 1934.

_____. *John J. Pershing: General of the Armies.* Harrisburg: Military Service Publishing Co., 1948.

Palmer, John M. *Washington, Lincoln, Wilson.* New York: Doubleday, Doran, 1930.

_____. *General Von Steuben.* New Haven: Yale University Press, 1937.

_____. *America in Arms: The Experience of the United States with Military Organization.* New Haven: Yale University Press, 1941.

Palmer, Robert, et al. *The Procurement and Training of Ground Combat Troops.* Washington: Department of the Army, 1948.

Pappas, George S. *Prudens Futuri: The U.S. Army War College, 1901–1967.* Carlisle: Alumni Association Army War College, 1968.

Pargellis, Stanley, ed. *Military Affairs in North America, 1748–1765.* New York: Appleton-Century, 1936.

Parker, Foxhall A. *The Battle of Mobile Bay.* Boston: A. Williams, 1878.

Parker, William H. *Recollections of a Naval Officer, 1841–1865.* New York: Scribner's, 1883.

Parkman, Francis. *Montcalm and Wolfe.* 2 vols. Boston: Little, Brown, 1884.

_____. *A Half-Century of Conflict.* Boston: Little, Brown, 1892.

Parton, James. *Life of Andrew Jackson.* 3 vols. New York: Mason, 1861.

Patrick, Rembert W. *Jefferson Davis and His Cabinet.* Baton Rouge: Louisiana State University Press, 1961.

Patterson, Samuel W. *Horatio Gates: Defender of American Liberties.* New York: Columbia University Press, 1941.

Patton, George S., Jr. *War as I Knew It.* Boston: Houghton Mifflin, 1947.

Paullin, Charles O. *The Battle of Lake Erie.* Cleveland: Rowfant Club, 1918.

Peckham, Howard H. *The War for Independence: A Military History.* Chicago: University of Chicago Press, 1958.

_____. *The Colonial Wars, 1689–1762.* Chicago: University of Chicago Press, 1964.

Peckham, James. *Gen. Nathaniel Lyon and Missouri in 1861.* New York: American News, 1866.

Pemberton, John C. *Pemberton: Defender of Vicksburg.* Chapel Hill: University of North Carolina Press, 1942.

Perry, Ralph Barton. *The Plattsburg Movement.* New York: Dutton, 1921.

Pershing, John J. *Final Report as Commander-in-Chief, American Expeditionary Force.* Washington: Government Printing Office, 1920.

_____. *My Experiences in the World War.* 2 vols. New York: Stokes, 1931.

Peters, Joseph P., comp. *Indian Battles and Skirmishes on the American Frontier.* New York: n.p., 1966.

Peterson, Harold L. *Arms and Armor in Colonial America.* New York: Bramhall House, 1956.

Pogue, Forrest C. *The Supreme Command.* Washington: Department of the Army, 1954.

_____. *George C. Marshall: Education of a General.* New York: Viking, 1963.

Polmar, Norman. *Soviet Naval Power: Challenge for the 1970's.* New York: National Strategy Information Center, 1972.

Pond, George E. *The Shenandoah Valley in 1864.* New York: Scribner's, 1883.

Porter, Horace. *Campaigning with Grant.* New York: Century, 1897.

Potter, E. B. *The United States and World Sea Power.* Englewood Cliffs, N.J.: Prentice-Hall, 1955.

Potter, E. B., and Nimitz, Chester W. *The Great Sea War.* Englewood Cliffs, N.J.: Prentice-Hall, 1960.

Preston, Richard A., and Wise, Sydney F. *Men in Arms: A History of Warfare and Its Interrelationships with Western Society.* New York: Praeger, 1970.

Price, William H. *The Civil War Centennial Handbook.* Arlington: Civil War Research Associates, 1961.

A Program for National Security: Report of the President's Advisory Commission on Universal Training. Washington: Government Printing Office, 1947.

Prucha, Francis Paul. *The Sword of the Republic: The United States Army on the Frontier, 1783–1846.* New York: Macmillan, 1968.

Puleston, William D. *High Command in the World War.* London: Scribner's, 1934.

_____. *Annapolis.* New York: Appleton-Century, 1942.

Quaife, Milo M., ed. *The Diary of James K. Polk.* 4 vols. Chicago: McClurg, 1910.

Quanbeck, Alton H., and Frye, Archie L. *Modernizing the Strategic Bomber Force.* Washington: Brookings Institute, 1976.

Randall, J. G. *Lincoln the President.* 4 vols. New York: Dodd, Mead, 1945–1955.

Randall, J. G., and Donald, David. *The Civil War and Reconstruction.* Boston: D. C. Heath, 1969.

Rawlyk, G. A. *Yankees at Louisbourg.* Orono: University of Maine Press, 1967.

Rees, David. *Korea: The Limited War.* New York: St. Martin's 1964.

Reeves, Ira L. *Military Education in the United States.* New York: Free Press, 1914.

Reilly, Robin. *The British at the Gates: The New Orleans Campaign in the War of 1812.* New York: Putnam, 1974.

Rentz, John N. *Bougainville and the Northern Solomons.* Washington: Marine Historical Section, 1948.

_____. *Marines in the Central Solomons.* Washington: Marine Historical Section, 1952.

Reynolds, Clark G. *The Fast Carriers: The Forging of an Air Navy.* New York: McGraw-Hill, 1968.

Reynolds, Grindall. *Concord Fight: April 19, 1775.* Boston: A. Williams, 1875.

Rhodes, James Ford. *History of the United States.* 8 vols. New York: Harper, Macmillan, 1896–1919.

Richardson, Albert D. *The Secret Service.* Hartford: American Publishing Co., 1865.

Richardson, James D., ed. *A Compilation of the Messages and Papers of the Presidents.* 10 vols. Washington: Bureau of National Literature and Art, 1904.

Richardson, Leon B. *William E. Chandler.* New York: Dodd, Mead, 1940.

Rickenbacker, Edward V. *Fighting the Flying Circus.* New York: Stokes, 1919.

Rickey, Don, Jr. *Forty Miles a Day on Beans and Hay: The Enlisted Soldier Fighting the Indian Wars.* Norman: University of Oklahoma Press, 1963.

Rickover, Hyman G. *How the Battleship Maine Was Destroyed*. Washington: Naval History Division, 1976.

Ridgway, Matthew B. *Soldier: The Memoirs of Matthew B. Ridgway*. New York: Harper, 1956.

Riedesel, Friederike von. *Letters and Journals*. Albany: J. Munsell, 1867.

Riling, Joseph R. *Baron von Steuben and His Regulations for the Order and Discipline of the Troops of the United States*. Philadelphia: Rilings Arms Books, 1966.

Risch, Irna. *Quartermaster Support of the Army*. Washington: Department of the Army, 1962.

Ripley, Roswell S. *The War with Mexico*. 2 vols. New York: Harper, 1849.

Roberts, Michael R. *The Military Revolution, 1560-1660*. Belfast: Boyd, 1956.

Robinson, William M. *The Confederate Privateers*. New Haven: Yale University Press, 1928.

Rodenbough, Theodore F., and Haskin, William L. *The Army of the United States*. New York: Maynard, Merrill, 1896.

Roland, Charles P. *Albert Sidney Johnston: Soldier of Three Republics*. Austin: University of Texas Press, 1964.

Roman, Alfred. *The Military Operations of General Beauregard*. 2 vols. New York: Harper, 1884.

Romanus, Charles F., and Sunderland, Riley. *Stilwell's Mission to China*. Washington: Department of the Army, 1953.

_____. *Stilwell's Command Problems*. Washington: Department of the Army, 1956.

_____. *Time Runs out in CBI*. Washington: Department of the Army, 1959.

Roosevelt, Theodore. *The Naval War of 1812*. New York: Putnam, 1882.

_____. *The Winning of the West*. 4 vols. New York: Putnam, 1894-1898.

_____. *The Rough Riders*. New York: Scribner's, 1899.

_____. *An Autobiography*. New York: Scribner's, 1913.

Ropes, John Codman. *The Army Under Pope*. New York: Scribner's, 1881.

_____. *The Story of the Civil War*. 2 vols. New York: Putnam, 1898.

Ropp, Theodore. *War in the Modern World*. Durham: Duke University Press, 1959.

Rosecrans, William S. *Report on the Battle of Murfreesboro*. Washington: Government Printing Office, 1863.

Rusling, James F. *Men and Things I Saw in Civil War Days*. New York: Methodist Book Concern, 1914.

St. Clair, Arthur. *Narrative of the Campaign Against the Indians, 1791*. Philadelphia: J. Aitken, 1812.

Samuel, Sigmund, comp. *The Seven Years' War in Canada*. Toronto: Ryerson Press, 1934.

Sapin, Burton M., and Snyder, Richard C. *The Role of the Military in American Foreign Policy*. New York: Doubleday, 1954.

Sargent, Herbert H. *The Campaign of Santiago de Cuba*. 3 vols. Chicago: McClurg, 1907.

Savage, Thomas. *An Account of the Late Action of the New Englanders, Under the Command of Sir William Phips*. London: Thomas Jones, 1691.

Schaff, Morris. *The Spirit of Old West Point, 1858-1862*. Boston: Houghton Mifflin, 1907.

_____. *The Battle of the Wilderness*. Boston: Houghton Mifflin, 1910.

Schaffter, Dorothy, and Mathews, Dorothy M. *The Powers of the President as Commander in Chief*. Washington: Government Printing Office, 1956.

Scharf, J. Thomas. *History of the Confederate States Navy*. New York: Rogers & Sherwood, 1887.

Schenck, David. *North Carolina, 1780–'81*. Raleigh: Edwards & Broughton, 1889.

Schley, Winfield S. *Forty-Five Years Under the Flag*. New York: Appleton, 1904.

Schnabel, James F. *Policy and Direction: The First Year*. Washington: Department of the Army, 1972.

Scott, Winfield. *Memoirs of Lieut.-General Winfield Scott*. 2 vols. New York: Sheldon, 1864.

Seager, Robert. *Alfred Thayer Mahan*. Annapolis: Naval Institute Press, 1977.

Sellers, Charles G. *James K. Polk*. 2 vols. Princeton: Princeton University Press, 1957–1966.

Semmes, Raphael. *Service Afloat and Ashore in the Mexican War*. Cincinnati: W. H. Moore, 1851.

_____. *Memoirs of Service Afloat*. Baltimore: Kelly & Piet, 1869.

Semple, Ellen C., and Jones, Clarence F. *American History and Its Geographic Conditions*. Boston: Houghton Mifflin, 1933.

Seymour, Charles, ed. *The Intimate Papers of Colonel House*. 4 vols. Boston: Houghton Mifflin, 1926–1928.

Shackford, James A. *David Crockett*. Chapel Hill: University of North Carolina Press, 1956.

Sheean, Neil, et al. *The Pentagon Papers as Published by the New York Times*. New York: Bantam, 1971.

Sheridan, Philip H. *Personal Memoirs of P. H. Sheridan*. 2 vols. New York: Webster, 1888.

Sherman, William T. *Personal Memoirs of General William T. Sherman*. 2 vols. New York: Appleton, 1875.

Sherrard, Owen A. *Lord Chatham: Pitt and the Seven Years' War*. London: Bodley Head, 1955.

Shindler, Henry. *History of the Army Service Schools*. Fort Leavenworth: Staff College Press, 1908.

Shy, John. *Toward Lexington: The Role of the British Army in the Coming of the American Revolution*. Princeton: Princeton University Press, 1965.

Sigsbee, Charles D. *The "Maine": An Account of Her Destruction in Havana Harbor*. New York: Century, 1898.

Sims, William S., and Hendrick, Burton J. *The Victory at Sea*. Garden City: Doubleday, Page, 1919.

Singletary, Otis A. *The Negro Militia and Reconstruction*. Austin: University of Texas Press, 1957.

_____. *The Mexican War*. Chicago: University of Chicago Press, 1960.

Smith, George Winston, and Judah, Charles, eds. *Chronicles of the Gringos: The U.S. Army in the Mexican War*. Albuquerque: University of New Mexico Press, 1968.

Smith, Holland, M. *Coral and Brass*. New York: Scribner's, 1949.

Smith, Justin H. *Arnold's March from Cambridge to Quebec*. New York: Putnam, 1903.

_____. *Our Struggle for the Fourteenth Colony*. 2 vols. New York: Putnam, 1907.

_____. *The Annexation of Texas*. New York: Macmillan, 1911.

_____. *The War with Mexico*. 2 vols. New York: Macmillan, 1919.

Smith, Louis. *American Democracy and Military Power*. Chicago: University of Chicago Press, 1951.

Smith, Page. *John Adams*. 2 vols. Garden City: Doubleday, 1962.

Smith, Robert Ross. *The Approach to the Philippines*. Washington: Department of the Army, 1953.

_____. *Triumph in the Philippines*. Washington: Department of the Army, 1963.

Smith, William H., ed. *Arthur St. Clair Papers*. Cincinnati: Robert Clark, 1882.

Soley, James Russell. *The Blockade and the Cruisers*. New York: Scribner's, 1883.

Sommers, Richard. *Richmond Redeemed: The Siege at Petersburg*. Garden City: Doubleday, 1981.

Spaulding, Oliver Lyman. *The United States Army in War and Peace*. New York: Putnam, 1937.

Spector, Ronald. *Admiral of the New Empire: The Life and Career of George Dewey*. Baton Rouge: Louisiana State University Press, 1974.

Spencer, Ivor D. *The Victor and the Spoils: Life of William L. Marcy*. Providence: Brown University Press, 1959.

Sprague, John T. *The Origin, Progress and Conclusion of the Florida War*. New York: Appleton, 1848.

Sprout, Harold, and Sprout, Margaret. *The Rise of American Naval Power, 1775–1918*. Princeton: Princeton University Press, 1944.

_____. *Toward a New Order in Sea Power*. Princeton: Princeton University Press, 1946.

Stacey, Charles P. *Quebec, 1759: The Siege and the Battle*. New York: St. Martin's, 1959.

Stallings, Lawrence. *The Doughboys: The Story of the A.E.F., 1917-1918*. New York: Harper & Row, 1963.

Steele, Matthew Forney. *American Campaigns*. Washington: U.S. Infantry Assoc., 1935.

Steere, Edward. *The Wilderness Campaign*. Harrisburg: Stackpole, 1960.

Steiner, B. C. *The Life and Correspondence of James McHenry*. Cleveland: Burrows, 1907.

Stephenson, Nathaniel W. *Texas and the Mexican War*. New Haven: Yale University Press, 1921.

Stevens, Frank C. *The Black Hawk War*. Chicago: F. E. Stevens, 1903.

Stevenson, Alexander F. *The Battle of Stone's River*. Boston: Osgood, 1884.

Stewart, Edgar I. *Custer's Luck*. Norman: University of Oklahoma Press, 1955.

Stine, J. H. *History of the Army of the Potomac*. Philadelphia: Rodgers, 1892.

Stockman, James R. *The Battle for Tarawa*. Washington: Marine Historical Branch, 1947.

Stone, William L. *The Campaign of Lieut. Gen. John Burgoyne and the Expedition of Lieut. Col. Barry St. Leger*. Albany: J. Munsell, 1877.

Strode, Hudson. *Jefferson Davis*. New York: Harcourt, Brace, 1955.

Stryker, William S. *The Battles of Trenton and Princeton*. Boston: Houghton Mifflin, 1898.

_____. *The Battle of Monmouth*. Princeton: Princeton University Press, 1927.

Swiggett, Howard. *War Out of Niagara: Walter Butler and the Tory Rangers*. New York: Columbia University Press, 1933.

Swinton, William. *Campaigns of the Army of the Potomac*. New York: C. B. Richardson, 1866.

Sword, Wiley. *Shiloh: Bloody April*. New York: Morrow, 1974.

Tan, C. C. *The Boxer Catastrophe*. New York: Columbia University Press, 1955.

Tanner, Robert G. *Stonewall in the Valley*. Garden City: Doubleday, 1976.

Tarleton, Banastre. *A History of the Campaign of 1780 and 1781 in the Southern Provinces of North America*. London: T. Cadell, 1787.

Taylor, Maxwell D. *The Uncertain Trumpet*. New York: Harper, 1960.

Thian, R. P. *Legislative History of the General Staff.* Washington: Government Printing Office, 1901.

Thomas, Benjamin P. *Abraham Lincoln: A Biography.* New York: Knopf, 1952.

Thomson, George G. *Problems of Strategy in the Pacific and Indian Oceans.* New York: National Strategy Information Center, 1970.

Thrapp, Dan L. *The Conquest of Apacheria.* Norman: University of Oklahoma Press, 1967.

Thwaites, Reuben Gold. *The Story of the Black Hawk War.* Madison: Wisconsin State Historical Society, 1892.

_____. *Original Journals of the Lewis and Clark Expedition.* 8 vols. New York: Dodd, Mead, 1904–1959.

Tierney, Richard. *The Army Aviation Story.* Northport, Ala.: Colonial Press, 1963.

Tinkle, Lon. *13 Days to Glory: The Siege of the Alamo.* New York: McGraw-Hill, 1958.

Titherington, Richard H. *A History of the Spanish-American War of 1898.* New York: Appleton, 1900.

Toland, John. *Battle: The Story of the Bulge.* New York: Random House, 1959.

Tompkins, Frank. *Chasing Villa.* Harrisburg: Military Service Publishing Co., 1934.

Townsend, E. D. *Anecdotes of the Civil War.* New York: Appleton, 1883.

Treacy, M. F. *Prelude to Yorktown: The Southern Campaign of Nathanael Greene.* Chapel Hill: University of North Carolina Press, 1963.

Tregaskis, Richard W. *Guadalcanal Diary.* New York: Random House, 1943.

Trevelyan, George Otto. *The American Revolution.* 4 vols. London: Longmans, Green, 1909–1914.

Truman, Harry S. *Memoirs.* 2 vols. Garden City: Doubleday, 1955.

Truscott, Lucian K. *Command Missions.* New York: Dutton, 1954.

Tucker, Glenn. *Tecumseh: Vision of Glory.* Indianapolis: Bobbs-Merrill, 1956.

_____. *High Tide at Gettysburg.* Indianapolis: Bobbs-Merrill, 1958.

_____. *Chickamauga: Bloody Battle in the West.* Indianapolis: Bobbs-Merrill, 1961.

_____. *Dawn Like Thunder: The Barbary Wars and the Birth of the U.S. Navy.* Indianapolis: Bobbs-Merrill, 1963.

_____. *Mad Anthony Wayne.* Harrisburg: Stackpole, 1973.

Tuleja, Thaddeus V. *Climax at Midway.* New York: Norton, 1960.

Turchin, John B. *Chickamauga.* Chicago: Fergus, 1888.

Turner, Gordon B. *A History of Military Affairs in Western Society.* New York: Harcourt, Brace, 1953.

Upton, Emory. *The Military Policy of the United States.* Washington: Government Printing Office, 1912.

U.S. Battle Monuments Commission. *First Division: Summary of Operations in the World War.* Washington: Government Printing Office, 1944.

U.S. Department of State. *In Quest of Peace and Security: Selected Documents on American Foreign Policy, 1941–1951.* Department of State Publication 4252. Washington: Government Printing Office, 1951.

U.S. Congress, Joint Committee on the Conduct of the War. *Report of the Joint Committee on the Conduct of the War.* 7 vols. Washington: Government Printing Office, 1863–1865.

Utley, Robert M. *Custer and the Great Controversy.* Los Angeles: Westernlore Press, 1962.

_____. *The Last Days of the Sioux Nation.* New Haven: Yale University Press, 1963.

_____. *Frontier Regulars: The United States Army and the Indian, 1866-1891.* New York: Macmillan, 1973.

Vagts, Alfred. *A History of Militarism, Civilian and Military.* N.p.: Meridian Books, 1959.

Vandiver, Frank E. *Rebel Brass: The Confederate Command System.* Baton Rouge: Louisiana State University Press, 1956.

_____. *Jubal's Raid.* New York: McGraw-Hill, 1960.

_____. *Black Jack: The Life and Times of John J. Pershing.* 2 vols. College Station: Texas A & M University Press, 1977.

Vaughn, Jesse W. *With Crook at the Rosebud.* Harrisburg: Stackpole, 1956.

_____. *Indian Fights: New Facts on Seven Encounters.* Norman: University of Oklahoma Press, 1966.

_____. *The Reynolds Campaign on Powder River.* Norman: University of Oklahoma Press, 1966.

Vestal, Stanley. *Sitting Bull: Champion of the Sioux.* Norman: University of Oklahoma Press, 1957.

Villard, Henry. *Memoirs of Henry Villard.* 2 vols. Boston: Houghton Mifflin, 1904.

Wagner, Arthur L. *Strategy.* Kansas City: Hudson-Kimberly, 1904.

Wagner, Ray. *American Combat Planes.* Garden City: Doubleday: 1968.

Walker, Francis A. *History of the Second Army Corps.* New York: Scribner's, 1891.

Wallace, Willard M. *Appeal to Arms: A Military History of the American Revolution.* New York: Harper, 1951.

_____. *Traitorous Hero: The Life and Fortunes of Benedict Arnold.* New York: Harper, 1954.

Waller, G. M. *Samuel Vetch: Colonial Enterpriser.* Chapel Hill: University of North Carolina Press, 1960.

Walworth, Arthur. *Black Ships Off Japan: The Story of Commodore Perry's Expedition.* Hamden, Conn.: Archon, 1966.

War of the Rebellion: A Compilation of the Official Records of the Union and Confederate Armies. 128 vols. Washington: Government Printing Office, 1880-1901.

Ward, Christopher. *The War of the Revolution.* 2 vols. New York: Macmillan, 1952.

Ward, Harry M. *The Department of War, 1781-1789.* Pittsburgh: University of Pittsburgh Press, 1962.

Warner, Ezra J. *Generals in Blue: Lives of the Union Commanders.* Baton Rouge: Louisiana State University Press, 1964.

Waugh, E. D. J. *West Point.* New York: Macmillan, 1944.

Webb, Alexander S. *The Peninsula: McClellan's Campaign of 1862.* New York: Scribner's, 1881.

Webb, Walter Prescott. *The Texas Rangers: A Century of Frontier Defense.* Boston: Houghton Mifflin, 1935.

Webster, John C., ed. *The Journal of Jeffery Amherst.* Chicago: University of Chicago Press, 1931.

Weems, John Edward. *The Fate of the "Maine."* New York: Holt, 1958.

Weigley, Russell F. *Quartermaster General of the Union Army: A Biography of M.C. Meigs.* New York: Columbia University Press, 1959.

_____. *Towards an American Army: Military Thought from Washington to Marshall.* New York: Columbia University Press, 1962.

_____. *History of the United States Army.* New York: Macmillan, 1967.

_____. *The American Way of War.* New York: Macmillan, 1973.

Werstein, Irving. *The Battle of Midway.* New York: Crowell, 1961.

Wesley, Edgar B. *Guarding the Frontier: A Study of Frontier Defense from 1815 to 1825.* Minneapolis: University of Minnesota Press, 1935.

West, Richard S., Jr. *Gideon Welles: Lincoln's Navy Department.* Indianapolis: Bobbs-Merrill, 1943.

_____. *Admirals of American Empire.* Indianapolis: Bobbs-Merrill, 1948.

_____. *Mr. Lincoln's Navy.* New York: Longmans, Green, 1957.

Whan, Vorin E. *Fiasco at Fredericksburg.* University Park: Pennsylvania State University Press, 1961.

Wheeler, Joseph. *The Santiago Campaign.* Boston: Lamson, Wolffe, 1898.

Whire, William C., and White, Ruth. *Tin Can on a Shingle.* New York: Dutton, 1957.

White, Howard. *Executive Influence in Determining Military Power in the United States.* Urbana: University of Illinois Press, 1925.

White, Leonard D. *The Jeffersonians: A Study in Administrative History.* New York: Macmillan, 1951.

Whitney, Courtney. *MacArthur: His Rendezvous with Destiny.* New York: Knopf, 1956.

Wigmore, Lionel. *The Japanese Thrust.* Canberra: Australian War Memorial, 1957.

Wildes, Harry E. *Anthony Wayne.* New York: Harcourt, Brace, 1941.

Wilkinson, James. *Memoirs of My Own Times.* 3 vols. Philadelphia: Small, 1816.

Willcox, William D. *Portrait of a General: Sir Henry Clinton in the War of Independence.* New York: Knopf, 1964.

Williams, T. Harry. *Lincoln and the Radicals.* Madison: University of Wisconsin Press, 1941.

_____. *Lincoln and His Generals.* New York: Knopf, 1952.

_____. *Americans at War.* Baton Rouge: Louisiana State University Press, 1960.

Willoughby, Charles A., and Chamberlain, John. *MacArthur, 1941–1951.* New York: McGraw-Hill, 1954.

Wilson, Frazer E. *The Peace of Anthony Wayne.* Greenville, S.C.: C. R. Kimble, 1909.

Wilson, Frederick T. *Federal Aid in Domestic Disturbances.* Washington: Government Printing Office, 1923.

Wilson, Herbert W. *The Downfall of Spain.* London: Sampson, Low, Marston, 1900.

Wilson, James Harrison. *Under the Old Flag.* 2 vols. New York: Appleton, 1912.

Wohlstetter, Roberta. *Pearl Harbor: Warning and Decision.* Stanford: Stanford University Press, 1962.

Wolf, John B. *The Emergence of the Great Powers.* New York: Harper, 1951.

Wolff, Leon. *Little Brown Brother: How the United States Purchased and Pacified the Philippine Islands.* Garden City: Doubleday, 1961.

Wood, W. Birkbeck, and Edmonds, James E. *A History of the Civil War in the United States, 1861–5.* New York: Putnam, 1905.

Wortham, Louis J. *A History of Texas.* 3 vols. Fort Worth: Wortham-Molyneux, 1924.

Worthington, Glenn H. *Fighting for Time: or, The Battle [of Monocacy] That Saved Washington and Mayhap the Union.* Baltimore: Day, 1932.

Wright, Albert H., comp. *The Sullivan Expedition of 1779.* Ithaca: Cornell University Press, 1943.

Wright, Quincy. *A Study of War.* 2 vols. Chicago: University of Chicago Press, 1942.
Wylie, J. C. *Military Strategy: A General Theory of Power Control.* New Brunswick: Rutgers University Press, 1967.

Young, John R. *Around the World with General Grant.* 2 vols. New York: American News, 1879.

Zimmerman, John L. *The Guadalcanal Campaign.* Washington: Marine Historical Branch, 1949.
Zook, David H., Jr., and Higham, Robin. *A Short History of Warfare.* New York: Twayne, 1967.

INDEX

WARREN W. HASSLER, JR., professor of American History, Pennsylvania State University, received the M.A. degree from the University of Pennsylvania and the B.A. and Ph.D. degrees from the Johns Hopkins University. He was presented the "Southern Book of the Year Award" for his *General George B. McClellan: Shield of the Union* (1957), and his subsequent books include *Commander of the Army of the Potomac* (1962); coauthor of *Civil War Books: A Critical Bibliography,* 2 vols. (1963); *Crisis at the Crossroads: The First Day at Gettysburg* (1970); and *The President as Commander in Chief* (1971). He is the author of the article on the American Civil War in the current *Encyclopaedia Britannica.*

Professor Hassler was appointed to the Secretary of the Army's Advisory Committee for the Military History Institute, U.S. Army War College, Carlisle Barracks, Pennsylvania (1969–1975); to the Morrison Chair of Military History, Command and General Staff College, Fort Leavenworth, Kansas (1975–1976); and to the Chair of Military History, U.S. Military Academy, West Point, New York (1979–1980). In 1981 he was awarded the Department of the Army's "Outstanding Civilian Service Medal" by the Secretary of the Army.